COGNITION, SOCIAL BEHAVIOR, AND THE ENVIRONMENT

COGNITION, SOCIAL BEHAVIOR, AND THE ENVIRONMENT

Edited by

John H. Harvey
Vanderbilt University

LEA LAWRENCE ERLBAUM ASSOCIATES, PUBLISHERS
1981   Hillsdale, New Jersey

Lawrence Erlbaum Associates, Inc., Publishers
365 Broadway
Hillsdale, New Jersey 07642

Library of Congress Cataloging in Publication Data
Main entry under title:
Cognition, social behavior, and the environment.

  Bibliography: p.
  Includes index.
  1. Social psychology—Addresses, essays,
lectures.   2. Cognition-Addresses, essays,
lectures.   I. Harvey, John H., 1943–
HM251.C64   302   80-28223
ISBN 0-89859-082-5

Printed in the United States of America

This book is dedicated to the
writers, editors, and publishers
who are recognizing, addressing,
and carefully creating meaningful
interfaces among disciplines and
areas in the social sciences.

Contents

Preface   **xv**

PART I: GENERAL PERSPECTIVES ON INTERDISCIPLINARY WORK

1. **An Environmental Psychologist's Perspective on
   the Interdisciplinary Approach in Psychology**
   Harold M. Proshansky   **3**
   Introduction   3
   Psychologists as Interdisciplinary Thinkers   5
   The Experimental-Laboratory Model   7
   The Mutual Isolation from Reality   11
   Independent and Dependent Variables   13 .
   Process versus Content   14
   The Question of Time   17
   Some Concluding Comments   18

2. **Ethnography as an Interdisciplinary Campground**
   Michael H. Agar   **21**

3. **Interaction of Language Use with Ethnography
   and Cognition**
   Roy Freedle   **35**
   The Cognitive Basis of Schemata   36
   Inquiring Systems as Schemata for Modeling Miscommunications   52

4. **Social Knowing from an Ecological-Event Perspective:
    A Consideration of the Relative Domains of Power
    for Cognitive and Perceptual Modes of Knowing**
    Reuben M. Baron **61**
    A Social-Knowing Continuum   63
    The Nature of the Relationship Between Perception
        and Cognitive-Based Knowing   73
    Emotions from an Ecological-Event Perspective   80
    A Concluding Statement   84

PART II: COGNITION AND THE ENVIRONMENT

5. **Cognition and Adaptation: The Importance of
    Learning to Learn**
    *John D. Bransford, Barry S. Stein, Tommie S. Shelton,
    and Richard A. Owings* **93**
    Initial Observations   94
    Some Problems of Understanding and Learning   95
    Successful and Less Successful Learners Revisited   99
    Learning to Learn   102
    Summary and Conclusions   108

6. **Cognitive Skill: Implications for Spatial Skill
    in Large-Scale Environments**
    William G. Chase and Michelene T. H. Chi **111**
    Cognitive Skills   112
    Map Drawing   122
    Spatial Knowledge and Cognitive Maps   129
    Summary   133

7. **Spatial Cognition and Reasoning**
    Perry W. Thorndyke **137**
    Types of Spatial Knowledge   139
    Knowledge Types and Spatial Judgments   143
    Individual Differences in Spatial Cognition   145
    Concluding Comments   147

8. **The Acquisition and Utilization of Spatial Knowledge**
    Keith Clayton and Mary Woodyard **151**
    A Proposed Framework   152
    An Experiment on Spatial Learning   157
    Summary   160

 9. **Hot Air: The Psychology of CO_2-Induced Climatic Change**
    Baruch Fischhoff **163**
    Interlude   165
    What's to Know?   166
    Low-Probability Events   169
    Recap   176
    What Else is There to Know?   177
    Cognitive Politics   181
    Conclusion   182

PART III: COGNITION AND SOCIAL BEHAVIOR

10. **The Interface of Cognitive and Social Psychology**
    Shelley E. Taylor **189**
    What is Social Cognition?   190
    The Social Psychology–Cognitive Psychology Interface:
        Social Psychology's Debt to Cognitive Psychology   196
    The Social Psychology–Cognitive Psychology Interface:
        Cognitive Psychology's Debt to Social Psychology   198
    Some Liabilities of the Cognitive–Social Interface   202
    Social Cognition's View of the Person:
        A Script for Camus?   205
    Conclusions   207

11. **The Role of Cognitive, Affective, and Social Factors
    in Attributional Biases**
    Gifford Weary **213**
    Focus of Attention as a Determinant of Causal Attributions   215
    Self-Focused Attention and Self-Attributions:
        Potential Mediating Processes   217
    Self-Serving Attributions and Personal Adjustment
        to Stressful Environments   221
    Conclusion   223

12. **Social Cognition and Affect**
    Susan T. Fiske **227**
    Definitions and Perspective   231
    Guides to the Role of Affect in Social Cognition   235
    A Role for Affect in Social Cognition   245
    Summary and Implications   255

13.   **The Story as a Social Environment: Children's Comprehension
and Evaluation of Intentions and Consequences**
Royal Grueneich and Tom Trabasso   **265**
Analysis of Motive and Intention Information   267
Review of the Standard or Traditional
   Moral-Judgment Literature   277
Story-Grammar Research   281
Summary and Conclusions   285

14.   **The Role of Cognitive Sets in Interpreting and
Remembering Interpersonal Events**
Kerry L. Yarkin, Jerri P. Town and John H. Harvey   **289**
Introduction   289
General Method for All Studies   294
General Results for All Studies   296
General Discussion and Conclusions   299
Framework of Processes Associated with the
   Perception of Social Events   302
Conclusion   306

15.   **Lay Analyses of Causal Forces on Behavior**
Gary L. Wells   **309**
Introduction   309
Causal Force   311
Original and Socialized Processing   312
The Relationship Between Perceived External and Internal Forces   317
Summary and Conclusions   320

16.   **On the Nature of the Question in Social Comparison**
William P. Smith   **325**
The Social Significance of Social Comparison   326
The Festinger Theory   326
Questions Social Comparison can Answer   328
The Question of Base Rate   335

17.   **The Relativity of Perception, Choice, and Social Knowledge**
Joseph S. Lappin   **341**
Overview   341
The Relativity of Knowledge: The Representation of
   Structure and Function   342
The Relativity of Choice Behavior   349
The Perception of Coherence in Dynamic Stimulus Patterns   353
Comments on the Role of Prior Knowledge in Perception   361

PART IV: SOCIAL BEHAVIOR AND THE ENVIRONMENT

18. **Crowding and Cognitive Limits**
    Susan Saegert **373**
    Effective Components of High-Density Settings   375
    Person–Environment Transactions in High-Density Settings   378
    Density as a Systemic Variable   382
    Crowding Theories and Cognitive Components   383
    An Ecology of Crowding Experiences   386

19. **A Cognitive Social Learning Approach to the Crossroads of Cognition, Social Behavior, and the Environment**
    Abraham Wandersman and Paul Florin **393**
    The Person–Situation Controversy—Personality Psychology
       as an Example   394
    A Cognitive Social Learning Approach to the
       "How" of Interaction   396
    Cognitive Social Learning Variables
       and Neighborhood Participation   398
    Concluding Comments   404

20. **Perceived Freedom and Control in the Built Environment**
    Richard D. Barnes   **409**
    Freedom and Control Constructs in the Design
       and Environmental Literatures   409
    Determinants and Consequences of Perceived Freedom and Control   411
    Problems with Perceived Freedom and Control Concepts   414
    Measuring Choice in the Built Environment   416
    Analysis of Choice Structure   418

21. **The Symbiotic Relationship Between Social Psychology and Environmental Psychology: Implications from Crowding, Personal Space, and Intimacy Regulation Research**
    John R. Aiello, Donna E. Thompson, and Andrew Baum   **423**
    Social Psychology   423
    Environmental Psychology   424
    Relationship Between Environmental and Social Psychology   425
    Crowding   427
    Personal Space   431
    Intimacy Regulation   434
    Summary   436

PART V: COGNITION, SOCIAL, BEHAVIOR, AND THE ENVIRONMENT

22. **People in Places: A Transactional View of Settings**
     Daniel Stokols and Sally Ann Shumaker   **441**
     Introduction   441
     Places: The Physical and Symbolic Context of Human Action   443
     Occupants: Their Composition, Organization, and Relationship to Place   453
     Settings: The Transactions Among People and Places   464
     Summary and Conclusions   478
     Describing and Classifying the Transactions
        Between People and Places: A Glossary   480

23. **The Perception of Neighborhood Change**
     Gary H. Winkel   **489**
     Introduction   489
     Background   490
     Change, Stability, and Environmental Manageability   493
     Environmental Manageability and Value Orientations   494
     The Judgmental Context for Manageability Assessments   498
     Neighborhood Structural Characteristics and Manageability   501
     Concluding Remarks   510

24. **Cognitive Mediation of Environmental Stress**
     *Andrew Baum, Robert J. Gatchel, John R. Aiello,
     and Donna Thompson*   **513**
     Social Density and Regulatory Control   514
     Social Density and the Development of Learned Helplessness   519
     Cognitive Mediation of Helplessness Conditioning   521
     Generalization of Learned Helplessness   526
     Environment, Cognition, and Behavior   529
     Summary   531

25. **Environmental Structure and Cognitive Structure**
     Anthony G. Greenwald   **535**
     The Self as an Organization of Knowledge   535
     Case Study of a Scientific Theory as a Knowledge Organization   541
     Environmental Structure and Memory Structure   545

PART VI: FINAL COMMENTARIES

26. **Social Cultural Prerequisites for Cognitive Research**
     John D. Bransford   **557**
     Experimentation and Social Contracts   558

Laboratory Research and Environmental Design   559
Laboratory Research and Rapport   560
Laboratory Experiments and Comprehension   561
Laboratory Research and Environmental Resources   562
The Concept of Ecology Validity   564
Summary and Conclusions   567

27. **The Need for a Cross-Cultural Perspective**
    Roy Freedle   **571**

28. **Benediction by an Anthropologist**
    Michael H. Agar   **575**

29. **No Man is a Discipline**
    Baruch Fischhoff   **579**
    Modes of Interdisciplinary Work   580

PART VII: EPILOGUE

30. **An Editorial Commentary on Interfaces in Psychology
    and the Social Sciences**
    John H. Harvey, Jerri P. Town, Kerry L. Yarkin   **587**
    General Conclusions   487
    Directions for Future Interdisciplinary Dialogue and Conferences   588
    Funding of Interdisciplinary Conferences   589

Author Index   **593**

Subject Index   **607**

Preface

Since the inception of psychology as a formal discipline, there has been a current of thought concerned with integrations of ideas and findings among subareas of psychology and between psychology and other disciplines. Indeed, an interdisciplinary emphasis was woven into the fabric of thinking and writing of such eminent pioneering psychologists as William James, Harry S. Sullivan, Kurt Lewin, and Fritz Heider. Thus, it may seem odd to some that the main objectives of this volume are to stimulate and nourish cross-disciplinary work in psychology and the social sciences in general. But that is the case.

This volume represents a commitment to examining and forging interfaces that have already begun to emerge and that may emerge in the future. Interestingly, also, a thrust of this volume involves critical scrutiny of links that may not be tenable now, or in the foreseeable future. Quite clearly, though, my belief as editor of this volume is that subareas of psychology and many disciplines within the social sciences have much more to offer one another than may previously have been recognized by specialists in the various subareas and disciplines. It is hoped that this volume will represent the first in a series of volumes reporting the proceedings of meetings concerned with interfaces in the social sciences to be held at Vanderbilt University in the 1980's.

This particular volume presents a set of original papers deriving from a crossdisciplinary conference held at Vanderbilt University from May 14–17, 1979. The contributors represent the areas of cognitive, environmental, and social psychology and anthropology. Each of the areas within psychology was represented by between seven and ten scholars. And, despite an attempt to include more anthropologists, only one anthropologist, Michael Agar, attended the meeting. In examining the breadth of this volume, one probably will be convinced of the value of anthropologists' talking to psychologists (see Agar's chapter—Chapter 2—and his final comments regarding the conference in Chapter 28).

In order for a large conference such as this one to be successfully planned and carried out, many people must work long hours and contribute in a variety of ways. I am indebted to John Bransford and John Aiello who, at the outset of our planning, provided thoughtful, expert input regarding possible combinations of participants. Tommie Shelton and Dorothy Timberlake contributed to the analysis of travel agendas and coordinated various important practical activities. Kerry Yarkin and Jerri Town helped in planning and executing all facets of the conference. Clearly, the event could not have been as successful as it was without their unending diligence. My secretary Connie Dyer Covert, as usual, was an invaluable helper; she typed all of the editorial correspondence and interstitial material and handled a variety of difficult tasks with aplomb. Finally, I thank the agency officials who believed in this project (see the final chapter in the book for a discussion of issues regarding funding of conferences) and provided generous support. Most importantly, these persons include Kelly Shaver and Joseph Young who, respectively, were directors of the social–developmental and memory and cognitive processes panels of NSF, and Ernest Q. Campbell, Dean of the Vanderbilt Graduate School and Chairperson of the Research Council. I am most grateful to NSF and the Vanderbilt University Research Council for providing funds to support this conference.

John H. Harvey

I
GENERAL PERSPECTIVES ON INTERDISCIPLINARY WORK

The four chapters in this introductory section are broad examinations of the value of interdisciplinary work and of concepts that will most likely be accorded central status in a fruitful pursuit of such work (e.g., ethnography and a continuum of social knowing). In the first chapter, Harold M. Proshansky speaks to the issues of interdisciplinary work with the sagacity of a scholar who was one of the founders of the field of environmental psychology—a specialty that draws heavily upon other areas of psychology as well as other social sciences. There is much to learn from Proshansky's statement, but the reader should be forewarned that Proshansky is not too sanguine about some current crossdisciplinary efforts, nor does he mince words in his criticism of various aspects of the field, including especially what he calls the experimental-laboratory model. Proshansky's chapter represents a challenge that other scholars eager to embark on interdisciplinary work must take formidable steps to meet—and, as he suggests in his conclusions, it is not an easy challenge.

Michael H. Agar, an anthropologist, presents a compelling case for considering ethnography as an empirical campground where a variety of different theoretical/ methodological mixtures can be integrated, modified, abandoned, or nourished. Agar discusses some of the important characteristics of ethnography and notes that, like most things in life, it is simple to do—badly! Agar indicates that ethnography implies the imposing task of development of prolonged relationships with group members in their natural settings. In a comment on Agar's chapter, Shelley Taylor suggests that Agar's ethnographic approach represents a dynamic interplay between phenomena and theory. Agar's overall posture is best summed up in his concluding comment that theory and the world must eventually meet in the social sciences.

Roy Freedle's treatment of ethnography involves a sophisticated discussion of people's development of cultural and perceptual schemata and of how these schemata interact with ethnographic differences in nonverbal behavior to form the basis for many communication failures. Freedle, as a writer–researcher and editor, has contributed in significant ways to crossdisciplinary dialogue, and his chapter bridges many areas, from experimental cognitive research to sociolinguistics to proxemics. Freedle's chapter represents an excellent example of the breadth of interdisciplinary scholarship; concomitantly, it reinforces Agar's argument that such scholarship requires in-depth training and work in a variety of disciplines.

In the final chapter in this introductory section, Reuben M. Baron provides a broad framework for viewing social cognitive processes. Although less extensive in scope than the first three chapters, Baron's chapter is a valuable integrative effort that involves an attempt to depict a continuum of social knowing, which, as stated before, will most likely be a core concept in interdisciplinary work in the social sciences. This continuum is bounded by a "direct knowing" at one end and an "indirect knowing" at the other end. The reader might note the similarity of some of Baron's arguments to those of Joseph Lappin on social perception in Chapter 17. Importantly, both of these theorists emphasize the role of basic perception in social-perception phenomena. Despite the recognized value of Heider's early writing and Gibson's work, contemporary work on social perception has given little attention to basic perceptual principles.

1 An Environmental Psychologist's Perspective on the Interdisciplinary Approach in Psychology

Harold M. Proshansky
Graduate School and University Center, CUNY

INTRODUCTION

Unlike other interdisciplinary conferences I have attended, this conference was organized by John Harvey and his associates in a rather open fashion rather than around some major social issue, urban problem, or impending crisis. What they have done is to bring us together to describe our research, discuss what problems we have, and, above all, to see both specifically and generally how our various efforts relate to each other in terms of conceptual linkages, empirical articulations, and theoretical integrations at the interface of our different disciplines. This is a good thing—in fact, it is downright refreshing. The fact is that we each go our merry way turning out research, writing papers and books, and then write more new research proposals, with no time to take pause, to reflect, and, most importantly, to ask: Does it fit with what's happening in other fields? Does it make sense? And even, is it worth it in terms of the cumulation of knowledge— or are we kidding ourselves? Like the Coca Cola sign of old, we should periodically invoke the motto "the pause that refreshes."

No great or stupendous things will come out of this conference. They never do and indeed they never can, given the amount of time, the numbers of people, and the difficulty of the objectives. Good things, however, can emerge if we first listen and learn what others are doing in other fields, and then answer the question of whether our own research findings and theoretical paradigms make as much sense seen from the point of view of what these other investigators in other fields are thinking, doing, and finding. Of course, each conference participant cannot do this with every other conference participant. Common conceptual and problem interests of individuals in the same and other fields will obviously dictate that we will listen, think about, and be more responsive to some conference participants than to others.

But—and you might have suspected a "But" would be coming—listening, learning, comparing, and integrating in the light of interface considerations can only be an important and useful enterprise if at the very start of this conference, and perhaps at points all along the way, we make ourselves aware of the hazards, restraints, and very real pitfalls involved in any attempt to establish a more comprehensive understanding of human behavior and experience by comparing, articulating, and integrating concepts, findings, and theoretical assertions across discipline boundary lines. Although it is true that my assigned task of providing a "perspective for interdisciplinary work" for this conference can be defined in a number of ways, the concern with hazards and restraints must be given the highest priority. Indeed, we may want to answer the critical question of whether it pays at this point to think in interdisciplinary terms or, even, are we ready for it? Before we become ecstatic over consistencies, articulations, and even integrations at the various interfaces of the three fields, or, on the other hand, sad and disappointed because it does not turn out as we hope or expect, we ought to try to trace the twists and turns and dangerous bumps and depressions we can expect to encounter as we make an attempt to move down the interdisciplinary road to cumulative knowledge.

Before I begin my task, it is important for you to know where I stand as I try to draw an interdisciplinary perspective for considering the relationships among and between the fields of cognitive, environmental, and social psychology. I began as a laboratory-oriented social psychologist interested in cognitive processes, but I eventually turned my attention to the concerns of the environmental psychologist—that is, to questions of the relationships between the built environment and human behavior and experience. For many environmental psychologists, including myself, the field is almost by definition interdisciplinary because it is conceived of as a *problem-centered* discipline concerned with major person/environment issues in the urban setting. Wittingly or unwittingly, it draws heavily on other fields of psychology, as well as on other behavioral sciences and the design professions.

Lest those at this conference who are unfamiliar with the field of environmental psychology get too excited about our theoretical and empirical interdisciplinary accomplishments, given the rather simple and self-assured way I defined the field, let me tell you quickly this is hardly the case. The field is new, our efforts inchoate, and in many instances—as we turn to other disciplines and they turn to us—it seems to be a case of the blind leading the blind. A large part of the problem, of course, lies in the fact that environmental psychology, indeed all behavioral sciences, are always ready to run, let alone walk, before they can crawl, given their great desire not only to solve both social and scientific problems, but also to achieve scientific respectability and prestige at the same time.

This is to be expected, but whatever our hopes, desires, and expectations, crawl we must, because our fields of specialization have a long way to go before we can say that we have a ''critical mass'' of cumulated knowledge, both theoretical and empirical. There are any number of genuine issues and problems that make it difficult for us even to crawl when we think, conceptualize, or attempt to undertake research in interdisciplinary terms. It is these issues and problems I would like to raise here, from, as I said before, the point of view of an environmental psychologist.

PSYCHOLOGISTS AS INTERDISCIPLINARY THINKERS

Having researchers from related but clearly different fields of psychology participate in an interdisciplinary conference is a very good thing because obviously it makes communication about interface issues much easier. That is particularly true of psychologists who have overlapping interests—for example, cognitive processes—in the sense of being concerned with similar problems or, even better stated, related conceptual and empirical issues. Having said at the beginning of this chapter how refreshing the idea of this conference was, I am, however, concerned at the same time that psychologists, given their sheer numbers, are going to be running the show. It will clearly make communication easier, but I am less certain about the level of interdisciplinary achievements that will occur despite this ease in communication. Indeed, it is because we tend to speak the same language and look at problems in a particular way that I suddenly found myself less delighted at the prospects of the conference with only one anthropologist present. We should not ignore the fact that there are sociologists, anthropologists, economists, and political scientists whose work and approaches are conceptually and empirically relevant to the processes and problems that concern cognitive, social, and environmental psychologists.

Do we have to have these other behavioral scientists present in our attempt to relate to and integrate our own area of specialization with each other? I would say yes, because there is a reality we ought to face from the beginning: Psychologists do not do very well when it comes to thinking, conceptualizing, or seeking empirical linkages in interdisciplinary terms. We not only tend to specialize narrowly on given research issues and thereby isolate our thinking from other problems in psychology—not to mention other behavioral science problems—but even when we do have interdisciplinary concerns about cognition, or attitudes, or learning, or motivation, in relation to complex human situations, they invariably reflect our almost ingrained bias and disposition toward *analyses at the psychological or individual level.* One way or another, whether we deal with interaction pairs, groups, communities, social organizations, the family, the classroom, or any of the other dynamic events involved in a complex human society, our reference point is always the person as the unit of analysis for describing, interpreting, and understanding these events expressed in and by the behavior and experience of people.

Lewin and his colleagues notwithstanding, we tend to stay at the psychological or individual level of analysis in our attempt to understand complex human phenomena that dictate and require our concern with events whose unique properties go beyond that level of analysis. This is not a case of being smug about our orientation or approach. It expresses our training and socialization as psychologists in the context of a "scientific discipline" that, like all other scientific disciplines, has normative, organizational, and value characteristics that serve to identify and, at the same time, carefully distinguish it from other fields of scientific endeavor. The solution, of course, is not the abandonment of our field, nor simply the creation of an interdisciplinary curriculum for training psychologists; psychologists must be trained to think as psychologists for, in fact, the individual level of analysis not only has a theoretical and empirical integrity of its own, but indeed must play a cornerstone role in any systematic attempt to cumulate knowledge about people as cognizing, adaptive, goal-directed social organisms.[1]

What we are saying, then, is that the need for interdisciplinary thinking in psychology is not one that challenges in any way the validity of the psychological level of analysis. What is to be challenged is how we use it in our thinking and research, as expressed by the way we define problems, the concepts we establish, and the kind of methodologies we employ, and in all these respects, by the implicit assumptions about "people" and "science" underlying these directed attempts to cumulate knowledge about human behavior and experience. As we attempt to demonstrate in our later discussion, it is these aspects of how we employ the psychological level of analysis that seems to isolate and cut us off from other dimensions and issues that should be included at the psychological level of analysis. Psychological analysis is a critical and fruitful way of thinking, but its full potential can only be realized—that is, deepened and extended—when the methods, techniques, and concepts it employs are evolved out of a broader analytical framework that recognizes its limitations in the totality of inter-related events that define and determine human behavior and experience.

When this happens, psychologists will still be looking at such behavior and experience as the psychological level of analysis, but with theories, data, and concepts that will reflect and express the nature and context of other than nonpsychological events that enter into the behavior and experience of people.

---

[1]Certainly I support the view of interdisciplinary training in addition to speciality training as recommended by John Harvey and Gifford Weary in another paper (1979). I have seen and been part of such training programs, and they work but often in a very limited way. Students in them know more and for a while become sensitive to the concepts and variables in the "other field," but when faced with a new issue, I am not sure they learn to think and analyze in interdisciplinary terms.

This is what we mean when we say that psychologists must learn to think at the individual level of analysis in interdisciplinary terms. Our reason for desiring other behavioral scientists at an interdisciplinary conference of this kind is that they provide a backdrop of ideas, concepts, and theories against which psychologists are then forced to look at the very specialized, isolated, and encapsulated nature of their approach. The fact is—and we have said this earlier—that it is not that we deal exclusively with the psychological level of analysis that encapsulates us, but rather the *way* in which we have dealt, and to a large extent continue to deal, with this level of analysis.

Because at this conference we are pretty much left to ourselves without the benefit of the perspective of other behavioral scientists, let me specify some of the factors in how we use the psychological level of analysis, such that it limits, indeed precludes, interdisciplinary analysis and integration. In effect, these are the problems and issues we alluded to earlier that we must face up to in any serious attempt to consider integrating data and concepts between and among the fields of psychology represented here. It cannot be stressed too strongly that the limitations in the way psychologists have defined and used the psychological or individual level of analysis has not only isolated them in an interdisciplinary sense—the inability to think, conceptualize, and do research in interdisciplinary terms—from other behavioral scientists, but from each other as well. We may speak the same language and feel quite comfortable communicating with each other because we work at the same level of analysis, but we really do not hear each other too well; nor can we, given our approach to problems at this level, an approach that inexorably limits and confines us to our own specialized concerns, thereby precluding the penetration of other views and conceptions that would extend and deepen our particular findings and ideas.

THE EXPERIMENTAL-LABORATORY MODEL

At the root of the problem of how psychologists think and do research at the individual level of analysis is the experimental-laboratory model and the assumptions underlying its use. The model continues to dominate both directly and indirectly the approach of psychology as a field of scientific inquiry. It is true that during the last three decades the model has increasingly been moved into field settings, employed with more complex formulations of problems and research designs, involved admixtures of laboratory and real-world research techniques and strategies, and has self-consciously worried about its use in university settings, with contrived social situations involving the use of deception in its research. Yet, its influence is as strong as ever, although perhaps more subtle than before. The crucial fact is that the model is far more than a research approach or a methodological strategy. Woven into its traditional scientific fabric of experimental controls, quantitative precision, and objective denotations is a set of assumptions about what science and human beings are all about; notwithstanding shifts in research techniques, strategies, problems, and research settings, these assumptions continue to exert influence, a great deal of influence, even in those directed attempts to break away from its influence.

The experimental-laboratory model and its underlying assumptions are not difficult to describe. I have described them before, as others have done, and indeed I suspect they will be the subject of much discussion over the next decade (Gergen, 1973; Gibbs, 1979; Proshansky, 1976). At root, the model seeks to establish cause and effect relationships between one or more specified variables seen as the causes of behavior and experiences in the person and, of course, one or more dimensions of those behaviors and experiences. Yet, the crucial point is that what guides the use of the model is an empirical orientation in which objectivity, precision of findings, and the use of controls are all essential to the valid use of the model. One way or another, all *other* factors on both sides of the equation, known or unknown, must be held constant so that the proposed relationship between the selected and defined independent and dependent variables can be truly tested.

Now let me make a simple point. The model that was borrowed from the physical and natural sciences is not only a perfectly sound one, but it has and will continue to have a critical and significant role to play in certain fields or problem areas of psychology. However, so much of its value depends on how, when, and for what kind of problem it is used that the problem is not the model but what psychologists have done with it. We not only misuse it, but we overuse it; above all, we have allowed it to overshadow, if not completely obscure, our view of what a science must do in its *creative* as well as its empirical endeavors in the search for a cumulative basis of knowledge. One of the more essential reasons we misuse and overuse it is that because of its success in the physical and natural sciences, we have allowed it to serve as our definition of science as an almost exclusively empirical and objective pursuit of understanding. In so doing, we have ignored the underlying assumptions not just about science, but about the human organism inherent not in the concept of the model itself, but in the way psychologists have made it *the* scientific method.

How do psychologists use the experimental-laboratory model—or perhaps better said, abuse it? Essentially we have turned it into a mechanism for formulating problems, evolving concepts, and indeed developing theoretical structures. Even now, if we review any of the research fields of psychology, the sovereignty of an experimental-laboratory empiricism as an approach still reigns supreme as it continually reflects and echoes the view that method must determine problems and theory. And indeed it does, in so many ways. For example, in the name of the method and its sacred goals of establishing knowledge that is objective and precise, the human organism is conceived of in *reductionistic* terms in many ways. First, the assumption is made that the apparent complexity of human behavior and experience need not stand in the way of reducing that complexity to a simplified orderliness of relating specific independent and dependent variables to each other in objective and precise terms. In effect, in the belief that there are a small or even a larger number of general and unitary underlying principles of behavior and experience, it is perfectly reasonable, therefore, to transcend both the complex nature and variability of people and situations or social contexts. Laboratory settings and even field settings, with proper manipulations and controls, will screen out and render inconsequential the "noise" introduced by these complexities and variations in the search for these simple and fundamental general principles.

This view is as true of social psychology, child psychology, personality psychology, industrial psychology, cognitive psychology, and others, as it is of the fields of experimental perception, learning, and motivation. The fact that the so-called "softer" fields employed more complex problems, settings, designs, and concepts does not nullify the "stripping of phenomena"—the manipulation of contexts, the use of contrived situations, and, above all, the belief that the principles are there. They can be extracted in the context of experimental research, and although so much of the complexity of people and situations is being left out, the principles in the end will be sufficient to explain and help us understand much if not all of this complexity. Whatever the rhetoric—because the real truth lies in what psychologists do in research and not in what they say or write—psychologists in all research fields, either directly or indirectly, assume that human behavior and experience is mechanistic, quantifiable, essentially far simpler to explain than it appears in its day-to-day complexity, and that whatever its "inner mysteries," we can have access to these mysteries by means of increasingly sophisticated methods and techniques of control and measurement.

The very great influence of the experimental-laboratory model even in the 1970's means that the field of psychology continues to be driven by empirical considerations at the expense of theory. Viewed from up close, theoretical conceptions play an almost negligible role in giving direction and meaning to research in a given field or problem area. The reader may quickly counter with the view that so much research and the attack on particular problems in the different fields are involved with conceptualizations, theoretical formulations, and even broader theoretical frameworks. We would not dispute this observation. What we would dispute is whether such theory plays any really meaningful or significant role. Theory, whether broad or specific, as a means of making creative breakthroughs in explaining the unknown—the hallmark of the continuing development of and the extraordinary achievements in the physical and natural sciences—seems completely absent from psychology as a field of scientific inquiry. To argue that we are too new a field and, thereby, give the usual lament of being in our infancy, simply begs the question. If we are advanced enough to use the experimental-laboratory model as if we were comparable to the physical and natural sciences, then why not some theoretical breakthroughs based on daring, speculative, and creative formulations. If we are so "young" that we are not ready for the latter, then this suggests that perhaps we are by no means ready for the former.

The fact is that we "talk" theory and "play" with it, but its role in our research, in the way we formulate problems, and indeed in how we train our students, is *secondary*. It would not be an exaggeration to say that implicitly, if not explicitly, we are antitheoretical. We seem to deal with theory in two ways.

To begin with, whether it was the early "schools of psychology" or the more modern approaches of the "cognitive psychologist," the "psychodynamic theorist," or those with a Skinnerian, Lewinian, Rogerian, or any other viewpoint, these were and are far more general theoretical approaches or orientations than "working" theoretical formulations. The "theory" was more a pronouncement of faith in one or more general assumptions, and was therefore so broad and general that its direct connection to the conceptualization of particular problems and issues was tenuous, to say the least. Such broad, so-called theoretical frameworks seem to hang out in space, and usually over time gradually float away, although intermittently they may be brought back for a renewal of the faith.

But this kind of broad, theoretical formulation is not so much the problem as is the question of what happens to our more directed attempt at theory—whether part of a general theoretical formulation or an ad hoc and specific one—when we deal with particular research problems or questions. Whether we are speaking of achievement motivation theory, cognitive dissonance, attribution theory, theories of crowding, or any number of others, the influence of the experimental-laboratory model is there—whether in the laboratory or the field—when psychologists begin to formulate these theories in the first place and certainly as they attempt to develop and extend them by means of systematic research. It would not be an exaggeration to say that research psychologists as a group always have at least one eye (and perhaps both) focused on method and research techniques in the very particular sense of establishing precise and objective cause and effect relationships between measurable variables.

It is small wonder that many problems and issues of human behavior and experience have only slowly entered the realm of scientific psychology—for example, love, hate, and envy (Berscheid, Christensen, Harvey, Huston, Kelley, Levinger, McClintock, Peplau, & Peterson, 1980)—or that our theoretical conceptions seem to be most often common-sense conceptions that may be more attractive than true because the methodological restraints and requirements for their test can be easily met by the experimental-laboratory model. But even when a daring and exciting theoretical formulation is put forth, the next step always seems to be "the experimental test." What ensues then is the transformation of the exciting ideas—whether then designated as intervening variables or hypothetical constructs—into concepts that are operational in nature and make empirical research possible. As we have said so many times before, the exciting conception or idea, and in particular the phenomenon that is its referent, become increasingly "peeled" until the integrity of both is completely eroded (for example, Proshansky, 1973, 1976). Our theories then, at the very beginning and certainly over time as we engage in more and more research to test them, are very often nothing more than camouflaged reflections of our preoccupations with the experimental-laboratory research methodology and techniques. Conflicting findings and discrepancies between "test" findings and the real world are never dealt with as a need to deepen and change our theoretical conceptions, but rather as problems in whether our research designs, methods, or techniques are comparable, reliable, or appropriate under given sets of conditions. If we consider attribution theory, cognitive dissonance theory, behavior modification theory, achievement motivation theory, or others, the outcomes always seem to be the same: The theoretical concepts and formulations and the research resulting from them become increasingly encapsulated as more refined, detailed, and specialized empirical procedures are elaborated to preserve the conception that the problems of cumulating knowledge in psychology lie in making the experimental-laboratory model work rather than in changing or discarding the theory.

I must remind the reader of a point made earlier. There is nothing intrinsic in the experimental-laboratory model that hinders the development of cumulative knowledge in psychology. Indeed, the importance of establishing an experimental basis of knowledge to some degree in a science cannot be overstated. But the question is when should it be used, for what problems, and at what stages in the development of a field of inquiry. The difficulty lies—as I have said before—in the overuse, misuse, and abuse of the model in psychology. This point of view does not imply that the "other" approach is the necessary panacea for building a cumulative body of knowledge. This "other" approach is research viewed as necessarily occurring in the real world under naturalistic conditions in which subjective or the phenomenal aspects of human behavior and experience are preserved. Merely to observe and record the "quality" of events in their pristine state is no more a solution to the problems of theory and data that have beset the field of psychology than is the pervasive use of the experimental-laboratory model. The matter of the two approaches is being discussed again and again because these problems continue to plague the field of psychology—and indeed some of the other behavioral sciences (Gibbs, 1979; Petrinovich, 1979).

THE MUTUAL ISOLATION FROM REALITY

To be interdisciplinary at the level of theory and research, whether between behavioral sciences or fields of psychology, means seeking to determine the relationships between different phenomena, concepts, and, indeed, existing explanations. Yet, to do all this presupposes that psychologists, the focus of interest here, begin their concerns with human behavior and experience in a direct and open fashion—that is, with a readiness and expectancy that these represent complex phenomena expressing a variety of person and environment influences that will have to be looked at long and hard in order to understand and get some grasp of the range and depth of this complexity. Of course, the fact is that this is precisely what is not done. The influence of the experimental-laboratory model not only programs the research psychologist to begin immediately to make the phenomenon methodologically manageable, devoid of all those complexities that express the influence of other relevant mediating events and phenomena, but in doing so he or she formulates the research questions so narrowly that not only is the integrity of the phenomenon often lost, but its relationships with related phenomena and other influences of importance not dealt with by the particular research question are completely obscured. What we often pack into our "all other things being equal" statement are just those events and phenomena that are dealt with by our colleagues in other fields or areas of specialization and that of course are the stepping stones or necessary linkages for interdisciplinary thinking and collaboration. They, in turn, do pretty much the same thing, so the isolation is mutual and complete.

In the context of the university laboratory, regardless of whether the human event is cognitive, social, environmental, or some mixture of these, there may be very little connection between it and the real-world phenomenon it is supposed to represent in whole or part. But even a university laboratory does not have to limit itself to the constraints and distortions of the experimental-laboratory model. It can do far better about reality than it does. We should be willing to look at crowding behavior, helping behavior, or even cognitive dissonance in laboratory settings in ways that would *maximize* the full expression of the complexities of these phenomena—that is, look at them without stripping them of so-called "error factors" by means of experimental controls. This would give an investigator the opportunity to be aware of and take note of the interdisciplinary or interface aspects of the phenomenon, those characteristics of it that would be more relevant to the interests and approaches of other kinds of investigators interested in the phenomenon. It would also allow the researcher to determine just how much the phenomenon could be experimentally defined and managed for purposes of systematic investigation without distorting it significantly.

The fact that investigators carry the experimental-laboratory model into realistic field settings does not necessarily resolve the issue of the imposed restraints on recognizing and responding to the interdisciplinary aspects of a problem. It should be evident then that the experimental-laboratory model, because it dominates our approach to theory and research, shapes our theoretical and methodological orientations so that we tend to be unaware of, insensitive to, and indeed uninterested in those other parts of the elephant experienced by the other blind people touching it. Interdisciplinary thinking in a meaningful sense does not come easy to psychologists because they have been systematically trained to simplify complex phenomena by ignoring or "peeling away" just those events and factors that represent other views and dimensions of the problem.

INDEPENDENT AND DEPENDENT VARIABLES

The difficulty with the experimental-laboratory model for interdisciplinary endeavors goes well beyond the issue that it camouflages so many important relevancies of a phenomenon in its commitment to objective and precise cause and effect relationships. As I have already suggested, this commitment often does havoc with the phenomenon itself by the need to define it and its hypothesized determinants as measurable dependent–independent variables respectively. The fact that these definitions may vary across fields often leads not only to inconsistent findings but to difficulties in making interdisciplinary analyses and integrations. There is no need to document the well-known fact that many firm findings in the laboratory tradition of social, personality, and other fields of psychology were not substantiated by more qualitative findings that emerged about the same phenomena in applied research efforts involved in solving problems in real-life settings. Once again, interdisciplinary efforts are bound to fail when those who come from the university laboratory seek contact with those in applied settings in order to consider problems and issues at the interface between disciplines or problem areas.

There is, however, a more critical problem that emerges from the independent–dependent variable nature of the experimental-laboratory approach. Indeed, it is a problem that one finds in correlational research as well as in the attempt simply to relate properties of people with properties of situations. The experimental-laboratory model, in its emphasis on independent–dependent variables and its constant concern with precise objective measurement (the operationalizing of variables), tends to ignore intervening states and processes—that is, that range of psychological and social factors that mediate and determine relationships between measurable variables. Certainly, sometimes such inner processes (for example, anxiety, stress, and so on) are introduced into theoretical formulations and the research that follows, but, as I suggested earlier, they too become defined by the experimental-laboratory model in operational terms to the extent that the integrity of these processes as phenomena in their own right is also lost.

To a large extent, however, linking or mediating processes tend to be ignored or avoided in experimental-laboratory research. They run counter to the demands of this model and its emphasis on objective and measurable independent and dependent variables. Thus, it is interesting to note that in his review of crowding research, Altman (1978) points out that there are beginning attempts to fill out the intervening psychological and social processes that relate, for example, consistent findings between density of crowding and particular personal and social outcomes. The failure to consider these conceptual linkages between human processes and environmental contexts also serves to reduce the possibilities of interdisciplinary analysis and integration.

The incredible preoccupation with linking up measurable independent and dependent variables, whether in the laboratory or out, leaves us with wide gaps in our understanding of how the individual functions not only as a psychological being, but as a sociocultural one as well. Interdisciplinary articulations are even more difficult between behavioral sciences than they are between fields within psychology itself. For example, between the cognitive characteristics of eco- nomically deprived children that may be related to their home environments and family settings we define as "lower class," there lies a labyrinth of unexplored events and processes representing different levels of analysis that undoubtedly relate the behavior and experiences of these children at the individual level to the properties of the family settings that define their day-to-day existence. On the other hand, the theoretical and research capacity to deal with these events and processes on an interdisciplinary basis, whether at a psychological level or be- tween levels of analysis, requires an approach to problems that puts the phenom- enon on display in a larger number rather than a smaller number of its dimensions and complexities, certainly before it is stripped and redefined to meet the de- mands of empirical operations and systematic measurement. As Agar's chapter in this volume (Chapter 2) notes, ethnography does in fact attempt to deal with human behavior and experience in these terms. It is by no means a simple methodological approach because there are questions as to what aspects of the human real-life events should be considered, as well as how does one go about interpreting the selected aspects of these events.

PROCESS VERSUS CONTENT

The search for general principles of behavior and experience of the person inexorably goes on in psychology. And, as noted earlier, the experimental- laboratory model is both seen and used as the approach par excellence for this purpose, because by definition such principles transcend the complexities and viabilities of people and situations. What this means, of course, is that the concern is primarily with process, specifically with such psychological processes as learning, motivation, emotion, thinking, feeling, and their complex inte- grations in the form of attitudes, values, cognitive structures, attributions, im- pression formations, and so on. Almost by definition, the *content* of human behavior and experience is left out, because both the precision and control requirements of the experimental-laboratory model and the search for general principles make this necessary. Of course, over the last two to three decades, particular motives, emotions, and attitudes have been studied, but essentially the concern was and still is with general principles rather than with the relationships of these specific psychological response systems to given behavioral and social contexts. As indicated earlier, much is left out in the search for precise, quantifiable variables by controlling so-called "error factors"; as we soon see, it is not just the complexities of social situations that are nullified in this "purifying" procedure. Even at the psychological level of analysis involving traditional psychological processes, a great deal of the *content* of these processes is controlled or excluded in the commitment to controlled measurement.

I get to this point in a moment. First, it is important to raise two questions about the efficacy, if not the validity, of the great emphasis on *psychological process* at the expense of psychological content. What must be stressed is that this emphasis is so great that even when content seems to enter into research on complex psychological processes, it is merely a vehicle to study psychological process in the laboratory; to this extent, many dimensions and contextual considerations that relate to the content of a given set of percepts, attitudes, or values are excluded or rendered neutral. One question that can be raised immediately is whether the search for general principles can safely assume, as it clearly does, that content and context have little, if any, influence on process. It may well be that we will require not a few but many principles of psychological process because of the mutual influences of content and context on the one hand and process on the other.

Of course, this view can be and often is countered with the argument that no one doubts the significance of content and context. However, not unlike the physical and natural sciences, insofar as psychological processes are concerned, there are embedded in the complexities and variabilities of human behavior and experience a smaller number of general principles that can be revealed in basic or pure research, omitting the covering and camouflage of particular people, meanings, places, and the like. These complexities, the argument continues, will fall into place once the basic principles are revealed and additional research is undertaken much later on "to get a fix" on just what "constants" are needed to handle the content and contextual complexities of everyday life. The weakness of this entire argument is twofold: First, it is an assumption based on a "faith" involving a rather indiscriminate adulation and emulation of the physical sciences—not to mention that given five decades of such devotion, it has yet to provide any substantive basis for a continuation of this faith; second, it ignores the very compelling possibility that getting at these smaller number of basic principles may require that we begin and stay with these complexities in order to preserve the integrity of the phenomena they characterize, because the principles may directly reflect these complexities. To stay with events as they are for long periods of time—regardless of laboratory considerations—may well at least tell us in time what we ought to study in the laboratory and what we could leave out in order to establish meaningful, precise cause and effect relationships. So much of what has been done and is done now is simply a reflection of the immediate demands of the experimental-laboratory model in conjunction with a range of implicit assumptions about how human psychological processes are organized and function in the person in relation to the person's behavior and experience in the complex contexts of everyday life.

Earlier, I indicated that even at the psychological level and in the study of traditional psychological processes, simple or complex, we omit still other important *content*. Perhaps it would be better to relate this content to activities designated as *human process* as opposed to *psychological process*. The latter, regardless of whether it is emotion, motivation, perception, learning, and so on, really represents a scientific designation of a recognized psychological function that serves the human organism by virtue of the integration of maturational biological capacities and developmental learning experiences. These designations, and the operational or denotative consequences that define them, must be distinguished from the human processes involved—that is, for example, the individual's perceiving or emoting as distinguished from the conceived function of "perception" or "emotion." The fact is that in these human processes, there is a vast *content* that is ignored again and again in the commitment to precise, measurable variables of psychological process. Whatever the process—for example, learning—there is a vast cognitive inner life that is ignored even when a person must commit a brief statement to memory. What does the person say to him- or herself? What words, pictures, or other devices are used? How does the person cope cognitively if something remembered suddenly gets lost?

Going to a more complex level, we have to ask if the questionnaire and attitude statements of our attitude-measuring instruments really match the percepts, ideas, fantasies, words, feelings, and so on, that the person may hold regarding an object (or may not even hold because the "attitude" may seem enduring on rational grounds for the researcher, but might be quite transient for the respondent). The folly involved in ignoring such content because it indeed "defies" the experimental-laboratory model—except if one wants "to peel" or to strip the content of psychological process until its fits the model—is perhaps best illustrated in Asch's early first-impression research, which led to a large number of investigations to test the hypothesis that such impressions were developed in a holistic or integrated fashion (Asch, 1946).

Not only did the "trait-list" methodology ignore content in a social sense completely—that is, what people were forming impressions of what other people for what purposes—but the phenomenal nature and context of the process by which individuals actually form first impressions was also ignored. First-impression formation is a highly complex cognitive process, and the trait-list methodology as a means of studying that process bears very little similarity to it, if any at all. Nor can we ignore the fact that forming first impressions varies in how, when, and where the impression formation takes place and that indeed it may not be one process, but a number of related, though different cognitive processes.

The failure to consider content in the particular sense just described is still another factor that makes interdisciplinary efforts among psychologists, at least those of us in the more or less ''soft'' fields of psychology, difficult. Whether we are interested in the same or different psychological processes or whether some of us are immersed in process and others in the complexities of such process in on-going social situations, the fact is we are cut off from each other. The search for general principles in the stripped-down, contrived human behaviors and experiences employed in the experimental-laboratory approach negates the following critical and very safe assumption for seeking interdisciplinary linkages and integrations: Human events, the behaviors and experiences of people, are complex on-going phenomena that transcend simplistic categories of description and explanation and as a result require analysis from the vantage point of a number of discipline and subdiscipline approaches; however, the objective is always that at various stops along the way in these pursuits, and ultimately, the resulting distinct ''categories of knowledge'' will fit together into a unified and coherent statement of understanding.

THE QUESTION OF TIME

So much research employing the experimental-laboratory model ignores the real and necessary question of time as a dimension in human behavior and experience. Perhaps it can be said that there is no single greater distortion resulting from the task of ''designing the person'' to fit this model. Of course, a concern with psychological processes conceived of as rooted in physiological mechanisms can for certain kinds of research render time as less than an important dimension. But beyond that, whether we are dealing with percepts, feelings, motivations, cognitive structures, attitudes, privacy, or the human being as a complex sociocultural organism, time is a crucial dimension. Indeed, it can be said now that stripping behavior and experience of its content to a large extent eliminates questions of change over time. But, not only does time enter in the fact that people experience and behave toward each other in given situations that begin, go on, and then end, but also basic psychological processes have time and change dimensions in them as well. Yet, for all of the pervasiveness of time as inherent in human existence and, therefore, as a critical dimension for understanding the person as a psychological being, we have only just begun to take it seriously and, clearly, it is not an easy problem to cope with in systematic research. But cope we must.

It should be evident that not unlike content, time also—if relegated into limbo as a dimension of human behavior and experience—cuts off or certainly minimizes interdisciplinary considerations. However, aside from the fact that eliminating the time dimension from many forms of complex behavior and experience minimizes many questions of an interdisciplinary nature, for those researchers who are concerned with human events as they occur in everyday life, the issue of time as a factor in the integrity of these events is clearly critical. But those who talk of process and general principle have little to offer those who are interested in processes and principles that have to do with individual change and the influence of a succession of events as they unfold from one point to the other over a period of time. It is only in the last two decades, with a growth of an interest in gerontology and the move away from the view that basic aspects of human personality are completely and fully established in childhood, that the view that development and change is a continuing process from birth until death has been given serious attention. The dilemma, of course, is that so much of our present-day "knowledge" of the behavior and experience of the person emerges from cross-sectional investigations involving a limited number of variables and is tied to, in many instances, highly contrived situations. There can be little question that one way or another, the ecological orientation of Brunswick (1956) and his focus on probabilistic functionalism will be the next steps for tying together a concern with process here and now and the sampling of that process over a variety of situations through periods of time.

SOME CONCLUDING COMMENTS

I have painted a pretty drastic picture of the pitfalls that confront psychologists interested in interdisciplinary collaboration because of the overuse and misuse of the experimental-laboratory model. Yet, I remind the reader that my purpose was to provide a perspective and not in any way to preclude a concern with the interrelationships between concepts, theory, and data at the interface of various disciplines in psychology. In effect, what has to be said is that being interdisciplinary in thought, analysis, and research—given our present state of knowledge—will not be easy. However, it will be far less difficult and certainly far more fruitful if we come to grips with at least some of the issues that I have raised in the previous discussion. Again, I must point out that I am not indicting the experimental-laboratory model. It is useful and significant as an approach to the study of human behavior and experience, but not when its use transcends the nature of problems and the view that theory and ideas must precede methods.

Perhaps what ought to be said is: Let's not kid ourselves. We have learned very little about cognitive processes, for example, that at the present time is useful in dealing with complex problems in the real world; in turn, our applied efforts in the real world, filled with content and the holistic character of experience, have given us few insights as to basic psychological processes that we can carry back to the laboratory. However, the perspective I have offered can be an optimistic one if, indeed, we are not only aware of the obstacles I have described, but in addition if we engage in a continuing analysis of what we have done, how far we have come, and where we are headed. Furthermore, we must stand ready to break away from the experimental-laboratory model and to worry less about objectivity and control and more about the very nature of the phenomena that we identify as critical and important. For interdisciplinary purposes, psychologists are going to have to learn many things; in my judgment, if can learn these things, then far greater progress in the development of cumulative knowledge will occur. Let me cite just a few of the things we are going to have to learn:

First, we must learn patience, to study a phenomenon over time and merely attempt to learn as much about it in the context in which it naturally occurs. Second, we will have to learn to sample and look at phenomena in a variety of situations and to allow that knowledge to determine what methods will be the best for studying that event close up in order to be able to make more objective and precise statements about it. Third, we are going to have to learn that the goal of general principles of behavior and experience may not be the order of the day for this century or perhaps even the next, and that because of the changing contextual character of the events we call human, we may have to rely more on situational and historical analysis than we ever have before. Fourth, we will also have to learn that theory and definition—even at the simplest level—must take precedent over "technology of strategy and research design." There can be nothing more profitable than an interdisciplinary approach that seeks to establish connotative and denotative relationships between and among concepts developed in different fields or in different problem areas of research. As an environmental psychologist, I can tell you that whether we begin with the concepts of privacy, territoriality, and crowding, or on the other side with cognitive dissonance, attribution theory, or cognitive structures, in every instance, these conceptions can be defined, for example, in terms of and implications for issues and problems that exist in the "other field." We will all have to learn all of these things, because without such changes in our conceptions and approach to human behavior and experience, the goal of cumulative knowledge in psychology will remain as elusive as it has been.

REFERENCES

Altman, I. Crowding: Historical contemporary trends in crowding research. In A. Baum & Y. M. Epstein (Eds.), *Human response to crowding.* Hillsdale, N.J.: Lawrence Erlbaum Associates, 1978.

Asch, S. E. Forming impressions of personality. *Journal of Abnormal and Social Psychology,* 1946, *41,* 258–290.

Berscheid, E., Christensen, A., Harvey, J., Huston, T., Kelley, H., Levinger, G., McClintock, E., Peplau, A., & Peterson, D. *The psychology of close relationships.* Book in preparation, 1980.

Brunswik, E. Perception and the representative design of psychological experiments. Berkeley: University of California Press, 1956.

Gergen, K. J. Social psychology as history. *Journal of Personality and Social Psychology,* 1973, *26,* 309–320.

Gibbs, J. C. The meaning of ecologically oriented inquiry in contemporary psychology. *American Psychologist,* 1979, *34,* 127–140.

Harvey, J. H., & Weary, G. The integration of social and clinical psychology training programs. *Personality and Social Psychology Bulletin*, 1979.

Petrinovich, L. Probabilistic functionalism: A conception of research method. *American Psychologist,* 1979, *34,* 373–390.

Proshansky, H. M. Theoretical issues in environmental psychology. *Representative Research in Social Psychology,* 1973, *4,* 93–108.

Proshansky, H. M. Environmental psychology in the real world. *American Psychologist,* 1976, *31,* 303–310.

2 Ethnography as an Interdisciplinary Campground

Michael H. Agar
University of Houston

In his recent book, Ulric Neisser (1976) calls for an understanding of cognition "as it occurs in the ordinary environment and in the context of natural purposeful activity [p. 7]." Harre and Secord, writing in social psychology (1972), argue that "at the heart of the explanation of social behavior is the identification of the meanings that underlie it [p. 9]." Nor is this "new" approach restricted to psychology. In sociology, for example, Glaser and Strauss (1967) argue that *verification* of theory has been stressed at the expense of its *generation,* grounded in the experience of the people about whom we theorize. Add to this the recent surge of interest in ethnography apparent in several different government agencies dealing with areas of life as diverse as work, education, and substance use.

At the same time, many anthropologists plea, with good reason, for a more systematic approach to ethnographic research. Their plea often involves more clearly stated hypothses, better operationalization of variables, and more attention to sampling. But in the rush to scientific control, some of the very characteristics of ethnography that now attract nonanthropologists are becoming endangered species. Some of this abandonment is fueled by the anthropological effort to move into jobs in the "real world." Many argue that real-world power spots are covered by the classic research approaches of the hypothesis testers, so if one wants to interact with that world, that is the way research had better be done.

At its best, such changes represent methodological convergence formed from such variously phrased oppositions as hypothesis testing versus ethnography, deductive versus inductive, quantitative versus qualitative, or contextual versus experimental. At its most destructive, the changes represent the last puff of social science smoke as the choices become an alienation so complete or an involvement so total that social science becomes an empty set.

For the moment, I want to take the optimistic view. I would like to take an approach to ethnography that might be appropriate for this conference. As I understand it, the purpose here is to allow psychologists of several different persuasions to sit together and work on the construction of a common framework within which they can comfortably and productively talk. I want to present ethnography as an empirical campground—a place where a variety of different theoretical/methodological mixtures can be integrated, evaluated, modified, abandoned, or grown.

Before making that argument, though, I need to discuss the nature of ethnography. This is not a simple task. In anthropology, there is a tradition of nontraining in ethnographic field work. There is a piece of folklore at Berkeley that goes something like this: A graduate student, at the end of her first year. was given a few hundred dollars and was told to go and study an Indian tribe. No one bothered telling her how to get there or what to do when she arrived. She nervously approached the door of Kroeber himself—one of the founders of American anthropology. Kroeber was typing (naturally) and continued doing so for a few seconds after her knock. She walked in and asked, with quavering voice, what she should do. Did Kroeber have any advice to offer before she embarked on her field trip? "Well," he advised professorially, "I suggest you buy a notebook and a pencil."

It does not matter whether the story is true or false. Like folklore often does, this story tells you something interesting about the group that generated it. In anthroplogy, traditionally, ethnography was not something one could train people for. Armed with the standard litany of participant observation, informal interviews, and field notes, one took the plunge, hopefully swam rather than sank, and then exchanged knowing glances with other initiates after the degree was granted.

In many ways, this prejudice is not unfounded. Ethnography is an experientially rich social science stressing the creative synthesis of widely divergent materials. In fact, a fully explicit ethnography is probably an impossibility. But the lack of specific discussions on ethnography as a process sometimes leads newcomers to assume that it is simple. Ethnography often gets tossed around in a cavalier fashion by outsiders. In the absence of detailed treatments of the process, one can hardly blame them. Besides, like most things in life, ethnography is simple to do—badly. I was recently approached by a friend of mine—a testing-oriented psychologist—to help him design an "ethnographic component" in a follow-up study. That component, he announced, was represented by a one-hour open-ended interview. The degree to which you see that statement as absurd is a function of your appreciation of the complexities of ethnographic research.

There is not time here to sketch the process in its entirety. There are a variety of recent treatments in both sociology and anthropology, and some first-person accounts have been written that give something of the feel of field work. (See, for example, Adams & Preiss, 1969; Agar, 1980; Bogdan & Taylor, 1975; McCall & Simmons, 1969; Spradley, 1979. Sample personal accounts are Powdermaker, 1966 and Wax, 1971.) What I hope to do here is give some sense of the core of an ethnographic orientation—not that all ethnographers would agree with it by any means. To begin to get a sense of this core, I would like to examine ethnography first by contrast, and then by example. Following that, ethnography as a theoretical campground can be discussed.

To define ethnography by contrast, it is instructive to examine conflict between ethnographers and nonethnographers. Conflict situations are useful because principles that usually lie implicitly in the background are brought to the surface. Let me give a couple of examples of articles containing critiques of survey studies by ethnographers.

The first example is taken from an article by Leach (1967). Leach is a British social anthropologist who worked in Sri Lanka, and his article criticizes a survey done in that country focusing on issues of land tenure. As an example of a specific criticism, the survey researchers isolated the basic unit of study as the "household," defined as those who eat from the same cooking pot.

But Leach notes that a knowledge of other aspects of village life leads to ambiguities in this apparently straightforward operational definition. First, Sinhalese girls marry rather young, and at the time of marriage, they receive their own cooking pot to prepare their husbands' meals. Leach also points out that inheritance tends to occur late in life. Now, argues Leach, imagine a situation where three married sons live with their parents. By the survey definition, this counts as three landless households and one landed household. In contrast, Leach would characterize it as three heirs to still-living parents.

Another criticism relates to the discussion of land. Land was characterized as high or low yield, but the researchers did not discuss the different kinds of land in Sinhalese villages. One kind, which Leach calls "traditional" lands, was measured using a traditional rule of thumb that, by Leach's estimate based on his field work, overestimated acreage by 50%. The other kind, called "acre" lands, was obtained from the crown after acreage was measured by standard survey techniques. The result is that traditional lands always look like lower yield lands, because their acreage is overestimated by one-half. When you add that most of the "acre" lands were purchased by wealthier villagers, you get results that suggest that wealthy landowners have all the high-yield land.

Leach makes other criticisms as well. It is worth digressing for a moment to point out that, in addition to serving as a useful case study in ethnographic criticism, the article also demonstrates the political consequences of methodological debate. If Leach is right, then the land situation in Sri Lanka is not nearly as bad as the survey shows. If Leach is wrong, then he is defusing an important study that shows a dramatic need for land reform. The different political implications of the argument make its resolution something more than a purely academic issue.

At any rate, before moving into a more general discussion of ethnography, let me offer a second example. An anthropologist named Kobben (1967) discussed problems in taking a census. Often census taking is considered a useful, nonthreatening thing to do in the early days of ethnographic field work. Kobben did his census, but later found out that it was distorted for a number of reasons.

First, people felt that large families aroused jealousy in others, so representatives of large families tended to deflate family size. In addition, mothers would underreport deceased children, because of fears of possible connections with witchcraft. Further, as Kobben put it, the people had "little sense of exactness." The anthropologist was asking for a kind of precision that was not called for in the group's daily life. And finally, the people joked about how difficult they were to count. The men were mobile, often having more than one family in one village.

Leach's and Kobben's articles are but two examples of a type of argument that I have encountered so frequently that I have come to think of it in its canonical form as "the ethnographic critique." It runs something like this: You (the hypothesis tester) have operationalized variable X using some kind of measurement procedure. Yet, your measurement X makes several assumptions about the perception and intent of the subject or respondent. I, the ethnographer, show that your assumptions are not in fact necessarily accurate when the same measurement is considered from the subject/respondent's point of view. Therefore, your analysis of aggregate data does not necessarily represent what you in fact think it does.

The key to the critique is in the phrase "from the subject/respondent's point of view." To use a currently fashionable term, the emphasis is on the *interpretation* of the world by members of the group under study. (For samples of recent uses of an interpretive focus, see Geertz, 1973; Gumperz, 1979; and Tyler, 1979.) To restate the ethnographic critique in terms of interpretation, an hypothesis tester brings to his research an interpretation that defines a small slice of behavior as significant. He also assumes something about the interpretation by subjects/respondents. The ethnographic critique shows that, either because of the way the slice was taken from the flow of life of subjects/respondents, or because of the transformation from one interpretation to another, or because of both, the abstracted slice does not consistently mean what the hypothesis tester thinks it does.

Let me illustrate this emphasis on interpretation by an example. In 1965, I worked in a small village in South India. Early in the work, I was preparing to leave to walk to a village some three miles away. The cook prepared a lunch for me, consisting of flat bread made from sorghum flour and some spinach. Just before he wrapped it in a cloth for me to carry, he placed a small lump of charcoal on top.

Now, if someone came up and asked me what happened, I would have to say something like, "hell if I know?" My sense of the charcoal would be that it might have something to do with filtering, flavoring, or cooking. I would have trouble constructing an interpretation of what had just occurred. But later, when I knew enough of the language, I would learn that the action of the cook made perfect sense.

I was travelling at midday, a time when spirits are particularly active. People travelling alone are particularly vulnerable to attack, especially when they are carrying food. However, charcoal is a spirit repellent, so the cook was protecting me before I left on the journey. What a rich interpretation of the same stream of behavior that I witnessed, one that any child in the village could have made.

Let me cite another example. In addition to my early work in South India, I have more recently worked with an exotic American tribe called "junkies." In 1974, I was working in New York on the use of methadone in the streets. Assume I am standing outside a methadone clinic, and a person walks in. Someone asks me what is going on. I might say, "Well, that guy is probably a patient in the program. He'll take his methadone and maybe stay awhile to visit a counselor or participate in a therapy group." The same person now turns to a junkie standing next to me, and asks the same question. The answer is: "He's going to cop."

My interpretation represents the "mainstream" view of methadone clinics. The junkie's much more succinct statement interprets the same behavior from a street point of view. "Cop" is a term junkies use specifically for the purchase of heroin from a dealer, and more generally in the sense of "get" or "obtain." By shifting to this interpretation, the "clinic" becomes the "dealer," the "medication" becomes the "dope," and what one goes through to get the dope becomes "copping." The differences in interpretation are made all the more subtle by the fact that the junke and I, to some extent, share the same language and are members of the same society.

Ethnography contains somewhere in its core the idea of learning new ways of interpretation. If this is so, then mamy of the features of field work follow from it. Frequent metaphors for the ethnographic role, for example, are those of "student" and "child." Both are subordinate learning rules whose occupants are expected to make mistakes and ask many questions. They are also expected to look to established group members for instruction and evaluation of their performance.

Such learning also implies prolonged, direct contact with group members, suggesting the importance of rapport and the complexity of the relationships established. It also implies contact in the natural context of group members, both because of the prolonged relationships and because of the need to participate in and observe the events being interpreted. Further, whatever else interpretation involves, it represents a complex web of interconnected ideas about the world that lead to what anthropologists call a "holistic" perspective. As an ethnographer learns, it also leads to the importance of constant comparison, as she continually refines her learning to find out whether certain interpretations cross people, situations, groups, communities, or cultures.

The emphasis on interpretation also helps understand the methodological problems. With the importance of learning and rapport, traditional sampling designs become difficult if not impossible to apply. In the beginning the ethnographer does not know what the relevant social types and their distribution are, nor does he know how to ask the right people the right questions in the right way. In the classic sense of the term, an ethnographer is often hypothesis free, since he doesn't yet know what the significant aspects of persons and situations are. If he thinks he does, he is not yet certain of how his notions relate, if at all, to the things people actually say or do. Early ethnographic work is not a place for the methodologically compulsive.

Yet, the alternative paradigm from hypothesis testing is not the appropriate way to approach the task of learning another way to interpret the world. Imagine taking a slice of life, or at least that part you attend to, and trying to imagine all the ways it might be interpreted, with a good chance that you cannot imagine the correct ways because they are outside your experience. You have to design some kind of experimental paradigm to eliminate all possibilities but one. No one would argue that such an approach was appropriate for the learning of another way to interpret the world, yet often it is seen as the only alternative to the fuzziness of traditional ethnography.

This is not the time or the place to discuss attempts to develop more systematic ethnographic methods. Let me just say that two basic strategies are involved. In the first, one tries to develop ways to more systematically document the ethnographic experience. In the second, one takes focal ethnographic conclusions and converts them into hypotheses for further testing. The problem is to maintain the breadth inherent in the idea of trying to comprehend how some group of people interpret reality, while at the same time focusing specifically enough so that it becomes humanly possible to treat the experiential base of an ethnographic conclusion in some publicly falsifiable manner. It is obviously no simple task.

For now, though, I want to return to ethnography as an attempt to learn another interpretive framework. "Interpretive framework" conceals a host of unresolved issues. The ethnographer is a translator writ large. Although she may do other things, the core of her work rests on the acquisition of an ability to interpret events in one of the possible ways that group members do. She tests her ability by using the group's language as metalanguage. Something occurs, and by her comments and the reactions of group members, or by her expectations of what group members comments might be, she decides she does or does not understand group interpretations.

Perhaps the best metaphor to describe this ability is the linguistic notion of paraphrase, though extended beyond its usual use. The ethnographer aspires to an ability to take in a range of verbal and non-verbal data from the stream of life and decode it. He then encodes the meaning into a string of statements, or metastatements, that group members accept as a possible account of what is going on.

But how does an ethnographer describe this ability to give interpretations. How do I explain to an outsider, for example, the charcoal incident in the South Indian village? In terms of the standard list of ethnographic categories, just this one example involved ideas about religion, economics, social relations, time, space, and food. Further, the interpretation must also be linked to other situations as well. Spirits also frequently attack new wives and migrant workers temporarily resident in the city. But other spirits speak through the village "god-men" as a direct line to the supernatural forces that control the world. Further, spirits are part of a system of knowledge that connects up with other kinds of supernatural entities, with ideas about the origin of the world and the group, and with some of the ceremonies that are conducted on religious holidays.

So, the first problem in interpretation is that the description must include the interrelated bundle of knowledge that one needs to comment on a particular event. The second problem is that some of that bundle will be event specific and some of it will be knowledge that applies to the interpretation of other events as well. The knowledge necessary to interpret events, in other words, must be presented both semantically and episodically, together with the procedures used by the ethnographer to interrelate the two.

A second problem in interpretation is that different interpretations might be given for the same event. This is really at least three problems. First, there may be systematic differences in how people interpret things. Landed villagers may talk about two men working in a field differently from landless villagers, for example. That kind of variability is to be expected. Second, there will be aspects of interpretation that an ethnographer learn from direct participation in events. He may notice patterns that no group member articulates, or that they specifically deny, especially when he begins looking for common threads in the interpretation of different events. That, too, is a normal part of ethnographic work.

But a third variation presents more problems, assuming for a moment that everyone in a group interprets using similar kinds of knowledge. What would constitute a minimal interpretation? What kinds of things would be the first to be mentioned in a more elaborate interpretation? What sort of ordering might there be to guide the production of interpretations? And, at the other end, when does an interpretation become overdone? What are the outer limits? An interpretation of an event in principle opens onto infinity—there is something that one can always add to an account one is giving. Group members, of course, would get impatient listening to an infinite interpretation. When does the amount of metatalk move from enough to too much?

Just to speculate for a moment, there is much work in psychology, linguistics, and anthropology to suggest that a minimal kind of interpretation would be to name the event of which the observed behavior is a part. "What's he doing?" comes the question. "Oh, he's writing a paper." Such an exchange might help explain to the Dean why staring out a window is not the unproductive activity he originally thought it was.

Perhaps the name is not enough, and more information needs to be given to interpret the observed behavior. How much is given—by one informant to another, by an informant to an ethnographer, or by an ethnographer to the readers of a report? The answer is, obviously, "it depends," but the specification of how and on what is far from clear. Interest in this problem perhaps helps explain the recent rediscovery of hermeneutics in anthropology.

Another important kind of interpretation, given that the event is known, might be a person's intent: "She's writing a paper to get tenure." "He's writing a paper because of unresolved Oepidal rivalry." "She's writing a paper because she loves to write anything." Obviously, intent is itself a complicated animal that comes in several species, but it is probably the kind of information that often occurs in interpretation.

Or, perhaps interpretation by intent has nothing to do with the event in group members' eyes. Perhaps the behavior is interpreted by reference to external rather than internal cause. Ethnographers' "whys" are often answered, for example, with what we might call interpretation from tradition—"That's just the way we do things." Or, returning to the South Indian spirits for another example, one may do things because a spirit has possessed him and he is no longer in control.

All of these examples are just quick introductions to a few of the problems that ethnographers face in working out a language for ethnographic work. It is a challenge, perhaps an impossible one, just because it must model what it is people think and do in the flow of life, including their contact with an ethnographer as a special case, such that the model suggests interpretations that make sense to them of what group members are about. It must also allow for multiple interpretations, and must explain why the different possibilities exist. It must show the relationships, if they exist, across the different interpretations of different events that make up life for the group. Further, because this connecting up will often involve statements that ethnographers infer rather than elicit, the language must produce statements that can be evaluated by a skeptical outsider. And finally, if all that were not difficult enough, it should do all this in a way that enables a specific group to be described, but also compared to ethnographic reports of other groups.

Where is such a language to come from—a language that allows the ethnographer to talk about the person, the situation, the interaction, and the natural surround in which it all occurs; a language that represents a variety of ways to assign meaning to the flow of life, some part of which will be useful in the characterization of a particular group; a language that will not only enable the ethnographer to do and report interpretations, but will suggest other possibilities that group members have never articulated.

Keeping this question in mind, consider the state of social science theory. The first strategy of theory development is simplification. A few slices of life are circled and defined as significant by the social scientist. Then, more often than not, some kind of behavior considered to be representative of the pieces in the flow of life is obtained from people in what for them is usually an artificial situation defined for the convenience and control of the social scientist. The relation of the isolated piece to the piece in situ, and the relation of the piece in situ to all the other things that are going on, are usually left as bothersome but untreated problems.

It is just this casual handling of the stuff of everyday life that inspires the ethnographic critique discussed earlier. And, it is in the crack between these two positions that I think an ethnographic language, as I have characterized it here, can play a mediating role. I am interested in ethnography for a variety of reasons. But one of them is that I think ethnographic work is an ideal ground for the evaluation, modification, and integration of different social-science traditions.

The general algorithm for this process would run something like the following: First, obtain an ethnographic grounding in the world of some group. Second, certain cross-situational, cross-personal aspects are singled out, with a knowledge of what the cuts mean and what has been left behind in the abstracting out. Third, relevant social-science theory is examined and evaluated as a potential resource for an ethnographic language to talk about these aspects. Fourth, returning to the leftover material, another aspect is isolated, and steps two and three are repeated. Fifth, having formed theoretically interesting ways to talk about the two aspects, figure out how those two ways of talking can be integrated into the overall language. Then start again at step two, gradually enriching the ethnographic language while at the same time evaluating, modifying, and perhaps abandoning the social-science traditions that were the original source.

Let me summarize the argument another way. I am using ethnographic language to represent the idea of a theory about how to talk about what the flow of life means to people. I like the term "ethnographic language" better than "ethnographic theory," because for me "language" better captures the idea of a multitude of concepts of a variety of types together with the rules that interlink them. A given social-science tradition then becomes a potential conrtibutor to the development of this language. The first question is whether or not it helps make sense out of the world of some group. A "no" here is not necessarily devastating, because as noted earlier not all parts of the language will be relevant to the discussion of all groups. However, at some point, it should be useful in discussing some subset of all the human groups on the planet.

The next question then becomes, what does it leave behind? The ethnographic language must expand to include them as well. At this point, other traditions might be drawn on. By the way, this kind of process also helps explain many of the arguments one hears on an interdisciplinary grant-review panel. In comes a hypothetical grant on the study of the relationship between drugs and crime. What about social class? says a sociologist. Do you know if a member of a criminal subculture will talk about crime the way the instrument suggests? says an anthroplogist. Don't you need to consider change in supply and demand over time to understand the responses? says an economist. Doesn't it matter whether a respondent attributes criminal activity to drug use or not? says a psychologist. If a person is drug free during an interview, does it mean anything compared to that person's state when under the influence? says a psychopharamacologist. And so it goes. Such arguments over proposals are the beginnings of the kind of process I am advocating here. The critics are all taking an area of experience that their tradition isolates as significant and they are asking why they have been left behind. Most often, though, such arguments occur in the spirit of academic adversity rather than ethnographic synthesis.

A final way of putting the argument might be to use the metaphor of Fourier analysis. I am not a mathematician, but the rough sense of Fourier analysis I learned is the decomposition of a complex wave into constituent regular wave patterns cooccurring over time. If for a moment you picture the flow of daily life as a complex irregular wave, then the development of an ethnographic language out of different social-science traditions is an attempt to specify the different regular waves and show their interactions produce the complex phenomenon we observed.

There are many examples that could be used to illustrate parts of the process, going back at least as far as Malinowski's critique of Freud or Mead's work on sex roles. For now, though, let us return to the case of the charcoal. First, we have the problem of understanding the interpretation. There are a variety of recent attempts to talk about the organization of the knowledge brought to the situation—attempts that go by such code words as frames, schema, scripts, and plans. In the case of the charcoal, action occurs because the enabling conditions are represented by considerations of time, space, and social isolation—spirit attacks occur more frequently at midday in open settings to lone people. The presence of food is a fact that increases the likelihood even further. Even though several external causes of spirit possession are present, no one must of necessity blindly submit to fate. A concerned person can take preventative measures, drawing on the knowledge that a lump of charcoal will repulse a spirit that might wander near.

The ethnographer was an idiot who did not know what dangers were present. The cook, knowing the situation, took the preventative action for him. Why? Was it because of a wish to protect someone he liked? Was it simple protection of a source of income? Or, because ethnographers draw crowds because of their continual bizarre behavior, was it because the cook did not want his fellow villagers to think he was negligent in protecting his employer? And, would he have done the same thing even if no one had been around? This question becomes more complicated when you consider that the cook–employer relation is much more than an economic one. To oversimplify for the present purposes, the relation is much more paternalistic, involving social and ritual obligations, personal loyalties, and so on.

Then, as we learn more and examine a range of spirit-related events, we begin to worry about explaining the interpretations. The key theme in the cases of spirit attack is the enabling condition of social isolation from the home village. Other cases include the new bride who had just moved to her husband's village and the worker temporarily resident in a distant city to earn some cash. This becomes even more interesting when we notice that if the spirit is successful in possessing the person, then that person returns to the village—his or her home territory— and, surrounded by neighbors and kin, receives folk cures, administered until the spirit is exorcised, under the supervision of a "god–man."

We learn that a variety of interpretations of spirit-related events involve social isolation. We now look for that theme in interpretations of other nonspirit related situations and find them there as well. There is the sad case, for example, of the old man whose elder brothers are dead. He had no sons and his daughters are in other villages with their husbands' families. Though he frequently visits his daughters, he likes to stay in his own village, but he is sad and pitied by the others. Again, the theme in interpreting his situation is the vulnerability of the social isolate—in this case isolated from his kin group.

Back another step, and we begin to think of the importance of this thread of social isolation in the interpretive schema of the villagers. Spirits are one of several cultural forms that strengthen the tie between an individual and the group by demonstrating the consequences of a lack of such ties. We now arrive at one of the great issues of social science—the relationship of the individual to society and culture. And we are now led to ask some interesting comparative questions, within the village, within the region, and among the variety of groups on the planet. In what kinds of groups, under what kinds of conditions is social isolation defined as a state of high personal vulnerability to danger? In what kinds of circumstances is it defined as a positive state, as in the vision quest of some traditional North American Indian tribes? In what kinds of situations is it a mixed blessing, as in the case of an urban junkie, who hustling alone gets to keep all he or she gets, though a single person cannot do certain lucrative hustles that require more than one person to successfully accomplish them?

We have come a long way from the charcoal. And only a few of the social-science traditions relevant to the ethnographic description of this small event have been brought in. Further, we have not even begun to play the reflexitivity game, wondering what these same traditions suggest about the ethnographer as well. For example, would an ethnographer who brought his or her own personal anxieties about social isolation into the field tend to notice that common interpretive thread more readily than one who was a loner? Would an ethnographer who grew up under continual threats of attacks by the devil understand the folk interpretations in the same way as one whose behavior was controlled by parental criticisms of personal failings?

But even in this limited example, I think the point has been made. Evaluation of theoretical differences usually occurs in the astral plane, in isolation from the stuff of everyday life. Yet a social-science tradition, at some point, should have something to contribute to our understanding of just that stuff, or at least part of it. We can then ask if the tradition helps at all. If it does, we can ask what else is going on that needs understanding. The uphill abstracting run is currently the most important in social science. At some point, we need to run downhill to see if what we think we have learned makes any sense in terms of the flow of everyday life.

To do so adequately requires an ethnographic orientation by a person conversant in a host of social-science traditions. That is an intimidating role to aspire to, given the information explosion. But, theory and the world must eventually meet in the social sciences. More often than not, the meeting is regulated by the social scientist in carefully controlled ways. But, if we aspire to a comprehensive understanding of the human situation, an exclusive reliance on such meetings is too sterile. In ethnography, multiple theories and multiple sources of data intermingle in a sort of intimate, multidimensional dialectic. As in the case of most intimacies, the results may be love, hate, or a mix of the two, but seldom will one leave feeling sterile.

ACKNOWLEDGMENTS

Support from NIDA Career Award K02 DA00055 is gratefully acknowledged. Helpful comments were provided by S. Scribner and A. Colson.

REFERENCES

Adams, R., & Preiss, J. J. (Eds.). *Human organization research*. Homewood, Ill.: Dorsey, 1960.
Agar, M. *The professional stranger*. New York: Academic Press, 1980.
Bogdan, R., & Taylor, S. J. *Introduction to qualitative research methods*. New York: Wiley, 1975.
Geertz, C. *The interpretation of cultures*. New York: Basic Books, 1973.
Glaser, B. G., & Strauss, A. L. *The discovery of grounded theory*. Chicago: Aldine, 1967.
Gumperz, J. J. Sociocultural knowledge in conversational inference. In 28th Annual Round Table Monograph Series on Language and Linguistics, 1979.
Harre, H., & Secord, P. F. *The explanation of social behavior*. Totowa, N.J.: Littlefield Adams, 1972.
Kobben, A. J. F. Participation and quantification. In D. G. Jongmans & P. C. W. Gutkind (Eds.), *Anthropologists in the field*. New York: Humanities Press, 1967.
Leach, E. R. An anthropologist's reflections on a social survey. In D. G. Jongmans & D. C. W. Gutkind (Eds.), *Anthropologists in the field*. New York: Humanities Press, 1967.

McCall, G. J., & Simmons, J. L. (Eds.). *Issues in participant observation*. Reading, Mass.: Addison-Wesley, 1969.

Neisser, U. *Cognition and reality*. San Francisco: Freeman, 1976.

Powdermaker, H. *Stranger and friend*. New York: Norton, 1966.

Tyler, S. R. *The said and the unsaid*. New York: Academic Press, 1979.

Spradley, J. *The ethnographic interview*. New York: Holt, Rinehart, & Winston, 1979.

Wax, R. *Doing fieldwork*. Chicago: University of Chicago, 1971.

3 Interaction of Language Use with Ethnography and Cognition[1]

Roy Freedle
Educational Testing Service
Princeton, N.J.

There will be four parts to this chapter. The first part attempts to describe the cognitive necessity of reducing complex experience into oversimplified categories. The results of this simplification process—cultural and perceptual schemata—are some of the cognitive sources of communication failure that occur, especially between members of bilingual-bicultural communities and monolingual-monocultural communities.

The second section of this paper will outline how cultures differ in their proxemic and kinesic behaviors; the ethnographic differences in these learned behaviors in interaction with the cognitive schemata already presented together form the basis for explaining many communication failures. The third section of this chapter will present a mathematical model along with data illustrating the interaction of differences in ethnographic use of English and Spanish in three bilingual populations and the effects these differences have in fitting a cognitive decision model to word association data. Finally, a mathematical decision theory is used to explore a richer descriptive model of the types of miscommunications described in the early sections of this chapter. Thus this paper first lays out a list of axiomatic constraints on cognitive behavior, shows how cultures differ in these constraints, and then introduces a methodology to more adequately track and model the rich nature of these schematic interactions between language and its social-cognitive realization.

The first section is almost a list of self-evident axioms. Because they are so basic, you may find reading them tedious. I ask for your indulgence because it is

[1]An earlier version of this paper was presented as part of an invited address at the American Psychological Association meetings, Aug.–Sept., 1979, held in New York City. Portions of this work were funded by a grant from NIE.

from these simple "facts" that we will be able to understand why members within an ethnographic community so often succeed in communicating, while members across different communities so often fail in communicating.

THE COGNITIVE BASIS OF SCHEMATA

The general assertions that follow are meant to apply to many aspects of behavior. After presenting these, we shall further argue that these constraints apply to language behavior in particular; we need this connection because language serves as a rich source for demonstrating the existence of these schemata.

The first self-evident fact is the following. It is impossible for our brains to keep track of all the nuances that take place in the environment. We psychologists have found (e.g., Miller, 1956) that we can handle a small amount of information thereby implying that we can make only a few decisions per unit time. How then do we manage to survive in this complex world? Part of the answer is, we do it by oversimplifying the world: We schematize it. Why does this work? It seems to work because the world is redundant and hence somewhat predictable; therefore these schematizations very often lead to correct and workable interactions with the environment. The only decision we typically have to make is which schema appears to be in operation at any one time. When we find the apparently correct one that fits the current situation, all we then must do is follow out the familiar steps of the schema in an almost automatic way. This greatly reduces the new decisions that have to be made at any one time. Furthermore, with a great deal of experience, we often decide that many of the nuances in the environment are not important for every task we perform. This simplifies some of the complexity still more. Also, we humans construct highly redundant sociocultural environments, probably in order to make the world even more predictable and less threatening. Our social structures and habitats are certainly highly predictable given that one has grown up within a particular culture and has experienced the natural groupings, values, and norms that make the community function smoothly. Such social organizations in all their redundancy is here interpreted to be a *consequence* of our limited processing capabilities. Cultural norms are schemata that are invented to help overcome cognitive overload.

Up to now I have suggested our human limitations and how this leads to schema formation. But we have strengths, too, which have import for schema functioning. In particular, with a great deal of practice, we are able to convert very complex tasks that originally required hundreds of decisions into virtually *automatic* tasks (e.g., piano playing a well-rehearsed piece is a virtually automatic activity). Paul Fitts (1964) was an early explorer in this realm. He found that learning the early phases of complex tasks greatly depended upon cognitive abilities, but later phases of these complex tasks were almost totally dominated by variance unique to the task itself (i.e., later task scores were uncorrelated with the cognitive test scores). Thus these complex tasks in their late phases were learned holistically and functioned as automatic gestalts. This is another way of saying that new schemata (new gestalts) can be formed no matter how complex the whole, and these schemata can be selected for their general usefulness within a particular cultural community. Thus even though we are cognitively quite limited in our computational powers for novel experiences, nevertheless, given a redundant cultural setting and given lots of time, we can build up an arsenal of complex schemata for handling all the useful functions for all the significant settings that a culture typically experiences. The rub in all this, is that cultures differ in what they consider useful, hence complex schemata can differ across cultural groups. As we shall discover later, these differences in schemata, especially those used in communication processes, will be the source of many miscommunications.

The general conclusion you are invited to draw at this point, is that oversimplification of the environment is inevitable; our finite capacities demand the construction of cognitive schemata that serve to bypass information overload. And, even though a large number of complex schemata can be learned and used in an almost automatic way, still error is inevitable, even within a community, because schematizations are necessarily incomplete representations of the environment.

A second general conclusion you are invited to make is that when the environment changes rapidly, as it certainly does in industrialized societies, our ability to make decisions is even more unstable. First there is less time to make decisions given a less redundant (i.e., changing) environment. Second we are no longer sure what decision should be made, because the changing environment calls into question the cultural values of any one community—it especially calls into question values that were the result of a prolonged and fairly steady-state culture associated with agriculturally based societies. Because we are no longer sure what decisions should be made, or find it difficult to define what the problem is, this too further undermines our weak capacity to make decisions. Our strengths in forming new complex and automated schemata are also interfered with. We are not sure which schemata to practice because our value system is no longer certain. Without practice and without the cultural motivation to internalize these complex routines, we become generally less skilled in coping with the ever-changing environment. This leads clearly to a vicious circle of ineptitude feeding upon ineptitude.

Some Comments on Language Schemata and Communicative Schemata

As I already suggested, the facts about behavior in general can also be applied to language in particular. Let me quickly cover these points. It is impossible to represent with any language all the nuances that can potentially be noted. Language is, in this sense, necessarily incomplete and ambiguous. We tend not to notice the ambiguity of language for as long as we operate within the well-rehearsed norms of a particular language community. That is, by virtue of being in a language community for many years, a large repertoire of complex linguistic and paralinguistic schemata can be learned, and can come to function in an almost automatic way. These linguistic and paralinguistic norms (intonation cues, eye-gaze patterns, junctures for discourse groupings, etc.) are further smoothly merged with social conventions and values that must be honored in communication within a community. The notion of communicative competence (Gumperz & Hymes, 1972) is applicable here. Because communities differ in how sociolinguistic competence is realized in speech, and because language is necessarily an incomplete representation of reality, the inevitable consequence is that error in communication is bound to occur. Hence miscommunications across cultures should be more prevalent than within cultures. Let's consider some of these examples.

Communication Breakdown: The Stresses of Cultures in Contact.   One might naively suppose that serious breakdown in communication occurs only when complicated topics are being discussed. The communications of interest here, though, are typically not of that type. In fact, the failures in communication especially between people who come from different cultural backgrounds (but all of whom know English) often involve some of the most mundane of topics: asking a question, trying to provide helpful information, and the like. It is also worth noting that the individuals who are involved in the communication failure are often puzzled and cannot explain what went wrong. This signals the largely automatic processes by which communication is effected. As we shall see, researchers have isolated some of the largely unconscious and subtle cues by which full-fledged language community members carry out their largely successful communications. Hence, when participants from outside this knowledge system bring a slightly different pattern of subconscious cues to bear for purposes of language comprehension, mismatches occur more frequently. The outcome of these mismatches, unfortunately, can often be unpleasant shouting, anger, wild accusations, and so on. Mutual avoidance is also a likely outcome.

Some Simple Examples of Miscommunication.   An Indian bus driver newly arrived on the job in London wishes to be polite and efficient. His customer steps into the bus. He says, ''Exact change, please.'' The customer apparently didn't hear and asks for a repetition. The driver responds with, ''Exact change [pause], PLEASE.'' The traditional British customer takes offense for what is regarded as an attempt to act superior or to be cheeky, even though there is nothing in the situation that would make such an interpretation plausible. In reserved British culture, emphasis is avoided unless especially necessary. In the Indian language, the emphasis that is here achieved by pausing and giving emphasis to the word ''please'' is customary in achieving clarification. A mismatch has occurred. The driver's job is now in jeopardy. Notice that the outcome of the mismatch, while not prescribed, is typically negative as it was above. This appears to be especially so when two strangers from different cultural backgrounds are involved. (The example is from Gumperz, 1977.)

Another example of interest comes also from Gumperz (1978). It involves an error in interpreting a "flat" intonation pattern used in pronouncing the word *gravy,* again with negative consequences. An Indian woman has been hired to serve gravy in a cafeteria line serving British workmen. The British worker probably expects some pleasant chit-chat possibly conveyed through the use of a dramatic intonation of words. The worker moves in place and approaches the woman serving gravy. Decorum in Indian society dictates that a woman remain reserved or "distant" in interacting with strangers. To accomplish conflicting demands, she merely inquires about whether the workman wishes gravy by uttering a flatly intoned "gravy." However, this puzzles the workman, who cannot decipher the intonation pattern according to the language norms of his community. He decides that she is trying to insult him. Again, a mismatch in communication patterns has led to a negative outcome although other options could have been invoked to avoid a confrontation.

Nix and Schwarz (1979) have presented some interesting examples of how individuals from the black subculture in New York City differ from white mainstream individuals in their interpretation of simple passages. They presented the following passage to individually tested black students in their New York classrooms. (Each student had to complete the passage by choosing which word made the most sense to him or her at the end of the passage: "Sally loved animals. She brought home every stray animal that she could find, no matter what it looked like. Her mother declared that she adopted any animal as long as it was: *A.* lively, *B.* alive, *C.* large, *D.* lame.")

Most members of the majority culture pick option B (alive); members of the minority subculture tended to choose option A (lively). To investigate why this happened, an extensive interview was carried out by Nix and Schwarz to see how each person justified his or her choice.

It is difficult in a review piece to do full justice to the novel analysis that the investigators bring to bear on their data, but the gist of their findings is that when option B (alive) was chosen, the passage was subjectively organized into a topic-comment discourse frame; but when option A (lively) was chosen, it was internally represented as an action-reaction discourse frame. More particularly, choosing the option *lively* rather than *alive* as correct was justified because *alive* represents a truism and should be rejected on that basis. But the majority mainstream choice of *alive* in contrast was justified by indicating that this represented a stance of hyperbole and exaggeration. Thus both groups evoked reasonable criteria for justifying their choices, but the frames that helped guide their original selection were clearly different. To further illustrate these differences in interpretive frames the students were asked whether the option "lame" would be correct. Those minority individuals who originally chose *lively* rejected *lame* because it is not a reasonable behavior for sensible people to waste money bringing home lame animals, whereas the group that originally chose *alive* accepted the possibility of choosing *lame* because "bringing home disabled animals is humane behavior sanctioned by the community." Thus the underlying frames differentiating the two groups was a pervasive sense of the scarcity or abundance of money. It is more difficult to pinpoint the frame that led to the topic-comment versus the action-reaction differentiation. But it seems reasonable to expect to point to the different cultural experiences as underlying the observed divergence in choices for purportedly the "same" surface utterances. This illustrates very clearly that language per se is ambiguous and that to comprehend a passage we must necessarily initiate interpretive frames to fill in the information that is unstated. Clearly, the two groups have filled in the missing information in different ways; hence, they must have used different interpretive frames in order to arrive at different justifications for their choices.

Not every interpretive difference is necessarily discovered by contrasting different culturally based groups. Even within a culture, deviations from normative use can be appropriate. For example, Frake (1975) suggests that on some occasions violations of a carefully prescribed ritual are used to communicate social messages such as solidarity and humor. Because members of the same community share the details of the proper ritual (i.e., have internalized a full schema of what it means to carry out the ritual in correct form), this shared knowledge (shared schemata) forms the background against which special meanings such as affection, humor, or hostility can be marked or called attention to. Yet even within a culture, such deviations from the norm may be misinterpreted. This is just another way of demonstrating that language forms and context are *necessarily incomplete* in specifying the full intentions of the actors and speakers. Miscommunication can therefore occur, albeit less frequently, within a language community, as well as across culturally different communities, whose members are attempting to speak the "same" language. An extreme case could therefore be made for claiming that no two people speak exactly the "same" language simply because the interpretive competencies of any two individuals, even members of the same language community, are in some details different. This extreme case can be justified by pointing out that instruction in becoming a member of a language community is never complete because we lack the conceptual tools for removing all sources of ambiguity from our attempts at instruction in the home and elsewhere.

The differences among individuals can be illustrated by reference to the concept of personal "themes" (Agar, 1979). Themes are similar to the notion of frame or schema, but Agar restricts the idea in his paper to presumably represent individual differences in world-view. The idea is that the personal philosophy and prevailing tendencies of an individual cause him or her to make sense of (interpret) the situations he/she encounters. Prolonged informal interviews with three individuals reveal striking differences in the details of their respective themes. The subthemes used by the first person highlighted three concepts: (1) social control and interaction is a problem, (2) admiration and respect if the social other demonstrates knowledge, and (3) social control is a problem *unless* there is a demonstration of knowledge, the coordination of the first two themes. Thus all three subthemes are interrelated for this person. A second person who was studied highlighted social independence. Yet another theme highlighted a lack of social independence. No third theme at the same "level" had yet emerged to successfully bridge these two contradictory themes. However, a third theme at an unspecified "level" did emerge: it involved the ability to "talk." To this person, talking need not imply social commitment; it is merely a way to have social contact without commitment. For the third person studied, the overwhelming theme in most aspects of the interactions involved his Chicano identity. This dominated the characteristics of subordinate themes such as family life, friends, religion, and occupation. Thus this third person had evolved a hierarchic system of main theme and subthemes different in structure from the first two individuals. Undoubtedly a study of all individuals in a particular community would reveal some striking differences in the organization of their personal themes that are habitually invoked to interpret and make sense of the world about them and their interactions with the world. Such idiosyncratic differences are also potential sources of miscommunication.

Erickson (1976) has written an important paper concerning the subtle ways in which nonverbal cues of eye-gaze can create the source of miscommunication across ethnic groups. Typically, when a black teacher speaks to a black student he/she maintains eye contact while speaking; while listening, each maintains only sporadic contact. Just the opposite holds for white teachers and students; that is, white speakers tend to allow their eyes to dart about while speaking, but when listening they maintain constant eye contact. This nonverbal communication habit would seem naively to be unimportant to *what* is being communicated and *how* it is being interpreted; but the naive view is wrong. When white teacher and black student were combined, their "conflicting" gaze patterns led to the following miscommunications. The black student appeared to be not listening or not understanding. This happened because the gaze mismatches led to a poor detection of the speaker's LRRM (Listener-Response-Relevant-Moment). This is a signal that some response from the listener, the black student, is expected to indicate (for example, clear understanding), and a similar signal from the black student was missed by the white teacher. The ultimate outcome of the miscommunication was, as before, a negative interpretation. The white teacher began to use one of two forms of hyperexplanation, either talking down to the student or giving repeated reasons for his assertions. The student interpreted this to mean that the teacher thought he/she was stupid. Again miscommunication has led to negative evaluation.

The "raw" material out of which a culture fashions nonverbal rapporttype communication signals is suggested by some reviews of Kempton (1978). Synchrony at the micro-level is demonstrated in the following wide range of behaviors: When someone speaks, the person exhibits self-synchrony, which means that the parts of their body move in synchrony with each other and with the speech. There is also interpersonal synchrony so that a speaker's movements are in synchrony with the listener's. Although different parts of the body move at different speeds and in different directions, yet they change direction at the same time. Condon and Sander (1974) have found self-synchrony even in newborns. Kempton also reports synchrony in primates. Dyssynchrony might occur in monkeys just before departure from the group. Dyssynchrony also has been reported in pathological behaviors such as schizophrenia, aphasia, epilepsy, autism, stuttering, etc. Most importantly for its cross-cultural implications in miscommunication, there is more synchrony observed between members of the *same* subculture including mothers and their infants, and men and women of the same culture. Once culture superimposes obligatory patterns on some of these movements (e.g., to cue an intended interruption or the like), these subconsciously processed contextualization cues become part of the interpretative apparatus that can lead to successful communicative interactions or to puzzling unsuccessful miscommunications, as between members from different subcultures.

With respect to educational settings one may detect an example of how different patterns of synchrony may alter the quality of teacher-student interactions. Byers and Byers (1972) studied the nonverbal interactions between a white teacher and two black and two white 4-year-old girls in a nursery school setting. The teacher appeared willing to interact equally with all students. But of the two most active students (one white, one black) only one was more successful at catching the attention of the teacher, the white student. Eight out of 14 attempts were successful in catching her attention; but for the black child only 4 out of 35 attempts to attract the teacher's eye were successful. Is this an example of mismatched patterns of synchrony? It seems likely for the following reasons. The white child timed her glances during those moments when the teacher was most likely to notice her; but the glances of the black child were timed when the teacher's attention was focused elsewhere so that she did not realize the child was attempting to interact. These researchers also report what can be labeled here as an example of affective asynchrony. The white student approached the teacher at times, which "naturally" led to the teacher's touching or hugging the child or having her sit on teacher's lap. But the black student made "inappropriate" (asynchronous) moves at crucial moments. This resulted in fewer nonverbal expressions of affection.

While Agar's (1979) study reveals persistent themes (schemata) at the level of individuals, Tannen's (1979) study reveals that there tend to be persistent themes for many members of a particular culture. These prevailing themes affect what significance is attached to everyday events, such as taking a bike ride past an orchard, encountering other individuals along the way, and the particular import of transferring food items. Of Tannen's many findings, the most relevant here in contrasting Greek and American groups are: (1) Americans comment on the film that they have seen by explicit reference to the film as a frame for guiding many aspects of their interpretations; the Greeks, however, seldom referred to the film per se in their comments; (2) there is a strong moral framework invoked in commenting on the film's actions by the Greeks, but this is infrequent among the American's comments; (3) Greeks drop more details than the Americans in one "falling" sequence. Tannen suggests that, in this last finding, such omissions may be tied to the Greeks' tendency to highlight interpretation and ignore details that did not fit the interpretation.

Here we see that frames exist at many levels that filter the "raw" data of the film into a prevailing way of organizing and making sense of sequences of actions. Such different orientations may lead to miscommunication when first-generation Greeks come to America, learn English, but persist in using these older interpretive frames to decide what is important to talk about and how one should realize this in speech. Tannen is currently engaged in analyzing data relevant to this last point.

Chafe (1977) suggests that there are wide differences in how cultures choose to structure details about a topic and how they make summarizing statements about the same topic. In conversation, he suggests that in Anglo culture people tend to begin by summarizing an event and then giving details. The Japanese, though, typically build up the details and then present the summary at the end. Such differences across speakers may contribute to disorientation or possibly impatience (e.g., "Get to the point, will you?").

Grimes (personal communication, 1978) has indicated that a difference in style exists even in Anglo culture among the various scientific disciplines in how they report their findings. He suggests that the rhetorical structure of articles in sociology and anthropology are oftentimes different from that of linguistics. A linguist tends to put his conclusions first and then gives details, much like a mathematician who presents his theorem first and then proceeds to prove it, whereas anthropologists discuss their methods and reasoning near the end of their papers. Such differences can create problems in smooth communication across disciplines.

Some Patterns of Communication Among Native Americans

Additional evidence concerning cultural frames that create communication problems across members of different language-culture groups comes from an early paper by Cazden and John (1971). Teachers often regarded Indian children as "shy" and "reluctant to talk." In the Anglo culture this might be interpreted negatively as possible evidence of retarded language development or psychological problems. The same behavior in Indian children probably has another explanation. Apache Indians consider it foolish to talk a great deal. Cazden and John indicate that in the Sunrise Dance representing the coming-of-age of young girls, the girl's grandmother places her hand over the girl's mouth to indicate that silence is a virtue. In their literature review (also see Cazden, John, & Hymes, 1972, pp. 331–394) they indicate that Navajos freeze up when looked at directly. Teachers might respond to the Indian child's bowed head (avoiding gaze) with such inquiries as "What's the matter? Can't you talk? Don't you even know your own name?" In addition, it has been reported that Navajos do not prefer to comment on a topic unless they regard themselves as highly proficient in it; to speak prematurely on a topic not fully mastered is considered a breach of intelligent behavior. Anglos, of course, have a different orientation since they regard practice as a prerequisite to obtaining full mastery. In other words, a mismatch in rules concerning when it is proper to talk exists across several Indian cultures in comparison with Anglo culture. Furthermore, a mismatch in presuppositions concerning the role of practice as a necessary step to attaining full mastery of a topic also exists. Both of these mismatches typically create negative assessments on the part of ill-informed teachers when faced with Indian children in their classrooms, even though a close examination of the sources of the miscommunication reveals that a negative evaluation is probably unwarranted.

Philips (1972) studied the speech behavior of Indian children inside and outside the classroom. In their community, interactions among participants do not recognize the Anglo distinction between a performer and an audience. Furthermore, there is no clear sense of "leader" of an activity (such as is assumed for the role of "teacher" in an Anglo community). Instead each person decides the degree to which he or she will participate in the activity at hand. All who are present are free to participate if they so choose. In the Anglo classroom studies by Philips (1972), however, there are four types of social-participant structures, some of which merge with the sociocultural rules of the Indian children and some of which violate these norms. The four structures are: (1) The teacher interacts with all the students, and it is always the teacher who decides whether to talk to just one person or to all. Also, a response from the student is obligatory and not a matter of individual choice. This clearly violates Indian norms. When the Anglo norms are violated, the child is probably labeled as "hostile" or "uncooperative." (2) A second structure used in the classroom involves the teacher interacting with only a subset of the class, such as special reading sessions. Participation is mandatory, and individuals are expected to perform verbally and singly rather than in chorus. The main purpose of this structure is to provide the teacher with an assessment of how much the student already knows of a certain skill. Hence, it presupposes incomplete mastery of a field, and also presupposes that individual responses will reflect incomplete mastery. This clearly violates Indian norms. Violation of the Anglo norms in such a case probably results in a student's being labeled as incompetent with respect to the knowledge domain being assessed. (3) The third classroom structure consists of all students working independently. The teacher is explicitly available to help, and this help is forthcoming if the student requests or initiates the interaction. The other students do not witness the details of the student-teacher interaction. This pattern does not contradict Indian norms for interaction. (4) The fourth interaction structure (which occurs infrequently in upper primary grades and very seldom in the lower grades) is also inconsistent with Indian interaction norms. It involves the students' being divided into small groups that are run by members of the group for the purpose of special "group projects." The teacher is still available for supervision if required.

In sum, it is clear that detailed ethnographic studies of the actual nature of structured interaction in these "naturalistic" settings within and outside the classroom clearly places Indian children at a disadvantage in terms of maximally benefiting from classroom activities that are structured in such a way as to violate norms instilled in the children from birth on. Not only does it fail to provide them with an optimal means for instruction, but it also alienates them with frequent negative evaluations given them by nonunderstanding but well-meaning teachers.

Weeks (1976) has presented a wealth of information concerning different patterns of language use among Yakima Indians that help to clarify additional sources of miscommunication. The native language of Yakima children is English. Yet school personnel complained that these children seemed to have "language problems" of a largely unspecified nature. Data analyzed by Weeks contrasted Indian children's use of language with non-Indian children who lived on the Yakima Reservation and also contrasted both with non-Indian children from Palo Alto, California.

Among the important findings are the following. Answers to questions are not obligatory, as it appears to be in Anglo culture. A question may be answered, perhaps at a later time. The typical pattern of Question, Answer, Confirmation (as in "What time are we to leave?" "At 6." "OK.") is therefore atypical in conversations with these Indian children. Furthermore, when they do answer questions, it is often in the form of a question. There is strong resistance to admitting to partial or no knowledge; hence these children typically will not say "I don't know." (It also helps to explain why they tend to answer a question with a question.) Yet this phrase is very common among Anglo children. This appears to be related to our earlier comments concerning the inappropriateness of speaking when one hasn't fully mastered some topic. Indian children are also not inclined to guess. They would lose face if their guessed-at answer proved to be wrong. This again is related to community norms which govern when one should speak on a topic. Guessing, however, is a frequent occurrence among Anglo students, and Anglo teachers appear to encourage it.

Weeks reports that for the language tasks she used to explore differences in language use between Indian and non-Indian children the following emerges. The Indian children depart from the stimulus pictures more and speak about related personal experiences. In presenting these experiences, they often quote previous conversations in what appears to be verbatim form, thus giving a narrative register form to their comments—e.g., "Grandma said, 'Tommy's going to get that boat and take us a ride on there. Waaaaay out there.''' ''Where?'' ''Waaaaay out there.'' [All produced by the same student.]

The Yakima children appeared to take control of the conversation by asking questions of the teacher. Anglo children rarely do this since it is assumed to be the role of the teacher to ask questions. Many of the questions asked by the Indian children were of a personal nature; Anglo children seldom asked personal questions. The Yakima children interpreted the interview as a friendly visit, whereas the Anglo children assumed that there was a special purpose behind the interview (''What am I supposed to say?''). Anglo children regularly corrected the teacher if the teacher appeared not to understand something they said. Indian children did not correct the teacher. Also, Indian children did not interrupt; in contrast, the Anglo children and the non-Indian children at Yakima often interrupted the teacher.

In terms of distribution of summary comments versus details, none of the children who were studied in the interview summarized as an adult might summarize. Yet the non-Indian children listed details in the pictures and began without any prompting by the teacher. The Indian children studied here picked up a picture and waited for the teacher to say something. When speaking, the Indian children often projected what might happen, whereas the Anglo children spoke of what was directly in the picture.

It is clear that there are complex presuppositions behind these conversations. If one cannot specify what they are, an Anglo teacher is likely to misinterpret the motivations and significance of the Indian children's statements. Such a teacher is likely to feel ignored (they don't acknowledge questions), or feel their authority has been usurped (they begin asking the teacher questions), or feel that they don't stick to the point (they project what might happen, and they use a narrative story-telling mode rather than just list facts). Yet all these misjudgments represent a failure to appreciate how cultures differently frame events, and differently frame when it is proper to speak and how one must present the information.

It is clear that culture molds and defines inevitable aspects of behavior more than one would believe is literally possible. That is, eye-glances, body angle, eye-blinks, head nodding, time intervals between movements (rate and frequency), vocal emphasis, variation in voice pitch, etc. These inevitable behaviors, however, are segmented and grouped differently by different cultures to signify and clarify more than words alone can convey. This is a critical part of coming to analytic terms with the problem of miscommunication.

The redundancy of shared context that pervades most discourse among members of the same culture is a protective agent against miscommunication. Repetitions of highly familiar events encourage casual cognitive monitoring of the significance of these events. But between cultures, verbal interactions tend to be brief and infrequent. Thus the protective aspect of redundancy in prolonged pursuit of a topic is typically absent in cross-cultural encounters. Hence it seems likely that suspicions that make these encounters brief in the first place also contribute to a negative interpretation of intentions when contextual cues fail to provide sufficient cues to guide correct interpretations.

We see that the notion of "frames" or "schemata" are ways of designating semiformalized knowledge that exists in gestalt clusters at many segments of culture. It represents ways to store and retrieve grammatical language *codes*, ways to represent *social* knowledge of *when* one is allowed to speak, *what* one could say, how one should say it (intonation patterns), whether one needs to answer questions, who has the right to ask questions. how to formulate some jokes (e.g., by violating language community norms where the violation is intentional and all present realize that; hence one is joking); and so on. The nuances of how we use this knowledge are seemingly endless. This raises in turn questions of how this highly particularized knowledge is ever learned (see Anderson, 1977; also see Freedle & Lewis, 1971; 1977; Lewis & Freedle, 1973).

Teachers may learn to become sensitive to these frames as they exist within the majority culture and as they exist within subcultures. In this way the teacher can minimize the many instances in which misunderstandings can occur through gestures, glances, intonation, choice of speech register (emphasis for clarity or for scorn), choice of discourse genre (story telling versus expository form), choice of language code, choice of whether or not to code-switch, and so on. Students may also be interested in learning how these various patterns of communication are employed in different cultures. This knowledge may help them to understand whether a teacher is necessarily abusing them or whether they have in turn misinterpreted the contextual cues of the majority culture. Perhaps the bright spot in this entire chapter is the surprise that people have upon discovering how they use these cues to interpret messages. This surprise can generate interest and be a cornerstone for generating very important classroom discussion. Furthermore, it may generate motivation for learning some of the skills that the majority culture values, be it reading, writing, or speaking in standard English.

A Specific Study Showing Influence of Ethnographic Language Use on a Language Task for Three Bilingual Populations

Freedle and Laosa (1979) recently presented some results that suggest that ethnographic differences in language use may possibly affect the types of cognitive representation that each language code has within a bilingual individual. They studied the simple word association task with stimulus words presented in English and Spanish, with language code being counterbalanced for order of presentation and with one week intervening between the two occurrences of the task. Four populations were contrasted because their use of English and Spanish in four different naturalistic settings were quite different. Three bilingual ethnic populations—the Cuban American in Miami, the Mexican American in Texas, and the Puerto Rican American in New York—and an Anglo population of

English monolinguals in Texas were tested. Naively one might think that since all three bilingual groups speak Spanish and English, that this should imply that the patterns of language use and the processing of bilingual information should be the same for each population. Laosa's work (1975) indicates that such a naive idea is clearly wrong. Naturalistic use of each language code by setting and social participant structure significantly alters the form of language that is used. For example, in one of the four settings—the classroom—he found that the three populations used a different proportion of English in this setting. Mexican Americans used 92% English, and 8% of Spanish or a mixture of the two languages; Cuban Americans used 42% English, while Puerto Rican Americans used only 26% English in this setting. One can then inquire whether such observed differences imply any differences in how English and Spanish are *accessed* in a controlled study carried out in this same setting. (Ideally of course one should like to explore whether the word associations patterns are themselves affected by changing the place the data is collected, say, in the family's home, or on the playground; one should also vary who the experimenter is—it could be the child's peer or his/her parent rather than an adult stranger; these suggestions are left for future work.)

With the word association data at hand, one can address several bilingual-cognitive issues that have been suggested by various authors over the years—see for example, Albert and Obler, 1978. The issue of whether the form of syntagmatic to paradigmatic (syn. to para.) shift is identical in each language code for a given bilingual population, is, in the light of the many factors that are known to influence language use, seen to probably depend upon the setting in which data are collected. Furthermore, since populations appear to use each language differently, one might well expect that the syn. to para. shift might be identical across languages for some groups, but not for other groups. In other words, the variations in naturalistic use across the three Hispanic populations suggests that a particular setting may induce different results in exploring the development of the syn. to para. shift. If true, this implies that *differences in ethnographic language use alter the form of developmental "laws" that we can uncover, and suggests that these "laws" may not be a fixed invariant entity, but may in fact be better stated as contextually dependent "laws" that vary from one setting to another for the very same individuals.*

The Freedle and Laosa report showed that the structure of word association data *is* different for each of the populations studied. To clarify the difference, two mathematical choice models were fitted to each of 21 "populations": Three grade levels by three bilingual populations by two languages of input yields 18 "populations." Three additional data populations come from the three grade levels of Anglo children tested in just English. One of the mathematical choice models (due to Luce, 1959) addressed the following problem. In word associations, nouns, verbs, and adjectives are the typical stimuli; the typical responses that a subject emits are also of the same three categories. Often, when a noun is given, a person will respond fairly often with another noun (paradigmatic response) but will also emit a verb (syntagmatic category) and sometimes an adjective (another syntagmatic category, given a noun as stimulus). Ditto when a verb or adjective is presented as a stimulus. The question that has never been addressed with word association data, to my knowledge, is: Is there a dimensional ordering to the three categories that can be used to explain why one word class is used more often as the response than another word class.

A similarity choice model suggests that if we place noun, verb, and adjective categories (three points in some space) along a one-dimensional scale, we can use such an ordering to explain why the stimuli evoke different frequencies of responses. The ordering noun-verb-adjective (with the noun point being to the left of the one-dimensional line, the adjective point being somewhere along the right-hand side of the line, and the verb point being somewhere between these two extreme points) implies that when a noun stimulus is presented, the subject is more likely to give a verb back as a syntagmatic response than he would an adjective because the verb is "closer" on the scale to the noun point than the adjective is. Similarly, for this same ordering, when an adjective is presented as the stimulus, the subject is more likely to give a verb back as the syntagmatic response than he would a noun because the verb point is closer to the adjective point than the noun point is. If in addition to knowing the ordering on the scale we also knew how far apart these three points were, we could then also indicate in very precise quantitative terms (using the choice model) exactly how frequently each three response categories would be used in response to each of the three stimulus categories.

There are two other ways to arrange three points on a line in deciding what the best underlying order is for a one-dimensional scale. If the order is verb-noun-adjective rather than noun-verb-adjective, this implies a slightly different pattern of syntagmatic use than just described. A third logically possible model (rejected by all the data and so is not discussed further here) is whether noun-adjective-verb is the ordering along a one-dimensional continuum.

A chi-square fit of both the noun-verb-adjective versus the verb-noun-adjective model was computed for each of the 21 "populations." The chi-square results showed quite clearly that the three bilingual groups are very different from each other. For example, model noun-verb-adjective best fit all of the data for the three grade levels of the Puerto Rican American group; this model furthermore was best regardless of whether English stimuli or Spanish stimuli were presented. Chi-squares for this model ranged from 17.63 to 66.47; whereas for the other model chi-square ranged from 80.97 to 719.64. The two remaining bilingual groups differed from the Puerto Rican American group in a very interesting way. When Spanish stimuli were presented, the Cuban American fit model verb-noun-adjective best for all three grade levels, but fit the other model best for all three grade levels when English stimuli were presented! The chi-squares ranged from 8.28 to 3.44 for model V-N-A when Spanish was presented and ranged from 38.84 to 80.10 for model N-V-A; when English stimuli were presented the chi-squares ranged from 45.14 to 64.16 for model N-V-A and from 60.48 to 111.60 for model V-N-A. This is a very important finding inasmuch as it suggests that the psychological similarity of nouns, verbs, and adjectives *within the same individuals* is different as a function of which language they are processing. A somewhat similar pattern across the two language codes was obtained for the Mexican American groups for all three age levels—that is, when Spanish stimuli were presented they fit model N-V-A best (ranging from 30.05 to 89.99 as contrasted with 81.19 to 195.54 for the competing model) but when English was presented model V-N-A fit the data better (chi-squares here ranging from 166.97 to 227.90 as contrasted with 248.38 to 300.18 for the competing model).

A close look at the Cuban American data versus the Mexican American data shows that while the pattern of results is similar, the degree to which the models fit the data is clearly different. Hence all three bilingual groups are different from each other qualitatively as well as quantitatively with respect to word association distributions.

Freedle and Laosa's paper also showed differences among the groups with respect to how often a response switched language codes in comparison with the stimulus of input. Switching from Spanish to English occurred in 40% of the cases for the Mexican American data but occurred very infrequently for the other bilingual groups. Very little code switching from English to Spanish occurred in any of the data. Differences were also found in the time it took to give a response; significant differences were very complexly related to the four ethnic populations, to age, and to language of input. The interested reader is referred to the original paper.

When the syntagmatic to paradigmatic shift was examined by Freedle and Laosa as a function of the language of input, only the Cuban Americans showed a distinctly different developmental curve across languages of input—they were developmentally more accelerated in Spanish than in English. (Remember, this result may vary when experimental setting and experimenter type are varied; this has yet to be studied.) The Puerto Rican and Mexican Americans showed a similar developmental curve regardless of language of input. Hence ethnographic experience appears to influence developmental "laws." A closer look at the data showed that for each language of input, two underlying pieces of the choice model could be examined for its developmental structure; that is, in fitting a particular ordering to the data, two distances had to be estimated—if the model was N-V-A, then the distance from N to V had to be computed and a second distance from V to A had to be computed. Each of these parameters generated its own developmental curve with respect to the syntagmatic to paradigmatic shift. With this in mind, it was found that the Puerto Rican and Mexican Americans differed in the degree to which paradigmatic shifts occurred for each of these two distance parameters. The Mexican Americans were more advanced (i.e., showed more paradigmatic shifts) for the noun to verb segment of the model, whereas the

Puerto Rican Americans were more advanced (para. shift) for the other parameter, the verb to adjective distance. Such a wide array of differences undermines any simple developmental ''law'' and instead suggests that it is *more appropriate to qualify such generic statements* in terms of ethnographic background, language of input, and the setting in which such developmental data are collected.

A Sketch of a New Methodology for Investigating the Structure and Function of Large-Scale Schemata

Several novel ideas will be sketched in this section: I will suggest that when schemata are invoked to interpret some situation, we implicitly are conducting a similarity match or are invoking semantic error detection and correction if new data fail to conform to the schema currently in operation. Both of these acts involve generating a likely or expected *set* of interpretations for an ongoing event; see Freedle (1972) for a discussion of these concepts in language comprehension.

The above is a somewhat novel view of what schemata can do for us; not only do schemata help us organize a vast array of elements into coherent wholes—thereby simplifying perception—but it also serves to correct apparent errors in the received information, this being achieved by making a judgment based on a similarity match of parts of the schema with the incoming information. Not only can we use a schema to detect and correct apparent errors, but we can also use it to fill in missing information. A few simple examples might help to clarify some of these processes.

With regard to error detection and correction, if the permissible range of elements has just two patterns, 00011 and 11100, but the pattern that is heard is 10011, we (1) decide that an error has occurred, (2) then search the permissible patterns for the pattern most similar to the received one (e.g., 00011 is more similar to 10011 than 11100 is), and (3) conclude that 00011 was the ''intended'' signal. We probably do *semantic* error correction when we listen to someone from a slightly different subculture: The knowledge routines that culture *x* knows may not perfectly match ours, but we apply a likelihood judgment in order to match the most likely pattern of permissible patterns to what we listen to. Thus in intonational-tone cluster matching, the English woman getting on the bus *matched* the slightly deviant tone-clusters produced by the Indian bus driver to an item in her set of permissible intonational patterns, and having made this likelihood match, she drew the incorrect conclusion concerning the driver's intentions. Note that in a sense she tried to correct the apparent error (the error being that the situation really did not call for hostility on the driver's part), but the closest match that she could find—given that she did not explicitly probe the situation further for obtaining new and crucial information concerning the driver's real intentions—was to assume that the intonation pattern was close enough to her set of intonational schema patterns to conclude that he very likely was trying to insult her. Thus error correction sometimes produces other errors, especially across cultures. The simplest way to reflect this complexity is to use schema theory on the set of possibilities. This is an important point—let me rephrase the argument. She scanned at a low level of relevance—the intonational. She did not think to scan at the larger situational level to realize that the situation did not really call for insult. Such a scan would have suppressed the "error" detection at the lower level or would have led to an overt questioning of intentions, "Have I offended you?"

Error correction attempts at the syntactic level are also made when we hear what seems like a grammatical error (e.g., "Don't nobody know" might be responded to by "Does that mean that someone knows?"). Again, an array of permissible alternatives within the listener's knowledge repertoire is scanned for the "closest" alternative, but in the above case the "error" was only apparent and no correction was necessary. Error detection and correction at the highest communicative level includes sudden shifts in apparent *intentions* (from pleasant to hostile or from pleasant to indifferent). One might also detect deviations (errors) in aesthetics ("Why are you being so crude?"), which is to say sudden shifts in *values;* sudden deviations in routes or *pathways* leading to a goal (e.g., "We want to get to route 22, why are you distracting me with your endless jokes?"); or sudden shifts in the *goal* itself ("I thought we came out to look at chairs; why are you looking at jewelry?"). Sudden detections and suggested corrections in real or apparent semantic-pragmatic errors at many levels of interaction can and do occur in communications between individuals who share different cultural backgrounds. For example, in some of the above we have seen that Indian children's intentions or goals might be misinterpreted if they asked the teacher too many questions, if they failed to answer questions directed to them ("Don't you want to learn?"), if the *pathways* they pursued were questioned ("Stick to the topic; give me just the facts"), or if the social values they had were questioned ("Don't you want to correct the answer that Mary gave?").

INQUIRING SYSTEMS AS SCHEMATA FOR MODELING MISCOMMUNICATIONS

In the preceding sections, I have repeatedly used a few concepts such as selection of a code from the repertoire or selection of a particular speech form (a question or imperative) from a set of possible forms to advance some goal, e.g., "Ask a *question* at the ticket counter if you want to know (goal) *when* the next train leaves." Notice too that the effect of carrying out a particular choice of language directed at a particular person in a particular location for a particular goal has an *outcome.* Some outcomes are *negative* following miscommunication with a further possible outcome of social isolation or verbal abuse. Other outcomes, however, are probably mildly successful achievements of goals and information exchange, especially between members who share a similar speech community (who share a similar schemata of what is significant in the world, what values must be placed on events, how events are to be segmented, etc.).

All of these terms—outcomes, sets of possibilities, values of outcomes, likelihood of a negative outcome, goals, settings, participants—all can be brought together in more organized fashion by considering how to use Inquiring System Theory as applied to human communication and human problem solving, be it through verbal or nonverbal channels (see Freedle, 1974, 1975, 1978, for a description of how to apply Inquiring Systems to developmental issues as well as to the analysis of dialogue and extended monologues). The original invention of Inquiring Systems was due to Churchman (1971), who sought a way to mathematize different kinds of problem-solving situations. He classified situations into five basic forms that I shall describe in the following: *Lo, Le, K, H,* or *S*.

To get an intuitive grasp of why such formulations can be useful in analyzing miscommunication, let us consider an example used earlier.

Bus driver: "Exact change, please."

Customer: "What did you say?"

Bus driver: "Exact change (pause) PLEASE."

Customer (acting insulted): "The nerve!"

We shall attempt to expand this seemingly simple exchange in terms that are of concern to Inquiring Systems, namely goals, problem-type, pathways to goal, sets of alternatives, outcomes of attempts, and value of outcomes (See Table 3.1).

From event 1 through event 8 we appear to have a cooperative principle in operation; both participants want to be helpful and to say things that are truthful and helpful. From event 9 through event 11 we have what may be a non-Gricean principle in operation since both participants are either angry or puzzled and are not communicating in order to be cooperative.

The cooperative stance of events 1 through 8 leads to problem states that are *socially* stereotyped and highly consensual—hence they are a gestalt *Lo* system.

The above two individuals though are both somewhat knowledgeable about each other's culture; the mismatches are traceable to "low-level" schema of intonation differences across their respective first languages. An example of a high-order schema difference will now be shown. Here we have two individuals who almost from the beginning of the conversation exhibit repeated failures to use the same molar organizing schema (inquiring system mode) in defining what problem they are dealing with and what types of responses are considered appropriate in solving the problem. The example comes from an interpretation (Freedle, 1975) I gave to a dialogue reported by Cole and Scribner (1974).

TABLE 3.1

Main Events (verbal and nonverbal) (covert & overt)	Representative of Culture 1 Bus Driver: participant 1 (P1)	Representative of Culture 2 Customer: participant 2 (P2)
1. P1 stops bus.		
2. P2 gets on.		
3. Covert event: P1 thinks a problem state may exist.	Covert problem: believes a problem state may exist P1 Goal: avert bad situation where P2 may expect P1 to break a large bill.	
4. P1 says something to solve problem.	Pathway activated: decides to avert possible problem by verbally saying "exact change please" spoken softly with no definite pause between words.	
5. Outcome — new covert problem because P2 couldn't hear clearly.		Outcome of 4 (neutral value) Subproblem: P2 didn't hear what P1 said. So, new Subgoal: ask for clarification. Pathway to goal: select from wide options of how to ask this: "What did you say?"
6. Says something to solve problem at 5.		
7. New problem state: how to satisfy the request for clarification	Perceives request for clarification as requiring a repetition of content but infers that he must speak more clearly and loudly (formal register under noisy background conditions). Hence, this is another subproblem: it has as its goal clarification; the pathway to this goal is chosen by repetition plus intonational clustering for emphasis and clarity according to his native cultural rules for speech: Hence he says: "Exact change (pause) PLEASE"	
8. Pathway to problem at 7.		
9. Outcome — new covert problem state. (Hegelian conflict)		Outcome of event 8 (negative value) Applying intonation rules appropriate to P2's socio-linguistic community; she believes P1 is trying to insult her (negative outcome). new goal: insult P1. Pathway to new goal: select verbal insult She says "The nerve!"
10. P2 tries to deal with event 9.		
11. P1 is puzzled by what P2 says.	Cover problem: Why did P2 say that? Why is she angry?	
12. P2 may plan (new goal) to file a formal complaint with the bus company.		Covert: I'm not going to let him get away with that.

GENERAL COOPERATIVE ORIENTATION

GENERAL CONFLICT ORIENTATION

54

Experimenter: "At one time spider went to a feast. He was told to answer this question before he could eat any of the food. The question is: Spider and black deer always eat together. Spider is eating. Is black deer eating?"

(*Comment:* This discourse format intends to establish a pure logic to the strong of propositions. The solution to the problem requires an inference.)

Subject: "Were they in the bush?"

(*Comment:* The subject does not follow the presumed logical format of the experimenter because this violates the cultural mode he typically uses. He attempts to place the premises on a *factual* basis not an abstract logical basis by concretizing information regarding location.)

Experimenter: "Yes."

(*Comment:* Here the experimenter appears to have accommodated to the subject's higher-order organizers for interpreting the flow of communication.)

Subject: "Were they eating together?"

(*Comment:* The *Le* inquiring system mode imposes a broad frame upon statements such that only a pure logical format must be used to arrive at answers to the problem, but the subject here again tried to make the assertion specific to a particular setting or occasion. Hence the subject is using a *K* mode that requires placing a data specific set of assertions in line with a more formal system of logical possibility.)

Experimenter: "Spider and black deer always eat together. Spider is eating. Is black deer eating?"

(*Comment:* The experimenter tries to reestablish a pure *Le* problem mode to link all the propositions together. To honor this frame one must produce a logical inference based upon the propositional information alone. Specific information concerning specific situations is irrelevant.)

Subject: "But I was not there. How can I answer such a question?"

(*Comment:* The subject again rejects the *Le* frame and reintroduces new factual information concerning his own absence from the event. Hence he reestablishes a *K* frame for linking his own propositions together and to link them with the assertions of the experimenter. What is important in this exchange is that the miscommunication has occurred at a level not typically found in members of minority groups who already live within a larger dominant majority culture (see Hall & Freedle, 1975, for other insights into this distinction).

Contextual cues across different communities may involve different systems of gesture, different intonation patterns, different fields of pragmatic interest. They may further vary in rules for which signal system *dominates* or combines with the values assigned to other signal systems. (Are eye-winks more important than verbal propositions in getting at what a person really thinks? Are "tense" body positions and a person's physical acts more important than verbal propositions in helping to decide how to interpret a person's attempts at communication?) Cultures probably differ in many ways in their rules of combination, rules of dominance, and number of possible systems that contribute to communication (e.g., some communities have "whistle" languages by which to communicate; others have a drum language). All of this needs further study.

Whether this must alter how educators are trained, whether it must alter whether social hierarchies (of teacher-student, king-servant) should be altered in dealing with students who come from less-hierarchical social systems are all questions for the future. They will not be easy to answer. Schemata operate in interpretation by allowing us to fill in missing (unspoken) slots of the Inquiring System. Thus if one is in a Hegelian (conflict) system, one uses the semantic slots appropriate to a *conflict-schema* in order to help guide the selection of *what* to say next (it alters the content), and *how* to say it (one might use direct rather than indirect means to convey information). For example, if irritated one may say "I told you to open the door, now open it and I don't mean maybe." but indirectly one might say in a cooperative stance "Please would you mind opening the door?" or "It's a little drafty in here."

Inquiring Systems as a Model for Studying Communication and Culture Change

Four of the five major systems will now be sketched. Each is intended to be a particular way to solve a problem.

The *Le* system is a formal symbolic system. It builds a formal mathematical representation of problems that start with a set of primitive analytic truths (axioms or propositions), and, from these, constructs a network of more general and formal propositional truths, much as proofs are derived from elementary axioms.

Lo systems represent experimental consensual systems. They build upon an empirical inductive representation of a problem by starting from a set of empirical observations (raw data, sense data) and construct a network of increasingly more general sets of facts, inductively arrived at. *Lo* systems are judged to be "true" or "factual" if there is widespread *social* agreement on a problem by a group of experts (the "experts" may be just ordinary members of a particular cultural group). Notice that *Le* systems are theoretically and deductively derived problems, whereas *Lo* systems are empirically and inductively derived problems. A "true" and correct decision in a *Le* system is a logical deduction, whereas a "true" or correct solution in a *Lo* system is an inductively arrived at social consensus.

K systems consist of mixtures of *Lo* and *Le* systems. When the two components, *Lo* and *Le,* are complementary, the total system is a standard *K* system; but when the two components are contradictory at various points, then we have an *H* system (a conflicting or Hegelian system).

"Truth" in a *K* system is the degree of correspondence between the *Lo* and *Le* subsystems; an example is a scientific problem that merges the theory (*Le* logical component) with the observed data (the *Lo* or empirical component). If the results agree with the theory, one is tempted to regard the theory as "true."

Many K systems are extremely complex and ill-structured (see Mitroff & Sagasti, 1973, for a discussion of inquiring systems). Many of the elements of a K system may be quantitatively unknown (e.g., the *probability* of certain events may not have been studied, and the likely *outcome* of performing a group of studies on a certain parameter may be unknown). Many social problems are ill-structured or "wicked" in this sense.

Conflicting H systems may have serious discrepancies between their subcomponents. For example, if we have two conflicting theories and want to assess which one is "better" with respect to some observations (data), we have a total H system. An example is the contrast between a Marxist theory and a capitalist theory in explaining an observed sequence of facts in the market place.

Now let's consider a system's view of analyzing language interactions. Facts of the environment (the empirical part) are interpreted through a cultural frame (a set of guiding assumptions [the theory part of the culture] and values about the world and about social structure); this subculture presents a K subsystem. The other culture that interacts with the first culture is another K' subsystem since members of this community also have a different set of guiding cultural assumptions (the "theoretical" component that guides everyday facts and situations typically encountered, the latter being the empirical elements of the K' subsystem). Together K and K' subsystems may form a Hegelian or conflicting H system when people try to communicate about very simple "facts." A larger representation of this would list different levels of *schema* that are *little systems unto themselves* since the regularities of the schema are ways to interpret "facts" encountered in the environment that are pertinent to that schema. Hence any given culture is really a *whole hierarchy* of K systems depending upon what sets of schemata are being looked at. Put together, the parts form a gigantic K system or, if the society is very complex, the subparts may together form a gigantic Hegelian or H system. This can easily occur in a complex industrial society which has a population representative of dozens of different counties and cultures. It is less likely to occur in small isolated communities, which are more likely to be represented by a K system.

As mentioned previously, Lo systems are strongly social consensual; hence "intimate" settings probably can also be designated as Lo systems; this decision carried with it an implicational network of appropriate values, pathways to goals, and outcomes that are appropriate to employment of that cultural schema. Given that other language community members also monitor at this broadly based gestalt level, they also apparently use the co-occurring contextual cues that are appropriate and specific to that schema. The failure of members from different communities to use the same schema, then, accounts for the breakdown of smooth communications; furthermore, the gestalt nature of many of these language schemata probably also accounts for the apparent inability of the speakers and listeners to know what went wrong with the communication—the gestalt patterns are learned holistically and tend to resist piecemeal analysis. (A scientist of language, however, is capable of breaking the gestalt down into its components. Thus there is no contradiction here in claiming that language communication can be fruitfully studied by means of inquiring system theory.)

Just labeling events in communication does not justify introducing these systems. But when we consider that *likelihoods* of choosing the best interpretation are under consideration, then we begin to see how the whole formal apparatus of a decision theory is needed to coordinate and *interrelate* in a sensible manner these many facets of communication (values, goals, outcomes, etc.), with the many facets of communication types (debate modes, joking sessions, fantasy sessions, rigorous rituals, etc.). Likelihood estimates are absolutely essential to bringing our scientific understanding of the *process* of communication to a fuller, more mature level. We especially need this increased level of complexity if we are to keep track of cultural mismatches and the many levels of frames that can contribute with various probabilities of occurrence to these miscommunications.

A decision theory of these five types has the breadth to handle most of the complexities that can occur in communication. The theory serves as a template against which to assess the *completeness* of an analysis. That is, have we accounted for values, goals, pathways, outcomes, and decision type in scoring our protocols, have we assessed the likelihoods of competing solutions from the participants in the communication setting, and have we determined other pathways, such as other variants or language strategies, that they might have pursued? By studying individuals and groups intensively one might be able, as did Agar (1979) and Tannen (1979), to characterize prevailing strategies of cognition, prevailing frequencies of employing each strategy, and so on. This, of course, is ambitious, but the next generation of language specialists may find that it is a necessary one in order to successfully build a theory of language comprehension that will have important and viable applications in the real world.

REFERENCES

Agar, M. Themes revisited: Some problems in cognitive anthropology. *Discourse Processes, a multidisciplinary journal,* 1979, *2,* 11–31.

Albert, M. L., & Obler, L. K. *The bilingual brain: Neuropsychological and neurolinguistic aspects of bilingualism.* New York: Academic Press, 1978.

Anderson, E. *Learning to speak with style: A study of the sociolinguistic skills of children.* Unpublished doctoral dissertation, Stanford University, December 1977.

Byers, P., & Byers, H. Nonverbal communication and the education of children. In C. B. Cazden, V. P. John, & D. Hymes (Eds.), *Functions of language in the classroom.* New York: Teachers College Press, 1972.

Cazden, C. B., & John, V. P. Learning in American Indian children. In M. Wax, S. Diamond, & F. Goring (Eds.), *Anthropological perspectives on education.* New York: Basic Books, 1971.

Cazden, C. B., John, V. P., & Hymes, D. (Eds.). *Functions of language in the classroom.* New York: Teachers College Press, 1972.

Chafe, W. Creativity in verbalization and its implications for the nature of stored knowledge. In R. Freedle (Ed.), *Discourse production and comprehension.* Norwood, N.J.: Ablex, 1977.

Churchman, C. W. *The design of inquiring systems.* New York: Basic Books, 1971.

Cole, M., & Scribner, S. *Culture and thought: A psychological introduction.* New York: Wiley, 1974.

Condon, W. S., & Sander, L. W. Synchrony demonstrated between movements of the neonate and adult speech. *Child Development,* 1974, *43,* 456–462.

Erickson, F. *Talking down and giving reasons: Hyper-explanation and listening behavior in inter-racial interviews.* Paper presented at the International Conference on Non-verbal Behavior, Ontario Institute for Studies in Education, Toronto, May 11, 1976.

Fitts, P. M. Perceptual-motor skill learning. In A. W. Melton (Ed.), *Categories of human learning.* New York: Academic Press, 1964.

Frake, C. O. How to enter a Yakan house. In M. Sanches & B. Blount (Eds.), *Sociocultural dimensions of language use.* New York: Academic Press, 1975.

Freedle, R. Language users as fallible information processors. In R. Freedle & J. B. Carroll (Eds.), *Language comprehension and the acquisition of knowledge.* Washington, D.C.: Hemisphere/ Wiley, 1972.

Freedle, R. O. A general systems view of the 1973 International Convention on Behavioral Development. *Human Development,* 1974, *17,* 235–240.

Freedle, R. Dialogue and inquiring systems: The development of a social logic. *Human Development,* 1975, *18,* 97–118.

Freedle, R. Human development, the new logical systems, and general systems theory: Preliminaries to developing a psychosocial linguistics. In G. Steiner (Ed.), *Piaget, and beyond.* Vol. 7 in the series: Psychology of the 20th century. Zurich, Switzerland: Kindler Verlag, 1978.

Freedle, R., & Laosa, L. *Development of word associations and lexical access time in bilinguals and monolinguals.* Paper presented at the meeting of the Eastern Psychological Association, Philadelphia, April 1979.

Freedle, R. O., & Lewis, M. *Application of Markov processes to the concept of state* (ETS RB 71–34). Princeton, N.J.: Educational Testing Service, 1971.

Freedle, R. O., & Lewis, M. Prelinguistic conversations. In M. Lewis & L. Rosenblum (Eds.), *Interaction, conversation, and the development of language.* New York: Wiley, 1977.

Gumperz, J. Sociocultural knowledge in conversational inference. In M. Saville-Troike, *28th Annual Roundtable, Monograph Series on Languages and Linguistics.* Georgetown: Georgetown University Press, 1977.

Gumperz, J. J. The conversational analysis of interethnic communication. In E. Lamar Ross (Ed.), *Interethnic communication.* Athens: University of Georgia Press, 1978.

Gumperz, J. J., & Hymes, D. (Eds.). *Directions in sociolinguistics: The ethnography of communication.* New York: Holt, Rinehart & Winston, 1972.

Hall, W. S., & Freedle, R. *Culture and language: The black American experience.* Washington, D.C.: Halsted/Wiley, 1975.

Kempton. In D. Tannen, *Sociolinguistic bibliography* (annotated). Unpublished manuscript, University of California at Berkeley, April 1978.

Laosa, L. Bilingualism in three hispanic groups: Contextual use of language by children and adults in their families. *Journal of Educational Psychology,* 1975, *67,* 617–627.

Lewis, M., & Freedle, R. Mother-infant dyad: The cradle of meaning. In P. Pliner, L. Krames, & T. Alloway (Eds.), *Communication and affect: Language and thought.* New York: Academic Press, 1973.

Luce, R. D. *Individual choice behavior.* New York: Wiley, 1959.

Miller, G. A. The magical number seven, plus or minus two: Some limits on our capacity for processing information. *Psychological Review,* 1956, *63,* 81–97.

Mitroff, I., & Sagasti, F. Epistemology as general systems theory. *Philosophy of the Social Sciences,* 1973, *3,* 117–134.

Nix, D., & Schwarz, M. Toward a phenomenology of reading comprehension. In R. Freedle (Ed.), *New directions in discourse processing.* Norwood, N.J.: Ablex, 1979.

Philips, S. U. Participant structures and communicative competence: Warm Springs children in community and classroom. In C. B. Cazden, V. P. John, & D. Hymes (Eds.), *Functions of language in the classroom.* New York: Teachers College Press, 1972.

Tannen, D. What's in a frame? In R. Freedle (Ed.), *New directions in discourse processing.* Norwood, N.J.: Ablex, 1979.

Weeks, T. E. *Discourse, culture and instruction.* Paper presented at the meeting of the American Educational Research Association, San Francisco, April 21, 1976.

4

Social Knowing from an Ecological-Event Perspective: A Consideration of the Relative Domains of Power for Cognitive and Perceptual Modes of Knowing

Reuben M. Baron
University of Connecticut

The basic approach I seek to promote can at one level be treated as a relatively innocent sounding empirical generalization: The *data base* of social psychology has broadened sufficiently with regard to what phenomena are of interest that it is now time to assess whether our current approaches to social knowing are still adequate. Specifically, I believe that as our data base has moved from short-term to extended interpersonal encounters (e.g., Levinger, 1974), from studying causal attribution on the basis of verbal vignettes to the use of dynamic displays that allow on-line changes in the focus of attention (e.g., Taylor & Fiske, 1978), from investigating social influence through verbal written materials to the persuasive possibilities of nonverbal communication (e.g., Albert & Dabbs, 1970), we have without realizing it crossed certain epistemic boundaries in regard to how people came to know their social environments.[1] The nature of this shift is well captured by B. R. Russell's (1948) incisive distinction between *knowledge by acquaintance,* a situation that increasingly describes the current paradigm, and *knowledge by description,* a situation that is characteristic of the old paradigm for social knowing. Given the validity of this type of distinction between knowledge based on "first-hand" or direct experience (knowledge by acquaintance) and knowledge based on vicarious or indirect encounters in which information about an event is conveyed through representation of the event, such as by verbal descriptions, modeling, pictures, and so on (knowledge by descrip-

---

[1]This change is, of course, relative; the research of social psychologists continues to lag well behind the work of ethnomethodologists in regard to studying the processes involved in knowledge by acquaintance (e.g., Garfinkel, 1967).

tion),[2] I propose that it is necessary to give increased recognition to the role that perceptual as opposed to cognitive processes play in knowing other people.

Minimally, such a situation will mean that we will have to recognize that higher-order judgments such as causal attributions can be biased at the level of registration in addition to or *perhaps instead of* being biased at the encoding or retrieval stages of the epistemic process. Although motivated at a more empirical and methodological level, this type of shift has already been advocated by McArthur (1981) and Newtson (1976). However, I believe that this level of concession to the importance of perceptual knowing is insufficient because it does not come to grips with the possibility that under certain conditions—for example, actively explored, temporally extended sources of stimulation—sensory *inputs may be able to convey directly accurate information about their sources in the environment. That is, to be fully adequate, the selectivity at registration view must deal with the problem of how it is that inputs can convey meaningful information at this level of organization.* In order to fully understand this proposition, it is necessary to turn to the ecologically oriented approach to event perception proposed by J. J. Gibson (Gibson, 1979; Shaw & Bransford, 1977). I do not, however, as becomes clear shortly, accept Gibson's (1977, 1979) view that we in effect banish inferential processes from the description of what goes on in ordinary knowing. Indeed, it is my hunch that one of the major values of taking a close look at how and what we know about other people is that it is going to turn out that even under ecologically valid event conditions certain aspects of social knowing will require that we go beyond the information available in even dynamically organized stimulus arrays.

Having made this rather heretical statement from the Gibsonian standpoint (albeit, I would argue, in a good ecological way), I hasten to add that most work in social perception has proceeded in the wrong direction. That is, one should not begin by denigrating the value of stimulus information but rather by attempting to see how far we can get with unelaborated stimulation before it appears necessary to appeal to higher-order cognitive processes. Viewed this way, we would begin by evaluating the adequacy of the informational support that exists in the stimulus structure of a given type of social encounter. The question then becomes how much, if any, additional cognitive elaboration is required for the perceiver to achieve a given type of social knowing, such as identification of emotions, causal attributions, and so on. That is, we begin by assuming that in most cases (1) there is valuable information in the temporally extended stimulus event; (2) any subsequent elaborations are superimposed upon this initial stimulus-based meaning.

---

[2]A good example of this distinction is available from a TV documentary called "Getting Straight," in which juvenile offenders distinguish between having the offenders see a TV version of what happened and being there in person to hear actual convicts talk about the horrors of prison life in a personally threatening way.

A SOCIAL-KNOWING CONTINUUM

The present view of the nature of how we come to acquire knowledge about the properties of other people differs from conventional interpretations in a number of ways. The basic premise of the interpretation I am advocating is that we cease to limit our descriptions of a given epistemic encounter to *either* a perception-based or a cognition-based interpretation. Such a dualistic formulation (e.g., Jones & Thibaut, 1958) precludes a whole range of interactions between perceptual and cognitive processes that I designate mixed mode processing—that is, I envisage a range of possibilities that includes (1) situations in which what is known based on perceptual knowing strongly biases the nature of higher-order cognitive judgments; (2) situations in which perceptual and cognitive modes are equally important; (3) situations in which the lower-order meaning is substantially transformed at a higher level of processing. I propose instead that we view actual social knowing as a *continuum* encompassing situations that entail no or minimal inference, moderate inference, or a great deal of inference. Here, inference means the utilization of constructive cognitive operations to clarify the meaning of a given event.

Traditional formulations are inadequate for a number of reasons. First, they fail to appreciate the possible value of knowledge based on unelaborated or minimally elaborated stimulus information (perception-based knowledge; see Fig. 4.1)—for example, the possibility that a person's internal states, such as his or her attitudes, emotions, intentions, and so on, may be isomorphically represented in manifest stimulus information that occurs over time, such as gait, posture, and various other expressive gestures of a spontaneous nature. Further, current formulations, even to the extent they recognize the possible importance of perceptual-based knowledge (e.g., Heider, 1958; Newtson, 1976), tend to treat a given phenomenon as *either* perception or cognition based. Such dualistic formulations are unable to encompass the fact that a *given phenomena of social knowing, such as impression formation or causal attribution, can be interpreted along the full range of the epistemic continuum depending on the conditions of knowing*

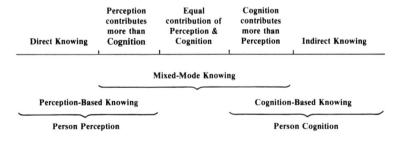

FIG. 4.1.   The social-knowing continuum.

available in any given encounter. For example, according to the present view, the epistemic process is likely to differ in regard to becoming increasingly *less* inferential when we shift from eliciting causal attributions in response to verbal vignettes (e.g., McArthur, 1972) to using dynamic visual displays such as videotapes or moving pictures (e.g., Heider & Simmel, 1944; McArthur & Post, 1977; Taylor & Fiske, 1975). That is, using verbal description as opposed to on-line displays of actual events in and of itself biases the epistemic process toward more mediated modes of knowing (see Kassin & Lowe, in press, for evidence regarding the developmental implications of the switch from verbal to visual displays).

Beyond its integrative value, the present type of continuum model is useful because it forces one to consider boundary conditions or appropriate domains of power for perception-based knowledge, cognition-based knowledge, and their interactive modes. In this regard, perception-based knowledge would at a first-order level of approximation appear to be yolked to knowledge by acquaintance, whereas inference-based knowledge would seem to be implicated in the indirect pick of information, as in knowledge by description (see also in this volume Wells' distinction between experience and socialization-based attributions—Chapter 15—and Thorndyke's distinction between navigation and survey-based knowledge—Chapter 7).

In addition to these general objectives, I hope that the introduction of this type of continuum will achieve two specific objectives in regard to the work being done in person perception. First, *I want to promote a deeper understanding of the nature of perceptual knowing in regard to the Gibsonian ecological-event perspective.* Second, *I hope to convince social psychologists of the value of this perspective for certain current issues in social knowing.* That is, a second line of defense against considering the role of perceptual processes in social knowing is to concede that they occur, but to question their importance (Jones & Thibaut, 1958). Specifically, I illustrate the value of the present approach in regard to two current lines of investigation in social perception–social cognition: the basis of causal attributions and the nature of the nonverbal communication of affect. Finally, it shoud be noted that in the course of developing the argument for a perceptual interpretation, the *minimal* thrust of such a view is that we pay more attention to the role of the temporally extended stimulus in social knowing—that is, analyses of social knowing should begin by specifying the possible stimulus-based informational supports for a given social judgment. The Gibsonian interpretation of the functional nature of such event-type information is presented in the following section.

Perception-Based Knowing

The role of perceptual knowing as we conceive of it is revealed most clearly as we go from direct knowing at the extreme left of the continuum through the point where perception-based knowledge dominates higher-order inferences. Before pointing to empirical phenomena that appear to be good candidates for a direct-perception interpretation, I would like to provide a brief overview of what it does and does not mean to adopt such a position.

At the most basic level, we take direct perception to mean that because environmental events structure light (e.g., ambient reflected light), sounds, and other physical parameters in ways specific to their sources in regard to properties of surface and substance, the information available for perception is already sufficiently rich that no additional cognitive elaboration is required to disambiguate its meaning. Such an interpretation transforms perception into an act of discovery or detection as opposed to construction. The metaphor Gibson (1968) offers is one of a radio receiver resonating to particular frequencies because of its particular structure: Given that many frequencies reach a receiver, a properly tuned receiver only resonates to some of the incoming signals and not to others (see Michaels & Carello, 1979, for an elaboration of this metaphor). Similarly, different species and different organisms within a species, because of differences in the nature of their sensory equipment and/or learning histories, resonate to different aspects of the information available about a given environment.

However, accepting this view of perception does not, as critics such as Shaver (1977) commonly assume, commit one to viewing perceivers as "passive and objective coders of stimulus information [p. 95]' "; nor is it correct to say that the stimulus structure can cause or determine what an organism perceives (cf. Gyr, 1972; Mace & Pittenger, 1975). These statements are inaccurate because they do not take into account the fact that Gibson has made two types of distinctions. The first deals with the distinction between the physical stimulus (e.g., radiant light) and information (ambient light—that is, light that is reflected off of cluttered terrestial surfaces). The second, and for our purposes more relevant, is Gibson's distinction between objective information (information about the world irrespective of perceiver properties) and useful information (information for animals). Specifically, one can talk of useful information only when the role of the perceiver is considered. Within the realm of useful information, the perceiver's contribution can, in turn, be specified at two levels.

The Meaning of an Active Perceiver.   At the simplest level, there is a confusion in regard to what a perceiver has to do to be considered active. I would claim that both the Gibsonian and information-processing approaches require an active perceiver but define active in two different senses. In the classic information-processing approach (Neisser, 1967), a perceiver is considered active if he or she engages in cognitive activities (e.g., inference, deduction, and so on) that serve to organize and give meaning to inadequate (e.g., fragmented and meaningless) sense data. In contrast to this "mental-constructivist" view of an active perceiver, Gibson's perceiver is less active "in the head" and more active "in the world"; active for Gibson means actively exploring—for example, manipulating or walking around the environment to put the sensory systems in contact with objects whose higher-order properties change over time. Further, in contradistinction to the constructivist information processor who is always in danger of exceeding his or her channel capacity, there is little danger of overload when information is obtained through exploration. Indeed, the more information that is available, the less confused the Gibsonian perceiver becomes. For example, the more perspectives one has on an object, the easier it is to know its essential identity; the more complete the rotation or the more contexts in which one sees an entity, the easier it is to establish what is invariant from what is changing (see the following discussion of the nature of events). Thus, the existence of overload may be more of a commentary on the lack of opportunity for adequate observation than any limitations of the perceiver.

It is, however, possible that these two positions are complementary. Is it not possible that a perceiver becomes a "constructivist" out of necessity when the sense data are inadequate because our typical experimental paradigm rules out active exploration? Perhaps the mind does the walking when our fingers or legs cannot. I would argue that by restricting the movements of the perceiver, by using static as opposed to dynamic displays, we cut the perceiver off from certain higher-order sources of information that are available to a more active perceiver in the form of texture gradients, transforming optic arrays, and so on (Gibson, 1979).

Affordances as Useful Information.   There is also a deeper level at which the stereotype of the passive, noncontributing perceiver is incompatible with an ecological perspective. Useful information is defined relationally; its very availability rests upon a compatibility between animal and environment. For example, snakes are superior detectors of thermal information, dogs and bats of auditory information, and humans of visual color information. Why this should be becomes clear when we realize that useful information is the information necessary for a given species to survive in a given environmental setting.

Information that specifies what behaviors can be engaged in with respect to a particular animal–environment ecosystem is referred to by Gibson (1977, 1979) as *affordance* information. The affordances of an environment are what opportunities for action—for example, walking, swimming, sitting, and so on—it offers (furnishes, provides) a particular type of animal. Such "offerings" or affordances require that we *consider jointly* the properties or contributions of the perceiving animal and the environment—for instance, the properties of surface and substance. The collaborative or ecosystem-like nature of affordance information may be illustrated at a number of levels including the sensory and response capabilities of animals as well as more transitory needs and attitudes.

For example, at the species level, "wallness" will have a different meaning for species such as flies, which are equipped for walking on walls, than for creatures such as humans who lack cup-like feet. Within-species variations also exist. A pencil can be perceived by an adult as being an instrument for writing meaningful prose; this potential use does not exist for a one-year-old child. With regard to transitory states, a piece of stale bread may appear edible to a hungry person, but not to a well-fed person.

Given this relational view of useful information, we cannot say that the stimulus structure causes or determines what the person will perceive, because what will be perceived *cannot* be specified independently of the perceiver's contributions, be they be his or her level of obtained stimulation in regard to active exploration or perceiver-state properties in regard to current attunements or "preparedness."

Finally, viewing information in affordance terms helps to specify limiting conditions for when perception will be direct. First, an unmediated view makes most sense in environmental settings in which what we want to occur is reasonably likely to occur; in such situations, the perceptual apparatus may be said to resonate to the structure of the environment. For example, under ordinary circumstances, a hungry frog on a lily pad will flick its tongue out at small, rapidly moving black objects. In such situations, it is unlikely that the frog requires higher-order mediation to disambiguate the meaning of the black darting object; for such a frog in such a setting, black, darting objects are for eating. Similarly, it is argued later that the meaning of certain human gestures may be equally directly available—for example, the meaning of clenched teeth and a raised fist. In such situations, the perceiver's allocation of attention matches the natural distribution of what will be perceptually salient.

From this perspective, mediational processes became necessary for events that are unusual, irrelevant, or insignificant for the interaction goals of given animals in given settings. *In this context, direct perception of the natural physical environment works because the sensitivities or attunements of animals have coevolved with changes in the properties of their habitual environments or niches.*[3] The challenge for future work is to establish whether similar synergistic relationships hold at the level of the social environment; for example, in a latter section of this chapter we explore the utility of treating aspects of emotion communication and causal attribution as social affordances whose meaning can be directly apprehended.

A second-order constraint on whether meaning can be achieved without higher-order cognitive elaboration is the nature of the informational support available in a given person–environment encounter. Direct perception is constrained on the one hand by *what it is necessary to know to function adaptively* and on the other hand *by the "goodness" of the information that is available about the environment.*

---

[3]This follows from viewing perception in ecosystem terms; from this perspective, organisms and their environments fit together in a manner such that each shapes the other. Thus, each species requires a particular environment and each environment will only support certain kinds of species.

Specifically, it is in the course of interacting with a *continually changing environment over time* that the information necessary for direct perception is generated. It is the information available in events—that is, it is the information telling us how change affects entities—that allows us to disambiguate the functional meaning of objects and object complexes. For the Gibsonian, it is the event, viewed as the smallest natural or ecologically valid unit of perception, that allows us to escape the frozen and fragmented stimulation that entails a constructive mode of knowing (Shaw, McIntyre, & Mace, 1974).

Finally, before moving on to a more detailed description of the nature of events, it should be understood that the nature of events and the nature of affordances are two sides of the same coin in that the structure of events is likely to follow the structure of affordances. In this regard, the *communication of long-term needs* is likely to require *morphological changes* of a relatively enduring nature to ensure that the need state will be constantly recognizable during a period of vulnerability or dependency. For example, recent discussions by Alley (1979) of how the dependency needs of young primates are communicated points to role of skin coloration and a "cuteness" configuration of the cranial–facial mask. Variable short-term needs, on the other hand, do not appear to generate slow, morphologically etched events. Here, a fast-event mechanism that is sensitive to rapid changes in the availability of food or the occurrence of danger is required. Perhaps this is a prototype for the fast-event properties of emotion signaling and nonverbal communication in general.

The Nature of Events

Before formally defining what a Gibsonian means by an event, we may note that events come in many varieties. They may be fast, such as walking or rotating a top, or slow, such as aging or illness. They occur to inanimate as well as animate objects. Further, events differ in what properties of objects they change; some events leave object shape alone—for example, rigid displacements such as rotation and translation; others are elastic—that is, they deform shape, such as by bending, stretching, flowing, squashing, bulging, and so on. In each of these cases, it may be noted that we are dealing with spatial–temporal change processes in regard to what properties or variables are changed or remain constant when certain operations are applied to a given entity or organization of entities.

Events as Transformations.   The best, albeit the most complex, formulation of the nature of events comes from the work of Robert Shaw and his associates (e.g., Shaw & Pittenger, 1977). In his research and theorizing about the nature of slow and fast changes, Shaw makes a number of bold assumptions that extend Gibson's basic insight that higher-order information is available in the optic array of light in regard to how entities characteristically deform light over time (e.g., Gibson, 1979).

In his interpretation of the nature of events, Shaw eschews the common-sense view that knowledge of change involves an inference based on stored information that ties together two isolated temporal experiences (e.g., Newtson, 1976). Instead, Shaw gives us a perspective on change that offers a very deep view of the relationship between variants and invariants—for example, between what variables of stimulation remain constant and what variables of stimulation change. Change according to this interpretation is best understood by trying to specify the properties of transformations that leave certain properties of objects constant while others change. Specifically, Shaw has proposed that the minimal description of a perceptual event involves two classes of invariants, structural and transformational.

Structural invariants are the properties of the world that remain constant over a given style of change. That is, some properties of a given object change and others remain constant (the structural invariants) over a particular type of change. For instance, the shape of an object remains constant over rotation as a form of change; the person's identity as ''John'' can still be perceived despite the fact that John undergoes elastic transformations such as aging and sickness.

Transformational invariants are global styles of change or mapping operations that remain constant while applied to any number of different structures; for example, many different types of entities can be rotated or transformed from a circle into an elipse. *Transformations both define and are constrained by the objects they change.* For example, an object will appear as a cube when rotated on its face only for certain periods out of a 360° rotation (four times or every 90° of rotation, giving a symmetry period of four). On the other side of the coin, the nature of a given transformation is partially defined by the objects it can be applied to; for example, only solid objects can be rotated.

Shaw goes on to make the assumption that the information specifying change and nonchange for a given entity can be directly perceived. This proposition becomes readily demystified if we simply modify it to read that the *effects* of different change processes—that is, their traces, records, or dynamic consequences—provide information about (1) the nature of the change that has occurred; (2) what the identity is of the entity undergoing change.

In the course of elaborating and demonstrating the value of his direct-perception view of events, Shaw has made two further claims that are central to his position. First, Shaw has proposed that the invariants specifying the nature of biological or elastic change are often of a sufficiently high order that they can only be described by non-Euclidean Geometries—that is, elastic change destroys basic metric properties such as the distance between two points, only preserving weaker topological properties such as connecticity and the ordering of points. In addition to being highly abstract, elastic transformations appear to be highly global in that a given form of change radiates over a number of substructures or local elements; for example, aging involves a characteristic style of deformation or remodeling that affects the whole body. Further, such transformations have high generality—that is, they retain their characteristic geometric properties over a wide range of entities; thus, the nature of aging as a topological transformation appears to be the same whether we view the aging process in humans, dogs, birds, and so on (Pittenger, Shaw, & Mark, in press).

Building on this view of the nature of the information specifying elastic-biological change (e.g., Pittenger & Shaw, 1975; Shaw & Pittenger, 1977), Shaw and his associates go on to make a second bold claim (see especially Pittenger, Shaw, & Mark, in press): Specifically, it is proposed that the *direct perception of change involves a strong isomorphism between the actual physical–biological properties of a given change phenomenon and the properties of the information necessary for a perceptual judgment.* For example, Pittenger, Shaw, and Mark (in press), when attempting to model the nature of the information used by people in making judgments of the age of a human face, looked at the actual properties of biological growth in regard to characterizing the geometric effects of aging on the cranial–facial complex. Based on these observations and on the earlier work of D'Arcy Thompson (1942), a particular type of topological transformation was selected as providing an isomorphic description of the physical growth process and the nature of the information used to make judgments about aging. Specifically, the primary aim of Shaw's research on the perception of craniofacial growth and aging has been the attempt to identify a mathematical transformation that models or produces the appearance of craniofacial growth when applied to the human head. A candidate transformation was identified in the form of a cardiodal strain deformation—that is, human growth, particularly during the first 20 years, appears to involve a global remodeling of the cranial–facial complex describable by a characteristic skewing of the relative size of the face to the head. The global character of such changes (which are somewhat analogous to transforming a circle into an elipse) are readily seen in Fig. 4.2.

The initial research involved applying different amounts of the candidate strain transformation and a competing transformation (affine shear) to the profile of a 10-year-old boy and comparing perceived age level for the two transformations. The outcome of the age-judgment task in experiment 1 (Pittenger & Shaw, 1975) shows that the cardiodal strain transformation had a marked effect on perceived age level whereas affine shear did not. A second study (Mark, 1979) compared the perceptual consequences of cardiodal strain and other prospective growth transformations to a sequence depicting actual growth using a variety of converging tasks including spontaneous judgments for which the subjects were not told age was the dimension of ordering. The results of these experiments and other studies that transform profile tracings of X rays of young children show that the perceptual and physical effects produced by cardiodal strain are nearly equivalent to those produced by actual growth. Related studies (e.g., Pittenger, Shaw, & Mark, in press) show the generality of the transformation by obtaining equiva-

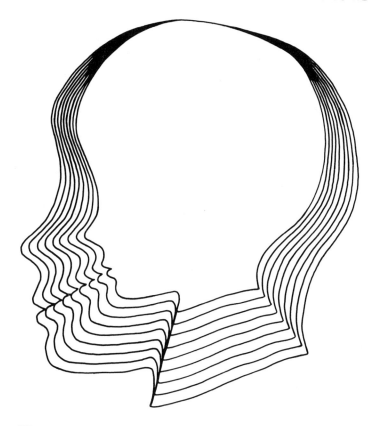

FIG. 4.2.   Examples of a cardiodal strain transformation for growth. (Adapted with permission from Todd, Mark, & Shaw, in press.)

lent perceived-age judgments for a range of animate and inanimate objects (e.g., human faces; faces of ducks, birds, and dogs; VW's, and chairs).

Although the studies of Shaw and his associates have thus far been limited to the investigation of slow-change processes, further support for the view that change can be perceived directly comes from the research of Johansson and his followers (e.g., Bassili, 1978; Cutting & Koslowski, 1977; Cutting, Proffitt, & Koslowski, 1978; Runeson, 1977) using *fast events* as stimulus displays.

The Point–Light Display.   Johansson (1973) has developed a fast-event paradigm for studying global dynamic events involving the perception of biomechanical movement. Johansson (1973) has shown that less than a dozen spots of light representing the movements of the main joints of the human body are sufficient for people to be able to identify both intensive and extensive properties of the display. People can not only correctly identify the mode of biomechanical movement—that is, whether people are walking, climbing, jumping, running, or dancing, and so on—but also the quality of the movement—the amount of effort expended in these activities.

Recent extensions of the Johansson technique are also noteworthy. Cutting and his associates (Cutting & Koslowski, 1977; Cutting et al., 1978) have utilized gait information of the Johansson type to demonstrate that people are able to identify personal and gender identity. Further, Bassili (1978) has recently demonstrated that movements of the face revealed through changes in points of reflected light are sufficient to disambiguate the meaning of the six primary emotions from posed displays presented dynamically. Applying the Johansson procedures to facial movement, Bassili was successful despite the fact that this technique obliterates local feature information.

Taken together, the Johansson-type studies suggest that in regard to fast events (1) judgments occur rapidly (e.g., in Johansson's research in less than a third of a second); (2) there is a high level of accuracy; (3) no extensive pretraining is required; (4) judgments occur without the person's being consciously aware of the type of information being used; (5) accurate identification occurs only when a *dynamic* as opposed to a static display is used; (6) global configurational information as opposed to local feature changes appears to be crucial.

Further, it may be noted that although fast and slow events provide the perceiver with different kinds of change information (kinematic and dynamic in regard to fast events; geometric in regard to slow events), a case can be made for the perceptual equivalence of these different types of information.[4] Specifically, it may be possible to directly apprehend the nature of slow events when the resultant geometric change has the form of a *spatial record of past kinematic and dynamic movements;* that is, the current geometric structure may spatially summarize the kinematic and dynamic changes that lead up to it (Shaw, 1978). For example, consider a photograph of the impact of a tornado such that as we move our eyes from left to right we literally see a ''trail of destruction.'' Here, change is sequentially manifested in a spatial translation of a temporal course of events. On the other hand, static displays of truly stationary objects give us pictures of things as opposed to events (e.g., a picture of a person versus a picture of a *new,* manufactured object).

Finally, it may be noted that the term *event* has been used at various levels of commitment to the importance of studying the perception of spatial–temporal change processes. First, it may be noted that at the simplest level, any research

---

[4]In this context, kinematic information refers to knowledge available from the direction, velocities, accelerations, and so on, of entities undergoing rapid change. Dynamic information refers to the information about change available in properties such as mass, energy, force, power, and so on. Geometric information is available from changes in the spatial organization of elements in a coordinate system.

that uses dynamic as opposed to static displays is implicating events at least at a methodological level. It is in this sense that much of the perceptual salience-causal attribution research of Taylor and Fiske (1975, 1978), because it uses videotapes instead of verbal materials, qualifies as event relevant. An event orientation at a somewhat deeper level of commitment treats events as objects of substantive interest either in their own right or as a way of studying other phenomena. Here, we would place the classic works of Michotte (1963) and Heider and Simmel (1944), as well as the recent unitization research of Darren Newtson (1976). Finally, there are those researchers, such as Shaw and Johansson, whose interest in events is at a deeper epistemological and perhaps even ontological level. Research is undertaken to demonstrate that events provide a basis for claiming that perception is direct—that is, sufficient information exists in the *display given the perceiver's state of preparedness or attunement* to enable accurate identification of the meaning of the event without recourse to higher-order constructive or mediational processes. Thus, any inquiry into the role that event-based perceptual knowledge plays should begin by distinguishing among *what information might be available (Gibson's objective level of information), what information can potentially be used (Gibson's affordance or useful information), and what information is typically utilized for a given type of social knowing (the present focus).*

THE NATURE OF THE RELATIONSHIP BETWEEN PERCEPTION AND COGNITIVE-BASED KNOWING

In this section, I would like both to motivate and describe situations in which one may have to invoke cognition-based knowing. As I view this problem, such situations range from what I have designated mixed-mode processing to primarily inference-based knowing where the impact of the initial stimulus-based knowledge is clearly secondary to the role of constructive processes in determining the ultimate social judgment.

At one level, the argument is trivial. From the Gibsonian perspective, mediation occurs when the person is prevented from access to the potential information in the environment—that is, when adequate informational support is not available. This situation may include everything from immobilizing the perceiver to presenting poorly illuminated or static stimulus displays. The importance of inference in such situations does not trouble Gibson (1979), because they do not reflect ecologically valid conditions of visual perception. They are but unusual special cases.

A more serious challenge to the direct-perception position is to argue that certain phenomena as they naturally occur under ecologically valid conditions require that the perceiver go "beyond the information given." This may in fact be the case in regard to knowing certain aspects of the social environment.

Specifically, I would claim at least provisionally that the story of how we know other people cannot be completely told in terms of direct perception. However, I also believe that it behooves us to see how far we can go in direct-perception terms before invoking cognitive mechanisms. I now specify the reasons for the position I have taken, both in general terms and in terms of two in-depth examples; causal attributions and emotion communication. These reasons should be viewed as an initial attempt to establish boundary conditions for different epistemic processes:

1. *The context of knowledge acquisition.* Although in regard to the physical world, it may be argued that knowledge by description is a less representative and ecologically valid way of learning about the environment, this does not appear to hold true in regard to the social environment. Specifically, second hand, representational, vicarious knowing appears to be both common and highly adaptive in regard to social knowing. I cite two examples. Bandura (1969, 1977), in his analyses of observational learning in regard to the impact of vicarious instrumental conditioning, points to the clear adaptive advantages of learning what behaviors will have positive consequences and what behaviors will have aversive consequences by observing other people as opposed to directly performing the actions. Second, Wells (Chapter 15 in this volume) does an excellent job of differentiating attributional knowledge based on socialization—for example, asking parents why events occur—from attributional knowledge based on direct observation of how events covary.

A less interesting version of the context of knowledge acquisition biasing the mode of knowing is simply to use experimental paradigms that diminish the person's possibility for first-hand experience with the other social entity. Such procedures typically eschew immediate judgment of on-going events. For example, one can reduce another person to a list of adjectives (e.g., Asch, 1946) or sentences (Hamilton & Leirer, 1979) and substitute delayed recall for on-line assessments (Ebbesen & Allen, 1979). Given such an impoverished informational support, the person has no recourse but to use memorial–inferential processes. Such situations simply demonstrate that knowledge-by-description is likely to entail cognition-based knowing.

2. *The instability of the social-stimulus display.* There are two senses in which the entities in the social world may create problems for a nonmediated view of knowing, even when viewed in event terms—for instance, as part of a face-to-face encounter over time. First, the simple presence of another person will alter the properties of a social stimulus—that is, the "Heisenberg phenomenon of indeterminancy" is likely to be much more acute in regard to the social than nonsocial environment. Specifically, both the properties of the perceiver and the perceived are continually changing on many dimensions, some reciprocal and some not. One possible solution in this regard is to assume that with increasing familiarity, social knowing becomes more direct. From a Gibsonian point of

view, what might be said to be occurring is an "education of attention" such that the relevant event information for perception does not exist until familiarity occurs. From this perspective, we simply need a broader event boundary for social than nonsocial events, an insight partially captured by Heider (1958) in his suggestion that social knowing is likely to involve more temporally extended perceptual fields. An alternative view is that initial social-impression formation at an existential level is relatively inferential and that only with extended acquaintance can we move to a more direct level of knowing. The analogy for this interpretation is one of skilled performance; initially, learning is highly monitored and then with mastery becomes automatic or nommediated.

3. *The "hidden"-meaning problem in social knowing.* Meanings can be hidden is social knowing for two reasons. First, it is possible to argue that certain properties of people are simply not capable of being recognized in terms of manifest physical-stimulus characteristics. Specifically, we may question Gibson's (1977, 1979) assertion that social affordances provide the same type of informational support as nonsocial afforances. For example, whereas one person's hostility may be overtly manifested in terms of clenched teeth, raised fists, and so on, is another person's compassion or guilt readily available in terms of physical-stimulus properties? At this point, we, of course, simply do not know; it is possible to argue that we are simply dealing with higher-order invariants, more abstract transformations that only become available after more extended interpersonal explorations.

Alternately, one can question whether complex social motives can be understood without at least mixed-mode processing; that is, perhaps we do pick up something useful on a direct level, but this has to be elaborated for us to achieve more complex levels of social meaning. Incidentally, I believe this view is a correct reading of Heider's (1958) position on social knowing (see Newtson, 1976, for a similar interpretation). This interpretation contrasts sharply with Jones and Thibaut (1958), who propose that social knowing is almost completely a matter of cognitive-based knowledge acquisition (see also Taylor & Fiske, 1978, for a straight social-cognition view).

Another variant of the hidden-meaning problem is the *case of deception.* Here, another person intentionally utilizes a deceptive self presentation—a possibility not likely to occur in regard to knowing the inanimate world. Because according to Goffman (1959) such deceptive interpersonal strategies are normative, their existence poses an interesting problem for the direct-perception view. That is, when self presentation is monitored, we are likely to be deceived so long as we take the other person's gestures at their "face value." Stated somewhat more generally, it is possible to claim that whereas illusions are atypical in the physical world, they are the very fabric of social interaction.

From this perspective, direct perception would only make adaptive sense for social properties that are difficult to falsify—for example, identity, age, gender, and, we argue subsequently, certain spontaneously expressed affective and motivational states. From a Gibsonian perspective, a possible rejoinder would be the assertion that deception can be disambiguated in terms of higher order transformations that differentiate a pseudoself display from a genuine one. For example, there is a suggestion from the work of Ekman and Friesen (1975) that the amount of time certain facial expressions are held differentiates between currently experienced and secondarily described emotions. Similarly, it might be argued that disambiguating a false self presentation is simply a problem in the education of attention; that is, we learn to shift our attention from channels where a high level of voluntary control exists—for example, the face—to other channels that are low in voluntary control—for instance, postural information.

Another version of how deception might be disambiguated from a direct-perception view is to argue that what is necessary is an extended event frame such that the person is seen in many contexts, playing many different roles. From a Gibsonian perspective, it may be argued that only by seeing a person from many different perspectives can one distinguish variants from invariants. This example nicely distinguishes the Gibsonian interpretation from the conventional overload view. According to the Gibsonian approach, the *more* perspective information obtained, the easier it is to detect the "true" meaning of the stimulus event.

In sum, at the risk of antagonizing advocates of both extreme positions, we have tried both to motivate problems for a Gibsonian direct-perception position as well as to suggest their possible rejoinders. One way to flesh out our argument is to examine two different current areas of social knowing—causal attribution and emotion communication—in depth with regard to the present "social-knowing continuum" (see Fig. 4.1).

Causal Attributions: A Many-Splendored Epistemic Act

Before analyzing the case for how we come to know about the motives, intentions, reasons, and so on, of others' actions, it is necessary to put this problem in perspective. First, I wish to reiterate that when Gibsonians use the term "direct perception," they do not refer to the phenomenological experience of direct knowledge; they refer to the possibility that tacit knowledge about the meaning of environmental events is potentially available in the structure of sensory input without the mediation of various constructive processes. Thus, the Gibsonian is *not* trying to predict a phenomenological criterion of directness; rather, he or she is concerned with whether there is an adequate informational support in the stimulus configuration for properly attuned perceivers to discern moods, intentions, views, attitudes, and perhaps even personality traits from observing the world of events. That is, because knowing the intentions of other people is obviously useful from an adaptive point of view—for example, it makes the other person's behavior understandable and predictable—there should exist information in the unfolding of social events to reveal underlying reasons, motives, intentions, and so on.

Given this proposition, one can proceed to establish how much can be known at a perceptual level. In terms of the present continuum, this type of question can involve either "pure" direct perception or perceptually biased cognitive judgments (e.g., Newtson, 1976). Each of these interpretations is discussed in turn.

The Direct Perception of Causality.   First, from an ecological–direct-perception point of view the problem should be formulated as follows: If the other person actually intends something towards a perceiver and is acting on this intent, how might this intention be specified in the world as opposed to in the perceiver's mind? That is, the intentions of another person are viewed as real properties of the person's interactions with the physical–social environment rather than attributes whose reality rests on inferences made by perceivers. For example, seeing someone struggle to move against a stiff wind would appear to allow the direct specification of a personal intent to move in a particular direction. Similarly, observing someone act cooperatively in a situation where other people are behaving competitively would appear to directly implicate the nature of a person's intentions (Hansen & Lowe, 1976). Indeed, there is evidence in the research of Kassin and Lowe (in press) that when Kelley's (1971) augmentation principle is presented in terms of dynamic visual displays in the mode of Heider and Simmel (1944) children can recognize the principle many years earlier than had come to be expected based on verbal vignette-type studies. That is, when on-line perceptual judgments are used, children as young as kindergarten age (5–6) are able to answer "why" questions (including forced choice, open-ended, and scaler ratings) in a way that indicates knowledge of augmentation effects. Previous research using stories and verbal-recall procedures (e.g., Shultz, Butkowsky, Pearce, & Stanfield, 1975) found no evidence of understanding below the eighth grade when kindergarten, fourth-, and eighth-grade students were compared. Such data suggest that contrary to Kelley's mediation interpretation, young children's interpretations of the augmentation principle are dominated by immediately given perceptual evidence rather than by higher-level cognitive inferences (Kassin & Lowe, in press).

In a similar vein, Runeson (1977) argues for a direct-perception interpretation of Heider and Simmel's original research. According to Runeson (1977), the original data suggest that "one immediately sees who is hunting whom, who hits whom, etc. It is also immediately seen who is aggressive and afraid [p. 17]." From the present perspective, immediate recognition data implies direct perception because it does not allow sufficient time for higher-order inference processes to have occurred. Another type of evidence in regard to the work of Heider and Simmel, which is relevant to the direct-perception argument, is Runeson's claim that the perception of causality is so strongly demanded by the stimulus events that causal judgments are resistant to preinformation. Here, the evidence appears mixed. An early attempt to modify such judgments by giving information about the nature of the forms did not have powerful effects on the impressions of dynamic relations (Shor, 1957). For example, *reversed preinformations did not reverse perceived causal relations.* However, a recent investigation (Massod, Hubbard, & Newtson, 1979) finds that causal judgments can be shifted if the set shifts patterns of unitization.

In one sense, however, the impact or lack of impact of preinformation is the wrong way to state the problem, because from a Gibsonian perspective all one would have to argue is that the preinformation should not be viewed as context but rather as requiring that a broader event that includes the preinformation be defined. However, from another perspective, the impact of preinformation does provide a useful way of demonstrating that a given phenomenon is perceptually as opposed to cognitively based.

This point is clearly recognized in Darren Newtson's research, which at a programmatic level seeks to demonstrate how a perceptual-level process, the fineness or style (the pattern) of the perceiver's segmentation or unitization of on-going stimulus events, biases higher-order cognitive judgments such as causal attribution. Specifically, from Newtson's type of perspective, a set will determine what aspects of a complex stimulus display will be seen as important. It can then be assumed that people will unitize more finely aspects of a display that are categorized as more important—that is, they will attempt to extract more information from important than unimportant aspects of a display (see J. C. Russell, 1979, for direct support for this proposition). Finally, following the analyses of Taylor and Fiske (1978), it may then be assumed that perceptually salient (for example, the more important aspects of a display) will be more readily available as loci for causal attributions. Thus, unitization may be linked to causal attributions because it identifies the nature of the person's distribution of attention.

General evidence relevant to the case for a perception-based interpretation of such higher-order judgments can also be found in the work of Zadney and Gerard (1974). This study demonstrates that preinformation affects subsequent judgments by operating at the level of registration as opposed to retrieval (a set is given both prior to viewing a scene and prior to a recall measure). A recent study by Cohen and Ebbesen (1979), although concerned with impression formation as opposed to causal attribution, is also supportive of the present position because it demonstrates that both the amount and pattern of unitization (1) are linked to an initial set; (2) are linked to the distal social judgment. A recent study by Newtson and his associates (Enquist, Newtson, & LaCross, 1979) is of particular relevance because it combines a Zadney-and-Gerard-type treatment and retrieval measurement procedure with a unitization measure.

Further, support for perception-based knowing in causal-attribution research would appear to exist in attempts to link perceptual salience with causal attribution (McArthur & Post, 1977; Taylor & Fiske, 1975, 1978). This domain of research is critical for a number of reasons. First, it is one of the few areas in person perception where dynamic-event information is the rule rather than the exception. Second, it is one of the few areas in person perception in which a systematic attempt has been made to identify the nature of the processes mediating causal attribution. The work of Taylor and Fiske (e.g., 1978) has been instrumental in generating both of these methodological advances. In particular, Taylor and Fiske (1978) make the claim that the relationship between perceptual salience and causal attribution is mediated at the encoding–retrieval level such that salient portions of the perceptual field are double encoded (iconically and verbally) and hence have become more available. The inability of Taylor to demonstrate such a mediation pattern despite an elegant and systematic program of research designed to demonstrate the presence of such higher order biasing raises the possibility that the biasing is more perceptual than Taylor and Fiske have been willing to accept up until now (see, however, Taylor, Crocker, Fiske, Sprinzen, & Winkler, 1979, for a more open position in regard to the possible impact of stimulus-based perceptual processes).

From the perspective of my earlier interpretation of the nature of the unitization–causal attribution linkage (see the section[11] in this chapter), one way to directly demonstrate the operation of perceptually based knowledge in this area is to collect both unitization and recall data and examine the causal paths for each in regard to causal attributions based on perceptual salience manipulations. That is, evidence for a perceptual-level processing would exist if we were able to demonstrate that varying perceptual salience affects the fineness and/or pattern of unitization, which, in turn, affects causal judgments (ideally in the same study, in which nonsignificant effects hold for retrieval-mediated paths). Such research is currently in progress in my lab (especially in regard to affect behaviors).

Before moving on to a discussion of the second substantive example, emotion communication, the unwary reader should be apprised of the fact that as I moved off of the Heider–Simmel-type paradigm, I changed the ground of my argument from direct perception to a mixed-mode variant of perception-based knowledge. I did this for two reasons: First, this is the level at which people like Newtson interpret the meaning of what they have done; further, simply being able to demonstrate that salience effects were primarily biased at a perceptual level would be a major contribution.

However, this would not be enough for the Gibsonian. What would be necessary is a demonstration that contrary to Newtson's inference-based image comparison view of "breakpoints," the perceiver is able to directly perceive the effects of the type of change that is occurring.

Presently in our own laboratory, two types of studies are being done to test a Gibsonian interpretation of unitization data. First, we are using the perceiver's points of consensual marking as a way of tracing where in the stimulus significant change is occurring. From this specification we are then attempting to characterize the type of change or deformation in the stimulus display that occurs during these temporal periods. Second, we are utilizing experimental manipulations designed to choose between an information overload and invariant pickup interpretation of the basis of breakpoints. The logic of this kind of study involves comparing a multiple perspective with a same perspective view of a given class of behavior and comparing the location and level of consensus for breakpoints. For example, the direct-perception view would predict more consensual breakpoints where over a sequence of inputs we view a given behavior from three different perspectives as opposed to seeing the behavior three times from the same perspective; that is, in the Gibsonian view, multiple perspectives should facilitate the pickup of invariants whereas in the information-processing view, it should strain channel capacity relative to a redundant viewing of the same perspective.

EMOTIONS FROM AN ECOLOGICAL-EVENT PERSPECTIVE

Because my own event research on the perception of emotion (e.g., Goodman, Baron, Shapiro, & Buck, 1978) is still at a point where it is more interesting from a methodological than a substantive standpoint, I would like to talk more about an event strategy than results. Looking back, I think my first reason for deciding to begin with the preception of emotion was my hunch that if there was direct perception in person perception it would be easiest to demonstrate for phenomena of strong adaptive relevance. The fact that Darwin (1872) had argued for the evolutionary significance of the communication of emotion along with the cross-cultural emotion-recognition data of Ekman (Ekman, Friesen, & Ellsworth, 1972) and Izard (1971) also made it easy to make a case for the ecological significance of emotion perception. Emotion at this level seemed to qualify as *useful information* or, in Gibson's terms, it seemed *possible to treat emotion as a social affordance.* That is, emotions appear to *convey information about the type of interactions* likely to be safely afforded by *both the physical and social environments.* Moreover, there is a suggestion that animals whose niche requires increased levels of social coordination—for example, the plain-dwelling baboon as opposed to forest-dwelling mandrill and drill baboon, humans versus all other primates—have a more mobile facial musculature for expressing emotion. Further, there is evidence that humans show a certain preparedness in regard to the pickup of emotion information in the sense of Seligman's (1970) biological boundaries. For example, Ohman and Dimberg (1978) have recently demonstrated human facial expressions of anger, as opposed to neutral or happy expressions, are more readily associated with aversive events in a conditioning paradigm.

From this type of social affordance analysis, it is possible to begin to derive the properties of emotion as an event. Specifically, emotions occupy a communication function analogous to that of variable needs; the pickup of information conveyed by emotion requires a fast-changing visual display system. In terms of the present thinking, then, emotions can be classified as fast events. Perceptually, this means that the changes wrought by emotions occur rapidly and are probably supported by kinematic and dynamic information. Thus, one level of description of different emotions would be in terms of movement parameters such as rate of change of different expressive features of the face, forcefulness of change, and/or direction of change (e.g., vertical versus horizontal). Such an analysis could perhaps be used to distinguish between positive and negative emotions.

In order, however, to begin to specify the information supporting the identification of different emotions within the positive and negative realms—for example, fear versus anger or joy versus interest—it will likely prove necessary to carry out a geometric level of analysis that investigates the face as a spatial coordinate system. If we follow the approach of Shaw and his associates, this means trying to establish what is in effect a psychophysical function between a biophysical specification of the style of change that has occurred and the information used by a perceiver to identify emotions.

A consideration of the properties of surface and substance of the face suggests that the dynamic changes that occur across the surface of the face in emotions are of a type that destroys Euclidean metric properties. Specifically, the changes created by emotions involve topological deformations such as stretching, squeezing, bulging, and so on; from this perspective, one could begin to describe different emotions in terms of differences in how the face and body are systematically deformed. For example, certain emotions might be analogous to deforming a circle into an elipse.

According to Shaw (e.g., Pittenger, Shaw, & Mark, in press; Shaw & Pittenger, 1977), characterizing a change in topological terms also implies a set of general transformational properties:

1. The changes characterizing emotions are likely to be highly abstract in nature. Bassili's (1978) finding that reasonably accurate identification of the primary emotions was possible even when local feature information was obliterated and the only information was the pattern of deformation revealed by changing points of light over a surface suggests that perceivers were responding to higher-order information such as relationships between relationships. Such a specification fits Gibson's (1979) view of people picking up on "formless invariants occurring over time [p. 167]." Further, in such situations, people are not aware of the information they are using (see also Cutting et al., 1978).

2. Emotions appear to involve *global* transformations—that is, changes that affect the appearance of local features, the total facial configuration, and the appearance of the body. The effects of a given style of change are manifested across as well as within subsystems.

3. The changes characterizing different emotions appear to be *highly general*—that is, they appear applicable to a wide variety of animate and inanimate objects. For example, the "drooping" properties of sadness can be applied to a wide variety of objects.

In addition to these properties of emotions as a style of change, we can also begin to analyze what properties of people are left unchanged by emotion and whether different emotions leave different properties unchanged. For example, it appears that structural invariants specifying personal identity, sex, and race are left unchanged by all emotion changes. On the other hand, it might be speculated that properties such as *perception of age* could be affected differentialy by different emotions. For example, *sadness* may make a person look older, whereas a happy expression may make a person look younger. Similarly, judgments of physical attractiveness may be systematically affected by different emotions. Emotions also appear to differ in terms of whether they primarily inform an observer about the perceiver per se or the current state of the perceiver's environment; for instance, an expression of fear suggests the presence of danger, an expression of happiness looks more inward.

Finally, emotions even more than most properties of the social environment appear to draw the perceiver into the nature of another's psychological state; that is, emotions appear to demand reciprocal behaviors. It is with this in mind that Ross Buck and I (Baron & Buck, 1979) have begun to differentiate between the spontaneous and intentional communication of emotion, proposing that the best case for direct perception resides in spontaneous communication. *Specifically, in spontaneous displays, the nature of the overt display appears to be highly isomorphic with the person's internal state.* Moreover, the type of gesture occurring in this type of display is characterizable as a *signal* as opposed to a symbol. With a signal, there is a natural relationship between the message and what is signified (e.g., a raised, clenched fist intrinsically signifies anger—the medium is the message). With a symbol, on the other hand, the relationship between the message and the referent is arbitrary. The use of verbal sarcasm or an upraised finger to convey anger is an example of a symbolized message. In general, we expect intentional displays to make greater use of symbols. Specifically, we propose that whereas spontaneous displays are more directly perceived, intentional communications involve mixed-mode processing of a more cognitive nature. General support for the relevance of this distinction can be found in the works of Jenkins, Jimenez-Pabon, Shaw, & Sefen (1975) and Buck and Duffy (1977), which suggest that although left-hemisphere–damaged persons are impaired in symbolic–intentional communication, damage to the right hemisphere appears to impair signal processing.

A further implication of the spontaneous–intentional distinction is the issue of whether it is correct to say that emotions are perceived as "happenings"—that is, events beyond voluntary control. Buss (1978) has made this claim in attempting to distinguish between happenings and purposive actions in regard to the use of reasons versus causes as modes of attribution. There is some empirical support for this distinction in McArthur's (1972) early work on causal attribution. There are three general questions that the present approach suggests in regard to these claims: First, is this true of all emotions?; are some emotions seen as more intentional than others—for example, *anger* as opposed to *disgust?* Second, if there are distinctions among emotions, can it be demonstrated that the modes of processing differ?; are intentional emotions processed more in the mixed-mode manner? Third, does Buss' distinction break down in situations in which it is clear there is a symbolic–intentional message being conveyed? Does the focus of attributions in regard to emotions change under conditions in which emotion displays appear under voluntary control, as in role-playing, certain self-presentation strategies, and so on.

In effect, a Gibsonian analysis would argue that there will be information in the stimulus display that a properly attuned person can use to differentiate the causal locus of emotion displays under voluntary as opposed to environmental control. For example, intentional displays may involve differences in kinematic properties such as rate of change and in dynamic properties such as the forcefulness of the display; for instance, the gestures may be exaggerated in an intentional display as in a forced smile. Because further spontaneous displays are likely to involve more subtle sources of information, they may require a longer event unit and/or more fine-grain processing in Newtson's sense.

Finally, it should be noted that our general research strategy in this area has been (1) to attempt to identify the basic event structure at a psychological level by using Newtson's unitization procedure; (2) to then, in a manner somewhat opposite in direction from the approach of Shaw and his associates (e.g., Shaw & Pittenger, 1977), use the person's event judgments as markers to begin to specify the physical–stimulus properties of the underlying events. That is, we go into the display in which a change in affect has been perceived and attempt to specify the physical nature of that change in regard to the type of geometric deformation that has occurred.

Further, we can go into the stimulus in a number of ways. For example, one can make still photographs of the displays and attempt to measure the static spatial properties of a given focal configuration in regard to geometric properties, such as differences in the angle between the nose and mouth (or eyes) for different emotions. In addition to or in lieu of stopping the displays and making stills, one can merely slow down the event process and attempt to map the phase relationships between different facial expressions. For example, what geometric changes occur at the point when a neutral expression becomes sad, when a smiling face becomes a frowning face, and so on? As a variant of this approach, we can let a perceiver control the speed of the display and measure how much and what information is needed for the person to identify changes in emotion state—for example, what is occurring when people slow down or speed up the event display? Further, one can combine the procedures of Newtson and Johansson in the context of the preceding approach by using perceived points of change (breakpoints) as foci for the placement of light markers (as opposed to placing lights randomly over the surface of the face).

A CONCLUDING STATEMENT

If this chapter appears to have a provocative cast, it is by intention; I explicitly seek to force both the mediated and nonmediated camps of knowing to reexamine their basic assumptions in light of the harsh crucible of social knowing (see Craik, 1979; Kolers, 1978; Neisser, 1976, for general discussions). I realize, however, that I have not been completely evenhanded in my epistemic analysis. Such a bias is, however, inevitable because I am trying to undo 20 years of denial of the importance of perceptual processes in social knowing. This denial is all the more disturbing in the light of powerful new empirical data that challenges the prevalent social cognition view. Here, I have in mind Leslie McArthur's (1981) recent conclusions regarding the greater importance of registration than encoding or retrieval effects for impression formation and causal attribution, the continued impressive data being amassed by Darren Newtson, as well as the manifest inability of Taylor and Fiske to find evidence for an encoding–retrieval mechanism despite the excellence and breadth of their research.

Almost as disturbing is the selective borrowing that has occurred from the cognitive-process area. The work of Johansson and Shaw or Neisser about 1976 is completely ignored in even otherwise highly scholarly works on social knowing (e.g., Schneider, Hastorf, & Ellsworth, 1979). Equally unfamiliar to students of social perception is the work in basic cognitive development by Odom (1978), which challenges the constructive view at its very origins. Specifically, Odom's (1978) perceptual salience research suggests that many of the " . . . basic and significant changes that occur in psychological development are primarily or exclusively based on the perceptual system's changing sensitivity to relations in the environment rather than on changes in cognitive processes that evaluate those relations [p. 128]." Thus, if social psychologists feel the need to borrow from general work in cognitive processes, they should be aware that there is published research in mainstream cognitive journals supporting alternatives to the constructivist–information processing view of the development, structure, and functioning of epistemic processes.

Further, I find it somewhat ironic that the constructivist approach, despite all its glorifications of higher-order cognitive processes, has recently led some of its adherents to conclude that people typically process information in a mindless manner (e.g., Langer, 1978; Taylor & Fiske, 1978). When an ecological analysis is applied (e.g., when behavior is viewed from a broader functional context in terms of its long-term utility), what looks from a limited time frame as a cognitive liability often turns out to be highly adaptive. Greenwald's analysis (Chapter 25 in this volume) of the long-term adaptive value of the ego's biases is an excellent case in point.

Although I may have reserved most of my negative comments for the mediated view, I have, if a reminder is necessary, raised some basic challenges for the Gibsonian position. I have, for example, challenged the general Gibsonian view that all knowing regarding useful information is nonmediational in nature. Specifically, I have suggested that Gibson is incorrect in assuming that "nothing new under the sun" happens when we move from nonsocial to social knowing. I have in particular emphasized the untrustworthiness of intentional displays, and the general problem of whether signal- and symbol-type processing lend themselves equally well to an unmediated view of knowing other people. In effect, I have proposed that whereas illusions do not provide a good model of how we know the nonpeople world, they come closer to capturing the often intentionally deceptive nature of social phenomena than any orthodox Gibsonian would care to admit. To put the issue somewhat grandly, the nature of the epistemic process may be tailored to how likely it is that things are what they appear to be; the key constraint for the evolution of epistemic processes may be the trustworthiness of our environmental data base.

The limitations of a purely nonmediated view are also apparent from a biological–evolutional prospective. First, it appears reasonable to argue that whereas the brain-stem situated old mind operated through a direct mode of perception, the indirect mode was a relatively late development with the advent of the cerebral hemispheres (e.g., Sagan, 1977). Further, given these new brain structures, the emergence of hemispheric specialization appears to pose a basic constraint on theories of knowing. May it not be argued that direct perception provides a much better description of right-hemispheric functioning than of left-hemisphere functioning? In this regard, at least one theory of the origins of hemispheric specialization suggests that the factor that led to specialization was the development of spoken language (e.g., Gazzaniga, 1970). Specifically, in line with our differentiation between spontaneous and intentional emotion communication, it appears that more complex types of social communication that involve multiple channels (i.e., verbal and nonverbal messages) require more inferential (e.g., mixed-mode) processing.[5]

A related argument is that the development of intentional, symbolic–linguistic processes not only facilitated social communication, it also opened up the possibilities for a conscious monitoring of one's behavior (e.g., Jaynes, 1977). In this connection, it may be recalled that I proposed earlier that conscious monitor-

---

[5]In fairness, it should be noted that contrary to the present argument, some neo-Gibsonians (e.g., Verbrugge, 1977) have attempted a direct-perception interpretation of aspects of sentence comprehension, using the metaphor as a bridge that allows one to assume a perceptual basis in past sensory experience for even spoken language.

ing often results in deceptive behavior that requires inferential strategies for disambiguation; for instance, conflicting cues from different sensory modes (speech is nonverbal; face versus body, and so on) have to be integrated in some way. Such integrations may, in turn, implicate a collaborative relationship between right- and left-hemisphere information processing that is analogous to my view of mixed-mode processing at the psychological level.

Finally, I should inform the reader that the use of hemispheric specialization as a means of bolstering my position was an afterthought in regard to my construction of a social-knowing continuum. This fact notwithstanding, I find it rather interesting that in some ways, at least, the study of the development and functioning of the hemispheres entails an approach to knowing that includes perception-based knowledge, cognitive- (e.g., symbolic-) based knowledge, and the interaction of these modes.

ACKNOWLEDGMENTS

I wish to thank John Harvey, Leonard Mark, and David Kenny for their helpful comments on an earlier draft of this chapter.

REFERENCES

Albert, S., & Dabbs, J. M. Physical distance and persuasion. *Journal of Personalized Social Psychology*, 1970, *15*, 265–270.

Alley, T. R. *Infantile colouration as an elicitor of carteaking behavior in old world primates.* Unpublished manuscript, Department of Psychology, University of Connecticut, 1979.

Asch, S. E. Forming impressions of personality. *Journal of Abnormal and Social Psychology*, 1946, *41*, 258–290.

Bandura, A. *Principles of behavior modification*. New York: Holt, Rinehart, & Winston, 1969.

Bandura, A. *Social learning theory*. Englewood Cliffs, N.J.: Prentice-Hall, 1977.

Baron, R. M., & Buck, R. *A Gibsonian event perception approach to the nonverbal communication of emotion.* Paper presented as part of a symposium on ''The Meaning of Nonverbal Communication,'' at the meeting of the American Psychological Association, New York, 1979.

Bassili, J. N. Facial motion in the perception of faces and of emotional expression. *Journal of Experimental Psychology: Human Perception and Performance*, 1978, *4*, 373–379.

Buck, R., & Duffy, R. *Nonverbal communication of affect in brain damaged patients.* Paper presented at the meeting of the American Psychological Association, San Francisco, 1977.

Buss, A. R. Causes and reasons in attribution theory: A conceptual critique. *Journal of Personalized and Social Psychology*, 1978, *36*, 1311–1321.

Cohen, C. E., & Ebbesen, E. B. Observational goals and schema activation: A theoretical framework for behavior perception. *Journal of Experimental Social Psychology*, 1979, *15*, 305–329.

Craik, F. I. M. Human memory. In M. R. Rosenzweig & L. W. Porter (Eds.), *Annual review of psychology* (Vol. 30). Palo Alto: *Annual Reviews*, 1979.

Cutting, J. E., & Koslowski, L. T. Recognizing friends by their walk: Gait perception without familiarity cues. *Bulletin of the Psychonomic Society*, 1977, *9*, 353–356.

Cutting, J. E., Proffitt, D. R., & Koslowski, L. T. A biomechanical invariant for gait perception. *Journal of Experimental Psychology: Human Perception and Performance,* 1978, *4,* 357–372.

Darwin, C. *Expression of the emotions in man and animals.* London: Murray, 1872.

Ebbesen, E. B., Allen, R. B. Cognitive processes in implicit personality trait inferences. *Journal of Personality and Social Psychology,* 1979, *37,* 471–488.

Ekman, P., & Friesen, W. *Unmasking the face.* Englewood Cliffs, N.J.: Prentice-Hall, 1975.

Ekman, P., Friesen, W. V., & Ellsworth. *Emotion in the human face.* New York: Pergamon Press, 1972.

Enquist, G., Newtson, D., & LaCross, K. *Prior expectations and the perceptual segmentation of ongoing behavior.* Unpublished paper, Department of Psychology, University of Virginia, 1979.

Garfinkel, H. *Studies in ethnomethodology.* Englewood Cliffs, N.J.: Prentice-Hall, 1967.

Gazzaniga, M. S. *The bisected brain.* New York: Appleton-Century-Crofts, 1970.

Gibson, J. J. What gives rise to the perception of motion? *Psychological Review,* 1968, *75,* 335–346.

Gibson, J. J. The theory of affordances. In R. Shaw & J. Bransford (Eds.), *Perceiving, acting, and knowing: Toward an ecological psychology.* Hillsdale, N.J.: Lawrence Erlbaum Associates, 1977.

Gibson, J. J. *The ecological approach to visual perception.* Boston: Houghton-Mifflin, 1979.

Goffman, E. *The presentation of self in everyday life.* Garden City, N.Y.: Anchor Books, 1959.

Goodman, N., Baron, R. M., Shapiro, B., & Buck, R. The perceptual organization of affect displays. Abstract of papers presented at A.P.A., Toronto, 1978. *Personality and Social Psychology Bulletin,* 1978, *4,* 354.

Gyr, J. W. Is a theory of direct visual perception adequate? *Psychological Bulletin,* 1972, *77,* 246–261.

Hamilton, D., & Leirer, V. O. *Organization of information in impression development.* Paper presented at the meeting of the American Psychological Association, New York, September 1979.

Hansen, R. D., & Lowe, C. A. Distinctiveness and concensus: The influence of behavioral information on actors and observers' attributions. *Journal of Personality and Social Psychology,* 1976, *35,* 294–302.

Heider, F. *The psychology of interpersonal relations.* New York: Wiley, 1958.

Heider, F., & Simmel, M. An experimental study of apparent behavior. *American Journal of Psychology,* 1944, *57,* 243–259.

Izard, C. *The face of emotion.* New York: Appleton-Century-Crofts, 1971.

Jaynes, J. *The bicameral mind.* Boston: Houghton-Mifflin, 1977.

Jenkins, J., Jimenez-Pabon, E., Shaw, R., & Sefen, J. *Schnell's aphasia in adults: Diagnosis, progress, and treatment.* Hagerstown, Md.: Harper & Row, 1975.

Johansson, G. Visual perception of biological motion and a model for its analysis. *Perception and Psychophysics,* 1973, *14,* 201–211.

Jones, E. E., & Thibaut, J. W. Interaction goals as bases of inference in interpersonal perception. In R. Tagiuri & L. Petrullo (Eds.), *Person perception and interpersonal behavior.* Stanford, Calif.: Stanford University Press, 1958.

Kassin, S. M., & Lowe, C. A. On the development of the augmentation principle: A perceptual approach. *Child Development,* in press.

Kelley, H. H. *Causal, schmeta and the attribution process.* Morristown, N.J.: General Learning Press, 1971.

Kolers, P. A. Light waves. Review of R. Shaw & J. Bransford (Eds.), Perceiving, acting, and knowing. *Contempory Psychology,* 1978, *23,* 227–228.

Langer, E. J. Rethinking the role thought in social interactions. In J. Harvey, W. Ickes, & R. Kidd (Eds.), *New directions in attribution theory* (Vol. 2). Hillsdale, N.J.: Lawrence Erlbaum Associates, 1978.

Levinger, G. A three-level approach to attraction. Toward an understanding of pair relatedness. In T. L. Houston (Ed.), *Foundations of interpersonal attraction*. New York: Academic Press, 1974.

Lorenz, K. *Evolution and the modification of behavior*. Chicago: University of Chicago Press, 1965.

Mace, W. M., & Pittenger, J. B. Directly perceiving Gibson: A further reply to Gyr. *Psychological Bulletin*, 1975, *82*, 137–139.

Mark, L. S. *A transformational approach toward understanding the perception of growing faces*. Unpublished doctoral dissertation, Department of Psychology, University of Connecticut, 1979.

Massod, C., Hubbard, M., & Newtson, D. Selective perception of events. *Journal of Experimental Social Psychology*, 1979, *15*, 513–532.

McArthur, L. The how and what of why: Some determinants and consequences of causal attribution. *Journal of Personality and Social Psychology*, 1972, *22*, 171–193.

McArthur, L. Z. What grabs you? The role of attention in impression formation and causal attribution. In E. T. Higgins, C. P. Herman, & M. P. Zanna (Eds.), *Social cognition: The Ontario Symposium* (Vol. 1). Hillsdale, N.J.: Lawrence Erlbaum Associates, 1981.

McArthur, L. Z., & Post, D. L. Figural emphasis and person perception. *Journal of Experimental Social Psychology*, 1977, *13*, 520–535.

Michaels, C., & Carello, C. *An introduction to the theory of direct perception*. Book in preparation, Department of Psychology, University of Connecticut, 1979.

Michotte, A. The perception of causality. London: Methuen, 1963.

Neisser, U. *Cognitive psychology*, New York: Appleton-Century-Crofts, 1967.

Neisser, U. *Cognition and reality*, San Francisco: W. H. Freeman, 1976.

Newtson, D. Foundations of attribution: The perception of ongoing behavior. In J. H. Harvey, W. J. Ickes, & R. F. Kidd (Eds.), *New directions in attribution research* (Vol. 1). Hillsdale, N.J.: Lawrence Erlbaum Associates, 1976.

Newtson, D., Rinder, R., & LaCross, K. Effects of availability of feature changes on behavior segmentation. *Journal of Experimental Social Psychology*, 1978, *14*, 379–388.

Odom, R. D. A perceptual-salience account of detalage relations and developmental change. In C. J. Brainerd & L. S. Siegel (Eds.), *Alternatives to Piaget: Critical essays on the theory*. New York: Academic Press, 1978.

Ohman, A., & Dimberg, V. Facial expressions as conditioned stimuli for electrodermal responses: A case of "preparedness"? *Journal of Personality and Social Psychology*, 1978, *36*, 1251–1258.

Pittenger, J., & Shaw, R. E. Aging faces as viscal-elastic events: Implications for a theory of non-rigid shape perception. *Journal of Experimental Psychology: Human Perception and Performance*, 1975, *1*, 377–382.

Pittenger, J., Shaw, R., & Mark, L. S. Perceptual information for the age level of faces as a higher-order invariant of growth. *Journal of Experimental Psychology: Human Perception and Performance*, in press.

Polanyi, M. *Personal knowledge: Toward a post-critical philosophy*. New York: Harper, 1964.

Runeson, S. *On visual perception of dynamic events*. Unpublished doctoral dissertation, Department of Psychology, University of Uppsala, 1977.

Russell, B. R. *Human knowledge, its scope and limit*. New York: Simon & Schuster, 1948.

Russell, J. C. Perceived action units as a function of subjective importance. *Personality and Social Psychology Bulletin*, 1979, *5*, 206–209.

Sackett, G. P. Monkeys reared in isolation with pictures as visual input: Evidence for an innate releasing mechanism. *Science*, 1966, *154*, 1468–1473.

Sagan, C. *The dragons of Eden*. New York: Random House, 1977.

Schneider, D. J., Hastorf, A. H., & Ellsworth, P. C. *Person perception*. Reading, Mass.: Addison-Wesley, 1979.

Seligman, M. E. P. On the generality of the laws of learning. *Psychological Review*, 1970, *77*, 406–418.

Shaver, K. G. *Principles of social psychology,* Cambridge, Mass.: Winthrop, 1977.

Shaw, R. Informal communication, 1978.

Shaw, R., & Bransford, J. Introduction: Psychological approaches to the problem of knowledge: In R. Shaw & J. Bransford (Eds.), *Perceiving, acting, and knowing: Toward an ecological psychology.* Hillsdale, N.J.: Lawrence Erlbaum Associates, 1977.

Shaw, R. E., McIntyre, M., & Mace, W. M. The role of symmetry in event perception. In R. B. McLeod & H. C. Pick, Jr. (Eds.), *Perception: Essays in honour of James J. Gibson.* Ithaca, N.Y.: Cornell University Press, 1974.

Shaw, R., & Pittenger, J. Perceiving the face of change in changing faces: Implication for a theory of object perception. In R. Shaw & J. Bransford (Eds.), *Perceiving, acting, and knowing: Toward an ecological psychology.* Hillsdale, N.J.: Lawrence Erlbaum Associates, 1977.

Shaw, R., Turvey, M. T., & Mace, W. Ecological psychology: The consequences of a commitment to realism. In W. Weimer & D. Palermo (Eds.), *Cognition and the symboloic processes.* Lawrence Erlbaum Associates, 1976.

Shor, R. E. The effect of pre-information upon human characteristics attributed to animated geometric figures. *Journal of Abnormal and Social Psychology,* 1957, *54,* 124–126.

Shultz, T. R., Butkowsky, I., Pearce, J. W., & Stanfield, H. Development of scheme for the attribution of multiple psychological causes. *Developmental Psychology,* 1975, *11,* 502–510.

Taylor, S. E., Crocker, J., Fiske, S. T., Sprinzen, M., & Winkler, J. D. The generalizability of salience effects. *Journal of Personality and Social Psychology,* 1979, *37,* 357–368.

Taylor, S. E., & Fiske, S. T. Point of view and perceptions of causality. *Journal of Personality and Social Psychology,* 1975, *32,* 439–445.

Taylor, S. E., & Fiske, S. T. Salience, attention, and attribution: Top of the head phenomena. In L. Berkowitz (Ed.), *Advances in experimental social psychology* (Vol. 2). New York: Academic Press, 1978.

Thompson, D. A. W. *On growth and form* (2nd ed.). Cambridge, England: Cambridge University Press, 1942. (Originally published, 1917.)

Todd, J. T., Mark, L., & Shaw, R. The perception of growth. *Scientific American,* in press.

Verbrugge, R. R. Resemblances in language and perception. In R. Shaw & J. Bransford (Eds.), *Perceiving, acting, and knowing: Toward an ecological psychology.* Hillsdale, N.J.: Lawrence Erlbaum Associates, 1977.

Zadney, J., & Gerard, H. B. Attributed intentions and informational selectivity. *Journal of Experimental and Social Psychology,* 1974, *10,* 34–52.

II

COGNITION AND THE ENVIRONMENT

All of the chapters in this section are concerned with cognition and change in the environment. In the first paper, Bransford, Stein, Shelton, and Owings examine the kinds of activities people may need to engage in to learn new information. These authors report some early findings deriving from a program of research concerned with successful and less successful learners. They demonstrate persuasively that the student's contribution to learning facilitates learning and that different types of intervention strategies may lead to enhanced learning on the part of less successful students.

The next three chapters in the section focus on how spatial cognition is acquired and used. In the first of these pieces, Chase and Chi ask, what kind of spatial knowledge is stored in memory and how is it used? The authors provide an informative review of work on visual-spatial skills and then examine map reading as an example of people's use of spatial knowledge.

In a commentary at the conference on the three papers concerned with spatial cognition, Reuben Baron suggested that Chase and Chi do not seem to be speaking of a literal cognitive map; rather, he views their use of ''map'' as a construct or heuristic device for understanding. On the other hand, Baron proposed that the authors of the next two papers, Perry Thorndyke and Keith Clayton and Mary Woodyard, seem to treat maps as literal images that people can retrieve more or less accurately. The reader will have to be the judge, though it is clear that all of these authors accord visual imagery a major role in spatial cognition processes.

In his paper, Thorndyke defines spatial knowledge as a collection of memories that may include images of geographic features, sequences of actions that define specific routes, images of area maps, and individual facts about specific objects or relationships. He describes recent research concerned with the idea that different categories of knowledge may be optimal for different spatial judgment tasks. Thorndyke also provides a useful discussion of individual differences in spatial cognition and reasoning.

Keith Clayton and Mary Woodyard emphasize the procedural properties of spatial knowledge and describes an experiment in which subjects attempted to learn a new physical environment. Clayton presents a provocative means-end-readiness framework that he indicates is a revision of some of Tolman's writings on cognitive maps.

Finally, this introduction to these papers on spatial cognition would be incomplete without report of Susan Saegert's interesting comments at the conference on this line of work. First, she called for more consideration of the affective component of learning an environment. Second, she expressed concern about the omission of attention to Kurt Lewin's ideas about psychological life space.

The final paper in this section by Baruch Fischhoff actually is a misfit. It could as reasonably be placed in the introductory or concluding sections as in any of the more specialized sections. The paper deals with cognition and adaptation, but in an indirect way. The paper represents a collection of well-informed facts and ideas that have relevance for a gamut of concerns represented in this volume, from how people make judgments and process and use information to the value of the social sciences in addressing major societal problems. As Fischhoff so aptly states, his interest in part is in recruiting some scholars to work on particular interfaces between psychology and the world. By using an analysis of CO_2-induced climatic change, Fischhoff makes a convincing case about the fraility of human judgment in light of an abstruse environment and our inadequate and impeachable information about it. Read carefully, this piece is a sobering reminder that however extensive are the developments in the fields represented at this conference, there still exists a real world with vast subtles that far supercede our current knowledge, and perhaps modes of knowledge acquisition.

5 Cognition and Adaptation: The Importance Of Learning to Learn

John D. Bransford
Vanderbilt University

Barry S. Stein
Tennessee Technological University

Tommie S. Shelton
Vanderbilt University

Richard A. Owings
Vanderbilt University

Certain issues are important irrespective of one's area of specialization. One involves understanding how people adapt to problems they confront. For example, why might people react differently to the same situation? One resident of a run-down neighborhood may give up in despair, whereas another may analyze the problem and elicit support in order to solve it. One would-be member of a social group may retreat because of feelings of discomfort, another may analyze the source of the discomfort and eventually resolve it. Solutions to problems such as these frequently require that people learn new information: information about the expectation of residents in one's neighborhood, the tacit rules of a social group, and so forth. The task of learning something new also represents a problem that people may react to in different manners; some may avoid tasks that require them to learn new information, whereas others may accept the challenge and approach the problem in effective ways.

In this chapter, we explore the kinds of activities people may need to engage in to learn new information. We focus on the activities that enable people to learn from written documents or texts. These activities (or set of skills), often identified with "literacy," involve understanding new information, remembering it, and effectively utilizing the information at later points in time. It is not surprising that our formal educational systems assign high priority to these skills. Some students become quite adept at learning new information by reading, whereas others experience much more difficulty. What are the successful students doing that the less successful ones are failing to do? What would it take to help the less successful students learn to learn? We feel that these questions are especially important because the ability to learn has pervasive effects on human behavior.

INITIAL OBSERVATIONS

The questions just described prompted us to begin observing how different people approach the problem of learning new information. We began with fifth graders: Teacher ratings and achievement-test scores were used to identify students in the top one-third and bottom one-third of a typical fifth-grade class. We selected passages designed for fourth graders that discussed topics such as boomerangs, camels, spiders, and so forth. Each child was asked to read a passage out loud, study it, tell us how he or she studied, and finally to answer questions about the passage. Each child was interviewed individually. All the children seemed enthusiastic about being in the experiment and appeared motivated to learn the materials and answer the questions. We helped all students decode (i.e., pronounce) any words that they found difficult and explained the meanings of any words that they did not know.

These interview sessions yielded two types of information that were helpful. First, the less successful students read more slowly, had more trouble decoding unfamiliar words, and were less familiar with some of the vocabulary used in the stories. Decoding problems have been documented by other researchers (e.g., Lesgold & Perfetti, 1978; Perfetti & Lesgold, 1977). The differences in vocabulary knowledge were also expected because this is one of the areas sampled by the achievement tests that were used to define the groups. The less successful students were also less accurate at answering questions about each passage. This, too, is hardly surprising; the teachers could have predicted this before we began our observations. If the less successful students are less familiar with the concepts discussed in each story, one would expect them to have greater difficulty understanding and remembering what they read (e.g., see Anderson, 1977; Bransford, 1979; Trabasso, in press).

Even though differences in available skills and knowledge may explain the performance differences between the successful and less successful students, it is important to understand why and how the successful students acquired more knowledge than the less successful students. It is possible that the only explanations are "differences in capacity" or "differences in prior exposure," but these explanations are not particularly illuminating. It appears reasonable to assume that people must do something in order to benefit from potential sources of information; perhaps the less successful students do not know what to do in order to learn.

We had hoped that children's descriptions of how they studied might reveal something about their general approach to learning. Our impression was that there were indeed differences between successful and less successful students' approaches to learning; however, these differences were hard to define. In general, the successful students seemed to take a much more active role in the learning process. Given a passage describing the phenomenon of rings around the moon, for example, several successful students stated that they asked themselves whether they had ever seen rings such as those the passage described and then compared their experiences with the written description. In a passage about boomerangs, several successful students noted that a small picture at the top of the page illustrated *one* of the two types of boomerangs described in the passage. Part of these students' study time was used to understand how the other type of boomerang would differ from the one in the picture. In contrast to the successful students, the less successful ones showed little tendency to relate the to-be-learned information to previous knowledge or to previously experienced information (e.g., a picture of one type of boomerang). Their primary mode of study seemed to be to reread the information they had previously read.

The interview data on study activities were suggestive but far from conclusive. We again encountered the problem that the less successful students seem to have acquired less knowledge than the successful students. The successful students mentioned more concepts and experiences that were relevant to the information they were reading, but this may simply reflect the fact that they had acquired more knowledge. It became clear that we needed a more precise understanding of the types of activities that underlie the acquisition of a knowledge base. For example, we asked ourselves what we did in order to gain expertise in an area that was initially unfamiliar. This problem is discussed next.

SOME PROBLEMS OF UNDERSTANDING AND LEARNING

In this section, we focus on a particular topic in order to illustrate some general problems of learning. The topic is "veins and arteries." What might a biological novice do in order to learn about a topic such as this? Assume that the novice reads a text stating that arteries are thick and elastic and that they carry blood that is rich in oxygen from the heart; veins are thinner, less elastic, and carry blood rich in carbon dioxide back to the heart. To the biological novice, even this relatively simple set of facts can seem arbitrary and confusing. Was it veins or arteries that are thin? Was the thin one or the thick one elastic? Which one carries carbon dioxide from the heart (or was it to the heart)?

Even the biological novice who is familiar with the terms "veins" and "arteries" may have difficulty learning the information in this passage. The problem the learner faces is that the facts and relationships appear arbitrary. We can create an analogous problem by using concepts that are familiar to everyone. For example, imagine reading 10 statements such as those listed here and then answering questions about them from memory:

> The tall man bought the crackers.
> The bald man read the newspaper.
> The funny man bought the ring.

College students do quite poorly when presented with these statements and asked questions such as "Which man bought the crackers?" (Stein & Bransford, 1979; Stein, Morris, & Bransford, 1978). The students rate each sentence as comprehensible yet have difficulty because the relationship between each type of man and the actions performed seem arbitrary. The biological novice is in a similar position because he or she sees no particular reason why an artery should be elastic or nonelastic, thick or thin.

There are several ways to deal with the problem of learning factual content that initially seems unfamiliar and arbitrary. One is simply to rehearse the facts until they are mastered; a more efficient approach is to use various mnemonic techniques. For example, the fact that arteries are thick could be remembered by forming an image of a thick, hollow tube that flashes "artery." The fact that arteries are elastic could be remembered by imagining that the tube is suspended by a rubber band that stretches and contracts, thereby causing the tube to move up and down. We could embellish the image by having red liquid (blood) plus round (like an "o") bubbles (oxygen) pouring out of the tube, and these could be moving in a direction away from an image of a Valentine's-day heart. This composite image could serve as a basis for remembering that arteries are thick, elastic, and carry blood rich in oxygen away from the heart. An alternate technique is to use verbal elaboration; for example, "*Art*(ery) was *thick* around the middle so he wore pants with an *elastic* waistband." There is a considerable amount of literature documenting the fact that the formation of images and linking sentences can facilitate retention (e.g., Bower, 1970; Bower & Clark, 1969; Paivio, 1971, Rohwer, 1966). Researchers have also explored the possibility of explicitly teaching various mnemonic techniques in order to improve people's abilities to learn (Weinstein, 1978).

It is important to note, however, that the problem of learning frequently involves more than just remembering facts. In order to use information that may be accessible, it is often necessary to understand why certain relationships exist and to understand the functions they serve. For example, imagine that people remember "Arteries are elastic" either by thinking of a rubber band holding a tube or "Art(ery) and his elastic waistband." What if these people are confronted with the task of designing an artificial artery? Would it have to be elastic? What are the potential implications of hardening of the arteries? Would this have a serious impact on people's health? Learners who used the previously mentioned mnemonics to remember that arteries are elastic would have little basis for answering these questions. Indeed, the "rubber band" and "waistband" mnemonics could easily lead to misinterpretations: Perhaps hardening of the arteries affects people's abilities to stretch their arms and legs.

Mnemonic techniques are useful for many purposes, but one must take a very different approach to learning in order to develop an understanding of veins and arteries. Effective learners attend to factual content, but they also seem to seek information about the *significance* or relevance of facts. For example, the passage about veins and arteries stated that arteries are elastic. What is the significance of elasticity? How does this property relate to the functions that arteries perform? An effective learner may seek information that can clarify this relationship. For example, our imaginary passage states that arteries carry blood from the heart—blood that is pumped in spurts. This provides one clue about the significance of elasticity—arteries may need to expand and contract to accommodate the pumping of blood. Some learners might then ask why veins do *not* need to be elastic. Because veins carry blood back to the heart, perhaps they have less of a need to accommodate the large changes in pressure resulting from the heart pumping blood in spurts.

Some learners may carry this process a step further. Because arteries carry blood *from* the heart, there is a problem of directionality. Why does the blood not flow back into the heart? This will not be perceived as a problem if one assumes that arterial blood always flows downhill; but, suppose our passage mentions that there are arteries in the neck and shoulder regions. Arterial blood must therefore flow uphill as well. This information might provide an additional clue about the significance of elasticity. If arteries expand from a spurt of blood and then contract, this might help the blood move in a particular direction. The elasticity of arteries might therefore serve the function of a one-way valve that enables blood to flow forward but not back. If one were to design an artificial artery, it might therefore be possible to equip it with valves and hence make it nonelastic. However, this solution might work only if the spurts of blood did not cause too much pressure on the artificial artery. Our imaginary passage does not provide enough information about pressure requirements so a learner would have to look elsewhere for this information. Note, however, that our learner realizes the need to obtain additional information. The learner's activities are not unlike those employed by good detectives or researchers when they confront a new problem. Although their initial assumptions about the significance of various facts may ultimately be found to be incorrect, the act of seeking clarification is fundamental to the development of new expertise. In contrast, the person who simply concentrates on techniques for memorizing facts does not know whether there is something more to be understood.

Can the general process of clarifying the significance of facts also facilitate remembering? To explore this question, it is useful to reconsider the set of factual statements discussed earlier, statements such as "The tall man bought the crackers" and "The bald man read the newspaper." We noted that those statements contain familiar concepts, yet are very difficult to remember; the relationships between the type of man and the actions performed seem arbitrary. This problem of arbitrariness is also faced by the biological novice who is trying to remember whether arteries are elastic or nonelastic and carry blood to or from the heart.

Note what happens when learners attempt to clarify the significance or relevance of factual content—for example, the significance of the fact that arteries are elastic. It is necessary to become aware of reasons for the elasticity of arteries that are related to the functions they perform. One can ask similar questions about the relationship between a tall man and cracker buying. What types of information might clarify the significance of mentioning that the man is tall? Consider the following elaborations of the statements that were presented earlier (we refer to the earlier statements as Base Sentences):

> The tall man bought the crackers that were on the top shelf.
> The bald man read the newspaper to look for a hat sale.
> The funny man bought the ring that squirted water.

When college students hear the 10 Base Sentences plus the extra information just illustrated, their ability to answer questions such as "Which man bought the crackers?" improves dramatically. However, it is possible that the addition of *any* meaningful information will help people remember what they hear or read.

This latter possibility can be evaluated by considering a different set of elaborations for the 10 Base Sentences:

> The tall man bought the crackers from the clerk in the store.
> The bald man read the newspaper while drinking coffee.
> The funny man bought the ring that was on sale.

College students who hear 10 statements such as these are poorer at answering questions such as "Which man bought the crackers?" than are students who hear the *Base Sentences alone* (Stein & Bransford, 1979; Stein, Morris, & Bransford, 1978). Clearly, only certain kinds of information help people grasp the significance or relevance of factual content. Information that the crackers were on the top shelf helps people understand the relevance of "tall man," information about the functions of the ring help people realize why a "funny man" might buy it. Students who hear the Base Sentences alone, or the Base Sentences plus uninformative elaborations, have no basis for understanding the significance of tallness, funniness, and so forth. This is analogous to a learner who knows only that arteries carry blood. Without more information about the nature of the blood flow (e.g., spurting, movement in one direction, even uphill), the fact that arteries are elastic appears to be an artibrary fact.

The previous data illustrate that memory is improved when people are *presented* with information that can clarify the significance of factual content, but effective learners must frequently do something in order to make information less arbitrary. Data from Stein and Bransford (1979) indicate that the activities learners perform are affected by the types of questions they are prompted to ask. College students were presented with Base Sentences such as *The tall man bought the crackers* and were asked to generate a phrase that completed each statement. Students in the first group generated phrases in response to the question "What might happen next?" Those in the second group answered the question "Why might each type of man perform a particular act?" Independent raters judged the degree to which each continuation clarified the significance of the information in each Base Sentence; they were able to agree with one another over 95% of the time. The students in the second group generated a greater number of precise continuations and this was reflected in their higher retention scores. The types of questions people ask themselves can therefore affect learning; for example, our analysis of learning about veins and arteries involved a search for the significance or relevance of facts.

SUCCESSFUL AND LESS SUCCESSFUL LEARNERS REVISITED

The purpose of the preceding section was to gain a clearer picture of what people must do in order to develop expertise in an area. Basically, they must ask themselves whether something they already know or have just read can clarify the significance of seemingly arbitrary facts. This approach to learning seems to facilitate memory for factual content as well as develop a basis for tackling new problems. The possession of a knowledge base that permits the clarification of arbitrary facts is undoubtedly an important part of this process. However, the development of such a knowledge base may be contingent on the learner engaging in activities such as those previously described.

In our earlier discussion of academically successful and less-successful students, we noted that the former seemed to have acquired more knowledge than the latter. However, we also felt that the less-successful students took a different approach to the problem of learning. Our efforts to analyze the process of learning about veins and arteries provided a clearer picture of what those differences might be. Less-successful students may be less likely to activate knowledge that clarifies the significance of factual content even though the necessary knowledge is potentially available. To explore this possibility, we needed to ensure that all the students had the potential knowledge to learn effectively; the important question involved the degree to which they utilized their potential. We therefore created materials that were much simpler than the reading passages used in the initial work.

Our first study (Owings, Petersen, Bransford, Morris, & Stein, in press) investigated the issue of "problem recognition." In order to deal with the problem of learning difficult factual content, for example, one must first realize that it is indeed difficult. To what extent would our academically successful and less-successful fifth graders realize that some materials were more difficult to master than others, and how would this affect their attempts to adapt to the task?

Based on our initial interview data, it seemed clear that even the less successful fifth graders could use some sources of information to assess learning difficulty. They knew that difficulty of vocabulary affected learning; the length of a passage was another cue that they used. However, suppose we used very simple vocabulary, kept passage length constant, and varied the arbitrariness of comprehensible factual content. Would the students realize that some materials were more difficult to master than others, and how would this affect their attempts to adapt to the task?

To explore this question, we created a set of simple stories that each had two versions. In one version, each statement was nonarbitrary or well motivated. In a story about boys discussing their activities, for example, The sleepy boy had taken a nap, The hungry boy had eaten a hamburger, and so forth. To create the arbitrary version, we repaired subjects and predicates with the constraint that each sentence still be comprehensible. For example, The sleepy boy had eaten a hamburger and The hungry boy had taken a nap. Similar versions were created for other topics. All students read one version of a story (either arbitrary or nonarbitrary), studied as long as they wished, read the opposite version of a second story about a different topic, and studied it. They were then shown both stories and were asked to state which one was harder to learn and why. Students then received a memory test (e.g., which boy had eaten a hamburger?). It is noteworthy that all the students in this study had participated in practice sessions and hence knew the type of test to expect.

The results indicated that the successful students were nearly perfect in their judgments of learning difficulty. They could also explain why the arbitrary stories were harder to learn. This knowledge seemed to guide their efforts to adapt to task difficulty; they studied stories that were hard to learn longer than those that were easy to learn. The academically less-successful fifth graders exhibited a very different pattern of performance. They were less accurate in their judgments of learning difficulty and studied the arbitrary stories no longer than the nonarbitrary stories. These children were able to use other cues to assess learning difficulty (e.g., passage length, difficulty of vocabulary), but failed to use arbitrariness of relationships as a cue. Nevertheless, their memory for the easier, nonarbitrary stories was much better than for the arbitrary ones, which suggests that the easier stories were indeed more congruent with their knowledge. Furthermore, at the end of the experimental session, we were eventually able to get the less-successful children to notice the differences among the stories, and they also became able to tell us how the arbitrary stories could be revised to make them easier. They therefore seemed to have the potential to differentiate the two types of stories, yet failed to do so until we explicitly prompted them.

The findings indicate that the less-successful students seemed less likely to spontaneously evaluate the arbitrariness of factual content than the successful students. However, the experiment provided no information about differences in the way that the two groups of students attempted to study the material; we were particularly interested in the degree to which students would activate knowledge that could clarify the significance of to-be-learned facts. We therefore conducted an additional study (Stein, Bransford, Owings, & McCraw, in preparation) with a different group of fifth graders. Students were presented with a list of sentences, such as *The tall man used the paintbrush, The hungry man got into the car,* and were asked to generate phrases that would help them remember each statement. The children were also shown that each statement dealt with a different type of man (e.g., hungry, tall, strong). Children were divided into three groups on the basis of teacher ratings and test scores: academically less successful, average, and successful. All were in regular classes in the fifth grade.

Five measures were used to assess performance. The first was the precision (i.e., nonarbitrariness) of student-generated elaborations (as judged by three independent raters). There were large differences among the groups, with the successful, middle, and less successful students receiving precision scores of approximately 70%, 50%, and 30%, respectively. Successful students generated continuations such as "The tall man used the paintbrush to paint the ceiling"; less successful students' continuations were more similar to "The tall man used the paintbrush to paint the chair." The second measure was cued recall (questions were of the form "Which man got into the car?"); again, there were large differences among the groups, with successful students performing best. The third measure was a conditional memory score: memory given that initial elaborations had been precise or imprecise. Precision had powerful effects on all three groups, with precisely elaborated statements being recalled best. The fourth measure assessed students' confidence in their answers during testing. We looked only at cases in which students had produced the correct answer and measured confidence as a function of whether the initial elaboration had been precise or imprecise. All groups were more confident given that their initial elaborations had been precise. The final measure assessed students' awareness of the relationship between their initial elaborations and subsequent retention. Did they seem to understand why they remembered the ones that they did? The majority of the successful students could explain this relationship, approximately 30% of the middle students could do so, and only one less successful student did so.

Overall, the results suggest that the successful students approached the task in a different manner from the less successful students. The successful students seemed to attend to the details of each statement and to activate knowledge that could make the facts less arbitrary. In contrast, the less-successful students produced continuations that could be true of any type of man but were not uniquely related to the particular type of man. These students seemed to have the potential to clarify the significance of the information (we document this later) yet failed to utilize their potential. If less-successful students take this approach in a wide variety of situations, it could have pervasive effects on their abilities to learn.

LEARNING TO LEARN

In this section, we move from problems of assessment to problems of intervention. If many students do indeed fail to activate potential knowledge that could clarify the significance of factual content, what might one do in order to help them learn to learn?

Note first that the problem of helping students learn to learn is not necessarily equivalent to the problem of helping them learn particular factual content. For example, we could have supplied our less-successful students with continuations of Base Sentences (e.g., The tall man used the paintbrush) that made them less arbitrary (e.g., The tall man used the paintbrush to paint the ceiling); this would undoubtedly have boosted the students' memory score. Similarly, an effective teacher or author could help students master certain materials by supplying information that makes relationships less arbitrary (e.g., The elasticity of arteries allows them to accommodate fluctuations in the pressure of blood, which is pumped in spurts by the heart). All of these procedures could help students learn a particular set of factual content, but they would not necessarily help them learn to learn.

The problem of helping students learn to learn can be illustrated by returning to the study in which fifth graders were asked to write continuations of statements such as *The hungry man got into the car*. We worked with a number of the less-successful students in order to bring them to the point where they would spontaneously activate knowledge that clarified the significance of the information in each Base Sentence. Our initial attempt at intervention was straightforward: We presented the students with examples of precise and imprecise continuations of Base Sentences and explained how the former could facilitate retention (e.g., we presented them with "The hungry man got into the car and drove to the restaurant" versus "The hungry man got into the car and drove to work" and explained how the first was more relevant to being hungry than the second). We then gave the students a list of 10 sentences and asked them to generate elaborations that would make the relationships less arbitrary (confusing) and easier to learn. We found that the training had little effect on the quality of elaborations generated by students (i.e., the degree to which they precisely clarified the significance of relationships). Not only did they fail to elaborate the new set of sentences precisely, but many also performed at chance when given a forced-choice test in which they were to choose which of two continuations of each sentence made the sentence less arbitrary and hence easier to learn.

In retrospect, the failure of this training procedure is understandable. If the less-successful learners were not engaging in the kinds of activities that would help them understand the potential significance of new information, then they would certainly have difficulty understanding the significance of our explanations and examples.

Our second attempt to help students generate informative continuations of Base Sentences focused on the importance of question asking. First, however, we wanted the children to experience the difficulty of remembering arbitrary facts. We therefore asked the children to help us evaluate why some things were harder to remember than others. Children were read a new list of 10 arbitrary Base Sentences (with no instructions to elaborate) and were then asked questions (e.g., Which man bought the milk?). As expected their memory performance was very poor, averaging only one or two items correct. This was not upsetting to the children because they were helping us evaluate the materials; they concluded that these materials were indeed hard to learn.

This experience set the stage for analyzing why each Base Sentence was so difficult to remember. Given a statement such as "The kind man bought the milk," for example, we first prompted students to ask themselves questions that would enable them to realize that the relationship was arbitrary. We might therefore ask "Is there any more reason to mention that a kind man bought milk than a tall man, a mean man?" This set the stage for the next step, which was to prompt students to activate knowledge that could make the relationship between "kindness" and "milk buying" less arbitrary (e.g., "Why might a kind man be buying milk?"). The third purpose of our intervention was to prompt students to evaluate their own continuations. For example, less successful students might write "The kind man bought the milk because he was thirsty." We would then ask: "What does this have to do with being kind?" "Wouldn't a mean man be just as likely to do the same thing?" Given these explicit queries, all the children were eventually able to write continuations that clarified the significance of kindness—for example, "The kind man bought the milk to give to the hungry child."

During the first few trials of the intervention, the students had to be explicitly reminded to ask themselves relevant questions. For example, they were eventually able to activate information that clarified the significance of the first Base Sentence (e.g., kind man), yet they rarely did this spontaneously for the Base Sentence presented on the second trial. After a few trials, however, the children began to internalize the process of question asking and to evaluate whether their elaborations clarified the significance of the facts. For example, given the Base Sentence "The rich man walked to the store," one student said "to buy some candy." She then remarked, "Wait, candy doesn't cost that much, I need something different," and after a brief pause said (smiling), "and bought the whole store." Many of the children's responses were quite creative, and they seemed to thoroughly enjoy the task.

After the children had elaborated the set of 10 Base Sentences, we administered the same memory test that they had done so poorly on earlier. Nearly all of them did perfectly. The most interesting data involved their excitement and pleasure; a task that had initially been extremely difficult became very easy to perform. We also gave the children the initial set of Base Sentences used in the *original* study and asked them to write phrases that made the facts meaningful and nonarbitrary. Over 90% of these elaborations were precise (i.e., clarified the significance of the factual content). These students' initial failure to activate relevant knowledge had therefore not been due to a lack of potential knowledge nor to some inherent "lack of verbal fluency." They needed help finding ways to evaluate whether information seemed arbitrary, to use their knowledge to make it less arbitrary, and to evaluate their attempts to meet this goal. By prompting the students to ask themselves relevant questions, we were able to observe a definite improvement in their performance on our experimental task plus a marked increase in their enthusiasm for the task.

We have observed additional situations in which less successful students improve when prompted to use potentially available knowledge to clarify the significance of factual content. Their performance on standardized comprehension tests represents a case in point. Many of the items on these tests are relatively simple; for example, children may read a statement such as "The child looked through the large round window" and may be asked to choose which of four pictures is most like the sentence. Many less-successful children make a considerable number of errors on this type of task.

We have tried to help children such as these evaluate the reasons for their choices. The first step is to help them clarify the nature of the task they are trying to perform. For example, we might present them with four pictures and ask "which one is best?" The purpose is to prompt them to evaluate the arbitrary nature of the question, to ask "What do you mean by 'best'?" We next show the students a sentence plus the four pictures and ask: "If you saw this sentence and these four pictures, what do you think the task would be?" A frequent response is "Find a picture that's like the sentence." This is a good description of the children's behavior when they take the comprehension test without being prompted; they frequently choose a picture that is partially correct, but not the one that is best.

The third step in our prompting procedure is to help the children evaluate task instructions more precisely. "Let's assume that the purpose of this task is to pick the picture that is most like the sentence. Do you think there will be one picture that could be correct, or more than one?" We proceed to ask: "Is the purpose of the task to find *a* picture that's like the sentence or find *the* picture that's most like the sentence?" Given this procedure, the children we have worked with are eventually able to understand the nature of the task.

Even given this general understanding, it is still frequently necessary to help children work through several problems in order to prompt them to evaluate their choices. After reading "The child looks through the large round window", for example, one less-successful fifth grader pointed to a picture of a child looking through a small round window. "Why did you pick that one?" asked the examiner. "Because the window is round," said the boy. The examiner then pointed to a picture of a child looking through the large round window and asked "Why not this one?" After a pause, the boy said "I guess it could be this one too." The examiner's next question was, "Did the sentence say anything else about the window that could help you choose between these two pictures?" Again there was a pause, and the boy closed his eyes while attempting to think. The examiner then said, "Look at the two pictures and decide what you would need to know to choose between them." Given this prompt, the boy quickly realized that he needed to know something about the size of the window; this was apparently sufficient to cue his memory, because he then realized that the original sentence had stated that the round window was *large*. When the boy began to internalize the process of asking himself what he would need to know in order to differentiate among the pictures, his performance on subsequent test items improved.

We have used similar prompting procedures in other situations—choosing a title that best describes a story, for example. Once again, we often find it necessary to help children clarify the nature of the task, to make it less arbitrary. They also need to be prompted to evaluate the choices they make. When choosing story titles, for example, we prompt children to ask what a story with a particular title would contain and then have them compare it to the story they just read (in this task, the original story is available for visual inspection). The children seem able to internalize these processes and to perform much better on subsequent tests of this type.

The improvements we have observed with the less-successful children may be specific to our experimental context and to certain sets of materials, of course. It seems clear that the less-successful children need a great deal of practice in many different contexts in order to learn to learn. The important point is that the failure of these students to utilize their potential is striking. They fail to spontaneously evaluate whether they understand the nature of the task, why one answer may be better than another, whether one set of materials is more difficult to learn then another, and so forth. Given this approach, it is hardly surprising that the less-successful children have difficulty in school.

Might the types of questioning and evaluative procedures we have emphasized affect students' abilities to learn and remember materials such as those presented in our initial interviews? In retrospect, the answer is "Yes." The successful students' descriptions of their study activities indicate that they were spontaneously engaging in questioning and evaluative activities similar to those we have just described. When studying a passage about boomerangs, for example, several successful students came to the part of the passage that distinguished returning from nonreturning boomerangs. They looked back at a picture of a boomerang at the top of the page in order to determine which kind it was. The picture was not labeled; the students were trying to use information from the story to decide which type it might be. We have no information about the details of the questions these children were asking regarding the two types of boomerangs, but they were at least asking themselves how the two types differed and were utilizing several sources of information (the picture plus descriptions from the passage) in order to make this comparison. These types of activities were rarely reported by the less-successful students. When reading about the boomerangs, for example, we assume that the less-successful children initially noticed the picture of a boomerang. However, there was no indication that they ever returned to the picture and asked themselves whether it was a returning or nonreturning boomerang, nor how and why the two types of boomerangs might differ visually. The primary mode of study for the less-successful children was to reread each passage a second time.

We found it instructive to analyze what we did in order to understand some of the passages we had presented to the students. For example, the passage about boomerangs was entitled "The trick is in the stick." The passage opened with "The 'whirling arm' used by Australian natives has amused and startled many people." The referent of "whirling arm" is unclear, so we had to search for more information to clarify what it meant. The next sentence specified that it was a boomerang. The paragraph went on to state that boomerangs are made of wood, are 1 to 3 feet long, and weigh about 8 ounces. These facts seemed reasonable, but what were we assuming in order to make them seem that way?

Here was an instance when facts could seem arbitrary unless one activated relevant knowledge; the learner needed to know something about the function of boomerangs, yet the passage had said nothing about what this was. We knew the function of the boomerangs, so we realized that boomerangs cannot be too long if someone is going to throw them; they also need to be relatively light. The fact that the boomerangs are made of wood rather than plastic, for example, made sense in light of our knowledge of Australian natives; they have no modern technology. In short, we had a considerable amount of knowledge that made these less-than-arbitrary facts. Students who knew something about boomerangs and Aborigines might therefore have an advantage over those who did not.

However, the second paragraph of the passage *did* provide information about the function of boomerangs. Students therefore had an opportunity to use this information to clarify the significance of various facts (e.g., size, weight). The passage proceeded to present information that we had not previously encountered, so we, too, found ourselves searching for information that could clarify its significance. The discussion of differences between returning and nonreturning boomerangs represents a case in point. The passage stated that the two types of boomerangs differ in size (it did not say how) and that nonreturning boomerangs are straighter, can be thrown a much greater distance, and are used for killing large animals as well as for combat. We were not familiar with nonreturning boomerangs, so we had to search for information that could clarify why they might have the properties that they do.

We assumed that nonreturning boomerangs are larger and heavier than returning boomerangs; this could account for their greater range as well as the fact that they are used for killing large prey and for combat. We are still unsure why nonreturning boomerangs are less curved than returning boomerangs. Perhaps it is harder to make them curved because they are larger and heavier (we are assuming that the Bushmen make them by hand); perhaps the design permits greater throwing accuracy over long distances. It is possible that nonreturning boomerangs are less curved because if they were not, they would return to the thrower before travelling a long enough distance. The important point is that we encountered information that was new for us. In order to learn about boomerangs, we therefore needed to do more than simply read the passage one time. Furthermore, our study activities involved much more than simply rereading the passage. We found ourselves asking how and why certain facts were relevant; study time was spent searching for information that could clarify the significance of various facts. The comments of our successful fifth graders became more meaningful after this exercise. It was very valuable to ask ourselves whether the picture at the top of the page was a returning or nonreturning boomerang and to try to imagine how and why the nonpictured boomerang would differ in design.

We undoubtedly asked ourselves a broader range of questions than did the successful fifth graders, who in turn seemed to ask more than their less-successful cohorts. Our ability to formulate relevant questions was probably affected by our knowledge base, but the important point is that the less-successful students seemed to have the potential to ask and answer a much greater number of questions than they did (the same is probably true of the successful students, but to a lesser degree). We could have explicitly prompted the less-successful students to ask themselves how they might clarify the significance of "whirling arm," the weight and size of returning boomerangs versus nonreturning boomerangs, and so forth. It seems clear that they had the potential to ask and answer many of the types of questions that we had asked ourselves. In order to learn to learn, these children need to develop their own procedures for evaluating the significance of factual content, for making it meaningful and relevant. This approach to learning is very different from simply rereading a passage a second time.

The act of merely rereading information is not only an inefficient way to learn the kind of material we presented to the children, but it can also be boring. If students are failing to ask themselves how various details may affect the performance of boomerangs, for example, they are missing the opportunity to discover some interesting facts. Imagine presenting the children with actual returning and nonreturning boomerangs, showing them how they work, letting them try them, and then discussing (at a simple level) why and how they work. What if they were much heavier, much longer, perfectly straight? How might someone have ever invented one, and who did (e.g., scientists)? It seems clear that most children would be delighted with a lesson such as this and would learn a great deal as well. We believe that effective learners can use written documents to at least approximate this type of experience. They seem able to place themselves in the role of an explorer or detective who searches for the significance of facts. Learners who fail to do this, who merely reread the sentences in a passage, for example, may find the experience uninteresting and tedious. The processes that underlie effective learning may therefore be related to those that capture students' interest, that motivate them to learn.

SUMMARY AND CONCLUSIONS

It seems clear that the ability to learn new information can be important for adaptation. We have focused on people's abilities to learn new information by consulting written documents and texts. Part of our discussion emphasized the difference between procedures that help one memorize facts (the use of mnemonics, for example) and those that help one clarify the significance or relevance of factual content. The latter processes seem to help one remember factual content and to develop a knowledge base that facilitates further understanding.

Our evidence suggests that academically successful and less-successful students may take different approaches to the problem of learning. The successful students seem more likely to evaluate the arbitrariness of factual content and to spontaneously activate knowledge that can make the information more meaningful and significant. This may be an important reason why they have acquired more knowledge than their less successful peers. When less-successful children are explicitly prompted to ask themselves relevant questions (e.g., what's the relationship between this fact and this activity?), their performance improves; so does their enjoyment of the task. Our work in the area of intervention is only preliminary, of course, but the evidence is at least consistent with the notion that the activities that underlie learning are subject to modification (see also Bransford, 1979; Brown, Campione, & Barclay, 1979; Campione & Brown, 1978; Feuerstein, in press; Kestner & Borkowski, 1979). The possibility that effective learning activities are related to the development of interest and motivation seems especially important to pursue (see Haywood & Burke, 1977).

The activities that appear to underlie effective learning are not unlike those that a good teacher or author engages in to make material easier to understand and learn. These activities involve evaluating the arbitrariness of relationships and clarifying their significance. The learner must perform a similar set of activities from his or her own perspective: Does this information seem arbitrary, and how could I make it make more sense? In order to develop these skills, learners must do more than simply listen to or read information that makes everything clearer; they must learn to evaluate and clarify on their own. These processes seemed to be facilitated by effective questioning; not questions that simply require a reiteration of factual content, but questions that prompt students to activate knowledge that helps them see the need to clarify the significance of facts. At a general level, questions need to help students evaluate information rather than merely regenerate it. When we read about veins and arteries or boomerangs, for example, we wanted to understand how differences in structure related to differences in function and not to merely memorize the information in the passages.[1] This led to an evaluation of the passages; we frequently discovered a need to look elsewhere in order to clarify the significance of various facts. Often, information from other sources helped us clarify information in the original passages, and vice versa. These activities involving evaluation and clarification seem important for developing knowledge in any type of problem domain.

ACKNOWLEDGMENTS

Aspects of the data and arguments discussed in this chapter were presented at the Society for Research in Child Development, March 1979; the Southeastern Psychological Association, May 1979, and the American Psychological Association, September 1979. We are grateful for the assistance of Dr. Edward Binkley, Director of Research and Evaluation, Metropolitan Public Schools, Nashville, Tennessee, and for the help of numerous principals, teachers, and students. Bill McCraw and Denise Wunderlich did an excellent job of helping us collect and analyze data. We also thank Drs. Carl Haywood and Ruth Smith for introducing us to their North American learning to learn project (Feuerstein's ''Instrumental Enrichment''); it is exciting and has had pervasive effects on our thoughts about learning to learn. Preparation of this chapter was supported in part by grants BNS 77–07248, NIE–G–79–0117 and by a University Research Council Fellowship awarded to John Bransford. The opinions, findings, conclusions, and recommendations expressed herein are those of the authors and do not necessarily reflect the views of the National Science Foundation or the National Institute of Education.

REFERENCES

Anderson, R. C. The notion of schemata and the educational enterprise. In R. C. Anderson, R. J. Spiro, & W. E. Montague (Eds.), *Schooling and the acquisition of knowledge.* Hillsdale, N.J.: Lawrence Erlbaum Associates, 1977.
Bower, G. H. Analysis of a mnemonic device. *American Psychologist,* 1970, *58,* 496–510.

---

[1]From our perspective, one goal of an effective learning-to-learn program is to help students develop criteria for evaluating the degree to which they understand new information. For example, we would help them become aware of the importance of asking themselves about relationships between structure and function; such questions can guide one's efforts to understand veins and arteries, boomerangs, reasons why particular animals have certain structural features, and so forth. When learning facts about camels such as ''can close their nose passages'' and ''have thick hair around their ear openings,'' for example, it is valuable to make these features less arbitrary by noting how they help camels survive desert sandstorms. This information can in turn help one understand why people who travel through deserts wear certain types of clothing (e.g., veils to protect their faces). Of course, there are a variety of additional perspectives that could guide one's efforts to understand topics such as those just mentioned. When the present authors try to understand boomerangs from the perspective of principles of aerodynamics, for example, it becomes clear that there is much more to be learned.

Bower, G. H., & Clark, M. C. Narrative stories as mediators for serial learning. *Psychonomic Science*, 1969, *14*, 181–182.

Bransford, J. D. *Human cognition; Learning, understanding and remembering.* Belmont, Calif.: Wadsworth, 1979.

Brown, A. L., Campione, J. D., & Barclay, C. R. Training self-checking routines for estimating test readiness: Generalization from list learning to prose recall. *Child Development*, 1979, *50*, 501–512.

Campione, J. D., & Brown, A. L. Toward a theory of intelligence: Contributions from research with retarded children. *Intelligence*, 1978.

Feuerstein, R. *Instrumental enrichment.* Baltimore, Md.: University Park Press, in press.

Haywood, H. C., & Burke, W. P. Development of individual differences in intrinsic motivation. In I. Užgiris & F. Weizmann (Eds.), *The structuring of experience.* New York: Plenum, 1977.

Kestner, J. & Borkowski, J. G. Children's maintenance and generalization of an interrogative learning strategy. *Child Development*, 1979, *50*, 485–494.

Lesgold, A. M., & Perfetti, C. A. Interactive processes in reading comprehension. *Discourse Processes*, 1978, *1*, 323–336.

Owings, R., Petersen, G., Bransford, J. D., Morris, C. D., & Stein, B. S. Spontaneous monitoring and regulation of learning: A comparison of successful and less successful fifth graders. *Journal of Educational Psychology*, in press.

Paivio, A. *Imagery and verbal processes.* New York: Holt, Rinehart, & Winston, 1971.

Perfetti, C. A., & Lesgold, A. M. Discourse comprehension and sources of individual differences. In M. Just & P. Carpenter (Eds.), *Cognitive processes in comprehension.* Hillsdale, N.J.: Lawrence Erlbaum Associates, 1977.

Rohwer, W. D., Jr. Constraints, syntax, and meaning in paired-associate learning. *Journal of Verbal Learning and Verbal Behavior*, 1966, *5*, 541–547.

Stein, B. S., & Bransford, J. D. Constraints on effective elaboration: Effects of precision and subject generation. *Journal of Verbal Learning and Verbal Behavior*, 1979, *18*, 769–777.

Stein, B. S., Bransford, J. D., Owings, R. A., & McCraw, B. *Individual differences in the spontaneous utilization of knowledge and skills.* Manuscript in preparation.

Stein, B. S., Morris, C. D., & Bransford, J. D. Constraints on effective elaboration. *Journal of Verbal Learning and Verbal Behavior*, 1978, *17*, 707–714.

Trabasso, T. On the making and assessment of inferences during reading. In J. T. Guthrie (Ed.), *Reading comprehension and education.* Newark, Del.: International Reading Association, in press.

Weinstein, C. E. Elaboration skills as a learning strategy. In H. F. O'Neil, Jr., (Ed.), *Learning strategies.* New York: Academic Press, 1978.

6 Cognitive Skill: Implications for Spatial Skill in Large-Scale Environments

William G. Chase
Carnegie-Mellon University

Michelene T. H. Chi
University of Pittsburgh

The central issue addressed in this chapter is why some people are better than others at getting around in large-scale environments. In general, people have a wide variety of spatial knowledge about their environment, including the spatial layouts of their houses, the neighborhoods in which they live, the routes they normally travel, and a great deal of other geographical knowledge. This chapter focuses on large-scale environments, environments that cannot be viewed from a single vantage point. In these environments, much of the spatial knowledge has to be inferred rather than perceived.

This chapter takes an information-processing approach to the analysis of spatial cognition. From an information-processing point of view, the important theoretical question reduces to how people represent large-scale environments, and what processes they use to operate on this knowledge—that is, what kind of spatial knowledge is stored in memory, and how is it used? Map reading is one example of people's usage of spatial knowledge. In order to understand a specific skill such as map reading, there are some additional complications concerning how people extract knowledge from maps to orient themselves in their environment. However, the central issue underlying map reading still remains one of knowledge representation.

In the analysis of spatial skills in large-scale environments, the chapter touches on three main topics. The first topic is a review of the literature on cognitive skills. Given the cognitive-skills literature, what can we expect to find in spatial skills? The second part of the chapter contains an experimental analysis of a common type of spatial error in map drawing, an error that has important implications for how spatial knowledge is represented. The final section of the chapter discusses the question of how cognitive maps are represented in memory in the light of the information-processing analysis of spatial skills.

COGNITIVE SKILLS

Chess and Other Game Skills

Probably the most relevant literature on visual-spatial skills is the research on skilled chess players. The early work on chess skill was done some 40 years ago, just prior to World War II, by Adrian de Groot (1965, 1966), who was able to study some of the very best chess players in the world, including two World Champions. The basic procedure that de Groot used was to present his subjects with a chess position and ask them to find the best move, and while they were doing so, to think aloud. De Groot hoped to discover the source of chess expertise by analyzing these thinking-aloud protocols. From his analysis, de Groot was able to dispel a few misconceptions. For example, Masters do not seem to search through the set of possible moves any faster than weaker players, nor do they "see" any further ahead than weaker players. In fact, if anything, chess Masters consider fewer possible moves than weaker players, and they analyze these moves to a lesser depth than weaker players. Typically, a Master might consider 30 to 50 moves in a difficult position, and search to a depth of two or three moves. It is unusual for a Master to consider more than 100 moves or search further ahead than five moves, and this is true of weaker players also. Thus, both Masters and weaker players search through a very small subset of the possible moves. Further, chess Masters and weaker players both use the same search strategies (depth first with progressive deepening). The one reliable difference between the Masters and the weaker players was that the Masters spent most of their time thinking about the consequences of good moves, whereas the weaker players spent a considerable amount of time analyzing bad moves. However, de Groot was unable to pinpoint the source of chess skill in the verbal protocols.

De Groot did, however, find a very striking difference between Masters and weaker players in a very different kind of task. He found that when chess Masters were shown a chess position for a very brief interval of time (5 to 10 seconds), they were able to recall the position almost perfectly from memory. Further, this remarkable ability dropped off very rapidly below the Master level. This result cannot be attributed to any kind of superior visual short-term memory capacity of the Masters because when the pieces are placed randomly on the chess board, recall is equally poor for Masters and weaker players (Chase & Simon, 1973b). Chess Masters have the same short-term memory limitations as everyone else.

What is it about this visual memory task that distinguishes Masters from weaker players? The fast presentation in this task eliminates any kind of complex analysis, and performance must rely on very fast recognition processes. What is the chess Master seeing when he looks at the chess board? In theory, the chess Master is seeing familiar patterns of pieces that he recognizes from experience, patterns that simply do not exist in the minds of less-experienced and less-skilled players. In a series of experiments, Chase and Simon (1973a, 1973b) set out to isolate and analyze the cognitive mechanisms underlying performance in this task; the first step was to devise a way to isolate these patterns. In these studies, two procedures were used. One procedure was simply to record, on video tape, the placement of pieces in the visual memory task, and then use the pauses during recall to segment the output into patterns. The second procedure was to have the subjects view a chess pattern in plain sight and reproduce the configuration on an adjacent chess board. In this second procedure, the subject was also video taped, and his head turns were used to segment the output into patterns.

Both of these procedures worked very well. Chess players did not recall whole positions in one smooth series of placements; rather, they recalled chess pieces in rapid bursts followed by long pauses (generally longer than 2 seconds). Similarly, when chess players reproduced a position in plain sight, they did so pattern by pattern with glances at the board position between patterns. Further, there was very good agreement between the two procedures as to what these patterns were.

When the Master's patterns were analyzed in detail, it turned out that he was remembering, for the most part, highly familiar, stereotyped patterns that he sees every day in his play and study of chess. Further, these patterns were very *local* in nature—that is, they consisted of circumscribed clusters of pieces in very localized regions of the chess board, and the pieces within a pattern were interrelated both by visual features (same color, proximity) and by chess function features (attack, defense). What was surprising about these patterns was how restricted they were, restricted both in terms of their visual–spatial properties and in terms of their stereotypy.

When memory performance was reanalyzed in terms of these patterns, it turned out that both the Master and the weaker players were recalling the same types of patterns, but that the Master's patterns were larger. When patterns are counted, rather than pieces, the Master's short-term memory recall is not so different from the novice's. On the same chess position, the Master recalled 20 to 30 pieces, divided into six or more patterns with three to six pieces per pattern, whereas the novice recalled only four to six pieces, and the novice's patterns consisted of single pieces.

In their theoretical account of chess expertise, Chase and Simon (1973a, 1973b) supposed that the chess Master has a very large repertoire of these patterns in long-term memory that he can quickly recognize, and that both Masters and weaker players are subject to the same severe short-term memory limitations. How many such patterns does the chess Master have in long-term memory? Simon and Chase (1973) considered several independent ways to estimate the size of the Master's pattern vocabulary, and they came up with an estimate of roughly 50,000 different configurations. In contrast, a good club player (Class A) seems to have a recognition vocabulary of about 1000 patterns, and a novice does not seem to recognize any patterns. Fifty thousand patterns seems like a large number, but if one considers how much time a chess Master has spent looking at chess positions (10,000–50,000 hours versus 1000–5000 hours of practice for a good club player), 50,000 patterns is not an unreasonable estimate, because with similar levels of practice, good readers build up comparable recognition vocabularies for words.

The differences found so far between Masters and weaker players reveal differences in memory organization of chess knowledge. How does this difference relate to the selection of moves? Chase and Simon (1973a) found other differences between Masters and weaker players that may address this issue. In one series of experiments, they found that the Master had a remarkable memory for a series of moves from a position, and indeed, the Master seemed to be able to remember a whole game after seeing the moves once at a rapid rate (5 sec/move). Further, the Master's recall of move sequences showed the same characteristic clustering as his recall of positions: Moves were remembered in bursts segmented by pauses, and the pauses seemed to come at breaks between sequences of stereotyped moves. In another experiment, the Master was extremely fast at executing a Knight's Tour puzzle as compared to weak players. In this puzzle, the task is to move a knight from square to square over a certain prescribed path. The Master's superior performance seemed to be related to his ability to perceive very rapidly the pattern of squares available to the knight. These results suggest that the selection of good moves occurs because good moves are associated with these patterns stored in long-term memory, or in some circumstances, patterns are simply associated with good or bad evaluations. For example, in the Knight's Tour task, the Master is able to find the move for the knight quickly because the pattern of squares available to the knight is associated with certain moves. Likewise, clusters of pieces forming patterns can also elicit potential (localized) moves. However, in order to understand the selection of moves with respect to the entire board position, we need to postulate that the clusters themselves form configurations of higher-level patterns. It is this configuration of larger regions of the chess board that may elicit sequences of moves, resulting in the segmentation of move sequences during recall.

This view of the organization of chess knowledge suggests that there are hierarchical orders of patterns in memory. That is, not only does the Master have localized structures of two to six pieces, but he may also have familiar configurations of chess-board positions consisting of several patterns. Although there is no direct evidence regarding the composition of the board patterns and their relation to the generation of good moves, it seems clear that chess expertise resides in the rapid "perceptual" recognition processes that tap the chess Master's long-term knowledge base. The if–then kind of logical processing that is revealed from de Groot's analysis of verbal protocols probably reflects relatively late mental operations on the output of the skilled "perceptual" recognition processes. Hence, the Master's expertise does not seem to lie in the slow, conscious, analytical processes that are apparent in verbal protocols. Contrary to popular opinion, the chess Master is a superior recognizer rather than a deep thinker.

This theoretical view can explain several phenomenal feats of the Master. First, the existence of familiar patterns, both at the localized level and at the higher board level, considerably reduces the processing load required for finding the best move, because the outcomes have been stored in long-term memory for immediate access rather than having to be discovered through time-consuming and costly analytic search. Second, this also explains why the chess Master seems to think of the best move, or at least a very good one, before he has had the time to analyze the consequences of it. And finally, it explains how a chess Master is able to defeat dozens of weaker players in simultaneous play: because for the most part the Master simply relies on his pattern recognition abilities— so-called "chess intuition"—to generate potentially good moves.

This analysis of chess skill is consistent with the rest of the literature on game skills. The visual memory effect with skilled chess players has been replicated many times (Charness, 1976; Ellis, 1973; Frey & Adesman, 1976; Goldin, 1978, 1979; Lane & Robertson, 1979), even with children (Chi, 1978). Further, the same effect has been found with experts in the games of go, gomoku, and bridge. In one study, Reitman (1976) was able to study the best non-Oriental go player in the world; this player's perceptual-memory performance with go patterns was virtually identical to that of the chess Masters. In another study, Eisenstadt and Kareev (1975) compared go and gomoku players on the very same patterns. Go and gomoku are played on the same lattice-like board with black and white stones, but the objects of the games are very different and the types of patterns that occur are also very different. (In go, the object is to surround the opponent's stones, whereas in gomoku, the object is to place five stones in a row.) Eisenstadt and Kareev (1975) showed that people who were trained to play go had superior memory for a briefly presented pattern taken from a game of go, but they did poorly on patterns taken from a gomoku game. They found just the reverse for the people they trained to play gomoku.

Nonperceptual Domains

We often refer to chess Masters' expertise as involving rapid "perceptual" recognition. It is important to ask how "perceptual" is this recognition system? By using the term "perceptual," we only mean it as a contrast with analytical. The recognition system is "perceptual" only to the extent that there is a direct association between the pattern configurations and the potential moves. It is not "perceptual" in the sense of being necessarily visual. For example, chess Masters can exhibit the same phenomenal memory feats even when the chess board is presented to them as a string of verbal statements. Similarly, one can examine another domain, such as the game of bridge, in which there is no obvious spatial component. Nevertheless, the research on bridge expertise has revealed the same visual-memory phenomenon. Charness (1979) and Engle and Bukstel (1978) have reported that bridge experts—those who have spent years playing tournament bridge and have mastered the game—can remember an organized bridge hand almost perfectly after viewing it for a few seconds. With unorganized hands, performance is uniformly poor for the experts and the less-experienced players. In addition, bridge experts were able to generate bids faster and more accurately, they planned the play of a hand faster and more accurately, and they had superior memory for hands they had played. Both articles concluded that bridge expertise, like chess, also depends on long-term knowledge, and that expertise depends on fast-access pattern recognition because these patterns are associated with strategies and correct lines of play.

In a totally different domain, physics problem solving, research is forthcoming that shows some effects analogous to those found in chess and related games, even though nonmemory tasks were used. That is, Simon and Simon (1978) and Larkin, McDermott, Simon, and Simon (1980) have discussed the phenomenon of "physical intuition," much like the chess Master's "chess intuition." Physical intuition is the capacity of the expert physicist to solve difficult problems rapidly, without a great deal of conscious deliberation, much like the nonanalytical nature of the chess Master's perceptual ability to find good moves. In a series of on-going studies, the mechanisms underlying this physical intuition are beginning to emerge. Using a categorization task, Chi and Glaser (1979) have found that expert physicists group physics problems as similar according to the underlying principles (e.g., Newton's Second Law), whereas novices group problems as similar according to the physical entities contained in the problems (e.g., a spring or an incline plane problem). This ability to categorize problems rapidly (45 seconds per problem, including reading time) suggests that there exists schemata of problem types, much like those found for algebra word problems (Hinsley, Hayes, & Simon, 1977). The most revealing finding, however, is that experts' schemata are organized around central physics principles, whereas the novices' schemata are organized around physical entities or objects. Furthermore, Chi, Feltovich, and Glaser (1979) are beginning to identify patterns of cues in the problem statements that can elicit directly the relevant underlying physics principles that should be applied to solve a given problem. Once a relevant schema is activated from the pattern of cues in the problem statement, the expert physicist can then proceed to work top-down in a more analytical manner within the activated schema to search for the appropriate procedure for solving a particular problem.

These physics results suggest the existence of a rapid perceptual mechanism for problem solving, not unlike the chess Master's ability to think of the good moves immediately followed by more analytical search. Hence, the extraordinary visual memory phenomenon of the chess Masters reflects not so much the perceptual nature of "intuition," but, rather, the knowledge and the organization of this knowledge that can facilitate the Master's ability to have a rapid "understanding" of the chess situation. Good understanding, according to Greeno (1977), is the ability of a problem solver to construct an adequate representation of the problem. The adequacy of an *initial* problem representation (that may be responsible for physical intuition) clearly depends on the nature and organization of the knowledge existing in memory. The fact that the expert physicist has a more coherent, complete, and principle-oriented representation of physics knowledge necessarily implies that his or her initial understanding of the physics problem must necessarily be better, leading more easily to a correct solution.

Higher-Level Organization

We have alluded earlier to the possibility that chess Masters may have higher-level configurations. Although Chase and Simon (1973a, 1973b) did not analyze the higher-level organization of chess patterns in any detail, they did report some evidence for between-pattern links based on conceptual and strategic aspects of the game (mostly coordinated attacks by patterns of pieces).

There are now stronger results relevant to this particular issue. Akin (1980) analyzed the recall of building plans by architects and found several interesting results. First, as with chess players, architects do not draw architectural plans from memory in one smooth output. Rather, architects recall plans pattern by pattern, and Akin was able to describe the nature of these patterns. Second, architectural plans are recalled hierarchically; that is, from an analysis of the pauses in recall, the nature of the elements recalled, and the order in which they were recalled, Akin was able to determine that these patterns were organized hierarchically with several levels. This is a very important property, and it should be further pointed out that a hierarchy is not universally the case. For example, Akin was able to show that under some circumstances in which the drawings were poorly encoded, the memory organization was less hierarchical and more fragmented, taking on more the property of a lattice than a tree structure. Finally, Akin was able to describe the nature of these patterns. At the lowest level in the hierarchy, these patterns are fairly small parts of functional spaces, such as wall segments, doors, table in a corner, and so on. The next higher level in the hierarchy contains rooms and other areas, and higher levels contain clusters of rooms or areas.

It is interesting to note that the fairly localized property of architectural patterns at the lowest level in the hierarchy is reminiscent of the localized nature of chess patterns. It is only at the next level in the hierarchy that architectural drawings take on the functional form of the architectural space: rooms, halls, and so on. It seems that architectural patterns are similar to chess patterns in that functional properties are more important at higher levels, whereas structural properties are more important at lower levels. What is striking about both the architectural and chess patterns is that at the lowest level, the memory representations are very localized.

Similarly, Egan and Schwartz (1979) have analyzed the recall of circuit diagrams by expert electronics technicians after a brief exposure (5–15 seconds) of the diagram. Egan and Schwartz reported the same visual memory effect, and they also found evidence of a higher-level organization for the skilled electronics technician. At the lowest level, the basic patterns were very similar to the chess patterns and architectural patterns in terms of their localized nature. The skilled technicians, however, were faster and more accurate with their between-pattern recall than the novices, which is good evidence in favor of higher-level organization. As Egan and Schwartz point out, to aid their recall, skilled technicians use their conceptual knowledge of what function the circuit was designed for. This is precisely the point that Akin made with respect to higher-level organization in the recall of building plans by architects. It is not yet clear, however, whether this higher-level organization of circuit diagrams is best described as a hierarchical tree structure or a flatter, lattice-like structure.

Analogous results are also emerging from research on physics problem solving. Chi, Feltovich, and Glaser (1979) are finding that physics knowledge can be organized at several levels. The lowest level contains "structural" or "physical" properties of the problem situation, such as a spring, a pulley, or an incline plane. The next higher level contains more complex situations that are usually not directly described in problem statements, such as a "before and after" situation. This refers to the states of energy or momentum of the total system before and after an event. The highest level of knowledge contains basic physics principles and procedures for their application. Expert physicists have elaborate knowledge at all levels, but their organization revolves around the principles, and their processing tends to be top-down. Novices have only developed elaborate knowledge structure of the lowest level, such as the relations among objects in an incline-plane situation. Their processing of problem situations appears to be more bottom-up.

The existence of higher-level functional knowledge in the more experienced individuals has also been demonstrated in the domain of baseball. Chiesi, Spilich, and Voss (1979) have found that the differential recall of baseball events by individuals with high- and low-baseball knowledge can be traced to their differential ability to relate the events to the game's goal structure; that is, high- and low-knowledge individuals are equally competent at recalling single sentences of domain-related information. However, high-knowledge individuals are better at recalling sequences of baseball events, presumably because they are better able to relate each sequence to the game's hierarchical goal structure of winning, scoring runs, and advancing runners.

To sum up the analysis so far, it appears that a large long-term knowledge base underlies skill performance in several varieties of spatial (as well as nonspatial) domains. Further, a very important component of the knowledge base is a fast-access pattern-recognition system, a system that greatly reduces processing load. In the game-playing examples and in physics problem solving, these patterns serve the purpose of retrieval aids for desirable courses of action. In the case of architects and electronics technicians, these patterns facilitate the perceptual organization of architectural drawings and circuit diagrams, respectively. What is striking among all these domains is the similarity in the hierarchical nature of the organization of knowledge. At the lowest level, the memory representations are very localized, containing ''structural'' properties, whereas at the higher levels, functional properties are more important.

Development of Cognitive Skill

It is important to ask how expertise is acquired in a given domain. The most obvious answer is practice, thousands of hours of practice, because it takes such a long time to acquire the necessary knowledge base. There may be some as yet undiscovered basic abilities that underlie the attainment of truly exceptional performance, such as a Grandmaster in chess. But for the most part, practice is by far the best predictor of performance in a majority of cases.

Practice can produce two kinds of knowledge. Practice enables the learner to build up a storage of patterns or lexicons. It can simultaneously also produce a set of strategies (or procedures) that can operate on the patterns. The presence of both types of knowledge can be demonstrated by examining exceptional mental calculators. Professor A. C. Aitken, for example, was perhaps the world's most skilled mental-calculation wizard. Hunter (1968) was able to show that Aitken's skill was primarily the result of two types of long-term memory knowledge. First, he possessed a tremendous amount of lexical knowledge about the properties of numbers. For example, he could ''instantly'' name the factors of any number up to 1500. Thus, for Aitken, all the three-digit numbers and a few four-digit numbers were unique and semantically rich, whereas for most of us, this is true only for the digits and a few other numbers, such as one's age. This knowledge alone provides a very substantial reduction in the memory load during mental calculation. Second, Aitken had gradually acquired a large variety of computational procedures designed to reduce the memory load in mental calculations. With years of intensive practice, these computational procedures gradually became faster and more automatic, to the point where Aitken's computational skills were truly astounding. For normal people, mental computations are severely limited by the capacity of short-term memory, and this limit is further compounded by the fact that most of us are taught only a few procedures that have very substantial storage overheads. For problems of any complexity, normal people have to resort to paper and pencil aids in order to store the results of intermediate computations. Professor Aitken (as well as other lightning calculators) gradually built up a long-term knowledge system that was capable of by-passing these constraints.

The acquisition of both types of knowledge can also be seen by tracing their development with time. Rayner (1958) analyzed the performance of six beginning players over a 5-week period as they learned the game of gomoku. He was able to describe the types of patterns that the players eventually learned to look for and the strategies dictated by each pattern. The patterns themselves are visually quite simple; the complexity arises in the number of moves required by the strategy to generate a win. The most complicated strategy that Rayner described was an 11-move sequence triggered by a fairly simple and innocuous-looking pattern of four stones. In his analysis of gomoku, Rayner described a process in which his subjects gradually switched from an analytic mode of working through the strategies to a perceptual mode in which they searched for familiar patterns for which they had already learned a winning strategy. In short, over a 5-week period in the laboratory, Rayner analyzed experimentally the perceptual learning process that is presumed to occur on a grand scale, over the course of years of practice, with the chess Masters.

The acquisition of both types of knowledge can be manipulated independently. In an on-going study, Ericsson and Chase (1980) were able to increase an average college student's memory span for digits from seven to 80 digits over a course of 2 years. How did this subject (S. F.) increase his digit span with practice? As it turns out, S. F. has a large knowledge base of running times for various races (e.g., 349 = 3 minutes and 49 seconds, near world-record mile time). Practice in this case did not produce the large data base of lexicons of running times. What the subject did with practice was to develop an elaborate mnemonic system in which he groups and segments the digits into hierarchical groups. In fact, unless he continually develops new hierarchical groups to code the digits, he would not be able to increase his digit span. Hence, this research suggests the following: First, the subject can independently develop a set of strategies to code and recall digits, when the digit patterns are already stored in memory. Second, there seems to be no limit to the extent to which a subject's memory span can be increased with extended practice. Finally, these data again reinforce the notion that memory-span limitation and short-term memory capacity are not synonymous. Memory span is limited both by the capacity of short-term memory and by the coding process. The more elaborate the coding processes a subject can develop, the greater will be the discrepancy between memory span and short-term memory capacity.

The three studies just cited suggest that cognitive-skill acquisition involves the development of extensive lexical and procedural knowledge. Such knowledge structures can take either the form of abstract–symbolic information (as in digits) or visual–spatial characteristics (such as a pattern of stones). Further, the principal mechanism underlying the development of such skill is extensive practice to build up the long-term knowledge base. And finally, there appears to be no limit to the extent to which cognitive skills can be developed, except perhaps for physiological processes such as aging. Elo (1965), for example, has computed an objective measure of tournament performance in world-class chess players, and has found a very regular relationship when this performance is plotted as a function of age. There is a steady, rapid improvement in performance from around age 14 through the 20's, followed by a peak at around age 35. Thereafter, there is a slow, regular decline in performance until, at age 65, performance has deteriorated to the same level as a 21-year-old.

It is perhaps instructive to review the major findings of the perceptual-motor skills literature to see what it can tell us about skill acquisition and cognitive skills. Probably the two most important generalizations to come out of that literature are (1) the *continuous* nature of skill acquisition; and (2) the *specificity* of acquired skills. If one looks at skilled performance as a function of practice, there seems to be a very lawful relation. Major gains in performance occur early in practice, followed by slower, steady gains over extended periods of practice. For a large number of speeded skills, if practice time and performance time are both transformed into logarithmic scales, the function seems to be linear. This result has led to mathematical theories of the learning process, which assume independent changes in a very large number of memory elements (Crossman, 1959; Lewis, 1978). Some such lawful relation is to be expected if skill acquisition involves a very large number of additions and modifications to the knowledge base.

Besides the smoothness of the learning curve, it is very surprising that improvements in less complex skills still occur after years of practice. In one industrial study, Crossman (1956) found a steady improvement, over a 2-year period, in the speed with which workers could operate a cigar-making machine. Beyond 2 years, the apparent asymptote in the workers' speed actually turned out to be a limit in the cycle time of the machine. What is really surprising about this study is that a seemingly simple motor skill, such as cigar making, can continue to show improvement with years of practice.

The continuous nature of motor-skill acquisition parallels the lack of any asymptotic limit to achievements in complex cognitive domains, such as mnemonic skills in digit span, mental calculations, and chess. It is typical to see steady improvements with years of practice. The only real limits seem to be a result of physiological limits such as aging.

The second important generalization from the perceptual-motor skills literature is that skills are so specific; that is, it has not been possible to predict individual differences in acquisition of complex perceptual-motor skills even in the face of large and reliable individual differences in those skills. This is true both from basic abilities and from other skills. That is, it has not been possible to predict performance on tennis, say, either from measuring the obvious basic abilities like eye–hand coordination, quickness, and so on, or from measuring performance on another closely related skill, say raquetball (Fitts & Posner, 1967; Marteniuk, 1974; Singer, 1968). The best predictor of future performance is present performance level. But even so, predicting performance at advanced levels from beginning levels of performance is not very reliable, presumably because, as Fleishman (1966) has shown, during the course of skill acquisition, there is systematic shifting of factors responsible for skilled performance. Presumably, at extremely advanced levels of skill, performance becomes more dependent on the contents of the knowledge base.

Both of these phenomena—the continuous improvement over long periods and skill specificity—are not unique to perceptual-motor skills. They also seem to be characteristic of cognitive skills, and for a very good theoretical reason. (There is not, in fact, much theoretical justification for differentiating perceptual-motor and cognitive skills.) Performance at high levels of a skill is dependent on a vast knowledge base of specific information about that particular skill. That is why practice is the major independent variable—because it simply takes so long to acquire the knowledge base—and transfer to other skills is for the most part ruled out because of the specificity of the knowledge.

To this point, this chapter has considered several principles of skilled performance. What seems to be common to all skills is the acquisition of knowledge in long-term memory, the purpose of which is to reduce processing load. A large component of this knowledge is visual–spatial pattern recognition because these patterns serve as retrieval cues for appropriate action. In the next section, skill differences in map drawing are analyzed in terms of how long-term knowledge is organized; the final section considers the question of how spatial skills in large-scale environments are organized.

MAP DRAWING

In this study, the phenomenon of interest is a revealing type of spatial error that often occurs when people draw maps. This error is interesting because it belongs to a class of normalizing errors that occur in large-scale environments, and an argument is made that these normalizing errors are the result of hierarchical organization of the memory representation.

Sixteen college students were asked to draw a map of the Carnegie-Mellon University campus, including 18 well-known buildings and street intersections. The 16 students consisted of 11 architecture undergraduates and five other undergraduates.

In order to eliminate problems associated with idiosyncratic drawing scales, each person's map was standardized in the x and y dimensions separately, and all subsequent analyses were based on z-scores. This transformation preserves individual distortions, but it does not allow differences in scale to enter into group averages.

Figs. 6.1 and 6.2 show the average maps for the architects and nonarchitects separately. The actual locations of the campus buildings are indicated by the squares, and the actual location of the roads surrounding the campus are also shown. The circles represent the average recalled location of the buildings in the subjects' maps, and the brackets at each location are ± 1 standard deviation between subjects in the x and y dimensions, separately. The dashed lines depict the errors—the discrepancy between the actual locations and the average drawn locations—and the legend contains the Root Mean Squared Deviation (RMSD), which is the standard deviation of these errors. There are three things to notice about these maps: (1) architects were significantly more accurate than nonarchitects (compare the RMSDs); (2) with one important exception, both architects and nonarchitects were very accurate in their placements; and (3) the one important exception involves an intersection of two streets that are not rectilinear with respect to the rest of the environment. The standard deviation for this one location was enormously large, as compared to the other locations. A closer examination of the individual maps revealed the source of the error. Most of the subjects (12) drew the streets of this intersection at right angles with respect to the rest of the environment, and they did so by forcing a 90° turn in one street or the other. Only four subjects, all architects, correctly drew these two streets at a 45° angle with respect to the rest of the environment.

Fig. 6.3 compares the actual street intersections with the three types of subjects. First, notice that the very large error in the location of the intersection (Figs. 6.1 and 6.2) is an averaging artifact caused by the mixture of the three types of subjects in the Fig. Second, even the map of the subjects who drew the intersection correctly is more rectilinear than the real map. Finally, a closer examination of Figs. 6.1 and 6.2 reveals systematic distortions at other campus locations. Most of the cases in which the reported location is more than 1 standard deviation away from the true location are situations in which the reported location is distorted toward a more rectilinear arrangement.

This error, it is argued, belongs to a class of normalizing errors that are the result of hierarchical organization of spatial knowledge. In this case, it appears that these errors are the result of a grid structure that people impose on their memory representations, and this grid structure can cause distortions in the location of local regions. Theoretically, it is assumed that people organize their geographical knowledge into sets of localized regions, and that these regions are organized hierarchically by a set of more global relations that link the more local regions together. For example, most people's geographical knowledge contains such relations as *California is west of Nevada*. In the present case, it is assumed that in the absence of specific global features, particularly in an urban environment, people automatically assume a rectilinear grid structure. This is precisely the assumption that Kuipers (1978) made in his elaborate formal model of spatial knowledge. There are a few instances of this type of error reported elsewhere in the literature. In one very interesting study, Milgram and Jodelet (1976) analyzed

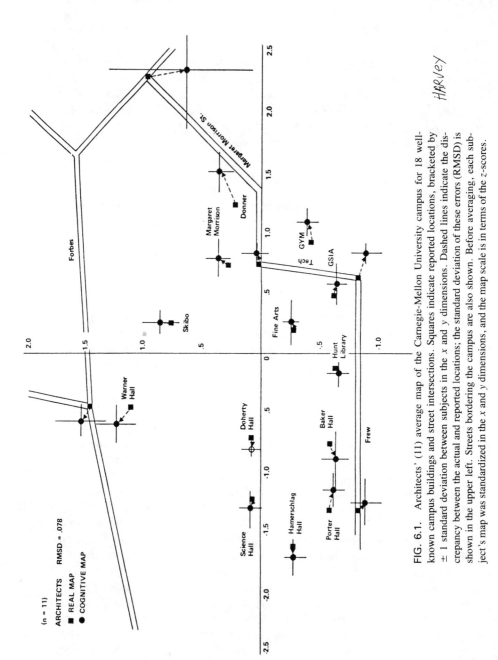

FIG. 6.1. Architects' (11) average map of the Carnegie-Mellon University campus for 18 well-known campus buildings and street intersections. Squares indicate reported locations, bracketed by ± 1 standard deviation between subjects in the x and y dimensions. Dashed lines indicate the discrepancy between the actual and reported locations; the standard deviation of these errors (RMSD) is shown in the upper left. Streets bordering the campus are also shown. Before averaging, each subject's map was standardized in the x and y dimensions, and the map scale is in terms of the z-scores.

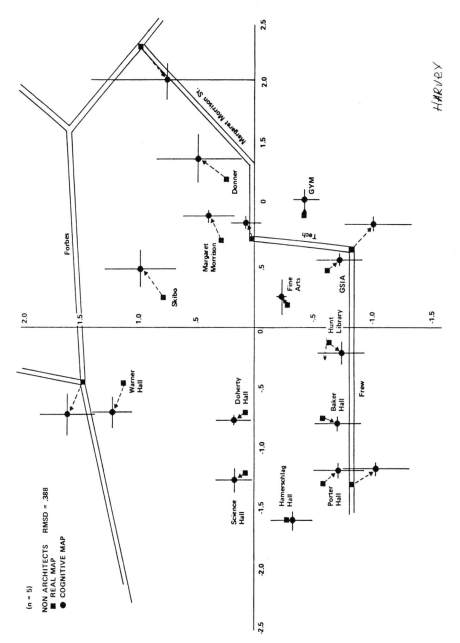

FIG. 6.2. Nonarchitects' (five) map of the CMU campus.

(n = 5)

NON ARCHITECTS   RMSD = .388
■ REAL MAP
● COGNITIVE MAP

HARVEY

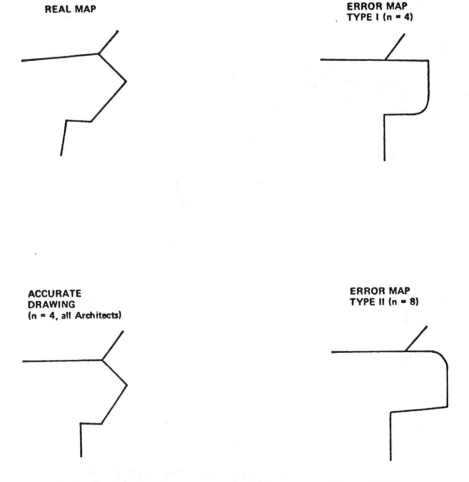

FIG. 6.3. Average maps for the only streets bordering the CMU campus, for three different types of subjects, depending on how they reported the one intersection at 45° with respect to the rest of the environment. The real map (upper left) is compared to the three types of subjects: (1) those who drew the intersection correctly (lower left, all architects); (2) those who forced Margaret Morrison Street to take a right-angle turn (upper left); and (3) those who forced Forbes Avenue to take a right-angle turn (lower right).

the hand-drawn maps of Paris by 218 Parisians; they reported that over 90% of their subjects underestimated the actual curvature of the Seine River. With the possible exception of the city limits of Paris, the Seine is probably the most prominent global feature of Paris. As Fig. 6.4 illustrates, however, in most people's minds, the Seine describes a more gentle and more regular curved path through Paris than is actually the case. Milgram and Jodelet (1976) conclude that this error ". . . reflects the subjects' experience. Although the Alma bend of the Seine is apparent in high aerial views of the city, it is not experienced as a sharp curve in the ordinary walk or drive through the city. The curve is extended over a sufficient distance so that the pronounced turn of the river is obscured [p. 109]." They further point out that because the Seine is usually drawn first, it introduces distortions in the locations of local regions, sometimes incorrectly displacing regions to the wrong side of the river or even eliminating certain districts altogether. In his informal interviews, Kuipers (1977) has also reported similar kinds of distortions caused by the curvature of the Charles River in Boston.

In the case of Paris, it is assumed that a prominent feature like the Seine River is used as a global (hierarchical) feature, and local regions are represented with respect to this global feature. As Milgram and Jodelet point out, people generally notice the curvature, but they fail to notice the irregularity, and the result is that they normalize the curvature in their memory representations. This kind of normalization can then serve as a serious source of error because people then incorrectly represent the relative locations of districts with respect to the more

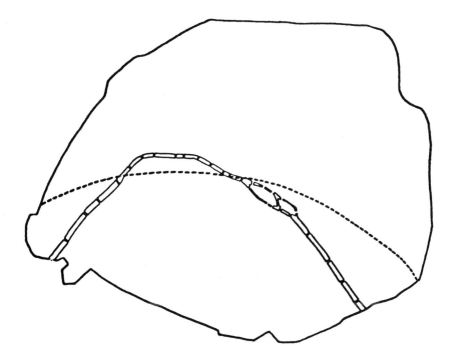

FIG. 6.4.   A comparison of the reported curvature of the Seine River (dotted line) and the actual course of the river through Paris. The dotted line represents the median curvature, based on 218 Parisians. From Milgram and Jodelet (1976). Reprinted by permission.

global feature. Notice the important implications of this assumption—that local regions are represented with respect to more global features: A great deal of spatial knowledge, perhaps most, is *inferred*. The relationship between two districts, say, is derived from their individual relationships to a global feature.

In another interesting study, Stevens and Coupe (1978) asked people to indicate the direction from one city to another, and they discovered several instances of large normalizing errors. In one particularly cogent example, they asked people who lived in San Diego to indicate the direction of Reno, Nevada. Virtually everyone indicated that Reno lies northeast of San Diego, when in fact it is northwest. As Stevens and Coupe point out, this type of error is symptomatic of hierarchical representation of spatial knowledge. To explain this error, it is assumed that people normally retrieve a set of spatial relations of the following sort from long-term memory:

1. Nevada is east of California.
2. San Diego is in the southern part of California on the West coast.
3. Reno is in the central part of Nevada on the California border.

Given this set of spatial relations, people *infer* that Reno is northeast of San Diego. These relations need not be verbal; most cognitive theorists would probably make the claim that spatial relations are abstract propositions (c.f. Clark & Chase, 1972). However, for the present purposes, the claim is simply that spatial knowledge is organized hierarchically without making any claims about the format. It is important to point out that even if one believes that spatial knowledge is stored as analogue images, this kind of spatial error is still the result of hierarchical representations; that is, suppose that an analogue image of California and Nevada is constructed in the mind's eye, and the relation of San Diego and Reno is "perceived" off the image. Still, the spatial knowledge needed to construct the image must come from somewhere; according to Kosslyn and Schwartz (1977), it must come from more abstract knowledge in long-term memory, from some kind of deep-structure representation of the sort illustrated in the preceding three spatial relations (1, 2, and 3). Regardless of whether the inferencing process is analogue or propositional, the strong claim is made here that the long-term memory representation is hierarchical. If spatial knowledge were not hierarchical in this case—if, say, the relationship between San Diego and Reno were stored directly—this kind of error would not occur.

Before moving on to the next topic, a couple of questions need to be addressed. First, why should spatial knowledge be hierarchical? The standard answer to this question is twofold. Hierarchies are efficient, and they are well suited for inference making. With hierarchical representations, it is not necessary to directly store every possible spatial relation; spatial relations that cut across regions can be inferred from more global knowledge. In addition, hierarchies in general are well suited for making abstractions, generalizations, and inferences (Chase, 1978).

A second question is why are these normalizing errors relevant with respect to everyday performance in the real world? People seem to navigate perfectly well in the city without being aware of variations in the global shapes of the routes they normally travel, as Thorndyke and Clayton and Woodyard have pointed out in their chapters in this volume (Chapters 7 and 8, respectively). If people can get around in their urban environments using known routes, what harm is there is not noticing, for example, that a turn is 45° rather than 90°? The answer is that sequential knowledge of known routes is very often sufficient to get around. Difficulties can quickly arise, however, if one attempts to use global features for navigation in these circumstances. For example, one can normally go around the block and get back to the same location by making four right turns, but not necessarily in cities like Pittsburgh or Boston! Serious navigational mistakes can also occur if one attempts to get from one neighborhood to the next with incorrect global representations such as those in Fig. 6.3. In the present study, it should be pointed out that some of the architects did exhibit superior knowledge of their large-scale environments, and this difference reflects real spatial skills. One of our primary research goals is to identify what constitutes spatial skills.

SPATIAL KNOWLEDGE AND COGNITIVE MAPS

What kind of spatial knowledge is activated when people think about their environment? This section attempts to deal with this question, and to explore the implications for cognitive maps. First, there is a substantial literature on this topic, and the reader is referred to several good reviews (Hart & Moore, 1973; Siegal & White, 1975; also see Chapters 7 and 8, by Thorndyke and Clayton and Woodyard, in this volume). For the most complete information-processing model of spatial cognition, the reader is referred to Kuiper's (1977, 1978) computer simulation. From a variety of sources in the literature, there is good evidence for the existence of at least two kinds of spatial knowledge. *Routes* refers to a local sequence of instructions that guides a person from one place to another along a known path. *Survey knowledge* refers to a more global structure containing a network of spatial relations that organizes more local regions. For example, if one knew that a desired location was to the north, say, of a prominent landmark, then a person's survey knowledge would allow one to get there without ever having travelled that route. From the developmental literature, it appears that there is an orderly progression in children's representations of large-scale environments with at least one important shift from route-type to survey-type representations, probably at the onset of Piaget's stage of concrete thought (around age 6). Some people even claim that when adults learn a new area, there is a recapitulation of these developmental stages, such that people first learn routes, and survey representations are subsequently built out of routes. (This latter statement is undoubtedly an oversimplification.)

This distinction between route and survey knowledge seems to be a fundamental one. In terms of performance, survey knowledge keeps people from getting lost when they leave a known route, and in terms of cognitive theory, the development of survey knowledge may be a very important advancement in the nature of representations.

What are some of the properties of this knowledge base? In the previous sections, an argument was made that (spatial) knowledge is hierarchical, and that local regions are interconnected by a network of global features. In the literature, there are also many references to the varied nature of this knowledge. In cities, this survey knowledge often takes the form of a grid structure, or a network of relative spatial relations with respect to some prominent landmark. Another important form of survey knowledge is a coordinate system based on cardinal directions (north, south, east, and west). It also seems quite evident that there are multiple frames of reference (coordinate as well as nested). For example, when a person emerges from the subway system onto the street, or a driver gets off an interstate system onto a local street network, there is a shift in the frame of reference.

Given this rich variety of representational knowledge, how is it used? From an information-processing point of view, what is the other half of the coin: What are the mental processes that people use to operate on these knowledge structures to actually get around in large-scale environments? There is understandably less written about process than structure in the literature, but there are still some good ideas in the literature. The reader is referred to the Chapters 7 and 8 in this volume by Thorndyke and Clayton and Woodyard, and to Kuiper's (1978) article. It is suggested that there is a fundamental distinction between two kinds of processes: automatic procedures and inference rules. In his model of spatial cognition, Kuipers (1978) only makes use of inference rules, but a strong case can be made that people use automatic procedures as well. An automatic procedure is used when someone follows a well-learned route. At each choice point along a well-travelled route, a decision must be made as to which way to go; this is normally accomplished smoothly, automatically, and unconsciously. Nevertheless, people must make use of some information from the environment to follow a route. The usual suggestion is that people use visual "images" or "icons"—that is, people have visual knowledge about each choice point stored in long-term memory, and as they approach these choice points, certain visual features serve to activate this knowledge. Associated with this knowledge are procedures that tell people what to do next. This is exactly the argument made earlier as to how chess players can think of good moves, good evaluations, or whole sequences of moves rapidly and seemingly unconsciously. In each case, procedural knowledge is built into long-term recognition memory, and if the right visual information appears, this knowledge is activated and appropriate action is taken.

The second kind of process that people use to operate on their spatial knowledge is the inference rule. In principle, these rules are used to derive knowledge that is not explicitly stored in memory. They may be used to fill in gaps in routes, to orient oneself in the environment, to perform geometric problem solving, and so on; Kuipers (1977, 1978) has provided a taxonomy of various types of inference rules for his model of spatial knowledge. A good example of the use of inference rules is provided by Stevens and Coupe's (1978) task. When someone is asked to indicate the direction of Reno with respect to San Diego, that person may or may not be conscious of some momentary mental image of California and Nevada, but in any case, he or she can easily generate an answer in a very few seconds. According to Stevens and Coupe (1978), people go through an inference process in which they derive the answer from the set of hierarchical propositions described earlier. Although Stevens and Coupe did not specify the inference rules needed to derive the answer, in principle, the types of rules described by Kuipers (1977, 1978) should work.

Given this rather elaborate information-processing theory of spatial knowledge, in what ways is skill manifested? Why are some people better than others at getting around in large-scale environments? From the earlier analysis of the cognitive-skills literature, one would have to say that the overriding consideration is the size of the knowledge base. People who have spent more time in a region, and who are more familiar with the area, should perform better. Perhaps a more interesting and less obvious question is why some people *acquire* spatial knowledge faster or better. Holding learning time constant, why are some people still superior? The standard answer in the literature seems to be that some people are better at using survey knowledge; certainly this is true developmentally in terms of why older children are better than younger children at getting around in large-scale environments. This was also true in the one skill difference reported in this chapter: Architects were superior to nonarchitects in their ability to accurately draw a map of their campus, and the biggest skill difference was due to that subset of architects who could correctly depict the global shape of the campus. Clearly, one would be interested in pursuing this issue further to determine if this performance is the result of some primary spatial ability for which architects are preselected, some aspect of their training, their curiosity about their environment, and so on. To summarize this issue, it seems fair to say that because there are many components involved in spatial knowledge, spatial skills could arise in many ways, and a full understanding will require more research.

The final issue addressed in this chapter is what are the cognitive components of cognitive mapping and cognitive maps. In the introduction to their influential volume, Downs and Stea (1973b) define these terms as follows: "Cognitive mapping is a construct which encompasses those cognitive processes which enable people to acquire, code, store, recall, and manipulate information about the nature of their spatial environment . . . a cognitive map is an abstraction which refers to a cross-section, at one point in time, of the environment as people believe it to be [p. xiv]." Thus defined, cognitive mapping is a good description for a cognitive model of spatial cognition, and this is precisely what Kuipers (1978) has attempted to implement; a cognitive map seems like a good way to characterize spatial knowledge. Two related problems, however, have arisen with respect to cognitive maps. One problem is what psychological significance to attach to cognitive maps, and the other problem is the operational difficulty of measuring the cognitive map.

As Downs and Stea (1973a) point out, researchers have tended to assume more psychological significance than is warranted to the cartographic properties of cognitive maps, and this has especially been true of geographers and cartographers. This misconception probably originated from Tolman's (1948) very influential article on cognitive maps. In this article, Tolman effectively dispelled the idea that the spatial behavior of animals (and people) could be explained in terms of stimulus–response connections. In its place, he substituted the notion that "something like a field map of the environment gets established in the rat's brain [p. 192]." By his very choice of terms—he entitled his article "Cognitive Maps in Rats and Men"—he developed the idea that there exists a two-dimensional map-like image in the head with topological or cartographic properties that people and animals use to navigate through their environment. From what we now know, this map metaphor has to be false. First, it seems clear from the cognitive literature that people do not have anywhere near the capacity to conjure up a complete image of a cognitive map. Certainly, chess Masters cannot imagine a whole chess board at once—they do it pattern by pattern. Architects, when drawing a plan from memory, only retrieve small subparts at a time, and the same is true of electronic technicians when working with circuit diagrams. In the map-drawing study, subjects worked on small subparts of maps when they drew maps, and they retrieved routes bit by bit. They seem to recall local pieces of routes and maps plus more global information about overall shape. Second, with respect to more permanent long-term memory knowledge, one is talking about vast amounts of knowledge of various kinds, probably organized hierarchically, that cannot possibly all appear in a cognitive map. In short, there does not seem to be any memory structure that corresponds to the cognitive map with the properties commonly ascribed to it.

The second problem concerns measuring the cognitive map. Given that a cognitive map is a useful abstraction that captures, at one moment in time, a cross section of people's perception of their environment, then it should be possible to obtain a "snapshot," so to speak, of this abstraction. This is exactly what Lynch (1960) tried to accomplish in his analysis of people's images of their city. Lynch used sketch maps, lengthy interviews, and field studies to construct composite maps of three U.S. cities: Boston, Jersey City, and Los Angeles. Lynch tried to abstract the key elements—paths, edges, landmarks, nodes, and districts—that were most memorable or imagable. The maps that Lynch constructed are very compelling and they seem to portray the essence and the character of each city. With his method, Lynch has captured an abstraction, an abstraction that seems to describe how people collectively view their city, how people of different ethnic backgrounds perceive their environments, and how the physical and sociological aspects of a city can affect people's representations of their environment. No wonder that Lynch's technique has had such a large impact on urban research.

But now a word of caution: These sociological maps should not be thought of as psychologically real. As previously pointed out, sketch maps or other derived maps cannot be thought of as measures of some internal cognitive map. Nor should they be thought of as aggregate maps. Nothing like these maps exist inside the heads of individuals. The averaging process does not somehow derive an ''average'' cognitive map.

This is an important but subtle point, and it is perhaps best illustrated with an example. In their analysis of sketch maps of Paris, Milgram and Jodelet (1976) plotted the 50 most frequent elements from their 218 subjects, and they found that the frequency of elements closely reflected the tourist Paris, the most famous sites of the city: the Seine, Arc de Triomphe, Notre Dame, Tour Eiffel, and so on. They therefore conclude that their data do not support the popular notion held by Parisians that there is a real Paris quite apart from the tourist Paris. But if Parisians take pride in the lesser known parts of Paris, especially if the Parisian's Paris is more idiosyncratic, it is not clear how their procedure would detect this aspect of Paris. By listing elements in order of frequency, they have in effect averaged out the private, idiosyncratic parts of individual maps. The net result is a sociological abstraction that is not characteristic of any one individual's sketch map. In this sense, these sociological maps are not psychologically real.

This is not to say that these maps are not useful sociological abstractions. This ''averaged'' map is undoubtedly a very useful index of the prominent parts of Paris, and as such could be very useful to urbanologists. In fact, these maps have already been demonstrated to be very useful research devices. It should simply be pointed out that the real psychological processes underlying spatial cognition reside in the short-term and long-term knowledge structures and processes described previously.

SUMMARY

This chapter has attempted to define the nature of spatial skill in large-scale environments. The first section of the chapter contained an analysis of cognitive skills in a variety of domains, and several characteristics of skill were revealed. One important characteristic of skills is that with practice, there is a shift from analytic reasoning to fast-access recognition processes, and this shift seems to be an inevitable result of severe short-term memory limitations. Analytic reasoning places too heavy a burden on short-term memory, and hence performance is serial and slow. To perform skills rapidly and efficiently requires ready access to large amounts of task-specific knowledge. People gradually acquire "preprogrammed" knowledge, knowledge that can guide skilled performance smoothly and efficiently without overloading short-term memory once it is triggered by the recognition system.

Another important characteristic of skills is the nature of this knowledge representation. It seems to be true for a wide variety of cognitive skills that knowledge is organized hierarchically. For visual–spatial skills, and perhaps for other skills as well, at the lowest level in the hierarchy, knowledge seems to be organized in very localized and stereotyped patterns. At higher levels, these local patterns are organized together by means of more conceptual or functional properties.

An analysis of the spatial-skills literature revealed that large-scale environments are generally thought of as hierarchically organized. People seem to have at least two distinct kinds of spatial knowledge: routes and survey knowledge. Further, there is very good evidence that geographic knowledge is organized in much the same way as other spatial skills, with local regions organized hierarchically around more global features. In cities, the hierarchy often takes the form of a grid structure. In one map-drawing study, it was found that skilled subjects were less likely to make normalizing errors on the hierarchical grid structure: in an environment that deviates from the grid structure, they were more likely to correctly code the deviation. This normalizing error, as well as other similar errors reported in the literature, is taken as strong evidence that geographical knowledge is organized hierarchically.

One final issue concerns the nature of cognitive maps. It was suggested that there is no cognitive structure corresponding to a "map in the head," as Tolman (1948) had originally supposed. From our analysis of cognitive skills, it was suggested that there is not enough short-term memory capacity to support an image of a map, and the vast, hierarchical long-term knowledge structures certainly are not organized like a map. The map metaphor is not a good model of how people organize their spatial knowledge.

One final word of caution. Cognitive mapping studies are a useful research technique for deriving sociological abstractions for urbanologists, but these "averaged" maps should not be thought of as psychological structures.

ACKNOWLEDGMENTS

Preparation of this chapter was supported by Grant #N00014-78-C-0375, NR 157-421 from the Office of Naval Research. We are indebted to Anders Ericsson for comments on an earlier draft.

REFERENCES

Akin, O. *Models of architectural knowledge.* London: Pion, 1980.

Charness, N. Memory for chess positions: Resistance to interference. *Journal of Experimental Psychology: Human Learning and Memory.* 1976, *2,* 641–653.

Charness, N. Components of skill in bridge. *Canadian Journal of Psychology,* 1979, *33,* 1–50.

Chase, W. G. Elementary information processes. In W. K. Estes (Ed.), *Handbook of learning and cognitive processes* (Vol. 5). Hillsdale, N.J.: Lawrence Erlbaum Associates, 1978.

Chase, W. G., & Simon, H. A. The mind's eye in chess. In W. G. Chase (Ed.), *Visual information processing.* New York: Academic Press, 1973. (a)

Chase, W. G., & Simon, H. A. Perception in chess. *Cognitive Psychology,* 1973, *4,* 55–81. (b)

Chi, M. T. H. Knowledge structures and memory development. In R. Siegler (Ed.), *Children's thinking: What develops?* Hillsdale, N.J.: Lawrence Erlbaum Associates, 1978.

Chi, M. T. H., Feltovich, P., & Glaser, R. *Physics problem solving by experts and novices.* Paper presented at the Psychonomic Society Meeting, Phoenix, Arizona, November 1979.

Chi, M. T. H., & Glaser, R. *Encoding process characteristics of experts and novices in physics.* Paper presented at the meeting of the American Educational Research Association, San Francisco, April 1979.

Chiesi, H. L., Spilich, G. J., & Voss, J. F. Acquisition of domain-related information in relation to high and low domain knowledge. *Journal of Verbal Learning and Verbal Behavior,* 1979, *18,* 257–273.

Clark, H. H., & Chase, W. G. On the process of comparing sentences against pictures. *Cognitive Psychology,* 1972, *3,* 472–517.

Crossman, E. R. F. W. *The measurement of perceptual load in manual operations.* Unpublished doctoral thesis, Birmingham University, 1956.

Crossman, E. R. F. W. A theory of the acquisition of speed-skill. *Ergonomics,* 1959, *2,* 153–166.

de Groot, A. *Thought and choice in chess.* The Hague: Mouton, 1965.

de Groot, A. Perception and memory versus thought: Some old ideas and recent findings. In B. Kleinmuntz (Ed.), *Problem solving.* New York: Wiley, 1966.

Downs, R. M., & Stea, D. Cognitive maps and spatial behavior: Process and products. In R. M. Downs & D. Stea (Eds.), *Image and environment.* Chicago: Aldine, 1973. (a)

Downs, R. M., & Stea, D. *Image and environment.* Chicago: Aldine, 1973. (b)

Egan, D. E., & Schwartz, B. J. Chunking in recall of symbolic drawings. *Memory & Cognition,* 1979, *7,* 149–158.

Eisenstadt, M., & Kareev, Y. Aspects of human problem solving: The use of internal representations. In D. A. Norman & D. E. Rumelhart (Eds.), *Explorations in cognition.* San Francisco: Freeman, 1975.

Ellis, S. H. *Structure and experience in the matching and reproduction of chess patterns.* Unpublished doctoral dissertation, Carnegie-Mellon University, 1973.

Elo, A. E. Age changes in master chess performance. *Journal of Gerontology,* 1965, *20,* 289–299.

Engle, R. W., & Bukstel, L. Memory processes among bridge players of differing expertise. *American Journal of Psychology,* 1978, *91,* 673–690.

Ericsson, K. A., & Chase, W. G. Acquisition of a memory skill. *Science,* 1980, *208,* 1181–1182.

Fitts, P. M., & Posner, M. I. *Human performance.* Belmont, Calif.: Brooks/Cole, 1967.

Fleishman, E. A. Human abilities and the acquisition of skill. In E. A. Bilodeau (Ed.), *Acquisition of skill.* New York: Academic Press, 1966.

Frey, P. W., & Adesman, P. Recall memory for visually-presented chess positions. *Memory & Cognition,* 1976, *4,* 541–547.

Goldin, S. E. Effects of orienting tasks on recognition of chess positions. *American Journal of Psychology,* 1978, *91,* 659–672.

Goldin, S. E. Recognition memory for chess positions. *American Journal of Psychology,* 1979, *92,* 19–31.

Greeno, J. G. Process of understanding in problem solving. In N. J. Castellan, D. B. Pisoni, & G. R. Potts (Eds.), *Cognitive theory* (Vol. 2). Hillsdale, N.J.: Lawrence Erlbaum Associates, 1977.

Hart, R. A., & Moore, G. T. The development of spatial cognition: A review. In R. M. Downs & D. Stea (Eds.), *Images and environment*. Chicago: Aldine, 1973.

Hinsley, D. A., Hayes, J. R., & Simon, H. A. From words to equations: Meaning and representation in algebra word problems. In P. A. Carpenter & M. A. Just (Eds.), *Cognitive processes in comprehension*. Hillsdale, N.J.: Lawrence Erlbaum Associates, 1977.

Hunter, I. M. L. Mental calculation. In P. C. Wason & P. N. Johnson-Laird (Eds.), *Thinking and reasoning*. Baltimore: Penguin, 1968.

Kosslyn, S. M., & Schwartz, S. P. A simulation of visual imagery. *Cognitive Science,* 1977, *3,* 265–296.

Kuipers, B. *Representing knowledge of large-scale space*. Unpublished doctoral dissertation, Massachusetts Institute of Technology, 1977.

Kuipers, B. Modeling spatial knowledge. *Cognitive Science,* 1978, *2,* 129–153.

Lane, D. M., & Robertson, L. The generality of levels of processing hypothesis: An application to memory for chess positions. *Memory & Cognition,* 1979, *7,* 253–256.

Larkin, J. H., McDermott, J., Simon, D. P., & Simon, H. A. Expert and novice performance in solving physics problems. *Science,* 1980, *208,* 1335–1342.

Lewis, C. W. *Production system models of practice effects*. Unpublished doctoral dissertation, University of Michigan, 1978.

Lynch, K. *The image of the city*. Cambridge, Mass.: MIT Press, 1960.

Marteniuk, R. G. Individual differences in motor performance and learning. In J. H. Wilmore (Ed.), *Exercise and sport sciences review* (Vol. 2). New York: Academic Press, 1974.

Milgram, S., & Jodelet, D. Psychological maps of Paris. In H. M. Proshansky, W. H. Ittelson, & L. G. Rivkin (Eds.), *Environmental Psychology* (2nd ed.). New York: Holt, Rinehart, & Winston, 1976.

Rayner, E. H. A study of evaluative problem solving. Part 1. Observations on adults. *Quarterly Journal of Experimental Psychology,* 1958, *10,* 155–165.

Reitman, J. Skilled perception in go: Deducing memory structures from inter-response times. *Cognitive Psychology,* 1976, *8,* 336–356.

Siegal, A. W., & White, S. H. The development of spatial representations of large-scale environments. In H. W. Reese (Ed.), *Advances in Child Development and Behavior* (Vol. 10). New York: Academic Press, 1975.

Simon, H. A., & Chase, W. G. Skill in chess. *American Scientist,* 1973, *61,* 394–403.

Simon, D. P., & Simon, H. A. Individual differences in solving physics problems. In R. Siegler (Ed.), *Children's thinking: What develops?* Hillsdale, N.J.: Lawrence Erlbaum Associates, 1978.

Singer, R. N. *Motor learning and human performance*. New York: Macmillan, 1968.

Stevens, A., & Coupe, P. Distortions in judged spatial relations. *Cognitive Psychology,* 1978, *10,* 422–437.

Tolman, E. C. Cognitive maps in rats and men. *Psychological Review,* 1948, *55,* 189–208.

7 Spatial Cognition and Reasoning

Perry W. Thorndyke
The Rand Corporation

During the second day of this conference, I was stopped while walking across the Vanderbilt campus by a couple who asked if I could direct them to the Holiday Inn. Although I was generally unfamiliar with the campus and its environs, I had walked between the Holiday Inn and the conference hall three times during the previous two days. Consequently, I was able to confidently point in the direction of the hotel and explain to them the best route to take in order to walk there.

This incident gave me particular satisfaction because I was able to analyze and understand my mundane (though by no means simple) behavior in that situation because of my research on spatial cognition, which, not coincidentally, is the topic of this chapter. I use the term cognition here not in its typical sense (as synonymous with "thinking"), but in its primary literal sense, which is the process of acquiring new knowledge.[1] Thus, as the title of this chapter indicates, I am concerned with how people acquire knowledge of their environment and how they use that knowledge to perform tasks such as, in the just-cited example, orienting oneself in the environment and giving directions.

Situations in which we acquire new spatial knowledge or use what we know to reason are ubiquitous in our lives. They range all the way from learning to get around in a new locale by acquiring knowledge about the names and locations of objects in the environment to reading a map to answer particular questions about the world (e.g., What's the name of that street? Where's the Pasadena Civic Center?). People also use the knowledge they acquire to perform such tasks as estimating distances between points or deciding how to get from one location to another by the shortest route.

---

[1] I am grateful to Frederick Hayes-Roth for pointing out this distinction.

Most people's spatial knowledge comes from a variety of sources. A frequent source of knowledge is a map, which provides a concise symbolism for a vast amount of geographic information, and so is particularly useful for finding information or answering questions rapidly. But most typically, people acquire knowledge from navigational experience. They travel through the world, observe objects, locations, and routes, encode that information in memory, and integrate it all into a coherent representation of the world. In this chapter, I propose some of the types of spatial knowledge that people have in memory, how they acquire that knowledge, and how particular knowledge types constrain performance on common spatial-reasoning tasks.

The question of how people perceive and respond to their spatial environment has concerned researchers from a wide range of disciplines, including geography, psychology, architecture, urban planning, and sociology. With the exception of a few isolated studies of spatial orientation (e.g., Tolman 1948; Trowbridge, 1913; Witkin, 1946), much of the psychological research on spatial cognition and reasoning has been conducted within the past 20 years. The bulk of this research has been in the area of environmental psychology (Downs & Stea, 1973, 1977; Golledge & Rushton, 1976; Lynch, 1960; Moore & Golledge, 1976; Proshansky, Ittelson, & Rivlin, 1970). However, as evidenced by the contributions of Chase and Chi (Chapter 6) and Clayton and Woodyard (Chapter 8) to this volume and by other recent articles in the literature (e.g., Allen, Siegel, & Rosinski, 1978; Kozlowski & Bryant, 1977; Stevens & Coupe, 1978; Thorndyke & Stasz, 1980), cognitive and experimental psychologists have begun to study this area of human behavior too.

The recent, "cognitive" approaches to human spatial reasoning (including the present chapter) differ somewhat from the traditional "environmental" approach. In both approaches, researchers are concerned with what types of spatial knowledge people acquire and, to some extent, how that knowledge is represented in memory. Such knowledge includes the identities of various geographic features (e.g., landmarks, paths or routes, boundaries, and regions), the locations of these features in the environment, the distances among them, and the knowledge necessary to orient oneself in the environment. Typically, environmental psychologists focus on how people derive such spatial knowledge from their day to day experiences. Such studies frequently employ correlational methods to relate personal variables such as socioeconomic status, mobility, attitudes, and preferences to individuals' environmental knowledge. Cognitive psychologists, in contrast, are considering maps, in addition to environmental experience, as sources of spatial knowledge. Further, instead of considering social variables as determinants of individual differences in spatial knowledge, cognitive psychologists are analyzing differences in spatial knowledge in terms of the processes individuals use to acquire, manipulate, encode, and retrieve information. Chase and Chi's contribution to this volume (Chapter 6) illustrates this approach. Such process analyses have also led cognitive researchers to consider the procedures by which people use their spatial knowledge to perform complex tasks such as memorizing maps, estimating distances, and selecting optimal routes between points.

The remainder of this chapter provides an overview to the approach my colleagues, Barbara Hayes-Roth and Cathleen Stasz, and I have been taking to the study of human spatial cognition. The chapter is organized around three main points that are illustrated and defended with a variety of formal and informal data. These points are:

1. People encode several types of spatial knowledge in memory.
2. Different types of spatial knowledge are optimal for different tasks.
3. Individuals vary in their strategies and abilities for acquiring spatial knowledge.

The following sections treat each of these propositions in more detail.

TYPES OF SPATIAL KNOWLEDGE

Our knowledge of the surrounding world comes from a variety of sources, including maps, movies and photographs, verbal descriptions, and direct perception during navigation. It seems reasonable, then, to suppose that a person's spatial knowledge is a collection of memories that may include images of geographic features, sequences of actions that define specific routes, images (perhaps fuzzy) of area maps, and individual facts about particular objects or relationships (e.g., the distance from San Francisco to Los Angeles is approximately 400 miles). Siegel and White (1975) have postulated three fundamental types of spatial knowledge: memory for landmarks (prominent geographic features), route representations (action sequences that connect separate locations), and configural representations (map-like, global organizations of object and route relationships). A variety of other researchers, using different terminologies, have made similar distinctions and have argued that a person's knowledge typically progresses from landmark to route to configural representations (Appleyard, 1969, 1970; Piaget, Inhelder, & Szeminska, 1960; Shemyakin, 1962; Siegel, Kirasic, & Kail, 1978).

I view these distinctions as defining categories of knowledge types, which I call landmark knowledge, procedural knowledge (knowledge of procedures for navigating between points), and survey knowledge (map-like configurations of points). Within these categories, I think it is possible to further refine the distinctions to capture differences in how detailed the knowledge is, how it is associated with related knowledge, and the form in which it is represented. Table 7.1 summarizes these knowledge types.

The different knowledge types may be thought of as stages in the representation of spatial knowledge. Like Clayton and Woodyard (Chapter 8 in this volume), I do not think that the acquisition of knowledge necessarily follows a

TABLE 7.1
Types of Spatial Knowledge

Knowledge Category	Form of the Memory Representation
Landmark ————————————→	Perceptual icons
Procedure ————————————→	⎧ Unordered productions ⎨ Ordered productions ⎩ Symbolic abstractions
Survey ————————————→	⎧ Schematized maps ⎩ Detailed maps

particular linear progression through these stages. Rather, people typically seem to have knowledge of each type about different portions of their environment. Exactly which stage best characterizes a person's knowledge depends on such factors as the extent of the person's navigational experience in the environment, the regularity of the geographic features in the environment, the person's motivation, whether or not the person has studied a map of the environment, and so on.

The first type of knowledge is the memory of familiar, previously experienced locations. Such knowledge may be thought of as *perceptual icons.* People most typically acquire these icons when first encountering a new environment, such as when visiting a new city or new area of a familiar city. As they travel through the region, they notice various objects and encode perceptual images that capture the visual scene. Repeated experience leads to the accumulation of a data base of these recognizable images of the area. Thus, people who have spent some time in a city can look through a set of photographs and determine which objects they have seen and the names of certain buildings and locations. One might acquire these memories independently of knowledge of the relative locations of the objects in the region or of the routes connecting them.

Much navigation behavior is goal directed; that is, people usually travel with a destination in mind. In novel environments, people begin to acquire route knowledge by associating with their perceptual icons behaviors they perform in order to reach a certain destination. Such associations are like production rules, or situation-action pairs of the form "if my destination is X and I am at recognizable location Y, then perform action Z." Clayton and Woodyard (Chapter 8 in this volume) refer to this type of knowledge as memory for actions in context. So, for example, if I am travelling in Los Angeles, my destination is The Rand Corporation, and my current view when I look around includes Synanon on my left, then I know I should turn right. Along the same route, another view I might have is an intersection with a traffic signal and the Royal Inn on the left. In this situation, I know I should turn left. People frequently acquire sets of such productions as a basis for navigating in an unfamiliar region using only memory of previous route traversals. For any particular route, the individual productions are independent in that they do not represent the order or occurrence along the route, nor is there any explicit association among them. In Table 7.1, knowledge of this type is referred to as *unordered productions*.

It is not unusual for a person to have extensive route knowledge of an environment comprising only these unintegrated route components. An acquaintance, MC, who is a native of Los Angeles, illustrates this point nicely. When asked to give directions for a moderately complex but frequently travelled route, she often replies, "I can't tell you how to get there, but I can take you there." This distinction between the ability to navigate and the ability to give directions potentially stems from two properties of the memory representation of unordered productions. First, the productions MC uses for navigation are independent and are organized in memory in no particular sequential order. So, even though MC can retrieve the appropriate action associated with each of the choice points, she cannot retrieve the order in which she will arrive at the points. Thus, once she arrives at a certain choice point, she knows the appropriate action to perform, but she cannot regenerate the sequence of choice points. A second reason for MC's inability to give directions may be due to an inability to recall or explain in sufficient detail the visual features of the locations where actions must be performed. Thus, although MC can recognize these locations when she arrives at them, the image of these locations may not be sufficiently strong for her to recall them.

A related type of procedural knowledge is listed in Table 7.1 as *ordered productions*. This knowledge is similar to unordered productions except that order information is represented by associations between productions. I may know, for example, that when I arrive at Synanon on my way to Rand, I should turn right, and that next I should use, say, production P46. P46, in turn, may state that when I arrive at the Royal Inn, I should turn left and then use production P81. Thus, sequential route knowledge is represented as an associative path through a set of individual productions.

As people become more familiar with the environment, they begin to replace their perceptual icons with *symbolic abstractions* of the region. Such symbolic information includes semantic knowledge about location names and approximate locations. This knowledge may supplant the perceptual information that was used previously for navigation. For example, one may learn that Rand is at the corner of Ocean Avenue and Colorado Boulevard, so that it is no longer necessary to be able to recognize the building. One needs only to know the name of the corner at which to turn. As such symbolic abstractions replace perceptual icons in people's route descriptions, less attention is given to the visual details of the environment. An interesting but as yet untested hypothesis following from this formulation is that as people become more experienced in an environment, they may actually become less sensitive to perceptual details due to an increasing reliance on symbolic abstractions.

In addition to learning these symbolic labels, people may also acquire spatial knowledge that cannot be perceived directly. Such knowledge includes distances between points and their relative compass bearings or orientations. One might learn these additional facts from a map, from another person, or by computing them from direct knowledge about routes connecting the points. This survey knowledge about relative spatial locations complements the procedural knowledge for navigating between locations. Thus, one might know not only how to get to Rand from Synanon, but that Synanon is one-half mile due south of Rand.

As the number of facts about spatial location, direction, and distance about a region grows, one builds what may be thought of as a network of spatial relations encoding knowledge about various locations. Stevens and Coupe (1978) have postulated that such knowledge is organized hierarchically in memory and that inferential processes operate on knowledge in the network to produce judgments about spatial relations. For example, one might have the following concepts and relations stored in memory: San Diego IS-PART-OF California, Reno IS-PART-OF Nevada, and California IS-WEST-OF Nevada. Using only this knowledge, one might infer, incorrectly, that San Diego is west of Reno. Stevens and Coupe have shown that people commonly make such errors in spatial judgment due to oversimplification of their stored relations.

People also appear to be able to represent and use survey knowledge in imaginal maps. Such a representation may come from a direct encoding of a physical map in some form, such as an image, that preserves the spatial relations among objects on the map, or it may be constructed out of numerous facts derived from direct experience in the environment. In either case, this type of memory is essentially visual, and it is most easily acquired by individuals who have vivid visual imagery and good visual-memory ability (Thorndyke & Stasz, 1980). Further, such imaginal maps can be examined, scanned, and manipulated in the same manner that one would use a physical map (Thorndyke, 1979).

Depending on the extent of people's knowledge of a region, their mental maps may vary in the amount of detail they contain. Individuals who have extensive navigational experience or who have studied a map may possess nearly veridical mental maps. I have referred to these in Table 7.1 as *detailed maps*. On the other hand, people frequently possess poorly developed maps containing normalized or oversimplified features. I refer to such maps as *schematized maps,* because they often contain a simple, prototypical configuration of elements. For example, Los Angeles contains a system of streets and freeways that approximate, although differ in significant ways from, a rectilinear grid. People who have lived in Los Angeles for a short time frequently assume that most streets are parallel or perpendicular to each other. When these individuals draw maps of the city, they make relational errors based on these assumptions of regularity. Further, they are surprised to learn that two streets that they had assumed to be parallel actually intersect. Chase and Chi (Chapter 6 in this volume) illustrate this phenomenon of systematic normalization of spatial relations in students' reconstructions of the map of the Carnegie-Mellon campus.

KNOWLEDGE TYPES AND SPATIAL JUDGMENTS

These distinctions among knowledge types become more salient when considering the estimates and judgments people make using their spatial knowledge. My colleague Barbara Hayes-Roth and I have developed the idea that the different categories of knowledge previously described may be optimal for different tasks requiring spatial judgments (Thorndyke & Hayes-Roth, 1978). Further, the method by which people acquire thei knowledge of the environment influences the type of knowledge that they have and the way in which it is represented. This suggests that people's performance on reasoning tasks depends on the type of experiences that have contributed to their spatial knowledge.

For example, navigational experience in a region leads directly to procedural knowledge. Such knowledge encodes the products of direct experience, including perceptual icons and the actions associated with those icons for traversing particular routes. The knowledge a person acquires directly about the space between two points when navigating comprises a sequence of turns at perceptible angles and the distance, experienced visually and kinesthetically, along each of the legs of the route. It is thus possible to obtain fairly precise local knowledge of the space and the route distance that connects the two points. In addition, as Tolman (1948) has demonstrated with rats and Kozlowski and Bryant (1977) with humans, navigational experience leads relatively rapidly to accurate orientation knowledge (the ability to point to unseen locations in the environment). This latter knowledge is particularly useful for dead reckoning in an unfamiliar environment and for locating oneself in the environment with respect to other objects or locations.

On the other hand, when people study a map of the same region, they have immediate access to the configural properties of the region. Because knowledge of the region is spatially rather than sequentially available, the global relationships among objects in the region are readily apparent. These relationships include the relative locations of and Euclidean (straight-line) distances between objects in the region. Thus, for example, if one views a map of Los Angeles, it is easy to discern whether UCLA or USC is closer to Rand and what their relative locations are. However, if one is restricted to driving among those points, the relative Euclidean distances and spatial locations may be quite difficult to ascertain.

The city of Boston provides an excellent environment with which to illustrate the distinction between reasoning from procedural and survey knowledge. Because the major geographic boundaries (the harbor and the Charles River) and many of the roads contain irregular curves, it is difficult to induce accurate survey knowledge of the city without looking at a map. In fact, it is not unusual for residents of the city to know how to navigate between points in the city along the best routes (which are not the shortest routes), but not be able to draw a map of the city that properly locates the same points.

Of course, Boston is an extreme example of the difficulty of inducing survey knowledge from navigational experience because of the severe irregularities of the common routes. In many regions, people can learn the spatial relationships well enough to draw a reasonably accurate map after a moderate amount of navigational experience. This illustrates another point about the acquisition of spatial knowledge: The type of knowledge a person has about an environment usually changes over time and increasing experience in the environment.

In an experiment designed to illustrate these points, Hayes-Roth and I tested various spatial reasoning skills of subjects who had had different learning experiences. We selected as our test environment the two buildings of The Rand Corporation, a maze of offices and hallways that most employees require a few weeks to master. Half of our subjects learned the Rand environment by memorizing a map of the floor plan of the two buildings. These subjects thus directly encoded a survey representation of the space. The map-learning subjects had never visited Rand prior to the experiment. The other subjects were Rand employees who had obtained their knowledge of the buildings by navigating through the hallways. We manipulated the amount of experience these subjects had had by selecting employees who had worked at Rand for either a month, 6 months, or 12 to 24 months.

We tested the spatial knowledge of our subjects on orientation, distance estimation, and object-location tasks. For the orientation task, we took subjects to various locations in the building and asked them to point in the direction of other unseen locations. Subjects with only 1 month of navigation experience performed more accurately on this task than subjects who had memorized the map. Furthermore, the longer individuals had worked at Rand, the more accurate their orientation judgments were. On the object-location task, subjects were given a piece of paper with two locations in the building specified and were required to mark the correct location of a particular third location. This test evaluated the accuracy of subjects' survey knowledge of the building. Subjects who had learned the map performed better than all navigation subjects, although the navigation subjects again improved with increasing experience. This result emphasizes the important distinction between the knowledge required to orient oneself in the environment and the knowledge required to reconstruct a survey representation.

Subjects performed two types of distance estimation between various sets of points: route distance (distance along the hallways between the two points), and Euclidean distance (straight-line distance). Subjects who had learned the map could readily compute from memory both types of distances; accordingly, they were equally accurate on both types of estimates. However, subjects with 1 month of navigation experience were far superior in their route estimates and inferior in their Euclidean distance estimates. Whereas direct navigational experience led to superior knowledge of the distances along travelled hallways, the survey knowledge subjects obtained from learning the map was optimal for computing Euclidean distances. Interestingly, performance on both estimation tasks improved with increasing experience, so that subjects with 12 to 24 months experience were equally accurate on both types of estimates and were superior to the map-learning subjects.

These results illustrate three important points about spatial cognition. First, different spatial-reasoning tasks require the use of different types of knowledge. Although survey knowledge, for example, may be appropriate for judgments of relative location and distances among objects, it is not optimal for judgments of spatial orientation. Second, different experiences induce, at least initially, different types of knowledge. This was illustrated in the performance differences of subjects who had studied a map and subjects who had travelled throughout the building. Finally, spatial knowledge evolves and changes with extensive navigational experience. Although such experience initially produces primarily procedural knowledge, increasing the amount of experience induces survey knowledge perhaps as accurate as that obtained from learning a map.

INDIVIDUAL DIFFERENCES IN SPATIAL COGNITION

The previous section outlined some general principles of spatial cognition and reasoning; an equally important source of variation in spatial-reasoning performance is the spatial-processing skill and style of the individual. These individual differences include both the strategies people use and the basic cognitive-processing abilities required to perform spatial cognition tasks. One of the first psychologists to study individual differences in the processes of spatial cognition was Trowbridge (1913), who investigated different strategies and individual abilities for orientation. In this section, I illustrate some of the dimensions of individual variation using the task of map learning, because maps are perhaps our most common source of survey knowledge.

An implicit assumption in the previous discussion of map representations in memory, one I have defended elsewhere (Thorndyke, 1979), is that learning a map entails the creation of a visual representation in memory. Creating a visual representation of a display as complex as a typical map depends both on learnable strategies for focusing attention on the display and organizing the visual field, and on more stable, fundamental skills such as encoding and manipulating visual information in mental images. In a series of experimental studies (Thorndyke & Stasz, 1980), Cathleen Stasz and I have been investigating the predictability of people's success at learning a map from their study strategies and spatial abilities.

Initially, we gave subjects a map to learn containing both spatial information (e.g., road patterns, rivers, building locations) and verbal information (named objects and locations). On each of six study/recall trials, subjects first studied the map for 2 minutes, attempting to learn as much of the map as they could. After the 2 minutes, subjects drew from memory as much of the map as they could remember. While subjects studied the map, they thought out loud about what they were looking at on the map, what techniques they were using to learn the information, what information they thought they had yet to learn, how they were deciding to change study strategies, and so on. By analyzing these verbal protocols for the set of "procedures," or study techniques, that subjects were using, we were able to relate speed of learning over trials to the set of study procedures subjects employed.

Three general types of procedures emerged from the protocols: attention, encoding, and evaluation. Attentional procedures included those by which subjects selected subsets of the map information on which to focus and those by which they decided the sequence of map elements to study. Encoding procedures included techniques for holding current information in working memory and techniques for elaborating the information and storing it in long-term memory for later retrieval. Predictably, the procedures that emerged from the protocols for encoding spatial information were different from those used to encode verbal information. The evaluation procedure comprised subjects' statements of whether or not they felt they had successfully learned the information on which they were currently focusing.

A comparison of the protocols of fast and slow learners revealed at least one difference in the use of procedures in each of the three categories. Good learners controlled their focus of attention on the map by isolating subsets of information and systematically learning the information in each subset before moving to a new one. Poor learners used more haphazard and unsystematic approaches to selecting information to learn. Good learners were more accurate in their self evaluations of what they knew or did not know than were poor learners. Further, when they decided that they did not yet know certain information, good learners were more likely to immediately attempt to learn that information than poor learners. Finally, and most importantly, good and poor learners differed in the encoding procedures they used to actually learn the information on the map. Although both good and poor learners were successful at learning the verbal information on the maps, good learners were far superior at learning the spatial information. They used a variety of techniques for learning spatial shapes and relationships, including visual imagery, encoding explicit spatial relationships between pairs of map objects (e.g., "the church is west of the fire station"), and naming a complex spatial configuration as a cue for reproduction of the shapes later (e.g., "this set of roads looks like a stick figure running to the west"). In contrast, poor learners were unable to learn much of the spatial information and used many fewer of the spatial-learning procedures.

Although the major difference between good and poor learners was in their success at learning spatial information, the relationship between performance and the use of study procedures was correlational. Thus, it was not clear that the use of effective learning procedures was the underlying determinant of the superior performance of good learners. Therefore, in another experiment, Stasz and I manipulated the procedures subjects used in order to assess directly the influence of particular procedures on learning success. We divided a sample of subjects into three groups, and gave each group a map to learn using its own techniques, as in the first experiment. We then trained the first group to use a set of six procedures that had been highly correlated with learning success in the previous experiment. Three of these procedures were techniques for learning spatial information, and included instruction in the use of visual imagery. The second group received training on six procedures that were uncorrelated with success in the first experiment. The third group received no training. Subjects then studied a second map on which they were instructed to use the procedures they had been taught. The group instructed in the use of the effective procedures improved their performance significantly more than the other two groups, indicating that the use of effective procedures contributed directly to subjects' learning success.

We also assessed the basic visual ability of all subjects by administering a psychometric test of visual memory. Essentially, this test measured subjects' ability to create, maintain, and retrieve a visual image in memory. We reasoned that the ability to encode visual information in memory might influence the benefit subjects derived from training in the use of spatial-learning procedures. An analysis of the posttraining performance of subjects in the effective-procedures group indicated that visual-memory ability *did* influence learning performance on the second map. In general, the higher a subject's visual-memory ability, the greater the improvement in performance over the first map. For subjects of high and medium ability, the extent of the improvement was significantly greater than for the subjects in the other two training groups. However, low-ability subjects improved no more than subjects in the other groups, indicating that they benefitted little from the effective-procedures training. Thus, both people's basic skills at using spatial information and the discretionary study techniques they employ play important roles in their spatial cognition.

CONCLUDING COMMENTS

In surveying some of the current research in spatial reasoning being conducted by cognitive psychologists, I have been motivated by two goals. The first goal has been to present and attempt to defend a few of the hypotheses about human spatial cognition that guide my research. In summary, these hypotheses are that (1) people have and use a variety of types of spatial knowledge; (2) the type of knowledge people have about a region depends on the nature of their experiences with the region; (3) for many spatial-reasoning tasks, performance is constrained by the type of knowledge available to the individual; and (4) people's low-level spatial-processing skills may limit the available forms of knowledge representation and task performance. The second goal has been to attempt to narrow the gap slightly between the concerns of cognitive and environmental psychologists studying spatial reasoning. Historically, this gap seems to have been due primarily to differences in problem domain and in methodology. Whereas environmental psychologists have, by and large, investigated real-world problems using observational or correlational methodologies, cognitive psychologists have traditionally conducted experimental studies of performance on simplified laboratory tasks. Although some of the tasks discussed in the previous sections used stimulus materials that were especially constructed for the experiments, the tasks themselves represented activities that people normally perform when learning and reasoning in their environment. In addition, an attempt was made to illustrate some alternative research paradigms that appear promising in the study of cognitive aspects of spatial behavior, including correlational methods such as protocol analysis used in conjunction with experimental studies. Inasmuch as the study of human spatial behavior is a growing concern in both disciplines, the exchange of knowledge across disciplines is clearly in the interest of researchers in both fields.

ACKNOWLEDGMENTS

This chapter was presented at the Conference entitled ''Cognition, Social Behavior, and the Environment,''held at Vanderbilt University in May 1979. The reported research was supported by the Office of the Director of Personnel and Training Research Programs, Psychological Sciences Division, Office of Naval Research, under Contract No. N00014-78-C-0042 with The Rand Corporation.

REFERENCES

Allen, G. L., Siegel, A. W., & Rosinski, R. R. The role of perceptual context in structuring spatial knowledge. *Journal of Experimental Psychology,* 1978, *4,* 617–630.

Appleyard, D. Why buildings are known. *Environment and Behavior,* 1969, *1,* 131–156.

Appleyard, D. Styles and methods of structuring a city. *Environment and Behavior,* 1970, *2,* 100–118.

Downs, R., & Stea, D. (Eds.). *Image and environment.* Chicago: Aldine, 1973.

Downs, R., & Stea, D. *Maps in minds.* New York: Harper & Row, 1977.

Golledge, R. G., & Rushton, G. (Eds.). *Spatial choice and spatial behavior.* Columbus, Ohio: Ohio State University Press, 1976.

Kozlowski, L. T., & Bryant, K. J. Sense of direction, spatial orientation, and cognitive maps. *Journal of Experimental Psychology,* 1977, *3,* 590–598.

Lynch, K. *The image of a city.* Cambridge, Mass.: MIT Press, 1960.

Moore, T. T., & Golledge, R. G. (Eds.). *Environmental knowing.* Stroudsburg, Pa.: Dowden, Hutchinson & Rose, 1976.

Piaget, J., Inhelder, B., & Szeminska, A. *The child's conception of geometry.* New York: Basic Books, 1960.

Proshansky, H., Ittelson, W., & Rivlin, L. *Environmental psychology: Man and his physical setting.* New York: Holt, Rinehart, & Winston, 1970.

Shemyakin, F. N. Orientation in space. In B. G. Ananyev et al. (Eds.), *Psychological science in the USSR* (Vol. 1, Pt. 1). U.S. Office of Technical Reports (#11466), 1962.

Siegel, A. W., Kirasic, K. C., & Kail, R. V. Stalking the elusive cognitive map: The development of children's representations of geographic space. In J. F. Wohlwill & I. Altman (Eds.), *Human behavior and environment: Children and the environment* (Vol. 3). New York: Plenum, 1978.

Siegel, A. W., & White, S. H. The development of spatial representations of large-scale environments. In H. W. Reese (Ed.), *Advances in child development and behavior* (Vol. 10). New York: Academic Press, 1975.

Stevens, A., & Coupe, P. Distortions in judged spatial relations. *Cognitive Psychology,* 1978, *10,* 422–437.

Thorndyke, P. Distance estimation from cognitive maps (R–2474). Santa Monica, Calif.: The Rand Corporation, 1979.

Thorndyke, P., & Hayes-Roth, B. *Spatial knowledge acquisition from maps and navigation.* Paper presented at Psychonomics Society Meetings, San Antonio, Texas, 1978.

Thorndyke, P., & Stasz, C. Individual differences in procedures for knowledge acquisition from maps. *Cognitive Psychology,* 1980, *12,* 137–175.

Tolman, E. C. Cognitive maps in rats and men. *Psychological Review,* 1948, *55,* 189–208.

Trowbridge, C. C. Fundamental methods of orientation and "imaginary maps." *Science,* 1913, *38,* 888–897.

Witkin, H. A. Studies in geographic orientation. *Yearbook of the American Philosophical Society,* 1946, 152–155.

8

The Acquisition and Utilization of Spatial Knowledge

Keith Clayton
Mary Woodyard
Vanderbilt University

In the literature on spatial knowledge, few papers begin without citing Tolman's classic paper entitled "Cognitive Maps in Rats and Men" (Tolman, 1948). In that paper, Tolman coined the term *cognitive map* and argued that rats, in the course of learning mazes, establish "something like a field map of the environment [p. 192]." In this chapter, we adopt some of Tolman's ideas and use them as a basis for outlining a contemporary framework for discussing spatial knowledge. The Tolman construct we choose to update, however, is not *cognitive map*. Rather, we propose a general framework by combining some modern work in memory with Tolman's construct of *means–end–readiness*. The distinction between *cognitive map* and *means–end–readiness* is similar to a contemporary distinction between *descriptive* as opposed to *procedural* representations of knowledge (e.g., Anderson, 1976). The procedural properties of spatial knowledge are therefore emphasized here.

An experiment is also described in which subjects learn a new environment. The experiment was not motivated by the theoretical framework, which remains incomplete and descriptive. Rather, the experiment was designed to test the feasibility of studying the acquisition of a simulated environment. The environment is simulated in a computer program and subjects learn the environment sitting at a terminal making movement commands and receiving descriptions of the consequences of their moves. The theoretical framework is described first and then used to separately discuss the acquisition and the utilization of spatial knowledge.

A PROPOSED FRAMEWORK

The construct of *means–end–readiness* evolved somewhat in Tolman's hands but the meaning adopted here was given in a paper published in 1959 (Tolman, 1959). In that paper, Tolman made his final attempt to provide a behavioristic alternative to S–R theory. No doubt, the substance of the paper was influenced by Spence's earlier claim (Spence, 1951) that Tolman's alternative was an S–S theory. According to Spence, Tolman assumed that what is learned is an association between stimuli. Tolman admitted that classical conditioning may be construed as S–S learning, but argued that maze learning involved S–R–S learning, and means–end–readiness was the construct used to characterize this learning. In Tolman's (1959) words: "a means-end-readiness . . . is a condition . . . equivalent to . . . a 'belief'. . . . to the effect that an instance of this *sort* of stimulus situation, if reacted to by an instance of this *sort* of response, will lead to an instance of that *sort* of further stimulus situations . . . [p. 113, Tolman's emphasis]."

In adopting the construct, we change the terms somewhat, substituting for stimuli and responses the terms situation, action, and outcome. Nevertheless, the major point is the same: The learner of a spatial environment can be considered to be learning that in certain situations certain actions will produce certain outcomes. Part of the motive for changing these terms is that it broadens the perspective. We prefer to consider spatial knowledge as a special case of general knowledge, and therefore prefer to characterize it in the same way that other kinds of knowledge may be described. As examples: "At this point, if I add two tablespoons of flour, the sauce will thicken." or "A racketball descending at this angle could be returned with a ceiling shot that will drop dead at the back wall." or "With temperatures in the reactor at this level, turning these feedwater valves should result in a decrease in the internal temperature."

Acquisition

As Thorndyke (Chapter 7 in this volume) points out, knowledge of a spatial environment may be acquired by direct experience or by studying a map. In this chapter, we focus on knowledge gained directly rather than symbolically and discuss four proposed components of such knowledge. These components are listed in Table 8.1, and they are ordered one through four. Although these components may be thought of roughly as "stages," we do not mean to imply that they are acquired serially. The fourth component may be acquired at the same time as the first, and knowledge of a given area of the environment may at the same time involve all four components.

The first component is the acquisition of memories for actions in contexts. The notion here is that encounters with the environment produce memories of situations and actions as well as associations between situations and actions. For

TABLE 8.1
Components of Spatial Knowledge

---

1. Memories of actions in contexts
     (situation–action pairs)
2. Means–end–readinesses
     (situation–action–outcome triads; S–A–O's)
3. Route maps from ordered sets of S–A–O's
     $S_1-A_1-O_1 \rightarrow S_2-A_2-O_2 \rightarrow S_3-A_3-O_3 \rightarrow$ etc.
4. Area maps from habitual spatial inferences

---

example, you may remember narrowly averting an accident on the interstate in Memphis or bumping into friends near your motel in San Francisco.

In treating situation–action pairs as the product of encounters with the world, it is important to emphasize that the "actions" referred to may be more than travel or movement actions. Stated another way, one component of our spatial knowledge involves associations between locations and actions, but the "actions" that become associated may include mental reactions and affective responses. For example, while travelling, we may inspect some of the buildings along the route in terms of their functional potential for later trips (Bransford, Nitsch, & Franks, 1977). These mental responses would thereby become attached to our memories of the trip. Similarly, we may be repulsed by the sight and smell of a garbage dump or we may experience stepping on chewing gum. These examples are trivial, but they speak to an important general point: If spatial knowledge originates from episodic encounters with the world, it contains much more than visual or graphic information and more than simple information about the relative positions of locations in space. An emphasis of this conference is on the importance of considering the interrelationship of cognition, social behavior, and the environment; we believe such a perspective arises easily from a treatment of spatial knowledge as evolving from an autobiography of *experiences* that happen to take place in space.

Once an association is formed between a situation–action pair and an outcome, we have a situation–action–outcome (S–A–O) triad, the equivalent of Tolman's means–end–readiness. Such triads amount to memories that at certain locations, particular actions had certain consequences. Consistent with Tolman, it is proposed that route knowledge—knowledge of how to find one location from another—may be characterized as a string, or ordered set, of S–A–O triads. For example, you may know your way from point *A* to point *B* by knowing how to leave *A*, which takes you to a new choice point from which you take a new path, resulting in another choice point, and so on. Conceiving route knowledge as an ordered set of S–A–O's is similar to conceiving of it as a set of ordered productions (Kuipers, 1977; Thorndyke, Chapter 7 this volume). However, we prefer the term S–A–O, because we intend to stress the point that *outcomes* of actions in the production chain serve as cues for succeeding actions. As is developed in the next section, utilization of spatial knowledge involves gaining access to that knowledge, and it is fruitful to keep in mind just how the knowledge may be cued.

It is also important to stress that in the string of S–A–O's tying A to B, the "actions" may be characterized in a very general way. For example, at a given place, one may know only that a particular action will take one *closer to the goal*, without being able to specify the outcome in any greater detail. In keeping with the spirit of this conference, we may note that the "actions" and "outcomes" of spatial knowledge may be as much social as spatial. Most of us, for example, have probably given campus directions of the form: Here is how to get to Sarratt Hall; when you get there, ask somebody nearby for further instructions. In the same way, our knowledge of a given spatial environment may be as anchored to social as to physical outcomes. Often, spatial knowledge is treated as if it were knowledge of points in physical space, a *geometric* knowledge. But spatial knowledge arises from *experience* and must have a social dimension.

Tolman distinguished between strip maps and area maps. The treatment so far is clearly more appropriate to the acquisition of strip maps (route knowledge) than area maps. Tolman offered few clues about how area maps may evolve from strip maps, but a feature of his theory in general is its emphasis on the learner's dynamic construction of provisional beliefs. Consistent with this characterization, it is proposed here that a fourth component of spatial knowledge be the products of inferences about what cannot be seen from what is seen. There are excellent analogies at this point from contemporary memory and cognitive map studies. For example, Bransford, Barclay, and Franks (1972) have studied memory for sentences of the form "Three turtles rested on a log and a fish swam beneath them," and showed that after having been exposed to such sentences, subjects are likely to erroneously judge that they had heard "Three turtles rested on a log and a fish swam beneath *it*." Bransford et al. (1972) argue that people make spontaneous inferences about spatial relations among objects as part of comprehending such sentences. In the same way, we want to claim that wayfarers spontaneously draw inferences about their environment as they proceed through it, and that these *additions* to experience serve as the basis for expectations about relationships among objects and routes. For example, if while walking down Main Street you find that Elm intersects at right angles, and further on find that Oak also intersects at right angles, you may infer that Elm and Oak are parallel. Similarly, you may assume that a turn in a town is a 90° turn. In the same way, students asked to draw a floor plan of their apartments are likely to make reasonable assumptions about the locations of structures that they cannot see (Norman, 1973).

We have said we like to think of these spatial inferences as being "spontaneous" although we prefer to think of them as "habitual." To expand on this a bit, these inferences may be thought of as more or less automatic cognitive habits that arise from initially conscious spatial-orienting responses. In a sense, they are cognitive skills developed and automatized with practice. In any case, if we draw inferences from local data about the nature of the region and if these inferences are *incorrect,* we may find that inferences from two different locations produce inconsistent knowledge about the region. These local inferences can be the basis of very substantial problems requiring solutions before the spatial knowledge is useful.

In summary, we have suggested that the acquisition of spatial knowledge involves the acquisition of four different components. These components have been described as growing out of episodic encounters with the environment evolving from situation–action associations into situation–action–outcome associations. Route information is treated as ordered sets of S–A–O's and additional knowledge, potentially incorrect, is produced by inferences drawn during the exploring of or exposure to the spatial environment.

Utilization

A prevailing theme in contemporary memory research, initiated largely by Tulving and his colleagues (Tulving & Thomson, 1973; Watkins & Tulving, 1975), is an increased recognition of the importance of the test environment in determining memory performance. In the same way, an understanding of spatial knowledge should benefit from an analysis of the test environment and of the relationship between that knowledge and various queries of that knowledge. There are a variety of kinds of tests of spatial knowledge: map drawing, direction giving, estimating distances between points in space, judging relative positions of locations, way finding, and so on. There are also many examples in the cognitive mapping literature of apparent discrepancies between the outcomes of different kinds of tests. Lynch (1960), for example, noted that Boston natives often failed to include the John Hancock building on their sketch maps of downtown Boston, even though they could easily locate it when directly asked to do so. These kinds of data are consistent with an expectation derived from contemporary memory research: Different queries of memory can be expected to differ not only in their likelihood of tapping the target knowledge, but also in the kinds of knowledge that they uncover. In the remainder of this section, spatial knowledge utilization is treated as an *access* problem and is discussed in terms of the componential analysis previously provided.

Consider Thorndyke's (Chapter 7, this volume) acquaintance, MC, who "can't tell you how to get there, but . . ." can take you. This example illustrates the striking difference between those cues available when giving directions and those available when travelling the route. When giving directions, the immediate cues are the name of the destination and the immediate environment. In contrast, the wayfarer is directly presented with the outcome of each action as a cue for the next. There are several possible sources for the difficulty to describe a traversible route. In order to describe a route in advance, one must be able to retrieve the outcome of each action. Thus, if at least one outcome in the S–A–O set has not been acquired, or cannot be recalled, the route cannot be accurately described. Another possibility is that the "outcome" as represented in the knowledge of the route is not the same as the "situation" needed to retrieve the next action. As noted earlier, the outcome may merely be represented as "nearer the goal," in which case the correct action would be known without being able to anticipate the next choice point.

Let us now contrast way finding and map drawing. Discrepancies are often reported between the maps people draw and the routes they take (Downs & Stea, 1973). Instances of this sort are also easy to find in the data of the experiment reported in the next section. Subjects often took a route inconsistent with their maps. Some of the discrepancies can be attributed to the same sources of differences between way finding and direction giving previously discussed. Actual travel provides exposure to the most effective cues of spatial knowledge. Some of the discrepancies are related to drawing skills—that is, to difficulties in decoding spatial knowledge into a graphic mode. Still other sources of discrepancy between maps and routes have been implied by the preceding remarks about habitual spatial inferences. Inferences drawn from two different locations can be inconsistent. For example, the inference previously made that Elm and Oak are parallel is reasonable only if they remain straight and Main has not turned between them. Some main streets of Nashville radiate from the center, much as spokes on a wheel, and this causes considerable difficulty for newcomers disposed to rectangular town designs. Similarly, the major streets bordering the Vanderbilt campus intersect at a 60° angle, causing problems for campus map drawers who assume they are at 90°. In this case, the map drawers are aware their maps are somehow wrong, because the parts do not fit together properly, but they do not know how to correct them. Within a region, their knowledge is valid, but across regions it is not.

So far, we have suggested that discrepancies between different tests of knowledge come from differences in the quality of the cues and from erroneous local inferences about relations among paths. Another source is related to the nature of the S–A–O itself. In particular, the "action" to be taken at a particular location may be defined without regard to arrival route. The wayfarer may arrive at a location, orient to the cues of the place, and on the basis of these cues decide on the next action. The "action" may be to "proceed down the tree-lined street" and may require a 45° turn to the right. But, in this particular example, the specification of the action does not include the angle of the turn, in which case the relative orientation of the incoming and outgoing paths is not a part of the S–A–O representation. As before, such knowledge would be sufficient for way finding, but would lead to difficulties in map drawing and in judgments about relationships among points and paths in space.

AN EXPERIMENT ON SPATIAL LEARNING

There are two general approaches to the study of the acquisition of a new environment. One could either have subjects become acquainted with a previously unexplored real spatial environment or one could attempt to simulate an environment. We were discouraged from having subjects learn a real environment because of the difficulty of manipulating characteristics of the environment and because recording the subjects' behaviors is not only difficult, but also requires constant monitoring by an observer. The alternative—having subjects learn a simulated environment—seemed attractive, provided we could make the task complex enough to be theoretically rich, realistic enough to appear to engage the same processes involved in the real thing, yet simple enough to be manageable.

We chose to have subjects learn a simulated environment under computer control. This not only offered a solution to the problem of how to simulate an environment that we could construct to our liking, but also gave us considerable leverage on data management. Our purposes for conducting the study, then, were twofold: First, we sought to assess the feasibility and potential of the training technique, and second, we wished to gain some exploratory data on spatial knowledge.

Method

The town we simulated is Carmel, California. It was chosen because it is small yet interesting, has natural boundaries, is basically rectangular with right-angle intersections (although some streets are curved and dead-ended), and because it is the well-known and well-loved hometown of the second author of this chapter, who wrote the computer program. It is bounded on the west by the bay, on the south by a lagoon, on the east by a major highway, and on the north by a golf course. Fig. 8.1 shows only some of the details in the town. The subject did not have access to this map during the experiment. The town is composed of 60 locations, 29 of which are street intersections. Each location is connected by a street or path to either one, two, three, or four other locations. Most locations are highly discriminable, having a distinctive building, house, or area, although a few intersections are very similar. The descriptions of the intersections depended on arrival route. For example, if the drugstore was described as being immediately on the right coming from one direction, it was described as across the intersection on the left coming from the opposite direction.

An example of a subject's interaction with the program is shown in Table 8.2. The subject used a CRT terminal, to prevent review of earlier moves, and typed in movement commands. After the movement command is typed, the computer displays a description of the location arrived at following the move. Movement commands that were accepted were RIGHT, LEFT, FORWARD, BACK; when

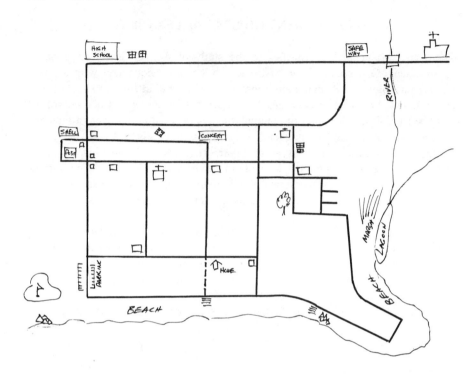

FIG. 8.1. Schematic map of town simulated by computer program. Most details omitted.

appropriate IN and OUT, for entering and leaving some buildings; UP and DOWN, when on a hill, and BEACH, when the beach was visible.

The subject's basic task was to learn the town by moving through it, without consulting a map. The experiment required 8 hours of training and testing; 16 subjects, receiving $2.50 an hour, completed the training. The experiment involved three separate phases. In the introductory session, the subject was given a "bus ride" into town, along Highway 1, left onto the major business street, left on the street to home. The subject was told that the town was a resort town and was instructed to explore the town with the goal of finding a grocery store (which had been passed on the bus ride) a post office (which had not been passed), and the beach (which had been described at one point in the distance).

The second phase of the training involved 16 20-minute sessions. Each session began with the subject at home, given the first goal. The subject was asked whether the location of the goal was known and was then instructed to find it. After the first goal was found, a second was given, and so forth, until 18 minutes had elapsed, at which time the subject was given 2 minutes to find the way home. The succession of goals was randomly chosen from a constant set of 16 locations in the town. These goals were uniformly distributed throughout the town and had

TABLE 8.2
An Example of Interaction Between Computer (Lower Case) and
Subject (Uppercase Commands)

You are on a tree-lined one-way street that runs along cliffs above the beach. Sandstone steps lead to
the beach behind you. There is a path through the trees ahead of you.
Which way?
RIGHT
The road above the beach turns from a narrow one-way road to a broader two-way road. In the middle
of the street behind you is a cement island planted with flowers and holding a WRONG WAY!
DO NOT ENTER sign.
Which way?
STRAIGHT
You're walking on the road above the beach. It takes a broad curve and you have a view of the whole
bay. A golf course is on the far side behind you.
You are on a road above the beach with a glass-fronted house ahead of you on your right. Steps
lead down to the beach to your right.
Which way?
STRAIGHT
You're walking along a road above a rocky coast. There are a few, very showy, houses to your
right, built over the ocean. The road makes a turn to your left.
The road makes a sharp bend here. You are on a rocky point looking over a bay, bordered by hills.
There is a red-roofed white building with a tower near the distant shore. Farther in the distance
the bay ends at a rocky peninsula.
Which way?
STRAIGHT
Which way?
LEFT
You are walking along a road above a yellow beach. The road curves at right angles to your right.
There is a parking lot next to a beach to your right. Beyond it, there is a lagoon, formed by the
river, which runs through the marsh ahead of you before it runs into the ocean behind you.
Which way?
LEFT

---

been selected to ensure eventual familiarity with all parts of the town. The
computer stored every movement command and recorded its latency.

The subjects took each of the 20-minute sessions at their own convenience.
The experiment was run at time-sharing terminals attached to a DEC–1099
system available 22 hours a day. After each session, the subject drew a map of
the town, which was returned immediately to the experimenters. In all, the
subjects drew 21 maps as training progressed, but no notes or diagrams were to
be consulted during training.

The third phase of the experiment involved a final session in which the subject
first drew a detailed map of the town. There was then a final test at the terminal in
which each subject was given a succession of seven goals (all subjects received
the same order). Three of these final goals were locations that had not been
among the original set of goals, but they had been passed on previous routes. One
route was designed to provide an *umwelg* problem—the subject found under

construction a road that had been previously unblocked and was forced to find a new route around the blockade. Finally, the subject filled out a questionnaire assessing other aspects of knowledge of the town and reactions to the training.

Results

The experiment produced a good-sized amount of data, which have been examined in a variety of ways. Surprisingly, it appears that the most heuristic results are not to be found in the details of movement commands and their latencies.

A majority of the subjects learned the town in considerable detail. From these kinds of results, we conclude that although the town is complex enough to be theoretically interesting, it can be learned in a period of time short enough to be experimentally useful. The technique also seems suitable for examining processes involved in using well-learned environmental knowledge. For example, we would be interested to know whether highly trained subjects asked to make distance judgments among pairs of locations in this simulated town would demonstrate the typical finding (Canter & Tagg, 1975) that the latencies to make real-world distance judgments are directly related to real-world distance.

One incidental finding was that 14 of the 16 subjects drew their final map with the same orientation (the same as Fig. 8.1). This particular result is highly unlikely, of course, if all four possible orientations were equally likely. We believe this result stems from the fact that each session, apart from the introduction, *began* from this orientation—that is, the subjects were oriented this way initially. Another observation that to us seems related was that, as we watched the subjects at their terminals, which we did during the first and final sessions, we noticed that their movement commands were sometimes preceded by fairly elaborate body movements, twisting in their chair, or turning their hands in front of their face. We speculate that these two serendipitous findings implicate a rather strong motor component to spatial acquisition.

SUMMARY

From a perspective of spatial knowledge as arising from episodic encounters with the environment, it has been proposed that spatial knowledge includes four components: (1) situation–action associations; (2) situation–action–outcome (S–A–O) associations; (3) path knowledge from sets of S–A–O triads; and (4) area knowledge from locally consistent inferences about relations among paths and locations. It is argued that components of spatial knowledge are differentially accessible, and that an understanding of comparisons among measures of spatial knowledge is aided by an analysis of cue-knowledge relationships. From this perspective, the causes of errors in spatial utilization are discussed, with special attention being given to errors in drawing maps. Finally, an experiment on spatial knowledge is described.

ACKNOWLEDGMENTS

The contributions of Mike Tarka, Karen Feinstein, and Julia Ford are gratefully acknowledged.

REFERENCES

Anderson, J. R. *Language, memory, and thought.* Hillsdale, N.J.: Lawrence Erlbaum Associates, 1976.

Bransford, J. D., Barclay, J. R., & Franks, J. J. Sentence memory: A construction versus interpretive approach. *Cognitive Psychology,* 1972, *3,* 193–207.

Bransford, J. D., Nitsch, K. E., & Franks, J. J. Schooling and the facilitation of knowing. In R. C. Anderson, R. J. Spiro, & W. E. Montague (Eds.), *Schooling and the acquisition of knowledge.* Hillsdale, N.J.: Lawrence Erlbaum Associates, 1977.

Canter, D., & Tagg, S. Distance estimation in cities. *Environment and behavior,* 1975, *7,* 59–80.

Downs, R. M., & Stea, M. (Eds.). *Image and environment.* Chicago: Aldine, 1973.

Kuipers, B. J. *Representing knowledge of large-scale space* (Tech. Rep. AI–TR–418). Cambridge, Mass.: Artificial Intelligence Laboratory, Massachusetts Institute of Technology, 1977.

Lynch, K. *The image of a city.* Cambridge, Mass.: MIT Press, 1960.

Norman, D. A. Memory, knowledge, and the answering of questions. In R. L. Solso (Ed.), *Contemporary issues in cognitive psychology: The Loyola Symposium.* Washington, D.C.: Winston, 1973.

Spence, K. W. Theoretical interpretations of learning. In S. S. Stevens (Ed.), *Handbook of experimental psychology.* New York: Wiley, 1951.

Tolman, E. C. Cognitive maps in rats and men. *Psychological Review,* 1948, *55,* 189–208.

Tolman, E. C. Principles of purposive behavior. In S. Koch (Ed.), *Psychology: A study of a science.* Vol. 2. *General systematic formulations, learning, and special processes.* New York: McGraw-Hill, 1959.

Tulving, E., & Thomson, D. M. Encoding specificity and retrieval processes in episodic memory. *Psychological Review,* 1973, *80,* 352–373.

Watkins, M. J., & Tulving, E. Episodic memory: When recognition fails. *Journal of Experimental Psychology: General,* 1975, *104,* 5–29.

9 Hot Air: The Psychology of CO_2-Induced Climatic Change

Baruch Fischhoff
Decision Research
A Branch of Perceptronics

Since 1957, the Mauna Loa Observatory has recorded a yearly increase of approximately one-third of 1% in the CO_2 (carbon dioxide) concentration of the Earth's atmosphere (Bacastow & Keeling, 1977). Although CO_2 concentrations are minute (on the order of 330 ppm), they play a major role in regulating the Earth's climate, particularly its temperature. Current projections indicate a doubling of CO_2 levels by the year 2030 with a consequent average warming (at the surface) of 3–4°C. Perhaps more important than the mean change is the differential warming at different latitudes, from 2°C at the equator to 11°C at the poles (Manabe & Wetherald, 1975). Reduction of the temperature gradient between different latitudes will likely mean a substantial reduction in atmospheric and oceanic circulation. One can anticipate marked changes in fisheries and agriculture, with a melting of the polar ice caps a distinct possibility.

Although point predictions are extremely unreliable at the moment, it seems to be a reasonable assumption that CO_2-induced variations in temperature and precipitation patterns will lead to "better weather" in some places and "worse weather" in others. If, for example, climatological patterns return to those characterizing the Altithermal Period 4000–8000 years ago, when the world was several degrees warmer than it is now, the habitability of the Canadian prairies and the Sahel would increase as the former became warmer and the latter wetter. On the other hand, reduced precipitation in the southern Great Plains of the United States would remove vast acreages from the stock of arable land (Kellogg, 1978). However, even areas with improved climate might be adversely impacted by such changes. The legacy of industrialization and colonialism has been the establishment of highly specialized and relatively inflexible land use and agricultural patterns. An underdeveloped equatorial country might have neither the time nor the capital to exploit the opportunity to shift from field crops to rubber and coffee; the hybridized grains used so successfully in the central United States might not prove as viable in the thinner soil of the upper Great Plains, which would then enjoy the best temperature–precipitation combination. International complications might prohibit some countries from exploiting their own technical ability to adapt. Iceland might be unable to pursue the fish on which its economy depends if shifts in ocean currents carried them within the 200-mile limits of other countries; power politics and local corruption might impede the flow of food stocks needed to tide some countries over as they adjust their agriculture to new conditions.[1]

Even where adaptations are technically and politically feasible, they may not even be attempted unless reasonable assurances can be given that they will be successful. A key piece of information in this respect is a guarantee that the climate is in fact changing. Unfortunately, the natural variability in climatic patterns is so great that it is difficult to identify either cycles or secular trends even in the absence of perturbations like that introduced by the increase in CO_2. The impact of changes in CO_2 is deduced with the help of general circulation models (GCM's), which simulate the results of overlaying such changes on approximations of today's climate. Unfortunately, these models must be based upon incompletely verified climatological theories and subjectively assessed model parameters (e.g., about oceanic currents and their interaction with the atmosphere). Not only are both present and future climates insufficiently understood, but they are also unlikely to yield clearly diagnostic signs that changes are afoot and action is needed. Indeed, for the 20 years that reliable CO_2 observations are available, global temperatures have actually been decreasing (*Climate Change to the Year 2000*, 1978; *World Climate Conference*, 1979).

Understanding and coping with the origins of the CO_2 build-up is fraught with the same problems as dealing with its impact. Measurement of the change itself is still part art, part science, although experts seem to be reaching consensus on acceptable procedures. No one is entirely certain that the recent upturn is not one leg of a natural cycle whose previous stages neither were observed nor are retrievable from geologic records. Current accepted wisdom is that the origins of the build-up are international. The two leading culprits are increased use of fossil fuels (CO_2 being a major by-product of combustion) and logging of forests, particularly in the tropics (with both burning of the trees and elimination of a natural CO_2 sink contributing to increased atmospheric concentrations). Because the benefits of the activities leading to the build-up are as unevenly distributed as

---

[1]A chilling reminder of economic constraints on cooperation in time of need is the fact that the massive starvation in the Sahel during the drought of 1968–1973 reflected a minor shortfall in the quantity of grain available. The needed grain was certainly available in the world market. The missing ingredients were adequate distribution systems and resources sufficient to allow the people of the Sahel to acquire the grain (Glantz, 1976).

the costs and benefits of its consequences, unprecedented international cooperation would be needed to halt the change. Deciding that such a halt was desirous
would require not only changes in attitudes toward nations, but changes in
attitudes toward nature. One prominent agronomist[2] has stated that even were a
CO_2-induced climate change in the offing, it would constitute ''not a problem but
an opportunity'' to master nature in new ways.

A final complication in establishing what is really happening lies in the
interface between the politics of science and of nations. For proponents of nuclear power, CO_2-induced climatic change is a consequence of using fossil fuels
that reduces the relative riskiness of the nuclear option. For students of the
atmosphere and oceans, concern over the problem potentially posed by CO_2
promises an outpouring of resources for the study of theoretical problems that
have now become quite actual. One can only speculate on the impact of this
context on the questions that are posed and the way answers are reported.

INTERLUDE

Why am I telling you all this? Because at least a portion of the natural scientists
dealing with this problem have realized that it cannot be managed without some
substantial recourse to social scientists. The origin, consequences, prevention,
and mitigation of this problem (if one exists) are all societal. All the natural
scientists can do is fill in the gap between CO_2 build-up and physical consequences. Even that they cannot do without some societal analysis indicating by
how much human activities are likely to upset the natural CO_2 balance, how
climatic changes are likely to affect that imbalance, and what information decision makers need to have as outputs from the climatologists' models.

In fact, the problem is acknowledged to be so complex that psychologists have
been asked for help (U.S. Department of Energy, 1980). This chapter is one
attempt to assess what psychologists do and can know about how people deal
cognitively with this environmental event with social causes and consequences. I
would consider it successful if I could (1) make a convincing case that psychologists do have something to offer; (2) identify in this context some issues that our
psychology has heretofore missed; (3) help define by example how one might
approach related problems; and (4) recruit some of you to work on this particular
interface between psychology and the world.

The prospect of CO_2-induced climatic change poses a series of interlocking
decisions to be made by individuals, groups, national, and international bodies.
At each level, people must decide whether the problem is worth attending to and,
if so, should efforts be made to prevent the build-up from happening (e.g., by

---

[2]Sylvan Witwer at the Department of Energy–AAAS Conference on CO_2-Induced Climatic
Change, Annapolis, Maryland, April 6, 1979.

drastically restricting the consumption of fossil fuels), to implement curative schemes (e.g., massive afforestation programs), to adapt to the new world we are creating (e.g., by developing new crops or moving large populations), or to promote the build-up (for those who hope to benefit from the change). Each decision requires an assessment of what is happening, what the possible effects are, and how well one likes them. The quality of these assessments at one level constrains the wisdom of the decisions made at others. Failure of the U.S. to adopt a coherent policy is likely to thwart any international effort. Absence of international cooperation may lead U.S. consumers to feel "why should we drive less when the Brazilians provide tax incentives for logging out the Amazon?" We are all in trouble if the climatologists seriously understate or overstate how much they know. How such assessments are made, by consumers, legislators, diplomats, or scientists, would seem to be eminently psychological questions.

WHAT'S TO KNOW?

Obviously, people respond to problems as they see them rather than to problems as they are. The importance of cognitive representations in coping with CO_2-induced climatic changes is particularly great because the evidence on causes, effects, and intermediary processes is almost entirely abstract. One cannot directly sense what is really important (e.g., CO_2 concentrations, atmospheric refraction), and what one can sense is often misleading (e.g., random weather fluctuations).[3] Both the content and quality of our response hinges on the validity of our (cognitive) understanding of what is happening to us and our world.

This chapter attempts a psychological analysis of the kinds of information that one must understand in order to be on top of the CO_2 situation. These generic types include very low probabilities, conflicts between technical experts, and descriptions of gradual changes buried in noise. A more extensive list appears in Table 9.1. Regarding each type of information, one should ask a series of questions:

1. What are its formal properties?
2. What are its observable signs?
3. How are those signs revealed to the individual?
4. Are they contradicted, supported, or hidden by immediate experience?
5. Do people have an intuitive grasp of such information?
6. To the extent that they do not have such a grasp, what is the nature of their misunderstanding?

---

[3]According to one leading climatologist, every time there is a major snowstorm in his area, the local news media call him to find out if this is the climatic change he has been predicting (Schneider, 1979).

TABLE 9.1
Nature of the Issues in CO_2-Induced Climatic Change

Properties of the Information
 High level of uncertainty
  Critical observations often missing or questionable
  Critical assumptions often unproven
 Uncertainty is poorly formulated
  Hard to assess·
  Hard to communicate
 Subject to distortion in transmission from experts to nonexperts
  Random error added
  Systematic error added
 Highly diagnostic information rare and unlikely
 Highly technical
 Enormous quantity
Properties of Process
 Component processes
  Many simple, established causal relations
  Many involve conjecture in the absence of historical or contemporary data
 Complex interactions between components
  Understood only through simulation models
  Future may arrive before models with desired sophistication to simulate it can be developed
 Hard to assess adequacy of theoretical approximations
 Superimposed on poorly understood natural changes and cycles
Properties of Effects
 Very low probabilities for many of most interesting
 Involve destabilization of entire ecologies
  Secondary and tertiary effects often unidentified (much less measured)
  Resilience of human controls uncertain
 Often completely unfamiliar
  Hard to imagine
  Hard to evaluate
 Long time span for many
  Until they are felt
  Until they can be undone (if not irreversible)
 Benefits and costs distributed at different points in time and to different people
 Incommensurable

7. How great are such misunderstandings and how severe are their consequences?
8. Does natural experience provide feedback highlighting misunderstandings and inducing improvement?
If we hope to improve as well as predict performance, we must also ask:
9. Can the understanding be enhanced, for example, by generating better evidence, developing superior presentations, or altering basic approaches to knowledge?

These questions ask how suitable people's cognitive ecology is for coping with the informational ecology within which they live. The accepted wisdom among many students of judgment and decision making under conditions of uncertainty is that the match is far from perfect. In this view, people have neither the cognitive capacity nor structures for coping with complex, probabilistic problems. As a result, they resort to judgmental heuristics or short cuts or rules of thumb that allow them to reduce such problems to simpler and more familiar terms. These strategies are adaptive in the sense that they always produce some answer and often that answer is moderately accurate. They are maladaptive in that they can produce highly erroneous judgments and in that the great facility with which they are applied inhibits the search for superior methods. Identification of these limits might be traced to Miller (1956) and Simon (1956); specification of how people get around them has involved Tversky and Kahneman (1974), among others.

Despite the considerable progress made by cognitive, social, and organizational psychologists in elaborating these concepts, and demonstrating their robustness, it is by no means trivial to apply them to a particular situation. One source of difficulty is that some heuristics might better be described as metaheuristics (Einhorn, in press). They provide not judgments, but ways to produce judgments. Thus, they are given to varying interpretations. For example, the availability heuristic leads people to judge events as likely to the extent that exemplars are easily available in memory or imagination. Deciding what constitutes exemplars, how the memory search is conducted, and how ease is measured requires a detailed analysis of the situation under consideration. A second problem is that we know little about the ecological validity of heuristics (e.g., how often and how badly do they lead us astray?). For example, are more likely events generally more available? If heuristics are valid, we can trust people's intuitive judgments more and our own ability to explicate these processes less. For, there are many ways to explain good judgments and many fewer to explain any particular pattern of errors.[4]

Presumably, there is no general answer to this question; the application and validity of judgmental strategies must depend on the situation. Whenever an answer depends on circumstances, we need a theory of circumstances. Analyzing the psychological details of particular situations like CO_2-induced climatic change is one path to developing a general capability for applying our theories.

Because there has been virtually no research on many of the kinds of information listed in Table 9.1, it seems most efficient to explore in depth what is and should be known about one kind of information that has been studied somewhat,

---

[4]Even though Kahneman and Tversky's research has come to be known for its identification of errors, they make no statement about how bad judgment is in general. They focused on errors both in hopes of finding one unique way to explain a pattern of errors than a pattern of success and because suboptimal behavior in conditions encouraging optimality suggests deep-seated cognitive tendencies.

that concerning low-probability events. This is done in the following section. Subsequent sections consider the possible results of similar analyses for other kinds of information, the implications of social realities on cognitive processes, the implications of cognitive processes on social realities, and the role of psychology in all this.

LOW-PROBABILITY EVENTS

One fortunate feature of our environment is that the most fearsome events happen fairly infrequently. Major floods are confined to small regions and typically are infrequent there; disastrous plagues have been the exception rather than the rule; even the most seismically active areas experience catastrophic tremors at long intervals. In the realm of hazards of human origin, life-threatening endeavors are usually constrained to have a low probability of leading to disaster. Even nuclear power plants, one of the most troublesome of hazards in many people's minds, do not melt down very often (although one might find any epsilon of probability unacceptable).

CO_2-induced climatic change involves natural effects of human origin. There, too, the worst effects seem to be quite unlikely. If one aggregated all expert opinions into a probability density function for the mean change in the Earth's temperature over the next 75 years, the result might be roughly bell shaped with a mean at $+1.5°C$ and 98% credible intervals at about $-2°C$ and $+7°C$. Thus, the most dire consequences seem quite unlikely. The probability of either a new Ice Age or rapid melting of polar ice caps accompanied by inundation of coastal cities is small, although nonnegligible. If the climatologists are to be believed, however, there is a good chance of some regional dislocations due to changed precipitation, increased variability of growing season, reduced need for space heating, and the like.

Although they may have great economic consequences, such changes are unlikely to threaten the viability of a society, particularly as long as other countries and regions can lend support. It is the low-probability–high-consequence events about which one must really worry. Mistakes in understanding them and preventing or mitigating their consequences could push a society beyond the limits of its resilience. Unfortunately, there are both statistical and psychological grounds for expecting such events to be poorly understood.

What Can Be Known?

At times, it is possible to identify a population of events from which an observed sample may be drawn as a step toward assessing the probability of a particular calamity. Most seismologists might argue that the United States Geological Survey (USGS), has perhaps 75 years of reliable records upon which to base assessments of the frequency of large earthquakes in various parts of the U.S. The copious records of ice-pack movements maintained in Iceland over the last millenium provide a clue to the probability of an extremely cold year in given future periods. The apparent absence of a full-scale meltdown in the 500–1000 years of nuclear reactor operation may allow setting some bounds on the probability of future meltdowns. Of course, extrapolation from any of these historical records is a matter of judgment. Changes in design, public scrutiny, and federal regulation may render the next 1000 reactor years appreciably different than their predecessors. The new conditions created by increased CO_2 concentrations may artificially change climate variability in a way that amplifies or dampens yearly or daily fluctuations.

Even if experts were to agree on the relevance of these records, a sample of 1000 reactor or calendar years may be insufficient. Given the magnitude of possible consequences, a .0001 chance of a meltdown might be deemed unconscionable, but we will be well into the next century and irrevocably committed to nuclear power and its consequences before we will have enough hands-on experience to assess the probability of a meltdown to the desired accuracy. We know that meltdowns are unlikely (in the present sense), but whether they are unlikely enough may not be known until it is too late, or it may not be known at all.

When no historical record is available upon which to base conjectures, one is left with conjecture alone. In the scientific community, the more sophisticated conjectures are based upon models. GCM's represent one such genre, the fault-tree and event-tree analyses of a loss-of-coolant accident upon which the "Rasmussen" Reactor Safety Study was based (Atomic Energy Commission, 1975) represent another. Each is composed of component processes and interactions between them that are known to some degree of precision.

The fault tree involves a logical structuring of what would have to happen for a core to melt down. If sufficiently detailed, it will reach a level of specificity for which we have relevant experience (e.g., the operation of individual valves). An overall probability of failure for the system is determined by combining the needed component failures. Unfortunately, some components are entirely novel or have never been used in these particular conditions; their performance parameters must be guessed. Furthermore, the logical structure and completeness of the tree are more or less matters of opinion.

GCM's share the same strengths and weaknesses. They attempt to predict the unknown world of heightened CO_2 concentrations on the basis of related observables and their hypothesized interconnections. These are, respectively, recorded atmospheric and oceanographic conditions and generally accepted theories of their dynamic interaction. As with fault trees, some of the data are uncertain and some of the logic is disputable.

Thus, critical low probabilities are often revealed through the filter of formal analyses rather than through direct experience. One's faith in the probabilities so revealed depends on the success of the analysts in identifying all relevant components, assessing their values, and understanding their interrelations. Recent psychological research suggests some likely bounds on their success and our faith. People apparently have limited ability to recognize the assumptions upon which their judgments are based, appraise the completeness of problem representations, or assess the limits of their own knowledge. Typically, their inability encourages overconfidence (Fischhoff, Slovic, & Lichtenstein, 1977, 1978).

One might hope that the results of this research conducted on laypeople could not be generalized to technical experts, that somehow their substantive knowledge and training would lead to improved judgment when forced to go beyond the available data. Unfortunately, a modicum of systematic data and many anecdotal reports suggest that this is not the case. As a case in point, a high-level peer review found that the Reactor Safety Study had greatly overstated the precision of its conclusions (Nuclear Regulatory Commission, 1978).[5] The unpleasant surprise at Three Mile Island demonstrated that it had not included all pathways to disaster[6] nor even explicitly raised a number of implicit and erroneous assumptions (e.g., that trained personnel would always be available). For their part, GCM's necessarily omit some aspects of the environment believed to be relatively unimportant (for the sake of manageability) and incorporate untested assumptions provided by other disciplines (e.g., that the rate of increase in CO_2 production of the last 20 years will continue unabated in the future, in a world that may have more or less nuclear power, war, recession, and environmental awareness than its predecessor). They seem poorly suited for even providing guesses at their accuracy.

If one reads such analyses and the rare subsequent evaluations with an eye to the psychology of the analyst, there seem to be generic sources of error and omission. These include: (1) failure to consider the imaginative ways in which human error can mess up a system (e.g., the Browns Ferry fire in which the world's largest nuclear power plant almost melted down due to a technician's checking for an air leak with a candle, a direct violation of standard operating procedures); (2) insensitivity to the assumptions an analysis makes about constancies in the world in which the system is embedded (e.g., no major changes in government regulatory policy); (3) overconfidence in current scientific and technological knowledge (i.e., assuming that there are no new chemical, physical, biological, or psychological effects to be discovered); (4) failure to see how the system functions as a whole (e.g., a system may fail because a back-up component has been removed for routine maintenance).

---

[5]A specific contribution of psychology to improving the practice of formal analysis is suggested by the experimental finding that the elicitation procedure used by Rasmussen's team for assessing failure rates produces judgments with particularly exaggerated precision (see Fischhoff, 1977).

[6]One intriguing limitation of fault-tree analyses is highlighted by the fact that it is something of a moot point whether or not the Three Mile Island sequence was included in the Reactor Safety Study (Whipple, 1979).

What Can They Tell Us?

Low-probability events reveal themselves to experts through systematic samples and formal models, each with their strengths and weaknesses. They reveal themselves to nonexperts through unsystematic experience and reports from the front by experts, seers, and the media that traffic in such reports.

To make use of what the experts tell us, we must understand both the substance of their message and the qualifications that (should) accompany it. An obvious limit on our ability to understand substance is having the report couched in unfamiliar technical terms. These can mislead (say, when technical terms have common-language counterparts with different meanings), confuse (perhaps leading us to think that we understand when we really do not), and dissuade us from even attempting to understand.

Obviously, most scientific problems afford opportunities for asserting some sort of elite control. However, even well-meaning attempts to inform the public may go astray. CO_2 issues make a terrific chalk talk, but their impact may be lost if care is not taken to draw causal links between the parts (Tversky & Kahneman, 1980), particularly those links connecting human behavior and climatological consequences. Without such explicit ties, a CO_2 crisis may appear implausible as well as improbable. On some level, it may be hard to believe that global cataclysm might be the result of such innocuous and sensible acts as lighting home fires and burning leaves. The CO_2 problem represents a global commons dilemma in which seemingly inconsequential individual decisions combine to produce universally averse consequences in the long run. Although moralizing might lead to more prosocial behavior (Dawes, 1980), it is likely to have little effect until recipients are convinced that a dilemma exists.

Even if people are willing to listen, it may be difficult to present low probabilities to them comprehensibly. Is, for example, the difference between .001 and .0001, so stated, meaningful to people? Scattered evidence suggests that people may ignore or exaggerate probabilities in that range (Lichtenstein, Slovic, Fischhoff, Layman, & Combs, 1978; Slovic, Fischhoff, Lichtenstein, Corrigan, & Combs, 1977). One alternative is to provide a concrete referent in the form of a familiar event with an accurately judged probability of similar magnitude. The efficacy of this (or any other) procedure for communicating low probabilities is still undocumented (Fischhoff, 1977).

As a guide to action, the uncertainty surrounding the experts' best guess may be as important as the substance of the guess. One wants to know ''Just how high could it be?'' and ''Do these experts know enough for me to take their best guess seriously?''. A good deal of evidence (e.g., Gettys, Kelley, & Peterson, 1973; Kahneman & Tversky, 1973) suggests that were such qualifications provided, they would not be used properly. In particular, people seem to be as confident making inferences from highly unreliable data as from reliable data, rather than less confident as statistical theory dictates.[7] If, as previously suggested, there is also a propensity for experts to exaggerate how much they know, one should expect a gap between the credibility afforded to scientific analyses and what they merit.

Another form of credibility problem arises when the integrity of the source is threatened. Most people probably have learned to discount what they see on TV because of its tendency to sensationalize. Whether they are aware of the subtle biases that can enter into scientific analyses may be another question. For example, the very raising of CO_2 questions rather than those surrounding other hazards of potentially greater magnitude[8] may reflect a desire to make life easier for one domestic energy industry (nuclear); not raising them may reflect a desire to obscure international energy issues (the fact that the industrialized countries are enjoying most of the benefits of creating the CO_2 imbalance whose costs will be borne by everyone). Whenever uncertainty is as rampant as it is with CO_2-related issues, there is ample opportunity to fudge results (say, by making small and, one hopes, unchallengeable changes in many parameters leading to a large overall effect) or manipulate the reported conclusions. For example, the executive summary of the Reactor Safety Study has been found to have limited fidelity to the body of the nine-volume report (Nuclear Regulatory Commission, 1978). Perhaps closer to home, climatologists, like psychologists, may often be tempted to describe their work so that firm conclusions seem close enough to merit funding but just far enough around the corner to prevent rigorous evaluation of the product.

What Can We Learn by Ourselves?

Unlike nuclear power, climate is directly experienced. That experience may set us wondering about the likelihood of major climatic changes (say, as did the recent West-coast drought and severe Northeastern winters). Once we are interested, that experience may support or contradict what the experts tell us (as the drought and cold seem to do, respectively), with regard to CO_2 projections. Often, personal experience will be all we have to go on.

How good are we at assessing low-probability natural events? A popular

---

[7]Glenn Schweitzer (1975), Director of the Office of Toxic Substances in the Environmental Protection Agency, has commented: "Too often lawyers and economists seize upon (statistically derived) numerical risk factors forgetting that these experimentally derived estimates may in fact have a very shaky relevance to the real world [p. 73]." See also Lodge (1976).

[8]Despite the enormous destructive potential of earthquakes in the U.S., and the fairly high likelihood of their occurrence, almost no research is going into improving human response. Seismological research designed to develop the capacity for earthquake prediction is, however, well funded, despite some serious suggestion (National Academy of Sciences, 1978) that the expected value of forecasts is negative, once one considers social reactions to them.

experimental design in the 1950's and 1960's had subjects try to learn the relative frequencies of successively presented events drawn from a multinomial distribution (usually binary events). As summarized by Peterson and Beach (1967), these studies found people to be quite good at the task. Unfortunately for the problem at hand, the target events in these studies were never of very low frequency or distributed over long periods of time amidst appreciable noise, as are natural hazards. Moving several steps in the right direction, Lichtenstein et al. (1978) asked people to judge the likelihood of a randomly selected individual dying from a variety of recognizable, but not necessarily common causes (e.g., botulism, tornadoes, cancer). They found that people (1) had a pretty good idea of the relative frequency of most causes of death; (2) substantially underestimated the differences in the likelihoods of the most and least frequent; and (3) persistently misjudged the relative likelihood of those causes of death that are unusually available (e.g., tornadoes) or unavailable (e.g., asthma). Slovic, Fischhoff, and Lichtenstein (1979) found a similar pattern of results in estimates of the fatalities from various technological hazards.[9]

Judgments of fatalities for unlikely events are, of course, not quite the same as judgments of their very low probabilities. In a study asking people about the lethality of some of these same causes of death (i.e., the probability of dying given that one was afflicted), we found that formally irrelevant changes in response mode produced appreciable differences in assessed probability (Fischhoff, Slovic, Lichtenstein, in press). For example, death rates derived from responses to the question "For every 100,000 afflicted, how many die?" were roughly two orders of magnitude greater than those in response to "For every individual who dies, how many are afflicted but survive?" These differences seem due in part to the effect response format has on how people access their knowledge, which is probably not naturally organized along these lines, and in part to variants of the well-known effects that the choice of numbers in magnitude estimation experiments has on the results of those experiments (Poulton, 1968).

Geographers' studies of lay assessments of the likelihood of (rare) natural hazards yield a mixed bag. For example, a survey by Hewitt and Burton (1971) found that residents of London, Ontario, had quite accurate judgments regarding the likelihood of hurricanes and tornadoes, typically overestimated the frequency of floods, and were split between overestimating and underestimating the frequency of ice storms and blizzards. Surveying a variety of such studies in various countries, Burton, Kates, and White (1978) concluded that the accuracy of judgments increases with length of time in the area, regularity of exposure to

---

[9]They also found that although laypeople agreed with most experts' assessments of the expected fatalities from nuclear power in an average year, they saw much greater likelihood for a major disaster and much greater consequences should one occur. Given the present state of uncertainty regarding nuclear power, it is unclear whose cognitive abilities are to be trusted more.

nature, periodicity of the hazard, and invulnerability from effects of hazard. These factors do not bode too well for responsiveness to CO_2. Furthermore, even in situations in which people have fairly accurate assessments, their notion of underlying mechanism may be quite different than the accepted scientific view. For example, an atypical period of rainy weather following the first agricultural settlements in the High Plains of the U.S. led to the belief (endorsed by the AAAS) that "rain follows the plow." The more normal and drought years following the breaking of the sod resulted in tragic disruption of lives and loss of topsoil (Kates, 1962; Opie, 1979).

Although many of the climatic fluctuations and meteorological events that may be affected by possible CO_2 changes have some natural, semiobservable frequency, the event itself does not. In fact, one directly sees little or nothing to indicate that some global dislocation may be on the way as a result of commonplace actions taken by all the Earth's denizens. Those who have not heard the cry of alarmed climatologists (e.g., Bryson, 1974; Schneider & Mesirow, 1976; Wigley, Jones, & Kelly, 1980) are doubtless worrying about other things. While everybody is doing something about the weather, no one is talking about it.

Do We Have to Know All This?

Given the complexity of the problem, one cannot expect anyone to know the future regarding these low-probability–high-consequence effects of a possible CO_2 build-up. Given our cognitive limitations, it may be unrealistic to expect very many people to have *optimal* judgments, properly incorporating all that could be known at present. Then, one must ask whether what we do understand is good enough. Is satisficing satisfactory?

In effect, one needs an error theory predicting the price paid for human frailty. Creating such a theory requires not just a consideration of the suitability of cognitive processes for understanding natural processes, but some idea of what decisions are to be made on the basis of our (mis)judgments. That is, what will be on the test? Without embarking on a detailed analysis of the personal and collective decisions that might be involved in trying to prevent a CO_2 crisis or mitigate its consequences, we might note a few general principles. The same reasons that make it difficult to assess low probabilities make it nearly impossible to evaluate those that we or others produce. As a result, spotting and correcting errors (i.e., learning) might be quite slow (Einhorn & Hogarth, 1978). In a consideration of formal risk-assessment procedures, Kastenberg, McKone, and Okrent (1976) found that assessments were extremely sensitive to outliers. Thus, the appropriateness of our decisions to take seriously or discount unusual events may be quite important. Von Winterfeldt and Edwards (1973) showed that under quite general conditions, modest inaccuracy in assessing probabilities (or utilities) should not have too bad an effect on decisions with continuous options (e.g., invest $X or increase production by $Y\%$). However, Lichtenstein, Fischhoff, and Phillips (1977) showed that such mistakes can be quite costly when decision options are discrete (e.g., operate/do not operate). When dealing with low probabilities, a modest underassessment may push the event below the threshold of concern; further underassessment may mean not only that nothing is done, but that the topic is not even monitored for future signals. On the other hand, overassessment may leapfrog the event over other low-probability–high-consequence events in our hierarchy of concerns and lead to the neglect of more important issues. Many advocates of nuclear power feel that its risks have been accentuated to the detriment of concern over the effects of fossil fuels (like CO_2-induced climatic changes).

Insensitivity of decision outcomes to errors would make it hard to go too far astray and hard to learn very much from experience. It is hard to tell when one has done a poor job of assessing very low probabilities; as a result, the skill may be lacking for those few instances in which one must get such assessments right. The difficulties of learning are exacerbated by the tendencies to state probabilities in vague, nonnumerical terms (Lichtenstein & Newman, 1967) and to reconstruct or misremember our own predictions to have been wiser than they actually were (Fischhoff, 1975). In the absence of any explicit instruction in dealing with low probabilities, any cognitive representations or manipulative skills that are not acquired naturally are not likely to be acquired at all.

RECAP

Thus, there are limits to what our natural and technological environment will reveal about the probability of the unlikely catastrophes it harbors. Not only does such information emerge of its own accord at a slow rate, but the best efforts of historians and modelers will not coax forth the whole story. This partial picture of an obscure environment reaches decision makers, be they legislators, regulators, industrialists, or laypeople, through the filters of science and the news media reporting them. Using that information requires some analysis of the physical limits on the acuity of its sources, as well as the random and systematic error that the filters might induce (e.g., through endemic overconfidence or self-serving biases). Decision makers must also integrate what they are told by the experts with what they are told by their senses and comrades.[10] This task is complicated by the facts that probabilities may be experienced and reported in forms that are hard to compare and that the definitions of relevant events and

---

[10]With the exception of social-comparison theory (Festinger, 1954), the role of indigenous social-support systems is generally ignored in the decision-making literature. Other people would appear to serve as an important source not only for information but also for decision rules (e.g., Kunreuther, Ginsberg, Miller, Sagi, Slovic, Borkan, & Katz, 1978). Discussion with others would also serve to expand an individual's information-processing capacity by externalizing some of the informational load, akin to human peripheral processors.

universes may be poorly specified. Finally, there is reason to suspect that we lack some of the cognitive repertoire needed to handle such information effectively and that our normal experience is poorly structured to inculcate such skills.

As mentioned, low probabilities were taken as a case in point for how one might develop the formal and psychological properties of a class of information encountered in various guises in CO_2 issues. Some hints at what analogous explorations with other kinds of information might reveal follow. The theoretical purpose of such analyses is to develop a broadly applicable theory of judgment based on the match between informational and cognitive ecologies. Doubtless there are other ways to characterize the situations within which individuals exercise their cognition. Informational types was chosen because of its generality and because it allows the exploitation of the many existing studies of responses to various kinds of information (albeit conducted without reference to their prevalence or distribution). Because psychologists have used information types in the past, one might expect them to be readily able to fill in the research gaps identified by an analysis like the present one. A conceptual scheme that raises answerable questions would seem to have something going for it.

The practical purpose of such an analysis is to anticipate people's perception of a situation as it naturally impinges upon them. This in turn should give us some idea of how and how well they would respond to it in the absence of any intervention. Finally, it should clarify somewhat the efficacy (or wisdom) of various manipulations designed to help people understand what is happening to them. From this perspective, it is not a foregone conclusion that ''expert'' intervention is superior to people's natural coping strategies. Nonetheless, it does seem that the world in which we, as individuals and as a species, have acquired our cognitive skills may be different from our present world, with its potential for socially induced climatic change and other forms of irreversible environmental degradation.

WHAT ELSE IS THERE TO KNOW?

Coping with CO_2-induced climatic change means comprehending a wide variety of information about possible effects and presumed underlying causes. Part of comprehension is an appraisal of the quality of that information. Having a low probability of occurrence is one quality of some possible effects, particularly the more drastic ones. Table 9.1 lists other formal or physical or objective properties of what one must know. The cursory discussions that follow sketch lines along which more protracted analyses might be conducted.

Properties of Information

As a guide to action, available information about climatic change has one most regrettable property: It is highly impeachable. This vulnerability stems from the same reluctance of the environment to reveal its secrets that plagues attempts to assess the probabilities of unlikely consequences. Scientific understanding of what is happening right now is limited by the embryonic stage of some theories, the absence of reliable data on some key parameters, and the small amount of data regarding others. Climatologists face the usual problems of discerning a weak (if ominous) signal amidst noise, created in this case, say, by unreliable measurement and meaningless local variations. Their task is complicated by the presence of systematic as well as random error in their observations. Climate is subject to poorly understood fluctuations that are large in their amplitude relative to the signal in question here. As a result, they can mimic or obscure the effects of CO_2 build-up. Climatologists' faith in eventual warming despite the cooling trend of the last 20 years reflects such a belief in the masking potential of cyclical fluctuations. Historical climatology provides some hope of reducing the heroism in this particular leap of faith by reconstructing past climates on the basis of documentary and physical evidence (Ingram, Underhill, & Wigley, 1978).

Evidence about the limits of evidence might reach nontechnical audiences in a number of ways (if it reaches them at all). One is through explicit statements of uncertainty; the problems of formulating and communicating such statements was discussed earlier. A second is through observation of disagreements between experts. Unless the audience has an appreciation of the naturally disputative and accretive character of science, its resolution of the conflict may not be a balanced and informed weighing of the sides. Alternative resolutions are doubting the probity of the disputants, siding with the most assertive (or colorful or optimistic or certain), or deciding that "anything goes" and that "my guess is as good as yours." Such potential for misleading or confusing the public by contradictory or premature pronouncements poses for climatology quality-control problems that most sciences are ill-equipped to handle. To take an example from another realm, even though most seismologists might agree that earthquake prediction is unfeasible at the moment, they would be hard pressed to cope with a freelancer publishing daily forecasts in the *L. A. Times*. Another path to recognizing uncertainty is through observing the conflict between one's own sensory experience and the pronouncements of climatologists. Our great facility for interpreting short-term fluctuations may seriously restrict the visibility of long-term trends (Fischhoff, 1980).

Properties of the Processes

Making sense of a natural or social process often means interpreting it in terms of some sort of causal scheme. If carefully explained, many aspects of CO_2-induced climatic change should make sense to most people. The causal agents are for the most part large, visible objects. Their interaction is through such physical processes as ice fields reflecting sunlight and wind mixing water. One can see how that works. Modest stretches of the imagination may be needed to visualize other aspects—for example, the large negative effects that minute concentrations of such a common chemical as CO_2 can have or the fact that many innocuous individual decisions can produce such an immense common dilemma. More difficult may be comprehension of causes whose impact has a very long lag time—for instance, the extent to which heavy capital commitment to some production and consumption patterns reduces social resilience and precludes many responses to crises, or the "time bomb" inherent in the enormous number of young people in the world today, with a lifetime of reproduction and overproduction of CO_2 before them.

Still other processes cannot by their nature be understood. GCM's are used because climatologists realize that one cannot simulate in one's head the interaction of a large number of systems, even if they are individually quite simple. After throwing everything into such a model, one must trust the results. What happens when those results are unwanted politically or counterintuitive (i.e., not believed) psychologically? There may be a strong temptation to try it again, adjusting the parameters or assumptions a bit. Any persistent tendency to yield to such temptation could generate a systematic and not easily detected bias in the results of modeling efforts. The debate arising out of Meadows, Meadows, Randers & Behrens' *Limits to Growth* (1972) or Forrester's *World Dynamics* (1973) may have petered out because there are no clear standards on the acceptability of models. Everyone agreed that the models in question were somewhat wrong and somewhat oversimplified, but no one could tell quite what that meant.

Properties of Effects

Because climate is part of our lives, we should, it would seem, have no trouble comprehending what the outcomes of CO_2-induced changes are (e.g., what it means to have an average increase of 2°C). There are, however, a number of reasons to doubt this presumption, all of which have analogues in the reasons for doubting the assumption that because we all live in society, we would be able to understand the meaning of a projected shift in one of its parameters (e.g., an increase in the median age or percentage of handicapped or price of fuel). One is that we do not experience our environment directly; rather, we have about us a series of defenses that regulate contacts so as to make them more pleasant and less demanding. Air conditioning and social norms are two obvious examples. We may have little idea of what life would be like if the conditions to which that veneer of civilization was adapted were changed.

A related reason for doubt is that we experience weather not climate, people not society. As a result, we seldom have to confront the complexity of the natural and social ecologies within which we live. We may not realize that an older world threatens the bankruptcy of the social-security system or that a warmer world will eliminate the hard freezes that keep pests from destroying susceptible crops in some regions. Although the connections are straightforward and comprehensible when drawn, one should not expect either experts or laypeople to recognize spontaneously the secondary or tertiary effects of projected changes.

Finally, no one knows how well people are able to imagine dramatic changes or, conversely, to what extent they are prisoners of their own experience. Do any of us who have not suffered that unmaskable pain of cancer know what it means? (If we did, would anyone start smoking?) What presumptions about unalterable aspects of human nature constrain our imaginations regarding, say, what awaits us in foreign countries or prison? Can we flesh out projections of climatic conditions outside of our species' experience? Can we really know what it will be like to live in the greenhouse? Without that experiential understanding, can we act appropriately to the possibility? A related argument is used by some foes of nuclear power who say that because we cannot grasp the time span during which some radioactive wastes must be stored, we should avoid the whole business; without basic comprehension, wise decision making is infeasible.

Understanding effects requires not only factual knowledge but also an evaluative assessment. Do we want this to happen? How badly? Such questions would seem to be the last redoubt of unaided intuition. Who knows better than an individual what he or she prefers? When one is considering simple, familiar events with which people have hands-on experience, it may be reasonable to assume that they have well-articulated opinions. Regarding the novel, global consequences potentially associated with CO_2-induced climatic change or nuclear meltdowns, that may not be the case. Our values may be incoherent, not thought through. In thinking about what are acceptable levels of risk, for example, we may be unfamiliar with the terms in which issues are formulated (e.g., social discount rates, miniscule probabilities, or megadeaths). We may have contradictory values (e.g., a strong aversion to catastrophic losses of life and a realization that we are not more moved by a plane crash with 500 fatalities than one with 300). We may occupy different roles in life (parents, workers, children) that produce clear-cut, but inconsistent values. We may vacillate between incompatible, but strongly held, positions (e.g., freedom of speech is inviolate, but should be denied to authoritarian movements). We may not even know how to begin thinking about some issues (e.g., the appropriate trade-off between the opportunity to dye one's hair and a vague, minute increase in the probability of cancer 20 years from now). Our views may undergo changes over time (say, as we near the hour of decision or the consequence itself) and we may not know which view should form the basis of our decision (Fischhoff, Slovic, & Lichtenstein, 1980).

If asked, people can usually find some way to evaluate almost anything. But if their values are poorly articulated, that way may tap only a part of what they feel and may lead to responses not in their own best interests. As a result, the particular or peculiar way that issues are posed by nature, scientists, politicians, and the media may have great power over just what responses emerge as apparent expressions of people's values.

COGNITIVE POLITICS

Real problems produce genuine conflicts of interests. Thinking about them might not only help protect our science from unwanted pressures, but also uncover some presumptions that are typically neglected.

One might start by asking "Why would anyone want to ask psychologists for their opinion about such policy issues?" A naive answer, doubtless with some truth, is that decision makers and natural scientists realize that they do not have all the answers; the source and resolution of this environmental problem lie in social and cognitive processes. If that is the case, one might ask "How far will they let us go?" For example, can we work on those topics traditionally in the stranglehold of economics or will our funds be restricted or, more ominously, will we censor our own inquiries to avoid areas in which we are not wanted? Are the natural scientists sufficiently committed to allow their people to work with us or do they maintain the prejudice that interdisciplinary research is the domain of people who cannot cut it in their own field and is thus a no-no for anyone interested in promotion and tenure? If that is the case, does it mean anything more than an ego-weakening rebuff or will restricted communication imperil the validity of our research?

A less naive answer to "Why did they ask us?" is that our basic paradigm embodies a political perspective appealing to some. Perhaps we are seen as contributing to a stratification with a technical elite near the top. Maybe experts are frustrated by the refusal of laypeople to believe their analyses, feeling "the public is crazy. Let's bring in some psychologists to solve this clinical problem." Our focus on individuals rather than social or political institutions may be conducive to some people of power. On the other hand, our interest in facilitating communication with laypeople may cast us as populists concerned with enfranchising and empowering nonexperts by increasing their ability to act in their own best interests. Our focus on what people can be taught to do may make us a healthy antidote to claims of lay incompetence (that stupid, emotive public). What we actually are probably lies between these extremes and depends on how we envision, shape, and disseminate our work. Again, even though names can never hurt us, labels can lead us to define our research task in ways that build in incapacities and blind spots that we could, in principle, avoid.

Although we may be invited at the behest of natural scientists and political decision makers, we should not hesitate to tell them how to run at least a part of their lives. We probably know some things about the foibles inherent in their modes of analysis that suggest altered approaches and reasons for caution (see the section "What Can Be Known" earlier in this chapter). We also may know something about what the body politic wants to know and how it might respond to various messages. Such information could serve as the basis for manipulating opinion or for making big science more responsive to the public that pays for it. For example, we might tell legislators never to order cost–benefit analyses because it is impossible to provide a clear exposition of their assumptions; we might tell climatologists that instead of trying to understand the full picture of what will happen, they should try to produce one clear diagnostic sign that something is really changing in the climate of sufficient magnitude to merit our attention.

CONCLUSION

Psychology has learned a fair amount about the minutiae of cognitive and social behavior in the constrained environments common to our various studies. The complexity of behavior and its sensitivity to subtle alterations in those environments has served as a source of both frustration and inspiration. Elaborating the effects of such shifts has led, at least in some cases, to a moderately inclusive understanding of very small worlds. The approach attempted here has been to look at the psychological equivalents of the environmental properties of a very large world. Such analyses might tell us (1) what we know and need to know about the application of existing results to the real world; (2) whether there are important tasks and phenomena out there that have yet to find their ways into our studies; and (3) what we know already with sufficient confidence to be able to contribute to policy making.

REFERENCES

Atomic Energy Commission. *Reactor safety study: An assessment of accident risks in U.S. commercial power plants* (WASH-1400). Washington, D.C.: Atomic Energy Commission, 1975.

Bacastow, R. B. & Keeling, C. D. Models to predict future atmospheric CO_2. In W. P. Elliott & L. Machta (Eds.) *Workshop on the global effects of carbon dioxide from fossil fuels.* Washington, D.C.: U.S. Department of Energy, 1977.

Bryson, R. A. A perspective on climatic change. *Science,* 1974, *184,* 753-759.

Burton, I., Kates, R. W., & White, G. F. *The environment as hazard.* New York: Oxford University Press, 1978.

Climate change to the year 2000. Fort McNair: National Defense University, 1978.

Dawes, R. M. Social dilemmas. *Annual Review of Psychology,* 1980, *31,* 169-194.

Einhorn, H. Learning from experience and suboptimal rules in decision making. In T. Wallsten (Ed.), *Cognitive processes in choice and decision behavior.* Hillsdale, N.J.: Lawrence Erlbaum Associates, 1980.

Einhorn, H. J., & Hogarth, R. Confidence in judgment: Persistence of the illusion of validity. *Psychological Review,* 1978, *85,* 395-416.

Festinger, L. A theory of social comparison processes. *Human Relations,* 1954, *7,* 117-140.

Fischhoff, B. Hindsight ≠ foresight: The effect of outcome knowledge on judgment under uncertainty. *Journal of Experimental Psychology: Human Perception and Performance,* 1975, *1,* 288-299.

Fischhoff, B. Cost-benefit analysis and the art of motorcycle maintenance. *Policy Sciences,* 1977, *8,* 177-202.

Fischhoff, B. For those condemned to study the past: Reflections on historical judgment. In R. A. Shweder & D. W. Fiske (Eds.), *New directions for methodology of behavioral science: Fallible judgment in behavioral research.* San Francisco: Jossey-Bass, 1980.

Fischhoff, B., Slovic, P., & Lichtenstein, S. Knowing with certainty: The appropriateness of extreme confidence. *Journal of Experimental Psychology: Human Perception and Performance,* 1977, *3,* 552–564.

Fischhoff, B., Slovic, P., & Lichtenstein, S. Fault trees: Sensitivity of estimated failure probabilities to problem representation. *Journal of Experimental Psychology: Human Perception and Performance,* 1978, *4,* 330–344.

Fischhoff, B., Slovic, P., & Lichtenstein, S. Knowing what you want: Measuring labile values. In T. Wallsten (Ed.), *Cognitive processes in choice and decision behavior.* Hillsdale, N.J.: Lawrence Erlbaum Associates, 1980.

Fischhoff, B., Slovic, P., & Lichtenstein, S. Lay foibles and expert fables in judgments about risk. In T. O'Riordan & R. K. Turner (Eds.), *Progress in Resource Management & Environmental Planning, Vol. 3,* Chichester: Wiley, in press.

Forrester, J. W. *World dynamics.* Cambridge, Mass.: Wright-Allen, 1973.

Gettys, C. F., Kelley, C. W., & Peterson, C. R. Best guess hypothesis in multi-stage inference. *Organizational Behavior and Human Performance,* 1973, *10,* 364–373.

Glantz, M. H. (Ed.). *The politics of natural disasters: The case of the Sahel drought.* New York: Praeger, 1976.

Hewitt, K., & Burton, I. *The hazardousness of a place: A regional ecology of damaging events* (Department of Geography Research Paper No. 6). Toronto: University of Toronto Press, 1971.

Ingram, M. J., Underhill, D. J., & Wigley, T. M. L. Historical climatology. *Nature,* 1978, *276*(23), 329–334.

Kahneman, D., & Tversky, A. On the psychology of prediction. *Psychological Review,* 1973, *80,* 237–251.

Kastenberg, W. E., McKone, T. E., & Okrent, D. *On risk assessment in the absence of complete data* (UCLA-ENG-7677). Los Angeles: University of California, 1976.

Kates, R. W. *Hazard and choice perception in flood plain management* (Department of Geography Research Paper No. 78). Chicago: University of Chicago, 1962.

Kellogg, W. W. Is mankind warming the earth? *Bulletin of the Atomic Scientists,* 1978, *23*(2), 10–19.

Kunreuther, H., Ginsberg, R., Miller, L., Sagi, P., Slovic, P., Borkan, B., & Katz, N. *Disaster insurance protection: Public policy lessons.* New York: Wiley Interscience, 1978.

Lichtenstein, S., Fischhoff, B., & Phillips, L. D. Calibration of probabilities: The state of the art. In H. Jungermann & G. de Zeeuw (Eds.), *Decision making and change in human affairs.* Amsterdam: D. Reidel, 1977.

Lichtenstein, S., & Newman, J. R. Empirical scaling of common verbal phrases associated with numerical probabilities. *Psychonomic Science,* 1967, *9,* 563–564.

Lichtenstein, S., Slovic, P., Fischhoff, B., Layman, M., & Combs, B. Judged frequency of lethal events. *Journal of Experimental Psychology: Human Learning and Memory,* 1978, *4,* 551–578.

Lodge, J. P. A risky road from hypothesis to fact. *Business Week,* June 21, 1976, 14–16.

Manabe, S., & Wetherald, R. T. The effects of doubling the CO_2 concentration on climate of a general circulation model. *Journal of Atmospheric Sciences,* 1975, *32,* 3–15.

Meadows, D., Meadows, D. H., Randers, J., & Behrens, W. W. *The limits of growth.* New York: Universe, 1972.

Miller, G. A. The magical number seven, plus or minus two: Some limits on our capacity for processing information. *Psychological Review,* 1956, *63,* 81–97.

National Academy of Sciences. *Committee on socio-economic effects of earth-quake prediction.* Washington, D.C.: National Academy of Sciences, 1978.

Nuclear Regulatory Commission. *Risk assessment review group report to the U.S. Nuclear Regulatory Commission* (NUREG/CR-0400). Washington, D.C.: Nuclear Regulatory Commission, 1978.

Opie, J. *America's seventy-year mistake: Settlement and farming on the arid great plains, 1870–1940.* Paper presented for Panel on Social and Institutional Responses, AAAS-DOE Workshop on Environmental and Societal Consequences of a Possible CO₂-Induced Climate Change, Annapolis, Maryland, April 1979.

Peterson, C. R., & Beach, L. R. Man as an intuitive statistician. *Psychological Bulletin*, 1967, *68*, 29–46.

Poulton, E. C. The new psychophysics: Six models for magnitude estimation. *Psychological Bulletin*, 1968, *69*, 1–19.

Schneider, S. Personal communication, April 3, 1979.

Schneider, S. H., & Mesirow, L. E. *The genesis strategy*. New York: Plenum, 1976.

Schweitzer, G. C. Toxic chemicals and regulatory decision making. In *Decision making for regulating chemicals in the environment*. Washington, D.C.: National Academy of Science, 1975.

Simon, H. A. Rational choice and the structure of the environment. *Psychological Review*, 1956, *79*, 427–434.

Slovic, P., Fischhoff, B., & Lichtenstein, S. Perceived risk. *Environment*, 1979, *21*(3), 14–20; 36–39.

Slovic, P., Fischhoff, B., Lichtenstein, S., Corrigan, B., & Combs, B. Preference for insuring against probable small losses: Implications for the theory and practice of insurance. *Journal of Risk and Insurance*, 1977, *44*, 237–258.

Tversky, A., & Kahneman, D. Judgment under uncertainty: Heuristics and biases. *Science*, 1974. *185*, 1124–1131.

Tversky, A., & Kahneman, D. Causal schemata in judgment under uncertainty. In M. Fishbein (Ed.), *Progress in social psychology*. Hillsdale, N.J.: Lawrence Erlbaum Associates, 1980.

Wigley, T. M. L., Jones, P. D., & Kelly, P. M. Scenario for a warm, high-CO_2 world. *Nature*, 1980, *283*, 17–21.

U.S. Department of Energy. *Carbon dioxide effects research and assessment program*, Washington, D.C., 1980.

von Winterfeldt, D., & Edwards, W. *Evaluation of complex stimuli using multi-attribute utility procedures* (Engineering Psychology Laboratory Tech. Rep. 011313-2-T). Ann Arbor, Mich.: University of Michigan, 1973.

Whipple, C. Personal communication, April 23, 1979.

World Climate Conference. Geneva: World Meteorological Organization, 1979.

III COGNITION AND SOCIAL BEHAVIOR

This set of eight chapters represents the largest set of focused papers in the book. Each piece is concerned with the relationship between cognitive and social processes. Also enmeshed in several of the papers is an examination of how basic perceptual, strong emotional and motivational, and memorial and comprehension processes interact with social perception.

As the reader considers these papers, certain combinations of themes may be evident. The first paper in the section by Shelley Taylor and the last paper by Joseph Lappin are both general, thought-provoking position statements. Taylor's paper represents a commentary on the nature of social cognition and how work in the area has developed. In her analysis, she discusses the pros and cons of the borrowing of ideas and methods by social psychologists from cognitive psychologists and vice versa. Taylor's statement is clearly a personal assessment of the social-cognitive linkage, written from the standpoint of a scholar who has an intimate knowledge of the "marriage" of social and cognitive psychology. Social perception researchers may benefit greatly from a careful study of Taylor's points and reasoning.

In his paper, Lappin discusses the relationship between individual knowledge and social environment from the perspective of research in perception and psychophysics.

This perspective may not be well-known to most social perception investigators. But it is an invaluable perspective as Lappin cogently argues. He reminds us early in the analyses that for Heider, undoubtedly one of the foremost pioneers of social perception work, there never was a serious divergence between cognitive and social psychology. As Lappin notes, Heider has defined cognition as "getting to know the environment." Lappin's conceptualization of change in the environment and the relativity of knowledge and choice behavior is a contribution that deserves study by social perception researchers.

Consensus on the consummation of this marriage addressed by Taylor is far from realized. This fact was made clear by Tom Trabasso's commentary at the conference on papers relating to social perception. Trabasso felt that considerable depth of understanding of other domain's theories must be achieved before concepts and methods are borrowed (or before much precise dialogue can occur?).

In the second and third papers in this section, Gifford Weary and Susan Fiske, respectively, provide an important service to this volume by focusing on the role of affect and motivation in social perception. As will be noted again in the last chapter, scholars concerned with interdisciplinary work in psychology cannot readily disregard the fact that strong emotions and motivations represent enduring and impactful aspects of human life.

Weary's paper is particularly unique in this volume in its focus on how motivational bias influences judgments. Also, her analysis is novel in its consideration of how attributional processes may be involved in personal adjustment to stressful environments. Fiske's paper is helpful in its attempt to differentiate cognitive and affective systems. While she acknowledges the overlap between these systems, she argues that purely cognitive systems stress memory and do not consider intensity or valence as major components. As implied above, while one may have reservation about this decided focus, Fiske's paper may be seen as required reading for a scholar who is interested in formulating a thoughtful view on the matter.

In the fourth and fifth papers in this section, first Grueneich and Trabasso and then Yarkin, Town, and Harvey provide discussions coupled with data presentations on comprehension and attribution. Although these chapters may appear to be disparate in content (e.g., the first focuses on variables associated with children's comprehension in the form of recall and evaluation; whereas the second focuses on variables associated with adults' attributions and recall), they have certain basic similarities. Each involves an examination of people's perception of others' intentions and motives and the consequences of other's behavior. Grueneich and Trabasso employ a story format, while Yarkin et al. employ a videotape presentation procedure. Also, each set of authors is concerned with the import of people's comprehension of and attribution about others as part of the *Gestalt* of understanding others that may include moral evaluation and effect. The fact that Grueneich and Trabasso's work represents an interesting example of and contribution to mainstream cognitive-developmental work reflects how much overlap often exists in contemporary work on cognitive, social, and developmental processes.

Finally, both the sixth and seventh papers in this section by Gary Wells and William Smith, respectively, are fundamentally concerned with people's more or less rational inquiries about and analysis of events in their social worlds. Wells presents a general model of observer attribution. His analysis of causal force borrows from Lewin's influential writings on topological psychology, and the reader may find interesting Wells' novel arguments about the concept of psycorrelation.

Smith's presentation on social comparison represents the only systematic treatment of this concept in the volume. His conception and the results he provides constitute one of the more extensive analyses of social comparison in social psychology in the 1970s. Unfortunately, there has not been as much attention given to social comparison phenomena in recent years as was the case in the late 1950s and 1960s. Such a fact is unfortunate because of the pervasiveness of social comparison in many aspects of social life (as highlighted by Kelley's and Schachter's writings on attribution and emotion, respectively).

In conclusion, it should be noted that both Wells and Smith provide useful discussion of issues in the domain of cognitive heuristics, a topical area of much popularity in contemporary work on social perception.

10 The Interface of Cognitive and Social Psychology

Shelley E. Taylor
University of California, Los Angeles

Early in 1975, when the Carnegie Symposium on Social Cognition was being organized, I was asked to comment on an eclectic set of papers that represented points of interface between cognitive and social psychology. Two of the papers came out of an artificial intelligence tradition; one was a cognitive model of parole decision making, and the fourth was a general piece on the fallibility of cognitive processes. As a relatively new Ph.D., with little experience in cognitive psychology, especially artificial intelligence, and little perspective on the social–cognitive interface, it was hard to find any common themes. The need to furnish a paper, however, quickly led to the discovery of some. At that time, I characterized the relationship between cognitive and social psychology not as a marriage, but as a series of flirtations (Taylor, 1976). Four years later, it is more clear, at least to me, that the relationship between social psychology and cognitive psychology may more properly be thought of as a marriage, and that we can reach some generalizations about how it is shaping up. Accordingly, I have three goals in this chapter: first, to outline what social cognition is and how it has developed; second, to describe some of the benefits of the social-psychology-cognitive-psychology liaison, of which there are many, and third, to discuss some possible liabilities and oversights created by too-liberal borrowing between social and cognitive psychology and by drawing on unquestioned assumptions about the relationship between cognition and social behavior. My description of the area and criticisms regarding its directions will no doubt meet with objections from some quarters. I offer the following as a personal assessment.

WHAT IS SOCIAL COGNITION?

As a term, "social cognition" is relatively new, having made its appearance within the last 5 years; it refers, broadly, to how people cognize their social world and their social relationships. The research in this area has typically focused on such questions as how people infer the attributes of another, decide on a course of action vis-a-vis other people, and represent the social environment in terms of their needs and attributions. Although the term social cognition itself is relatively recent, the interface of cognitive psychology and social psychology is not.

Over the last 20 years, there have been three identifiably different thrusts within social cognition, dominant during different time periods, with clear differences in theoretical focus and empirical directions. Early research focused on the *person as a consistency seeker,* driven by a motive to achieve consistency within the cognitive system. Later work, indicative of a pendulum shift away from this motivational emphasis, considered the *individual as an information processor* who uses data in a logical fashion and whose errors are traceable primarily to motivational factors. Finally, we have come to a view of the *person as a cognitive miser,* characterized by a research emphasis on how people simplify information so as to make judgments quickly and efficiently.

Thus, in many respects, social psychology has always been cognitive. For some purposes, we can trace the development of social cognition to Kurt Lewin's 1936 work.[1] Lewin was concerned with how the mind ascribes properties to and organizes incoming stimulation in social situations. He developed field theory, a quasimathematical model of movement of forces in fields as a function of change in the value of those stimuli. In that theory he specified two structural elements, cognitions and motivations. His research endeavors concentrated on attitudes in particular and spawned the field of attitude change, perhaps the first major empirically oriented "social cognition."[2]

The Person as Consistency Seeker

From the mid-1950's to the mid to late-1960's extending into the present, the dominant research focus in social psychology was attitude change, and the dominant theoretical framework within social psychology was a view of people as cognitive consistency seekers. According to this view, people are motivated to

---

[1]It is difficult to date the beginning of social cognition. One can begin with Aristotle, or alternatively, one can begin with attribution theory in 1972. However, I would like to adopt a middle position and suggest that we can trace the development of social cognition directly to Kurt Lewin's 1936 work.

[2]The perceptual readiness literature (e.g., Bruner & Goodman, 1947) is also clearly social cognition and should be considered another empirical point of departure.

maintain consistency within their belief systems and between their beliefs and behaviors. A number of specific consistency theories developed, most notably Festinger's (1957) consonance/dissonance principle, Heider's (1958) balance and imbalance principle, and Osgood and Tannenbaum's (1955) congruity/incongruity principle. The heuristic value of cognitive consistency theory is easily documented in the huge number of experimental studies that was generated. Though this work was heavily motivational in its emphasis on a purposive drive model of behavior, the work was also heavily cognitive in that the social world was assumed to be represented by cognitive units called attitudes: a mental and neural state of readiness to respond organized through experience exerting a direct or dynamic influence on behavior (Allport, 1935).

What is perhaps most important about the dominance of the consistency principle was that it not only spawned attitude-change research, but it pervaded approaches to virtually every other substantive content area researched at this time (e.g., attraction, achievement, the self). A classic study on self concept (Aronson & Mettee, 1968), for example, demonstrated that when an individual's self esteem has been lowered by negative feedback, this self esteem will generalize, leading to cheating behavior in a completely different situation. Work on achievement by Aronson and Carlsmith (1962) demonstrated that people will alter their performance, whether good or bad, to be consistent with their expectations of their performance, as established by feedback on prior tasks. Research on interpersonal attraction (see, for example, Byrne & Blalock, 1963) maintained that people are attracted to similar others because those similar others validate the goodness of one's own beliefs. Thus, the impact of consistency theory on social psychology was enormous.

Eventually, consistency theories fell into disfavor. They were criticized on a number of grounds (see Kiesler, Collins, & Miller, 1969). First, there were simply too many of them that were virtually indistinguishable from each other, and second, they shared a number of common weaknesses. None was able to specify precisely what constituted cognitive inconsistency, and none included adequate provisions for quantifying degree of inconsistency. The question of what relationship between objects or people is required for consistency even to be an operating principle was not clear. Accordingly, most of the models suffered from a lack of specific predictions.

By far the more important question was, Are we on the right track when we talk about consistency? Where exactly does consistency fit in? Is it a wired-in, cold, nonmotivational rule of the cognitive system? Are we motivated to achieve consistency because inconsistency is an aversive drive state? Is consistency an overload mechanism that only operates if too much information is coming in at once? Is consistency simply functional, or is it a value, not intrinsic to the cognitive system at all, but rather derived from the cultural context in which beliefs are expressed? Once research questioned the consistency principle, it became clear that people are able to maintain high degrees of inconsistency among their attitudes and between their attitudes and behavior. People compartmentalize sufficiently that they simply fail to perceive inconsistencies where, to an outside observer, an inconsistency clearly exists.

As cognitive consistency began to be questioned, a number of new issues began to emerge. First, there was a movement away from the macrotheoretical approach. It became clear that broadly established principles of consistency were subject to numerous qualifications depending on such factors as situational forces and other attitudes. As a result, research became more conservative, represented in part by a shift away from macrotheory to a minitheoretical approach (a small set of semilinked hypotheses). There was also a movement away from the view that truth lies in main effects to a view that truth lies in interactions. Processes that had heretofore been considered single processes, like attitude change, came to be viewed as multiple processes. McGuire's (1968) important piece on attitude change is the best example of this trend; he reconceptualized attitude change in terms of a series of stages (e.g., attention, comprehension, yielding, and acceptance), each influenced by a host of different factors.

The Person as Information Processor

The third trend, and by far the most important for current purposes, was a movement away from motivationally based models of attitudes and behavior toward so-called information-processing models, models that paralleled the newly developing field of cognitive psychology. This change has to be considered a substantial metatheoretical shift within social cognition. It represented a movement away from a view of people as rationalizing, motivating, face-saving, and justifying, to a view of people as naive scientists and problem solvers. (Indeed, many people would date the beginning of the field of social cognition as this point.) More effort was directed toward the conscious, precise, and formal consideration of cognitive processes as determinants of human development and behavior. Research was characterized by efforts to conceptualize and in some cases even measure the intervening states. Social behavior from this perspective was viewed as the product of rational, though not infallible, information-processing strategies, which direct the coding, storage, and retrieval of information, as well as the analysis of it and actions taken as a result of it.

Much of the work in this area can be characterized as borrowing cognitive hypotheses and exploring their implications for social situations. For example, the work on cognitive aspects of stereotyping draws heavily on the categorization literature as bases for its predictions (see, for example, Brewer, 1979; Tajfel, 1972; Taylor, Fiske, Etcoff, & Ruderman, 1978; Wilder, 1981).

The best example of this new trend in social cognition has been attribution theory. Attribution theory, of course, drew from the Brunswick lens model, which formed the background for Heider's early work. In paralleling developments in cognitive psychology, attribution theory was concerned particularly with how experience is mediated, and how it is then represented and used as a basis for inference and action. The key assumption of attribution theory is that common-sense psychology can tell scientists a great deal about behavior, and that simply looking at how people conceptualize causal relationships within their environment will tell a great deal about how people perceive causality to operate within the social world.

The early attribution approaches borrowed a number of assumptions from early cognitive psychology, including the idea that people are essentially rational decision makers. It was assumed that if an individual has enough time and enough capacity, he or she will take in information logically, combine the information in some specifiable and reasonably complex fashion, and make generally good and accurate decisions, dismissing some factors and incorporating other information into causal schemas. Paralleling Lewin's distinction between cognition and motivation and harking back to the consistency models of previous years, a sharp difference was assumed to exist between the answers provided by cognitive processes and those provided by motivational ones. When people depart from what would be expected as a reasonable decision, it was maintained, motivation and emotional factors have undoubtedly interfered in the process. Thus, cognitive processes were seen as giving good and right answers, and motivation as interfering with reasonable decision making.

Embodying these developments, both Kelley's (1967) and Jones and Davis' (1965) attribution theories posit rational problem-solving or naive-scientist models of information processing. Kelley's theory maintains that, under certain circumstances, individuals sample across time, modality and persons for the purpose of making stable attributions in their environment. The cornerstone of Jones and Davis' theory involves the analysis of noncommon effects in which a perceiver generates the possible outcomes for a number of alternative decision courses and then infers correspondent inferences on the basis of what effects are produced that possible alternatives would not have produced.

Despite the centrality of Kelley's and Jones and Davis' models of attribution, no dominant theoretical model emerged in attribution theory. Kelley's and Jones and Davis' work was joined by Schachter and Singer's (1962) work on the attribution of emotional states, Rotter's (1966) scale work on locus of control, and Bem's (1972) self-perception theory, all of which made quite different theoretical assumptions. The consequence of no dominant formal theory is that attribution ''theory'' can be considered little more than a collection of ideas that share some common attributes: concern with the mediation between the stimulus and the response as a critical determinant of that response (in other words, how the individual construes meaning from stimuli); a view of the organism as actively constructing and interpreting experience much as a naive scientist would; as doing so in substantially causal terms, and in an essentially nonmotivational fashion (see, Shaver, 1975).

Not surprisingly, attribution theory shortly produced critics of its own, and many of the criticisms hinged around the absence of a formal theory. When one uses an individual's naive theory to construct formal theory, there are no formal constraints, as there are when a theory has been developed deductively. The absence of formal constraints on theory leads to an absence of consistent operating assumptions across empirical investigations, thereby building in an ability to explain away inconsistencies. Indeed, attribution theory has an embarrassing power to explain just about everything (see Sheil, 1974). Furthermore, although attribution theory gave the causal attribution central mediational status, no good, formal mediational arguments and corresponding methodological efforts to test those mediational arguments resulted. Perhaps the most severe problem for attribution theory, however, came from gradually accumulating evidence that individuals do not go through the kinds of formal scientific-like processes that are hypothesized to underlie the attribution process. Rather, individuals seem to make judgments much more quickly using much less information and showing much clearer biases than had been thought.

The somewhat disturbing and seemingly pervasive penchant of the social perceiver to depart from virtually all normative models of adequate thought gave rise to a brief period in social psychology that can be called the errors and biases period. Some of the most interesting work that has ever been done in social psychology was done during this period (see, for example, Miller & M. Ross, 1975; L. Ross, 1977), and interest in this set of problems persists. I see it, however, as a transition period in that it derives its focus from the inadequacies of an old way of looking at a problem—namely, the naive-scientist model—without fully bringing into sight a new way of looking at the problem. I think this transition has now been completed and that we can articulate the current metatheory that drives social cognition.

The Person as Cognitive Miser

These insights have now led to what I would call the third trend in social cognition research, one that marks the field today: the view of the person as a cognitive miser. The developments that led to this view began in cognitive psychology. Whereas guiding principles of early cognitive psychology had advanced the position that the cognitive system follows rational, orderly principles, what became clear after just a few years of cognitive research was that not only are people's judgments and decisions less complete and rational than was thought, but that not all errors can be traced to motivational factors. Even in the absence of motives, judgments were found to be made on the basis of scanty data that was seemingly haphazardly combined and strongly influenced by preconceptions. Dawes (1976), for example, reviews evidence that decision makers believe that they are combining a great deal of information in a complex way, when they are in fact making decisions on the basis of one or two highly salient cues, which are not weighted in the ways they think they are weighting them. Indeed, research on issues such as clinical diagnosis and admissions decision making suggests that if an algorithm could be agreed upon, one would be better off turning the problem over to the computer than leaving it with the fallible information processor (Dawes, 1976). As a consequence of these observations, the person came to be seen as capacity limited, capable of dealing accurately with only a little data at a time. Rather than being viewed as a naive scientist who optimizes, the person was said to "satisfice" (cf. Simon, 1957) and use short cuts that would produce decisions and judgments efficiently and accurately— hence, the view of the person as a cognitive miser.

One of the ground-breaking and most provocative contributions to this revised view of cognitive processes has been Kahneman and Tversky's writings on cognitive heuristics (Kahneman & Tversky, 1973; Tversky & Kahneman, 1974). According to Tversky and Kahneman (1974), heuristics are used under conditions of uncertainty—that is, the unavailability or indeterminacy of important information. Uncertainty derives primarily from the fact that information relevant to a particular judgment is almost always incomplete. The factual material may be inaccessible, it may not be gathered in time to bear on the decision, or it may be too voluminous to be properly utilized in the judgment task.

Within social cognition, this viewpoint has also achieved prominence, first, because the pieces by Kahneman and Tversky have been so influential within cognitive psychology, and second, because the naive-scientist models of human behavior proved to be useful normative but not useful descriptive models of behavior. Because the social world is at least as complex as the object world, it stands to reason that just as in making decisions about nonsocial events, the social perceiver will use heuristic strategies and short cuts to make judgments about social events.

Although not specifically labeled as studies of the social perceiver as a heuristic user and cognitive miser, a number of trends within social cognition fit nicely into this emphasis. For example, recent work on the impact of salient stimuli (Taylor & Fiske, 1978) suggests that in forming impressions of others and making judgments about social situations, people often seize upon one or two salient cues and use those as a basis for organizing their impressions. The work on mindlessness (Langer, 1978) suggests that many decisions are made with virtually no thought at all, but are rather made automatically. Nisbett and his colleagues (for example, Hamill, Wilson & Nisbett, 1978; Nisbett & Borgida, 1975) suggest that vivid case information is more influential than more reliable, but pallid, statistical evidence. This most recent trend, the person as cognitive miser, perhaps represents the clearest evidence that there is now a marriage between social psychology and cognitive psychology.

To summarize, then, any work that emphasizes how an individual cognizes his or her social world can be thought of as social cognition. Within the field, there have been three distinct trends: the person as consistency seeker, a view that was heavily motivational; the person as cold information processor, a view that is still prevalent within many parts of social psychology; and the most recent view of the person as cognitive miser who uses heuristics to reach decisions as quickly as possible. These trends, of course, are gradual ones and the evolution of the field is not yet completed. One can see each of these emphases still reflected in the current literature. Nonetheless, these themes seem to capture the transitions and directions in which the field of social cognition has been moving. What have been the benefits of this interface?

THE SOCIAL PSYCHOLOGY–COGNITIVE PSYCHOLOGY INTERFACE: SOCIAL PSYCHOLOGY'S DEBT TO COGNITIVE PSYCHOLOGY

The question "What contributions have derived from this cognitive–social interface?" is easy to answer. If we ask "What has cognitive psychology given to social cognition?" the answer is "Just about everything": metatheory, theory, hypotheses, paradigms, variables, and measures. Social psychologists have clearly been the heavy borrowers in the social–cognitive relationship. One rarely sees theory and hypotheses going the other way. Has this been beneficial to the field? For the most part, I think it has.

Take the shift toward process models. People not only talk process models now, but they actually make efforts to measure process in as complete ways as is possible. Social psychologists are now being more cautious about speculating on what is going on in people's heads. Rather than making sweeping claims regarding the cognitive processes of subjects (what I referred to in my 1976 paper as S–R methodology to test S–O–R relationships), instead, there is an effort to define much more precisely the process that is going on and an effort to use the measurement procedures and the paradigms adopted by cognitive psychologists to actually examine process arguments. We have seen greater use of cognitive measures (e.g.; reaction time, recall, organization of recall, requests for additional information, eye movements and scanning, and verbal-protocol analysis); these tools have provided us with some interesting results and clues. Reaction-time measures have been used successfully by Smith and Miller (1980), by Pryor and Kriss (1977), and by Lingle and Ostrom (1979) to specify the nature of subjects' inferences in person perception. (See Lingle & Ostrom, 1979, for a criticism of the reaction-time method.) Organization of recall, particularly clustering, has been used quite successfully by Hamilton, Katz, and Leirer (1980) to infer how people process person information differently under impression-set versus memory-set instructions. Requests for additional information have been used successfully by Garland, Hardy, and Stephenson (1975) to test predictions generated by Kelley's attribution theory. Looking time has been used in our research (see Langer, Taylor, Fiske, & Chanowitz, 1976) in marginally successful efforts to examine the extent to which salient stimuli impact judgment. Verbal-protocol analysis in social experimentation has to my mind not been terribly successful. I am willing to be corrected, but I have seen few successful efforts to code subjects' verbal responses to social situations into meaningful terms that have provided a fruitful theoretical or empirical outcome.[3] People seem to have the capacity to talk about social material endlessly and in diverse ways that defy coding efforts. Recall has had a more checkered history, which I return to later. (See also Taylor & Fiske, 1981).

Parenthetically, one might note that although cognitive psychology has provided many of the techniques for measuring the assumed mediating processes, it has done little by way of furnishing adequate methods of data analysis suitable to inferring mediation. Analysis of variance is still the dominant method of data analysis, and it is inappropriate for examining mediation (see Taylor, 1976). Social psychologists have begun to use causal modeling (see Kenny, 1979) to this end, and in some cases, results of the two techniques (ANOVA and causal modeling) differ greatly, indicating that the ANOVA approach is giving us misleading results (see Fiske, Chapter 12 in this volume). Cognitive psychologists might consider data analysis an area in which they can "borrow back" from social psychologists, and incorporate these analytic techniques into their own efforts to test mediation (Greenwald, 1979).

Returning to the issue at hand, social psychology's debt to cognitive psychology is also reflected at the metatheoretical level. This higher level of borrowing also seems to be well placed. Departures from normative decision making (see, for example, Slovic & Lichtenstein, 1971) and attributional (see, Kelley, 1967) models have been so glaring, so extreme, and so persistent that a descriptive model is needed. That descriptive model, the person as cognitive miser, is not fully fleshed out, but suggests that people are capacity limited and must draw on already-stored knowledge to a greater extent than had been previously considered.

By implication, this metatheoretical shift should move us toward examining how knowledge is stored—that is, we can think of heuristics as knowledge-module getters and as sets of rules for going through the modules. What do the modularized knowledge structures (or schemas) look like? Despite the current popularity of the term "schema," research on schemas, particularly their content, has not for the most part materialized. The term has been invoked to explain certain processing phenomena, but actual focus on what the schemas look like and how social knowledge is stored has been almost completely lacking. An exception to this general pattern is the impressive work by Schank and Abelson (1977).[4] Their shift away from what is going on on-line to what modularized knowledge looks like is, I think, a good focus. An unfortunate aspect of the

---

[3]The apparent lack of success of verbal-protocol analysis in social–psychological investigation stands in sharp contrast to its success in other areas, such as cognitive research (see, for example, Newell & Simon, 1972), in ethnomethodology (Garfinkle, 1967), and in anthropology (Agar, 1980).

[4]The work of Gordon Bower and his colleagues on scripts and stories is also a significant exception (see, for example, Bower, Black, & Turner, 1979).

Schank and Abelson work is that because this job is so very difficult and because so many of the issues raised are specific to the method involved—namely, artificial intelligence—rather than the problem involved—namely, social knowledge—the issues that currently occupy people in artificial intelligence are likely to be of little, if any, interest to social psychologists. Thus, whereas the emphasis of the people in artificial intelligence seems to be well placed, their products, at least at the present, are of limited value to us.

Does this mean that we should take on the schemas problem using our own methods and research? It is not clear. At least one prominent psychologist in social cognition has suggested that there will be little payoff in trying to study the structure of schemas. He suggests (L. Ross, 1979) first that such knowledge is too idiosyncratic to be studied across persons because it would have little generalizability. He also suggests that we should study what we can study, and that at this point neither our methods nor our thinking is sufficiently well developed to enable us to make any reasonable statements about the structure of knowledge. My own feeling is that we really have not made much of an effort to do this yet, and that before we become too pessimistic about the usefulness of research on schemas, we should at least see whether or not there is enough commonality in knowledge structures to make it advantageous to study them. One particularly promising direction in this line seems to be looking at incomplete versus complete knowledge structures (see, for example, Fiske & Kinder, 1981).[5]

To summarize, social psychology's debt to cognitive psychology is substantial and reflected at all levels of the research endeavor. The interface of the two fields is also helping to point out new directions for theory and research.

THE SOCIAL PSYCHOLOGY–COGNITIVE PSYCHOLOGY INTERFACE: COGNITIVE PSYCHOLOGY'S DEBT TO SOCIAL PSYCHOLOGY

The debt that cognitive psychology owes social psychology may be less apparent. I see three major contributions of social psychology to cognitive psychology: first, the benefits of testing cognitive hypotheses in real-world settings; second, the discovery of important cognitive constructs such as the causal attribution and beliefs about control that have significance in social environments; third, the

---

[5]There are at least two ways of approaching this problem; one would be to study the development of schemas as individuals are acquiring more and more information. Another would be a cross-sectional analysis of schemas based on individual experience. In other words, if we focus on people at different stages of learning in knowledge structures, we may thereby have some greater sense of how knowledge structures develop and change with experience (see Taylor & Crocker, 1981, for a review of this literature).

ability of social psychology to act as a translator between cognitive psychology and other, more applied disciplines.

Perhaps social psychology's greatest contribution to cognitive psychology, one that is not yet fully exploited, is its ability to test out a number of important cognitive relationships with ecologically valid stimulus materials. In cognitive experiments, stimulus materials are typically impoverished, and it is difficult to know the extent to which stimuli, dependent measures, and findings can be generalized to real-world settings. Social-psychological research has suggested that many can. In our work, for example, we have borrowed from the literature on attention and salience (see, for example, Kahneman, 1973) and have applied these ideas to understanding perceptions of distinctive or unusual people in the social environment, for example, solo Blacks or women in token integration situations or physically disabled people (Taylor, Fiske, Close, Anderson, & Ruderman, 1975). Hamilton and Gifford (1976) have suggested that illusory correlation can explain some aspects of stereotyping social groups.

However, cognitive psychology could be borrowing more from social psychology in this area than it has. Occasionally, I detect in my cognitive colleagues a bemused tolerance of social cognition, as if cognitive research were the "real" hard stuff, and social cognition the fluff that does little more than show how cognitive phenomena generalize. In fact, as Greenwald (1979) points out, social extensions of cognitive phenomena are essential to the cognitive endeavor; without them, it is impossible to know if the results of cognitive experiments reflect anything real about behavior or are merely artifacts of the stilted laboratory paradigms employed.

Unfortunately, social psychologists, too, have not always recognized that one of the chief contributions they make to cognitive psychology is testing out relationships in ecologically valid settings. Rather, in some cases, we have borrowed not only the constructs and the metatheory from cognitive psychology, but the stimulus materials as well. Although in some cases this has paid off in precision of inferences, to the extent that contrived, reduced materials persist as a substitute for the exploration of a socially rich phenomenon, we may miss a great deal that is important. At the risk of irritating a number of friends, I would suggest that person-memory experiments are a particularly good example of a procedure with low ecological validity that has failed to provide us with particularly good information about how people are actually perceived and represented by others. For example, some recent work (Cantor & Mischel, 1979; Taylor, 1981) suggests that people may perceive others more in terms of roles than traits, but because person-memory experiments typically involve learning lists of trait adjectives about a hypothetical person, this paradigm would miss the level at which persons are being categorized (see also Hamilton, Katz, & Leirer, 1980, for an expansion of these criticisms). Thus, what we may have done in many person-memory studies is borrowed the paradigm from cognitive psychology with few of the advantages of the social application. If cognitive paradigms are to be employed in elucidating some defined problem, we should define the range of phenomena that can be studied successfully through these stilted paradigms and develop alternative paradigms that can be employed simultaneously to tap some of the more rich and more social qualities of the same problem.

A second advantage of using social settings to test cognitive hypotheses is that, by virtue of their complexity, they provide the potential for helping to define the boundaries of the cognitive phenomena. For example, a given hypothesis can be examined in a number of social settings to see how well it holds up or to see what the characteristics of the settings are in which the relationship is strongest and weakest. As a consequence, social investigations also expand the range of dependent variables that are studied. In a cognitive experiment on object perception, only a certain number of dependent variables are appropriate. It does not make sense to ask, for example, whether objects are perceived as causally important in the environment, but it does make sense to ask that question about people. In our salience research, for example, we find that people are seen as more prominent and more influential in their social environment when they have been salient. Thus, social psychologists can expand the range of judgments that are relevant to a given cognitive phenomenon to address important social issues such as causal attributions, evaluations, and impressions.

Perhaps most important in this context, the social arena often provides a setting for examining behavioral consequences of social inferences. Ultimately, we want to predict not only other cognitions but behaviors as well. Because cognitive judgments frequently do not predict behavior very well (e.g., Schuman & Johnson, 1976), it is especially important to be able to determine the circumstances when they do.

Finally, taking cognitive hypotheses into the social environment often elucidates intrinsically interesting social phenomena as it tests theory. For example, work on perceived control has illuminated the plight of the institutionalized aged (Langer & Rodin, 1976; Schulz, 1976). Work on attributions of responsibility has informed us about the world of paraplegics and quadriplegics (Bulman & Wortman, 1977), and our own work on salience has addressed the dynamics of token integrations (see, for example, Taylor, Fiske, Close, Anderson, & Ruderman, 1975).

A second major contribution of social psychology to cognitive psychology has been the development of a unique set of theoretical constructs for understanding how people cognize their world. Within the cognitive literature, emphasis has focused on such judgments as predictions and frequency estimates. The social psychologists have contributed at least two central constructs—one being the causal attribution, and the other being the perception of control. The causal attribution has been found to mediate perceptions in a wide variety of situations ranging from interpersonal attraction (see Kelley, 1967), loneliness (see Peplau, Russell, & Heim, 1979), victimization (see Wortman, 1976), physical symptoms (see Pennebaker & Skelton, 1978), and achievement behavior (see Weiner,

1974). For example, from the Peplau et al. (1979) work, we know that lonely people who attribute their loneliness to personal failings report making fewer efforts to meet people than those who do not. Attributions of perceived control and whether or not one has control can affect reactions to emotional disorders (e.g., Ross, Rodin, & Zimbardo, 1975), to physical disorders (Johnson & Leventhal, 1974), and to institutionalization (Langer & Rodin, 1976; Schulz, 1976). For example, we know that people who understand the rationale for a noxious medical procedure and hence feel in control tolerate its noxious side effects somewhat better (Johnson & Leventhal, 1974). A review of these literatures is prohibitive here, but they have generated more excitement and research in social psychology than any other phenomena of recent years.

The payoffs of these ideas for cognitive psychology, however, may be indirect. There is little, if any, evidence that cognitive psychologists have jumped on either the attribution or the control bandwagon. In fact, the concepts are not particularly appropriate ones for understanding cognitive judgments about simple stimulus materials. However, a number of other disciplines have borrowed heavily from control and attribution literatures and, by implication, from cognitive psychology as well. Clinical psychologists have maintained that judgments of control and attribution are important elements in whether or not an individual is likely to be improved by treatment (Johnson & Leventhal, 1974; Ross, Rodin, & Zimbardo, 1975). Bandura's (1977) model of self efficacy gives cognitive judgments regarding one's ability to engage in certain skills, central status. Hardly a week goes by without someone from another discipline, such as medicine, education, or social work, asking me to recommend attribution or control articles that they can use to understand some specific social problem. For example, just recently, I had a call from a physician asking me what there was on patients' attributions for their illnesses, because he felt that the tone of the initial clinical interview was strongly determined by patients' causal preconceptions about their illnesses. Thus, social psychology has functioned as a way station or a translator, putting cognitive hypotheses into terms that are usable by other disciplines.

It may be, then, that we are fated always to borrow in one direction. The social psychologists borrow from the cognitive psychologists without being able to give as much back, but they are in turn able to pass on the advantages of a cognitive perspective to practically oriented and applied disciplines such as medicine, education, or more relevant to this conference, architecture and planning.[6]

Having sung the praises of the social–cognitive liaison, the next task is to probe its potential liabilities, particularly those that result from inadvertently adopting implicit assumptions.

---

[6]To borrow a metaphor from the Nashville night life, we can think of the relations among the field as that among gypsies, tramps, and thieves, the cognitive psychologists acting as the gypsies, the social psychologists as the tramps, and the more applied disciplines as the thieves.

SOME LIABILITIES OF THE COGNITIVE–SOCIAL
INTERFACE

The extent to which social cognition has found its way into other disciplines is tremendously exciting, but it also gives cause for nervousness. Our constructs may not be able to deliver everything we say they can. For example, I am particularly nervous that we are holding out the same hope for the attribution that we once did for the attitude, as to its ability to predict behavior, and that this will be problematic in the applications of the attribution construct. For example, Abramson, Seligman, and Teasdale (1978) have given the causal attribution a central role in their revised theory of learned helplessness. Barsky and Stoeckle (1977) have suggested that attributions for a disease may be a primary determinant of how patients react to their illness. Many of these analyses are theoretically elegant and extremely promising in their behavioral implications. However, if we have learned anything from the attitude change literature, and more specifically from the attitude-behavior relationship, it should be that there is a very low correspondence between the two. If we look at the attribution–behavior relationship in even the most stilted of laboratory studies, it is clear that exactly the same situation exists. The relationship is weak; we have known this for years. As early as 1972, Nisbett and Valins attempted to salvage the attribution-behavior relationship with reference to the concept of hypothesis testing, and empirical evidence continues to suggest that the attribution–behavior relationship is extremely weak.

Wortman and Dintzer (1978) raise this point in their gentle but telling critique of Abramson et al. (1978), warning that something as apparently fragile as an attribution may not be the best central explanatory concept for a phenomenon as persistent and powerful as depression. I would like to underscore their point here and suggest that, under most circumstances, attributions do not predict behavior very well. Accordingly, we must be extremely cautious when we act as a translator to more applied disciplines and remind them that these constructs are not likely to do everything for them that they hope.[7]

A second general problem in social-cognition research is, exactly what is mediating what? Put another way, exactly why do we assume that cognitive judgments mediate affective ones? For illustrative purposes, consider the dependent variable of recall. Recall has had a fairly interesting fate in social-psychological experiments.[8] Researchers have used recall as an effort to measure

---

[7]That causal attributions or beliefs about control are very fragile can be seen if one thinks about an important situation, such as a personal relationship; the enormous number of explanations one can come up with for its rough or smooth course at any given time and the great fluidity of one's take on the issue that comes from talking it over with others or thinking about it suggests that most important events will be attributionally overjustified.

[8]Interestingly enough, the imaging construct has had a fate almost identical to that of recall in the social-cognition literature. Originally invoked as the possible mediator between stimuli and corre-

attention and the amount of information absorbed about a particular portion of the environment. A straightforward cognitive argument is that volume of recall should mediate subsequent judgments, such as the extremity or the confidence with which they are held. A number of efforts to look at recall as this kind of mediator have failed. Research by McArthur (1981), by Taylor and Fiske (summarized in 1978), by Anderson and Hubert (1963), and by Dreben, Fiske, and Hastie (in press) all suggest that recall measures are, at least under some circumstances, relatively autonomous of affective judgments. Because most of these investigations have begun with the assumption that volume of recall is mediating subsequent judgments, the absence of a correlation between the two is, to say the least, problematic (see also Fiske, Chapter 12 in this volume).

This point raises two additional issues, one having to do with what constitutes a good test of mediation and the other having to do with whether or not cognitive processes mediate affective judgments. On the first point, many of the experiments that have employed cognitive measures as well as more social, affective measures have found predicted changes in both. Because the investigation begins with the assumption that cognitive processes are mediating the affective ones, parallel differences on both kinds of measures have been taken as support for that position. However, no evidence for mediation beyond this point has been presented. It may be that affective processes are in fact mediating the cognitive ones, or that both the cognitive and the affective judgments are mediated by some third set of variables. Accordingly, we have been a little lax in testing specific elements of our mediational models, a problem that should be redressed if we propose to continue assuming that cognitive processes are mediating social judgments.

The second reason for attending closely to the failure of recall to covary with social judgments is that it may raise serious questions for the general relationship between cognitive and affective variables. Zajonc (1979), for example, has conducted a series of studies indicating that affective judgments are made more quickly and with greater confidence than cognitive ones. For example, he shows that people can answer the question, "Do you like this?", an evaluative judgment, faster than they can answer the question, "Have you see this before?", a simple cognitive judgment of recognition. Data like these, which suggest the temporal priority of affective judgments, make it very unlikely that recognition is mediating liking.[9] More generally, we have always assumed that cognitive pro-

sponding strong impressions (see Taylor & Fiske, 1978), measures of success of imaging and measures of social perception presumably mediated by imaging have shown virtually no relationship to each other (see Fiske, Taylor, Etcoff, & Laufer, 1979).

[9]Zajonc has taken a particularly strong stand in the interpretation of these data and has suggested that the affective system and the cognitive system may be relatively independent of each other in the brain. If this is true, it would cause us to seriously requestion the nature of our cognitive models of social behavior.

cesses are mediating more evaluative ones. We may well have to rethink that relationship.

A third general set of criticisms of the social–cognitive liaison focuses on the type of research and theory social cognition has generated. One liability of social cognition is that it is easy to do badly. There are lots of cognitive hypotheses lying around that can be directly applied to interesting social situations. Accordingly, it is simple to do an interesting piece of research by taking a rather commonplace cognitive hypothesis and applying it in a rather interesting social situation. Thus, the borrowing can be rather straightforward without much creativity involved on the part of the researcher. More effort could be devoted to examining precisely what factors in the social situation are not addressed by the cognitive hypothesis or what is uniquely social about the manifestation of this process, rather than simply relying on cognitive psychology to provide theory, constructs, paradigm, and measures, reserving only the setting as social.

A second problem is that we have not adequately defined the domain of situations to which our cognitively based hypotheses apply. This is less problematic in cognitive settings, because one is not tempted to make widespread, far-reaching associations on the basis of a simple cognitive experiment. However, when one tests a cognitive hypothesis in a social environment, the *apparent* generalizability of the effects may be extremely great and, accordingly, people may be more likely to overgeneralize the phenomena. We need to do a better job of binding our phenomena and defining the contextual factors that influence the powerfulness of the phenomenon in a given domain.

A third problem in social cognition is the lack of theory. Despite the fact that cognitive consistency theory may not have a particularly good scorecard at this stage, it had the effect of defining a number of research directions, a heuristic function of generating research, and the potential to give rise to a number of intrinsically interesting subphenomena. The dictum that there is nothing as practical as a good theory was never more fully represented as in the consistency literature. The presence of at least a working theory, if not a good theory of cognitive consistency, also provided grounds for disconfirmation of the theory, and although cognitive consistency theory eventually produced its own downfall, at least it built in the criteria for so doing. The fact that we have no overarching theoretical approach in social cognition at this point, but rather only a metatheory, suggests that although we may have the bases for generating considerable research in interesting social settings, we have not built in the basis for falsifying our own phenomena. Accordingly, the current state in social cognition can proliferate unimpeded until such time as we are able to formulate an adequate theory that will lead to its own downfall. This is one area in which we could borrow from the cognitive psychologists but have not. Cognitive psychologists do a lot more model testing and competitive model testing (see Estes, 1975) than we do, and pressure to do so forces them to specify their models more fully than we do. Our theories, such as they are, are too loose.

Finally, in our haste to borrow relationships from cognitive psychology, we are not letting substantive content direct social psychology as much as we might. There are intrinsically interesting social phenomena that ought in themselves to constitute the basis of empirical inquiry. However, we in social cognition tend to let the cognitive relationships direct the focus of the research rather than the substantive content area. Perhaps social psychology needs to return to grounded theory (Glaser & Strauss, 1967), an in-depth analysis of the phenomena themselves as the basis for the development of theory, instead of allowing the phenomena to be selected as possible examples of the particular cognitive phenomenon (cf. Agar, Chapter 2 in this volume). Obviously, one cannot reasonably argue for one to the exclusion of the other, but perhaps social psychology should strive for more of a balance between the two.

SOCIAL COGNITION'S VIEW OF THE PERSON: A SCRIPT FOR CAMUS?

The next issue I would like to discuss in some detail, because it addresses a set of interrelated concerns I have about social cognition. The focus of this concern is: As characterized by the research in social cognition, what kind of creature is our social perceiver? I see him as something out of a Camus novel: alone, bereft of language, without emotion, looking backwards at where he has been.

First, an old but still important theme is the issue of the role of affect in judgments. When the most significant events that happen in one's own life are affective ones, it is hard to justify an exclusively cognitive professional orientation. Furthermore, having moved away from the position that motivations and emotions are responsible for the errors in the cognitive system to a viewpoint that cognitive processes are responsible for many of these errors, we seem captivated by those cognitive errors and somewhat reluctant to study the motivational and emotional bases of either error-free or biased processing. A cold model of social behavior cannot persist very long. Continuing to ignore the important role of affect and motivation is likely to result in a pendulum swing back toward heavily motivational models, rather than in a synthesis of cognitive and motivational factors. If we can make further efforts toward bringing motivational factors back into our fundamentally cognitive analyses, we can hopefully avoid yet another swing of the social–psychological pendulum.[10]

A second problem in social cognition is our tendency to become less and less interactive. Presumably because cognitive psychology is noninteractive, social cognition is also noninteractive. We need to move beyond the conceptualization

---

[10]In actual fact, social cognition has always maintained at least a partial interest in "hot cognition," and so this criticism applies more strongly to cognitive psychology, especially work in artificial intelligence, than it does to our own efforts.

of the other person as a thing to models that can begin to specify elements of interaction and how we should go about understanding those. Indeed, we often forget that there are other ways of dealing with problems than thinking about them, particularly when those problems involve social interaction. What kinds of social problems are solved how? Particularly lacking in our models is a specification of the circumstances under which we think about problems to make judgments versus when we communicate about problems to make judgments.

Suppose I come home from my office one day and find a pair of dirty socks in the middle of my living room. How do I conclude who left them there? I can conceivably use Kelley-like processes to solve this problem and try to infer who left the socks there on the basis of who has been present when the socks have been left there before, has she or he always been present, and so on. Or, I could use heuristic processes and see whose name leaps to mind as I stare at the socks in the middle of my floor. Alternatively, I can yell, ''Who the hell left these socks in the middle of the living room?'' Put simply, there are a lot of circumstances in which the social perceiver is not mute; she or he will ask the questions that need asking.

I do not think this is as commonplace a criticism as it may sound. The features that would characterize a communications-based model of social cognition are very different from those that characterize a perceptual model, what we have at present. The former model is interactive and recursive, with feedback provided by one participant to another. Kidd (1978) has characterized this kind of approach as a ''negotiation model'' of social cognition. One can see easily that the questions that are posed by such an approach are different from those of a perceptual model. To take the specific example of script theory (Schank & Abelson, 1977), a perceptual model leads one to ask questions like, ''What is the script that an individual uses for this situation?'' An interactive model is more likely to ask, ''What will be the consequences when two participants in a situation have different scripts for it?'' Ethnographers and cognitive anthropologists often adopt this position, and the thrust of their efforts might be welcomed by social psychologists (cf. Freedle, Chapter 3 in this volume; Agar, Chapter 2 in this volume). A new focus on communication, then, is needed in social cognition (see, for example, Higgins, 1981), and we may well see a renaissance of interest in group process.

Finally, I am disturbed by how many of our theories in social cognition are reflective, rather than progressive. It is as if the social perceiver were always walking backwards, commenting on things that have already happened. We rarely adopt a future orientation that inquires as to our subject's goals and plans for reaching them. It is worth noting, in this context, that artificial-intelligence efforts to model social behavior conceive of the social perceiver as a goalful, planful being who is future oriented. My own work has now shifted to this focus and I am struck by how many very fundamental assumptions about social knowledge are questioned once this perspective is adopted.

My final feelings about social cognition represent little more than a vague unease, but I feel compelled to share them anyway. There seem to be a great many circumstances when we are doing one thing and our minds are off completely on their own doing something else. I am not merely saying that we are "mindless" about much of our behavior; much mindlessly performed behavior can be made mindful by simply catching oneself up. I am talking about the circumstances under which we are doing something and have absolutely no idea why. Perhaps I sound dangerously psychodynamic, but I see two possible bases for unease. One source of unease is a practical one. Although cognitive models do not require subject awareness or ability to verbalize what is going on either as a theoretical or as a methodological tool, many approaches in social cognition require both. Social-cognition researchers tend to rely rather heavily on cognitive constructs that are verbalizable (such as the causal attribution or beliefs about control), both because such constructs have theoretical significance (we have not yet acknowledged the unconscious causal attribution) and because on methodological grounds, arguments for mediation are more persuasive if there is independent evidence that the mediator exists. Because there is some basis for questionning whether people have conscious access to the reasons underlying their behavior (see Nisbett and Wilson, 1977), relying on verbal reports for evidence of mediation is risky. The second source of unease is more existential. I am convinced (as, I think, are some others in social cognition) that the mind continually keeps itself entertained and that perhaps we should not take it quite so seriously. It is always working, thinking a few profound thoughts and a great many remarkably silly ones. Many of these thoughts are accordingly completely inconsequential (albeit highly entertaining). To my mind, then, this poses a broader question, "When do we need social cognition and when should we ignore it?" I do not pretend to have any answers to this dilemma—I raise it as a caution. In short, not only do we need to bound our cognitive phenomenon, we may need to better define the boundaries of cognition itself.

CONCLUSIONS

To summarize, compared with 1975 when I first wrote about the interface of social and cognitive psychology, I now feel that there is much clearer evidence that such a marriage has actually taken place. It is not such a bad marriage either, although one partner is clearly more involved than the other. There have been a number of important developments in the field of social psychology that owe an enormous debt to cognitive psychology. If cognitive psychology correspondingly owes social psychology a major debt, that is less apparent, although there are clear ways in which cognitive psychology could profit from drawing on social psychology more. At present, social psychologists seem to be acting effectively as translators of cognitive relationships into social phenomena that are then used by other disciplines. However, it is also apparent that a number of problems in social cognition are being ignored as a result of the heavy borrowing from cognitive psychology. This is not in and of itself a basis for radically altering social cognition as a field; however, just as many marriages can be improved by greater independence between the partners, perhaps this one can too.

ACKNOWLEDGMENTS

Part of this chapter was written while the author was still at Harvard University. The chapter has been heavily influenced by David Hamilton, Reid Hastie, Richard Nisbett, David Sears, and Beau Sheil. However, these people do not share in the opinionated expression of these ideas, only in their genesis. I am also grateful to Tony Greenwald and Hsiao-Ti Falcone for their extended criticisms of an earlier draft. Preparation of this manuscript was facilitated by a grant from the National Science Foundation to the author (BNS 77-09922).

REFERENCES

Abramson, L. Y., Seligman, M. E. P., & Teasdale, J. D. Learned helplessness in humans: Critique and reformulation. *Journal of Abnormal Psychology*, 1978, *87*, 49–74.

Agar, M. H. *The professional stranger: An informal introduction to ethnography.* New York: Academic Press, 1980.

Allport, G. W. Attitudes. In C. Murchison (Ed.), *Handbook of social psychology.* Worcester, Mass.: Clark University Press, 1935.

Anderson, N. H., & Hubert, S. Effects of concomitant verbal recall on order effects in personality impression formation. *Journal of Verbal Learning and Verbal Behavior*, 1963, *2*, 379–391.

Aronson, E., & Carlsmith, J. M. Performance expectancy as a determinant of actual performance. *Journal of Abnormal and Social Psychology*, 1962, *65*(3), 178–182.

Aronson, E., & Mettee, D. R. Dishonest behaviors as a function of differential levels of induced self-esteem. *Journal of Personality and Social Psychology*, 1968, *9*, 121–127.

Bandura, A. Self-efficacy: Toward a unifying theory of behavioral change. *Psychological Review*, 1977, *84*, 191–215.

Barsky, A. J., & Stoeckle, J. D. *Explaining the cause of illness: Attribution in the tasks of care.* Unpublished manuscript, Harvard Medical School, 1977.

Bem, D. J. Self-perception theory. In L. Berkowitz (Ed.)., *Advances in experimental social psychology* (Vol. 6). New York: Academic Press, 1972.

Bower, G. H., Black, J. B., & Turner, T. J. Scripts in memory for text. *Cognitive Psychology*, 1979, *11*, 177–220.

Brewer, M. B. In-group bias in the minimal intergroup situation: A cognitive–motivational analysis. *Psychological Bulletin*, 1979, *86*, 307–323.

Bruner, J. S., & Goodman, C. C. Value and need as organizing factors in perception. *Journal of Abnormal and Social Psychology*, 1947, *42*, 33–44.

Bulman, R. J., & Wortman, C. B. Attributions of blame and coping in the "real world": Severe accident victims react to their lot. *Journal of Personality and Social Psychology*, 1977, *35*, 351–363.

Byrne, D., & Blalock, B. Similarity and assumed similarity of attitudes between husbands and wives. *Journal of Abnormal and Social Psychology*, 1963, *67*, 636–640.

Cantor, N., & Mischel, W. Prototypes in person perception. In L. Berkowitz (Ed.), *Advances in experimental social psychology* (Vol. 12). New York: Academic Press, 1979.

Dawes, R. Shallow psychology. In J. Carroll & J. Payne (Eds.), *Cognition and social behavior*. Hillsdale, N.J.: Lawrence Erlbaum Associates, 1976.

Dreben, E. K., Fiske, S. T., & Hastie, R. Impression and recall order effects in behavior based impression formation. *Journal of Experimental Social Psychology*, in press.

Estes, W. Some targets for mathematical psychology. *Journal of Mathematical Psychology*, 1975, *12*, 263-282.

Festinger, L. *A theory of cognitive dissonance*. Stanford, Calif.: Stanford University Press, 1957.

Fiske, S. T., & Kinder, D. R. Involvement, expertise, and schema use: Evidence from political cognition. In N. Cantor & J. Kihlstrom (Eds.), *Personality, cognition, and social interaction*. Hillsdale, N.J.: Lawrence Erlbaum Associates, 1981.

Fiske, S. T., Taylor, S. E., Etcoff, N., & Laufer, J. Imaging, empathy, and causal attribution. *Journal of Experimental Social Psychology*, 1979, *15*, 356-377.

Garfinkle, H. *Studies in ethnomethodology*. Englewood Cliffs, N.J.: Prentice-Hall, 1967.

Garland, H., Hardy, A., & Stephenson, L. Information search as affected by attribution type and response category. *Personality and Social Psychology Bulletin*, 1975, *1*, 612-615.

Glaser, B. G., & Strauss, A. L. *The discovery of grounded theory: Strategies for qualitative research*. Hawthorne, N.Y.: Aldine, 1967.

Greenwald, A. G. Personal communication, May 17, 1979.

Hamill, R., Wilson, T. D., & Nisbett, R. E. Insensitivity to sample bias: Generalizing from atypical cases. *Journal of Personality and Social Psychology*, 1980, *39*, 578-589.

Hamilton, D. L., & Gifford, R. K. Illusory correlation in interpersonal perception: A cognitive basis of stereotypic judgments. *Journal of Experimental Social Psychology*, 1976, *12*, 392-407.

Hamilton, D. L., Katz, L. B., & Leirer, V. O. Organizational processes in impression formation. In R. Hastie, T. Ostrom, E. Ebbesen, R. Wyer, D. Hamilton, & D. Carlston (Eds.), *Person memory and encoding processes*. Hillsdale, N.J.: Lawrence Erlbaum Associates, 1980.

Heider, F. *The psychology of interpersonal relations*. New York: Wiley, 1958.

Higgins, E. T. The "Communication Game": Implications for social cognition. In E. T. Higgins, C. P. Herman, & M. P. Zanna (Eds.), *Social cognition: The Ontario symposium* (Vol. 1). Hillsdale, N.J.: Lawrence Erlbaum Associates, 1981.

Johnson, J., & Leventhal, H. Effects of accurate expectations and behavioral instructions on reactions during a noxious medical examination. *Journal of Personality and Social Psychology*, 1974, *29*, 710-718.

Jones, E. E., & Davis, K. E. From acts to dispositions: The attribution process in person perception. In L. Berkowitz (Ed.), *Advances in experimental social psychology* (Vol. 2). New York: Academic Press, 1965.

Kahneman, D. *Attention and effort*. Englewood Cliffs, N.J.: Prentice-Hall, 1973.

Kahneman, D., & Tversky, A. On the psychology of prediction. *Psychological Review*, 1973, *80*, 237-251.

Kelley, H. H. Attribution theory in social psychology. In D. Levine (Ed.), *Nebraska symposium on motivation* (Vol. 15). Lincoln: University of Nebraska Press, 1967.

Kenny, D. A. *Correlation and causality*. New York: Wiley, 1979.

Kidd, R. Personal communication, March, 1978.

Kiesler, C. A., Collins, B. E., & Miller, N. *Attitude change: A critical analysis of theoretical approaches*. New York: Wiley, 1969.

Langer, E. J. Rethinking the role of thought in social interaction. In J. H. Harvey, W. J. Ickes, & R. R. Kidd (Eds.), *New directions in attribution research* (Vol. 2). Hillsdale, N.J.: Lawrence Erlbaum Associates, 1978.

Langer, E. J., & Rodin, J. The effects of choice and enhanced personal responsibility for the aged: A field experiment in an institutional setting. *Journal of Personality and Social Psychology*, 1976, *34*, 191-198.

Langer, E. J., Taylor, S. E., Fiske, S. T., & Chanowitz, B. Stigma, staring and discomfort: A novel stimulus hypothesis. *Journal of Experimental Social Psychology,* 1976, *12,* 451–463.

Lewin, K. *Principles of topological psychology.* New York: McGraw-Hill, 1936.

Lingle, J. H., & Ostrom, T. M. Retrieval selectivity in memory-based impression judgments. *Journal of Personality and Social Psychology,* 1979, *37,* 180–194.

McArthur, L. Z. What grabs you? The role of attention in impression formation and causal attribution. In E. T. Higgins, C. P. Herman, & M. P. Zanna (Eds.), *Social cognition: The Ontario symposium* (Vol. 1). Hillsdale, N.J.: Lawrence Erlbaum Associates, 1981.

McGuire, W. J. Nature of attitudes and attitude change. In G. Lindzey & E. Aronson (Eds.), *Handbook of social psychology.* Reading, Mass.: Addison-Wesley, 1968.

Miller, D. T., & Ross, M. Self-serving biases in the attribution of causality: Fact or fiction? *Psychological Bulletin,* 1975, *82,* 213–225.

Newell, A., & Simon, H. A. *Human problem solving.* Englewood Cliffs, N.J.: Prentice-Hall, 1972.

Nisbett, R. E., & Borgida, E. Attribution and the psychology of prediction. *Journal of Personality and Social Psychology,* 1975, *32,* 932–943.

Nisbett, R. E., & Valins, S. Perceiving the causes of one's own behavior. In E. E. Jones, D. E. Kanouse, H. H. Kelley, R. E. Nisbett, S. Valins, & B. Weiner (Eds.), *Attribution: Perceiving the causes of behavior.* Morristown, N.J.: General Learning Press, 1972.

Nisbett, R. E., & Wilson, T. D. Telling more than we can know: Verbal reports on mental processes. *Psychological Review,* 1977, *84,* 231–259.

Osgood, C. E., & Tannenbaum, P. H. The principle of congruity in the prediction of attitude change. *Psychological Review,* 1955, *62,* 42–55.

Pennebaker, J. W., & Skelton, J. A. Psychological parameters of physical symptoms. *Personality and Social Psychology Bulletin,* 1978, *4,* 524–530.

Peplau, L. A., Russell, D., & Heim, M. An attributional analysis of loneliness. In I. Frieze, D. Bar-Tal, & J. Carroll (Eds.), *Attribution theory: Applications to social problems.* San Francisco: Jossey-Bass, 1979.

Pryor, J. B., & Kriss, M. The cognitive dynamics of salience in the attribution process. *Journal of Personality and Social Psychology,* 1977, *35,* 49–55.

Ross, L. The intuitive psychologist and his shortcomings: Distortions in the attribution process. In L. Berkowitz (Ed.), *Advances in experimental social psychology* (Vol. 10). New York: Academic Press, 1977.

Ross, L. Personal communication, April, 1979.

Ross, L., Rodin, J., & Zimbardo, P. G. Toward an attribution therapy: The reduction of fear through induced cognitive–emotional misattribution. *Journal of Personality and Social Psychology,* 1975, *32,* 245–254.

Rotter, J. B. Generalized expectancies for internal versus external control of reinforcement. *Psychological Monographs,* 1966, *80,* 1–28.

Schachter, S., & Singer, J. Cognitive, social, and physiological determinants of emotional state. *Psychological Review,* 1962, *69,* 379–399.

Schank, R., & Abelson, R. *Scripts, plans, goals, and understanding: An inquiry into human knowledge structures.* Hillsdale, N.J.: Lawrence Erlbaum Associates, 1977.

Schulz, R. The effects of control and predictability on the psychological and physical well-being of the institutionalized aged. *Journal of Personality and Social Psychology,* 1976, *33,* 563–573.

Schuman, H., & Johnson, M. Attitudes and behavior. In A. Inkeles (Ed.), *Annual review of sociology* (Vol. 2). Palo Alto, Calif.: Annual Review, 1976.

Shaver, K. G. *An introduction to the attribution processes.* Cambridge, Mass.: Winthrop, 1975.

Sheil, B. A. *Theories of naive psychology, or naive theories of psychology? An analysis of the attribution movement.* Unpublished manuscript, Harvard University, 1974.

Simon, H. A. *Models of man.* New York: Wiley, 1957.

Slovic, P., & Lichtenstein, S. Comparison of Bayesian and regression approaches to the study of human information processing in judgment. *Organizational Behavior and Human Performance,* 1971, *6,* 649–744.

Smith, E., & Miller, F. Salience and the cognitive mediation of attribution. *Journal of Personality and Social Psychology,* 1979, *37,* 2240–2252.

Tajfel, H. Social categorization. In S. Moscovici (Ed.), *Introduction à la psychologie sociale.* Paris: Larousse, 1972.

Taylor, S. E. The development of cognitive social psychology. In J. Carroll & J. Payne (Eds.), *Cognition and social behavior.* Lawrence Erlbaum Associates, 1976.

Taylor, S. E. A categorization approach to stereotyping. In D. L. Hamilton (Ed.)., *Cognitive processes in stereotyping and intergroup behavior.* Hillsdale, N.J.: Lawrence Erlbaum Associates, 1981.

Taylor, S. E., & Crocker, J. Schematic bases of social information processing. In E. T. Higgins, P. Herman, & M. P. Zanna (Eds.), *Social cognition: The Ontario symposium* (Vol. 1). Hillsdale, N.J.: Lawrence Erlbaum Associates, 1981.

Taylor, S. E., & Fiske, S. T. Getting inside the head: Methodologies for process analysis in attribution and social cognition. To appear in J. Harvey, W. Ickes, & R. Kidd (Eds.), *New directions in attribution research,* Vol. 3. Hillsdale, N.J.: Lawrence Erlbaum, 1981.

Taylor, S. E., & Fiske, S. T. Salience, attention, and attribution: Top of the head phenomena. In L. Berkowitz (Ed.), *Advances in experimental social psychology* (Vol. 2). New York: Academic Press, 1978.

Taylor, S. E., Fiske, S. T., Close, M., Anderson, C., & Ruderman, A. *Solo status as a psychological variable: The power of being distinctive.* Unpublished paper, Harvard University, 1975.

Taylor, S. E., Fiske, S. T., Etcoff, N., & Ruderman, A. The categorical and contextual bases of person memory and stereotyping. *Journal of Personality and Social Psychology,* 1978, *36,* 778–793.

Tversky, A., & Kahneman, D. Judgment under uncertainty: Heuristics and biases. *Science,* 1974, *185,* 1124–1131.

Weiner, B. (Ed.). *Achievement motivation and attribution theory.* Morristown, N.J.: General Learning Press, 1974.

Wilder, D. A. Categorization and intergroup bias. In D. L. Hamilton (Ed.), *Cognitive processes in stereotyping and intergroup behavior.* Hillsdale, N.J.: Lawrence Erlbaum Associates, 1981.

Wortman, C. B. Causal attributions and personal control. In J. H. Harvey, W. J. Ickes, &. R. F. Kidd (Eds.), *New directions in attribution research.* Hillsdale, N.J.: Lawrence Erlbaum Associates, 1976.

Wortman, C. B., & Dintzer, L. Is an attributional analysis of the learned helplessness phenomenon viable?: A critique of the Abramson-Seligman-Teasdale reformulation. *Journal of Abnormal Psychology,* 1978, *87,* 75–90.

Zajonc, R. B. Feeling and thinking: Preferences need no inferences. *American Psychologist,* 1980, *35,* 151–175.

11 The Role of Cognitive, Affective, and Social Factors in Attributional Biases

Gifford Weary
Ohio State University

Attribution theories frequently view people as logical information processors, "intuitive scientists," gathering information and drawing inferences in an attempt to understand the causes of their own and others' behaviors. Moreover, all attributional approaches to self and other perception assume that the underlying causes of behavior can be inferred with some degree of validity from an examination of the behavior and the context in which it occurred.

Frequently, however, attributional processes appear to be less than logical and, in fact, appear to be systematically biased (see Ross, 1977, for an overview of attributional biases). For example, Jones and Nisbett (1972) have suggested that due to differences in information and visual perspective, "there is a pervasive tendency for actors to attribute their actions to situational requirements, whereas observers tend to attribute the same actions to stable personal dispositions [p. 80]." Although evidence suggests that this hypothesized actor–observer bias may not be quite as pervasive as Jones and Nisbett originally suggested (Monson & Synder, 1977), it has received considerable empirical confirmation (Harvey, Harris, & Barnes, 1975; Nisbett, Caputo, Legant, & Maracek, 1973). Other biases in causal judgments have been suggested in the literature, but have not been systematically investigated. For example, Jones and Davis (1965) proposed that the attribution process may be distorted by the attributor's personal needs. These authors suggested that attributors are more likely to make dispositional inferences about an actor if the actor's behavior (1) is uniquely conditioned by the attributor's presence; or (2) is hedonically relevant (i.e., results in positive or negative consequences) to the attributor.

The investigation of such biases in causal attributions is of importance primarily because it may help us to elucidate basic attributional processes. It is, therefore, not surprising that much recent theoretical and empirical work has been concerned with the source and operation of systematic biases in attributions of causality (e.g., Miller & Ross, 1975; Ross, 1977; Taylor & Fiske, 1978; Weary Bradley, 1978). Perhaps because attribution theorists have emphasized the fundamentally cognitive nature of mechanisms involved in self and interpersonal perception, most writers interested in attributional processes have stressed the importance of informational as opposed to motivational sources of bias. This information-processing approach to understanding attributional biases has received considerable sympathy. Indeed, Lee Ross (1977) has advocated that we *abandon* motivational concerns and concentrate on informational, perceptual, and cognitive factors that may account for systematic biases in attributions of causality. Other writers, however, have urged a more balanced approach in investigating potential mediating causes of attributional biases, noting that the most reasonable theory of the causal inference process will most likely involve a precise articulation of the interaction of motivation and cognition (e.g., Shaver, 1975; Weary Bradley, 1978).

Much of the controversy surrounding the existence of cognitive versus motivational distortions in attributional processes has focused on research related to the tendency for actors to assume greater causal responsibility for positive than for negative outcomes attendant to their behaviors. The operation of self-serving, or defensive, motivations has generally been used to explain these positive-negative outcome asymmetries in self-attributions (Weary Bradley, 1978). That is, it has been argued that under certain conditions, individuals may be able to enhance or protect their esteem by taking credit for good outcomes and by denying blame for bad outcomes attendant to their behaviors.

This chapter examines several cognitive, affective, and social factors that may account for apparently self-serving attributional biases. Focus of attention has been proposed as one possible explanation of systematic distortions in self-perception and attribution (Duval & Wicklund, 1973; Taylor & Fiske, 1978). It has been suggested that the locus of causal attribution is primarily a function of focus of attention. According to this attentional hypothesis, if attention is directed toward the self, self-attributions of causality for an outcome should be exaggerated regardless of the affective quality, or valence, of the outcome. One purpose of this chapter is to examine the empirical evidence for and against the proposed relationship between self-focused attention and self-attributions. This chapter also discusses how focus of attention may act in conjunction with biases in availability of information and motivational processes to influence attributions of causality. Finally, because self-serving attributions presumably function to enhance and protect self-esteem, empirical evidence suggesting that self-serving attributional biases play a role in individuals' adjustments to stressful environmental conditions is examined.

FOCUS OF ATTENTION AS A DETERMINANT OF
CAUSAL ATTRIBUTIONS

In an important paper, Taylor and Fiske (1978) have argued that the locus of perceived causality is determined primarily by where one's attention is directed within the environment and that attention is itself a function of what information is salient. According to this "psychology of salience," then, one's self-attributions of causal influence will be exaggerated to the degree that one regards himself or herself as the object of his or her own attention (i.e., to the degree that the self is made salient).

Duval and Wicklund (1973) also have proposed that the locus of causal attribution is primarily a function of focus of attention. These authors (Duval & Wicklund, 1973) have proposed that conscious attention is directed either toward the self, resulting in a state of objective self-awareness, or toward external events. According to Duval and Wicklund, the direction of conscious attention is determined (1) by social and nonsocial stimuli that draw attention inward, such as reflections of the self or the attention of an audience on some aspect of the self; and (2) by stimuli that draw attention outward, such as distracting lights or sounds. To the extent that a stimulus draws attention toward the self and creates a state of objective self-awareness, self-attribution of causality will presumably be exaggerated (Duval & Wicklund, 1973).

The findings of studies designed to test the focus of attention-locus of causal attribution hypothesis have provided some support for the general notion that self-focused attention leads to greater self-attributions of causal influence. In an early study, Duval and Wicklund (1973) tested their focus of attention hypothesis by asking subjects to estimate the extent to which they were responsible for the negative outcomes of several hypothetical situations. In all situations, either the subject or another person was potentially responsible for the hypothetical outcome. As predicted, subjects who were exposed to a stimulus designed to increase self-focused attention (mirror condition) attributed significantly greater responsibility for the hypothetical outcomes to themselves than did subjects who were not exposed to the stimulus (no mirror condition).

In a second study, Duval and Wicklund (1973, Study 2) examined the relationship between self-focused attention and self-attributions of causality for positive and negative outcomes. Specifically, under conditions of high or low self-focused attention, subjects were asked to estimate the extent to which they were responsible for positive or negative outcomes of several hypothetical events. As predicted, under conditions of high self-focused attention, subjects attributed more causal responsibilitiy to themselves than did subjects under conditions of low self-focused attention, regardless of the valence of the outcome.

Although the results of Duval and Wicklund's (1973) study suggest that focus of attention will influence attributions independent of the affective quality, or valence, of the outcome of an event, a study conducted by Federoff and Harvey

(1976) casts some doubt upon the generality of this focus of attention hypothesis. In their study, Federoff and Harvey used a highly involving, behavioral situation to examine the effects on attributions of causality of subjects' expectancies about the outcome of an event and observation of the actual outcome while in a state of high or low self-focused attention. Specifically, in the presence (high self-focused attention) or absence (low self-focused attention) of a camera, subjects delivered therapeutic instructions that were expected to have a positive or a negative effect and that produced a positive or negative effect on supposedly phobic patients. Federoff and Harvey (1976) reported that in high self-focused attention conditions, subjects' self-attributions of causality were greater for positive than for negative observed therapy outcomes. In the low self-focused attention conditions, subjects' self-attributions did not differ as a function of expected or observed outcome. Overall, the data showed no evidence for a main effect of focus of attention upon attributions of causality to self.

In discussing their findings, Federoff and Harvey (1976) suggested that self-focused attention may have exaggerated the arousal of self-esteem motives produced by the observed outcome manipulation. As a consequence, subjects in a state of high self-focused attention accepted more credit for a positive than for a negative outcome (i.e., made more self-serving attributions), whereas these tendencies may have been much less pronounced when subjects experienced a state of low self-focused attention.

In another experiment, using a procedure similar to that used by Federoff and Harvey, I (Weary, 1980) manipulated therapist subjects' perceptions of expected (positive or negative) and actual (positive or negative) therapy outcomes. In addition, subjects were asked to deliver the therapeutic instructions in the presence (high publicity) or absence (low publicity) of an observer. Although this study was not designed specifically to test the relationship between self-focused attention and self-attribution, it should be noted that the presence of an audience has successfully been used to create a set toward self attention (Carver & Scheier, 1978; Wicklund, 1975).

As predicted from a self-esteem model of responsibility attribution, I found that subjects accepted more causal responsibility for positive than for negative outcomes (i.e., subjects made seemingly self-serving attributions). Moreover, these positive–negative outcome attributional differences were more pronounced under high publicity (high self-focused attention) conditions. This was due primarily to the observed tendency for high publicity subjects to accept less responsibility than low publicity subjects for the negative outcome.

Hull and Levy (1979) also have reported a study that demonstrates that the locus of causal attribution is not determined by self-focused attention per se, but rather depends on the evaluative aspects of the attributional environment. Specifically, these authors (Hull & Levy, 1979) argued that self-awareness "involves an increased sensitivity to the situationally defined meaning of one's actions and, as such, entails a greater responsivity to the presentational constraints and evaluative connotations of self-attributed responsibility [p. 766]." In line with this emphasis on the influence of the attributional context, two recent studies (Frey, 1978; Weary, Harvey, Perloff, Schweiger, & Olson, 1979) have provided evidence suggesting that when performance outcomes and attributions are known and may be called into question by others, individuals feel vulnerable about reporting attributions that appear self-serving. Under such conditions, individuals tend to accept more responsibility for negative outcomes than they do when their performance outcomes and interpretive activities are more private. According to Hull and Levy (1979), self-awareness should be associated with a heightened sensitivity to just these kinds of self-presentational and defensive concerns. The effects of self-awareness, then, should vary as a function of the publicity of causal judgments (i.e., the self-presentational character of the attributional context) and should not be expected to exert a unidirectional influence on causal attributions.

In their study designed to test these notions regarding the relationship between self-awareness and publicity of causal judgments, Hull and Levy (1979) used a procedure similar to that used by Duval and Wicklund (1973, Study 1). More specifically, subjects in a state of high or low objective self-awareness were asked to estimate the extent to which they were responsible for the negative outcomes of several hypothetical situations. In addition, half of the subjects were asked to write their names and social security numbers on the experimental questionnaires and to anticipate a brief discussion of their responses at the end of the experiment (public attribution condition). The remaining subjects were asked to put their unsigned, completed questionnaires in a large pile of previously completed experimental materials (private attribution condition). Hull and Levy predicted, and found, that in the public attribution conditions, subjects in a state of high objective self-awareness attributed more responsibility for the negative outcome to themselves than subjects experiencing a state of low self-awareness. However, this pattern of results was reversed in the private attribution conditions.

In summary, research using a variety of techniques to manipulate self-attention leaves little doubt about the importance of focus of attention as a determinant of the locus of causal attributions (see Duval & Hensley, 1976, for a review). However, the studies by Federoff and Harvey (1976), Hull and Levy (1979), and Weary (1980) suggest that more work is needed to determine how focus of attention operates in conjunction with other processes, such as motivational concerns, to influence causal judgments.

SELF-FOCUSED ATTENTION AND SELF-ATTRIBUTIONS: POTENTIAL MEDIATING PROCESSES

The evidence reviewed so far suggests that there may be important limiting conditions to the general notion that causal attributions will follow the focus of attention; however, there is considerable evidence that focus of attention can be a significant determinant of the locus of causal attributions (Duval & Hensley, 1976; Duval & Wicklund, 1972, 1973; Wicklund, 1975). In this section, I examine two processes that have been proposed as possible mediators of the attention–attribution relationship. In particular, I examine how focus of attention may operate in conjunction with availability of information and motivational processes to influence self-attributions of causality.

Attention and Availability of Information

Taylor and Fiske (1978) have suggested that biases in the availability of information in memory may mediate between focus of attention and locus of causal attribution. These authors have proposed that as a result of differential attention to a salient stimulus (including the self), information about that stimulus is more available, or stored in a more easily retrieved form. When the perceiver is asked to make a causal judgment about an event involving the salient stimulus, more information is retrieved and, consequently, more causal influence is attributed to that stimulus.

Much of the evidence cited by Taylor and Fiske (1978) as support for the attention–availability– attribution links is not directly relevant to self-perception and self-attribution. However, Ross and Sicoly (1979) recently reported a series of five experiments designed to assess the occurrence of egocentric biases in availability of information in memory and self-serving causal attributions for events that occurred during group interaction. The data of these experiments provided consistent evidence for egocentric biases in availability and attribution; that is, subjects' own contributions to a joint product were more frequently recalled, and individuals accepted more responsibility for a group product than other participants attributed to them. Moreover, Ross and Sicoly found significant correlations between the magnitude of the bias in availability and the magnitude of the bias in responsibility (Ross & Sicoly, 1979, Study 1).

Most pertinent to the present chapter was the final experiment reported by Ross and Sicoly (1979). In this study, graduate students were stimulated to focus cognitively on either their own contributions to their B.A. theses or on the contributions of their supervisors. The authors assumed that this focus of attention manipulation would result in differential availability of self or supervisor contributions. As predicted, subjects accepted significantly more responsibility for their theses in the self-focus than in the supervisor-focus condition. Although availability of information was not assessed directly in this fifth experiment, the results are consistent with the attention–availability– attribution relationship proposed by Taylor and Fiske (1978).

Ross and Sicoly (1979) suggested four processes that might have accounted for the observed egocentric biases in availability of information and in attributions of causal responsibility. First, these authors argued that for several reasons, one's own inputs may be facilitated by differential encoding and storage of self-generated inputs. For example, individuals may rehearse or repeat their own ideas or actions, thereby increasing the retention of their own inputs. Second, egocentric biases in availability and attributions may result from differential retrieval of information from memory (cf. Taylor & Fiske, 1978). That is, individuals may try to recall their own contributions and inappropriately use this information to estimate their *relative* contributions without adequately considering the inputs of others. Third, informational disparities may mediate egocentric biases in recall. For example, individuals may have greater access to their own internal thoughts and strategies than do observers.

Overall, Ross and Sicoly (1979) believed their results supported selective retrieval as the mediator of biases in availability of information; however, they also noted a fourth process that may account for egocentric biases in availability and attributions: Such cognitive biases may be determined by motivational influences. For instance, positive feelings about the self may be enhanced by focusing on or weighting more heavily one's behavioral contributions for an action. In an attempt to investigate this motivational interpretation of the availability bias, Ross and Sicoly (1979, Experiment 2) had pairs of subjects work jointly on a social awareness task. Several days later, subjects were led to believe that their group had performed well or poorly. The authors hypothesized that self-generated inputs to a group product should be more available after success than after failure if the bias in availability is caused primarily by the motivation to enhance self-esteem. Consistent with this hypothesis, Ross and Sicoly (1979) reported that subjects attributed a significantly greater proportion of recalled comments to themselves after success than after failure. In addition, subjects' evaluations of the other person's comments were significantly lower in the failure than in the success condition. This latter finding suggests that subjects attempted to shift the blame for failure onto their partners. In summary, the results of Experiment 2 provided evidence consistent with the notion that the bias in availability of information was influenced by the affective quality of the subjects' outcomes.

Although not directly concerned with causal inference processes, several other investigators have examined the relationship between affective states and availability of information in memory. For example, Isen, Shalker, Clark, and Karp (1978) induced positive or negative affective states by having subjects win or lose a computer game (Study 2). These investigators reported that subjects who won the game were better able to recall positive material in memory. Although recall of negative material by subjects who failed the game was not found, the authors argued that negative mood is probably a more complex event than positive mood; consequently, an expectation of symmetry between positive and negative affective states may not be warranted. In a similar vein, Mischel, Ebbesen, and Zeiss (1976) found that individuals who had been exposed to positive-expectation–inducing feedback (i.e., subjects in whom a positive feeling state had been induced) were less able to recognize information about their negative qualities than about their positive qualities in a test of memory. In general, the studies reported by Mischel et al. (1976) and Isen et al. (1978), as well as the second experiment reported by Ross and Sicoly (1979), suggest that availability of information in memory may be affected by the mood state at the time of recall.

Attention and Self-Evaluation

As previously noted, both Taylor and Fiske (1978) and Duval and Wicklund (1973) have contended that focus of attention influences causal attributions. Whereas Taylor and Fiske propose an informational mediator (i.e., availability), Wicklund's (1975) most recent statement of the theory of objective self-awareness involves a strictly motivational mediator of the attention–attribution relationship. More specifically, the theory of objective self-awareness is a theory of self-evaluation. All effects resulting from self-focused attention are presumed to be motivated by the individual's affective reaction to the discrepancy between his or her attainments and aspirations. During states of high self-focused attention, an individual will experience either positive or negative affect depending on whether attention is directed toward a positive (behavior exceeds aspirations) or negative (behavior fails to meet aspirations) discrepancy (Wicklund, 1975). If positive affect follows self-focused attention, the individual presumably will be motivated to assume responsibility for the behavioral outcome. If negative affect follows self-focused attention, the individual initially will accept responsibility for the behavior. Following this self-critical reaction, however, objective self-awareness theory postulates that the individual will be motivated to reduce the negative affect by directing his or her attention toward external events or by reducing the negative discrepancy. In an attempt to explain why self-focused individuals sometimes make lower self-attributions for negative outcomes, Wicklund (1975) suggested that one means of reducing a negative discrepancy (and, concomitantly, negative affect) is to deny responsibility for a behavioral outcome. If this mode of discrepancy reduction is used, the general hypothesis that self-focused attention leads to exaggerated self-attributions of causality will not be confirmed; in this case, greater self-focused attention will lead to *lower* self-attributions of causality for the negative outcome. Although the proposed attention–affect attribution links have not been investigated directly,[1] the previously discussed studies by Federoff and Harvey (1976) and Weary (1980)

---

[1]It should be noted that, in a series of experiments, Scheier and Carver (1977) have found that self-focused attention increases the individual's responsiveness to his or her transient positive and negative affective states. However, in these studies, affective states were produced by having subjects view slides of nude women or read mood statements. Because these affective reactions were not the result of positive or negative outcomes attendant to subjects' own actions, and because attributions were not measured, these studies are not considered here.

are consistent with the notion that self-attributions may be used to enhance positive self-evaluations or to mitigate the impact of negative self-evaluations.

SELF-SERVING ATTRIBUTIONS AND PERSONAL ADJUSTMENT TO STRESSFUL ENVIRONMENTS

Few psychologists would argue with the idea that self-esteem is essential to emtoional well being. Indeed, a number of clinical psychologists have argued that a positive regard for self is a prerequisite for mental health and that a major goal of psychotherapy is to foster such regard in clients (e.g., Rogers, 1951). Because self-serving attributions presumably enhance or protect self-esteem, it seems reasonable to ask whether such attributional biases play a role in individuals' adjustments to stressful environmental situations (i.e., whether self-serving attributions are in fact effective in maintaining self-esteem).

There are surprisingly few empirical studies concerned with the effects of self-serving biases in causal judgments upon subsequent behavior and/or feelings or self-worth. However, the research that does exist suggests that self-serving attributions do serve a defensive or protective function. For example, several investigators have found that such attributions are associated with more positive and less negative affective states (Nicholls, 1975; Riemer, 1975; Weary, 1980) and greater feelings of self worth (Weary, 1980). In addition, a study by Weiner and Sierad (1975) suggests that inducing external attributions for failure may help low-achieving students lessen the aversive consequences of failure on esteem maintenance and reduce subsequent performance decrements. A similar point has been made by Klein, Fencil-Morse, and Seligman (1976), who provided evidence that learned helplessness was not exhibited when depressives were induced to attribute prior failure to an external cause (task difficulty); however, when depressed subjects were induced to attribute failure to an internal cause (ability), subsequent performance deficits emerged.

Whereas the study by Klein et al. (1976) manipulated depressed individuals' causal ascriptions for their performance outcomes, a recent study by Kuiper (1978) examined depressives' and nondepressives' *typical* patterns of attributions for successful and unsuccessful outcomes. Specifically, in this study, depressed and nondepressed college students performed a word association task and then received feedback indicating they had answered 20%, 55%, or 80% of the items correctly. Following task performance, students were asked to assign causal responsibility for their performance outcomes to effort, ability, task difficulty, and luck. The results indicated that nondepressives made internal attributions (ability, effort) for success and external attributions (task difficulty, luck) for failure. In accord with Klein et al.'s (1976) findings suggesting that learned helplessness is dependent on exposure to failure *and* the attribution of helplessness to internal causes, Kuiper reported that depressives made internal attributions for failure.[2] Contrary to expectations, depressives also made internal attributions for successful outcomes. In discussing these findings, Kuiper (1978) speculated that:

> nondepressives' external attributions for failure may represent an effective strategy (i.e., the operation of a self-protective bias) for preventing the occurrence of depression. On the other hand, the depressive's tendency to make a personal attribution for failure may be a very ineffectual strategy for preventing the occurrence of depression.... For instance, it is possible that blaming oneself for failure may contribute to other features of depression, such as feelings of unworthiness, guilt, self-devaluation, and loss of self-esteem [p. 243].

The notion that self-attributions for one's negative behavioral outcomes may be implicated in the etiology and maintenance of maladaptive behavior patterns also has been suggested by Storms and McCaul (1976). In their model of emotional exacerbation of dysfunctional behavior, these authors proposed that individuals first perceive some undesirable aspect of their own behavior for which they make a self-attribution. This self-attribution of unwanted dysfunctional behavior presumably leads to negative self-evaluations and an increase in anxiety that exacerbates the unwanted emotional behavior. Storms and McCaul noted that this exacerbation model should be applicable to any emotional disorder in which the primary symptomatic behavior is increased by anxiety.

In a test of their exacerbation model, Storms and McCaul (1975) examined the role of subjects' attributions about their speech disfluencies upon subsequent disfluency rates. More specifically, normal-speaking subjects were asked to make two tape recordings of their speech. After subjects completed the first recording, the experimenter informed all subjects that they had displayed a very high number of disfluencies such as repetitions and stammers. Next, half of the subjects were told that their disfluency rate was a normal result of situational factors such as being in an experiment; the remaining subjects were told that their disfluency was a symptom of their own personal speech pattern and ability. All subjects then were asked to make the second tape under conditions of high or low situational stress (i.e., subjects were told that their second tape either would or

---

[2]Several investigators have found evidence indicating that individuals exaggerate their causal responsibility for uncontrollable, negative outcomes attendant to their behaviors. It has been suggested that such causal attributions may serve to enhance feelings of control over the environment (see review by Wortman, 1976). Although such evidence may appear to be inconsistent with the self-serving bias formulation, Miller and Norman (1975) have suggested that such a control motive may be one manifestation of the need to view oneself positively. Furthermore, I have argued elsewhere that under certain conditions, esteem needs may be best served by accepting responsibility for negative behavioral outcomes (Weary Bradley, 1978). Clearly, more research is needed to identify the behaviors for and the conditions under which individuals will accept greater responsibility for positive or negative outcomes and the effects of such causal judgments on subsequent behavior and feelings of self worth.

would not be played with identifying information to a psychology class). Storms and McCaul (1975) predicted, and found, that self-attribution– high-stress subjects exhibited significantly greater increases in stammering than all other groups. The results of this study, then, provide support for the notion that the internalization of a negative self-attribution may lead to exacerbation of dysfunctional behavior.

CONCLUSION

In summary, systematic distortions in attributional processes has been a topic of much theoretical and empirical concern (e.g., Ross, 1977, Taylor & Fiske, 1978; Weary Bradley, 1978). In the preceding sections of this chapter, the general hypothesis that self-focused attention will exaggerate self-attributions of causality has been examined. There is considerable empirical evidence that focus of attention is an important determinant of causal attributions. However, several studies suggest some important limiting conditions to the focus of attention hypothesis; specifically, several studies have found that increased self-attention leads to increased self-attributions of causality following positive outcomes but that increased self-attention leads to decreased self-attributions following negative outcomes, at least when attributional judgments are relatively private (cf. Hull & Levy, 1979). Recent empirical investigations have offered support for two potential mediators of this relationship between self-focused attention and self-serving causal attributions; that is, the relationship between focus of attention and self-serving biases in attributions may be mediated by biases in availability of information (Ross & Sicoly, 1979), or by more motivational processes (Wicklund, 1975). A third and quite reasonable possibility is that motivational influences and availability of information jointly result in self-serving attributions of causality (e.g., Ross & Sicoly, 1979). Currently, we are unable to rule out any of these possibilities.

Finally, research relevant to the notion that self-serving causal attributions play a role in individuals' adjustments to stressful environmental situations and to personal failure has been examined in this chapter. Although there is a substantial body of literature documenting the pervasive tendency for individuals to accept more causal responsibility for their own positive than for their own negative behaviors, there are very few studies concerned with the effects of such causal asymmetries upon individuals' subsequent behaviors and/or feelings of self worth. However, the research that does exist suggests that self-serving attributions foster self-esteem and are important to personal adjustment. Further examination of the relationship between self-serving causal attributions and personal adjustment to stressful events and situations is a natural and necessary direction for future research. Moreover, such research programs would represent interfaces among cognitive, environmental, and social psychology and would highlight the continued need for the type of interdisciplinary dialogue that has been the goal of this conference.

ACKNOWLEDGMENTS

The author wishes to thank Andrew Baum, Susan Fiske, John Harvey, and Kelly Shaver for their helpful comments on an earlier version of this chapter.

REFERENCES

Carver, C. S., & Scheier, M. F. Self-focusing effects of dispositional self-consciousness, mirror presence, and audience presence. *Journal of Personality and Social Psychology,* 1978, *36,* 324–332.

Duval, S., & Hensley, V. Extensions of objective self-awareness theory: The focus of attention–causal attribution hypothesis. In J. H. Harvey, W. J. Ickes, & R. F. Kidd (Eds.), *New directions in attribution research* (Vol. 1). Hillsdale, N.J.: Lawrence Erlbaum Associates, 1976.

Duval, S., & Wicklund, R. A. *A theory of objective self-awareness.* New York: Academic Press, 1972.

Duval, S., & Wicklund, R. A. Effects of objective self-awareness on attribution of causality. *Journal of Experimental Social Psychology,* 1973, *9,* 17–31.

Federoff, N. A., & Harvey, J. H. Focus of attention, self-esteem, and attribution of causality. *Journal of Research in Personality,* 1976, *10,* 336–345.

Frey, D. Reactions to success and failure in public and private conditions. *Journal of Experimental Social Psychology,* 1978, *14,* 172–179.

Harvey, J. H., Harris, B., & Barnes, R. D. Actor–observer differences in perceptions of responsibility and freedom. *Journal of Personality and Social Psychology,* 1975, *32,* 22–28.

Hull, J. G., & Levy, A. S. The organizational functions of the self: An alternative to the Duval and Wicklund model of self-awareness. *Journal of Personality and Social Psychology,* 1979, *37,* 756–768.

Isen, A. M., Shalker, T. E., Clark, M., & Karp, L. Affect, accessibility of material in memory, and behavior: A cognitive loop? *Journal of Personality and Social Psychology,* 1978, *36,* 1–12.

Jones, E. E., & Davis, K. E. From acts to dispositions: The attribution process in person perception. In L. Berkowitz (Ed.), *Advances in experimental social psychology* (Vol. 2). New York: Academic Press, 1965.

Jones, E. E., & Nisbett, R. E. The actor and the observer: Divergent perceptions of the causes of behavior. In E. E. Jones, D. Kanouse, H. H. Kelley, R. E. Nisbett, S. Valins, & B. Weiner (Eds.), *Attribution: Perceiving the causes of behavior.* New York: General Learning Press, 1972.

Klein, D. C., Fencil-Morse, E., & Seligman, M. E. P. Learned helplessness, depression and the attribution of failure. *Journal of Personality and Social Psychology,* 1976, *33,* 508–516.

Kuiper, N. A. Depression and causal attributions for success and failure. *Journal of Personality and Social Pscyhology,* 1978, *36,* 236–246.

Miller, D. T., & Norman, S. A. Actor–observer differences in perceptions of effective control. *Journal of Personality and Social Psychology,* 1975, *31,* 503–515.

Miller, D. T., & Ross, M. Self-serving biases in the attribution of causality. Fact or fiction? *Psychological Bulletin,* 1975, *82,* 213–225.

Mischel, W., Ebbesen, E., & Zeiss, A. Determinants of selective memory about the self. *Journal of Consulting and Clinical Psychology,* 1976, *44,* 92–103.

Monson, T. C., & Snyder, M. Actors, observers, and the attribution process: Toward a reconceptualization. *Journal of Experimental Social Psychology,* 1977, *13,* 89–111.

Nicholls, J. G. Causal attributions and other achievement-related cognitions: Effects of task outcome, attainment value, and sex. *Journal of Personality and Social Psychology,* 1975, *31,* 379–389.

Nisbett, R. E., Caputo, C., Legant, P., & Maracek, J. Behavior as seen by the actor and as seen by the observer. *Journal of Personality and Social Psychology,* 1973, *27,* 154–164.

Riemer, B. S. Influence of causal beliefs on affect and expectancy. *Journal of Personality and Social Psychology,* 1975, *31,* 1163–1167.

Rogers, C. R. *Client-centered therapy.* Boston: Houghton Mifflin, 1951.

Ross, L. The intuitive psychologist and his shortcomings: Distortions in the attribution process. In L. Berkowitz (Ed.), *Advances in experimental social psychology* (Vol. 10). New York: Academic Press, 1977.

Ross, M., & Sicoly, F. Egocentric biases in availability and attribution. *Journal of Personality and Social Psychology,* 1979, *37,* 322–336.

Scheier, M. F., & Carver, C. S. Self-focused attention and the experience of emotion: Attraction, repulsion, elation, and depression. *Journal of Personality and Social Psychology,* 1977, *35,* 625–636.

Shaver, K. G. *An introduction to attribution processes.* Cambridge, Mass.: Winthrop, 1975.

Storms, M. D., & McCaul, K. D. *Stuttering, attribution, and exacerbation.* Unpublished manuscript, University of Kansas, 1975.

Storms, M. D., & McCaul, K. D. Attribution processes and emotional exacerbation of dysfunctional behavior. In J. H. Harvey, W. J. Ickes, & R. F. Kidd (Eds.), *New directions in attribution research* (Vol. 1). Hillsdale, N.J.: Lawrence Erlbaum Associates, 1976.

Taylor, S. E., & Fiske, S. T. Salience, attention, and attribution: Top of the head phenomena. In L. Berkowitz (Ed.), *Advances in experimental social psychology* (Vol. 11). New York: Academic Press, 1978.

Weary, G. An examination of affect and egotism as mediators of bias in causal attributions. *Journal of Personality and Social Psychology,* 1980, *38,* 348–357.

Weary Bradley, G. Self-serving biases in the attribution process: A reexamination of the fact or fiction question. *Journal of Personality and Social Psychology,* 1978, *36,* 56–71.

Weary, G., Harvey, J. H., Perloff, R., Schweiger, P. K., & Olson, C. T. *Effects of performance outcome, anticipated future performance and publicity of interpretive activities on causal attributions.* Unpublished manuscript, Ohio State University, 1979.

Weiner, B., & Sierad, G. Misattribution for failure and enhancement of achievement strivings. *Journal of Personality and Social Psychology,* 1975, *31,* 415–421.

Wicklund, R. A. Objective self-awareness. In L. Berkowitz (Ed.), *Advances in experimental social psychology* (Vol. 8). New York: Academic Press, 1975.

Wortman, C. B. Causal attributions and personal control. In J. H. Harvey, W. J. Ickes, & R. F. Kidd (Eds.), *New directions in attribution research* (Vol. 1). Hillsdale, N.J.: Lawrence Erlbaum Associates, 1976.

12 Social Cognition and Affect

Susan T. Fiske
Carnegie-Mellon University

In social psychology, the research pendulum has accelerated toward cognitive methodologies and theories to account for social phenomena. This chapter argues that the pendulum has swung far enough, and that an exclusive focus on social cognition now can be tempered by more consideration of affect. The current explosion of research in social cognition enables us to study affect in a cognitively informed fashion, to pay attention to the *processing* of affect. Process-oriented research measures events at the center of the stimulus–organism–response chain, with results useful to social psychology. Rather than simply manipulating stimuli, measuring responses, and inferring processes, social research has returned profitably to the black box of cognition. Building on this approach, recent cognitive and cognitive-social research illuminate a role for affect in social cognition, a role that acknowledges the area's growing insights into cognition.

This new cognitive sophistication generally has modeled human beings as information processors of limited capacity, with a concomitant necessity for cognitive economy. As mirrored by the information-processing approach, research has focused on how the impossible tasks of social cognition are possible. It has become commonplace to acknowledge in chapter introductions that the object and social worlds overwhelm people's ability to cognize all the information available. Cognitive and cognitive-social psychology have focused on how the consequent selectivity operates; the processes of attending, combining, inferring, and retrieving have supplemented previous concern with psychological products, outcomes such as judgment and evaluation. Recent explorations detail the processes that facilitate cognitive economy in the face of an objectively overwhelming environment. In an historical perspective, the current work views perceivers as cognitive misers who emphasize processing efficiency at all other costs (Taylor, Chapter 10 in this volume). As a result of this metatheoretical approach, new insights are being gained on social perception and cognition: The economical encoding, organization, and retrieval of person information is increasingly understood, drawing in large part on the cognitive-miser view.

Much of social cognition, then, focuses on the efficient organization of knowledge about people, drawing on cognitive psychology's work both in processing strategies and in knowledge structures or schemas (see, in this volume, Bransford, Stein, Shelton, & Owings, Chapter 5; Grueneich & Tabasso, Chapter 13; or more generally, J. R. Anderson, 1976; Rumelhart & Ortony, 1977; Thorndyke & Hayes-Roth, 1979). The bulk of social-cognition research relies heavily on memory measures to tap the organization of social knowledge into generic structures sometimes labeled schemas. (For examples of this type of approach see, in this volume: Greenwald, Chapter 25; Yarkin, Town, & Harvey, Chapter 14; for a review, see Taylor & Crocker, 1981, and for current collected overviews, see Cantor & Kihlstrom, 1981; Hastie, Ostrom, Ebbesen, Wyer, Hamilton, & Carlston, 1980; Higgins, Herman, & Zanna, 1981. But also see Baron, Chapter 4 in this volume, for a dissenting view.) Whatever the conceptual underpinings, all this work emphasizes cognitive structure and process, guided by the requirements of cognitive economy.

Despite its by now clear utility, the cognitive-miser view omits a vital social phenomenon: affect. Unlike most purely cognitive stimuli, social information is dramatically colored by affect, and in the current enthusiasm for borrowing from cognitive psychology, that fact tends to be forgotten. Social cognition intrinsically involves the perceiver's self concept and uniquely concerns stimuli with needs, wishes, and opinions of their own (cf. Higgins, Kuiper, & Olson, 1981; Zajonc, 1980a); consequently, it pulls in affective reactions. These distinct features of social cognition require methodological and theoretical concerns that social psychology cannot afford to neglect, because these concerns are intrinsic to social phenomena.

Although social cognition has ignored affect, the rest of social psychology never has. The field boasts an illustrious history of addressing affect in interpersonal settings. Depending on one's conception of affect—and the current usage is defined shortly—social psychology's mainstreams always paid attention to affect. Attitude research as early as Hovland, Janis, and Kelley (1953) addressed the effects of emotion (fear) on persuasive communication; dissonance theory (Festinger, 1957) fundamentally relies on motivated tension reduction, and recent research focuses on, for example, whether dissonance requires an aversive state of arousal (Higgins, Rhodewalt, & Zanna, 1979; Zanna, Higgins, & Taves, 1976). Attitudes themselves are usually defined as having a major affective component (see, e.g., Himmelfarb & Eagly, 1974). In person-perception research, the nonverbal area almost entirely concerns the expression and communication of emotion (see Schneider, Hastorf, & Ellsworth, 1979, for a recent overview), and the impression-formation area prominently includes work on evaluations of others (N. H. Anderson, 1974). Interpersonal attraction intimately hinges on affective responses (Berscheid & Walster, 1978). Stereotyping also fundamentally pulls in affect-laden reactions to others (Ashmore & Del Boca, in press). As this partial listing illustrates, the field as a whole certainly does not neglect affect.

But most attention to affect thus far has not been cognitively oriented, and, of course, it did not aim to be. Given the timing of the most recent cognitive revolution, explorations into affect so far have been ill-equipped to address cognition. In contrast, the recent mushrooming of social-cognition research uniquely suits that area to entertain a cognitively sophisticated view of affect. Given what is rapidly being learned about social cognition, we are in a position to consider how social cognition might inform the study of affect. The companion point is that affect forces new considerations onto social cognition, and it is high time that it do so. As a consequence of both these points, this chapter defines a role for affect in social cognition. Specifically, this chapter argues that cognition and affect are in part separate systems, with distinct features. Of course, there is also overlap, and that interface is detailed in the pages that follow. But this effort primarily describes ways that affect systematically differs from cognition.

As an illustration of this fundamental distinction, consider a major guiding metaphor in social cognition. The cognitive-miser approach to social cognition derives from information-processing theories, and both emphasize the ways that people compensate for limited cognitive capacity. Both draw on the digital-computer model of human cognition. That computer metaphor represents cognitive processes rather well. For example, memory research profitably builds on the binary feature of digital computers: Something is either "on" or "off," in memory or not, and remembering it is largely a process of access within complex memory structures (e.g., J. R. Anderson, 1976). So the representation of individual items in memory nicely fits into binary code. But the digital metaphor does not as usefully capture affect, which is not a neatly binary variable. A better metaphor for affect is the analog computer, which continuously registers changing inputs by varying voltages. Like affect, analog processes more directly preserve the relationship between input intensity and the internal representation. Digital processes, in contrast, invoke intermediate symbolic transformations. The analog metaphor is limited,[1] but serves to emphasize that intensity is a major

---

[1]Analog models have been suggested for affectively laden variables before, by N. H. Anderson (1974) and by Zajonc (1980b). And, an analog–digital controversy is raging in cognitive psychology over the representation of mental imagery, although it is not clear that this debate is resolvable (see J. R. Anderson., 1978; but compare Hayes-Roth, 1979; Pylyshyn, 1979; and J. R. Anderson's 1979 reply). However, the controversy concerning mental imagery highlights the fact that digital representations may not completely suit some psychological phenomena that are importantly continuous. Of course, digital computers can be made to simulate affect (or any other "analog" variable), and Lehnert, Roseman, & Abelson (1980) recently have addressed precisely this issue.

feature of affect qualitatively different from binary logic. In addition to intensity, direction is also a major feature of analog systems. Direction is intrinsic to affect as well; affects are intrinsically valenced. As with a number line, slide rule, or analog computer, direction and intensity capture the essential features of affect. To anticipate the major point of the separate systems argument, purely cognitive approaches stress memory and do not consider intensity or valence as major structural features; in contrast, affect demands both as minimal structural features. At the least, cognition and affect differ in fundamental ways. To the extent that they are wholly separable systems, they have allowed independent investigation. But to the extent that they interact, cognitive-social psychology must examine that interface. Given the dramatically social features of affect and its venerable history within social psychology, recent gains in cognition enable us to construct a role for affect in social cognition.

This chapter describes such a role. The first section defines some crucial terms: affect, cognition, and social. The field of emotion is enormous and unruly, spanning at least a century of research and theory. Little of that massive literature directly informs social cognition, but even the useful portions have been neglected and deserve not to be. The major definitional task is devoted to affect, because affect is a relatively novel problem for cognitive-social research. To describe a role for affect in social cognition, further specification of cognition also proves helpful. In the flurry of social research on that topic, we forget to stand back and examine what we mean by cognition. In operational terms, social cognition has almost entirely concerned social memory, frequently omitting even plausibly "cognitive" variables such as attention and interpretation. To remedy that in part, their role is addressed here directly, as they bear an affect.

After defining terms, the subsequent section focuses on existing guides to the role of affect in social cognition. Selected research on conceptions of the self and others illustrates the place of prior social knowledge and experience in the processing of affect. Such accumulated and abstracted experience goes under the name of schemas. Affect interfaces with social cognition—and this is the central point—by way of schema-driven interpretation. These structured, generic expectations not only cue knowledge, as is currently assumed, but also cue affect. Schemas organize both affect and cognition, the latter in terms of criteria that are increasingly understood (cf. Hastie, 1981; Taylor & Crocker, 1981). Affect is less known from this perspective, but this chapter argues that its structure may be summarized first in terms of valence. This inherent structural feature of affect fundamentally distinguishes it from cognition. Intensity is the other vital feature of affect discussed here. In ways forshadowed by the analog metaphor and to be discussed more fully, affect's intensity results from input intensity. Specifically, alerting, attention, and arousal are implicated in the extremity of affective reactions. As in other conceptual analyses here, these points are buttressed by available data. Overall, then, this chapter aims to distinguish features of cognition and affect and to examine their interplay in social settings.

DEFINITIONS AND PERSPECTIVE

To define a role for affect in social cognition, one should clarify what is meant by affect, and by cognition.

Cognition

Cognition is understanding; it involves a perceiver's internal processes that mediate between stimuli and responses, or more fashionably, inputs and outputs. Cognition includes processes of attention, interpretation, storage, and retrieval. In discussing the proposition that cognition and affect are independent, it is important to be clear about where among those varied cognitive processes independence plausibly could and could not lie. Clearly, attention—which may be seen as a cognitive process—precedes both cognitive and affective outputs. Minimal processing must occur before any reaction, however immediate, can be made. Thus, affect and cognition cannot plausibly be separate until stages that follow on attention and immediate perception. This chapter addresses the processing of affect at the immediate stages, where it is not distinguished from cognition, as well as at later stages, where affect and cognition do separate.

Affect

Defining affect requires a more extended discussion, given the novelty of its application to social cognition. Defining affect also requires great selectivity, given the eclectic history of emotion in psychology, which has spanned perspectives ranging from physiological to behavioral to phenomenological (for a comprehensive and clear overview, see Strongman, 1978). This chapter's usage of affect focuses narrowly on its role in social cognition. Consequently, physiology, behavior, and phenomenology are only brought in where inextricably tied to cognition. As Simon (1969) and others have argued, science can proceed independently at different levels of explanation, integrating only when each level has developed sufficiently to warrant export to other levels.

In the context of social cognition, affective reactions are distinguished by the specificity of their targets. This buys a contrast between mood (or feeling states) and other emotions (cf. Ewert, 1970). Mood has no specific affective target but rather suffuses all one's experiences, even though directed at none in particular. Recent work has shown that good moods cue associations to positive retrievals, thus possibly reinforcing the mood state (Clark, Goldin, & Isen, 1979). Work on mood explores such issues as how moods are labeled (e.g., Nowlis, 1970), as well as their influence on retrieval (e.g., Bower, Monteiro, & Gilligan, 1978; Isen, Shalker, Clark, & Karp, 1978). Such research on mood deals with generalized affective states, whereas other research on affect deals with more specifically targeted affective reactions. Because the current analysis concerns the role of affect in social—that is, interpersonal—cognition, the most appropriate feelings to consider are feelings directed toward other people. (See Clark & Isen, in press, for a discussion of mood and cognition.)

The Structure of Affect. These exclusions made, we can turn to the main definitional task. Defining interpersonal affect inherently implicates structure. In this regard, a troublesome and fundamental concern is the extent to which emotions are complexly differentiated or simply equivalent to valence. Does the structure of affect in social cognition need to encompass more than valence? Does social cognition require a taxonomy of affect? The roots of this problem can be traced to James' (1884) distinction between judgments of pleasantness or interest, and his primary concern, which was with more discrete emotions, seen as tied to different bodily symptoms (see McDougall, 1928, for another early discussion of this). The contrast between preference—usually evaluation as good or bad—and more differentiated affective response is an important one. To what extent do interesting and researchable problems lie in preferences, such as "I really dislike Laura," and to what extent do they lie in richer emotional reactions, such as "Laura makes me furious"? Preferences, evaluations, and simple judgments of personal impact lend themselves to analysis as mere positive-negative appraisal. Whether such preferences fall on a single positive-negative continuum or on two separate dimensions need not concern us at present (cf. Kanouse & Hanson, 1971). The crux of the distinction is that such preferences and evaluations seem qualitatively different from more rich, complex emotions, which might seem to require more than one or two dimensions. For example, although shame and anger are both intense negative emotions, it has seemed to many theorists a travesty to reduce them both simply to negative feelings.

The distinction between simple evaluation and rich differential emotion has plagued the affect area for some time and has hinged in large part on physiological concerns, which are relevant here only to the extent that it is known how physiology influences cognition. On the antecedent side, based on a careful review of available evidence, Mandler's (1975) resolution of the differential-emotions problem supports the view that the causes of emotion are not physiologically differentiated. He concludes that *undifferentiated* autonomic arousal best characterizes physiology's contribution to emotion. On the consequent side, the case for differential emotions is simple and, on the face of it, convincing: Scientists and other people do, in fact, distinguish among different patterns of emotional response. But is there a difference that makes a difference to social cognition? This question can be answered by considering the evidence for differentiated emotional response, data that are introspective, on the one hand, and empirical on the other.

First, lay introspection asserts that emotions have discrete qualities that go beyond mere preference judgments. However, the phenomenology of emotion has a long (and checkered) career as scientific evidence and inspiration. For example, James, in the tradition of his day, drew heavily on introspection for his germinal insights into emotion. More recently, however, Mandler (1975) has argued persuasively that ordinary language—and by implication, ordinary insights—are not a sufficient basis for a science of emotion:

> Consider the adequacy of distinguishing between heavy and light packages, loud and soft noises, and angry and joyous feelings for most communicative purposes. But the heavy–light and the loud–soft distinction are totally inadequate for scientific purposes. Why, then, should we expect angry–joyful to be adequate [p. 9]?

In a more general context, Nisbett and Wilson (1977) have argued that perceivers often do not have insight into their own psychological processes; if that holds for affective processes, then introspection will not do as evidence for the differentiated processing of affect, however intuitively appealing that conclusion may be. Introspection provides particularly poor data in the case of affective processing, relying as such analysis usually does on retrospective reporting or hypothetical prediction. Such conditions have been analyzed as those most heavily inference laden and inaccurate (Ericsson & Simon, 1980), and so the science of emotion cannot proceed on the basis of ordinary intuitions such as these.

Besides introspection, the second basis for objecting to simple evaluation as capturing affect is empirical. One empirical basis for distinguishing emotions derives primarily from clinical observation of the differential functions served by emotions, which do not reduce to mere valence. Izard (1977), building on Tomkins (e.g., 1965), argues specifically that a simple positive–negative dimension potentially distorts, because "any emotion (e.g., joy, fear) may be positive or negative if the criteria for classification are based on the adaptiveness or dysadaptiveness of the emotion in a particular situation [p. 18]." But, the business of social cognition is not clinical judgment, which sheds little light on the processing of affect. Clinical insight potentially does inform us about the intrapsychic functions of emotion, but it does not contribute to our understanding of affective processing.

Still on the consequence side, another empirical basis for distinguishing several emotions derives from data on the clear differentiation of facial and behavioral concomitants of affect (e.g., Ekman, 1972; Izard, 1977; James, 1884; Plutchik, 1970). But these theorists, whose primary grounding lies within the field of emotion, are all ambiguous with respect to the role of cognition in affect. There need be no disagreement that the factors they consider are important, but cognitive-social psychology is best equipped to focus more closely on affective structure and process.

The third and final empirical argument for differential emotion lies in previous theoretical accounts labeled cognitive within the field of emotion. Among them, the two major theorists rely centrally on the notion of appraisal. In this view, people constantly evaluate the personal impact of the environment, and any nonneutral evaluations generate emotion. Arnold (1970) defines emotion entirely in terms of cognitive appraisal: "a felt tendency toward anything appraised as good, and away from anything appraised as bad [p. 176]." Her theoretical approach in effect falls closer to the simple view of emotions than to the rich, differentiated view, because she musters no firm evidence for differentiated affect. Lazarus (e.g., Lazarus, Averill, & Opton, 1970) extends Arnold's view of appraisal and action tendencies to argue that cognitive appraisal generates differing bodily and physiological response syndromes; these serve to identify differing emotions, much as symptoms identify but do not explain diseases. His program of research, focused especially on stress, directly and indirectly manipulates perceived personal relevance of threatening stimuli, for example, via the narrative framing of a gory film, the immediacy of anticipated shock, and clinical assessment of long-term defensive styles. Essentially, this research supports the conclusion that personal relevance of unpleasant stimuli catalyzes negative emotion, but the underlying cognitive processes are ambiguous. Both Lazarus and Arnold assert that cognitions cause differentiated affective and physiological responses, but do not describe precisely how the cognitive process operates. And, although each holds that more complex emotions than mere appraisal will eventually be distinguished by discrete bodily responses, the analysis of neither Arnold nor Lazarus makes a clear case for differential emotions. Each explicitly considers only simple emotions—that is, positive–negative evaluation.

A recent cognitive theory of emotion explicitly does address the differential emotions problem. Roseman (1979), drawing on an analysis of goal states (cf. Schank & Abelson, 1977), creates a cognitively driven taxonomy of emotion, in which he identifies the antecedent psychological events that trigger 13 separate emotions. A prominent dimension is evaluation or desirability; others are availability of the goal object, perceived probability, causal agent, and legitimacy. An innovative feature of this taxonomy is the expressly cognitive nature of the five dimensions. To date, Roseman's taxonomy is the most promising effort from a cognitive perspective, but it awaits empirical validation. Pending such support, it seems premature to count on the role of particular dimensions. The taxonomy in any case supports the idea that valence (evaluation) is a necessary component for defining the structural features of affect. Valence emerges repeatedly as the single dimension overlapping varied taxonomies of emotion (e.g., Davitz, 1970; Plutchik, 1970; Schlosberg, 1954; Wundt, 1897). And, it also appears persistently in semantic judgments (Osgood, Suci, & Tannenbaum, 1957), in small group evaluations (Bales, 1970), and in person perception (Schneider et al., 1979). Recent evidence favors the view of affect as valence plus arousal (Russell, 1978). To put it simply, interpersonal affect certainly includes at least valence, but the extent to which other dimensions are required remains open to empirical test. Certainly, valence will do as a conceptual starting point.

As yet, there is no firm empirical basis for requiring differentiated emotions in cognitive approaches to interpersonal affect. Not only is it premature for social cognition to tackle differential emotions, there are no apparent a priori reasons why the role of affect in social cognition should differ across discrete emotions, beyond the positive–negative breakdown provided by ''mere'' evaluation. Consequently, research and theory focused on evaluation (preference judgments) sheds light on the most vital part of affect. Valence constitutes a preliminary working definition of affect, although it may seem barren to some.[2]

There is another way that cognitive approaches to interpersonal affect seem at first to define affect in a limited fashion. Strongman (1978), in his comprehensive review, criticizes cognitive approaches such as those of Lazarus and Arnold for neglecting the intensity brought on by arousal; they only deal with mild (i.e., low-arousal) emotions. But, if cognition and arousal are both essential to affect, then it is a useful task to study those cognitive preferences, whatever their intensity. Lukewarm evaluations and preferences may not capture the entire phenomenon of affect, but they do focus on an essential and researchable part of it.

Strongman raises another and more telling critique of cognitive approaches to affect. He points out that cognitive approaches use S–R methodology as if it can establish intervening processes (cf. Taylor, 1976, for a similar critique of early social-cognition research). Recent advances in the study of cognitive processes make this criticism potentially obsolete, in that one can now more directly assess the intervening links. Evidence from social-cognition research contributes in precisely this fashion to clarify processes at the affect–cognition interface. The remainder of this chapter addresses the interplay of cognition with interpersonal affect, in ways informed by cognitive research.

GUIDES TO THE ROLE OF AFFECT IN SOCIAL COGNITION

As we have seen, even ''cognitive'' approaches to affect have been ambiguous in their analyses of process and their cognitive assumptions have not yet been substantiated empirically. The introductory section argued that social psychology, with its growing cognitive sophistication, is now suited to consider affect at the level of processing. Although it mostly has ignored the issue up to now, social cognition does give a few precedents for the cognitively informed study of

---

[2]Kinder, in a personal communication (1979) regarding affective responses to politicians, has suggested that hypothetical stimuli may not elicit differentiated affect, but evaluation only, whereas real stimulus people, with a history of impact on the perceiver, may elicit clearly differentiated affect. Consistent with this suggestion is the fact that clinicians, who deal with real people, argue for differential affects, whereas experimental psychologists, who do not, are more likely to ignore differential affect. New data may resolve this fundamental issue and ultimately the distinction between affect and evaluation may prove useful. For the moment, affect and evaluation are used interchangeably here.

interpersonal affect. Exceptions to the neglect of affect surface in work on perceptions of the self and others. Two currents run through this work: First, cognitive interpretations based on prior experience structure affect, structure that mainly lies in valence, according to evidence available so far. The second theme in the research to date indicates that, where attention is measured or manipulated, it intensifies affect.

Self Knowledge and Affect

Research on self-focused attention (''objective self awareness'') demonstrates that both mood and interpersonal affect are exaggerated by attention directed to the self (Scheier & Carver, 1977; Wicklund, 1975, 1978). A process model specific to self-focused attention is being developed (Carver, 1979); it suggests that cognitive assessment provides the valence of expectancies for one's own behavior. And the resulting valenced expectations have affective consequences (Carver, Blaney, & Scheier, 1979). Such assessment must be based on stored knowledge about previous experience in that situation. So, the store of knowledge about one's self ultimately cues affect. And those affects are intensified by self attention.

A related version of the cognitive-interpretation theme also emerges in work on self concept and psychopathology. Kuiper and Derry (1981) propose a schema-driven model of depression, in which persistent and perhaps inaccurate self knowledge triggers long-term affective consequences. Again, the affective result of (depressive) self knowledge seems to be intensified by the chronic self-preoccupation characteristic of psychopathology. In both clinical and normal populations, then, self attention intensifies the affective consequences of stored knowledge.

Interpretations structure affect in another set of paradigms related to self inference. Attribution research represents a major cognitive thrust in social psychology, in its focus on how people think about their own and other people's behavior. Despite this focus, the research and theory only sometimes specify cognitive processes. Where cognitive variables are measured rather then inferred, research supports the idea that self attributions cue affect, at least in achievement-related contexts (Bradley, 1978; Weary, 1979; Weiner, in press; Weiner, Russell, & Lerman, 1978, 1979). That attributions have emotional consequences has been pitted against information-based explanations (e.g., M. Ross & Sicoly, 1979; Taylor & Fiske, 1978). Motivational perspectives hold that people assign causality in ways that protect their self esteem and their public image (see, e.g., Federoff & Harvey, 1976; Hull & Levy, 1979; Wicklund, 1975), whereas cognitive perspectives argue that people assign causality to salient factors that engulf their attention or are easily retrieved (see, e.g., McArthur & Post, 1977; L. Ross, 1977; M. Ross & Sicoly, 1979). Weary (Chapter 11 in this volume) provides an overview of that debate, sensibly concluding that affect and cognition probably both contribute to attribution (cf. Shaver, 1975).

Certainly, attribution theory's motivational–cognitive debate deserves to be finished. A viewpoint that resolves it, and that is relevant here, may lie in the following: Salience effects operate by exaggerating attributions in whatever direction they already tended (see, e.g., Taylor, Fiske, Close, Anderson, & Ruderman, 1977). Under some circumstances, defensive strategies predict the valence or direction of attributions. For example, directing attention to the self exaggerates the self-serving tendency not to take credit for failures. Cognitive perspectives have lacked a basis for predicting the direction of salience effects, mainly predicting that salient stimuli elicit extreme judgments (see Taylor & Fiske, 1978). Conversely, motivational perspectives have lacked a basis for predicting the extent and domain of self-serving biases. Combined, the two perspectives complement each other: Salience acts as an amplifier of affect-based attributions, for which motivation can determine valence. The exact processes that guide the direction and extremity of attributions remain to be specified, because most work hints at but does not completely clarify either the affective or cognitive component. Although much attribution work, both cognitive and motivational, only suggests intervening processes, recent work begins to fill this gap, in ways that are discussed shortly. For the present, the point is that a much-studied genre of cognitive interpretation, the attribution of causality, can have distinct affective consequences, and these consequences, further, are intensified by attention. As with self-awareness research, so with self-attribution research: Cognitive interpretations have affective consequences that are intensified by attentional focus.

Labeling of Emotion

The cognitive interpretation framework is not entirely new to the study of affect. Schachter's classic work on emotion (Schachter, 1971; Schachter & Singer, 1962) made a related point: Cognitions have affective consequences; specifically, they provide the label for emotion. As in research on self attribution and on self awareness, Schachter argued that cognition provides the perception of emotional states, and operationally, that perception was mainly either positive or negative. Schachter's original point was that social situations supply such interpretative labels given ambiguous arousal. The well-known manipulation of epinephrine-induced arousal may or may not have caused subjects to label their own emotions according to the situational cues given by the confederate's euphoric or angry behavior (for critiques, see Izard, 1977; Plutchik & Ax, 1967; Schneider et al., 1979), but the initial insight remains provocative. It paves the way for the first detailed cognitive analysis of interpersonal affect. Even in the work of Schachter's most recent critics (Marshall & Zimbardo, 1979; Maslach,

1979), some agreement surfaces. Both sides agree that ambiguous arousal must be interpreted, either in terms of the situation or in terms of prior personal experience with ambiguous arousal. Maslach argues that unexplained arousal itself biases interpretation toward negative emotional labels, based on a priori expectations about unexplained arousal. Schachter and Singer (1979) reply that the interpretation is entirely determined by context. But what guides interpretation in either model? In both cases, cognitive interpretations of emotion rely on one form or another of accumulated experience that provides appropriate emotional labels. A major feature of those labels is their valence.

The arousal component of Schachter's model is important too, regardless of whether arousal does or does not constrain its cognitive interpretation. On both sides of the controversy, arousal triggers cognitive interpretation, and together they constitute affect. This point implicitly parallels the earlier conclusion drawn from self-attribution and self-awareness work. There, attention combined with cognition to produce affect. Here, arousal is implicated as the partner to cognitive interpretation. This is not inconsistent; attention and arousal are closely linked (e.g., Norman, 1976); arousal has well-known attentional concomitants, serving to facilitate focused cognitive activity (e.g., Easterbrook, 1959; Kahneman, 1973). Their roles intermingle in the current analysis. If attention exaggerates affect, as implied by the research reviewed so far, and if attention and arousal covary, then arousal also can exaggerate affect.

Arousal and, consequently, attention serve two functions in the current analysis: First, arousal and attention both exaggerate affect, as just suggested, and second, they trigger interpretation, as implied by the work of Schachter and Maslach. This dual effect of the attention–arousal pair is clarified further by describing a recent cognitive model of emotion.

Like Schachter, Mandler (1975) argues that arousal and cognitive interpretation constitute emotion. Mandler clarifies the triggering role of arousal by agreeing with Schachter that arousal triggers cognitive interpretation ("meaning analysis"), but adds that, conversely, cognitions also can cause arousal.[3] Not only do a fluttery heart and a queasy stomach cause a person to wonder why, but internally provoked wondering why sometimes causes butterflies and palpatations. Thus, arousal finds its place in a system of mutual causality that outputs emotion (see Fig. 12.1). Both arousal and interpretation are necessary to emotion.

If cognitive interpretation is cued by arousal, what cues arousal? Arousal is sometimes cued by cognition, but sometimes it is cued by the environment. In Mandler's view, arousal is most importantly caused, however, by the interruption of highly organized activities (again, see Fig. 12.1). Interruption signals a

---

[3]Other relevant examples of this phenomenon lie in recent dissonance work showing that inconsistent cognitions cause arousal (Higgins et al., 1979) and further, that such arousal is aversive (Zanna et al., 1976). Cognitions clearly can generate arousal.

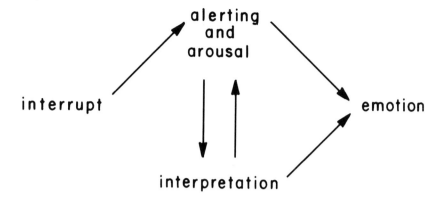

FIG. 12.1.   A general model of affect and cognition, interpreted from Mandler (1975).

change in the environment, readying the organism for cognition and action. Two types of interruption are specified, both relying on expectations about external stimuli: Either the expected does not occur or the unexpected does. Either a loud explosion or the absence of an expected explosion can cause butterflies and palpatations.

Such interruption, then, sets trouble-shooting in motion, with a few possible consequences, according to Mandler. If the problem is quickly (automatically) resolved, no emotion is attached to the interruption and ensuing arousal. (That loud explosion was only a neighbor's door slamming.) If the interruption constitutes easily integrated novelty, it is evaluated as good. (That loud explosion was my friend opening a surprise bottle of champagne.) Finally, if the interruption and arousal cannot be solved easily, if coping will be difficult, the interruption is evaluated as negative. (That loud explosion was a delinquent shooting my cat.) Mandler reviews a range of evidence on the interruption–arousal linkage. Relative to other aspects of his model, the mechanism seems undeveloped whereby ease of coping would cause the valence of affect. But the interrupt–arousal link itself usefully clarifies a major antecedent of emotion. Among other precursors to this aspect of Mandler's model, Simon (1967) proposed a related view of emotion as a mechanism functional for interrupting highly organized on-going activities. In his model, emotion adaptively forces an immediate response to urgent events such as intense external stimuli, impending physiological needs, and disturbing cognitive associations. Both Mandler and Simon view interruption and arousal as integral to emotion and they elaborate its antecedents in ways neglected by Schachter.

Mandler also embellishes Schachter's description of the other component necessary to emotion—that is, cognitive interpretation. Mandler's discussion of "meaning analysis" relies on expectations and prior knowledge. Such stored concepts about what to expect and how to interpret incoming stimuli may be framed as schemas—that is, generic knowledge abstracted from prior experience. Schemas contain associations to attributes and relationships among attributes for a given concept (e.g., R. C. Anderson, 1977; Bobrow & Norman, 1975; Rumelhart & Ortony, 1977); cognitive psychology of late has emphasized the importance of theory-driven processing, and Mandler's meaning analysis fits with that emphasis. Meaning analysis locates inputs with respect to organized knowledge structures and stops searching when a prior structure adequately accommodates the current events. Meaning analysis is similar to appraisal (i.e., Arnold, 1970; Lazarus et al., 1970), but does not reduce to simple evaluation according to Mandler.

In the context of emotion, schema-driven cognitive interpretation is novel, although it is hardly new elsewhere. Much current work in cognitive and cognitive-social psychology employs the schema notion, which is integral to the more general view of people as cognitive misers. As yet, though, none of this work has integrated affect. Mandler's analysis provides the conceptual base for that integration. Although Mandler's model is compelling, it is too general at present to serve as a framework for examining the role of affect in interpersonal settings. It suggests that unexpected events cue arousal, that arousal together with meaning analysis creates emotion. But it remains to social cognition to embellish and specify that model with respect to interpersonal affect. Mandler, like Schachter, is primarily concerned with the labeling of emotional states and not specifically with emotion directed toward other people, to which the discussion now turns.[4] Using the concept of schema-driven interpretation of affect, social cognition can, then, pursue a view of people as indeed cognitive misers, but not necessarily as emotional paupers.

Before pursuing this view, a caveat is in order: A major conceptual issue lies in the schema notion, which all too often is so broadly defined as to be not falsifiable. A related question is whether schemas are conceptually old wine in a new bottle (see Taylor & Crocker, 1981, for a discussion of both issues). In this particular context, the schema notion emphasizes the cognitive features of the current analysis. All the roughly comparable terms in analyses of affect carry their own unique excess baggage (e.g., meaning analysis, appraisal, ideoaffective structure, expectation), and schemas simply carry cognitive connotations of general and recent vintage. Within cognitive analyses, other possible terms each

---

[4]Leventhal (1974) has hypothesized a related process for the labeling of affect. Prewired expectancies and their confirmation or disconfirmation drive the emotional arousal system and generate simple pleasant or unpleasant reactions; interpretation or meaning separately guides the differentiation of affects. In his research (e.g., Leventhal, Brown, Shacham, & Engquist, 1979), Leventhal focuses particularly on the interaction of expectations and attention at the level of immediate encoding—that is, perceptual schemas. His work suggests an earlier site for emotional encoding than that described here, but his underlying reliance on attention, arousal, and expectation as combining to produce emotion is complementary to the current viewpoint.

have their own other excess meanings: Some are domain-specific schemas, such as frames (visual), scripts (event sequence), stereotypes (person); some have specific structural implications, such as feature list, network of associations; some tie in mainly irrelevant literatures—that is, set, expectancy; and some address only a subset of the issues—that is, prototype, chunk. But the underlying point is that particular affective knowledge is tied to an organized set of associations that can be triggered as a coherent whole; affective interpretation is an active process based on experience, rather than being wired-in or disorganized or responsive to each new encounter or totally veridical or any other possibility not informed by recent advances in cognition. Thus, the term schema focuses the analysis on the general problem of cognitive, structural, and processing variables related to affect.

Interpersonal Affect

Although not typically interpreted as affect, research on evaluations of others (impression formation) sheds some light on affect in social cognition. Given the previous argument that simple evaluations constitute a manageable and crucial portion of affect, regardless of their dimensional simplicity and low intensity, research on simple evaluative reactions to others potentially aids the exploration of interpersonal affect. Among person perception researchers, Norman Anderson (e.g., 1974) most thoroughly investigates evaluation: He provides a model of how perceivers distill an overall likability response from the mass of another person's attributes. Anderson depicts the process as reducing each attribute to its evaluative component—that is, on a positive–negative continuum—which is not unlike the notion of cognitive appraisal raised by Arnold and Lazarus. Anderson goes several steps further than they do, in that he directly speculates about the cognitive processes of evaluation. His averaging model portrays the person as an analog computer, converting a series of stimulus evaluations into a weighted summary, a process not unlike the metaphor previously suggested.

However, although Anderson's model hints at underlying cognitive processes that might produce interpersonal affect, he has not directly measured those processes. He addresses neither how individual attributes are evaluated prior to their integration into the overall evaluation, nor exactly how affect and cognition are processed in person perception. However, extensions of his basic approach do address these issues, as the next section demonstrates, in reviewing our research on evaluations and recall.

In contrast to Anderson, the recent work of Robert Zajonc (1980b) does directly address the processing of affect and cognition in evaluative judgments. Zajonc asserts that affect and cognition are processed differently, that compared with cognition, affect is basic, effortless, inescapable, irrevocable, subjectively valid, implicates the self, is difficult to verbalize, and may be separated from content. Most innovative in his current contribution to social cognition is his proposal that affect can come first, that after minimal sensory processing, a preference is formed—essentially a pleasant or unpleasant judgment. Cognitive processes, such as feature discrimination and recognition, proceed separately and more slowly. Moreland and Zajonc (1977, 1979) provide the most relevant evidence that underlies the separate-systems view of affect and cognition. Specifically, using Japanese ideographs, they find clear evidence that mere exposure effects on evaluation are not mediated by stimulus recognition. Further, affective judgments are faster and more memorable than purely cognitive judgments (see Zajonc, 1980b, for a review of other evidence). Affect, then, may precede and be independent of cognitive judgments. This proposal radically departs from prevailing assumptions in social psychology and in previous work on affect. As reviewed so far, "cognitive" research and theory in affect have assumed that cognition precedes affect (e.g., N. Anderson, 1974; Arnold, 1970; Lazarus et al., 1970; Mandler, 1975).

Zajonc's provocative proposal demands closer conceptual and empirical investigation because, in light of the affect research reviewed earlier, Zajonc has focused on a particular aspect of the affect–cognition problem. First, his conceptual analysis explicitly revolves around preference—that is, it remains to extend his analysis to more intense affective reactions. Second, the empirical base of Moreland and Zajonc's work is entirely attitudes toward inanimate objects. It remains to apply the analysis to perceptions of people. Finally, Zajonc primarily focuses on the consequence side of affect and cognition—that is, judgments and recall as outputs. But it is informative to consider the processing of affect and cognition at earlier stages, such as inputs; the framework discussed here considers earlier stages as well.

Zajonc has issued a conceptual challenge: Are affect and cognition separate? Or, if and when they meet, what might characterize their interface? In fact, Zajonc does not assert that affect always precedes cognition, simply that it can do so. It would be strange if there were absolutely no contact, in light of the work reviewed so far—that is, work on the cognitive appraisal of emotion, on affective consequences of self evaluation and self attribution, and on impression formation.

Before proceeding to evaluate social-cognition research that bears directly the separate-systems view of affect, it is helpful to summarize where the analysis has come so far. Work on feelings about oneself and on the labeling of emotion suggests in general that cognitive interpretations have important affective consequences. Analyses from cognitive approaches to some of the same phenomena hint that attention exaggerates the affective consequences of such interpretations.[5] Other work suggests that attention and arousal are both tied to affect: Schachter's model for the labeling of emotional states first adds the role of

---

[5] Izard (1977) and others view attention as a single specific affect. In contrast, the current view of affect as valence-plus-intensity incorporates attention into all affects.

arousal to analyses of affect. Mandler's model elaborates the causes of arousal (interrupts) and describes the interplay of arousal with cognitive interpretation, which then produces emotion. As a model for social cognition, however, Mandler's analysis is insufficiently specified. However, it does provide a compelling precedent for viewing affect as driven by cognitive interpretation. Turning from the general problem of labeling of emotion to specifically interpersonal affect, work on evaluations of others is sparse in cognitive insight. Zajonc, however, has proposed that some types of cognitions may follow on affect rather than vice versa.

As an important qualification to the current view, cognitive interpretation as guiding affect does not imply that cognitions all precede affect. Attention and minimal processing, specifically the fit to prior experiences, easily can precede both affective judgments and "cognitive" processes such as recognition.[6] Further, schema-driven interpretation can be either automatic and immediate or more deliberate and controlled, without challenging the cognitive-interpretation view. Affect is cued off stimuli by their fit to prior experiences, and it may well be cued before other more "cognitive" schema-based knowledge. For example, if a person's former sweetheart drove a blue VW bug, instant affect can surface at the sight of one. Such experience-based affective reaction can occur prior to other "cold" knowledge that surrounds blue VWs—for example, that the exsweetheart has since sold the car, that it had a grey interior, that such a car gets good mileage. Similarly, one can react strongly to blue VWs, or to people, for that matter, simply because they remind one of somebody, but such a reliance on prior experience as cuing affect does not presuppose awareness. In sum, then, regardless of relative timing, speed, or awareness, prior knowledge structures can be usefully viewed as cuing both affect and cognition. Thus, this analysis does not necessarily conflict with, and in fact does not primarily evaluate, the problems of affect–cognition sequence, relative speed, or awareness. Rather the focus here is how each is processed: How might cognitive misers deal with affect?

To anticipate the position taken here, cognitive misers process affect the way they process anything else—efficiently. If new information can be fit to old affectively laden knowledge, then the cognitive miser has available an immediate affective response, without laboriously calculating all the pros and cons of any particular new input (cf. N. Anderson, 1974). In this sense, then, affect is schema driven. Using the term schema for this process has the advantage of emphasizing cognitive structure: organized knowledge abstracted from prior encounters with individual instances. But using the term schema also has liabilities. As a concept in social cognition, it is not always specified well enough to be falsifiable. Its usage in the research that is described is fairly concrete, however. Its more general role in the model lies in its propensity to elicit process-level

---

[6]Zajonc implies this, but it is easy to miss, in light of his provocative central thesis.

mechanisms. A further implication of schema-driven processing of affect is that affect and cognition do connect at the level of interpretation, although they separate elsewhere. The final section returns to this issue.

Before finally proceeding to research that pursues the schema-driven role of affect in social cognition, a last comment is in order, regarding generalizations across paradigms. The work reviewed so far and the research that is discussed span a range of judgments: overall evaluation, likability, specific feelings, causal attributions. Some are more obviously affective than others. The definitional section of this chapter argued that evaluation or mere valence serves as a first approximation to affect and that firm empirical data do not yet support a more differentiated view. Certainly valence is the single most important dimension of affect, and it provides a starting point for cognitive analyses of affect. Thus, evaluations are a useful temporary surrogate for affect.

Attributions are less obviously affective judgments. In contrast to affect, attributions may seem purely "cold" semantic judgments, might seem to be measured only in uninvolving settings, and might seem to be influenced by entirely separate factors than, for example, evaluations. In certain circumstances, however, attributions carry clear affective overtones. Attributions for achievement outcomes recently have been shown to have definite affective consequences (Weiner, Russell, & Lerman, 1978, 1979). Locating causes for success and failure has clear evaluative implications for one's self image, and Weiner has shown that different affects emerge from different dimensions of attribution for achievement.[7] Attributions of dominance similarly carry affective overtones, for several reasons. First, much of the research on perceived causality ensures that attributions are not easily reducible to pure semantic judgment, by using videotaped or live conversations (e.g., Taylor & Fiske, 1975). Because perceivers are making attributions to real people, they must draw on accumulated experience in judging actual behavior, rather than on simple verbal association. Second, such attribution affects operate *more* clearly for involved than for uninvolved subjects (Taylor, Crocker, Fiske, Sprinzen, & Winkler, 1979, Study 2). So "cognitive" attribution affects are not confined to affectively uninvolving settings. And, finally, strongly evaluative measures (e.g., how friendly) are influenced by attentional manipulations just as impressions of dominance are; such evaluations of people are exaggerated in proportion to the person's relative salience (see Taylor & Fiske, 1978, for a review). The concomitant polarization of attributional and evaluative judgments is further evidence that attributions of this type strongly parallel affect. That is, deciding who dominated whom in a conversation and who was friendly both carry affective implications. Varied data show, then, that attributions are affectively significant judgments. The implica-

---

[7]This line of research forms an exception to the general lack of social-cognitive evidence for differential emotions. However, this developing line of research at present focuses mainly on achievement situations and so awaits generalization.

tion of the preceding argument is this: Some attribution research potentially illuminates affective processes and so is admissible evidence in constructing a role for affect in social cognition. The next section draws heavily on attribution data.

There is a final argument for casting a wide net to include evaluations, affect, and some attributions in the same framework. Social cognition's major neglect of affect requires drastic measures, and any potential evidence is useful, if it is cognitive in orientation. Moreover, all these affectively laden judgments do indeed reveal convergent principles for assessing where affect and social cognition separate and where the systems connect.

A ROLE FOR AFFECT IN SOCIAL COGNITION

To this point, the discussion has centered on previous research consistent with an evolving model for social cognition and affect, but not on research that directly supports such a model. This section discusses the research that provoked, at first, the separate-systems view of cognition and affect. Later, this research effort evolved to specify where cognition and affect might separate and where they might connect. This section works through data that apply directly to stages in the processing of interpersonal affect. The general framework provided by the theory and research reviewed so far suggests three separable stages: interrupts, attention, and schema-driven interpretation.

Interrupts

The beginning part of the model concerns environmental interrupts—unexpected events or salient features—that attract attention. Some of the antecedents of selective social attention are interpersonal parallels to selective attention toward objects. For example, novel people elicit attention, and people wearing bright colors draw attention. As discussed by McArthur (1981) and by Taylor and Fiske (1978), ample evidence indicates that salient social stimuli, defined a priori, will attract attention. Certain types of people will stand out in the environment by virtue of being unusual: Social outcasts—such as gypsies, tramps, and thieves or, less exotically, handicapped people—will elicit staring (Langer, Taylor, Fiske, & Chanowitz, 1976). Such novel people stand out on account of their statistical rarity in the culture. In a particular setting, solo or token individuals within an otherwise homogeneous group also attract attention by virtue of contextual rarity (Taylor et al., 1977).

Other antecedents of social attention are more uniquely raised by social perception than by object perception. The general principle here is that people focus attention on the most informative cues, which are also the most unusual ones. In person perception, it is well established that most information is slightly positive, due to the prevailing Pollyanna-type expectations people have about others (see Kanouse & Hanson, 1971). Given a standard, moderately positive expectation, negative information will stand out by virtue of being rare. So will extremely positive information. The expected distribution of positive and negative person information is depicted in Fig. 12.2. First, the horizontal axis depicts the evaluative impact of information. The neutral point of evaluation is indicated by the dotted vertical line. The vertical axis depicts the expected frequency of varying levels of evaluation. If people expect most social information to be slightly positive, then the distribution should bulge to the right of the neutral point, as shown; most information is slightly positive. Negative information and extreme positive information will be more rare, if the bulk of social information is seen as slightly positive.

Consider an example. If a friend describes someone as nice, or says that the person pats dogs occasionally, that is uninformative because it is fairly common. But if the person feeds every stray dog in the neighborhood, that is positive and extreme, so it is informative. On the other hand, if this person regularly kicks dogs, that is informative because it is negative; it is unexpected. And, if the person runs over dogs at every opportunity, that is especially informative; it is not only negative, but extreme. By systematically varying the extremity and valence of standard photographs (replicated over two behavioral dimensions and 16 stimulus people), a study by Fiske (1980) tested the hypothesis that extremity and negativity have disproportionate impact. Subjects consistently looked longest at extreme negative stimuli, about equally at moderate negative and extreme positive photos, and least at moderate positive photos. As predicted, the stimuli that were theoretically the most informative indeed elicited more attention. Thus, the moderate positivity bias in person perception implies that nega-

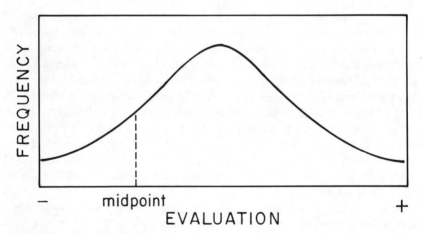

FIG. 12.2. Theoretical frequency distribution of person attributes at differing levels of evaluation (Fiske, 1980).

tive and extreme attributes will stand out by virtue of being unexpected; such attributes do elicit exaggerated looking times. In sum, then, people pay attention to extreme and negative social information, because it is rare and informative. Within a single individual, principles of social perception predict the direction of attention.[8]

All these studies of social novelty hinge on the perceivers' schemas, which may be defined as people's highly organized conceptions of what the social environment usually contains. Although these studies measured attention and not arousal, attention (specifically, the orienting response) has previously been linked to arousal (e.g., Berlyne, 1960), and so it is likely that arousal is triggered in a similar fashion (see Taylor & Fiske, 1978, for more discussion of social attention and alerting). The first stage of affective processing, interruption, functions to direct attention to unexpected environmental features, in social as well as inanimate settings, and so to alert the perceiver to potentially significant stimuli. Unusual events are more likely to require focused coping and thus to be affectively significant. Thus, the salience–attention link interrupts perceivers to alert them automatically to the stimuli most likely to affect them importantly.

Attention

Extremity.   Attention, in its turn, intensifies affective judgments, as previous work has hinted. Given exaggerated attention, evaluations and attributions become polarized—that is, the same stimulus elicits more extreme judgments when salient than when not salient. As argued earlier, in the discussion of defensive attribution effects, attentional focus intensifes affect, thus determining extremity of reactions. If attention determines intensity—that is, exaggerates judgments in whatever direction they already tended—then the same stimuli that attract attention should also carry the most weight in affective judgments. Earlier work bears on this issue. Several studies converge to show that attention provides evaluative intensity. For example, as noted earlier, directing subjects' attention to one member of a conversation will polarize their evaluations in whatever direction the judgments already tended (see Taylor & Fiske, 1978). Other research already cited (Fiske, 1980) shows that when attention is measured rather than manipulated, it corresponds nicely to evaluative weight. The more attention received by a particular attribute of a person, the more weight it carries in the overall evaluation. Thus, intensity is contributed by the attentional response. It is quite possible that more extreme intensity than is usually found in experimental social research is contributed by measurable physiological arousal. But even at minimal levels of

---

[8]Another dramatically social variable that predicts attentional focus is interpersonal outcome dependency (Berscheid, Graziano, Monson, & Dermer, 1976); despite measuring attention, the single relevant study did not address cognitive or affective variables beyond that stage, and so the finding is difficult to integrate into the entire framework proposed here.

arousal, the alerting response in the form of selective attention exaggerates affective responses.

Cuing interpretations. Attention-determined intensity is only part of the story. Attention not only cues intensity, it also sets interpretation in motion. The major gap in this model lies in the causal connection between attention and interpretation. This link cannot be evaluated here because social-cognitive research does not bear directly on it,[9] and there is no particular reason why it should. The attention–interpretation link is not a uniquely social phenomenon and in fact, requires more basic research in cognition. Moreover, because the attention–interpretation causality is hypothesized to go both ways, only connection, not cause, needs to be established. That much, at least, is supported by previous research (see Mandler, 1975). Of greater interest to social cognition is the nature of schema-driven affect, to which we now turn.

Schema-Based Interpretation

Thus far, the processing of affect has been described with respect to environmental interrupts (salient stimuli) as cuing attention, and in turn, attention as both exaggerating evaluative responses and cuing interpretation. Interpretation is a necessary process, because attention-driven intensity without direction or content is not itself affect. The interpretation of incoming stimuli determines the valence or direction of affective judgments. This evaluation must be made on the basis of abstract rules generalized from previous experience, and such generic knowledge may be characterized as schemas. In this context, the schema concept emphasizes two processing results: cognitive and affective. Because the cognitive effects of social schemas are the main on-going focus of much other analysis, only the outlines of that work are summarized here. Far more discussion is devoted to the novel problem of schema-driven interpretation of affect and to the interface between cognitive and affective responses.

Schema-Based cognition.   In this context, the schema notion brings in a few particular concepts. The first is inference: the fit of new instances to prior experience and the consequent assumptions made about the new instance. In ways well documented elsewhere, schemas allow for gap filling in the cognitive realm; given the applicability of a particular schema, people infer thematically related attributes that are never given (e.g., Bower, Black, & Turner, 1979; Cantor & Mischel, 1979). The second concept generated by the schema notion is organization. Schemas structure the relevance and consistency of incoming in-

---

[9]The Berscheid et al. (1976) study cited in footnote 8 tangentially applies here, in that cognitive interpretation (a person's role as a date or not a date) cued attention. But the application to the current framework is not entirely firm.

formation with respect to prior theories (see, e.g., Hastie, 1980). Schemas provide researchers with a sensible way to think about relevance and consistency, because schemas are people's informal theories about how the world should operate (consistency) and about what goes with what (relevance). The pair of concepts—inference and organization—emphasizes the impact of prior knowledge on new inputs—that is, schema-based interpretation (see Taylor & Crocker, 1981, for a review of the cognitive effects of social schemas).

Interplay of Affective and Cognitive Responses: Supporting the Null Hypothesis.   A program of research bears on the affect–cognition interplay in the model. At preliminary stages, we had assumed that cognitive and affective responses would be inextricably linked. It seemed reasonable to assume that intensity of affective reactions would covary with memory for the relevant inputs. Then, early research results and the provocative proposal made by Zajonc (1980b) suggested that the affect–cognition link was not obvious, and in fact, the null hypothesis seemed to be supported: Affectively laden judgments and recall persistently were unrelated.

One set of efforts was prompted by impression-formation research (N. H. Anderson & Hubert, 1963) that first hinted at separate systems of interpersonal affect (evaluation) and cognition (recall). The essential problem attacked was whether liking people hinges on memory for the data on which the liking is based (Dreben, Fiske, & Hastie, 1979). The question revolves around whether attributes that stand out in making an affectively laden judgment also stand out in memory. Within the impression domain, one can solve for the relative weight of individual items in a likability judgment and simultaneously calculate the probability of recall for those items. Specifically, people were presented with sentences describing behavior. These included, for example, "John rudely insulted the woman who found his wallet on the sidewalk where he dropped it," and "Frank drove 30 miles by himself to help his friend whose car had broken down on an empty dirt road." Each subject saw a series of such sentences for each stimulus person and made likability ratings. Previous person-perception work has indicated that serial position of information contributes to its relative weight (N. H. Anderson & Farkas, 1973; Jones & Goethals, 1971). Usually this emerges as primacy, but various response conditions produce recency. Some of the task conditions that cause serial position weights to vary enabled us to calculate weight as a function of serial position. Primacy emerged where primacy is predicted and recency where that is usually obtained in evaluative judgments.

More interesting to the affect–cognition problem are the recall curves calculated for the same data. It might seem sensible to predict that people remember the same attributes they weight heavily. If information has an impact on judgment, it should stand out and be remembered particularly. However, that is not at all the case. The serial position curves for recall were all U-shaped, a standard memory result showing both primacy and recency. The likability weights, in contrast, had showed *either* primacy or recency, but never both in the same condition. Moreover, correlations between recall and weight were about zero. So the obvious link between an affective judgment and recall of the data on which it was based just is not present. Recall and affective weights were completely unrelated. This, then, is suggestive evidence that recall—a cognitive process—is governed by mechanisms distinct from likability judgments—affective reactions to people.

This effect or, strictly, noneffect replicated in our finding a similar lack of relation between cognition and affect in another domain. Fiske, Taylor, Etcoff, and Laufer (1979) were interested to see whether one can mimic actual salience effects in stories that depict relative salience. In other words, if people read a story and take a particular character's perspective, will they construct an imaginary scene and show exaggerated attributions as a function of *imaginary* stimuli that engulf their attention? One story involved a taxi driver, with a passenger in the back seat, driving out of a tunnel and onto a main street. Visual images from the cabbie and passenger's vantage point concluded damp, glistening titles, green and white exit signs, and the bright sunlight in contrast to the dark tunnel interior. Coming toward the tunnel exit ramp—that is, down the main street from the opposite direction—were a motorcyclist and a driver in a Toyota. Images best seen from their perspective on the main street included a hitchhiker with a knapsack, a boarded-up gas station, and the Toyota driver's purple and white hat. The exiting cab encountered a stalled truck in its path and swerved into the motorcyclist's lane. The motorcyclist, who was not concentrating, did not see the cab, and they crashed into each other.

The story had two actors and an observer who shared each actor's imaginary vantage point. Subjects were assigned to one of these four roles. Their recall was measured as a function of imaginary perspective, and defensive attributions on behalf of their character were measured—that is, motorcyclist role takers should blame the cabbie for the accident, and vice versa. The role-taking manipulations of visual perspective did have a huge effect on recall for vantage-relevant information in the story. But the vantage-relevant visual recall bore no relationship to attributions of causality.[10] Again, we came out for the null hypothesis.

The lack of relationship between affective judgments and recall carried over to attributions made about live interactions. In modeling the effects of attention on attribution, Fiske, Kenny, and Taylor (1979) consider several possible relationships between recall and attribution. One possibility would be that when salient stimuli attract attention, this perceptual focus results in encoding more details about the salient aspects of the environment. If a perceiver takes in a greater quantity of details about, for example, the salient actor in a conversation, the

---

[10]Bower (1977) did find a connection between affect-laden attributions and vantage-relevant recall. But those studies confounded actor–observer role with visual perspective, so interpretations of the relevant covariation are ambiguous.

person can access more instances of the salient actor causing the conversation than instances of the nonsalient actor being causal, so the perceiver assigns relative influence accordingly. About half the studies that measure both recall and attribution find that they are positively correlated, whereas half get no relationship, and none gets a reversal (see Taylor & Fiske, 1978). The implication, then, is that something about memory covaries with attribution, but it has not been specified well, or else the recall–judgment link would be clearer. This motivated the consideration of various likely specifications of recall.

The first candidate considered follows from the nature of attention in the salience studies. In one study, people's ability to take in the verbal content of the conversation was completely disrupted, but salience affects remained intact (Taylor, et al., 1979, Study 1). Some observers of a dyadic conversation observed unencumbered, whereas others were assigned to count the total number of pronouns as they watched. The pronoun counters remembered virtually nothing of the conversation's verbal content, and yet they showed salience effects on attribution that were just as strong as the effects shown by the control observers. Thus, the critical attentional process seemed able to operate solely in a visual mode. Consider how this might work: At a cocktail party, one witnesses someone else's conversation, which cannot be heard because of the din of fascinating chatter all around. Essentially deaf to the conversation between these two people, one is observing over the shoulder of one of them, enroute to the hors d'oeuvres table. Although unable to hear a word they say, the observer might well pick up an impression of who is dominating the conversation, on the basis of gestures, talking time, who interrupts whom, who seems to be asking the questions, and who seems to be a passive, attentive listener.[11] Our subjects were in precisely this situation, and in fact, they managed to come up with impressions of influence. Deaf to the conversation content, they were left with vivid images of the salient person animatedly talking and carrying on. Accordingly, they rated that person as more influential, perhaps because more images of that person came to mind. Because the visual channel alone can produce salience effects, visual recall might well connect to impressions of influence.

However eminently plausible visual images might be as a mediator, and despite significant effects of attention on both visual recall and on attributions, the relationship of visual recall to attributions simply did not exist. In two studies, the mediating link between visual recall and attribution was directly assesed; in neither study was it of a size worth mentioning. As a methodological aside, we would have been misled had we only relied on the ANOVA results—that is, the significant effects of attention on visual recall and on attribution. To demonstrate mediation, it is not sufficient to show the effect of the manipulation (attention) on both the mediator (recall) and the dependent measure (attribution).

[11]This example is not to be confused with the "cocktail-party phenomenon" in attention, whereby one is distracted to varying degrees by competing aural stimuli.

Investigating mediation, then, requires establishing the link between the mediating variable and the main dependent measure. Typically, social psychologists do not precisely test such crucial mediating links, because of our usual analyses of variance; these simply test the effect of the manipulation on both the mediating variable and the effect of interest, treating both as dependent variables. Consequently, our research used alternative analysis methods for testing mediation models, specifically structural modeling techniques, which are more commonly used in sociology and political science with nonexperimental data. Examining patterns of correlations to assess their consistency with specified models, the techniques involve a combination of path analysis and factor analysis (Jöreskog, 1973; see Kenny, 1979, for an in-depth discussion of these methods applied to social-science research). Structural modeling, then, disabused us of visual recall as a potential mediator of the attention–attribution relationship. Yet again, we came out for the null hypothesis in exploring the interplay of affect and cognition.

Because quantity of visual recall does not connect well to impressions of influence, another specification of recall was considered, which also seemed a likely candidate. Sheer quantity of recall seemed to be unrelated, but ease of recall might be the crucial link. That is, people may take in equivalent amounts of information, but impressions of influence may be formed from the most available data (see Kahneman & Tversky, 1973). In this view, impressions are formed from data stored at the top of the mental heap, data stored in an easily retrievable form. To summarize the results of our foray down a rather reasonable path, availability of visual recall does not reject the null hypothesis. Easily recalled visual evidence does not connect to impressions.

At this point, there were two alternative routes; we could give up and come out for the null hypothesis as best describing the affect–cognition interface. But that is an unsatisfactory resolution, partly because proving the null hypothesis is an impossible task and partly because it is no resolution. We cannot ever claim no relationship between every kind of recall and impressions. Someone will always dream up a kind of recall we did not measure. And, there remains a scientist's dissatisfaction with giving up. So, there is a second possibility; the studies can be refined by using more subtle measures. Undaunted, we made another foray.

Interplay of Cognitive and Affective Responses: Schema-Driven Processing.   The final cognitive–attribution link derived from causal schemas: people's informal hypotheses about what causes what. As discussed by Tversky and Kahneman (1980), perceivers focus on data that resemble (are representative of) causality, regardless of their logical relevance to the actual causal process. For example, if an observer believes that confident people are influential, then the perceiver will use confidence as evidence for influence, regardless of its actual impact on the observed interaction. Perhaps, then, evidence that people perceive as relevant is a likely candidate for linkages between recall and impressions of influence.

That was exactly the case. When people went back to their recall output and tagged those items that they saw as relevant to their attributions, a clear relationship emerged between recall and impressions of influence. People's memory for what they consider relevant evidence and their impressions of who caused what clearly showed the appropriate mediating link. What developed here is that the affectively laden impressions are highly correlated with memory for data perceived as relevant. The schema concept usefully defines relevant evidence, and what is more, in these studies, it defines evidence relevant to affectively laden impressions. In sum, the role of schemas in affect is yet to be specified fully, but these studies provide preliminary evidence, and we can speculate further.

Schema-Based affect.   Other research bears on schematic processing of affective judgments. Defensive attributions, as argued, are based jointly in cognitive and affective processes. Salience effects exaggerate attributions in whichever direction the perceiver is pushed motivationally. But how to describe the directional biasing effects of motivation? Structured sets of rules, built up from previous experience, could determine affect-based self attributions—for example, "When I succeed, I caused it; when I fail, it's not my fault" (Frieze, 1977; Weiner, Frieze, Kukla, Reed, Rest, & Rosenbaum, 1971; Weiner et al., 1978); or "I've always been a responsible person; I could never cause an accident like that" (Duval & Hensley, 1976); or "I'm responsible for all the bad (and good) things that happen to me; whatever I get is my fault (Kuiper & Derry, 1981). Self schemas do not have to contain only cold cognitive information, nor do the contents of schemas all have to be rational and right.

Evaluations may be schema based in ways suggested by another realm. Consider stereotypes. Knowledge could structure stereotyped evaluations in two ways. First, current research on stereotypes indicates that people categorize others on the basis of salient social features (Taylor, Fiske, Etcoff, & Ruderman, 1978), misperceive stereotype-consistent covariation (Hamilton & Rose, 1979), misremember information that fits with their stereotyped expectations (e.g., Cohen, 1977; Snyder & Uranowitz, 1978), and organize recall on the basis of stereotypes (Fiske, Piaget, & Dunn, 1970). Stereotyping is well explained by normal cognitive processes (see Hamilton, 1979, for a review), typified by schema research. Stereotypes may be considered simply one kind of person schema (cf. Ashmore & DelBoca, 1981; Taylor & Crocker, 1981), and they typically have been studied in the cognitive-miser paradigm, relying on memory measures. But social schemas can contain derogatory or laudatory information about others and that feature captures the recently neglected affective feature of stereotyping. Consider comments like "Oh yeah, I recognize that type; we never get along," or "This prospective student reminds me of Smedley, who stuck around 10 years and never finished; I'm against admitting this one" (cf. Abelson, 1976). Stereotyping especially points out that cognitive misers have feelings too, and they discover them just as they do cognitive "knowledge": by drawing on preconstructed evaluations tied to previously established patterns of knowledge.

Another hypothesis concerning schema-based interpretation and affect also stems from stereotyping research. Linville (Linville, 1979; Linville & Jones, 1980) has suggested that evaluations are more polarized, the less complex one's schema is. Thus, a single piece of information carries less evaluative weight when one already possesses a complex set of knowledge, compared to when one knows very little. Evaluations of outgroup members, for example, would be more influenced by one extremely positive or extremely negative instance than would evaluations of one's own group, about whom one knows so much more. Linville's predictions are supported for immediate evaluations of simplistically perceived people and objects. Tesser (e.g., Tesser, 1978; Tesser & Leone, 1977) finds that such evaluations become more polarized over time, if the schema is sufficiently developed to provide further evaluations buttressing the direction of the original moderate reaction. In impression formation, N. H. Anderson's set size effect (e.g., 1974) makes a prediction similar to Tesser but without elaborating the cognitive underpinnings. In any case, this research all provides preliminary evidence that schema complexity is important in shaping the extremity of affect.

To summarize various speculations about schemas and affect, suggestive evidence from attribution and stereotyping argues that prior knowledge and expectations (schemas) structure affectively significant information; such schemas cue valence in affective reactions.

Summary

Fig. 12.3 summarizes the role advanced for affect in social cognition. Starting at the left, salient features of the social environment generate interrupts. Just as in object perception, novelty and contrast attract attention. Further, person information may attract attention by virtue of being evaluatively rare. Extreme and negative information have been shown to attract attention because they are unexpected events. Thus, salient social information causes alerting and attention. (This, if anything, is the "environmental" relevance of the model.) In turn, attention provides intensity to affective reactions. Evaluations of people, judgments of influence, preferences, and likability are argued to be affectively laden, and these judgments have all been shown to be exaggerated or intensified by attention. Moving to interpretation, several lines of research and theory argue that affects are interpreted by fit to prior experience. Such experience accumulates to form generic knowledge, or schemas, that structure new information of both an affective and cognitive sort. Moving to outputs, the most crucial struc-

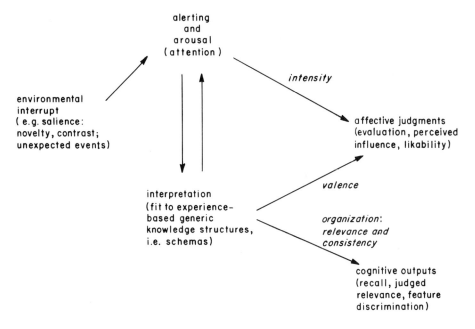

FIG. 12.3.   An embellished model of interpersonal affect and social cognition.

ture for affect is valence. The most relevant organizing structures for cognitive variables are relevance and consistency. As is becoming well established, prior cognitive structures organize cognitive reactions such as recall, judged relevance, and feature discrimination. This chapter argues that prior cognitive structures also organize interpersonal affect. In short, schemas cue emotion.

SUMMARY AND IMPLICATIONS

This chapter began with the observation that the burgeoning literature on social cognition neglects affect. Exceptions to this rule lie in work on defensive attribution, self knowledge, and impression formation. Research in these areas hints at a role for affect in social cognition, but does not focus on the structure and processing of affect. One analysis that does emphasize the processing of affect emerges in Zajonc's proposal—stemming from research in attitudinal mere exposure—that affect can be independent of cognition. Recent data from person perception also show that affectively laden judgments (attributions and evaluations) are uncorrelated with some seemingly relevant cognitive responses (recall for the items on which the judgment was based). These results all conspire to support a separate-systems view of interpersonal affect and cognition.

Closer examination of the separate-systems hypothesis requires definition of both affect and cognition. What exactly characterizes the pair of psychological phenomena that so unexpectedly separate? Definition of structure and specification of process clarify the role of affect in social cognition. The structure of affective and cognitive responses differ in ways that shed light on their interplay. Affect may be structurally defined and characterized based on literature somewhat unfamiliar to many social psychologists. In social cognition, affect may be usefully distinguished into mood, evaluation, and emotion. Mood is unfocused affect, not targeted at particular causes or consequences. Evaluation is affect focused on particular objects, and is limited to valence that varies in intensity but not over multiple dimensions; evaluation characterizes the simple view of affect as positive/negative appraisal. Emotion, also, is focused affect, but is importantly differentiated beyond mere evaluation. Differential emotions have not been addressed here, first, because the evidence bearing on differential emotions is uneven, and so it seems premature to count on the presence of any particular dimension in interpersonal affect. Second, no striking evidence insists that the role of affect in social cognition will differ across dimensions other than positive and negative affects. Thus, the essential defining structure of interpersonal affect is valence. And valence, by definition, has no particular role in solely cognitive responses.

Intensity is the other vital structural facet that differentiates affect and cognition.[12] Intensity is contributed to affective judgments by attention and arousal. In analyses by Mandler, by Schachter and Singer, and even by their critics, it is clear that arousal prompts cognitive interpretation of affective states. Furthermore, person-perception work indicates that a usual concomitant of arousal, attention, intensifies affective judgments. The exact role of attention and arousal in interpersonal affect requires further clarification, but this much is clear: Intensity matters to the structure of affect in ways not paralleled by more purely cognitive variables such as memory; distinctions between affect and cognition, then, include at least the structural features valence and extremity as fundamental to affect.

Affect and cognition differ also in features of their processing that are fundamentally separate. Close examination indicates stages at which cognition and affect must overlap and stages at which they are independent. Clearly, attention—which may be seen as a cognitive process—precedes other responses, both affective and cognitive. Minimal processing must occur before any reaction, however immediate, can be made. Attention and minimal processing, then, is a

---

[12]Intensity clearly could be considered intrinsic to cognition—for example, related to levels of activation within particular cognitive structures (e.g., Collins & Loftus, 1975)—but at present, social psychology's borrowing of cognitive variables does not draw heavily on such inherently continuous aspects of cognitive representation.

stage at which affect and cognition cannot sensibly be distinct. At the interpretation stage following on attention, affect and cognition still overlap. Both are cued by abstracted prior knowledge. Schemas cue valence in affect and other types of structure in cognition—that is, such variables as relevance and consistency. A possible distinction in processing may lie in valence's being cued more quickly than other more "cognitive" knowledge; valence, being simpler and adaptively more important, may be a more automatic judgment than cold cognitions. In sum, the processing distinctions between affect and cognition, then, lie in the stages that follow on attention and interpretation. Once inputs are fit to prior experience, affect and cognition diverge in response structure and possibly in speed. Thus, an answer to the separate-systems question is: Yes, affect and cognition do differ. Their structure is fundamentally different, and further, affect is amplified by input intensity in ways cognition is not.

Looking ahead to the future role of affect in social cognition, several issues will persist as problems for research and analysis. First, salient social stimuli clearly cause attention and quite possibly cue arousal. But the mechanisms by which they do so remain unclear and ripe for investigation. Second, although attention intensifies affect, again, the mechanisms are unclear. Third, patterned knowledge or schemas cue at least the valence of affect and define the relevance and consistency of cognitive variables such as memory. But neither the structural features nor the processing mechanisms are at all obvious in the case of affect. Finally, in developing a cognitively informed study of interpersonal affect, further research will doubtless focus on whether and how differential affects matter to social cognition. Defining a role for affect in social cognition requires in all cases close analyses of process.

Given the context of this conference volume, a final caveat is in order: Basic research in social cognition is prone to ignore behavior, because the main concern lies with events inside the organism. But, affect has important behavioral antecedents and consequences and several emotion theorists have discussed such affective response syndromes (e.g., Izard, 1977; Lazarus et al., 1970; Miller, Galanter, & Pribram, 1960). An exception to the usual neglect of behavior in cognitive approaches to affect lies in Roseman's (1979) and Abelson's (1979) newly developed analyses of affect in terms of goals and plans; these are the foundations for a cognitively informed view of affectively based behavior.

Social-cognition researchers in affect will be propelled toward accounting for behavior by a more general set of forces, in addition. As the field becomes increasingly tied to other fields, particularly as it becomes increasingly applied, social and cognitive psychology, in their various mixtures, will be forced to account for behavior better than we do now. If we take seriously the application of social cognition and affect to other fields—for example, to legal psychology (e.g., Penrod & Hastie, 1979), medical psychology (e.g., Taylor, 1979; Wortman & Dunkel-Schetter, 1979), political psychology (Fiske & Kinder,

1981), or environmental psychology (this volume)—then research and theory cannot continue ignoring behavior. In this volume's application to environmental psychology, the contributions severally draw on the whole healthy range of variables: affective, cognitive, and behavioral. This makes sense; real world consumers of social cognition and affect will demand behavioral consequences.

In closing, this chapter does not argue for an entirely new pendulum swing over to affect and away from cognition. The systems are too entwined to allow that. Rather, social cognition can spiral: The return to affect can move forward simultaneously, if it brings with it the recent advances in theory and methods of cognitive psychology.

However, our models need not be limited to the computer metaphor that drives much of that work. Memory in general, and schemas in particular, are represented well by the binary digital-computer model, and that model has propelled parts of the field for some time. But, if affects are better considered via an analog metaphor, where will that push social-cognitive research and theory? Very simply, it forces one to consider both intensity, constantly changing depending on intensity of the inputs, and valence, determined by the sign of the inputs.

Both together are minimal conditions to the consideration of interpersonal affect. If we concentrate on only valence or only intensity, we will work with a caricature of affect. Consider how a sole reliance either on valence or on intensity creates a peculiar portrait of a person. In the movie ''Manhattan,'' Woody Allen sorts people into heroes and villains, with no degrees in between. More specifically, he sorts women into heroines and villainesses. We all know people whose emotional life is black and white, for whom the sole affective structure is positive or negative, with no shades of grey. Conversely, there are people for whom the major dimension in life is intensity. Such people seem to respond to others solely on the basis of intensity, regardless of whether it is positive or negative. In the same movie, Diane Keaton says to Allen, ''You were hostile and I found that very attractive.'' He responds, ''Really?'' and notably, he is more delighted than surprised. She was responding only to intensity of experience. Both Keaton and Allen are to some extent affective caricatures, in their respective reliance on only valence or only intensity. (Perhaps that explains why they did not get along, in the end.)

In any case, movies and real life deal with affect in ways neglected by social cognition. No model of the social human being as cognitive digital computer, however complex, will explain smoothly Keaton's fascination with intensity in that movie, nor Allen's sole reliance on valence. Although explaining Keaton and Allen is not anyone's main purpose here, more consideration of affective reactions would take us beyond the affectively barren cognitive-miser model. Perhaps we can marry that emotional pauper to one of the tragicomedians Keaton or Allen, both of whom are rich in pleasure and pain.

ACKNOWLEDGMENTS

Portions of this chapter were presented at a symposium on Social Cognition and Affect, the American Psychological Association, 1979. I would like to thank Eugene Borgida, Margaret Clark, John Harvey, Reid Hastie, Charles Kiesler, Patricia Linville, Shelley Taylor, and Robert Zajonc for their comments on an earlier draft.

REFERENCES

Abelson, R. P. Script processing in attitude formation and decision-making. In J. S. Carroll & J. W. Payne (Eds.), *Cognition and social behavior*. Hillsdale, N.J.: Lawrence Erlbaum Associates, 1976.

Abelson, R. P. *The affect structure of the persuasive appeals of public affairs organizations*. Paper presented to American Psychological Association, New York, 1979. (a)

Abelson, R. P. *Comprehension of feelings*. Manuscript in preparation, Yale University, 1979. (b)

Anderson, J. R. *Language, thought, and memory*. Hillsdale, N.J.: Lawrence Erlbaum Associates, 1976.

Anderson, J. R. Arguments concerning representations for mental imagery. *Psychological Review*, 1978, *85*, 249–277.

Anderson, J. R. Further arguments concerning representations for mental imagery: A reply to Hayes-Roth and Pylyshyn. *Psychological Review*, 1979, *86*, 395–406.

Anderson, N. H. Information integration: A brief survey. In D. H. Krantz, R. C. Atkinson, R. D. Luce, & P. Suppes (Eds.), *Contemporary developments in mathematical psychology* (Vol. 2). San Francisco: W. H. Freeman, 1974.

Anderson, N. H., & Farkas, A. J. New light on order effects in attitude change. *Journal of Personality and Social Psychology*, 1973, *28*, 88–93.

Anderson, N. H., & Hubert, S. Effects of concomitant verbal recall on order effects in personality impression formation. *Journal of Verbal Learning and Verbal Behavior*, 1963, *2*, 379–391.

Anderson, R. C. The notion of schemata and the educational enterprise. In R. C. Anderson, R. J. Spiro, & W. E. Montague (Eds.), *Schooling and the acquisition of knowledge*. Hillsdale, N. J.: Lawrence Erlbaum Associates, 1977.

Arnold, M. B. Perennial problems in the field of emotion. In M. B. Arnold (Ed.), *Feelings and emotions: The Loyola symposium*. New York: Academic Press, 1970.

Ashmore, R. D., & Del Boca, F. K. Conceptual approaches to stereotypes and stereotyping. In D. L. Hamilton (Ed.), *Cognitive processes in stereotyping and intergroup behavior*. Hillsdale, N.J.: Lawrence Erlbaum Associates, 1981.

Bales, R. F. *Personality and interpersonal behavior*. New York: Holt, Rhinehart, & Winston, 1970.

Berlyne, D. W. *Conflict, arousal, and curiosity*. New York: McGraw-Hill, 1960.

Berscheid, E., Graziano, W., Monson, T., & Dermer, M. Outcome dependency: Attention, attribution, and attraction. *Journal of Personality and Social Psychology*, 1976, *34*, 978–989.

Bersheid, E., & Walster, E. H. *Interpersonal attraction*, 2nd ed. Reading, Mass.: Addison Wesley, 1978.

Bobrow, D. G., & Norman, D. A. Some principles of memory schemata. In D. G. Bobrow & A. Collins (Eds.), *Representation and understanding: Studies in cognitive science*. New York: Academic Press, 1975.

Bower, G. H. *"On injucting life into deadly prose": Studies in explanation-seeking*. Paper presented to the Western Psychological Association, Seattle, 1977.

Bower, G. H., Black, J. B., & Turner, T. J.   Scripts in memory for text. *Cognitive Psychology,* 1979, *11,* 177–220.

Bower, G. H., Monteiro, K. P., & Gilligan, S. G.   Emotional mood as a context for learning and recall. *Journal of Verbal Learning and Verbal Behavior,* 1978, *17,* 573–585.

Bradley, G. W.   Self-serving biases in the attribution process: A reexamination of the fact or fiction question. *Journal of Personality and Social Psychology,* 1978, *36,* 56–71.

Cantor, N., & Kihlstrom, J. F. (Eds.).   *Personality, cognition, and social interaction.* Hillsdale, N.J.: Lawrence Erlbaum Associates, 1981.

Cantor, N., & Mischel, W.   Categorization processes in the perception of people. In L. Berkowitz (Ed.), *Advances in experimental social psychology* (Vol. 12). New York: Academic Press, 1979.

Carver, C. S.   A cybernetic model of self-attention processes. *Journal of Personality and Social Psychology,* 1979, *37,* 1251–1281.

Carver, C. S., Blaney, P. H., & Scheier, M. F.   Focus of attention, chronic expectancy, and responses to a feared stimulus. *Journal of Personality and Social Psychology,* 1979, *37,* 1186–1195.

Clark, M. S., Goldin, S. E., & Isen, A.   *Positive mood and retrieval of material from memory.* Paper presented to the American Psychological Association, New York, 1979.

Clark, M. S., & Isen, A. M.   Toward understanding the relationship between feelings states and social behavior. In A. Hastorf & A. Isen (Eds.), *Cognitive social psychology.* New York: Elsevier North-Holland, in press.

Cohen, C. E.   *Cognitive bases of stereotyping.* Paper presented to the American Psychological Association, San Francisco, 1977.

Collins, A. M., & Loftus, E. F.   A spreading-activation theory of semantic processing. *Psychological Review,* 1975, *82,* 407–428.

Davitz, J. R.   A dictionary and grammar of emotion. In M. B. Arnold (Ed.), *Feelings and emotion: The Loyola symposium.* New York: Academic Press, 1970.

Dreben, E. K., Fiske, S. T., & Hastie, R.   The independence of item and evaluative information: Impression and recall order effects in behavior-based impression formation. *Journal of Personality and Social Psychology,* 1979, *37,* 1758–1768.

Duval, S., & Hensley, V.   Extensions of objective self-awareness theory: The focus of attention-causal attribution hypothesis. In J. Harvey, W. Ickes, & R. Kidd (Eds.), *New directions in attribution research* (Vol. 1). Hillsdale, N.J.: Lawrence Erlbaum Associates, 1976.

Easterbrook, J. A. The effect of emotion on cue utilization and the organization of behavior. *Psychological Review,* 1959, *66,* 183–201.

Ekman, P.   Universals and cultural differences in facial expressions of emotion. In J. Cole (Ed.), *Nebraska symposium on motivation, 1971.* Lincoln: University of Nebraska Press, 1972.

Ericsson, K. A., & Simon, H. A.   Verbal reports as data. *Psychological Review,* 1980, *87,* 215–251.

Ewert, O.   The attitudinal character of emotion. In M. B. Arnold (Ed.), *Feelings and emotions: The Loyola symposium.* New York: Academic Press, 1970.

Federoff, N. A., & Harvey, J. H. Focus of attention, self-esteem, and attribution of causality. *Journal of Research in Personality,* 1976, *10,* 336–345.

Festinger, L.   *A theory of cognitive dissonance.* Stanford: Calif. Stanford University Press, 1957.

Fiske, S. T.   Attention and weight in person perception: The impact of negative and extreme behavior. *Journal of Personality and Social Psychology,* 1980, *38,* 889–906.

Fiske, S. T., Kenny, D. A., & Taylor, S. E.   *Structural models for the mediation of salience effects on attribution.* Unpublished manuscript, Carnegie-Mellon University, 1979.

Fiske, S. T., & Kinder, D. R.   Involvement, expertise, and schema use: Evidence from political cognition. In N. Cantor & J. Kihlstrom (Eds.), *Cognition, social interaction, and personality.* Hillsdale, N.J.: Lawrence Erlbaum Associates, 1981.

Fiske, S. T., Piaget, A. & Dunn, D.   *The cognitive organization of stereotypes in memory.* Unpublished manuscript, Carnegie-Mellon University, 1980.

Fiske, S. T., Taylor, S. E., Etcoff, N. L., & Laufer, J. K.   Imaging, empathy, and causal attribution. *Journal of Experimental Social Psychology,* 1979, *15,* 356–377.

Frieze, I. H.   Causal attributions for success and failure: Advances in theory and applications. Paper presented to the Midwestern Psychological Association, Chicago, 1977.

Hamilton, D. L.   A cognitive–attributional analysis of stereotyping. In L. Berkowitz (Ed.), *Advances in experimental social psychology* (Vol. 12). New York: Academic Press, 1979.

Hamilton, D. L., & Rose, T.   *The role of associatively-based illusory correlation in the maintenance of stereotypic concepts.* Unpublished manuscript, University of California at Santa Barbara, 1979.

Hastie, R.   Schematic principles in human memory. In E. T. Higgins, C. P. Herman, & M. P. Zanna (Eds.), *Social cognition: The Ontario symposium.* Hillsdale, N.J.: Lawrence Erlbaum Associates, 1981.

Hastie, R., Ostrom, T., Ebbesen, E., Wyer, R., Hamilton, D., & Carlston, D. (Eds.).   *Person memory.* Hillsdale, N.J.: Lawrence Erlbaum Associates, 1980.

Hayes-Roth, F.   Distinguishing theories of representation: A critique of Anderson's "Arguments concerning mental imagery." *Psychological Review,* 1979, *86,* 376–382.

Higgins, E. T., Herman, C. P., & Zanna, M. P. (Eds.).   *Social cognition: The Ontario symposium* (Vol. 1). Hillsdale, N.J.: Lawrence Erlbaum Associates, 1981.

Higgins, E. T., Kuiper, N. A., & Olson, J. M.   Social cognition: A need to get personal. In E. T. Higgins, C. P. Herman, & M. P. Zanna (Eds.), *Social cognition: The Ontario symposium* (Vol. 1). Hillsdale, N.J.: Lawrence Erlbaum Associates, 1981.

Higgins, E. T., Rhodewalt, F., & Zanna, M. P.   Dissonance motivation: Its nature, persistence, and reinstatement. *Journal of Experimental Social Psychology,* 1979, *15,* 16–34.

Himmelfarb, S., & Eagly, A. H.   Orientation to the study of attitudes and their change. In S. Himmelfarb & A. H. Eagly, *Readings in attitude change.* New York: Wiley, 1974.

Hovland, C. I., Janis, I. L., & Kelley, H. H.   *Communication and persuasion.* New Haven: Yale University Press, 1953.

Hull, J. G., & Levy, A. S.   The organizational functions of the self: An alternative to the Duval and Wicklund model of self-awareness. *Journal of Personality and Social Psychology,* 1979, *37,* 756–768.

Isen, A. M., Shalker, T. E., Clark, M., & Karp, L.   Affect, accessibility of material in memory, and behavior: A cognitive loop? *Journal of Personality and Social Psychology,* 1978, *36,* 1–12.

Izard, C. E.   *Human emotions.* New York: Plenum, 1977.

James, W.   What is an emotion? *Mind,* 1884, *9,* 188–205.

Jones, E. E., & Goethals, G. R.   Order effects in impression formation: Attribution context and the nature of the entity. In E. E. Jones, D. E. Kanouse, H. H. Kelley, R. E. Nisbett, S. Valins, & B. Weiner (Eds.), *Attribution: Perceiving the causes of behavior.* Morristown, N.J.: General Learning Press, 1971.

Jöreskog, K. G.   A general method for estimating a linear structural equation system. In A. S. Goldberger & O. D. Duncan (Eds.), *Structural equation models in the social sciences.* New York: Seminar Press, 1973.

Kahneman, D.   *Attention and effort.* Englewood Cliffs, N.J.: Prentice-Hall, 1973.

Kahneman, D., & Tversky, A.   On the psychology of prediction. *Psychological Review,* 1973, *80,* 237–251.

Kanouse, D. E., & Hanson, L. R.   Negativity in evaluations. In E. E. Jones, D. E. Kanouse, H. H. Kelley, R. E. Nisbett, S. Valins, & B. Weiner (Eds.), *Attribution: Perceiving the causes of behavior.* Morristown, N.J.: General Learning Press, 1971.

Kenny, D. A.   *Correlation and causality.* New York: Wiley-Interscience, 1979.

Kinder, D. R.   Personal communication, September 1979.

Kuiper, N. A., & Derry, P. A.   The self as a cognitive prototype: An application to person perception and to psychopathology. In N. Cantor & J. F. Kihlstrom (Eds.), *Personality, cognition, and social interaction.* Hillsdale, N.J.: Lawrence Erlbaum Associates, 1981.

Langer, E. J., Taylor, S. E., Fiske, S. T., & Chanowitz, B.   Stigma, staring, and discomfort: A novel stimulus hypothesis. *Journal of Experimental Social Psychology,* 1976, *12,* 451–463.

Lazarus, R. S., Averill, J. R., & Opton, E. M.   Toward a cognitive theory of emotion. In M. B. Arnold (Ed.), *Feelings and emotions: The Loyola symposium.* New York: Academic Press, 1970.

Lehnert, W., Roseman, I., & Abelson, R. P.   *Affect analysis and text comprehension.* Paper presented to Cognitive Science Society, New Haven, 1980.

Leventhal, H.   Emotions: A basic problem for social psychology. In C. Nemeth (Ed.), *Social psychology: Classic and contemporary integrations.* Chicago: Rand-McNally, 1974.

Leventhal, H., Brown, D., Shacham, S., & Engquist, G.   Effects of preparatory information about sensations, threat of pain, and attention on cold press or distress. *Journal of Personality and Social Psychology,* 1979, *37,* 688–714.

Linville, P.   *Dimensional complexity and evaluative extremity: A cognitive model predicting polarized evaluations of outgroup members.* Unpublished doctoral dissertation, Duke University, 1979.

Linville, P. W., & Jones, E. E.   *Polarized appraisals of outgroup members. Journal of Personality and Social Psychology,* 1980, *38,* 689–703.

Mandler, G.   *Mind and emotion.* New York: Wiley, 1975.

Marshall, G. D., & Zimbardo, P. G.   Affective consequences of inadequately explained physiological arousal. *Journal of Personality and Social Psychology,* 1979, *37,* 970–988.

Maslach, C.   Negative emotional biasing of unexplained arousal. Journal of Personality and Social Psychology, 1979, *37,* 953–969.

McArthur, L. Z.   What grabs you? The role of attention in impression formation and causal attribution. In E. T. Higgins, C. P. Herman, and M. P. Zanna (Eds.), *Social cognition: The Ontario symposium* (Vol. 1). Hillsdale, N.J.: Lawrence Erlbaum Associates, 1981.

McArthur, L. Z., & Post, D. L.   Figural emphasis and person perception. *Journal of Experimental Social Psychology,* 1977, *13,* 520–535.

McDougall, W.   Emotion and feeling distinguished. In C. Murchison (Ed.), *Feeling and emotion: The Wittenberg symposium.* London: Oxford University Press, 1928.

Miller, G. A., Galanter, E., & Pribram, K.   *Plans and the structure of behavior.* New York: Holt, Rinehart, & Winston, 1960.

Moreland, R. L., & Zajonc, R. B.   Is stimulus recognition a necessary condition for the occurrence of exposure effects? *Journal of Personality and Social Psychology,* 1977, *35,* 191–199.

Moreland, R. L., & Zajonc, R. B.   Exposure effects may not depend on stimulus recognition. *Journal of Personality and Social Psychology,* 1979, *37,* 1085–1089.

Nisbett, R. E., & Wilson, T. D.   Telling more than we can know: Verbal reports on mental processes. *Psychological Review,* 1977, *84,* 231–259.

Norman, D. A.   *Memory and attention: An introduction to human information processing* (2nd ed.). New York: Wiley, 1976.

Nowlis, V.   Mood: Behavior and experience. In M. B. Arnold (Ed.), *Feelings and emotions: The Loyola symposium.* New York: Academic Press, 1970.

Osgood, C. E., Suci, G. J., & Tannenbaum, P. H.   *The measurement of meaning.* Urbana: University of Illinois, 1957.

Penrod, S., & Hastie, R.   Models of jury decision making: A critical review. *Psychological Bulletin,* 1979, *86,* 462–492.

Plutchik, R.   Emotions, evolution, and adaptive processes. In M. B. Arnold (Ed.), *Feelings and emotions: The Loyola symposium.* New York: Academic Press, 1970.

Plutchik, R., & Ax, A. F.   A critique of "Determinants of emotional state" by Schachter and Singer (1962). *Psychophysiology,* 1967, 4, 79–82.

Pylyshyn, Z. W.   Validating computational models: A critique of Anderson's indeterminancy of representation claim. *Psychological Review,* 1979, *86,* 383–394.

Roseman, I.   *Cognitive aspects of emotion and emotional behavior.* Paper presented to the American Psychological Association, New York, 1979.

Ross, L.   The intuitive psychologist and his shortcomings: Distortions in the attribution process. In L. Berkowitz (Ed.), *Advances in experimental social psychology,* (Vol. 10). New York: Academic Press, 1977.

Ross, M., & Sicoly, F.   Egocentric biases in availability and attribution. *Journal of Personality and Social Psychology,* 1979, *37,* 322–337.

Rumelhart, D. E., & Ortony, A.   The representation of knowledge in memory. In R. C. Anderson, R. J. Spiro, & W. E. Montague (Eds.), *Schooling and the acquisition of knowledge.* Hillsdale, N.J.: Lawrence Erlbaum Associates, 1977.

Russell, J. A.   Evidence of convergent validity on the dimensions of affect. *Journal of Personality and Social Psychology,* 1978, *36,* 1152–1168.

Schachter, S.   *Emotion, obesity, and crime.* New York: Academic Press, 1971.

Schachter, S., & Singer, J. Cognitive, social, and physiological determinants of emotional state. *Psychological Review,* 1962, *69,* 379–399.

Schachter, S., & Singer, J. E.   Comments on the Maslach and Marshall–Zimbardo experiments. *Journal of Personality and Social Psychology,* 1979, *37,* 989–995.

Schank, R., & Abelson, R.   *Scripts, plans, goals, and understanding: An inquiry into human knowledge structures.* Hillsdale, N.J.: Lawrence Erlbaum Associates, 1977.

Scheier, M. F., & Carver, C. S.   Self-focused attention and the experience of emotion: Attraction, repulsion, elation, and depression. *Journal of Personality and Social Psychology,* 1977, *35,* 625–636.

Schlosberg, H.   Three dimensions of emotion. *Psychological Review,* 1954, *61,* 81–88.

Schneider, D. J., Hastorf, A. H., & Ellsworth, P. C.   *Person perception* (2nd ed.). Reading, Mass.: Addison-Wesley, 1979.

Shaver, K. G.   *An introduction to attribution processes.* Cambridge, Mass.: Winthrop, 1975.

Simon, H. A.   Motivational and emotional controls of cognition. *Psychological Review,* 1967, *74,* 29–39.

Simon, H. A.   *The sciences of the artificial.* Cambridge, Mass.: MIT Press, 1969.

Snyder, M., & Uranowitz, S. W.   Reconstructing the past: Some cognitive consequences of person perception. *Journal of Personality and Social Psychology,* 1978, *36,* 941–950.

Strongman, K. T.   *The psychology of emotion.* New York: Wiley, 1978.

Taylor, S. E.   Hospital patient behavior: Reactance, helplessness, or control? *Journal of Social Issues,* 1979, *35,* 156–184.

Taylor, S. E.   Some frameworks to bridge cognitive and social psychology: Discussion. In J. Carroll & J. Payne (Eds.), *Cognition and social behavior.* New York: Wiley, 1976.

Taylor, S. E., & Crocker, J.   Schematic bases of social information processing. In E. T. Higgins, C. A. Herman, & M. P. Zanna (Eds.), *Social cognition: The Ontario symposium* (Vol. 1). Hillsdale, N.J.: Lawrence Erlbaum Associates, 1981.

Taylor, S. E., Crocker, J., Fiske, S. T., Sprinzen, M., & Winkler, J. D.   The generalizability of salience effects. *Journal of Personality and Social Psychology,* 1979, *37,* 357–368.

Taylor, S. E., & Fiske, S. T.   Point-of-view and perceptions of causality. *Journal of Personality and Social Psychology,* 1975, *32,* 439–445.

Taylor, S. E., & Fiske, S. T.   Salience, attention, and attribution: Top of the head phenomena. In L. Berkowitz (Ed.), *Advances in experimental social psychology* (Vol. 11). New York: Academic Press, 1978.

Taylor, S. E., Fiske, S. T., Close, M., Anderson, C., & Ruderman, A.   *Solo status as a psychological variable: The power of being distinctive.* Unpublished manuscript, Harvard University, 1977.

Taylor, S. E., Fiske, S. T., Etcoff, N. L., & Ruderman, A. J.   Categorical and contextual bases of person memory and stereotyping. *Journal of Personality and Social Psychology,* 1978, *36,* 778–793.

Tesser, A.   Self-generated attitude change. In L. Berkowitz (Ed.), *Advances in experimental social psychology* (Vol. 11). New York: Academic Press, 1978.

Tesser, A., & Leone, C. Cognitive schemas and thought as determinants of attitude change. *Journal of Experimental Social Psychology,* 1977, *13,* 340–356.

Thorndyke, P. W., & Hayes-Roth, B. The use of schemata in the acquisition and transfer of knowledge. *Cognitive Psychology,* 1979, *11,* 82–106.

Tomkins, S. S. Affect and the psychology of knowledge. In S. Tomkins & C. E. Izard (Eds.), *Affect, cognition, and personality.* New York: Springer, 1965.

Tversky, A., & Kahneman, D. Causal schemata in judgments under uncertainty. In M. Fishbein (Ed.), *Progress in social psychology.* Hillsdale, N.J.: Lawrence Erlbaum Associates, 1980.

Weary, G. Self-serving attributional biases: Perceptual or response distortions? *Journal of Personality and Social Psychology,* 1979, *37,* 1418–1420.

Weiner, B. A cognitive (attribution)-emotion-action model of motivated behavior: An analysis of judgment of help-giving. *Journal of Personality and Social Psychology,* in press.

Weiner, B., Frieze, I. Kukla, A., Reed, L., Rest, S., & Rosenbaum, R. M. Perceiving the causes of success and failure. In E. E. Jones, R. E. Nisbett, S. Valins, & B. Weiner (Eds.), *Attribution: Perceiving the causes of behavior.* Morristown, N.J.: General Learning Press, 1971.

Weiner, B., Russell, D., & Lerman, D. Affective consequences of causal ascriptions. In J. H. Harvey, W. J. Ickes, & R. F. Kidd (Eds.), *New directions in attribution research* (Vol. 2). Hillsdale, N.J.: Lawrence Erlbaum Associates, 1978.

Weiner, B., Russell, D., & Lerman, D. The cognition–emotion process in achievement-related contexts. *Journal of Personality and Social Psychology,* 1979, *37,* 1211–1220.

Wicklund, R. A. Objective self-awareness. In L. Berkowitz (Ed.), *Advances in social psychology* (Vol. 8). New York: Academic Press, 1975.

Wicklund, R. A. Three years later. In L. Berkowitz (Ed.), *Cognitive theories in social psychology.* New York: Academic Press, 1978.

Wortman, C. B., & Dunkel-Schetter, C. Interpersonal relationships and cancer: A theoretical analysis. *Journal of Social Issues,* 1979, *35,* 120–155.

Wundt, W. C. H. Judd (trans.). *Outlines of psychology.* New York: Stechert, 1897.

Zajonc, R. B. Cognition and social cognition: A historical perspective. In L. Festinger (Ed.), *Four decades of social psychology.* Oxford: Oxford University Press, 1980. (a)

Zajonc, R. B. Feeling and thinking: Preferences need no inferences. *American Psychologist,* 1980, *35,* 151–175. (b)

Zanna, M. P., Higgins, E. T., & Taves, P. A. Is dissonance phenomenologically aversive? *Journal of Experimental Social Pshchology,* 1976, *12,* 530–538.

13

The Story as a Social Environment: Children's Comprehension and Evaluation of Intentions and Consequences

Royal Grueneich
Hamilton College

Tom Trabasso
University of Chicago

In her review of the research concerning the development of social cognition, Shantz (1975) discusses how children come to understand the thoughts, emotions, intentions, and viewpoints of other people. This understanding is inferential in nature because much of the content cannot be directly observed and a child must "go beyond the information given" (Bartlett, 1932). Although several studies involve perceptual processing, such as in investigations of role taking (Flavell, 1968) or film understanding (Flapan, 1968), the vast majority of studies in developmental social cognition are primarily verbal and rely extensively on the use of *stories* as their main source of information about social inferences.

Stories serve many functions in communication. They summarize events concerning happenings to people. They tell us about the goals, plans, behavior of and outcomes for others. They involve conflict and conflict resolution. They attempt to socialize children by providing examples of desirable behavior that is rewarded and undersirable behavior that is punished. They often are succinct summaries of social events generated by a naive theory of psychology (Heider, 1958), especially of human intentionality.

In this chapter, we consider the story as a representation designed for children of the personal–social world. An analysis of children's ability to comprehend the structure and content of stories should tell us much about what they know about this world.

Our focus is on what has been called "moral-judgment" research, in which children are asked to make evaluative inferences about a story, the protagonist's intentions, and/or the consequences of the protagonist's actions. A substantial amount of this research was initially stimulated by Piaget (1932). According to Piaget, children exhibit two types of moral thought: objective and subjective responsibility. In objective responsibility, which is the less developmentally advanced type of thought, an actor is evaluated solely or primarily on the basis of the consequences of his or her behavior rather than on the intentions behind performing the behavior. By contrast, for subjective-responsibility judgments, which represent the more developmentally advanced thought, the actor is evaluated solely or primarily on the basis of his or her intentions, rather than on the consequences of the behavior. Having observed that the same child would often make objective-responsibility judgments at one time but subjective judgments at another, Piaget did not believe that objective and subjective responsibility represented different stages of development, but he nevertheless did claim that these two types of moral thought followed a developmental trend, with objective-responsibility judgments decreasing and subjective-responsibility judgments increasing with age.

In his classical paradigm for assessing these two types of judgments, Piaget presented a pair of stories to each child. One of the stories in the pair depicted a protagonist who acted from ''good'' intentions but accidentally produced a large amount of damage, whereas the other story portrayed a protagonist who acted with ''bad'' intentions but produced only a small amount of damage. After listening to both stories, the child was asked to indicate which of the two protagonists he or she thought was naughtier. If the child judged the protagonist who produced the greater damage as naughtier despite the ''good'' intentions, the child was classified as giving an objective-responsibility response. However, if the child evaluated the character who produced less damage but acted from bad intentions as naughtier, he or she was scored as giving a subjective-responsibility response.

Piaget's seminal work stimulated activity on two questions, one having to do with children's comprehension of motives and intentions, and the other with how information about motives and intentions influences chilren's moral judgments (Keasey, 1978). The two questions are related in that children obviously must have at least some awareness and understanding of intentions before they can make moral judgments that are based on them. However, they are independent in that children may know about intentions but not consider them when making moral judgments. As Keasey has also pointed out, Piaget meant objective and subjective responsibility to pertain to whether a child *used* intention information to make moral judgments, not to whether the child was aware of intentions. Piaget, in fact, even reported that children who made objective-responsibility judgments often were aware of the actor's intentions. Piaget's original claims notwithstanding, the subsequent literature has pursued both questions, even though the distinction between them has not always been recognized or dealt with appropriately.

ANALYSIS OF MOTIVE AND INTENTION INFORMATION

Despite the substantial amount of effort that has been devoted to investigating children's comprehension of motives and intentions, very little consideration has been given to *how* information about motives and intentions is portrayed for children. This is unfortunate because even a cursory examination of the literature indicates that investigators have depicted motives and intentions in a great variety of ways. Although it has frequently been recognized that the type of information presented to a child is likely to have an important effect on the child's understanding of a character's motives and intentions, there has been little direct analysis and systematic investigation of this problem. This section of the chapter attempts to fill in part of this lacuna, with the following discussion being motivated by the fact that children's understanding of motives and intentions has usually been assessed in terms of their responses to stories or story-like materials (Shantz, 1975). Accordingly, the focus here is on how motive and intention information is conveyed in narratives and on the effects that this might have upon the child's comprehension. We consider how motives and intentions are depicted in filmed or videotaped episodes as well as in verbal stories, because the former also have a story-like character, in that the sequence of events portrayed in this format usually parallels that of stories. It may be that there are intrinsic differences between the two media that dramatically affect the comprehension of motives and intentions, but we ignore this possibility here and instead concentrate on their similarity in event structure.

Story-Grammar Analysis

Recently, several investigators (e.g., Mandler & Johnson, 1977; Rumelhart, 1975; Stein & Glenn, 1979; Thorndyke, 1977; Warren, Nicholas, & Trabasso, 1979) have developed *story grammars* and inference taxonomies to analyze the structure of simple stories. Because the story grammar proposed by Stein and Glenn (1979) seems to be well suited for dealing with the type of goal-motivated activity that is commonly depicted in moral-judgment research, our focus is on this grammar and, most particularly, on those of its aspects that are relevant to analyzing motive and intention information.

Stein & Glenn's grammar, like the other story grammars, has two major components: categories of information, which specify the different types of information contained in the story, and logical relations, which specify how the categories are connected or related to each other. The key structure in the grammar is the episode, or behavioral sequence, which consists of six main categories plus the relations that connect them. The first category is the *setting,* which introduces characters, provides background information, sets the locale and time, and describes personal traits and dispositions. This is followed by the *initiating event,* which is some event or happening that begins a character's behavior sequence. The initiating event can be an event external to the protagonist, such as the action of another person (e.g., getting punched by someone), or it can be an action or internal event originating in the actor (such as the experiencing of pain or hunger). The initiating event evokes some type of *internal response* in the protagonist, which is the third major category in the episode. Internal responses include affective or emotional responses, goals or desires, and thoughts or cognitions. The internal responses then motivate the protagonist to make some sort of *attempt* to satisfy his or her goals and desires. The attempt category represents the overt actions that the protagonist performs in order to satisfy goals. The protagonist's attempt, in turn, results in some kind of *direct consequence.* The direct-consequence category indicates whether or not the protagonist attained his or her goals and suggests other changes in the event sequence that result from the attempt. The direct consequence also initiates or causes a *reaction* on the part of either the protagonist or some other character. Reactions most commonly indicate how the protagonist feels, thinks, or behaves in response to direct consequences, but they may also specify how other characters are affected by direct consequences.

The complete grammar of Stein and Glenn (1979) actually contains a great deal beyond what is presented here. However, most of that is not critical to this discussion, as nearly all of the stories used in the moral-judgment literature can be analyzed in terms of the single-episode structure just described. For a simple example of how this episode structure can be used to analyze these stories, consider the following story used by Costanzo, Coie, Grumet, and Farnill (1973):

> Michael was playing in the toy room. He noticed that the toys were in a big mess and decided to straighten them up. He emptied the toy box onto the floor in order to sort and arrange the toys properly. Just then Mrs. Green came into the room and said, "Oh, Michael. We're going to have company in a few minutes and now you've messed the room all up [p. 156]."

In this story, the setting presents Michael at play in the toy room, and the initiating event is his observation that the toys are in a mess. This event leads to Michael's decision to straighten up the toys, which is an internal response. This, in turn, motivates him to empty the toys on the floor, which is an attempt. The direct consequence resulting from Michael's attempt is not explicitly stated in the story, but it is most likely that the toys are lying in some sort of haphazard arrangement on the floor. Whatever its exact nature, the direct consequence initiates the reaction of displeasure by Mrs. Green when she walks in the room and sees the toys scattered on the floor.

Although a "well-formed" or "ideal" story will contain all six of the categories in an episode, in reality, stories often do not explicitly express all of the categories. For example, Stein and Glenn (1979) note that folk tales often omit the internal response and reaction categories, probably because these categories are strongly implied by the information specified in the other categories. The stories used in moral-judgment research also typically omit one or more of the categories; the reaction category is probably the one most often omitted, although initiating events are also omitted quite frequently. However, even when a category is not explicitly expressed in a story, the grammar implicitly represents it and thus calls attention to its existence.

Two different claims can be made about a grammar. One is that the categories and relations in the grammar represent the internal structures or cognitive schemata that the subject uses to encode and organize information during story comprehension (Stein, 1979). The other, more modest claim is that the grammar is a useful tool for analyzing the information that is contained both explicitly and implicitly in a story and, therefore, for constructing and analyzing stimulus materials.

Extension of Grammar to Account for Motives and Intentions

By itself, Stein and Glenn's (1979) story grammar does not adequately account for many of the ways in which motive and intention information are conveyed in stories. Consequently, we need to supplement their grammar with a more extensive analysis of the problem. In doing so, we borrow from three main sources. One involves spelling out in greater detail some of the implications of the grammar itself. Another comes from some of the ideas of social psychologists who have contributed to the development of attribution theory (Heider, 1958; Jones & Davis, 1965; Kelley, 1972; Kruglanski, 1975). And the third comes from an examination of some of the various stimulus materials that have been used in the literature.

Before proceeding, it is important that we give some attention to the distinction between the concepts of motive and intentionality (Berndt & Berndt, 1975; Heider, 1958; Keasey, 1978; Shantz, 1975). Briefly, the concept of motive refers to the goal of an actor's behavior or to the particular reason the person has for performing an action, whereas the concept of intentionality refers to whether an action and/or its consequences were intentionally or accidentally produced by the actor. These two concepts are partially interdependent, because the attribution of a motive to an action implies, of course, that the act was intended, and the attribution that an action or behavior was accidentally performed implies that it cannot be accounted for in terms of a motive (i.e., one does not attribute a motive to an actor for accidentally losing balance and falling down). Nevertheless, the two are not identical. An act may be accounted for by a particular motive, and thus be intended, but its consequences may not have been intended. Thus, the attribution of a motive to an act does not necessarily imply that all or indeed any of the actual consequences of the act were intended. Because there seem to be good conceptual and empirical reasons for distinguishing between motives and intentions (see especially Keasey, 1978), we attempt to maintain this distinction wherever it is relevant.

Story information about a character's motives and intentions can come from six main sources, which very closely parallel the categories of the Stein and Glenn (1979) grammar. One source is information about the internal states of the character, which corresponds with the internal-response category of the Stein and Glenn grammar. According to the grammar, this information can relate to the character's goals or desires (e.g., "Mary wanted to hit John"), her feelings or affective responses (e.g., "Mary was very angry"), or to her thoughts or cognitions (e.g., "Mary thought John was obnoxious"). A second source of information, corresponding to the attempt category in the grammar, concerns the actor's behavior (e.g., "Mary hit John"). A third source, corresponding to Stein and Glenn's direct-consequence category, is about the immediate consequences or results of the act (e.g., "John got a black eye from Mary"). Although actions and consequences are viewed as separate sources of information here, it should be noted that in the natural-language description of event sequences, information about actions and consequences is very often conveyed simultaneously rather than separately. For example, the statement, "Frank killed a rat," indicates both that Frank acted in some violent way against the rat and that the consequence of his action was the death of the rat. In this kind of case, it is difficult to make a clean distinction as to whether actions or consequences are being described. The previous story example from Costanzo et al. (1973) is another example of this. A fourth source of information, which parallels the reaction category in the grammar, is how the actor reacts or responds to the consequences that his or her actions produce—that is, whether the actor feels surprised, happy, upset, or guilty (e.g., "Mary felt glad when she hit John"). A fifth source of information concerns what kinds of situational or external forces are operating upon the actor and how these influence him or her (e.g., "Mary's mother told her to hit John"). A final source is the setting itself, in which the character's habitual actions or states supply motives for subsequent actions. For example, "Mary and John were enemies" allows one to infer a reason for why Mary later hits John— namely, Mary disliked John and wanted to harm him.

Each of these sources of information may by itself or through explicit or implicit relationships with other sources allow one to infer what are a character's motives and intentions. Consider information about the character's internal states, which is obviously important for identifying a character's motives and intentions. Internal-state information can be provided in various ways in a story or video episode. For example, it may be explicitly given, as when a story contains a statement such as "Bill wanted to help his friend," or when a character verbally expresses desires or feelings (e.g., "Bill said, 'I want to help

Mother' ''). This latter technique seems to be a common way of depicting motives and intentions for audio–visual stimuli. Internal states are also often conveyed in the video format through facial expressions, tone of voice, body position and movement, and soon, with the explicitness of these cues varying from being very clear (e.g., making an emphatic expression of fear and horror) to being very subtle (e.g., showing slight signs of uneasiness). Subtle and inexplicit cues about internal states obviously should be less likely to be detected or used to infer intentions and motives than should clear and explicit information.

Motives and intentions are also specified by the relationships between internal-state information and other sources of information. One of the most important of these relationships is that between internal states and actions. Information about internal states and actions is often redundant, so that information about one may imply or suggest information about the other. Thus, knowing that an actor desires to harm another person, we expect such actions as hitting, pushing, punching, and so on. Similarly, knowing that an actor is angry, we are not surprised when that person hits someone. Conversely, if an actor hits someone, we readily infer that he or she wanted to hurt that person, was angry at that person, and so on. This predictability between internal states and actions is, of course, not perfect. Several actions may be consistent with a particular internal state, and vice versa. The goal of helping someone, for example, can be expressed through a diversity of behaviors, including such things as giving money, performing services, giving advice, and so on. Further, internal states and actions may often be related in unusual ways. For example, a mother's desire to help her child might lead to her hitting the child. Her behavior would then seem inconsistent with her goal until it were realized that she acted to prevent the child from running into the street and getting struck by traffic.

Because the concept of motive refers to the goal of a particular behavior, the tendency toward having predictable or natural associations between internal states and actions leads to the formulation of a very simple rule for determining an actor's motive: *When information about internal states and actions is consistent (i.e., the character's goals, feelings, and thoughts are consistent with subsequent actions), then the goal that is stated in or implied by the internal-state information is perceived as accounting for the actor's motive for behavior.* An example from one of the film episodes used by Hewitt (1974) should illustrate this rule. In this episode, one boy says to another, "I'm going to get you for calling me that," and then lets a table fall on the other's leg. In this case, the actor's behavior should be attributed to a motive of revenge, because this is the goal that he expresses verbally and because his action of letting a table fall on the other boy is consistent with that goal.

When internal-state information is concerned not with the character's goals but with feelings and cognitions, the attribution of a motive often can still be made by inferring a goal that is consistent with both the actor's cognitions or feelings and an action. For example, consider the following statements:

Karen was angry. She hit Judy.

In this instance, it will readily be inferred that the motive for Karen's behavior was to hurt Judy, because anger is very consistent with the desire to hurt, as is the behavior of hitting.

When inferences are being made about intentionality, as opposed to motivation, the relationship between internal states and consequences is extremely important because part of the definition of intentionality is that the outcome or the consequences of an actor's behavior be those that the person wanted or desired to produce. This suggests that an important rule for inferring whether the consequences of a character's actions were intentionally or accidentally produced is the extent to which those consequences are consistent with the character's goals as stated or implied by the available internal-state information. *If the consequences are consistent with the stated or implied goals of the actor, an inference that the consequences were intended is likely. If, on the other hand, this information is inconsistent, an inference that the consequences were accidentally produced would become more likely.* An example of this can be seen from one of Piaget's (1932) stories:

> A little boy who was called Augustus once noticed that his father's ink-pot was empty. One day that his father was away he thought of filling the ink-pot so as to help his father, and so that he should find it full when he came home. But while he was opening the ink-bottle he made a big blot on the tablecloth [p. 118].

Because Augustus' goal of helping his father is not consistent with getting a big blot of ink on the tablecloth, he probably did not intend this to happen.

Another internal-state–consequence relationship of particular relevance to the making of inferences about intentionality is that between the knowledge that the actor has about the possible consequences of an action and the actual consequences produced by the behavior. Heider (1958) and Jones and Davis (1965) have noted that consequences that an actor could not have foreseen cannot have been intended by that person. Accordingly, one rule governing the attribution of intentionality is that *when the consequences of an actor's behavior are those that he or she expected or knew could occur, he or she probably intended those consequences; if the actor was not expecting the consequences, he or she produced them accidentally.* Again, one of Piaget's (1932) stories illustrates the application of this rule:

> A little boy who is called John is in his room. He is called to dinner. He goes into the dining room. But behind the door was a chair, and on the chair there was a tray with fifteen cups on it. John couldn't have known there was all this behind the door. He goes in, the door knocks against the tray, bang go the fifteen cups and they all get broken [p. 118]!

Because John had no knowledge that his opening of the door would break the cups, he had to have broken the cups accidentally. Information concerning an actor's knowledge about the consequences that his or her actions will produce may be explicitly stated or only implied in a story. Piaget's story, for example, explicitly states that John did not know that the tray of cups was behind the door. However, even if the statement about John's lack of knowledge was deleted from the story, we would still probably infer that he broke the cups accidentally, because a door usually does not have cups behind it, and no indication is given that John is aware of this unusual situation.

Another relationship that may specify intentionality is that between actions and consequences. For a particular action, some consequences are more likely to result than others. For example, some plausible consequences of hitting a person are that the person will get a black eye, a bloody nose, a bruise, and so on. On the other hand, it is unlikely that the hitting will improve the victim's physical condition or make the victim feel good. Although this association between actions and their likely consequences is not perfect and is stronger for some action–consequence links than others, it is still often strong enough to provide information about whether an actor intended the consequences that his or her behavior produced. *Therefore, the greater the extent to which an action produces consequences not usually associated with it, the more likely it is that those consequences were unintended, provided, of course, there is not information that the actor was expecting the unusual consequences to occur.* One of Elkind and Dabek's (1977) stories demonstrates this rule:

> Larry is playing with a ball in the park. He throws the ball and when it comes down it hits and breaks his friend's glasses that are on the bench [p. 519].

Because throwing a ball and letting it land does not ordinarily result in glasses being broken, Larry probably did not intend to break the glasses.

In some cases, information about actions alone may specify intentionality. This is because certain characteristics of an action, such as its form, persistence, or intensity, often provide cues as to whether it is being intentionally or accidentally performed. With respect to its form, actions are sometimes described in a story or depicted in a film sequence in such a way that unintentional activity is indicated. For instance, involuntary actions such as "tripped," "slipped," "fell," and "bumped" indicate that unintentional activity is involved. In video presentations, the manner in which an actor performs a behavior may convey information about whether the activity is intentional or accidental. For instance, an actor in a video episode constructed by Farnill (1974) showed fumbling and shaking motions as he dropped a flowerpot, indicating that this action was unintended.

Another informative set of cues about the intentionality of a behavior concerns its persistence and intensity. Because intention implies effort (Heider, 1958), the greater the persistence and the intensity of a behavior, the more likely it is that the behavior is intended. If a child were to break one dish, we could believe this to be accidental; but if the child were to break five dishes, one after the other, we would readily infer that the breaking of the dishes was intentional. Finally, it is important to note that when an action is judged to have been accidentally performed, this means that the consequences of that action could not have been intended by the actor.

How the actor reacts to the consequences of his or her behavior may also help to specify motives and intentions. People generally react positively when the consequences of their behavior are consistent with their goals and negatively when they are not. Thus, if a character expresses dissatisfaction with the consequences of his or her behavior, it is not likely that the person performed the behavior in order to produce those consequences. If, in contrast, the character expresses satisfaction, it is more likely that he or she intended the consequences. Further, certain reactions are specially informative about the actor's intentions. For example, a reaction of surprise strongly suggests that a consequence, or at least the magnitude of it, was not expected. This relationship between consequences and reactions is obviously not a perfect index of motives and intentions, because an actor may be pleased when his or her actions fortuitously result in good outcomes or be dissatisfied when his or her behavior produces consequences that he or she had known might occur but hoped would not. Nonetheless, an actor's reactions to the consequences of his or her actions often serve as good indices of the intentions underlying behavior. The following description of a film segment used by Flapan (1968) demonstrates how reactions to consequences can give cues about a character's motives and intentions:

> She tries to "show him" how she will shoot by throwing a rock at the squirrel. The rock kills the squirrel, which surprises and grieves the girl. Crying, she says she didn't mean it [p. 14).

In this sequence, several of the girl's reactions indicate that she had not intended to kill the squirrel—for example, her expression of grief and surprise, crying, and saying that she had not meant to do it.

Still another way of specifying motives and intentions is by providing information about the external forces operating upon the actor and the effect that these forces have upon behavior. Kelley's (1972) discounting principle expresses one important rule for using this type of information to infer a character's motives. The discounting principle states that a given cause is less likely to be inferred as producing an effect if it is known that there are also other causes that may have produced the effect. From the discounting principle, we can derive the rule that *when a behavior is preceded by an external initiating event, an explanation of the behavior in terms of an alternative internal cause should become less likely.* For instance, we are less likely to infer that a child's motive for washing dishes is to help his or her mother when we know that the mother has ordered the child to do the dishes.

An actor's motives will also be reflected in the way that he or she responds to external forces. Kruglanski's (1975) analysis suggests another rule for connecting an actor's responses to external forces with his or her motives: *When an actor is motivated by a particular goal, attempts to satisfy that goal will not be influenced by situational factors that neither change the goal nor affect the possibility of achieving it.* That is, an actor's behavior will be affected only by situational forces that are pertinent to the goals that that behavior expresses. Thus, by seeing how an actor's behavior covaries with different situations, we can obtain important information about the motives behind it. For instance, one way of determining the reason a woman is marrying a wealthy man (whether it is because she loves him or because she is interested in his money) is to observe how she responds when her suitor suddenly loses his wealth. If her real motive is love, then she will still marry him because the loss of his wealth will not affect her motive. On the other hand, if her motive is monetary, she will call off the marriage because her desire will then have no chance of being satisfied. A corollary of the preceding rule is *that when an actor's attempt to satisfy a goal is blocked by the situation, that person will tend to continue making other attempts to satisfy that goal.* Continuing the previous scenario, if the woman's real motive for marriage is monetary, she can be expected to look for another wealthy suitor if her current one loses his wealth. Another source of inferring intentionality is in setting information where a character's habitual actions or states imply salient, long-term goals. For example, if a story depicts a character who intensely dislikes school, and if the story states that the student is not in school one day, the inference will be made that the student was not because he or she did not want to be, and not because he or she was ill. The rule here is that *habitual actions or states imply goals that account for the specific actions and outcomes depicted in a story unless other information indicates otherwise.*

Applications of the Motive and Intention Analysis

One of the advantages of the preceding analysis is that it focuses the researcher's attention on the character of the information contained in the stimulus materials. Doing an explicit analysis of stimulus materials is important, because it is common to find in the moral-judgment literature stories and film episodes that are poorly constructed. In addition, characters' motives and intentions are often ambiguously portrayed. The following story, employed by Piaget (1932), illustrates these problems:

> There was a little boy called Julian. His father had gone out and Julian thought it would be fun to play with his father's ink-pot. First he played with the pen, and then he made a little blot on the table cloth [p. 118].

In this story, it is, first of all, unclear whether Julian's motive for playing with his father's pen and ink-pot was bad or merely neutral. Because Julian was playing with the writing instruments when his father was gone, this suggests that he may have been doing something he was not supposed to do. However, the story fails to make a clear connection between Julian's playing and his father's absence, so it is also reasonable to infer that Julian was not engaging in any forbidden activity. Second, the story provides virtually no relevant information for determining whether Julian intentionally or accidentally made the ink blot. For this sort of story, in which information about consequences is clearer and more salient than that about motives and intentions, it is not hard to see why a young child might emphasize the former more than the latter in making moral judgments.

The extended story-grammar analysis is also useful for investigating the effects that variation of stimulus information has upon children's understanding and motives and intentions. For this kind of research, several degrees of difficulty with respect to inferring motives and intentions from story information can be identified at a gross level. The easiest case should be when the actor's motives and intentions are explicitly stated. The following story, employed by Leon (1979), provides such an example:

> John was very mad at one of his friends. He saw his friend coming. He picked up a rock and threw it at his friend. The rock hit John's friend on the leg and made a bruise [p. 79].

It is quite clear that John's motive for throwing the rock is to hurt his friend and that the damage to his friend is intentional. This is because the internal state, action, and consequence information in this story are strongly and consistently related. Throwing a rock implies the desire to harm, and this is, in turn, consistent with the internal state of being mad and with the consequence of bruising his friend's leg.

As information about motives and intentions is made less explicit and relationships between categories of information weaken, making inferences about motives and intentions become more difficult. Compare, for example, the following story also used by Leon (1979):

> Mike and a friend were throwing rocks against a wall. Mike threw a rock against the wall. The rock bounced back toward Mike's friend. The rock hit Mike's friend on the leg and made a bruise [p. 79].

In this story, there is little explicit information about motives and intentions. For example, there is no information about Mike's internal states—that is, whether he is angry at his friend, wants to hurt him, or has any expectations about what will happen when he throws the rock against the wall. The description of the action suggests that the consequences were probably unintended: When a thrown

object is deflected and then hits someone, it is likely that this happened accidentally. Still, it is possible that Mike was throwing rocks against the wall in the
hope that one would bounce back and hit his friend. Consequently, these inferences appear to be harder to make than those for Leon's previously cited story.

The most difficult situation for making inferences may be when different
categories of information are inconsistent or in conflict with each other. Warren
et al. (1979) provide an example of this:

> Chris wanted to help his mom. Chris broke all the eggs in the refrigerator. Chris
> finished in time for supper [p. 48].

In this sequence, there is an inconsistency between Chris' motive to help his
mother and his breaking of the eggs. Warren et al. suggest that one way the
comprehender might try to resolve this inconsistency is to infer a plausible
rationale for relating Chris' goal and his behavior plus its consequences; for
example, that as he went to the refrigerator to take out the milk, he accidentally
knocked over a carton of eggs. Attributions of motives and intentions may be
especially difficult when there are contradictions between categories of information, because the contradictions must not only be detected, but must also be
resolved in some way, which requires a search for plausible means of resolution.

The foregoing discussion implies a program of research that tests the validity
of the rules as well as developmental differences in rule knowledge and usage.
Studies by Harris (1977) and Sedlak (1979) are suggestive because they assessed
children's understanding of Heider's (1958) levels of responsibility attribution.
Because their stories represent multidimensional combinations of several factors
such as causal relations, goals, foreseeability, and external constraints, interpretations of their findings are not simple. Both studies found, however, that older
children and adults were more sensitive to the factors subsumed under Heider's
levels than were the younger children who either did not differentiate causal
attributions across levels (Harris) or were more affected by outcomes (Sedlak).

REVIEW OF THE STANDARD OR TRADITIONAL
MORAL-JUDGMENT LITERATURE

The discussion to this point has emphasized that children's understanding of
motives and intentions is likely to depend heavily on the nature of the stimulus
materials used to assess this comprehension. Another hypothesis that is
suggested by our analysis is that younger children's comprehension should be
influenced more than older children's by variation in stimulus content. These
developmental differences in comprehension should be a function of the salience
and explicitness of motive and intention information. Although these issues and
hypotheses have frequently been discussed in the literature (e.g., Chandler,
Greenspan, & Barenboim, 1973; Leon, 1979), they have rarely been dealt with
in an explicit manner. Consequently, any review of research that provides data

relevant to these issues must be limited. Nevertheless, some studies provide informative or suggestive data. A brief and selective review of these studies would seem to be of value.

Bearison and Isaacs' (1975) study represents an attempt to investigate the effects of providing explicit versus implicit motive and intention information. Six- and 7-year-old children heard two story pairs that varied according to three conditions. For the story pairs in the ''intention-inferred'' condition, the children had to infer the character's motives and intentions from the narrative description of the character's overt behavior. In the ''intention-explicit'' condition, statements that reported the characters' intentions were added to the stories. The stories used in the intention-asked condition were identical to those in the intention-inferred condition. However, after hearing each pair of stories, the children in this condition were asked if each of the characters ''meant to do a bad thing?'' The purpose of this type of probe question was to induce the children to think about the character's intentions. The results indicated that the children made significantly more subjective responsibility judgments in the intention-explicit and intention-asked groups than in the intention-inferred group.

In interpreting these results, however, some limitations of Bearison and Isaacs' study should be noted. First, their description of their stimuli was not detailed enough to allow for a very precise determination of what the difference was between the stories in which motives and intentions had to be inferred and those in which they were made explicit. Second, it is possible that the questions that were used in the intention-asked condition (i.e., whether the character ''meant to do a *bad* thing?'') biased the subjects' subsequent judgments.

Consistent with Bearison and Isaacs' results are some of the data collected by Leon (1979). In this study, first through seventh grade children and college students were asked to judge how much punishment characters should receive in stories that orthogonally combined different levels of intent with different levels of negative outcomes. The subjects heard both a set of simple and a set of complex stories, with the intention information being explicitly stated in the simple stories but only implicitly provided in the complex stories. Whereas for the simple stories there were no significant age differences in evaluation as a function of the intention of the story characters (i.e., the younger children's judgments were as much intention-based as were the college students'), for the complex stories, intention had a greater influence on the adults' judgments than it did on the children's judgments. Thus, Leon concluded that the age differences in judgments for the complex stories were due to the children's not extracting the same intention information as adults.

An issue that has received a significant amount of attention in the moral-judgment research concerns the effects of using verbally presented versus filmed stimuli. Although both types of media have been used, only two studies have directly compared them. Chandler et al. (1973) found that first graders gave more intention-based judgments for video as compared to verbal story pairs. In contrast, Berndt and Berndt (1975) generally found better *comprehension* of motives and intentions for their stories than for their films, although *evaluations* seemed to be slightly more intention-based for the films. Unfortuantely, neither Chandler et al. nor Berndt and Berndt described their videotape and verbal materials in enough detail to provide a good idea of how the two media compared in terms of the motive and intention information that was portrayed. This, rather than any intrinsic differences between the media, may be the most important determinant of comprehension and evaluations. For example, one possible argument would be that motive information can be conveyed more directly in stories than in filmed episodes, because motives can be explicitly stated in stories but they cannot be depicted visually because they are internal states. For example, in a study comparing motives inferred from picture stories with motives explicitly stated in verbal stories, Asp, Johnson, and Trabasso (1979) found that children 5 to 8 years of age spontaneously recalled more internal-state (motive) information from the verbal stories than from the picture stories. Perhaps this kind of result could be offset by other factors. For example, a character in a film can verbally express desires or portray feelings that strongly imply particular motives. In this way, information about motives may be conveyed as clearly in a video format as in a story. Whether or not this particular speculation is correct, comparisons between the two media cannot be meaningful unless a careful analysis is made of the information that is being conveyed by the stimuli used to represent each medium.

Another relevant class of studies comprises those that have directly assessed children's comprehension motives and intentions. For example, a major study performed by Flapan (1968) investigated 6-, 9-, and 12-year-old children's understanding of social interaction depicted in filmed episodes. The children's understanding of the interaction was assessed through their recall of the episodes and from their answers to a set of probe questions.

Several significant age trends emerged in the analysis of children's recall data. The 6-year-olds gave fewer explanations that accounted for an action in terms of the just-preceding events or the present setting than did the older children. Also, 6-year-olds made fewer statements that indicated inferences about feelings and about thoughts and expectations. In general, Flapan noted that those 6-year-olds who did give explanations expressed these in terms of situations and actions and not in terms of psychological factors such as feelings, intentions, thoughts, or interpersonal perceptions. An example of this that Flapan gives is that a 6-year-old typically would say, "She was crying because the squirrel was dead," whereas a 12-year-old would say, "She started crying because she felt sorry for killing the squirrel."

For probe questions about feelings, 6-year-olds often said that they did not know the answer, or answered incorrectly. Most of the 9-year-olds' answers concerned obvious, uncomplicated feelings that were mentioned in the dialogue or were clearly depicted in the expressive behavior of the characters. The 12-year-olds, on the other hand, mentioned a complex combination of feelings, inferred feelings that were not explicitly mentioned or depicted in the dialogue or action, or answered by naming a feeling and then elaborating in terms of the actor's thoughts, intentions, or expectations. For questions that required some sort of explanation, the 6-year-olds often said that they did not know, gave inappropriate answers, or answered in terms of the preceding action or the current situation. The 9-year-olds explained primarily in terms of the preceding action or the existing situation, but occasionally explained in psychological terms. The 12-year-olds, in contrast, usually explained in psychological terms.

Although Flapan's results support the hypothesis that there are developmental differences in children's ability to understand and infer motives and intentions, this statement probably needs to be qualified because of some limitations in her data. First, her recall data must be interpreted cautiously, because she noted that many times, the psychological aspects of the situation that were not mentioned by the children in giving their own accounts of what happened were mentioned in response to specific questioning. Thus, *the recall data appeared to underestimate the children's comprehension,* and *it is possible that they did this more so for the younger than the older children* (see also Stein & Glenn, 1979). In addition, the results were summed over a great deal of variance with respect to how difficult the interaction was to understand. Because Flapan gave a fairly detailed description of the content of the episodes, it is possible to get some idea of how motives and intentions were portrayed in her films. Some of the information seemed to have been quite clear and explicit. For example, the characters often verbally stated their intentions, as when one character indicated his desire to use another's pair of skates by shouting at her, ''I want a turn.'' Expressions of affect or feeling also seemed to be a common way of conveying internal-state information, although it is not possible to determine how clearly these were portrayed. Conversely, a complete understanding of much of the interaction seemed to require inferences about rather complicated motives and intentions, and these often involved a character's perceptions of another character's feelings and motives. Thus, Flapan's stimuli involved a very heterogeneous array of motive and intention information. Her results would have been much more informative had there been some breakdown of the developmental trends in terms of the type of film information.

Berndt and Berndt (1975) showed preschoolers (mean age = 4-11), second graders, and fifth graders videotaped episodes that depicted four types of intentions: instrumental aggression (i.e., aggression that obtained an object that the actor wanted for himself or herself), accidental action, displaced aggression, and altruism. For each of the episodes, both an immediate cause (near motive) and a more distant cause (far motive) were portrayed. For instance, the actor in one of the episodes wanted another boy's airplane (near motive) so he could play airport (far motive). For each filmed episode, a story that corresponded to it in form but not in content was constructed.

The analysis of the children's understanding of motives indicated that there were no age differences for understanding of the near motives for the instrumental aggression and accidental episodes. However, the younger children understood the near motives in the other two episodes and the far motives in all episodes significantly less well than did the older children. Because it appears from the description that Berndt and Berndt provide of their video episodes that the actors verbalized their near motives in the instrumental-aggression and accidental episodes but may not have done so in the other two episodes, one possible explanation for these results is that the near-motive information for the instrumental-aggression and accidental episodes was explicit enough that even the young children understood these motives. From the description of the episodes, it also appears that the far motives were not very relevant to understanding the on-going activity, and that information about them may have been less clear and explicit than that about the near motives. In response to questions about intentionality, the older children performed significantly better than the younger children for all except the instrumental-aggression episode, where there were no developmental differences.

Studies by Leifer, Collins, Gross, Taylor, Andrews, and Blackmer (1971) and by Collins, Berndt, and Hess (1974) also found significant developmental differences on measures of children's understanding of motives and intentions. Leifer et al. showed a movie of an adaptation of a familiar fairy tale to 4-, 7-, and 10-year-olds, and Collins et al. showed an edited version of an action–adventure television program to kindergarten, second-, fifth-, and eighth-grade children. Although neither set of investigators described the type of motive and intention-information portrayed in their films, much of this information was probably fairly subtle and complex.

This brief review highlights some of the problems in the existing literature. There are compelling reasons to believe, despite the paucity of relevant data, that the nature of the information that is conveyed by stimulus materials has a critical effect upon children's comprehension and evaluations. Research to date, however, has failed to deal effectively with this problem. Stimulus construction, for the most part, seems to have proceeded haphazardly, with the probable consequence that stimulus materials often fail to answer the questions that they are intended to address. For example, many of the findings in the literature concerning age differences in moral judgments or evaluations may have their basis primarily in developmental differences in the ability to infer critical information from a given set of stimulus materials, rather than in differences in the judgment process per se. If this is indeed the case, then much of the research in this area has not provided meaningful data on the development of the moral-judgment process.

STORY-GRAMMAR RESEARCH

In this section, we review some studies concerning children's comprehension and inferences or internal states that have been generated within the framework of story grammars. These studies assume that memory for story information, as assessed either via retelling of the story or by answering probe questions, is an index of comprehension. Their value is that, in contrast to most of the traditional developmental research using stories, memory and comprehension are assessed in terms of specific information about goals, attempts, and consequences, using recall as well as systematic interview or probe questions.

In a seminal study, Stein and Glenn (1979) presented a set of simple stories to first and fifth graders. In one experiment, children's comprehension of the stories was assessed through their recall of the stories; in another experiment, it was assessed by their answers to probe questions about why things happened as they did in the story. For the recall data, internal responses tended to be recalled less frequently than other categories of information, and the fifth graders recalled significantly more internal responses than the first graders. Although most of the first graders made some references to the intentions or feelings of the characters, they more frequently concentrated on the outcomes of the action. However, developmental differences were less common for the probe questions. The majority of the children's answers were correct for both age groups—81% for the first graders and 94% for the fifth graders. Although the older children gave more statements in response to the questions, the younger children mentioned internal responses in their answers as frequently as did the older children. In fact, both younger and older children answered the causal probe questions predominantly in terms of internal responses. In addition, many of the internal responses that were infrequently recalled in the first study were often mentioned by both younger and older children in response to the probe questions. The relatively good performance of the younger children in this study as compared to some of the other studies is probably due to the fact that motive and intention information tended to be quite clearly specified in Stein and Glenn's stories.

A recent study by Nezworski, Stein, and Trabasso (1979) has explored how well children are able to infer and use information from different story-grammar categories in making moral judgments. The important aspect of the Nezworski et al. study is that the authors controlled for the semantic *content* of the information as it varied over the different story-grammar categories.

In order to illustrate how this was done, one of the three stories is shown in Table 13.1. This single-episode story was written such that the protagonist would

TABLE 13.1
Nezworski, Stein, and Trabasso (1979) Secret-Trip Story

Setting	Once there were two children named Peter and Mary who lived across the street from one another.
Initiating Event	One morning Peter called Mary and asked her to come over to play.
Internal Response	But Mary wanted to go shopping and she didn't want to tell Peter where she was going.
Attempt	So she told Peter she was sick and could not come over to play.
Direct Consequence	Then Mary went shopping and bought a brand new skateboard.
Reaction	Mary thought it was a special toy and was glad she kept the shopping trip a secret from Peter.

be judged as "naughty." One group of 12 5-year-olds and one group of 12 7-year-olds heard three such stories and, after each hearing, made moral-judgment ratings, justified the ratings, and then recalled the story. The judgments were decidedly negative, averaging 1.22 and 2.19 for the 5- and 7-year-olds, respectively, on a 7-point scale.

In each of five other conditions within each age group, 12 children heard three stories, which were modified by adding two sentences. The two sentences contained special information that would allow the child to *reinterpret the motives* of the protagonist. This special information contained essentially the same semantic content across stories, but was systematically varied as to which story-grammar category it belonged. Table 13.2 illustrates the special-information categories for the Secret-Trip Story.

Note that across the five categories, the same key concepts occur: it is about to be Peter's birthday, and Mary may obtain a present for him.

For the five special-information conditions, the content from Table 13.2 was inserted in the appropriate location of the category for the story of Table 13.1. For example, the Internal-Response condition Secret-Trip Story would read:

> Once there were two children named Peter and Mary who lived across the street from one another. One morning Peter called Mary and asked her to come over to play. Mary knew that the next day was Peter's birthday and she thought about a birthday present. Mary wanted to go shopping and she didn't want to tell Peter. So she told Peter she was sick and could not come over to play. Then Mary went shopping and bought a brand new skateboard. Mary thought it was a special toy and was glad she kept the shopping trip a secret from Peter.

After each child in each condition heard each of three different stories (each of which had appropriate special information inserted in appropriate locations), he or she rated the protagonist, justified the rating verbally, and recalled the story.

In comparison to the Normal (no special information) version in Table 13.1, the addition of the special information significantly increased the moral judgment ratings in a positive direction for both age groups. Furthermore, there were *no* significant differences between the special-information conditions with each

TABLE 13.2
Special Information Categories of Secret-Trip Story

Setting	The next day was Peter's birthday and Mary always gave Peter a birthday present.
Initiating Event	Mary's friend told her that the next day was Peter's birthday and that he might like a birthday present.
Internal Response	Mary knew that the next day was Peter's birthday and she thought about a birthday present.
Direct Consequence	Mary gave Peter a present on his birthday the next day.
Reaction	Mary was excited about giving Peter a present on his birthday the next day.

TABLE 13.3
Moral-Judgment Ratings[a]

Special-Information Condition	Grade	
	Kindergarten	Second
None	1.22	2.19
Setting	3.13	3.69
Initiating Event	3.06	3.83
Internal Response	3.42	3.64
Direct Consequence	3.25	3.81
Reaction	3.50	4.06

[a]Data from Nezworski, Stein, and Trabasso, 1979.

grade and there was no grade x condition interaction. Table 13.3 summarizes the moral-judgment data.

Thus, the children in both age groups did equally well in being able to infer and make use of information about motives from five different sources of information. As long as the content was the same, the sources of information as classified by the story grammar did not appear to matter.

A content analysis of children's justifications for their ratings also reflects children's ability to use the special-category information to infer intentions. In Table 13.4, the proportion of children who justified their rating by (1) citing

TABLE 13.4
Classification of Justification for Moral Judgments by Conditions and
Grade Level[a]

	Type of Justification				
		Evaluative Inferences			
	Citation of Acts	Negative	Mixed Polarity	Positive	N
Condition					
Normal	.38	.54	.03	.00	72
Special Category	.12	.26	.38	.20	360
Grade					
Kindergarten	.23	.34	.22	.15	216
Second	.09	.28	.42	.19	216

[a]Data from Nezworski, Stein, and Trabasso, 1979.

the protagonist's actions (e.g., "She didn't tell Peter she was going shopping"); (2) making exclusively negative evaluative inferences (e.g., "She lied"); (3) including mixtures of positive and negative evaluative inferences (e.g., "She lied but surprised Peter with a present"); or (4) exclusively stated positive evaluative inferences (e.g., "She gave Peter a skateboard for a present") are shown for both the conditions and grades. With respect to the special-category conditions, one can see that the addition of the special-category information increased the number of evaluative inferences in the mixed and positive polarity categories by 55%. The main differences between the younger and older children's justifications are that the younger children gave actions whereas the older children gave mixed polarity inferential justifications.

SUMMARY AND CONCLUSIONS

Our review indicates that the moral-judgment literature has been plagued by serious methodological problems. A large measure of these difficulties stem from the fact that stimulus materials used to assess children's comprehension and evaluations have tended to be poorly constructed. Because of this, children have often dealt with stimuli that lacked critical categories of information or that failed to clearly specify important connections between categories of information. Further, stimulus materials have focused on only a small part of the information that potentially affects the judgment process. Although these problems have been recognized by several investigators, attempts to deal with them have generally been unsuccessful and ineffective, probably because researchers have had little else besides intuition to guide them.

Several solutions to the problems of stimulus construction can be suggested. At a minimum, investigators should provide a detailed descriptions of their stimuli, a practice that unfortunately has often not been followed. For stories, this should usually involve presenting the complete stories; for filmed material, researchers should provide as careful and complete a description of the film content as possible. Also, it would probably be useful to have some standardization of stories across studies, because variation in story structure and content probably accounts for a great deal of the inconsistency of results in the literature. Use of the extended story-grammar analysis would also help to reduce some of the problems of stimulus construction. This analysis can serve several functions. First, because it provides an explicit analysis of stimuli, it is useful for constructing stimulus materials that contain the kinds of information that the researcher wishes to depict for his or her subjects. Second, it may suggest manipulations of stimulus content that have interesting effects upon comprehension or evaluations. And third, it may identify some of the types of information that have important effects upon children's moral judgments but that might otherwise be overlooked.

ACKNOWLEDGMENTS

This research was supported by the National Institute of Child Health program project grant (5 Pol HD05027) to the University of Minnesota's Institute of Child Development, and by National Institute of Education grant NIE–G–77–0018 to T. Trabasso. In addition, T. Trabasso was supported as a visiting scholar at the Center for the Study of Reading, University of Illinois, by the National Institute of Education under Contract No. US–NIE–C–400–76–0116.

REFERENCES

Asp, S., Johnson, L., & Trabasso, T. *How does the mode of presentation effect story comprehension?* Paper presented at the annual meeting of the American Educational Research Association, San Francisco, April 1979.

Bartlett, F. C. *Remembering: A study in experimental and social psychology.* Cambridge, England: Cambridge University Press, 1932.

Bearison, D. J., & Isaacs, L. Production deficiency in children's moral judgments. *Developmental Psychology,* 1975, *11,* 732–737.

Berndt, T. J., & Berndt, E. G. Children's use of motives and intentionality in person perception and moral judgment. *Child Development,* 1975, *46,* 904–912.

Chandler, M. J., Greenspan, S., & Barenboim, C. Judgments of intentionality in response to videotaped and verbally presented moral dilemmas: The medium is the message. *Child Development,* 1973, *44,* 315–320.

Collins, W. A., Berndt, T. J., & Hess, V. L. Observational learning of motives and consequences for television aggression: A developmental study. *Child Development,* 1974, *45,* 799–802.

Costanzo, P. R., Coie, J. D., Grumet, J. F., & Farnill, D. A reexamination of the effects of intent and consequence on children's moral judgments. *Child Development,* 1973, *44,* 154–161.

Elkind, D., & Dabek, R. F. Personal injury and property damage in the moral judgments of children. *Child Development,* 1977, *48,* 518–522.

Farnill, D. The effects of social-judgment set on children's use of intent information. *Journal of Personality,* 1974, *42,* 276–289.

Flapan, D. *Children's understanding of social interaction.* New York: Teachers College Press, 1968.

Flavell, J. H. *The development of role-taking and communication skills in children.* New York: Wiley, 1968.

Harris, B. Developmental differences in the attribution of responsibility. *Developmental Psychology,* 1977, *13,* 257–265.

Heider, F. *The psychology of interpersonal relations.* New York: Wiley, 1958.

Hewitt, L. S. Children's evaluations of harm-doers as a function of intentions and consequences. *Psychological Reports,* 1974, *35,* 755–762.

Jones, E. E., & Davis, K. E. From acts to dispositions: The attribution process in person perception. In L. Berkowitz (Ed.), *Advances in experimental social psychology* (Vol. 2). New York: Academic Press, 1965.

Keasey, C. B. Children's developing awareness and usage of intentionality and motives. In C. B. Keasey (Ed.), *Nebraska symposium on motivation* (Vol. 25). Lincoln: University of Nebraska Press, 1978.

Kelley, H. H. Attribution in social interaction. In E. E. Jones, D. E. Kanouse, H. H. Kelley, R. E. Nisbett, S. Valins, & B. Weiner (Eds.), *Attribution: Perceiving the causes of behavior.* Morristown, N.J.: General Learning Press, 1972.

Kruglanski, A. W. The endogenous–exogenous partition in attribution theory. *Psychological Review*, 1975, *82*, 387–406.

Leifer, A. D., Collins, W. A., Gross, B. M., Taylor, P. H., Andrews, L., & Blackmer, E. R. Developmental aspects of variables relevant to observational learning. *Child Development*, 1971, *42*, 1509–1516.

Leon, M. Coordination of intent and consequence information in children's moral judgment. In F. Wilkening, J. Becker, & T. Trabasso (Eds.), *The integration of information by children*. Hillsdale, N.J.: Lawrence Erlbaum Associates, 1979.

Mandler, J. M., & Johnson, N. S. Remembrance of things parsed: Story structure and recall. *Cognitive Psychology*, 1977, *9*, 111–151.

Nezworski, T., Stein, N., & Trabasso, T. *Story structure versus content effects on children's recall and evaluative inferences* (Tech. Rep. No. 129). Urbana, Ill.: University of Illinois, Center for the Study of Reading, June 1979.

Piaget, J. *The moral development of the child*. Glencoe, Ill.: Free Press, 1932.

Rumelhart, D. E. Notes on a schema for stories. In D. G. Bobrow & A. Collins (Eds.), *Representation and understanding: Studies in cognitive science*. New York: Academic Press, 1975.

Sedlak, A. J. Developmental differences in understanding plans and evaluating actors. *Child Development*, 1979, *50*, 536–560.

Shantz, C. U. The development of social cognition. In E. Hetherington (Ed.), *Review of child development research* (Vol. 5). Chicago: University of Chicago Press, 1975.

Stein, N. How children understand stories: A developmental analysis. In L. Katz (Ed.), *Current topics in early childhood education* (Vol. 2). Hillsdale, N.J.: Ablex, 1979.

Stein, N. L., & Glenn, C. G. An analysis of story comprehension in elementary school children. In R. R. Freedle (Ed.), *New directions in discourse processing* (Vol. 2). Hillsdale, N.J.: Lawrence Erlbaum Associates, 1979.

Thorndyke, P. W. Cognitive structures in comprehension and memory of narrative discourse. *Cognitive Psychology*, 1977, *9*, 77–110.

Warren, W. H., Nicholas, D. W., & Trabasso, T. Event chains and inferences in understanding narratives. In R. R. Freedle (Ed.), *New directions in discourse processing* (Vol. 2). Hillsdale, N.J.: Lawrence Erlbaum Associates, 1979.

14

The Role of Cognitive Sets in Interpreting and Remembering Interpersonal Events

Kerry L. Yarkin
Jerri P. Town
John H. Harvey
Vanderbilt University

INTRODUCTION

One of the major themes of this volume is the potential benefits associated with an integration of ideas, concepts, and methodology drawn from social and cognitive psychology. In recent years, work on social cognition has been vigorously developed and now represents a focal line of inquiry in contemporary social psychology. Social psychologists working in this area have borrowed considerably from cognitive psychologists in their conceptualizations and methodologies. For example, social psychologists have begun using dependent measures that include reaction time, recall, organization of recall, requests for additional information, and eye movements and scanning (see Taylor, Chapter 10 in this volume). Also, cognitive psychologists, as reflected by some of Bower's (1976) recent writings as well as that of some of the contributors to this volume (e.g., Bransford; Grueneich & Trabasso), have begun to write about the value of social-psychological concepts in their work. Bower (1976) suggests that readers understand prose material by using the same causal, motivational schema they use to understand people. To date, social-psychological concepts borrowed by cognitive investigators largely derive from the person-perception and attribution-research literatures.

The early result of this empirical and theoretical exchange shows promising integrative links between the specialities of social and cognitive psychology. Illustrative work at this interface includes research on how the accessibility, availability, and salience of information are related to attentional and memorial processes (Bregman, 1968; Pryor & Kriss, 1977; Taylor & Fiske, 1978), how recall and attention are related in an interpersonal-attraction situation (Berscheid, Graziano, Monson, & Dermer, 1976), how cognitive tuning sets influence perceptual, attributional, and memorial processes (Harkins, Harvey, Keithly, & Rich, 1977; Harvey, Harkins, & Kagehiro, 1976; Zajonc, 1960), and how people reconstruct memorial representations of others to fit stereotypic beliefs (Snyder & Uranowitz, 1978).

The theoretical and empirical work discussed in this chapter represents a further contribution to the presently rather embryonic field of social cognition; our particular focus is on variables influencing observers' interpretation and recall of interpersonal events. An important distinction concerning work at this interface of cognitive and social psychology centers on the stimuli employed in our work as compared to those employed by cognitive theorists studying understanding and comprehension and, in general, by social psychologists probing social cognition. Although all of these researchers are examining understanding, the independent variables used in the majority of cognitive and social-cognitive studies have been operationalized via written passages, sentences, and trait lists. However, our work utilizes what we view as more naturalistic social-interaction episodes presented via videotape. There has been, though, a recent emergence of some work in the cognitive area (Bates, Maslin, & Kintsch, 1978; Kintsch & Bates, 1977) employing more naturalistic stimuli in the examination of memory for linguistic material.

According to Heider (1958), in the course of observing everyday events, people quickly and easily make numerous attributions about individuals involved in events and the causes of their behavior. He further proposes that this activity occurs spontaneously, whether or not observers are specifically queried about their attributions. Following this line of reasoning, in our work we explored whether certain cognitive sets and their locus of administration elicit, in a spontaneous way, a high degree of interpretation and also affect memory, as people observe interpersonal situations.

Methodological Importance of Present Work

One of the most notable features of this work concerns its relevance for methodology in attribution research. The idea that people spontaneously engage in considerable inferential activity as they observe various interpersonal events has rarely been investigated in the attribution area. Typical designs in this area involve explicit solicitation of attributions of a particular degree to certain sources of causality presented by an investigator. However, the request that a person make an attribution may influence the interpretive act in a manner that would not ordinarily be characteristic of a naturalistic interpretation of the event observed. Recently, Wong and Weiner (1979) also have adopted a methodology that appears to be relatively naturalistic in format. Their attribution-dependent variable consisted of a self-questioning measure that asked people to report what questions they would most likely ask themselves given certain outcomes.

In our work, we were interested in assessing whether, as a function of experimental manipulations, people would respond to an open-ended question about what they observed and how they felt with a set of clearly identifiable cause–effect and dispositional statements. Thus, the design essentially involved an "incidental-attribution" paradigm in which people are not directly asked to make any kind of attribution to any particular person or situation. Our main attribution-dependent variable was number of interpretations, referred to as degree of unsolicited attribution, made by subjects (secondarily, we also examined the type of attributions made). In the three studies discussed here, Study 1 involved subjects freely listing their thoughts, whereas Studies 2 and 3 involved the adoption of a thought-listing measure similar to the technique advanced by Greenwald (1968) and Petty, Wells, and Brock (1976) in measuring cognitive responses to persuasive messages in the attitude area. In the last two studies, this technique was used because of its potential for enhancing the replicability of research on unsolicited attributions.

Involvement

One of the basic assumptions underlying our work is that interpretive activities will be engaged in a more elaborate fashion and that memory activities will be engaged in a more precise way, the more involved the observer is in the situation being observed. At this point, it is essential to define carefully our theoretical construct of involvement. Involvement, within the boundaries of our research paradigm, relates to the observers' interest in understanding the interpersonal dynamics of the observed event. This conception of involvement on the part of the observer might be understood better by imagining the captivating phenomenal experience felt by an audience in watching a stimulating theatrical production (e.g., an excellent movie or play). In this situation, it is highly likely that observers symbolically and perhaps vicariously participate in the observed event in their attempt to understand its content.

It is essential to distinguish our usage of the concept of involvement from past research focusing on this same concept. In particular, work in the attitude area concerned with "issue involvement" (Kiesler, Collins, & Miller, 1969), "ego involvement" (Sherif, Sherif, & Nebergall, 1965), "personal involvement" (Apsler & Sears, 1968), "response involvement" (Zimbardo, 1960), or "task involvement" (Sherif & Hovland, 1961) has dealt with factors influencing people to adopt positions in attitude-change contexts, and the attitudinal issue had varying levels of practical importance for the subjects. Our subjects were not participating in a direct way in the event, and only one of the cognitive-set variables (e.g., future interaction) related to a matter that might have been functionally important to our subjects. In the final study, a measure was included to probe indirectly subjects' degree of interpretive involvement. Involvement was expected to be enhanced in situations with considerable attributional activity and recall accuracy.

Cognitive Sets

We assumed further that the presence of cognitive-set information would increase subjects' interpretive involvement in the observed event and provide them with an organizational framework for interpreting the event. The concept of cognitive set has a long history in the field of psychology (see Neisser, 1967). This concept (*"Einstellung"*) was emphasized by Gestalt theorists in their analyses of perception (Wertheimer, 1958). They observed in early work that psychological needs (e.g., hunger), values (e.g., aesthetic and ethical), and emotions (e.g., fear) all determined, in various ways, the range and frequency of perception (e.g., Allport, 1955; Bruner & Goodman, 1947). Subsequent research on perceptual sets, arising from the need in social psychology to recognize the role of perception in guiding action, was concerned with the manner in which organization and selectivity indirectly regulate cognitive activity in order to serve various functions (Bruner, 1973). The phenomena most often studied in this research involved the identification of complex patterns in ambiguous stimulus presentations. An analogy can be drawn between these types of stimuli and the inherently ambiguous nature of socially rich phenomena studied by social psychologists. In the present work, our emphasis was upon various sets as orienting devices or motivators of individuals' interpretive involvement in dramatic events that they observed on videotape.

In the three studies presented here, the effects of three different cognitive sets on interpretation and memory were examined. These sets included one to empathize with the actors depicted in the event (versus a set to remain detached), a set to anticipate future interaction with an actor in the videotape (versus no set), and an attributional set relating to the emotional problems of one of the stimulus persons presented in the event (versus no set). Each of the set variables was assumed to stimulate the subjects' involvement within our experimental context while they observed the event.

Locus of Administration of the Set Variable

In the third study, we specifically examined the effect of the locus of administration of the cognitive-set variable on attribution and recall activity. We have argued thus far that various cognitive sets affect subjects' interpretive involvement in understanding and remembering aspects of various interpersonal events. But what is the effect of the timing of the set information on subjects' attributional and recall activity?

It has been suggested that cognitive-tuning sets affect the flexibility of an individual's cognitive structure, which might in turn affect impressions formed about others (Bower, 1978; Harkins et al., 1977). Work by Harkins et al. (1977) found greater attribution of causality to plausible sources when set information was given prior to an event that involved an extreme outcome than when it was given subsequent to observing the event. They suggested that sets administered prior to the observation of an event may have affected the manner in which an event was observed and encoded.

There is conflicting evidence in the memory literature concerning the effects of locus of administration on recall accuracy. For example, some researchers have found that information that facilitates assimilation of a prose passage when presented prior to the event does not enhance recall when presented after the passage (Bransford & Johnson, 1972; Dooling & Mullet, 1973). Other work has suggested that postinput cuing can facilitate reconstructive recall (Hasher & Griffin, 1978; Miller, 1976). We expected that subjects receiving set information prior to viewing an event would encode more information and make more attributions than those receiving this information after observing an event. We also expected more accurate recall in conditions in which subjects were given a set prior to observing the event.

Other Independent Variables

Additionally, a manipulation concerning the seriousness of the event observed was included in the first two studies.[1] Research has shown that behavior leading to relatively extreme outcomes is associated with high dispositional attribution to the actor involved (Chaiken & Darley, 1973; Harvey, Harris, & Barnes, 1975). The effect of this variable on freely occurring attributional activity, however, has not been previously examined. Similar to the foregoing reasoning concerning the cognitive-set manipulations, we assumed that more serious outcomes would lead to more involvement in trying to understand the event. The prediction concerning this variable was that individuals exposed to an event having a serious outcome would make more unsolicited attributions and exhibit more accurate recall than individuals exposed to an event having a moderate outcome.

Finally, a manipulation investigated only in the third study was time of measurement. A major reason for including this variable was to investigate whether the results of differences in interpretive involvement would reveal lasting effects over a period of time. With the exception of some early work by Bartlett (1932) and a few other investigators (e.g., Snyder & Uranowitz, 1978), research has given minimal attention to variables influencing both memorial and attributional processes over time in either cognitive or social psychology.

In terms of the time variable, no strong a priori predictions were made concerning the effects of the set and locus manipulations on interpretation and recall

---

[1]In the first two studies, which manipulated seriousness of outcome, this variable always involved consequences that were relatively negative in nature (this is less clearly so in the moderately serious condition). Most research in attribution using this variable has been concerned with negative outcomes. However, we must emphasize that the results presented here are not necessaryily generalizable to outcomes that are positive in outcome. In our stimulus presentation, it is not possible to separate effects due solely to seriousness relative to effects due solely to negativity.

performance. Perhaps, as Bartlett (1932) suggested, regardless of the experimental manipulations, all subjects might be expected to adopt over time short and concise packages of impressions of the original event. On the other hand, there is evidence from work in the memory area employing a time variable that the theme of an event is the attribute with the greatest memory strength and that has the highest probability of being remembered after some time interval (Hasher & Griffin, 1978). Further, in terms of recall after a temporal delay, Underwood (1969) has suggested that material learned well originally will show less decay over time relative to material learned less well. We expected that if the set and locus manipulations lead to a differential degree of interpretation and accuracy of recall immediately upon testing (hence a greater learning of details of the event), these effects would remain relatively consistent over a 2-week period.

It may be helpful to reiterate the experimental hypotheses for the three studies:

1. We expected that in all three studies, subjects receiving cognitive-set information would make more unsolicited attributions and exhibit greater recall accuracy than subjects receiving no such information.

2. In the first two studies employing a seriousness of outcome manipulation, we expected an increase in attribution and recall activity as severity of outcome increased.

3. In the third study, we expected that subjects receiving the set before observation of the event would make more attributions and display greater recall accuracy than set-after subjects. No-set subjects were expected to engage in the least interpretive activity and exhibit the poorest recall.

4. In the third study, we expected that results obtained at the first time of measurement would remain relatively similar at the 2-week measurement period.

GENERAL METHOD FOR ALL STUDIES

Subjects and Design

The subjects in Study 1 were 80 male and female undergraduates. A 2 (empathy or detached set) × 2 (moderate or serious outcome) between-subjects factorial design was employed. In Study 2, the subjects were 64 undergraduates. A 2 (anticipated interaction set or no set) × 2 (moderate or serious outcome) between-subjects factorial design was used. Finally, 42 college students participated in Study 3 (22 female, 20 male). The design was a 3 (set before, set after, or no set) × 2 (immediate and later period of measurement) factorial with one between-subjects factor (set) and one within-subjects factor (time of measurement).

Procedure

The overall procedure employed in these studies involved variations on a single theme. In each of the three studies, subjects were told that the study concerned people's perceptions of interpersonal events and that they would view a short videotape. At this point, subjects received the cognitive-set manipulations.

The first of the three studies employed an empathy set—subjects in this condition were asked to imagine that they were close friends with the stimulus persons; in another set of conditions, subjects were asked to be detached. The second study involved an anticipated future interaction set. Subjects were told that they would later meet with an unidentified person from among the stimulus persons, or they were given no such set. Finally, the third set manipulation involved an attributional set—subjects were told that one of the women whom they were about to see had severe emotional problems and had received inpatient psychiatric help for depression. This last study also employed the locus of administration manipulation. The attributional set information was given to subjects either just prior to viewing the tape or immediately following viewing. A third condition did not receive any set information.

Three different videotapes of interpersonal events were examined in these studies. In all cases, the videotape consisted of a 6-minute stage presentation by amateur actresses and actors. Pilot work indicated that in each of the tapes, the actors' physical attractiveness was quite similar and that they gave equally skillful performances. The first tape was used only in Study 1, and it involved a discussion between a college couple about their various activities over spring break. The second videotape, employed in Study 2, provided a richer stimulus situation with four persons discussing their divergent views concerning appropriate sexual conduct. In the third study, the videotaped stimulus event involved a discussion between two old friends, in which one of the women expressed considerable depression and dissatisfaction with her life. In this study, a single tape involving a serious outcome, as determined by pilot ratings, was employed.

Seriousness of the outcome of the situation was varied in the first two studies only. This variation was carried out via the use of two separate versions of the same interpersonal encounter. The seriousness of the outcome was manipulated by the actors' display of emotion through nonverbal cues. Amount of eye contact, the actors' tone of voice, and body orientations were varied to provide a more, or less, serious outcome. The actual verbal dialogue was almost identical in the serious- and moderate-outcome versions. For each of the tapes, pilot work indicated that the two versions did indeed reflect the intended variations in outcome severity; also, the tapes were rated as highly naturalistic.

In all cases, after completion of the tape, each subject was taken to a second experimenter who collected the dependent-variable evidence. First, the subjects were asked to recall in writing what they had seen and heard as well as to note any thoughts or feelings they may have had while viewing the tape. This represented the unsolicited attribution-dependent measure in the studies.

The number of unsolicited interpretations made on the attribution measure in all studies was calculated by trained raters who were unaware of the experimental hypotheses. The coding criteria for what constituted an attribution were phrases and clauses denoting or connoting dispositional attributes of the stimulus persons or causal relations for specific effects occurring in the episode. The interrater reliability in the coding of attributions across all three studies ranged between .87 and .96. The attribution score for each subject was an average of the raters' calculations divided by the total number of thoughts.

In the first study, it was also necessary for the raters to code the total number of independent thoughts produced by subjects on the free-response format. However, the second and third studies introduced a more refined technique in measuring unsolicited attributions. In these two studies, subjects listed their thoughts and feelings in marked-off boxes on a page, with a thought being defined by what the subject wrote in each box.

One might wonder why no memory evidence was obtained from the subjects' written responses. The reason is that pilot work showed that it was virtually impossible to code these written statements for correct reports of details of the observed event and to find differences in accuracy as a function of the experimental manipulations. Unlike the attributional statements that were coded, almost any written statement about some aspect of the event could be coded as a correctly recalled item. Thus, only a cued recall measure was used to probe memory.

After completing the attribution measure, all subjects were given a cued recall test. It should be pointed out that this recall test contained questions directly related to details of the event and physical characteristics of the actors, and not directly relevant to the content of the sets. Some examples of the questions we included are: "How many posters were on the wall?; "Which person in the tape was wearing a flannel shirt?" In Study 3, in which time of measurement was of interest, subjects returned after a 2-week period and completed the identical questionnaires received earlier.

GENERAL RESULTS FOR ALL STUDIES

The results of the first two studies are discussed together because the findings from these investigations were parallel in patterning, and then the third study is examined separately. In the first two studies, the effectiveness of the set and severity variables was clearly supported by manipulation check evidence. All participants reported receiving the proper set instructions. The outcome variation in these studies was shown to be effective by subjects' responses to manipulation checks, which reflected the intended variation in seriousness. Outcome was held constant at a serious level in the third study, and evidence was obtained indicating that subjects thought that the outcome of the event was quite serious.

Means for the index of attribution are presented in Table 14.1. For the first two studies, in terms of the attribution measure, with the attribution score equivalent to the number of attributions reported divided by the total number of reported thoughts, there was a main effect for set and seriousness of outcome. These findings were consistent with the predictions that set and severity would stimulate a greater amount of interpretive activity. No other significant differences were found. These data provide support for the predictions for both set and the seriousness of outcome variables.

In terms of recall, there was only a main effect for set. The pattern of data for severity provides only directional evidence that serious-outcome subjects would exhibit greater recall accuracy than moderate-outcome subjects (see Table 14.1).

For the third study, means for the measure of attribution are presented in Table 14.2. There was a significant main effect for set on attribution at the immediate time interval, and no significant changes for any of the three conditions over the temporal delay. Individual comparisons (Dunn's Test) revealed differences that supported the hypothesis that set-before subjects would make more attributions than set-after subjects, and that both set-condition subjects would make more attributions than no-set subjects. No other significant dif-

TABLE 14.1
Studies 1 and 2:
Means and Variances for Index of Number of Attributions Made and
for Accuracy of Recall

	Observational Set			
	Empathy Set		*Detached Set*	
	Moderate Outcome	*Serious Outcome*	*Moderate Outcome*	*Serious Outcome*
Index of number of	.42	.57	.32	.44
attributions made	(.027)[a]	(.025)	(.029)	(.029)
Number of correctly recalled	10.6	10.7	9.2	10.2
items (out of 14 total)	(2.0)	(2.6)	(3.0)	(2.8)
	Anticipated Interaction Set		*No Anticipated Interaction Set*	
	Moderate Outcome	*Serious Outcome*	*Moderate Outcome*	*Serious Outcome*
Index of number of	.76	.80	.57	.69
attributions made	(.025)	(.018)	(.029)	(.030)
Number of correctly recalled	13.6	13.8	11.6	12.9
items (out of 18 total)	(1.5)	(2.5)	(2.1)	(3.3)

[a]Numbers in parentheses are variances.

TABLE 14.2
Study 3:
Means and Variances for Index of Number of Attributions, Accuracy of
Recall, and Degree of Involvement

Index of Number of Attributions Made	Set Variable		
	Set Before	Set After	No Set
Immediately after observation	.92[a]	.68[b]	.50[c]
	(.009)	(.01)	(.04)
Two weeks after observation	.94[a]	.70[b]	.45[c]
	(.02)	(.04)	(.04)
Recall (number of correctly recalled items out of 15 total)			
Immediately after observation	10.0[a]	9.1[b]	8.4[b]
	(1.6)	(1.5)	(2.2)
Two weeks after observation	9.5[a]	8.0[c]	6.9[d]
	(1.4)	(1.0)	(1.2)
Involvement			
Immediately after observation	6.2[a]	4.7[b]	3.2[c]
	(1.4)	(1.8)	(1.0)
Two weeks after observation	6.4[a]	5.3[b]	3.0[c]
	(.81)	(2.2)	(1.7)

[a,b,c,d]Means with identical superscripts are nonsignificant by Dunn's Test; numbers in parentheses are variances.

ferences were found; there were no pronounced differences across conditions concerning the types of attributions made by subjects in any of the studies.

In terms of recall in the third study (see Table 14.2), there was a significant main effect for both set and time. At the immediate interval, set-before subjects recalled more items than both set-after and no-set subjects. However, at the 2-week period, the results supported the prediction that set-before subjects would recall more than set after subjects, and that both set-condition subjects would recall more than the no-set condition subjects.

For the time variable, within both set-after and no-set conditions, there were significant decreases in recall accuracy. No such findings were obtained for the set-before condition.

Means for the involvement measure are also presented in Table 14.2. It can be seen from these results that set-before subjects reported feeling more involved in the situation than did set-after subjects, and both set-condition subjects reported feeling more involved than did the no-set subjects. Involvement was measured on a Likert-type scale(0 to 8) that asked subjects to indicate the degree to which they felt involved in understanding the overall stimulus situation, with high numbers representing high involvement. There was a significant main effect for the set variable on the involvement measure. Individual comparisons showed that at both the immediate and 2-week measurement periods, set-before subjects indicated significantly more involvement than did set-after subjects and that subjects in both set conditions showed significantly more involvement than did the no-set subjects. Results for the time variable showed no significant changes in subjects' reported involvement within any condition.

Finally, in all three studies there was a modest correlation ($rs \cong .30$) between attribution and recall. Correlational evidence obtained from the third study indicated positive relationships among attribution, cued recall, and interpretive involvement ($rs \cong .40$).

GENERAL DISCUSSION AND CONCLUSIONS

In this chapter, we have described three studies that reveal consistent results concerning the effects of different cognitive sets on a measure referred to as unsolicited attribution and on accuracy of cued recall. The results of these studies generally provide strong support for the hypotheses advanced.

In each of the three studies, subjects receiving set information made more unsolicited attributions and exhibited greater recall accuracy than subjects receiving no such information. Three different cognitive sets and three different videotaped interpersonal events were examined. Seriousness of the outcome of the event (manipulated only in Studies 1 and 2) also lead to an increase in attributional activity as the seriousness of the outcome increased. However, this variable did not influence the recall measure in either study.

The third study extended our investigation of set effects on interpretation and recall by including two additional variables: locus of administration of the set and time of measurement. In this study, the effect of receiving the cognitive-set information prior to viewing the stimulus event was found to result in an increase in both attributional activity and recall accuracy when compared to conditions in which the set was received subsequent to viewing. Both set-before and set-after subjects showed greater attribution relative to the no-set subjects, and this pattern of results remained consistent over the 2-week period. In the data for recall, the only unexpected finding was that the set-after subjects showed recall similar to that of no-set subjects on immediate testing, but they showed less of a decrement in recall than the no-set subjects 2 weeks later. It should be pointed out that although the set information provided in this experiment appears to have been relevant to fostering interpretive activity (because it contained information regarding personal problems of one of the stimulus persons), this information probably had little direct relevance in stimulating recall accuracy because the information clearly was not semantically related to questions presented in the cued-recall questionnaire.

In the last study, we also included a measure of reported involvement. It was assumed that attribution and recall effects would be directly influenced by subjects' involvement in trying to understand the nature of the observed event. The results on this measure provide indirect support for this contention by showing that involvement reported by subjects was influenced by the independent variables in a manner quite similar to the effects of these variables on attribution and recall.

Finally, in all three studies, modest significant correlations were found between attribution and recall. In the final study, involvement also was found to be correlated with both attribution and recall.

The Unsolicited-Attribution Technique

The results of this work indicate the efficacy of the incidental-attribution paradigm in measuring freely occurring interpretive activity. Given some apprehension among attribution researchers that interpretive activity may not occur very often unless people are specifically asked to make attributions, the demonstration of the viability of this technique (including the attitude-type thought-listing refinement in Studies 2 and 3) would seem to represent a useful contribution to future research in attribution.

The results obtained in this series of studies demonstrate that interpretive activity can be elicited in the context of individuals observing an interpersonal encounter. Although type of attribution did not systematically differ across conditions, subjects in all conditions spontaneously produced written responses that could be reliably coded as dispositional or situational statements. It was found that approximately 85% of the attributions reported by subjects, across all conditions, were dispositional in nature. It may be useful to provide some examples of the types of attributions made by subjects after observing the social episodes used as stimuli in these studies. These attributional statements included: "I thought he was weird."; "She was extremely old-fashioned."; "I think she will never be happy with her life."; "It's no wonder she never dates—she is really unattractive."; "Her views on premarital sex were ridiculous."; "He acted like a phoney liberal."; "She overreacted because she felt insecure."

Alternative Explanations

We have interpreted the data deriving from these studies as consistent with an assumption that the attribution and cued-recall effects were mediated by subjects' involvement in trying to understand the bases of the events observed. But are there other possible explanations for the attribution and recall data and other theoretical possibilities relating to the data that need to be examined? One issue is that the task of listing thoughts and feelings during the subjects' completion of the attribution measure might have provided additional encoding of information that subsequently influenced the cued-recall measure. However, this argument is weakened by consideration of the correlations between the total number of thoughts listed and the cued recall in all of the studies ($rs < .07$).

An explanation that might be advanced to account for the results across studies is that of experimental demand (Orne, 1962). But such a possibility seems improbable. It would appear to be highly unlikely for subjects in between-subjects designs to infer that the experimenter expected a specific amount of free-response interpretive activity or a particular amount of recall accuracy as a function of the experimental manipulations.

Is it likely that the independent variables influenced attribution and recall because they stimulated more cognitive work? This explanation, although plausible, is weakened because neither the total amount of thoughts reported by subjects, nor the time spent on the attribution measure was significantly affected by the experimental manipulations in any of the studies. This argument, of course, does not rule out an explanation that emphasizes amount of thought that was not or could not be reported by subjects.

Another possible alternative explanation concerns a differential degree of attention exhibited by subjects in all of the three studies. An interpretation in terms of attention seems to overlap somewhat with the explanation we have suggested concerning interpretive involvement. Furthermore, if attention were the principal mediator, and if recall is an adequate index of attention, in the first two studies, both the set manipulation and seriousness of outcome should affect recall of aspects of the event. Seriousness, however, did not consistently influence recall, although it did influence attribution. In the third study (in which locus was examined), the recall data for immediate versus later measurement periods for the *set-after* subjects are difficult to understand via an attentional interpretation, per se. But attention cannot be ignored. It does seem reasonable to suggest that attention may be viewed as a specific component of the more general interpretive-involvement concept advanced in this work.

We have argued that the data in these studies may be understood in terms of subjects' involvement in trying to understand the interpersonal dynamics of the observed event. As the preceding discussion suggests, our work is not conclusive in pinning down this mediation process. Attention, probably involving differences in the amount of information processed and some type of facilitative organizational process, may be facets of this more general involvement concept. It is also possible that some type of affective or emotional component may enter into the subjects' involvement. Thus, much more work remains to be done in order to reveal more conclusively the nature of the mediation process.

Attribution and Recall

Do these studies provide much information about the relationship between attribution and recall? There are several features of the data that provide suggestive ideas about linkages between the two dependent variables investigated in this work. First, these studies all demonstrated the effects of cognitive set manipulations on both amount of unsolicited attribution and accuracy of cued recall.

Second, locus of administration of an attribution-set variable was shown to affect cued recall. Additionally, modest to moderately strong correlations were found across studies for the relationship between amount of interpretive activity and accuracy of recall. Thus, the data point toward meaningful links between the two variables in our research paradigm.

In this work, it has been argued that subjects' involvement in trying to understand the stimulus events presented to them lead to the predicted effects on both attribution and recall. As was previously mentioned, it may be assumed that interpretive involvement subsumes other factors relevant to the encoding and/or organization of information as people observe interpersonal events. At the intuitive level, it seems likely that some degree of relationship between attribution and recall should be expected even if this is the case only because various aspects of events may be stored in memory in a way that is at least partially overlapping and available for both attribution and recall responses. However, the theoretical nature of this linkage is not clear from this work beyond an elementary level of analysis.

Also, it is important to note that recent research investigating this linkage has yielded equivocal results. For example, see Fiske, Taylor, Etcoff, and Laufer (1979) who report little or no association between total recall and attribution versus Smith and Miller (1979) who report a more substantial relationship. These two reports present two different positions regarding the possible relationship between interpretative and memorial processes. The former supports a position that would suggest that evaluation of a person and recall of details upon which the evaluation is based are stored in separate memory systems. On the other hand, the latter paper presents an argument, based on cognitive research in understanding and comprehension, that attributional processing may take place either at the time of encoding and storage of information or at the time of its retrieval from memory. In this case, a strong relationship between attribution and recall would be expected. Although our results and interpretation are more consistent with the second position presented here, the current research does not permit us to make any definitive statement regarding the resolution of this issue.

Finally, it is important to emphasize that there are substantial methodological differences between the present work and previous work concerned with this relationship. Careful analysis of other methodologies in which the attribution-recall relationship has been investigated (see Taylor & Fiske, 1978) will reveal a diversity of research paradigms, with none approaching the degree of rich social content found in the "soap-opera" type stimuli used in our work.

FRAMEWORK OF PROCESSES ASSOCIATED WITH THE PERCEPTION OF SOCIAL EVENTS

In this chapter, we have introduced the concept of interpretive involvement as an important mediator of interpretation and recall of interpersonal events. At this point, it might be instructive to outline the processes that have been investigated

FIGURE 14.1

A SCHEMATIC REPRESENTATION OF PROCESSES INVOLVED IN PERCEPTION OF SOCIAL EVENTS

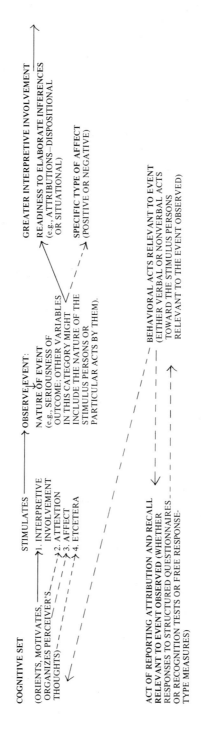

NOTE: DOTTED LINES INDICATE EXTENSIONS TO THE RESEARCH PRESENTED IN THIS CHAPTER.

in this work, while also mentioning other possible processes that deserve examination in future research. The proposed stream of processes is hardly exhaustive but does provide an attempt to describe a typical sequence of analysis. The model presented in Fig. 14.1 depicts a sequence from the introduction of cognitive-set information to attribution and also significantly to later behavior.

From the outset of this discussion, we should emphasize that we do not necessarily view the events in the proposed sequence as occurring in the temporal order shown. We believe that such an order reflects our results fairly well. However, we do not know, for example, if interpretive involvement preceded affect, or vice versa, or for that matter if affect was even stimulated by our operations. Another caveat is that we have little insight about the various strengths of the proposed causal connections. As an illustration, a set's ultimate impact upon a behavioral act relevant to an event may be filtered through so many other processes that it is relatively weak. On the other hand, the set's effect upon interpretive involvement as the event is observed or immediately thereafter may be quite substantial. In general, we recognize that even with a relatively simple proposed sequence such as the present one, there are an infinite number of possible complexities in terms of ordering of events, causal connections, strength of connections, and so on. And this recognition is concomitant to the recognition that the particular events chosen may be incomplete or wrong in major ways. Caveats aside, theoretical representations are meant to facilitate understanding of empirical phenomena, and we believe that a framework such as the one proposed is consistent with that objective.

As shown in Fig. 14.1, the first stage of the proposed sequence represents the induction of cognitive sets. Cognitive sets have been extensively examined by both social and perception investigators (Asch, 1946; Bruner, 1973; Kelley, 1950; Zajonc, 1960). The research in this chapter represents one approach for studying the role of cognitive sets. Our analysis suggests that cognitive sets stimulate subjects' interpretive involvement in the event. Other important processes such as selective attention and affect may also be stimulated by sets. As subjects observe particular social events, both set information and the specific nature of the event (e.g., seriousness of outcome) is proposed to increase involvement leading to more pronounced readiness to engage in inferential activity as well as to recall aspects of the event. Other recent approaches used in investigating set effects (e.g., Massad, Hubbard, & Newtson, 1979; Messé, Stollak, Larson, & Michaels, 1979; Newtson, 1976) have examined the relationship of particular sets of perceptual organization of action sequences and social behavior. In this focus on sets, we concur with Baron (Chapter 4 in this volume) who has stressed the import of a more careful analysis of the perception component of the social perception–cognition sequence.

In this volume, Fiske (Chapter 12) has pointed out that affect is a variable that has been conspicuously neglected in the realm of social cognition. As illustrated in Fig. 14.1, we would like to suggest further that the content of set information provides an impetus that may ultimately be associated with a particular type of affect that, in turn, may be related to subsequent attributional activity. In terms of the relationship between affect and recall, Bower (1976) has suggested that a reader's emotional mood affected which character in a story he identified himself with, and when asked to recall everything in a neutral mood, recalled more facts about the character with whom he identified (see also Isen, Shalker, Clark, & Karp, 1978). Additional work relevant to the proposed sequence has examined links between specific affect induction and interpersonal perception (Izard, Nagler, Randall, & Fox, 1965) and behavior (Exline & Winters, 1965). We are presently engaged in research designed to investigate types of attributions (whether positive or negative, dispositional or situational, etc.) associated with particular sets and particular processes such as the perceiver's mood and involvement.

The present framework broadens the conception of attributional influence to include appropriate behavioral consequences. Several scholars working in social psychology have recognized and emphasized the need to explore possible relationships between attribution and behavior (Deaux, 1976; Kelley, 1973; Snyder, 1976; Weary, Chapter 11 in this volume); Weiner, Frieze, Kukla, Reed, Rest, & Rosenbaum, 1972). It is apparent that research investigating the relationship between attribution and behavior is at an early stage of development (e.g., see Smith & Knowles, 1979). Nevertheless, this relationship is worthy of much empirical and theoretical attention because it represents a core issue in our understanding of the importance of cognitive activities in naturalisitc streams of activity. This relationship, too, is of central interest in our current program of work.

Our schematic representation of the proposed sequence of events involves the possibility of a circular causality loop. It is likely that within social interactions, behavioral acts will provide a foundation for other operations. They may, for example, contribute to the formation of sets toward events or affect the report of attributions, memories, and so on. This presumed feedback relationship may be considered somewhat analogous to Bem's (1972) theory of self perception in which he assumes that individuals infer self attributes on the basis of their own overt behavior.

Finally, it should be evident that any research designed to systematically probe the interactions of the various processes discussed here will require careful theoretical enunciation and the implementation of ingenious methodological and statistical technology. Currently, methods of causal modeling and path analysis are beginning to be employed in the explanation of the relationships among complex social processes (e.g., Fiske, Kenny, & Taylor, 1979). Presently, there is a major need for studies examining the usefulness of advanced and multiple methodologies in this area of work. As McGuire (1973) has so eloquently stated:

> In our actual cognitive and social systems, effects are the outcomes of multiple causes which are often in complex interactions; moreover, it is the rule rather than

the exception that the effects act back on the causal variables. Hence, students of cognitive and social processes must be encouraged to think big, or rather to think complexly, with conceptual models that involve parallel processing, nets of causally interrelated factors, feedback loops, bidirectional causation, etc. [p. 452].

CONCLUSION

In conclusion, consistent with the underlying theme of this volume, it is important to emphasize the similarities and benefits likely from a merging of ideas in the areas of cognitive and social psychology. But, it is also important to recognize that the models adopted in the cognitive area may not always be appropriate for social psychologists exploring understanding of interpersonal events, such as our videotaped scenarios. Similarly, social-cognition concepts may be inappropriate for understanding the types of phenomena examined by cognitive theorists. If cognitive psychologists are examining comprehension and memory for stimuli related to people and their relations, more refinement in their techniques and ideas may be offered by social psychologists. By the same token, social psychologists studying comprehension and memory have much to learn from cognitive theorists who have meticulously developed an extensive body of knowledge on memory processes. It is apparent from research in these areas that each provide substantive contributions to the emerging area of social cognition. However, if this merger is to be fruitful for all involved, neither field can assume superiority. The likelihood of success depends greatly on a broad perspective and appropriate theoretical and methodological exchanges—as we believe have begun to occur in many recent forums, including the present volume.

ACKNOWLEDGMENTS

This work was supported by grants from the Vanderbilt Research Council and the Spencer Foundation to the last author. The authors thank Bibb Latané, Jean Lightner, John Bransford, Keith Clayton, Darren Newtson, William Smith, and Gifford Weary for advice and comments on this work.

REFERENCES

Allport, F. H. *Thories of perception and the concept of structure.* New York: Wiley, 1955.
Apsler, R., & Sears, D. Warning, personal involvement, and attitude change. *Journal of Personality and Social Psychology,* 1968, *9,* 162–166.
Asch, S. E. Forming impressions of personality. *Journal of Abnormal and Social Psychology,* 1946, *41,* 258–290.
Bartlett, F. C. *Remembering: A study in experimental and social psychology.* Cambridge, England: Cambridge University Press, 1932.

Bates, E., Masling, M., & Kintsch, W. Recognition memory for aspects of dialogue. *Journal of Experimental Psychology: Human Learning and Memory*, 1978, *4*, 187–197.

Bem, D. J. Self-perception theory. In L. Berkowitz (Ed.), *Advances in experimental social psychology* (Vol. 6). New York: Academic Press, 1972.

Berscheid, E., Graziano, W., Monson, T., & Dermer, M. Outcome dependence: Attention, attribution, and attraction. *Journal of Personality and Social Psychology*, 1976, *34*, 978–989.

Bower, G. H. Experiments on story understanding and recall. *Quarterly Journal of Experimental Psychology*, 1976, *28*, 512–537.

Bower, G. H. Experiments on story comprehension and recall. *Discourse Processes*, 1978, *1*, 211–231.

Bransford, J. D., & Johnson, M. K. Contextual prerequisites for understanding: Some investigations of comprehension and recall. *Journal of Verbal Learning and Verbal Behavior*, 1972, *11*, 717–726.

Bregman, A. S. Forgetting curves with semantic, phonetic, graphic, and contiguity cues. *Journal of Experimental Psychology*, 1968, *78*, 539–546.

Bruner, J. S. *Beyond the information given*. In J. M. Anglin (Ed.), New York: Norton, 1973.

Bruner, J. S., & Goodman, C. C. Value and need as organizing factors in perception. *Journal of Abnormal and Social Psychology*, 1947, *42*, 33–44.

Chaikin, A. L., & Darley, J. M. Victim or perpetrator? Defensive attribution of responsibility and the need for order and justice. *Journal of Personality and Social Psychology*, 1973, *25*, 268–275.

Deaux, K. Sex: A perspective on the attribution process. In J. H. Harvey, W. J. Ickes, & B. F. Kidd (Eds.), *New directions in attribution research* (Vol. 1). Hillsdale, N. J.: Lawrence Erlbaum Associates, 1976.

Dooling, D. J., & Mullet, R. L. Locus of the thematic effects in retention of prose. *Journal of Experimental Psychology*, 1973, *97*, 404–406.

Exline, R. V., & Winters, L. C. Affective relations and mutual glances in dyads. In S. S. Tompkins & C. E. Izard (Eds.), *Affect, cognition, and personality*. New York: Springer, 1965.

Fiske, S. T., Taylor, S. E., Etcoff, N. L., & Laufer, J. K. Imaging, empathy, and causal attribution. *Journal of Experimental Social Psychology*, 1979, *15*, 356–377.

Fiske, S. T., Kenny, D. A., & Taylor, S. E. *Structural models for the mediation of salience effects on attribution*. Unpublished manuscript, 1979.

Greenwald, A. G. Cognitive learning, cognitive response to persuasion and attitude change. In A. G. Greenwald, T. C. Brock, & T. M. Ostrom (Eds.), *Psychological foundations of attitudes*. New York: Academic Press, 1968.

Harkins, S. G., Harvey, J. H., Keithly, L., & Rich, M. Cognitive tuning, encoding, and the attribution of causality. *Memory and Cognition*, 1977, *5*, 561–565.

Harvey, J. H., Harkins, S. G., & Kagehiro, D. K. Cognitive tuning and the attribution of causality. *Journal of Personality and Social Psychology*, 1976, *34*, 708–715.

Harvey, J. H., Harris, B., & Barnes, R. D. Actor–observer differences in the perceptions of responsibility and freedom. *Journal of Personality and Social Psychology*, 1975, *32*, 22–28.

Hasher, L., & Griffin, M. Reconstructive and reproductive processes in memory. *Journal of Experimental Psychology: Human Learning and Memory*, 1978, *4*, 318–330.

Heider, F. *The psychology of interpersonal relations*. New York: Wiley, 1958.

Isen, A. M., Shalker, T., Clark, M., & Karp, L. Affect, accessibility of material in memory and behavior: A cognitive loop? *Journal of Personality and Social Psychology*, 1978, *36*, 1–12.

Izard, C. E., Nagler, S., Randall, D., & Fox, J. The effects of affective picture stimuli on learning, perception and the affective values of previously neutral symbols. In S. S. Tompkins & C. E. Izard (Eds.), *Affect, cognition, and personality*. New York: Springer, 1965.

Kelley, H. H. The warm–cold variable in the first impressions of persons. *Journal of Personality*, 1950, *18*, 431–439.

Kelley, H. H. The process of causal attribution. *American Psychologist*, 1973, *28*, 107–128.

Kiesler, C., Collins, B., & Miller, N. *Attitude change*. New York: Wiley, 1969.

Kintsch, W., & Bates, E. Recognition memory for statements from a classroom lecture. *Journal of Experimental Psychology: Human Learning and Memory*, 1977, *3*, 150–168.

Massad, C. M., Hubbard, M., & Newtson, D. Selective perception of events. *Journal of Experimental Social Psychology*, 1979, *15*, 513–532.

McGuire, W. J. The yin and yang of process in social psychology: Seven koan. *Journal of Personality and Social Psychology*, 1973, *26*, 446–456.

Messé, L. A., Stollak, G. E., Larson, R. W., & Michaels, G. Y. Interpersonal consequences of person perception processes in two social contexts. *Journal of Personality and Social Psychology*, 1979, *37*, 369–379.

Miller, K., Sr. *Memory reactivation in children: The importance of instructions.* Unpublished doctoral dissertation, Temple University, 1976.

Neisser, U. *Cognitive psychology.* New York: Appleton-Century-Crofts, 1967.

Newtson, D. Foundations of attribution: The perception of ongoing behavior. In J. H. Harvey, W. J. Ickes, & R. F. Kidd (Eds.), *New directions in attribution research* (Vol. 1). Hillsdale, N.J.: Lawrence Erlbaum Associates, 1976.

Orne, M. T. On the social psychology of the psychological experiment: With particular reference to demand characteristics and their implications. *American Psychologist*, 1962, *17*, 776–783.

Petty, R. E., Wells, G. L., & Brock, T. C. Distraction can enhance or reduce yielding to propoganda: Thought disruption versus effort justification. *Journal of Personality and Social Psychology*, 1976, *34*, 874–884.

Pryor, J. B., & Kriss, M. The cognitive dynamics of salience in the attribution process. *Journal of Personality and Social Psychology*, 1977, *34*, 49–55.

Sherif, M., & Hovland, C. *Social judgment.* New Haven: Yale University Press, 1961.

Sherif, C. W., Sherif, M., & Nebergall, R. E. *Attitude and attitude change.* Philadelphia: W. B. Saunders, 1965.

Smith, R. J., & Knowles, E. S. Affective and cognitive mediators of reactions to spatial invasions. *Journal of Experimental Social Psychology*, 1979, *15*, 437–452.

Smith, E. R., & Miller, F. D. Salience and the cognitive mediation of attribution. *Journal of Personality and Social Psychology*, 1979, *37*, 2240–2252.

Snyder, M. Attribution and behavior: Social perception and social causation. In J. H. Harvey, W. J. Ickes, & R. F. Kidd (Eds.), *New directions in attribution research* (Vol. 1). Hillsdale, N.J.: Lawrence Erlbaum Associates, 1976.

Snyder, M., & Uranowitz, S. W. Reconstructing the past: Some cognitive consequences of person perception. *Journal of Personality and Social Psychology*, 1978, *36*, 941–950.

Taylor, S. E., & Fiske, S. T. Salience, attention, and attribution: Top of the head phenomena. In L. Berkowitz (Ed.), *Advances in experimental social psychology* (Vol. 11). New York: Academic Press, 1978.

Underwood, B. J. Attributes of memory. *Psychological Review*, 1969, *76*, 559–573.

Weiner, B., Frieze, I., Kukla, A., Reed, L., Rest, S., & Rosenbaum, R. M. *Perceiving the causes of success and failure.* New York: General Learning Press, 1972.

Wertheimer, M. Principles of perceptual organization. In D. Beardslee & M. Wertheimer (Eds.), *Readings in perception.* Princeton, N.J.: Van Nostrand, 1958.

Wong, P. T., & Weiner, B. *When people ask why questions and the temporal course of the attribution process.* Unpublished manuscript, Trent University, 1979.

Zajonc, R. The process of cognitive tuning in communication. *Journal of Abnormal and Social Psychology*, 1960, *61*, 159–167.

Zimbardo, P. H. Involvement and communication discrepancy as determinants of opinion conformity. *Journal of Abnormal and Social Psychology*, 1960, *60*, 86–94.

15

Lay Analyses
of Causal Forces
on Behavior

Gary L. Wells
University of Alberta

> *"Happy is he who has been able to learn the cause of things."*
> *(Virgil, Georgics, Book II)*

INTRODUCTION

Few scientists would disagree with Virgil's claim as it applies to themselves. Discovering cause–effect relations is a cornerstone of scientific knowledge and represents one of the three basic elements of scientific theory construction (Marx, 1951). Analogously, attribution researchers think of the layperson's *perception* of cause–effect relations as a potential cornerstone of lay knowledge, and of perceived cause–effect relations as a basic element of social cognition. Knowledge of cause–effect relations in our physical environment is clearly a necessity for everyday existence. We know that pressure applied to a light switch causes the onset and offset of light in a room, we know that the application of force to a door will close the door, and so on. Similarly, people have beliefs about cause–effect relationships in the social environment, such as the force of threats or peer pressure on overt behavior. Attribution theorists are concerned with the latter process—how people as participants and observers perceive the causes of behavior.

Traditionally, the attribution question in experimental social psychology has focused on the issue of how the attributor ascribes the locus of behavioral causality to something external to the actor/behaver (e.g., money, peer pressure) or to something internal to the actor (e.g., attitudes, traits). This internal–external dichotomy is not totally descriptive of the multidimensional nature of attributions. The dichotomy does not, for example, map directly onto attributions of responsibility, freedom, or intent (Wells, 1976). The dichotomy, however, is not employed out of sheer simplicity, but is presumed to be of potential import for the observer's ability to predict and perhaps act in the social world. Recent evidence, for example, shows that internal versus external attributions for an aggressive act affect retaliatory behavior (Dyck & Rule, 1978).

One of the approaches to attribution taken by experimental social psychologists has involved analyzing attributions of causality by the actor (the one whose behavior is to be explained) versus an outside observer. I believe that the central thrust for the actor–observer approach to attribution stems from Daryl Bem's concept of how the individual infers his or her attitudes from his or her behavior much as would an outside observer (Bem, 1965, 1967). This notion was carried on by Kelley (1967). Jones and Nisbett (1971) modified the actor–observer notion by focusing on a discrepancy in which the actor tends to attribute causality more to external events than does the observer, and maintained that the *process* of attribution is different for the actor and the observer; the discrepancy is due primarily to the differential information available to actors and observers. I do not question here whether the self-attribution process is identical to the observer-attribution process. However, the actor–observer literature does not leave one with a clear impression of the relationship between actors' and observers' attributions (see Harvey, Arkin, Gleason, & Johnson, 1974; Johnson, Feigenbaum, & Weiby, 1964; Sherrod & Farber, 1975; Snyder, Stephan, & Rosenfield, 1976; Streufert & Streufert, 1969; Wells, Petty, Harkins, Kagehiro, & Harvey, 1977; Wolosin, Sherman, & Till, 1973; Wortman, Costanzo, & Witt, 1973). It is my intention, therefore, to not use actors' attributions as a data point on which to build a model of observer attribution. Although I do not believe that the attribution notions proposed in this chapter are restricted to observers, variability in actors' attributions does not make actors a convenient reference point at this time.

Fortunately, we have learned a great deal about observer attribution. At the risk of oversimplification, I can summarize a partial list of reliable independent variables that affect attribution. We have learned that behaviors that are associated with a large number of desirable effects (i.e., outcomes for the actor) are attributed more to external factors and less to internal characteristics of the actor than are behaviors associated with fewer desirable effects. Not surprisingly, this relationship reverses when the desirable effects are *foregone* rather than obtained (Jones & Davis, 1965; Newtson, 1975; Wells & Ronis, 1979). Similarly, the desirability of the effects obtained (foregone) is negatively (positively) related to internal attributions (Jones & Davis, 1965). It is also clear that actions occurring in the context of salient external stimuli are attributed less to internal factors than are actions not associated with salient external stimuli (Taylor & Fiske, 1978). Fewer internal attributions are made to an actor whose behavior is in the direction of role constraints than when the behavior is out of role (Jones, Davis, & Gergen, 1961). Also, behaviors that are distinctive (that is, not performed by the actor in other stimulus situations) are attributed less to internal factors than are nondistinctive behaviors (Kelley, 1967; McArthur, 1972, 1976). Consensual behaviors (i.e., behaviors that are or would be performed by others in that stimulus situation) are attributed less to internal factors than are nonconsensual behaviors (Kassin, 1979; Kelley, 1967; Wells & Harvey, 1977, 1978). This does not exhaust the list of independent variables that appear to affect causal attribution. But, the list is sufficient to make an important point. Specifically, there are two routes to take in the future development of an observer-attribution literature: Continue adding to the list of independent variables or integrate these variables into a common framework. This chapter attempts to take the latter option.

General Assumptions

Before introducing a general model of observer attribution, certain assumptions should be noted. Most of the empirical studies in observer attribution have involved attributions regarding the behavior of a stranger. This practice is defendable on two grounds. First, it assures methodological control over certain types of prior information. Prior information about the nature of the actor (e.g., if the person is a friend) may not only create statistical noise for the hypothesis under consideration, but may also make certain manipulations (e.g., the nature of the act) impossible to manipulate or incredulous for the observer. More importantly, however, attributions regarding a stranger's behavior presumably reflect the basic processes that operated in the original development of prior knowledge about friends. Thus, it is not that attributions toward strangers generalize only to strangers, but that attributions toward strangers represent "time one" in the development of behavioral attribution.

Because we are primarily dealing with attributions toward people for whom we have no prior information, the attribution to internal and external causal loci must be based on only two bits of information: the behavior itself and the context (or environment) in which the behavior occurred. As obvious as it may seem, it must be remembered that the observer cannot directly see traits, attitudes, or any other potential internal forces that may be responsible for the behavior. Similarly, I would argue that although the observer can directly perceive environmental stimuli that might be influencing the behavior, the observer is not born with any knowledge of the force that these stimuli (the action context) exert on behavior. In other words, the observer's mind is originally a blank tabula rasa on which causal schema will be etched by experiential contact with the dynamic social and physical environment.

CAUSAL FORCE

When confronted with an event to be explained, whether that event is physical (e.g., a felled tree) or behavioral (e.g., conformity), the attributor must consider the existence of certain causal forces. The remainder of this chapter sketches out how the perceiver of a behavioral event learns to assign *causal-force* values to various entities. A causal force is defined as any internal entities (e.g., traits, attitudes) or external stimuli (e.g., other people, money) that are perceived to influence behavior (cf. Lewin, 1943).

Before addressing the important issue of how causal-force values are developed, it should be noted that an attributor's assignment of a causal-force value to some internal entity or external stimulus need not reflect reality. Just as a nonmechanic may erroneously believe that a battery is a necessary causal force for running a car, a lay attributor may believe that personality traits are necessary causes of human behavior. The auto mechanic knows, and can experimentally demonstrate, that a car battery serves only to start an engine and, beyond that, serves no role in the powering of an automobile. Similarly, the psychologist may demonstrate that traits have a relatively minor role in the "driving" of human behavior (Mischel, 1973). The important issue, however, is not that human assignments of causal force are nonveridical, but instead, how to predict the causal-force estimates of the lay attributor.

It can be argued that external causal-force values are higher when the effects of an action are desirable rather than undesirable, when the desirable effects are many rather than few, when the external stimuli are salient rather than nonsalient, when the behavior is in the direction of role constraints rather than opposed to role constraints, when the response to the external stimulus is consensual rather than atypical, when the action is distinctive to the stimulus rather than nondistinctive, and so on. However, simply arguing that causal force is a mediating construct for the variables of desirability, salience, role, and so on, is to some extent only a tautological observation. Understanding the causal-force concept requires an understanding of the processes by which lay attributors develop estimates of causal force for environmental and internal entities.

ORIGINAL AND SOCIALIZED PROCESSING

The model presented here begins with a distinction between two sources of knowledge about causal force. One source is termed "socialized processing." The other source is termed "original processing." Socialized processing is something that attribution theorists and researchers have almost totally ignored. It refers to the obvious fact that much of our knowledge about the "causes" of events is learned through language-based communication. I have very little to say about socialized processing except to note that it is prototyped by the 3–5-year-old's infamous characteristic of asking "why" questions. For example, while my 4-year-old son and I were driving a stretch of interstate highway, he asked how the singers on the radio always knew when we were going under a bridge. The cooccurrence of the bridges to the loss of an AM radio signal triggered an attributional inquiry that then required education or socialized information to instill an alternative causal schemata in the child. The ''Why this?'' and ''Why that'' questions are inquiries that are direct attempts to acquire rules in the art of attribution. It is difficult for anyone who has raised a child to deny the pervasive influence of socialized processing that surely surfaces as causal schemata that originate through *secondary* sources such as parents; that is, not all of an individual's knowledge regarding cause and effect is obtained through direct observation. Even though socialized processing may be an important determinant of knowledge about causal forces at one level, it nevertheless begs the question. How is it that the parents knew an answer? The issue is circular. This is precisely the reason that one must consider a more basic factor—namely, original processing.

Original processing refers to the *direct* observation of relationships between environmental elements and behavioral response. Original processing is a data-driven process in which the observer takes in, stores, and retrieves information regarding the extent to which certain classes of events cooccur. The general proposition is that the causal force or force field that is perceived to characterize a given element is a function of the extent to which that element is perceived to covary with the response under consideration. That statement, of course, is a reiteration of Kelley's (1967) general thesis. It is difficult to deny that our *everyday knowledge* about cause and effect was originally based on observations about the cooccurrence of events. Granted that this knowledge may have an ancestral base (that was the point of mentioning socialized processing), but the *origin* of our knowledge about causal force is still there. Furthermore, it can be argued that much of our *individual* knowledge about causal force operates on the same basis.

The general model being developed here is that knowledge about causal forces originates through the observation of cooccurrence between events. For example, human fear responses cooccur more with large than with small dogs. Eventually, these observations lead to an inference about causal forces. As outlined later, the resultant causal-force values develop considerable autonomy from the original perceiving the causal strength of the environmental elements. For a fairly large domain of environmental elements, modern humanity has shortcut this process through socialized processing so that the child need not experience all stimuli in order to have a feel for their causal-force values. Although socialized processing accounts for much of the individual's knowledge of causal force, it is nevertheless the case that original processing accounted for the cultural or common knowledge that was passed down via socialization. Thus, the remainder of this chapter deals with original processing in more detail.

The Nature of Original Processing

First, it needs to be pointed out that even though original processing is based on a concept of correlation between two or more events, the cognitive mechanisms of the perceiver are not identical to the mechanics involved in a scientist's methods of collecting, storing, and retrieving information for purposes of calculating a correlation. Original processing is, therefore, more appropriately defined as a process of estimating perceived relations or "psycorrelations" rather than correlations. One of the characteristics of psycorrelations is that early observations of cooccurrence are not as strongly modified by later observations as would be found in a normative revision model. This has been observed by Edwards (1968) and others in various contexts. This is a type of primacy effect that is central to a general model of observer attributions. Recall that I earlier argued that original processing gives rise to perceptions of causal force that are somewhat autonomous from the original data. That is, the observer quickly develops a "feel" for causal strength, which produces a lowered reliance on new data. Another way of describing the development of knowledge regarding causal force is to say that it becomes less data driven with increased experience. In attribution and the psychology of prediction, there are various documentations of this. Specifically, people have been shown to be data driven by such things as consensus or base rates when the stimuli impinging on the actor (i.e., environmental elements) are not known through socialized or previous original-processing (e.g., Ajzen, 1977; Caroll & Siegler, 1977; Hansen & Lowe, 1976; Zuckerman, 1978). However, when people have already established causal-force values for the events under consideration, either through original or socialized processing, their attribution and prediction judgments are somewhat autonomous from the data available at the time of judgment (e.g., Nisbett & Borgida, 1975; Miller, Gillen, Schenker, & Radlove, 1974).

There are a couple of studies that deserve mention here. First, a recent unpublished study by Jennings, Amabile, and Ross (1978) used a paradigm in which bivariate distributions were presented sequentially to subjects. For example, tones of various durations and letters from A–Z were presented and the relationship or correlation was manipulated. The subjects' task was to estimate the correlation—that is, the dependent measure was a psycorrelation. The results (Jennings et al., 1978) revealed that "the task proved very difficult . . . at least that was the seeming implication of the very large standard error associated with the group's covariation estimate [p. 395]." Basically, the results show that only when the correlation is very high or very low do subjects' estimates show close correspondence to reality.

The analysis that I have presented, however, suggests that the primacy effect would lead subjects to use the *first few presentations* to develop an early pyscorrelation and either ignore the subsequent presentations or selectively encode later presentations so as to be supportive of the quickly derived psycorrelation. In line with this, I manipulated the correlation between two events both for the first few presentations of event pairings and for the overall correlation. Specifically, subjects were given sequential presentations of pairings of noise intensity and lighting intensity. There were five levels of noise presented over headphones and five levels of lighting presented by slide displays. The correlation conditions were

+.90, +.70, +.50, +.30, +.10, and there were 40 pairings per subject. Crossed with these five levels of overall correlation were these same five levels presented on the *first few* trials. The results revealed that: (1) the primary determinant of the psycorrelations was the first few trials; (2) except in extreme cases (e.g., .10 for the first few pairings and .90 overall), there was little modification of psycor-relations resulting from later trials; (3) the psycorrelations were, in the case of congruence between first few and later trials, extremely close to the actual correlations. In fact, in cases of congruence, the correlation between actual correlations and psycorrelations was +.86. Thus, it appears that observers' psycorrelations were data driven, but overly represented by early observations.

Note that this type of primacy effect is more than simply a reduction of impact for a given data point as a function of the number of data points that have already been processed. That is, if one were to fit a Bayesian statistical analysis, which is a statistically optimal descriptor of the degree of reduced impact that a new data point should have, the fit would be very poor. Rather than describing the psycor-relator as irrational, however, it is more fruitful to consider him or her as *different* from formal, statistical models.

One of the implications of this primacy effect in original processing is that it is sometimes difficult to demonstrate in the laboratory that people are responsive to data-based logic when they derive attributions. The central problem, however, stems from the fact that the laboratory subject has an entire lifetime of non-laboratory experience in which theories regarding causal force have already developed. This is similar to one of the problems inherent in laboratory-produced attitude - change research in which arguments delivered to the recipient of the persuasive communication have impact to the extent that prior, nonlaboratory arguments are absent and the persistence of any attitude change is a function of subsequent exposure to nonlaboratory communications.

Another cognitive mechanism involved in original processing that differs from scientifically derived estimates of correlation if that the human processor tends to treat data that is presented sequentially differently than she or he treats simultaneous presentations. For example, it appears that *sequential* presentation of base rates has a stronger effect in revising prior psycorrelations than does *simultaneous* presentation (Feldman, Higgins, Karlovac, & Ruble, 1976; Manis, 1977). Of course, the human observer has little experience with simultaneous presentations of data. More typical of nonlaboratory experiences is the unfolding of data over time. Similarly, lay observers' typical experiences with data involve relatively small samples, something that seems to be perceived as almost as trustworthy as large samples (Tversky & Kahneman, 1973).

Another factor involved in the psychological processing of correlations was noted by Kahneman and Tversky (1973). They noted that people do not adequately consider the role of statistical regression in explanatory and predictive domains. Therefore, one would expect that reward (an environmental element that is typically used in conjunction with good performance) and punishment (which is typically used in conjunction with poor performance) would not be perceived to be equally correlated with altered behavior. That is, because good performance is subject to statistical regression downward, any effects of reward must operate *against* statistical regression. Because poor performance is subject to statistical regression upward, however, any effect of punishment is *helped* by regression. Therefore, the psycorrelation between reward as an environmental element and performance alteration would be less than the psycorrelation between punishment and altered performance. This in turn should lead people to overestimate the causal force of punishment relative to reward. In line with this, a recent study showed that people attributed a person's action that was performed under the contingencies of reward more to the internal characteristics of the actor (attitude) than the same behavior performed under a punishment contingency (Wells, 1980). This was true even though the reward and punishment contingencies were equally correlated with the action—that is, the reward and punishment elements were equal in their causal force. It was further shown that this asymmetry between reward and punishment was greatly reduced by explicitly provided information that the rewarding and punishing stimuli were equally effective in producing the response (Wells, 1980).

Another factor that operates in determining psycorrelations, which in turn affects causal-force perception, is that events that are more likely to be represented in memory are also overrepresented as data points in psycorrelations. There are a number of demonstrations of this in the work of Chapman (1967), Hamilton and Gifford (1976), and others. This means that salient environmental elements are going to be perceived to be highly correlated with behavior because one's memory for such cooccurrences is enhanced by the characteristics of the environmental stimuli. This in turn leads to salient stimuli having high causal-force values.

The preceding discussion of salience is not a particularly satisfactory description of the issues involved in salience. In fact, no theory that includes the concept of salience will escape the criticism that it is a tautology until it specifies the origin of salience—that is, what makes a particular stimulus salient in the first place? Ortony (1979) assumes that "salience can be operationally defined in terms of subjects' estimates of the prominence of a particular attribute with respect to a concept to which it does or could apply [p. 162]." Ortony therefore suggests that a salient attribute of a stimulus cluster is salient because of its relationship or correlation with another entity or event. This appears to have some definitional value. My 4-year-old son, for example, was recently watching a television show in which the protagonist walked around a corner and was mugged. My son's response was, "If I had heard that kind of music, I wouldn't have gone around the corner." Clearly, it was through direct processing of the correlation between music type and event outcome that made the music salient enough to enter into memory. This is consistent with Fiske, Kenney, and

Taylor's (1979) notion that salience effects operate by directing attention to schema-relevant data, which are then overrepresented in recall.

A factor that is similar to, but importantly distinct from, salience is cognitive accessibility. Cognitive accessibility refers to the ease of recall of some bit or cluster of information. Priming a bit or cluster of information (i.e., drawing information into a short-term memory store), may make that information dominate in the subsequent attributional judgment. Ferguson and Wells (1980), for example, presented subjects with a behavioral scenario followed by questions that primed cognitive access to either consensus, consistency, or distinctiveness characteristics of the behavioral scenario. The results were consistent with an access-dominance notion of attribution—for example, the priming of high-consensus information led to strong stimulus attributions and the priming of high-distinctiveness information led to strong person attributions. Thus, even though the scenario was identical for all subjects, their attributions depended in part on which type of information was recently primed into high-cognitive access.

Much of what I have outlined here can be found in previous models. Certainly, the concept that people use perceived covariance information was the central tenet of Kelley's (1967) model of attribution. However, it should be noted that covariance is only part of a complex model. First, I tried to point out how psycorrelations are responsible for the *original* processing of information about cause and effect, but often get passed along indirectly through language-based communication or *socialized* processing. I also tried to outline how original processing operates and how it is dependent on certain limitations of human performance. It was also argued that there is some storage of the information by identifying certain classes of elements in the environment as having *causal force* for certain behaviors. To the extent that the perceiver has developed a causal-force schema for the situation and behavior being observed, further data-based information that was effective at the original-processing level is minimally utilized. Finally, internal causal forces, which are never directly seen, are inferred to exist to the extent that external causal forces are absent in the context of an action. It is this final point that I now address in more detail.

THE RELATIONSHIP BETWEEN PERCEIVED EXTERNAL AND INTERNAL FORCES

One of the major issues with which attribution theorists and researchers have not come to grips is the relationship between internal and external attributions. Some researchers have constructed a single attribution index by separately measuring internal and external attributions and subsequently taking a difference score between the two (e.g., Storms, 1973; Wells et al., 1977). Others have measured the dichotomy by placing internal on one end of the measurement scale and external on the other end of the measurement scale (e.g., Duval & Wicklund, 1974; Feather & Simon, 1971; Nisbett & Borgida, 1975; Ruble, 1973). Such measurement procedures are more than questions of methodology. The two procedures previously mentioned imply a theoretical perspective in which internal and external attributions have an inverse linear relationship. However, studies that have reported internal and external attributions separately (e.g., Arkin & Duval, 1975; Enzle, Hansen, & Lowe, 1975; Harvey, Harris, & Barnes, 1975; Miller, 1975; Sherrod & Farber, 1975; Taylor & Koivumaki, 1976) do not necessarily show such a relationship (see Solomon, 1978).

Although it is clear that the relationship between internal and external causal forces is not so simple as an inverse linear relationship, internal and external attributions are not independent. The major proposition is that: *Internal attributions are represented by a decelerating inverse function when mapped against external causal forces.* Note that the critical distinction between this proposition and the relationship that was discredited in the previous paragraph is that the former describes a relationship that is linear whereas the latter describes a quadratic function. The rationale for this proposition is rather straightforward. Specifically, internal causal forces (which can never be directly observed) need only be ascribed to the actor up to a certain logical point—namely, the point at which the external causal forces are adequate to explain the action. Beyond that point, additional external causal forces will not continue to reduce internal attributions. At and beyond the point where the external forces are perceived to completely account for the action, internal attributions will be at a level that would be expected had the observer–attributor not known about the behavior of the actor. That is, because the action is totally accounted for by external forces, the observer has learned nothing about the actor's unique internal forces and the attributor can only assume internal forces to be as strong or weak as the typical actor in that population.

Fig. 15.1 presents empirically derived data points I collected. These data were collected by having subjects observe a videotaped scenario in which an actor is shown slamming desk drawers, cursing, and, finally, kicking the desk. The external forces were manipulated across seven levels by describing the context of the action in various ways. These seven levels were selected on the basis of pilot testing on a separate sample of subjects who were asked to sort among a large sample of frustrating external experiences. The result of the pilot testing produced seven levels that were, in the view of the pilot subjects, equal distances apart on a subjective-frustration scale. At the highest level of the seven external forces, it was said that the actor had just been fired from his job and fined $1000 by his professional association for something that he did not do. The lowest external force described the force on the actor as having been unable to find a paper clip. The dependent measure in the main experiment was a composite index of three measures (e.g., "To what extent was Tom's reaction due to his

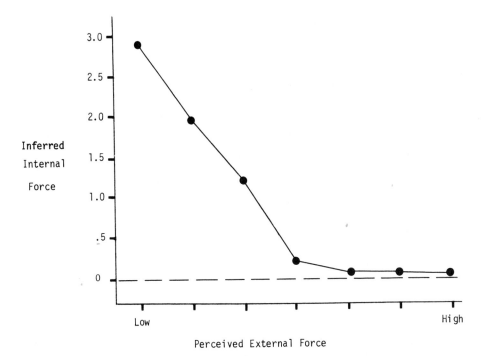

FIG. 15.1.   Relationship between perceived external force and inferred internal
forces.

dispositional intolerance to frustration?''). The zero point on the internal-force
scale theoretically represents the point at which the external forces adequately
account for the action. Operationally, this represents the scale average for the
three internal-force measures given by observers who did not know of the behavior of the actor nor of the external forces impinging on the actor (i.e., the
average "tolerance for frustration" in the population). The zero point was actually 4.2 on the 15-point scale (where high numbers represent less tolerance) and
distances along the internal-force axis represent standard deviations from this
zero point.

One of the implications of the decelerating negative relationship between
internal and external forces is that alterations in external causal force need not
affect internal attributions. Thus, studies that attempt manipulations of internal
attributions by increasing external attributions will not be effective if the attributor has already decided that the primary causal locus resides externally (e.g.,
Nisbett, Borgida, Crandall, & Reed, 1976, a depressive mood study).

There is one qualifying element involved in the decelerating negative relationship proposition. Kelley (1971) has noted that one of the principal problems in
specifying the relationship between attribution variables is one of "constancy of
effect." That is, when the observer is faced with an attribution dilemma under

one condition (e.g., two external causal forces are present) versus another condition (e.g., one external causal force is present), it is assumed that the *effect* (i.e., behavior) to be explained is identical in the two situations. Suppose, for example, that the data for Fig. 15.1 were collected by describing the action as "overt frustration" rather than explicitly showing the action via videotape. This probably would have led the attributor to assume that the action was not severe (e.g., frown) in the "paper-clip" condition and very severe in the "fired-and-fined" condition. This in turn might have led to relatively equal internal attributions across levels of external force. Similarly, failure to adequately describe the external force although manipulating the extremity of the action might produce an increase in *both* internal and external attributions across conditions.

SUMMARY AND CONCLUSIONS

Although much of the lay observer's knowledge of behavioral causality is obtained through socialized processing (i.e., taking advantage of language-based communication channels to adopt cultural and parental hypotheses), the socialized knowledge was at one time based on direct observation.[1] Novel behaviors and/or novel environments, which provide poor transfer of socialized knowledge, engage direct or original processing in the form of psycorrelations (perceived correlations). Unlike scientists' methods of obtaining correlational data, the lay observer's sampling techniques are not necessarily random or representative of the population to which the observer generalizes. Instead, psycorrelations are influenced by extra weights being assigned to both salient stimuli and early data points, and little or no consideration of statistical subtleties (e.g., statistical regression).

A given psycorrelation need not have been either *specifically* taught at the socialized processing level or directly experienced for a given individual. Instead, the psycorrelation can exist because of stimulus generalization (leading to stimulus categories) at either the original-processing level or the socialized-processing level. The magnitude of psycorrelation, whether it matches a scientific estimate of the true correlation or not, determines the level of causal force perceived to characterize the stimulus under consideration.

A given behavior initiates a search in the environment for a stimulus element for which there is a psycorrelation. Identifying such an element leads to the assignment of causality for that element. Identifying multiple psycorrelated ele-

---

[1]It is not unusual, however, to find socialized or cultural "knowledge" being based on timely theorizing by a small number of influential people rather than on direct observation. "Experts," for example, have created socialized schema that dictate that much behavior is determined by unconscious battles being fought between psychodynamic forces. Whatever the merit of this type of causal-force notion, it is safe to say that it was at no time based on direct observation, yet has probably influenced lay analyses of causal force in the 20th century.

ments leads to a division of causality among the elements in proportion to the magnitude of the psycorrelations. Identifying elements that have negative psycorrelation values leads to the augmentation (see Kelley, 1971) of causal assignments to any positive psycorrelation elements. Failure to perceive a sufficient psycorrelation element leads to the inference that internal causal forces (e.g., attitudes or traits) characterize this specific actor more than the average actor in the population.

Several problems in the observer-attribution area remain unsolved. First, although many independent variables have been identified and shown to reliably affect the extent to which internal versus external attributions are made, little progress has been made in specifying when observers will make one type of internal attribution versus another type. For example, when will an observer make an attitudinal attribution to a target actor versus a trait attribution versus a mood attribution? All three are internal attributions that presumably increase with decreasing external causal forces. A related question concerns how the observer decides which specific property *within* a type of internal attribution should apply to the target actor. For example, assuming the observer attributes the target-actor's behavior to something about the actor's traits, which specific traits are involved? Most attribution researchers choose trait-dependent measures on the basis of the researcher's intuitions about which traits are most likely to be affected. But, a preferable approach would involve a priori specification of which traits will be affected. This should be derived from a model that does not rely on the investigator's intuitions.

Finally, there is some concern among attribution theorists regarding the balance between theory and data. Some attribution researchers appear to believe that theory has outstripped data, whereas others argue that data outstrips theory. In reality, it seems clear to me that neither is the case. Instead, there may be adequate amounts of both data and theory, but there is a problem with the extent to which the data are relevant to the theories, and vice versa.

REFERENCES

Ajzen, I. Intuitive theories of events and the effects of base-rate information on prediction. *Journal of Personality and Social Psychology,* 1977, *33,* 733–742.

Arkin, R. W., & Duval, S. Focus of attention and causal attributions of actors and observers. *Journal of Experimental Social Psychology,* 1975, *11,* 427–438.

Bem, D. J. An experimental analysis of self persuasion. *Journal of Experimental Social Psychology,* 1965, *1,* 199–218.

Bem, D. J. Self perception: An alternative interpretation of cognitive dissonance phenomena. *Psychological Review,* 1967, *74,* 183–200.

Caroll, J. S., & Siegler, R. S. Strategies for the use of base rate information. *Organizational Behavior and Human Performance,* 1977, *19,* 392–402.

Chapman, L. J. Illusory correlation in observational report. *Journal of Verbal Learning and Verbal Behavior,* 1967, *6,* 151–155.

Duval, S., & Wicklund, R. A. Effects of objective self-awareness on attribution of causality. *Journal of Experimental Social Psychology,* 1974, *9,* 17–31.

Dyck, R. J., & Rule, B. G. Effect on retaliation of causal attributions concerning attack. *Journal of Personality and Social Psychology*, 1978, *36*, 521-529.

Edwards, W. Conservatism in human information processing. In B. Kleinmuntz (Ed.), *Formal representation of human judgment*. New York: Wiley, 1968.

Enzle, M. E., Hansen, R. D., & Lowe, C. A. Causal attribution in the mixed-motive game: Effects of facilitory and inhibitory environmental forces. *Journal of Personality and Social Psychology*, 1975, *31*, 50-54.

Feather, N. T., & Simon, J. G. Attribution of responsibility and valence of outcome in relation to initial confidence and success and failure of self and other. *Journal of Personality and Social Psychology*, 1971, *18*, 173-188.

Feldman, N. S., Higgins, E. T., Karlovac, M., & Ruble, D. N. Use of consensus information in causal attributions as a function of temporal presentation and availability of direct information. *Journal of Personality and Social Psychology*, 1976, *34*, 694-698.

Ferguson, T. J., & Wells, G. L. Priming mediators of causal attribution. *Journal of Personality and Social Psychology*, 1980, *38*, 461-470.

Fiske, S., Kenney, D., & Taylor, S. Structural models for the mediation of salience effects on attribution. Unpublished manuscript, Carnegie-Mellon University, 1979.

Hamilton, D. L., & Gifford, R. K. Illusory correlation in interpersonal perception: A cognitive bias of stereotype judgments. *Journal of Experimental Social Psychology*, 1976, *12*, 392-407.

Hansen, R. D., & Lowe, C. A. Distinctiveness and consensus: The influence of behavioral information on actors' and observers' attributions. *Journal of Personality and Social Psychology*, 1976, *34*, 425-433.

Harvey, J. H., Arkin, R. M., Gleason, J. M., & Johnson, S. Effect of expected and observed outcome on the differential causal attributions of actor and observer. *Journal of Personality*, 1974, *42*, 62-77.

Harvey, J. H., Harris, B., & Barnes, R. D. Actor-observer differences in perceptions of responsibility and freedom. *Journal of Personality and Social Psychology*, 1975, *32*, 22-28.

Jennings, D., Amabile, T. M., & Ross, L. *The covariation detection problem: Theory-driven vs. data-driven estimates of association*. Unpublished manuscript, Stanford University, 1978.

Johnson, T. J., Feigenbaum, R., & Weiby, M. Some determinants and consequences of the teacher's perception of causation. *Journal of Educational Psychology*, 1964, *55*, 237-246.

Jones, E. E., & Davis, K. E. From acts to dispositions: The attribution process in person perception. In L. Berkowitz (Ed.), *Advances in experimental social psychology* (Vol. 2). New York: Academic Press, 1965.

Jones, E. E., Davis, K. E., & Gergen, K. J. Role playing variations and their informational value for person perception. *Journal of Abnormal and Social Psychology*, 1961, *63*, 302-310.

Jones, E. E., & Nisbett, R. E. The actor and the observer: Divergent perceptions of the causes of behavior. In E. E. Jones, D. Kanouse, H. H. Kelley, R. E. Nisbett, S. Valins, & B. Weiner (Eds.), *Attribution: Perceiving the causes of behavior*. New York: General Learning Press, 1971.

Kahneman, D., & Tversky, A. On the psychology of prediction. *Psychological Review*, 1973, *80*, 237-251.

Kassin, S. M. Consensus information, prediction, and causal attribution: A review of the literature and issues. *Journal of Personality and Social Psychology*, 1979, *37*, 1966-1981.

Kelley, H. H. Attribution theory and social psychology. In D. Levine (Ed.), *Nebraska symposium on motivation*. Lincoln: University of Nebraska Press, 1967.

Kelley, H. H. Attribution in social interaction. In E. E. Jones, D. Kanouse, H. H. Kelley, R. E. Nisbett, S. Valins, & B. Weiner (Eds.), *Attribution: Perceiving the causes of behavoir*. New York: General Learning Press, 1971.

Lewin, K. Defining the "field at a given time." *Psychological Review*, 1943, *50*, 292-310.

Manis, M. Cognitive social psychology. *Personality and Social Psychology Bulletin*, 1977, *3*, 550-566.

Marx, M. H. The general nature of theory construction. In M. H. Marx (Ed.), *Psychological theory: Contemporary readings*. New York: Macmillan, 1951.

McArthur, L. A. The how and what of why: Some determinants and consequences of causal attribution. *Journal of Personality and Social Psychology*, 1972, *22*, 171–193.

McArthur, L. A. The lesser influence of consensus than distinctiveness information on causal attributions: A test of the person–thing hypothesis. *Journal of Personality and Social Psychology*, 1976, *33*, 733–742.

Miller, A. G. Actor and observer perceptions of the learning of a task. *Journal of Experimental Social Psychology*, 1975, *11*, 95–111.

Miller, A. G., Gillen, B., Schenker, C., & Radlove, S. The prediction and perception of obedience to authority. *Journal of Personality*, 1974, *42*, 23–42.

Mischel, W. Towards a cognitive social learning conceptualization of personality. *Psychological Review*, 1973, *80*, 252–283.

Newtson, D. Dispositional inference from effects of actions: Effects chosen and foregone. *Journal of Experimental Social Psychology*, 1975, *11*, 205–214.

Nisbett, R. E., & Borgida, E. Attribution and the psychology of prediction. *Journal of Personality and Social Psychology*, 1975, *32*, 932–943.

Nisbett, R. E., Borgida, E., Crandall, R., & Reed, H. Popular induction: Information is not always informative. In J. S. Carroll & J. W. Payne (Ed.), *Cognition and social behavior*. Hillsdale, N.J.: Lawrence Erlbaum Associates, 1976.

Ortony, A. Beyond literal similarity. *Psychological Review*, 1979, *86*, 161–180.

Ruble, T. L. Effects of actor and observer roles on attributions of causality in situations of success and failure. *The Journal of Social Psychology*, 1973, *90*, 41–44.

Sherrod, D. R., & Farber, J. The effect of previous actor–observer role experience on attribution of responsibility for failure. *Journal of Personality*, 1975, *43*, 231–247.

Snyder, M. L., Stephan, W. G., & Rosenfield, D. Egotism and attribution. *Journal of Personality and Social Psychology*, 1976, *33*, 435–441.

Solomon, S. Measuring dispositional and situational attributions. *Personality and Social Psychology Bulletin*, 1978, *4*, 589–594.

Storms, M. D. Videotape and the attribution process: Reversing actors' and observers' points of view. *Journal of Personality and Social Psychology*, 1973, *27*, 165–175.

Streufert, S., & Streufert, S. C. Effects of conceptual structure, failure, and success on attribution of causality and interpersonal attitudes. *Journal of Personality and Social Psychology*, 1969, *11*, 138–147.

Taylor, S. E., & Fiske, S. T. Salience, attention, and attribution: Top of the head phenomena. In L. Berkowitz (Ed.), *Advances in experimental social psychology* (Vol. 11). New York: Academic Press, 1978.

Taylor, S. E., & Koivumaki, J. H. The perception of self and others: Acquaintanceship, affect, and actor–observer differences. *Journal of Personality and Social Psychology*, 1976, *33*, 403–408.

Tversky, A., & Kahneman, D. Availability: A heuristic for judging frequency and probability. *Cognitive Psychology*, 1973, *5*, 207–232.

Wells, G. L. *On the equivocality of dependent variables in attribution*. Paper presented at a meeting of the Midwestern Psychological Association, Chicago, 1976.

Wells, G. L. Asymmetric attributions for compliance: Reward vs. punishment. *Journal of Experimental Social Psychology*, 1980, *16*, 47–60.

Wells, G. L., & Harvey, J. H. Do people use consensus information in making causal attributions? *Journal of Personality and Social Psychology*, 1977, *35*, 279–293.

Wells, G. L., & Harvey, J. H. Naive attributors' attributions and predictions: What is informative and when is an effect an effect? *Journal of Personality and Social Psychology*, 1978, *36*, 483–490.

Wells, G. L., Petty, R. E., Harkins, S. D., Kagehiro, D., & Harvey, J. H. Anticipated discussion eliminates actor–observer differences in the attribution of causality. *Sociometry*, 1977, *40*, 247–253.

Wells, G. L., & Ronis, D. L. *A causal-force conceptualization of attribution*. Unpublished manuscript, University of Alberta, 1979.

Wolosin, R. J., Sherman, S. J., & Till, A. Effects of cooperation and competition on responsibility attribution after success and failure. *Journal of Experimental Social Psychology,* 1973, *9,* 220–235.

Wortman, C. B., Costanzo, P. R., & Witt, T. R. Effect of anticipated performance on the attribution of causality to self and others. *Journal of Personality and Social Psychology,* 1973, *27,* 372–381.

Zuckerman, M. Use of consensus information in prediction of behavior. *Journal of Experimental Social Psychology,* 1978, *14,* 163–171.

16

On the Nature of the Question in Social Comparison

William P. Smith
Vanderbilt University

In this chapter, I hope to characterize a view of how people use performance information from other people to make inferences about their own abilities. This is a view that stresses the importance of understanding the nature of the question a person asks before we can interpret the significance of the answer, a stress that appears elsewhere in this volume. In so doing, I argue that more than one question may be involved in self assessment of ability, and that knowing which question is being asked may be very important in understanding social comparison. This is a view that has been intimated by a number of investigators, including Singer (1966) and Jones and Regan (1974). I hope to explore it more systematically than others have. In any case, it is a view very different from that expressed in the theory that has dominated research in this area for 25 years, Festinger's (1954) theory of social comparison processes. According to the Festinger theory, if I am uncertain about my ability, I will seek to compare myself with others who are similar in ability; if I find them, I will develop a subjectively accurate and precise judgment of my ability; if I find only others of different ability, I remain uncertain, and continue my search. This seems a bit overgeneralized from a perspective 25 years after the fact. My own approach has involved taking a fresh intuitive look at just what questions a person might answer about his or her own ability through information about another's task performances, and then applying some simple information-processing models to understand how the information is used.

However, I would first like to give a brief overview of the place of social comparison concepts in psychology. I then proceed to an examination of the Festinger theory as it applies to ability judgment, and a brief look at relevant research related to that theory. After presenting my own view, I discuss some experiments, mostly conducted in my laboratory, relating to different questions people may ask about ability through social comparison. These experiments draw on models related to decision making under risk, and the psychology of judgment. Finally, I turn the tables and talk about a methodological contribution social psychology might make to the study of the psychology of judgment.

THE SOCIAL SIGNIFICANCE OF SOCIAL COMPARISON

Concepts of social comparison abound in theories of social behavior, both in sociology and in social psychology. We are said to obtain our notions of appropriate sexual behavior and political attitudes through knowledge of the behaviors and attitudes of relevant reference groups, to decide whether we deserve the quality of our treatment by others in areas of life ranging from the economic to the romantic—through comparing our fates with those of others—and to judge our worth and competence in the world of work through comparison of performances with others. All of these theories, including reference groups, relative deprivation, status congruence, equity, and comparison theory per se assume that much of our knowledge about ourselves and the world is mediated through the examination of the acts, statements, and fates of others. However, most of these theories are concerned with the relationship between various macrosocial arrangements, and the expression of social discontent. Consequently, these theories, with the exception of distributive justice in the guise of equity theory, have little elaboration with respect to the cognitive processes involved in social comparison. The Festinger theory of social comparison processes differs from the others mentioned in that it focuses on judgment rather than discontent, but it shares their lack of elaboration of the cognitive processes involved.

THE FESTINGER THEORY

The Festinger (1954) theory is elegant and simple. It consists of a set of propositions, most of which apply to both opinion and ability evaluation. It begins with the proposition or assumption that people have a drive to evaluate their opinions and abilities. Festinger (1954) goes on to propose that evaluations of opinions and abilities is sought through comparison respectively with the opinions and abilities of others when "... objective, nonsocial means are not available [p. 118]." The core of the theory resides in the similarity hypothesis and its several corollaries and derivations. This hypothesis (Festinger, 1954) proposes that "... the tendency to compare oneself with some other specific person decreases as the difference between his opinion or ability and one's own increases [p. 120]." The implications of this hypothesis are, first, that people choose to compare with similar others when they have a choice, and that comparison with similar others results in subjectively precise and stable evaluations of one's opinions and abilities. On the other hand, if only very different others are available for comparison (Festinger, 1954), "... the person will not be able to make a subjectively precise evaluation [p. 121]," and there are tendencies to change either self evaluation or the other's position. In short, if one does not find similarity, one seeks to create it. However, Festinger explicitly recognizes the differential malleability of opinions and abilities. Hence, differences between people are seen as likely to result in social influence in the case of the more malleable opinions, whereas they result in further efforts to locate similar others in the case of the less malleable abilities. Indeed, with respect to abilities, the theory becomes a theory of selective association.

Unfortunately the Festinger theory is silent about the nature of the cognitive processes involved in ability evaluation; it does not indicate just how comparison with another of similar ability results in stable, precise self-evaluation. There is a very mechanical aspect to the theory: uncertainty about ability leads to objective test, or comparison with a similar other, either of which reduces uncertainty. Hence the theory fails to tell us just what comparison with a similar other could tell a person about his or her abilities, and why it should enhance confidence or stability in self-assessment. In fact Jones and Regan (1974) have suggested that there is a logical inconsistency in the similarity hypothesis as applied to ability evaluation. They ask how one knows another is similar without comparison, and if one does know, why comparison is necessary. They resolve the issue by pointing to two different questions which may be involved in the social evaluation of ability; I shall return to this point shortly.

The vast majority of the research on the social comparison of abilities has been concerned with the issue of whom a person will select for performance comparison, rather than with variables more directly characterizing judgment itself, such as uncertainty and quality of judgment. The results of this research have been very mixed. While there is some evidence for preference for similar others, variously defined (e.g., Jones & Regan, 1974; Martens & White, 1975; Wheeler, 1966; Zanna, Goethals, & Hill, 1975), this evidence is not very striking in many cases, and evidence for choice of comparison with those better off (e.g., Wheeler, 1966; Wilson & Benner, 1971), those worse off (e.g., Hakmiller, 1966), and for extreme performers at both ends of a performance dimension (e.g., Wheeler, Shaver, Jones, Goethals, Cooper, Robinson, Gruder, & Butzine, 1969) has been obtained under various conditions. It is difficult to determine from this research just what conditions generally favor choice of a similar other versus choice of different others because experimental paradigms have varied widely. For example, the choice to compare has taken the form of options to view other's performances, to affiliate with others without restriction, and to compete with others. I do not intend to review this research in detail, but the data hardly support any monolithic hypothesis of preference for similar other in ability comparison.

QUESTIONS SOCIAL COMPARISON CAN ANSWER

Prediction of a Task Outcome

Perhaps it is useful at this point to ask from an intuitive perspective just what it is that information about the task performances of another person can offer us in our attempts to judge our own abilities. Before we can answer this question, it may be necessary to ask just what people mean when they ask what their abilities are. It seems clear that there are at least two distinguishable meanings of the question. One is a simple, specific question about performance outcomes likely to result when we attempt to grapple with the set of environmental contingencies we call a task. Examples of such questions are, Can I play the ''Moonlight Sonata'' of Beethoven? It implies a temporally stable capacity of the person to obtain a certain level of outcomes from a task if he or she makes a motivated attempt. If I can play the Sonata today, I can do so tomorrow; if I can run a mile in 8 minutes today, I can do it tomorrow. This also implies an effective way of inferring ability in this sense: Simply try the task. The level of outcomes I obtain tomorrow will be the same as the level I obtained today.

If an effective means of inferring ability in this sense is to attempt the task of interest, we can reasonably ask what role the comparison or observation of the performances of others could play here. Jones and Regan (1974) have answered this by suggesting that people can learn how they themselves will fare on a novel task by observing the task outcomes another person of similar ability obtains from that task. This is possible because the ability concept connotes generality of the performance capacity over a domain of tasks, and temporal stability in the ordering of any group of people with respect to that ability. In short, what is stable about ability across tasks in the domain of any given ability is the ordering of performances of any given set of persons across that domain.

Let me illustrate this point with the way in which we assess our ability in a domain that has become increasingly important to academic people: running ability. My ability to run is conceived by me in general terms: If I am a good runner, I run well on a track, or cross country, on flat land, or uphill and downhill. Yet, the generality is not contained in any specific index of running skill in any given situation. First, knowing that I can run a mile in 8 minutes on a flat track does not tell me how fast I can run an undulating mile cross country. Further, it does not tell me whether I am a good runner. My goodness as a runner is always defined by how fast or how long other people run. I am a good runner if I can run as fast or faster than those other persons with whom I compare myself. Further, I assume that my rank order in my chosen group of referents will be stable across all of the tasks in the domain of running ability—for example, running on a track as well as running cross country. In addition, if I know I am *equal* to a given other in running under a given set of conditions—for example, on a track—I will assume I shall be equal to that other under other conditions—for example, running cross country. Hence, if I have established my equality of ability with another person under one set of conditions, I can predict specifically how well I will do under other, unfamiliar conditions by observing that other's outcome under those conditions. If my friend and I both run a mile in 8 minutes on a track, and my friend tells me she has run a mile cross country in 10 minutes, I can expect to run a mile cross country in 10 minutes, despite never having actually tried it myself. We might then expect that a person interested in predicting his or her specific outcome on an unfamiliar task to be interested in observing the performances on that task of someone already established as similar in ability. Jones and Regan (1974) have demonstrated this point very nicely in an experiment. Their subjects were faced with the decision of choosing among a set of unfamiliar tasks, all presumably tapping the same ability, but varying in level of difficulty. They were shown that in order to maximize their monetary payoffs, they should choose the hardest task they could master. They were then given the opportunity to choose another person for discussion of the task; their choice was between someone described by the experimenter as similar and someone dissimilar to them in the relevant ability. In some cases, the other had already completed the monetary task, and received the outcomes; in other cases, the other had not attempted the task. They found subjects to be more interested in talking with the similar other when the others had completed the task than when they had not.

The use of observation of a similar other's task outcomes implies that the observer already knows his or her standing on ability with respect to others—or at least knows that his or her standing is equal to that of the observed other. This implies the second use of others' performance outcomes: the comparison of performance with others in order to determine ability standing. In other words, in order to make use of the outcome I observe another receiving from a task novel to me, I must know my ability standing relative to that other. One means, and in some sense the ultimate means of making that determination is to compare performances with that other on another task within the same ability domain.

Turning to the question of just when a person might be interested in observing another's performance outcomes, and when he or she might be interested in performance comparison, the answers are obvious: We wish to observe another's performance on a novel task when we want to predict our own performance on that task, and have no direct experience with it. When we wish to determine our ability standing relative to another person, we are interested in comparing performances with him or her. Perhaps a more interesting meaning of this issue concerns the conditions under which we are interested in one or the other of these questions. Following Jones and Regan (1974), I would agree that we are interested in answering these questions when the answers are relevant to important decisions we face. That is, we are not eternally looking over each other's shoulders to examine each other's fates, nor do we continually compare ourselves with others—though a stronger case can be made for ubiquitous interest in comparison. We are interested when the answers inform immediate decisions that imply important rewards and costs for us.

Some kinds of decisions clearly are informed by knowledge of how one is likely to fare against a given task or tasks. Decisions such as whether to apply for medical school, or whether to try to lift the air conditioner out of a second-story window are informed by such knowledge. In general, information that enables a person to predict his or her outcome from a specific task is helpful in choosing an appropriate task, and in adjusting aspects of life that are contingent on task outcome. Although trying the task oneself is informative, it may be very costly, as in the medical-school and air-conditioner examples. Hence, I may seek to observe the outcomes of others whom I believe to be similar to me in relevant abilities in making my decisions.

Assessment of One's Standing in A Group

However, evaluation of one's *standing* on important ability dimensions in a group has utility beyond telling a person whose performance outcomes he or she should observe in order to predict performance on a novel task. One's ability rank in a group tells one how he or she will fare in future competition with others, but also to whom one should turn for advice, help, and instruction, and from whom one can expect requests for help, instruction, and advice. It also predicts one's share of esteem and approval from others, and indeed how valued one is as a group member, and how one should value others. For example, knowing one's wilderness skills not only enables one to determine whether or not one should attempt a given overnight trip—through observing the outcomes of similar others who have just returned from a similar trip—but it also enables one to determine whom one should take along, how tasks should be allocated, and whose tents one will have to help pitch. These outcomes beyond task-outcome prediction per se might be called social-response outcomes, and knowledge of them is obviously valuable even if one is not interested in task prediction itself.

This line of argument suggests a pervasive interest in one's standing in the groups within which one's life is lived. Now, let me turn to the issue of just how one determines standing. At first, it would seem that one might cast about at random for comparison within any important group, and this may be the case where one is totally ignorant of how others perform. However, a careful examination of the problem of inferring ability differences suggests a different picture.

If we view ability in the context of a set of motivated performances on a simple task, ability can be coordinated to the mean of the task performances. In that vein, Joe Schwartz and I suggested, in a 1976 paper (Schwartz & Smith, 1976), that the problem of determining one's ability standings relative to that of another person be seen as analogous to the statistician's problem of determining whether two means are significantly different. We plunged further, and suggested that the degree of interest in comparing with a particular other would depend on just how difficult the problem of discriminating ability was. Using the analogy of the t-test for two means, we pointed out that the difficulty of the discrimination depended on such matters as the size of the variance in each sample, but more importantly, it depends on how similar the means are! We included the additional simple bit of statistical knowledge contained in the t-test, which every undergraduate major knows: that increasing the size of the n facilitates the discrimination of difference between two means. From this analogy, we argued that large differences are easily discriminated—that is, require little information—a small n, but smaller differences require more information. Hence, we predicted that given some minimal comparative-performance information, people should be more interested in further comparison with a similarly performing other than with another whose performances are very different from their own.

This model for ability discrimination as we termed it turns out to be highly similar to a model of decision making under risk proposed by Frank Irwin and another William Smith (Irwin & Smith, 1956). It has two interesting implications. One is that if you have no information at all about your standing in a group, and little opportunity to sample performances, selecting those you think may be extreme performers as your sample may be a good strategy. In this way, you can discover whether there are any meaningful differences in the group: It takes only a small sample of performances to determine a difference in ability if the means are very different. This may explain just why range finding, the choice of extreme performers, appears as a comparison strategy in several studies of social comparison (Gruder, 1971; Wheeler et al., 1969).

The other implication is that if you *do* have even a little information about the performances of others, you will already have a feel for who is much better or much worse than yourself: Few data are necessary for the discrimination. Those whose performances are not so different from your own present more of a problem: In order to discover whether there really are differences, you need a larger sample. Hence, given some comparison information about fellow group members, the preference for comparison should increasingly converge on those with performances similar in level to those of the comparer.

Joe Schwartz and I conducted two experiments to examine this approach, and published the results in 1976. We told our subjects that we were studying the ability of persons to extract relevant information from complex stimulus arrays, an ability that is of obvious importance in many areas of life, from shopping for the best buy in a supermarket to coordinating the movement of air traffic at an airport. We asked subjects to perform on a task that we said tapped this ability. This task involved the subjects' examining a display of nine numbers, which were printed in different colors, and summing those printed in a particular color named at the bottom of the display as quickly as they could. They were told the time they required to accomplish this was an index of their complex information-processing ability. They then had 20 trials of this task without feed-back. They were then told that a second purpose of our experiment was to determine how good people were at detecting differences between themselves and others in ability, and that for that purpose they would get to see feedback from their own performances and those of another person on the complex information-processing task. They were then given 20 sheets of paper, placed face down on a table in front of them, and were told that each sheet contained a score for one trial of the task for themselves, and a score for another person—always the same other person over trials.

The scores contained the experimental manipulations in each experiment. The scores of the other were of either high or low in variance, and the mean difference was either large—four points—or small—one point. In addition, the other's mean was either higher or lower than the subject's.

In one experiment, we informed subjects that their skill at detecting differences in ability was indexed by the amount of information they required to make a confident judgment of whether there was a difference, and its direction if there was a difference. They were then told to turn over one sheet of feedback information each time there was a signal from the experimenter, until they reached a confident judgment. At that time, they were to fill out a judgment form at their sides. We predicted that subjects would persist longer at comparison when variance in performances was high than when it was low, and longer when the mean difference in performance between self and other was small than when it was large. Both these predictions received strong support: Subjects persisted for over 10 trials of feedback when performance variance was high, and for slightly over eight trials when it was low; they looked at over 11.5 trials when the other's performance was similar to their own, but less than eight when it was different. Both these differences were significant beyond the .01 level. Direction of the difference between self and other's performances had no detectable effect.

The fact that people were more interested in comparing with a similarly performing other than a differently performing other suggests vindication of the Festinger (1954) similarity hypothesis, though Festinger is silent on the role performance variance might be expected to play. However, we argued that similar others are of interest because their very similarity creates uncertainty, whereas Festinger argued the opposite: Similar others are sought because they uniquely invest one's judgments with certainty. The second experiment we conducted was designed to answer the question of the impact of comparative performance information on certainty.

This experiment had the same design and procedure as the first, except that subjects were instructed to look at all 20 trials of performance feedback, stopping to answer questions about their ability relative to the other after trials 1, 5, 10, 15, and 20. These questions requested that they give a probability rating for the truth of each of three statements: that they were the same as the other in ability, were less able, or were more able than the other. We predicted that the probabilities assigned to the appropriate judgment—that is, greater ability when the subject's performance mean was higher than the other's, less ability when the other performed better—would increase over trials, but that this increase would be more dramatic when variances were low rather than high, and more dramatic when the mean difference was large rather than small. In fact, probabilities increased over trials, and were significantly higher when the other was dissimilar than when he or she was similar to the subject in performance. Variance also showed the expected pattern, though in interaction with trials and direction. The direction effect suggested simply that subjects were more reluctant to make a high-probability statement that they were less able than the other than a similar statement that they were more able.

Let me add here that the t-test analogy we proposed in this work is most appropriate in cases in which subjects enter a comparison situation with weak or no preconceptions of their ability relative to the other. We have found that subjects with an expectancy to do better or worse than the other are more interested in comparative performance information from the other when that expectancy is disconfirmed than when it is confirmed. Some version of Bayes' theorem is probably a more apt general analogy.

Assessment of One's Standing in a Social Category

As I have noted before, this research has been concerned with the process whereby a person comes to infer his or her ability level relative to another, given that this is the question to be answered. As part of the procedure, we demanded that subjects address themselves to that question. We have assumed that a person recurrently encounters situations that demand that he or she assess his or her standing on some ability dimension within some specific group or aggregate— demand in the sense that such information is adaptive for the person in that situation. However, when an ability is seen as having some general relevance to one's fate across a number of particular groups and situations, it seems likely that one will have an abiding interest in one's standing on that ability in the broader group or social category from which these particular groups are drawn. For example, the new member of the college debating society is interested not only in how his or her skills at rhetoric and argument compare with other members', but with members of societies on other campuses, and indeed with other students in general; this skill not only predicts one's esteem within the debating society, it bears on such questions as the likelihood of success in numerous fields, including law, politics, and even science. Indeed, most skills have some general application, and are subject to such interest; there are exceptions, such as skill at speaking and writing in a secret code used only by some particular club of which one is a member. But in general, it seems likely that people are interested in their standing on most abilities within a broader community or category within which their fates will be worked out. For college students, one such group is likely to be the general category of other college students: These are the people with whom they will compete for jobs and for professional-school admissions, not to mention mates; these are the people with whom they will socialize in country clubs and religious organizations. Thus, it seems reasonable that people will make efforts to discover their standing in these broader social categories.

But how is such information obtained? Rarely are we given an opportunity to examine our standing in a large distribution on some general ability dimension. Receiving an IQ score is one of the few occasions of this sort. For the most part, we must take bits and pieces of information where we find them. Each time a tennis player has a game, data relevant to general standing in a relevant population are provided. The question I would like to raise is just how people use such information in inferring their general standing. The problems of inferring the characteristics of large populations from small samples is well known to statisticians and psychologists; not only is there the problem of possible systematic bias in any given sample, there is the problem of just how representative any small sample is of the larger population from which it is drawn. However, there is reason to believe that people are quite willing to make dramatic generalizations from small samples, and although obvious bias in a sample may be taken into account, the mere possibility of bias seems uninfluential in the willingness of people to generalize.

There is considerable evidence on the willingness of people to generalize from small samples. Perhaps the most dramatic example is found in the Davis (1966) "frog pond" study, discussed by Pettigrew (1967). Davis looked at occupational aspirations of recent college graduates from a sample representing all graduates in the year 1961. Briefly, he found that grade standing in school was a far more important determinant of occupational choice than school quality. In other words, students with good grades from a mediocre school aspired to the same careers as those with good grades from high-quality schools. The result suggests that equally talented people will have different aspirations, depending on the sample of others available for comparison.

In general, this seems to illustrate one aspect of what Tversky and Kahneman (1974) have called the heuristic of representativeness, or more specifically, the law of small numbers. They argue that people treat any sample, no matter how small, as representative of the larger population from which it is drawn.

Some of the experiments we have conducted on social comparison appear to demonstrate this phenomenon. Given that we described complex information-processing ability plausibly as an ability of general importance, this seems reasonable. The two experiments I would like to discuss were conducted by Sal Soraci, Joseph Schwartz, Shirley Maides, and me. In each experiment, subjects were asked to assess their complex information-processing skills relative to one other person. In one experiment, the comparison other was described as another student. Subjects received comparative performance information from two tasks, both said to tap the ability. They found that they did either consistently better than the other, consistently worse, or did better on one task, and worse on the other. After comparison, among other items on a questionnaire was an 11-point rating scale requesting that subjects rate their complex information-processing ability relative to other undergraduates in general at their university. The midpoint of the scale designated equality, and subjects who had performed above the other on one task and below the other on the other task rated themselves as slightly better than the average student at their university, whereas those performing consistently below the others rated themselves slightly below the university average, and significantly lower than subjects with mixed-performance feedback. Those who performed consistently above the other rated themselves above the university average, and somewhat but not significantly higher than subjects with mixed feedback. Hence, it seems that subjects were quite willing to infer their standing in a population of university undergraduates from comparison with a single other member of it.

The other experiment provided what is perhaps a more dramatic example. Here, subjects compared with one person on one task tapping complex information-processing ability; however, this person was *not* an undergraduate at their university. For some subjects, the other was said to be a theoretical mathematician, and for other subjects the comparison person was said to be an assembly-line worker. Subjects were given information prior to comparison suggesting that theoretical mathematicians in general were very good at this sort of task, much better than the average college student, and that assembly-line workers were typically very poor at this task, much worse than college students. Subjects in each of these conditions found that they did either better or worse than the other. After comparison, subjects who did better than an assembly-line worker or worse than a theoretical mathematician estimated their own abilities as about equal to the average student in their university. However, those who did worse than the assembly-line worker estimated their ability as worse than other students as well, and significantly lower than those who had performed better than the assembly-line worker or worse than the mathematician. In addition, those who did better than the mathematician estimated their ability above the student average, though not significantly higher than those who did better than the worker or worse than the mathematician. In other words, subjects were willing to estimate their abilities relative to a significant group even when they had compared with a person from a *different* group, presumably through transitivity assumptions. If a subject believed that mathematicians were generally more able than students, who were in turn more able than workers, he or she also believed that performance inferior to a worker implied ability inferior to other students.

THE QUESTION OF BASE RATE

So far, I have discussed the utility for social psychology of some simple information-processing notions that are drawn from, or have their parallels in, cognitive psychology. Now I am so bold as to suggest that social psychology has something to offer in the study of cognitive processing. More particularly, I refer to certain kinds of methodological issues to which social psychologists are particularly sensitive. The specific issue of interest to me is the issue of how to ask a question. I am aware that cognitive psychologists are concerned with the conceptual issue of how one asks a question, as John Bransford eloquently demonstrated in his contribution to this volume (Chapter 26). However, I am concerned with a more mundane, methodological issue.

The particular area of cognitive psychology of interest is the psychology of judgment, and the issue I wish to address is that of the role of base-rate information in social judgment. This is an issue related to social comparison, but here I wish to deal with it in its own right. Kahneman and Tversky (1973) published some data relating to the neglect of base-rate information in social judgment. Their argument, very briefly, was that people are strongly influenced by data that they regard as representative of some population, so strongly influenced that they ignore base-rate data in making inferences or predictions. For example, if I believe lawyers are somewhat more likely than engineers to be sharp dressers, and I encounter a stranger in a Pierre Cardin jacket in my suburban bank branch, I will likely decide that he is a lawyer, even if I know that only 10% of the people in that suburb are lawyers. Social psychologists interested in attribution processes found this a controversial point once they translated base rate into consensus, and saw its implications for the Kelley (1967) cube model for attribution. Kahneman and Tversky provided several experimental demonstrations of this point. One experiment (Kahneman & Tversky, 1973) involved presentation of the following instructions to subjects:

> A panel of psychologists have interviewed and administered personality tests to 30 engineers and 70 lawyers, all successful in their respective fields. On the basis of this information, thumbnail descriptions of the 30 engineers and 70 lawyers have been written. You will find on your forms five descriptions, chosen at random from the 100 available descriptions. For each description, please indicate your probability that the person described is an engineer, on a scale from 0 to 100.
>
> The same task has been performed by a panel of experts, who were highly accurate in assigning probabilities to the various descriptions. You will be paid a bonus to the extent that your estimates come close to those of the expert panel. [p. 241].

All subjects were then given a set of five descriptions of people in the set. A sample description (Kahlneman & Tversky, 1973) was:

> Jack is a 45-year-old man. He is married and has four children. He is generally conservative, careful, and ambitious. He shows no interest in political and social issues and spends most of his free time on his many hobbies which include home carpentry, sailing, and mathematical puzzles.
> The probability that Jack is one of the 30 engineers in the sample of 100 is _____ % [p. 241].

Subjects were asked to estimate the probability that each person described was an engineer or lawyer. Subjects also got a null description (Kahneman & Tversky, 1973):

> Suppose now that you are given no information whatsoever about an individual chosen at random from the sample.
> The probability that this man is one of the 30 engineers in the sample of 100 is
> _____ % [p. 241].

Without going into detail, let me say that Kahneman and Tversky found that base rate had little influence, but the description had a great deal of influence on the assigned probabilities. Perhaps the most damning finding was that subjects provided with the null description *did* use the base rate for prediction, but those given an obviously worthless description simply estimated probability at 50%, regardless of base rate. The worthless description (Kahneman & Tversky, 1973) read:

> Dick is a 30-year-old man. He is married with no children. A man of high ability and high motivation, he promises to be quite successful in his field. He is well liked by his colleagues. [p. 242].

Much of the literature that has accumulated in social psychology bearing on this issue shows that base rates can be strong determinants of prediction given the appropriate conditions. However, I would like to suggest that there was a basic problem in the methodology of the Kahneman and Tversky experiment. I suggest that in their instructions, they unwittingly asked their subjects a question that rendered the base-rate information irrelevant whenever a description of the target person was provided. After giving base-rate information, they told subjects that a panel of experts "... were highly accurate in assigning probabilities to the various descriptions"! Note that it is the *descriptions* the panel was said to assess so accurately. Further, subjects were offered a bonus for coming close to the panel's judgment per se! It seems to me that their information converts the question from one of discovering who this fellow described is, in the base-rate context, into a question of whether the subject can find the answer that obviously must be in the description. In other words, if experts were highly accurate in deciding who the information in the description described, there must be a right answer in that description. If as a subject I think I detect that answer, I should give a high probability rating to whatever category—lawyer or engineer— the answer suggests. If not, I must say it could go either way—50/50. The base-rate data are irrelevant.

To go beyond speculation here, Sal Soraci and I devised a test of this hypothesis. We used a probability-rating approach much like that of Kahneman and Tversky. We used three levels of base rate information in the design: The set contained 10%, 30%, or 50% lawyers. We used two levels of representativeness

TABLE 16.1
Rated Probability that Stimulus
Person is a Lawyer, By Base Rate
and Instructional Set

	Base Rate		
Set	10%	30%	50%
Expert	51.69	49.62	65.36
No Expert	32.56	52.04	63.88

in our descriptions, low and high. The low information stated that the person, at a convention, missed his children and looked forward to meeting an old friend. The high-representativeness information stated that the person was active in the PTA and had been on his college debating team. Finally, for half of the subjects in each of these conditions, we inserted a statement that experts had been highly accurate in assigning probabilities to these descriptions, whereas the other half had no such statement. Each subject was asked to rate the probability that the person described was a lawyer.

Two findings of this experiment are of interest. First was an interaction of the presence–absence of the expert statement with base rate, $p < .049$. We found that when the expert statement had been deleted, probabilities assigned were strongly affected by base rate, but when the expert statement was included, base-rate effects were much weaker (see Table 16.1).

The other was an interaction of presence–absence of the expert statement with representativeness of the description, $p = .021$. When representativeness was low, whether the expert statement had been included made little difference, but when representativeness was high, subjects with the expert statement gave higher probability estimates than did those without it (see Table 16.2). We would, of course, have preferred that subjects with expert information give a higher probability for low-representative information than those with no expert information. Nonetheless, the data strongly suggest that the strength of base-rate effects very much depends on whether you ask subjects to use the information, or to ignore it.

TABLE 16.2
Rated Probability that
Stimulus Person is
a Lawyer, By
Representativeness
and Instructional
Set

	Representativeness	
Set	Low	High
Expert	36.65	74.47
No Expert	39.37	59.62

On the basis of this one example, I cannot argue that social-psychological sophistication in asking questions can generally make contributions to cognitive-psychological research, but I suspect it may. Fischhoff's (1976) question as to why social psychologists' subjects seem so rational, and the subjects of those studying the psychology of judgment so irrational, may in some small measure be answered through the way in which the respective groups of investigators frame their questions.

REFERENCES

Davis, J. A. The campus as a frog pond: An application of the theory of relative deprivation to career decisions of college men. *American Journal of Sociology,* 1966, *72,* 17–31; quoted in Pettigrew, T. F. Social evaluation theory: Convergences and applications. In D. Levine (Ed.), *Nebraska symposium on motivation, 1967.* Lincoln, Neb.: University of Nebraska Press, 1967.

Festinger, L. A theory of social comparison processes. *Human Relations,* 1954, *7,* 117–140.

Fischhoff, B. Attribution theory and judgment under uncertainty. In J. H. Harvey, W. J. Ickes, & R. F. Kidd (Eds.), *New directions in attribution research* (Vol. 1). Hillsdale, N.J.: Lawrence Erlbaum Associates, 1976.

Gruder, C. L. Determinants of social comparison choices. *Journal of Experimental Social Psychology,* 1971, *7,* 473–489.

Hakmiller, K. L. Threat as a determinant of downward comparison. *Journal of Experimental Social Psychology,* 1966, Supplement *1,* 32–39.

Irwin, F. W., & Smith, W. A. S. Further tests of theories of decision in an expanded judgment situation. *Journal of Experimental Psychology,* 1956, *52,* 345–348.

Jones, S. C., & Regan, D. T. Ability evaluation through social comparison. *Journal of Experimental Social Psychology,* 1974, *10,* 133–146.

Kahneman, D., & Tversky, A. On the psychology of prediction. *Psychological Review,* 1973, *80,* 237–251.

Kelley, H. H. Attribution theory in social psychology. In D. Levine (Ed.), *Nebraska symposium on motivation, 1967.* Lincoln, Neb.: University of Nebraska Press, 1967.

Martens, R., & White, V. Influence of win–loss ratio on performance, satisfaction, and preference for opponents. *Journal of Experimental Social Psychology,* 1975, *11,* 343–362.

Pettigrew, T. F. Social evaluation theory: Converges and applications. In D. Levine (Ed.), *Nebraska symposium on motivation, 1967.* Lincoln, Neb.: University of Nebraska Press, 1967.

Schwartz, J. M., & Smith, W. P. Social comparison and the inference of ability difference. *Journal of Personality and Social Psychology,* 1976, *34,* 1268–1275.

Singer, J. E. Social comparison—progress and issues. *Journal of Experimental Social Psychology,* 1966, Supplement *1,* 103–110.

Tversky, A., & Kahneman, D. Judgment under uncertainty: Heuristics and biases. *Science,* 1974, *185,* 1124–1131.

Wheeler, L. Motivation as a determinant of upward comparison. *Journal of Experimental Social Psychology,* 1966, Supplement *1,* 27–31.

Wheeler, L., Shaver, K. E., Jones, R. A., Goethals, G. R., Cooper, J., Robinson, J. E., Gruder, C. L., & Butzine, K. W. Factors determining choice of a comparison other. *Journal of Experimental Social Psychology,* 1969, *5,* 219–232.

Wilson, S. R., & Benner, L. A. The effects of self-esteem and situation upon comparisons choice during ability evaluation. *Sociometry,* 1971, *34,* 381–397.

Zanna, M. P., Goethals, G. R., & Hill, J. F. Evaluating a sex-related ability: Social comparison with similar others and standard setters. *Journal of Experimental Social Psychology,* 1975, *11,* 86–93.

17

The Relativity of
Perception, Choice,
and Social Knowledge

Joseph S. Lappin
Vanderbilt University

OVERVIEW

The purpose of this chapter is to discuss the relationship between individual knowledge and the social environment from the perspective of research in perception and psychophysics. In the compartmental organization of topics and methods of contemporary psychology, social cognition and psychophysics rarely come in contact, but of course that does not mean these topics are unrelated. Although their common ancestry is not immediately detectable in the superficial appearances of modern research, they do share an intellectual heritage as aspects of the general study of perceptual organization. To Kurt Lewin and Fritz Heider, for example, the theoretical commonalities between the perception of physical relations and the perception of social relations were apparent long ago. My aim is to adopt a similarly broad perspective of psychophysics and social cognition as aspects of the organization of an individual's knowledge of the environment. I outline what I see as a general framework for the study of perception that might also be applicable to the study of social cognition. Although my conception of these topics derives in part from a Gestalt orientation similar to that of Lewin, Heider, and Gibson, some of the concepts are taken from statistical theories of communication and decision. My intent is not merely to advertise the value of perceptual research for social psychologists, but also to consider the impact of social environment on the functioning of perceptual processes.

This chapter is based on three postulates: The first and most important is an epistemological assumption about the representation of knowledge, which might be called the *relativity of knowledge*. The assumption is that all knowledge consists of relationships among objects, events, and actions rather than of individual symbols, stimuli, or responses as such. The perception and cognition of humans as subjects and the theories and models of humans as scientists may be characterized as mappings from one set of relationships to another.

A second, corresponding assumption is what I call the *relativity of choice behavior*. All behavior is choice behavior; actions are choices from the available alternatives. The conception is similar to what Fishbein (colloquium at Vanderbilt University, 1979) has called "a theory of reasoned action." As in studies of signal detection, I consider human actions as reasoned responses to available information, and use statistical decision theory as a normative model for these actions.

The third postulate is an hypothesis about the operation of the perceptual systems. Specifically, the perceptual systems are hypothesized to behave under many environmental conditions as linear systems—where their output can be represented as a weighted combination of each of the input components, introducing in the output no new features associated with interactions among the initial input components. Thus, the perceptual information is a simple reflection of the environmental information, permitting an essentially undistorted reconstruction of it.

The general implication of these postulates is that the organization of perception reflects the organization of the environment and the person's role within it. A primary objective of contemporary research on human information processing has been to analyze the characteristics and limitations of the processes that are presumed to operate on the components of stimulation. In contrast, the focus of the present chapter is on the organization of the environmental information. I develop the idea that prior knowledge is tacitly involved in virtually all of the acquisition and use of knowledge about the environment. The role of prior knowledge, however, is neither to modify nor supplement the processing of information, but to anticipate generalized relationships in the pattern of stimulation and to anticipate the functions and consequences of actions.

Two years ago, at a conference at Vanderbilt University honoring Fritz Heider and his contributions to social psychology, Heider was asked to discuss his conception of the processes involved in perception and social relations. Heider's discussion was based on concepts from Gestalt psychology that may have sounded somewhat passé from the perspective of contemporary social and cognitive psychology. Following his discussion, someone in the audience asked Heider what he understood by the term "cognition." His answer (as I remember it) was that "cognition is getting to know the environment." The present chapter pursues the same approach.

THE RELATIVITY OF KNOWLEDGE: THE REPRESENTATION OF STRUCTURE AND FUNCTION

Perhaps the most fundamental characteristic of the world we observe is that it changes. It varies from place to place and from time to time. Sometimes, the changes are gradual, coherent, and continuous over space and time; sometimes, they are abrupt, irregular, and unconnected, jumping from one position in space–time to another. Variation is the essence of physical events, and it is the essence of information.

The remarkable thing is that we recognize patterns within these changes. If we know anything at all, it is that the changes are often coherent. If variation is the essence of physical events and information, then invariance is also their essence. Replications, symmetries, similarities, isomorphisms, and other correspondences are continually detected in the patterns of our observations. Indeed, could it be otherwise?

Construction of the appropriate representation for the observed stability and coherence of the world constitutes a fundamental problem in epistemology. Simple as it might seem, this representational problem has generated major philosophical controversies. The problem is crucial, for it provides the material and tools with which subsequent descriptions of perception and knowledge are built. Two divergent representations, which I refer to as *analytic* and *functional,* lead toward fundamentally different conceptions of the content and process of knowing. A comprehensive review and critique of the philosophical background of these two epistemological approaches is given by Cassirer (1923/1953). Much of the subsequent discussion is guided by Cassirer's analysis.

The analytic approach is based on the Aristotelean theory of *concepts.* Supposedly, generalized concepts are derived from the common properties of a set of diverse objects. Classifications of similar objects are presumed to result from an analytic comparison of the objects and isolation of their common features. Thus, the basic mental process is presumed to be the abstraction of common elements from the diversity of the larger forms in which they appear. The substance of a concept is defined by the set of common features that are abstracted from a collection of observations. Presumably, the one fundamental relationship is similarity, as defined by shared elements. Thus, the acquisition of knowledge is construed as the development of a taxonomy—a scheme for classifying the objects of the world.

This intuitively natural epistemology is implicit in many of the conventions of ordinary thought and language, both casual and scientific. Flowers and trees, fishes and birds, faces and personalities are conveniently described by their shared and distinguishing features.

Analytic conceptions of perception and cognition have long prevailed in psychological thinking. British associationism and introspective structuralism were two programs explicitly devoted to the application of this epistemology. A corresponding rationale occurs in a variety of forms in contemporary cognitive psychology: Memory is commonly regarded as a set of symbols stored at discrete loci, conceptual systems are frequently modeled as taxonomic networks of objects and nodes (Anderson & Bower, 1973), and pattern recognition is frequently described as the detection and classification of distinctive features (Reed, 1973). In what is known as the information-processing approach, perceptual and cognitive processes are modeled as sequences of operations on discrete inputs to the sensory channels.

A fundamental assumption in all of these conceptions is that stimulus information may be represented by sets of discrete symbols or elements. Such a representation might seem theoretically justified by the 20th-century work on information theory and coding—in which the informational content of a symbolic code explicitly depends only on the consistency of the mapping between the set of symbols and the set of objects, independently of the physical attributes of the symbols or objects. Such a symbolic representation now seems so intuitively reasonable that alternatives are difficult to remember.

There is, however, a more general and powerful method for representing the coherent aspects of our changing observations. The alternative, referred to here as a *functional* approach, is based on the representation of objects and events in terms of *relationships*. Whereas the analytic approach defines stable structures in terms of recurrent substantive components, the functional approach regards *change* itself as fundamental and defines stable structures in terms of invariance under transformation. Without the change, the unchanged is unknowable. In the analytic approach, relations are restricted to the sharing of common elements, but in the functional approach, any relationship might in principle be used to represent objects and events. Relationships can be defined physically over space and time, by comparison with structures not actually present, or in some abstract numerical, algebraic, or symbolic space.

The distinction between functional and analytic representation derives from the fact that relations can be defined independently of the particular characteristics of the component elements involved in the relation. For example, the relations *less than, between, connected,* or *same* might apply to numbers, points in a geometrical space, musical notes, semantic relations, friendships, managerial options, or community housing patterns. The generality of mathematics owes to the isomorphism of various algebraic, numeric, and geometric relational systems to countless other physical and conceptual systems. The artistic expression of poems and paintings owe to correspondences between relationships in the artists' materials and relationships in other media. Communication and representation in general—by neural events, perception, memory, language, mathematics, arts, or science—may be regarded as mappings from one relational system to another.

If the fundamental terms of a representation are taken as relationships rather than as substantive elements, then what are the implications for definitions of the units and complexity of stimulus arrays? What are the implications for descriptions of the capacities and processing characteristics of the perceptual and cognitive systems that operate on these inputs?

Consider, for example, the set of symbols

a 1 z b 2 . . .

There are several potential ways to describe this set, corresponding to alternative inductions of expanded sequences. Thus, the sequence a 1 z b 2 z c 3 z d 4 z . . . .

Whereas the shorter sequence might have been represented as five independent symbols, the longer sequence can be represented as an alternation between two ordered series and one constant symbol. The symbol in position n can be generated from the symbol in position $n-3$ by the relation *next* defined on the appropriate list. Similarly, we can compare the latter sequence with others containing the same initial components, such as

a 1 z b 2 K b A 2 1 z K 2 k 1 8 Z a . . .

to see that the representation of any given set of components depends on the organization of the context in which it is embedded. The complexity of the representation required for any given set of stimulus elements depends not on the number of components it contains, but on the organization of relationships within that set and within the context in which it occurs. An infinitely large set of elements might have a simple description by the recursive application of a single function that transforms one element into another. The set of positive integers, for example, can be parsimoniously represented by a recursive function of the form

START $(x) = 1$; NEXT $(x) = x + 1$.

The small set of transformations *repeat, transpose* (i.e., shift, add, next), *reflect* (mirror, invert), and *identity* constitutes a transformational group that has found repeated applications in representing a variety of both artificial and natural patterns of symbols, music, and visual forms (Babbitt, 1961; Greeno & Simon, 1974; Shubnikov & Koptsik, 1974; Simon & Sumner, 1968; Weyl, 1952). The perceptual and cognitive validity of such representations has been well established (e.g., Brown, 1971; Restle, 1970; Simon, 1978; Simon & Kotovsky, 1963).

Insofar as stimulus arrays are represented this way in terms of relationships, the concept of a stimulus "unit" (feature, etc.) would seem to have no prior meaning, because the definition would always have to depend on the global organization of the context. (Although the preceding examples and many of the published experiments have involved discrete, physically unrelated symbols, the components of naturally occurring patterns are typically physically similar and interconnected.) Correspondingly, the capacity of the system in which such stimulus inputs are processed becomes difficult to define if the amount of input cannot be quantified in numbers of components. Indeed, the whole history of psychophysics provides almost no evidence that *any* physically definable stimulus component serves as a functional unit for perception independently of the context in which it occurs. The recent work of Julesz (Caelli & Julesz, 1978; Caelli, Julesz, & Gilbert, 1978) appears to provide the best available evidence for feature detection in human perception, although the presently documented features involve topological relationships (e.g., quasilinearity) and constitute only a tiny fraction of the input for human form perception.

If we cannot meaningfully define units of stimulation nor capacities for processing them, then how are we to represent stimulus patterns and their perceptions? If representation is by functional relations, then what are the relevant relations and how are they determined by the stimulus pattern? What is the observer's contribution to the perceptual process?

With regard to the specification of the appropriate relationships, it should be noted that three different levels of relationships are relevant to the representation of any given stimulus pattern. First, there are *internal physical* relationships defined by the distribution of energy and other elementary physical attributes (chromatic wavelength, acoustic frequency, molecular concentration, etc.) over space and time. Because a pattern is describable as a function over space and time, groups of simple geometric transformations such as translation, rotation, reflection, and dilation within Euclidean spaces are appropriate for representing the physical organization of most visual and auditory patterns. In many cases, a more appropriate representation can be obtained from simpler ordinal or topological relations such as connectedness and betweenness. The main point is that the perceptual complexity of a stimulus depends not on the number and character of its physical components as such, but on their *pattern* in space and time. A simple pattern is one whose space–time distribution can be described by a small number of parameters. In Fig. 17.1, for example, the pattern on the left is obviously less complex than the pattern on the right, although both have the same number of components. This simplicity may be considered as internal property of the pattern, because it can be represented as a correspondence (e.g., autocorrelation) of the pattern with itself—that is, as symmetry or invariance under transformation.

It is worth emphasizing that the great majority of stimulus patterns are dynamic events, changing not only in space but in time as well. The motions of both objects and observer produce transformations of the physical patterns of

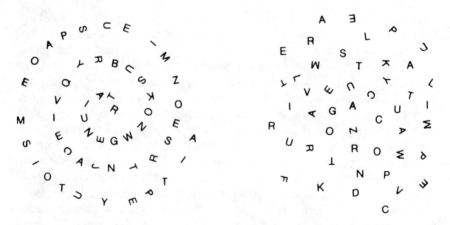

FIG. 17.1.   Two patterns with the same components but different complexity.

stimulation on the receptors. The perceptual systems are designed to detect not only the transformations, but also the structural relations that remain invariant under the transformations. (I discuss evidence for this in a later section.)

A second level of relationships is what might be called *statistical*—involving relations with alternative events that might potentially occur. The significance of any particular stimulus event depends on the context of alternatives. This was, of course, the point of information theory: The amount of information associated with the occurrence of any given stimulus event is a function of its *probability* in relation to the alternatives that might have occurred in its place. (A rose is not a rose independently of other objects that might appear in its stead.) This is by now a familiar idea in psychology, but familiarity sometimes breeds neglect. The idea is regularly forgotten in much of the research and theory aimed at describing the cognitive processes that operate on a given stimulus input. Certainly, it is not intuitively obvious that a stimulus may be held physically constant while its effective sensory characteristics are altered by changing its alternatives. It is important to notice that this aspect of the stimulus depends on the observer's prior knowledge and expectations, and is therefore not necessarily determined by the external characteristics of the environment as separated from the observer. Moreover, the specification of the set of alternatives and their probabilities may be quite fuzzy. Nevertheless, these statistical characteristics are a fundamental aspect of the stimulation that an observer receives.

A third level of relationships are what might be called *semantic*—involving (1) groupings of present patterns with other objects and events of the past and future; and (2) isomorphisms or analogies with other "similar" patterns. Such relationships determine the "meaning" of a stimulus pattern. Because these groupings and isomorphisms with other patterns are only constrained but not determined by a given stimulus pattern, the knowledge of a given pattern can generally be organized in a variety of schemas. The organizational repertoire that an observer employs is derived primarily from relationships with the social environment—from communications with other people, from the demands and opportunities of commerce with social institutions, from language and other symbolic media, from educational paradigms, from cultural values, and so on. The patterns of relationships that are detected within the spatial and temporal array of objects and events are heavily conditioned by the sociocultural system in which they occur. Different members of different groups within different cultures will have different understandings of the collage of symbols in Fig. 17.2. What is noticed by one person may be undetected by another.

Of course, these three different levels of relationships typically are intermingled. The semantic level may overlap with the physical level, insofar as many of the relations between objects widely separated in time may be considered the results of slow but continuous transformations, as in the case of growth from child to adult. The dynamics of a large social system involve many such prolonged events extending over centuries. Similarly, statistical relationships are

348

applicable to the spectrum of events extending from the microscopic physical to the macroscopic semantic level.

THE RELATIVITY OF CHOICE BEHAVIOR

Following the same functional approach for representing behavior as for knowledge in general, it is important to consider the relationship between a response and its alternatives. Just as perceptual processes involve implicit discriminations among alternative stimulus events, so too behavior involves implicit choices among alternative responses. The postulate that I call "relativity of choice behavior" is that *all behavior is choice behavior,* and can be understood only in relation to the alternatives from which it is chosen. The use of overt behaviors for the study of perceptual and cognitive processes necessarily involves the control and analysis of the decision strategies that contribute to the choice of behavior. The unit of analysis is not an individual stimulus—response pair, but multiple stimuli and multiple responses: The tendency of a given stimulus to produce a given response must be interpreted by comparison with the tendency of the same stimulus to produce other responses and the tendency of other stimuli to produce the same response.

The assumption that all behavior is choice behavior seems to lead naturally to the conception of humans as rational decision makers, weighing evidence before choosing options. Without insisting that humans are admirably wise or even consistent in their decisions, it is nevertheless plausible to assume that their actions are if not rational, then reasoned—based on some evaluation of evidence and some anticipation of the consequences of alternative actions. Moreover, theories of rational decision procedures can serve as models for certain aspects of real human choice behavior.

The relativity of choice behavior constitutes an important working assumption adopted in a large segment of phychophysical research. Separation of the contributions of decision strategies from those of perceptual processes is crucial in drawing inferences from overt responses to stimulus information. The best-known and perhaps best-developed theoretical and methodological paradigm for dealing with this problem is the theory of signal detectability (TSD). Although many of the details of this theory apply to a restricted class of experimental problems, dealing primarily with the detection of well-defined physically simple stimuli, the general concepts are much more widely applicable. A brief review of the basic ideas in TSD is helpful in conceptualizing the role of the choice process in other situations.

There are two basic components of TSD: (1) a model of an ideal observer; and (2) the analysis of receiver operating characteristics (ROC curves). The first component comprises a model of the statistical properties of the stimulus, which are presumed to be the sole limiting factor on the performance of an ideal observer who might employ any of a variety of decision procedures. In general, the optimal decision rule is defined on the likelihood ratio

$$L(x) = \frac{P(e \mid H_i)}{P(e \mid H_j)} \; ,$$

where e is a random variable representing the observed event that provides the evidence on which a decision is based, and H_i and H_j are two alternative and mutually exclusive hypotheses about the distal stimulus category that might have produced the observed event. Because the proximal physical events occurring at the sensory receptors of an observer are presumed to be variable, a decision about which distal stimulus category produced a specific proximal event must consider the conditional probabilities, $P(e|H_i)$, that the event might have occurred in the various alternative stimulus categories. In many cases, these conditional probability distributions may reasonably be assumed to be normal, though this certainly is not a necessary assumption. The appropriate probability distribution is determined by the specific stimulus environment. The point is that perceptual observations are construed as statistical. Predictions about the performance of ideal or real observers in a given detection task must be based on the statistical characteristics of the stimuli in that task.

In most of the simple laboratory detection tasks to which TSD has been applied, there are only two alternative stimuli and two alternative responses, and in this case, the observed events, or more generally the likelihood ratios, can be regarded as distributed along a single vector that best discriminates between the two alternative categories. In many real detection and recognition tasks, however, there may be more than two alternative stimuli and the observer may be uncertain about the specific parameters that define a given category. In such cases, the relevant evidence is distributed along several different physical vectors, so that there may be several different likelihood ratios associated with a single event, and the observer may be faced with the additional problem of deciding on the most appropriate attributes to use in making a decision. Such increases in uncertainty about the stimulus parameters lead to a decline in the performance of even the hypothetical ideal observer. Thus, prior knowledge about the potential stimulus parameters is intimately associated with the statistical evidence on which decisions must be based.

A second and more familiar component of TSD is concerned with the analysis of ROC curves as a technique for distinguishing the contributions of perceptual and decision processes in overt responses. Theoretically, the decision about any specific stimulus event depends on two logically separate influences: (1) the likelihood ratio associated with that event, which summarizes all of the sensory information about the stimulus; and (2) the decision criterion, which is a critical value of the likelihood ratio that must be exceeded by the observed value in order to decide in favor of the corresponding hypothesis. Whereas the likelihood ratio is determined by the proximal stimulus event, the decision criterion can be adjusted to any value, depending on the probable consequences of the alternative responses. Specifically, the decision criterion is presumed to depend on the following factors: (1) the prior odds in favor of the hypothesis before any evidence is observed, $P(H_i)/P(H_j)$; (2) the relative utilities (costs and benefits) of the alternative responses under each of the hypothetical stimulus conditions; and (3) the goal of the decision strategy (e.g., maximize expected value, minimize maximum risk, etc.). In most applications, it is not necessary to assume that observers make the wisest use of these factors to pick the decision criterion that is truly optimum; it suffices that the decision criterion is adjustable in response to these factors.

For a given pair of alternative stimuli, as the decision criterion for a response R_i is set at successively lower values, the conditional response probabilities, $P(R_i|H_i)$ and $P(R_i|H_j)$, the "hit rate" and "false alarm rate," both increase together. The functional relationship between these two response measures is the ROC curve—describing the change in performance under varying decision criteria with a fixed pair of stimulus alteratives. Thus, the ROC curve is an invariant performance characteristic that measures the observer's capability for discriminating between the two stimuli. Considerable research demonstrates the validity of this technique for distinguishing the effects of decision criteria from those of the discriminability of the stimuli in a wide variety of sensory, perceptual, and cognitive tasks (see Swets, 1973). Evidently, human observers do utilize the statistical information associated with observed stimulus events and do adjust the decision criterion in response to changes in stimulus probabilities and response contingencies. The success of TSD in conceptualizing the role of the decision process in the performance of detection and recognition tasks may be regarded as one of the most important contributions of research in perception and psychophysics to the general understanding of human behavior.

The application of statistical decision theory as a normative model with the study of knowledge and action in social settings. The conception is essentially similar to Fishbein and Ajzen's (1975) conception of the role of beliefs, attitudes, and intentions in behavior. Recently, Fishbein has referred to this theoretical approach as a "theory of reasoned action." As in statistical decision theory, a fundamental premise is that actions are elicited not simply as responses to particular beliefs or attitudes, but that they are chosen in relation to alternative actions on the basis of their anticipated effectiveness in satisfying a variety of objectives and values.

Clearly, an individual's choices of action are constrained by cultural values, by relationships with social and economic institutions, by roles within familial groups, by the opportunities for interactions with significant others, and so on. These constraints are imposed both by the values and consequences associated with alternative actions and by the availability of information about the potential choices.

Evaluations of the relative merits of alternative actions are tantamount to anticipations of effectiveness, as defined in any of a number of qualitatively different biological, selfish, social, or economic contexts. Typically, these contexts overlap to a considerable degree. The individual knowledge structures that serve to anticipate the effectiveness of actions are representations of these contexts, extended over space and time and embodying the spatio–temporal continuities of the self, objects, and actors within the individual's "life space." Thus, the effectiveness of any given action is characterized by its potential impact in some such spatio–temporal context or life space. Sometimes, the effectiveness of actions may be measured in such concrete terms as the economic utility for the individual—by monetary costs and benefits and by probabilistic risks and opportunities. More often, however, the effectiveness must be judged by the functional compatibility of the action within the processes of some larger social system. The range of choices may be quite different depending on the structure and purpose of the particular social organization and depending on the individual's role within it.

Because the functional effectiveness of a given choice by a given individual might be evaluated within a number of different contexts, the mutual compatibilities among these various contexts reflect the likelihood that the value of an action for an individual will conflict with its value for a particular social organization. That is, many of an individual's actions are social interactions; the coherence of an individual's knowledge and actions reflects and in turn affects the coherence of a social organization.

From an epistemological viewpoint, it is crucial to understand that many of an individual's actions are exploratory—aimed at the discovery of additional information about the environmental theater in which the actions are staged. Thus, actions and the knowledge by which they are guided are bound in a continuing feedback loop. Actions are chosen on the basis of preconceptions of their effects, but then serve to modify those conceptions. Neisser (1976) refers to this as a "perceptual cycle." Similarly, the continual accommodation and assimilation between the organization of individual knowledge and the organization of the environment has long fascinated Piaget as an analogue of biological adaptation. Moreover, many of an individual's actions have the effect of restructuring the environment to better fit and facilitate subsequent actions. Greenwald (Chapter 25 in this volume) provides excellent illustrations of this point. Thus, choices are guided by knowledge structures both internal and external to an individual's head.

The organizational partnership between knowledge, action, and environment may be illustrated by the visual–motor coordinations that occur as a running tennis player maneuvers and swings to return an oncoming tennis ball away from an anticipating opponent. Despite its competitive aspects, the game demands elaborate mutual adaptations among the knowledge and actions of two intercoordinated individuals.

The evolution of individual knowledge within the dynamics of a social system involves similar coordinations among knowledge, action, and environment. Indeed, the boundaries between these three subsystems grow increasingly vague with the passage of time and increasing mutual adaptation. All might be considered parts of the same general decision system that guides the choice of behavior.

THE PERCEPTION OF COHERENCE IN DYNAMIC
STIMULUS PATTERNS

How is an individual's knowledge obtained by the perceptual processes? How is the stability of perceptual experience derived from the changing complexities of physical stimulation at the sensory receptors? How can constant percepts of moving objects, of dynamic events, be obtained by moving observers? How can a rose be seen as a rose independently of its surroundings and position in relation to the observer?

A given distal stimulus object in the three-dimensional environment may be represented by an infinite variety of proximal stimuli at the two-dimensional surfaces of an observer's sensory receptors, depending on the relative position and motion of the observer and depending on the context of other stimuli in the environment. The recognition of a distal stimulus object would seem to demand the intervention of sophisticated processes for translating the apparently unreliable sense data into a meaningful interpretation of the environment. Knowledge of the environment would seem unobtainable directly from the sensory events; presumably, it could only be constructed indirectly by inferences from the cues contained in the proximal stimulus arrays. Such inferences would seem to demand heavy reliance on the observer's prior knowledge and memory of environmental structure.

One commonly adopted hypothesis about how reliable knowledge can be obtained from unreliable sense data is that recognition is based on detection of distinctive features that are presumed to characterize a stimulus independently of its context. That is, a given distal stimulus object might be regarded as a unique combination of features that remain invariant under the addition and subtraction of features belonging to other stimuli and under the projective transformations associated with changes in the relative positions of object and observer. The specification of these distinctive features must be predetermined by the structures and states of the observer's perceptual system, for the explanatory value of this approach requires a prior definition of features that does not rely on previous identification of the global stimulus in which they appear. Thus, the perceptual representation of a stimulus array would typically be molded by the set of features to which the system has been tuned by its genetics, by its previous experience, and by the objectives and strategies of the observer. Accordingly, contemporary research on perception and cognition has usually focused on the information-handling processes that are presumed to construct a representation of the world from the cues available in the sensory images.

It has been frequently but prematurely assumed that reconstruction of the whole visual pattern from a featural description would pose no great theoretical problem. However, such a reconstruction now appears incapable in principle of accounting for the demonstrated achievements of human observers in recognizing patterns and resolving spatial relations. One compelling theoretical argument follows from the work of Minsky and Papert (1969) and Abelson (1977) on the limitations of the computational devices known as "perceptrons." The perceptron is a device that decides whether any given pattern is a member of a particular class by testing whether a weighted combination of binary features (that are satisfied or not as all-or-nothing properties) is above a threshold criterion. Minsky and Papert seriously dampened early optimism about the capabilities of such devices as general pattern-recognition systems by revealing their inability to decide such basic geometric relations as connectedness. Abelson extended these negative results by showing that *any* computations based on the outputs of a finite number of such perceptrons would not be able to reliably recognize any topological invariant or to reliably recognize nontrival figures embedded in extraneous contexts. These limitations of linear threshold decision functions can be taken to apply to hypothetical feature-detection systems in general: If the featural properties are permitted to assume a continuous range of values, then the system simply provides a linear transformation of the input, and its performance will be essentially the same under any orthogonal transformation of the underlying basis set of "features" or even the same as if there were no specified feature analyzers at all, so that the concept of a feature loses its meaning.

An alternative, functional hypothesis is that knowledge of the structures and events of the environment is obtained directly from the spatio–temporal variations of the proximal stimulation at the receptors. This, of course, is the conception of perception voiced principally by James Gibson (e.g., 1950, 1966, 1979). In contrast to the conventional view that the perceptual construction of the world from knowledge of sensory data requires the mediating operations of various mechanisms, memories, or inferences, the alternative Gibsonian view is that the origin and content of perceptual knowledge *is* the organization of space–time relationships in the patterns of stimulation. The spatio–temporal organization of proximal stimulus patterns is a reflection of the structures and events of the observer's environment, and the spatio–temporal organization of neural events is a reflection of the organization of the stimulus patterns. The organization of one is coordinated with that of the other. To understand the sense in which this is true, however, it is necessary to represent stimulation and knowledge in terms of relationships over space and time and to represent the environment in terms of its constraints on the observer's actions. As a concrete illustration, consider the symmetries and coordinations within and between environment, perception, and action in the playing of a game of tennis.

We turn now to illustrative experimental evidence on the perception of coherence in dynamic visual patterns. The general points to be made from these experiments are the following:

1. The perceived structure of dynamic visual patterns is their invariance under projective transformations. The transformations determine the perceived invariance.

2. Under many conditions, depending on the organization of the stimulus patterns, vision operates as a linear system in which the output signal/noise ratio is proportional to the input signal/noise ratio. Thus, the general picture is that the origin and content of perception is the coherence of the spatio–temporal patterns of stimulation.

One experimental paradigm employed extensively in my laboratory involves the presentation of a rapid sequence of two or more computer-controlled displays of random dots that may be correlated and shifted in relation to each other. The observer's task is to detect the *relationship* (which appears as movement) between successive displays. Each display consists of a large number of randomly positioned dots—typically, 512 dots are randomly positioned in half the cells of an imaginery 32 × 32 matrix. The duration of each display is usually about 100 msec., and the time between the displays may be varied from 0 to 100 msec. When successive displays are shifted in relation to each other, the outside boundaries remain fixed, so that detection of the displacement must be based on the global correspondence of the microstructure rather than on the local correspondences of the outside contours of the pattern. The rationale of this task is analogous to the "cyclopean" methodology devised by Julesz (1971) for the study of stereopsis—where the information required for the performance of the task is available only in the relationship between separate patterns, each of which is uninformative in isolation.

An initial and clear result of such experiments is that observers are readily able to detect the coherent relationship between just two such random-dot displays, provided that the temporal and spatial separation between the two is not large (not more than about 50 msec. and shifted not more than about three rows or columns) (see Lappin & Bell, 1976). If there is no intervening time between the two displays, if the shift is only one column, if the displays are fully correlated (each dot and each empty space remains in the same relative position except for the shift), then all observers clearly see the pattern as moving and make essentially no errors in identifying the direction of the shift. Accuracy declines rapidly with increasing temporal or spatial separation. It is noteworthy that masking does not occur with such patterns, despite the incoherent pattern that would correspond to the simple unshifted superposition of the two displays. Evidently, the visual system is adept at detecting the correspondence between the successive patterns at different points in time and space.

The performance of this task improves with the number of elements in the pattern, contrary to what one might expect if the process involved a limited-capacity memory-storage system. As a first approximation, the signal/noise ratio of the observers' detections (as indexed by the TSD measure d') increases in direct proportion to the square root of the number of elements in the pattern, just as in statistics the standard error of the mean decreases with the square root of the sample size. Hence, the phenomenon seems to resemble a statistical correlation more than a memory storage (Lappin & Bell, 1976).

At a descriptive level, the detection of coherence in these dynamic patterns seems to involve a process similar to *autocorrelation*, which measures the organization of the pattern by cross-multiplying the pattern with a transformation of itself. A general formula for the autocorrelation of a continuously defined pattern in two dimensions is the following:

$$A(T) = \int \int f(x,y) \cdot T[f(x,y)] \; dxdy$$

where $f(x,y)$ is the spatial pattern in Cartesian coordinates and $T(f)$ is a transformation of the pattern. It is important to note that the autocorrelation is defined over the space of transformations rather than in the XY coordinates of the original pattern. Often, the formula of this autocorrelation is expressed in terms of additions and subtractions to the XY Cartesian coordinates—the group of translations in the plane—but the autocorrelation can be defined on any transformation that maps the pattern onto itself.

A second important property of the autocorrelation is that it is a linear operation, which preserves the organization of the pattern to which it is applied. By definition, a linear operation is one that satisfies the superposition principle: If f and g are two input patterns, and a and b are arbitrary positive scalars, and L is the function that specifies the output of the system, the operation L is linear if:

$$L(a \cdot f + b \cdot g) = aL(f) + bL(g)$$

In other words, each input reappears as an addition to the output of the system, independently of the context to which it is added.

Brian Kottas and I (Lappin & Kottas, 1977) have tested this hypothesized linearity of the visual system more directly in other experiments. In one of these experiments, we measured the detectability of coherent motion as a function of the number of sequential display frames and of the correlation between successive frames. We found that detectability increased in direct proportion to the interframe correlation and the square root of the number of samples in time (one minus the number of display frames). Moreover, the effects of both variables were interchangeable and describable by a single parameter, as if each coherent event in time or space added independently to the overall coherence of the whole pattern. Thus, the output signal/noise ratio of the observers' performance (d') was approximately proportional to the input signal/noise ratio. This spatial and temporal linearity means that the perceived organization was simply a reflection of the coherent organization of the stimulus patterns.

This linearity is compatible with the hypothesis that the visual system employs some process akin to autocorrelation. However, the linearity is dependent on the nature of the organization of the pattern. For example, if two patterns moving simultaneously in opposite directions are spatially superimposed, then the detectability of coherence in one of the patterns decreases inversely with the coherence of the other pattern, as if the two organizations compete destructively. Such competitive interaction clearly violates the superposition property. Evidently, the underlying system is not truly linear, although it has a remarkable capability for behaving that way under many conditions. A vast amount of vision research demonstrates an approximate linearity in tasks ranging from the psychophysical detection of simple spatial patterns to electrophysiological responses of single cells in the visual systems of the crab, cat, and monkey (see Cornsweet, 1970; Graham & Ratliff, 1974; Sekuler, 1974). Evidently, a stable organization of neural activity is one in which multiple elements act as independent parallel channels, with the intercorrelations among their response patterns shaped by the organization of the stimulus patterns rather than genetically preshaped by the anatomical organization.

When one pauses to consider the functions that a perceptual system must provide in order for an animal to accommodate its behavior to the demands and opportunities afforded by unanticipated environmental events, then it seems obvious that its response patterns must reflect the organization of environmental events rather than the prior organization of the nervous system. The potential power associated with the detection of coherence by autocorrelating the pattern with itself is suggested by the fact that a correlation can be defined over any group of transformations that maps the stimulus onto itself. In the preceding experiments, the transformations were simply planar translations, in an *XY* Cartesian coordinate system. This is not a privileged coordinate system, however; performance is very similar when patterns are rotated in a polar coordinate system (Bell & Lappin, 1979). The generality of this visual correlation procedure is suggested by the following demonstrations.

We wondered whether observers were capable of detecting three-dimensional structure and motion in random-dot patterns subjected to projective transformations. This group is of special interest because it is associated with the changes in perspective produced by objects and observers in three-dimensional space. The perceptual phenomena traditionally known as shape constancy and size constancy refer to the apparent invariance of perceived three-dimensional structures under projective transformations.

Jon Doner, Brian Kottas, and I (Lappin, Doner, & Kottas, 1980) have presented two successive displays (about 200 msec each) of 512 dots randomly positioned as if distributed with uniform probability density over the surface of a transparent sphere and then projected (with perspective) onto the plane of a computer-controlled CRT screen. This is suggested schematically in Fig. 17.3. The projective transformation is accomplished by shifting the dots as if the sphere were rotated 5.6 degrees about a vertical axis through the center of this sphere. When there is no interval between the successive displays, only two displays are sufficient for most observers to obtain a compelling impression of a solid sphere rotating in three-dimensional space! To verify that the three-dimensional structure and motion are not merely subjective impressions, we have asked observers to discriminate between patterns of differing degrees of correlation, choosing the more coherent or more spherical of two alternative patterns. We hypothesized that if the invariant three-dimensional structure and motion constituted a stable visual organization, then discriminations between patterns of

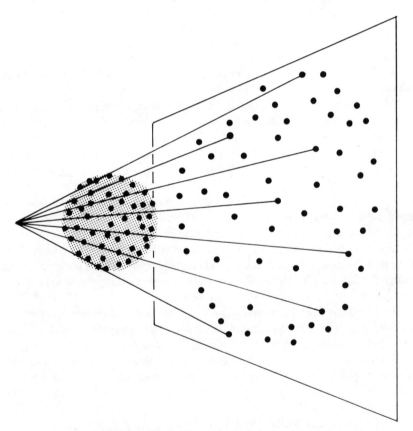

FIG. 17.3.   A schematic illustration of a projection of a dotted sphere onto a plane. In the actual experiment, 512 dots were randomly distributed with uniform density over the surface of the sphere. (Reprinted with permission of authors and publisher. Lappin, et al., *Science*, 8 August 1980, *209*, 718. Copyright, 1980.)

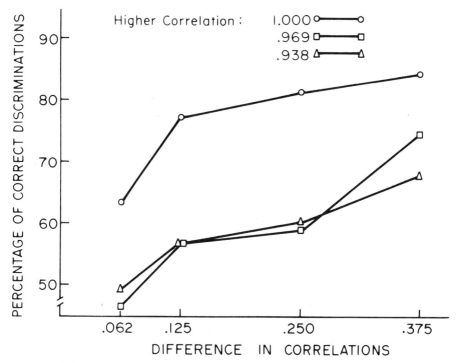

FIG. 17.4. Discrimination accuracy (two-alternative, forced-choice) as a function of the difference in correlation (proportion of dots remaining in the same relative positions in two successive displays) of two projected spherical patterns. There were two alternative correlations for a block of trials, both of which were presented on each trial. The parameter distinguishing among separate curves is the higher of the two alternative correlations. (Reprinted with permission of authors and publisher. Lappin, et al., *Science*, 8 August 1980, *209*, 718. Copyright, 1980.)

differing coherence might be more accurate when one of the patterns was a perfectly correlated sphere than when neither pattern was highly correlated. Indeed, that is what happened. The results are shown in Fig. 17.4. Lowering the correlation of the sphere by only 3% was sufficient to greatly diminish performance. Additional decrements in the correlation had little or no effect on performance.

This experiment demonstrates that the projective relationship between only two successive displays of random dots in two dimensions provides sufficient information for the detection of an invariant three-dimensional relationship. These results are compatible with the remarkable demonstrations by Johansson (1975) and by Kozlowski and Cutting (1977) that dynamic patterns of less than 10 spots of light attached to the ankles, knees, wrists, and so on, of walking humans and exposed for less than 1 second can provide sufficient information for the identification of the specific person wearing the lights, even though nothing but the lights can be seen!

The picture that emerges from these experiments is one of an astonishing capability for detecting coherent relationships in changing visual patterns. Evidently, what is perceived in these patterns is their *symmetry*, or invariance, under transformation. (For a discussion of the concept of symmetry and its application in perception, see Shaw, McIntyre, & Mace, 1974.) That is, the origin and content of the perception are coherent relationships over space and time, rather than absolute values of the patterns at particular points in space and time. Apparently, those relationships are detected that best preserve the organizational simplicity of the environmental events under changes in the perspective from which they are viewed.

The speculation that change, or transformation, is the origin of the substantive content of perception is closely associated with the conception of a *group* as the fundamental form of perception and knowledge, as explicitly discussed by Cassirer (1944). The specific relationship that remained invariant under the projective transformations in the preceding experiments is the three-dimensional Euclidean distance between two points. Even though this distance cannot be directly represented in a stationary plane projection, it can in general be recovered as an invariant under projective transformation, and evidentially that is just what the visual system accomplishes.

Now the projective group is similar to the Lorentz group that characterizes the special theory of relativity in physics. The special theory of relativity can be regarded as a symmetry principle that must be satisfied by the velocity of light (and indeed by all physical laws)—namely, that the velocity of light remains invariant under the position and motion of an observer moving at a constant velocity. Analogously, we might speculate that the perception of motion of environmental objects is invariant under the motion of the observer. Many examples of athletic performance, such as an outfielder sprinting to catch a fly ball, or a scrambling quarterback passing to a distant running receiver, as well as such everyday feats as guiding a car through freeway traffic, seem to illustrate an analogous ability of moving observers to perceive motion of objects in the environment. Development of this analogy between physical relativity and vision must be saved for another paper (Lappin, in preparation), but there is a variety of evidence that points to its validity.

The visual tendency to see those structures and events that best preserve the organizational simplicity of the dynamic stimulus patterns seems analogous to similar tendencies toward economy of description in social perception and cognition (e.g., Buckhout, 1974). Indeed, such phenomena are suggested by nearly all theories of attribution and cognitive balance. Perhaps many of these phenomena originate in the organization of the stimulation as much as in the processes of the mind (cf. Baron, Chapter 4 in this volume).

COMMENTS ON THE ROLE OF PRIOR KNOWLEDGE IN PERCEPTION

A fundamental problem in the study of perception, cognition, and social relations concerns how the perception of present events is influenced by the observer's prior knowledge. To what extent is new information filtered and prejudged at the outset by the standards of past experience? Whether one is interested in the recognition of physically defined stimulus patterns, the development of individual knowledge, the attribution of causal factors in social relations, attitude change, or the diffusion of information in social communities, a central (perhaps *the* central) problem involves the specification of how present knowledge derives from the conjoint contributions of prior knowledge and present information. If there is any common ground in the domains of psychophysics and social cognition, then it is based upon this general problem.

Enthusiasm about perceptual research in the so-called "new look" paradigm during the 1950's (see Bruner & Klein, 1960) was concerned with the prospect of revealing the influence of social values, personality, and motivation in the selectivity of an observer's perceptual "set." Although the understanding of many of the "new look" phenomena was deeply altered by the development of theories of decision and choice behavior, and although contemporary perceptual research has developed in different directions, there remains a potentially large latent interest in the problem, implicit in the very active research and theory on *selective attention.* If observers are considered active seekers and selectors rather than passive recorders of new information, then the object and motivation for their perceptual activity must often involve social relations. Moreover, such selective phenomena are of major significance in the sociology of knowledge: To the extent that individuals selectively seek and attend to limited classes of information, this selection process must play a determining role in the diffusion of information, beliefs, and attitudes in social communities.

A second privotal aspect of the interface between perception and social cognition involves phenomena of *interpretation*—the attribution of causal relations and the generalization of environmental characteristics not directly represented in the proximal stimulus patterns. Almost by definition, interpretive and attributional phenomena would seem to involve, in Bruner's (1957) words, "going beyond the information given."

In investigating selective and interpretive phenomena, the primary focus of contemporary research has been on the perceptual and cognitive processes of the observer. That is where the main action has seemed to lie—not in the information provided by the environment, but in the selective and interpretive processes occurring in the observer's head after reception of the information, going beyond the information given directly by the environment.

There is important justification, however, for reexamining the organization of environmental information and the shaping influence that it exerts on the knowledge an observer obtains from it. "Explanations" for the organization of social knowledge might not always require the intervention of special psychological mechanisms for selecting and interpreting stimulus information; many of these cognitive phenomena might be better understood in terms of the dynamics of the partnership between person and environment. As Mace (1977) suggests, an alternative strategy might be to "ask not what's inside your head, but what your head's inside of."

One of the conceptual conveniences that tends to constrain our understanding of many psychological phenomena is the dichotomy between person and environment. Implicitly, the individual person is considered as a closed system bounded by skin, receptors, effectors, and so on. By definition, the environment is supposed to be what is outside the person. A "stimulus" is regarded as a causal event produced by the environment, independent of the animal that receives it. In principle, the stimulus is supposed to be the proximal stimulus, physically definable at the sensory receptors, although in practice, of course, most researchers usually find it more convenient to refer to the distal stimulus, defined in terms of the environment that is functionally effective for the observer. Inside the person are sensory receptors that transduce the physical stimulus events, sensory nerves that encode and transmit neural representations, and unspecified brains mechanisms that associate the sensory representations with information in memory, construct interpretations of environmental conditions, the select appropriate responses. The implicit but widely accepted assumption is that observers can directly experience only the mediating neural events, as stated, for example, in Muller's doctrine of specific nerve energies. This conception implies the philosophical doctrine of idealism, or perhaps even solipsism, as Fodor (1980) has recently concluded (approvingly).

An alternative realist position—that the objects of perceptual experience are actually the objects and events of the environment—can be developed from two premises: (1) perception and knowledge are defined on relationships over time and space rather than on the proximal stimulation of neural activity at a specific point in time and space; (2) person and environment do not constitute two functionally or logically separate systems, but (according to Shaw & Turvey, in press) are "two complementary subsystems" that function as "reciprocal contexts of mutual constraint." The fundamental idea that perception must be considered an aspect of the functional relationship between person and environment is what James Gibson has been insisting for the past several years (see Gibson, 1979), and it is an important basis for Neisser's (1976) efforts to reformulate cognitive psychology.

As Shaw and Turvey point out, implicit in this ecological approach is a conception of scientific explanation that differs from the traditional mechanistic conception of most psychologists, substituting for the traditional notion of cause–effect chains the more modern and more general notion of symmetry principles that describe the cooperative relations between functionally interdependent subsystems. Thus, the environmental context constrains in both a probabilistic and functional sense the alternative perceptions and actions that are viable for a person within that environment, while the relevant aspects and events of that environment are defined, selected, and modified by the functioning of the person—as in the mutual coordinations of perception, knowledge, and action between two boxers, between husband and wife, among a community of automobile drivers, between a computer user and the technology and personnel of a computer center, or even (as Greenwald observes in Chapter 25 in this volume) between a person and a drawer of clothes. Thus, explanations for the derivation and content and a person's knowledge should be based on the functional relation between person and environment as coordinated components of a larger ecosystem.

It is useful to note that the functional integrity of person and environment was an important aspect of the early social cognitive theories of Lewin and Heider. For example, Lewin (1936) writes that:

> the transition from Aristotelean to Galilean concepts demands that we no longer seek "the cause" of events in the nature of a single isolated object, but in the relationship between an object and its surroundings. It is not thought then that the environment of the individual serves merely to facilitate or inhibit tendencies that are established once and for all in the nature of the person. One can hope to understand the forces that govern behavior only if one includes in the representation the whole psychological situation. . . . It is necessary to find methods of representing person and environment in common terms as parts of one situation [p. 11–12].

Further, with regard to the role of past experience in controlling present behavior, Lewin (1936) demanded by his principle of "contemporaneity" that the effective past must be represented in terms of the organization of the present life space, an approach that contrasts sharply with most modern analyses:

> From the point of view of systematic causation, past events cannot influence present events. Past events can only have a position in the historical causal chains whose interweavings recreate the present situation. This fact has often not been given enough consideration in psychology. [p. 35].

Similar themes are explicit in Heider's (1959) writing about the relation between the perceived distal environment and proximal stimulation:

> Since perception is adapted to the environment, it is obvious that we must be familiar with the environmental structures to which it is adapted if we are to get a comprehensive understanding of it. . . . one has to go beyond the mere statement that the proximal stimulus is caused by the distal stimulus. One has to use concepts

which have to do with the coordination of manifolds, with order and disorder, with the domination of one system by another, and with constraints: that is, one has to use the concepts which have been elaborated and sharpened in recent years by the new developments of information theory and cybernetics [p. ix].

In contrast to many contemporary conceptions, attributions of causality were attributed by Heider (1944) not to particular cognitive mechanisms within the person, but to the phenomenological organization of the whole perceptual field:

It is the thesis of this paper that the principles involved in these studies [of organization of the perceptional field] can be applied profitably to the perception of other persons and their behavior, and that one of the features of the organization of the social field is the attribution of a change to a perceptual unit.... Such causal effects often play the role of data that can be thought of as *proximal stimuli* [emphasis mine] through which are mediated to us properties of the origins which belong to the stable relevant psychological environment [pp. 358–359].

The idea that prior knowledge is inherent in the characteristics of present proximal stimulation is a less radical idea than might at first appear. Indeed, it is implicit in the technical definition of *information*. Recall that by Shannon's definition the amount of information associated with the occurrence of events from some set of alternatives is measured by a transformation of the *probabilities* of the events:

$$H = -\sum_i p_i \log p_i, \qquad \text{where} \sum_i p_i = 1.$$

That is, the amount of information conveyed by a given event depends not on its physical properties as such, but on the receiver's prior uncertainty about those properties. As Garner (1974) expresses the idea, "information is a function not of what the stimulus is, but of what it might have been, of its alternatives [p. 194]." Like the physical measure of entropy in thermodynamics, information derives from the organizational complexity or randomness in a collection of events. The complementary concept of *redundancy* is a measure of the degree of organization or constraint on the events that occur in a system. Thus, any constraints on an observer's uncertainty about the potential stimulus events that may occur in a given environmental context are reflected in a fundamental way in the information associated with these events.

Ironically, what is known as the information-processing approach to perception and cognition usually relies on a different and theoretically incorrect concept of information—in which information is an absolute quality of the individual stimulus rather than a relative quality defined in the context of alternatives. The concern has been with the processing rather than with the information.

It is further instructive to examine the logic of the Bayesian formulation of the transformation from prior to current knowledge effected by present stimulus information. If e represents a given proximal stimulus event, and if H_i and H_j are two mutually exclusive hypotheses about the environmental conditions that produce the event, then the functional relation between current knowledge, present stimulus information, and prior knowledge can be expressed by the following formula, which is a familiar version of Bayes' theorem:

$$\frac{P(H_i \mid e)}{P(H_j \mid e)} = \frac{P(H_i)}{P(H_j)} \times \frac{P(e \mid H_i)}{P(e \mid H_j)}$$

The three terms, from left to right, are known as the posterior odds, the prior odds, and the likelihood ratio favoring hypothesis H_i over H_j. The information provided by the stimulus event e is fully summarized by the likelihood ratio, whereas the prior odds are independent of this event. The elegance of this equation is perhaps more evident in its logarithmic transform, which becomes the simple additive relation: Log posterior odds equals log prior odds plus log likelihood ratio. Thus, in arriving at any given level of confidence about the existing environmental conditions, prior knowledge and present stimulus information are weighted equally and added together. As prior knowledge is increased, then correspondingly less stimulus information is required to obtain a given level of performance or confidence.

Several implications of this theoretical relation between prior knowledge and present perception bear mention. As expected, when the prior odds in favor of some stimulus event are experimentally increased or decreased, subjects in a variety of detection, recognition, and speeded performance tasks will correspondingly lower or raise their criteria for choosing the appropriate response (cf. Green & Swets, 1966; Lappin 1978; Swets, 1973). Such changes in performance with changes in prior odds do not require any change in the perceptual process, merely a change in the decision criterion for choosing a response. The failure to distinguish the role of the decision criterion in controlling the amount of perceptual information required for a given response vitiates the interpretation of much of the research on perceptual set conducted in the "new look" program. A change in the prior odds of some stimulus *should* lead to a change in the behavior of a rational decision maker, irrespective of any effects on the available perceptual information. In most cases, the effect of "readiness" for a particular stimulus is most parsimoniously attributed to a change in decision criterion rather than a change in perception.

This conceptual distinction between perceptual and response processes is most meaningful in experimental tasks involving the presentation of brief stimuli on discrete trials; the distinction between perception and response becomes blurred as the stimulus environment becomes more complex and continually available. When observation is continuous, present information and prior knowledge may be combined in an on-going feedback loop, in which the observer's search for new information shapes the effective stimulus environment.

Despite the conceptual distinction between prior odds and present likelihood ratio, the likelihood ratio does depend in a fundamental way on certain aspects of the observer's prior knowledge about the environment. This dependence has not been widely recognized in cognitive research, but it is theoretically important for it affects the degree to which performance changes resulting from changes in prior knowledge should be attributed to the information-processing characteristics of the observer rather than to the information being processed.

First, it is fairly obvious that computation of likelihood ratios depends on the observer's previously acquired knowledge of the correlations between e and the various alternative H_i. If the observer has not yet had the opportunity to learn these correlations, then of course the likelihood ratio for any given event will tend toward 1.0, favoring no particular hypothesis very strongly.

Dependence of the likelihood ratio on the observer's prior knowledge extends to a deeper level, however. Consider the common situation in which a number of physically distinct alternative stimuli are associated with the same response category. Suppose, for example, that a stimulus might occur at any one or another of several alternative spatial locations, and that the observer is required only to detect ("yes" or "no") the occurrence at any location. In other words, suppose that the observer is uncertain about the specific parameters or dimensions of the stimulus. Because the observer does not know beforehand which of several alternative locations or dimensions is operative on a given trial, then the likelihood ratios of each of several independent events are potentially relevant and must be considered in deciding whether the target stimulus has occurred. As a result, the signal/noise ratio corresponding to the actual stimulus event is effectively diluted by the inclusion of additional noisy information from other nonstimulus events. As the number of alternatives increases, there is an increasing chance that one of the nonstimulus alternatives will be mistaken for the true target stimulus. The performance of even an ideal observer with an unlimited attention span will be diminished by the demand to combine the likelihood ratios corresponding to additional potential stimuli. It should not be surprising that the speed and accuracy of real observers are similarly adversely affected (e.g., Green & Birdsall, 1978; Kinchla, 1977; Lappin, 1978; Lappin & Uttal, 1976).

Because uncertainty about the stimulus parameters will lead to a decline in performance even without any limitations on attention span, then obviously evidence of such a decline is not sufficient to conclude that the capacities of human observers are limited in attending simultaneously to several separate events. Nevertheless, this fact has been forgotten in a considerable body of research on human information processing, where such effects have often been attributed to attentional or memory-search processes with limited capacity. Such special-purpose mechanisms may be unnecessary if the proximal stimulus information has already been altered by changing the number of stimulus alternatives. The point is that "the stimulus" is not defined solely by its proximal physical characteristics, but depends on the context in which it is presented.

If we hold to the idea that stimulation and perception are defined on relationships, then the complementarity between environmental stimulus events and the observer's knowledge of the patterns in which they are embedded may be seen to extend to a broad spectrum of potential relationships. In the preceding discussion of information and likelihood ratio, the relationships were only stochastic—defined on merely categorical differences between alternative stimuli—but other relationships among objects and events at separate points in time and space should also vary in salience depending on the physical and social context in which they are embedded. The pointing of a toy gun by a child of 6 has different meanings in Indianapolis, Johannesburg, or Belfast. The passage of a second of time encompasses the perception of different numbers of events in the interval between stimulus and response in a reaction-time experiment, after plunging from a plane and before pulling a cord to open a parachute, or in the arms of a lover.

Although it may be doubted that the social environment significantly alters the sensitivity to most physical relationships between closely neighboring points in space and time, many culturally significant patterns involve components that have little or no direct physical relationship. One important example is provided by printed text, where words are constructed from physically unrelated component characters whose shapes are essentially arbitrary. The rapid identification of such patterns—roughly 250 words per minute, give or take 100 or more—by a skilled reader indicates that specific combinations of these arbitrary alphabetic components have rapidly recognized significance. Joshua Staller and I (Staller & Lappin, 1979) have recently found in a speeded visual search task that three-letter targets forming words were detected more accurately than were meaningless permutations of the same letters, even after thousands of trials of searching for the same target pattern. Apparently, the word-targets were more readily distinguished from the multitude of irrelevant background characters by virtue of the observer's past experience with the cultural functions of these patterns. An analogous highlighting of significant patterns of relationships must be fostered by the organization of the person's social transactions.

If prior knowledge is a characteristic of the person's on-going relationship with the environment, then it is inherent in virtually all of the commerce between person and environment. The function of such knowledge need not be regarded as selectively facilitating or inhibiting the processing of certain information nor supplementing the interpretation of sensory data. Rather, prior knowledge may be regarded as an anticipation of the consequences of actions. These anticipations originate from constraints on environmental events and or the person's functions within the environment.

ACKNOWLEDGMENTS

Preparation of this chapter was supported by NSF 78-05857 Research Grant.

REFERENCES

Abelson, H. Computational geometry of linear threshold functions. *Information and control,* 1977, *34,* 66–92.

Anderson, J. R., & Bower, G. H. *Human associative memory.* Washington, D.C.: V. H. Winston, 1973.

Babbitt, M. Set structure as a compositional determinant. *Journal of Music Theory,* 1961, *5,* 72–94.

Bell, H. H., & Lappin, J. S. The detection of rotation in random-dot patterns. *Perception &Psychophysics,* 1979, *26,* 415–417.

Brown, E. R. *Abstraction and hierarchical organization in the learning of periodic sequences.* Doctoral dissertation, Indiana University, 1971.

Bruner, J. S. Going beyond the information given. In H. Gruber, et al. (Eds.), *Contemporary approaches to cognition.* Cambridge, Mass.: Harvard University Press, 1957. (Also in J. S. Bruner. *Beyond the information given.* New York: Norton, 1973.)

Bruner, J. S., & Klein, G. S. The functions of perceiving: New Look retrospect. In B. Kaplan & S. Wapner (Eds.), *Perspectives in psychological theory.* New York: International Universities Press, 1960. (Also in J. S. Bruner. *Beyond the information given.* New York: Norton, 1973.)

Buckhout, R. Eyewitness testimony. *Scientific American,* December, 1974.

Caelli, T. M., & Julesz, B. On perceptual analyzers underlying visual texture discrimination: Part I. *Biological Cybernetics,* 1978, *28,* 167–175.

Caelli, T. M., Julesz, B., & Gilbert, E. N. On the perceptual analyzers underlying visual texture discriminations: Part II. *Biological Cybernetics,* 1978, *29,* 201–214.

Cassirer, E. *Substance and function.* New York: Dover, 1953. (Originally published in Chicago, by Open Court, 1923.)

Cassirer, E. The concept of group and the theory of perception. *Philosophy and phemonenological research,* 1944, *5,* 1–35.

Cornsweet, T. N. *Visual perception.* New York: Academic Press, 1970.

Fishbein, N., & Ajzen, I. *Belief, attitude, intention, and behavior.* Reading, Mass.: Addison-Wesley, 1975.

Fodor, J. A. Methodological solipsism considered as a research strategy in cognitive psychology. *Behavioral and Brain Sciences,* 1980, *3,* 63–73.

Garner, W. R. *The processing of information and structure.* Hillsdale, N.J.: Lawrence Erlbaum Associates, 1974.

Gibson, J. J. *The perception of the visual world.* Boston: Houghton-Mifflin, 1950.

Gibson, J. J. *The senses considered as perceptual systems.* Boston: Houghton-Mifflin, 1966.

Gibson, J. J. *The ecological approach to visual perception.* Boston: Houghton-Mifflin, 1979.

Graham, N., & Ratliff, F. Quantitative theories of the integrative action of the retina. In D. H. Krantz, R. C. Atkinson, R. D. Luce, & P. Suppes (Eds.), *Contemporary developments in mathematical psychology* (Vol. 2). San Francisco: Freeman, 1974.

Green, D. M., & Birdsall, T. G. Detection and recognition. *Psychological Review,* 1978, *85,* 192–206.

Green, D. M. & Swets, J. A. *Signal detection theory and psychophysics.* New York: Wiley, 1966.

Greeno, J. G., & Simon, H. A. Processes for sequence production. *Psychological Review,* 1974, *81,* 187–198.

Heider, F. Social perception and phenomenal causality. *Psychological Review,* 1944, *51,* 358–374.

Heider, F. On perception, event structure, and psychological environment. *Psychological Issues,* 1959, *1*, (Monograph No. 3)

Johansson, G. Visual motion perception. *Scientific American,* June 1975.

Julesz, B. *Foundations of cyclopean perception.* Chicago: University of Chicago Press, 1971.

Kinchla, R. A. The role of structural redundancy in the perception of visual targets. *Perception & Psychophysics,* 1977, *22,* 19–30.

Kozlowski, L. T., & Cutting, J. E. Recognizing the sex of a walker from a dynamic point-light display. *Perception & Psychophysics,* 1977, *21,* 575–580.

Lappin, J. S. The relativity of choice behavior and the effect of prior knowledge on the speed and accuracy of recognition. In N. J. Castellan, Jr. & F. Restle (Eds.), *Cognitive Theory* (Vol. 3). Hillsdale, N.J.: Lawrence Erlbaum Associates, 1978.

Lappin, J. S. *Some analogies between the special theory of relativity and visual perception.* Paper in preparation.

Lappin, J. S., & Bell, H. H. The detection of coherence in dynamic random-dot stimuli. *Vision Research,* 1976, *16,* 161–168.

Lappin, J. S., Doner, J., & Kottas, B. L. Minimal conditions for the visual detection of structure and motion in three dimensions. *Science,* 1980, *209,* 717–719.

Lappin, J. S., & Kottas, B. L. Spatial and temporal linearity in detecting coherent structure in dynamic random-dot patterns. *Investigative Ophthalmology and Visual Science, ARVO Abstracts,* 1977, p. 10.

Lappin, J. S., & Uttal, W. R. Does prior knowledge facilitate the detection of visual targets in random noise? *Perception & Psychophysics,* 1976, *20,* 367–374.

Lewin, K. *Principles of topological psychology.* New York: NcGraw-Hill, 1936.

Mace, W. M. James J. Gibson's strategy for perceiving: Ask not what's inside your head, but what your head's inside of. In R. Shaw & J. Bransford (Eds.), *Perceiving, acting, and knowing.* Hillsdale, N.J.: Lawrence Erlbaum Associates, 1977.

Minsky, M., & Papert, S. *Perceptrons: An introduction to computational geometry.* Cambridge, Mass.: M.I.T. Press, 1969.

Neisser, U. *Cognition and reality.* San Francisco: Freeman, 1976.

Reed, S. K. *Psychological processes in pattern recognition.* New York: Academic Press, 1973.

Restle, F. Theory of serial pattern learning: Structural trees. *Psychological Review,* 1970, *77,* 481–495.

Sekuler, R. Spatial vision. *Annual Review of Psychology,* 1974, *25,* 195–232.

Shaw, R., McIntyre, M., & Mace, W. The role of symmetry in event perception. In R. B. MacLeod & H. L. Pick, Jr. (Eds.), *Perception essays in honor of James J. Gibson.* Ithaca, N.Y.: Cornell University Press, 1974.

Shaw, R., & Turvey, M. T. Coalitions as models for ecosystems: A realist perspective on perceptual organization. In M. Kubovy & J. Pomerantz (Eds.), *Perceptual organization.* Hillsdale, N.J.: Lawrence Erlbaum Associates, in press.

Shubnikov, A. V., & Koptsik, V. A. *Symmetry in science and art.* New York: Plenum, 1974.

Simon, H. A. Induction and representation of sequential patterns. In E. L. J. Leeuwenberg & H. F. J. M. Buffart (Eds.), *Formal theories of visual perception.* New York: Wiley, 1978.

Simon, H. A., & Kotovsky, K. Human acquisition of concepts for sequential patterns. *Psychological Review,* 1963, *70,* 534–546.

Simon, H. A., & Sumner, R. K. Pattern in music. In B. Kleinmuntz (Ed.), *Formal representation of human judgment.* New York: Wiley, 1968.

Staller, J. D., & Lappin, J. S. Observers detect higher order relations in visual search for letters. *Bulletin of the Psychonomic Society, Program for the Twentieth Annual Meeting,* 1979, pp. 258–259.

Swets, J. A. The relative operating characteristic in psychology. *Science,* 1973, *183,* 990–1000.

Weyl, H. *Symmetry.* Princeton, N.J.: Princeton University Press, 1952.

IV SOCIAL BEHAVIOR AND THE ENVIRONMENT

The four papers in this section of substantive chapters focus on central concepts of environmental psychology, especially crowding, stress, freedom, and control and their link to social behavior. In the first paper, Susan Saegert examines the role of cognitive limitations in experiences of crowding and also limitations in cognitive theories designed to explain these experiences. In particular, she analyzes the cognitive overload interpretation for various effects of high density environments. Saegert's analysis is rich in propositional content as well as commentary regarding appropriate methodology for investigating complex environmental events (e.g., notice her emphasis on path analytic procedures and descriptive research—not unlike that discussed by Agar).

In the second paper, Wandersman and Florin describe a field study which uses a cognitive social learning approach to study the person-situation interaction. They focus on the role of certain cognitive processes in mediating variables involved in this interaction and call upon Mischel's extensive writings in the development of their conception. Wandersman and Florin discuss early data from a field study of participation in neighborhood type organizations. As noted by Baruch Fischhoff in commenting on this work at the conference, an interesting implication of their findings is that the prosperity of neighborhood groups may hinge on economic factors that have not been studied extensively in environmental research, such as the presence or absence of redlining.

In the third paper, Richard Barnes provides a useful discussion of the role of the concepts of freedom and control in design and environmental literatures. Barnes' presentation is particularly valuable in its address of the frequent communication gap between environmental and other researchers and designers. Similar to Saegert, Barnes provides some perspectives on methodology involved in studying perceived freedom and control in the built environment. Barnes presents an important challenge to researchers in this area when he says, "If the concepts of perceived freedom and perceived control are to be meaningfully applied to design problems, there must be a way of linking them to specific decisions made in the course of a person-environment interaction."

In the final paper in this section, John Aiello, Donna Thompson, and Andrew Baum present a case for the view that environmental and social psychology are complementary areas and that the thoughts, feelings, and behavior of people can best be understood by including a consideration of the context within which these thoughts, feelings, and behavior occur. As the reader will note, the argument here is similar to the one presented by Baum et al. in the last section of the book. The present paper includes an explicit discussion of the two areas of environmental and social psychology and of how these areas can be linked meaningfully in environmental-social research. Kurt Lewin's influence is pinpointed as a singularly major factor in furthering this linkage. Aiello et al. briefly discuss various domains of work to illustrate their logic.

18 Crowding and Cognitive Limits

Susan Saegert
City University of New York

The title of this chapter can be seen as a double entendre in that the topic I wish to address concerns not only the role of cognitive limitations in experiences of crowding, but also the limitations of cognitive theories in explaining these experiences. Most of the research I have done on crowding takes as its starting point the physical and psychological restrictions an individual encounters in understanding and acting in high-density environments (Langer & Saegert, 1977; Love & Saegert, 1978; Saegert, 1973, 1975, 1978; Saegert, Mackintosh, & West, 1975). The most obvious property of a crowded environment is that it constrains movement and leaves a person open to physical interference from others (cf. Heller, Groff, & Solomon, 1977; Saegert, 1973; Schopler & Stockdale, 1977; Stokols, 1972a). Clearly, this is not a cognitive variable, yet it may be viewed as setting a problem that an individual must handle cognitively. Stokols (1972a, 1972b, 1978) has differentiated the experience of crowding from physical density conditions and argued that perceived crowding mediates stress and triggers coping responses. Worchel and Teddlie (1976) have applied an attribution theory model to crowding in which they postulate a two-page process: First, close proximity to others induces arousal; then, under some circumstances this is labeled as crowding.

The two theoretical approaches just mentioned emphasize spatial restriction as the significant physical determinant of crowding experiences and labeling as the main cognitive issue. A third theoretical position, and the one that I have pursued, has focused on cognitive overload as the chief explanatory mechanism for various effects of high-density environments (Cohen, 1978; Desor, 1972; Milgram, 1970; Saegert, 1973, 1975, 1978). The assumption is made that people can attend to only a certain amount of information at a time. Excessive demands on attention capacity are created by intense, unpredictable, uncontrollable, or simply extremely numerous environmental events. Thus, large numbers of other people become a source of potential overload: They create a setting with numerous constituent elements and they are often unpredictable and uncontrollable.

These assumptions of cognitive overload have provided the intuitive underpinnings for social theorists as early as LeBon in 1865 (LeBon 1895-1964). However, he and more recent sociological theorists did not tie the effects of this sort of overload to any particular setting. LeBon believed that merely participating in large groups such as parliaments or mass political parties leads to cognitive impairment. In these situations, he concluded that people take leave of their common sense and fall prey to various forms of simple-minded and primitive thinking, or perhaps fail to think for themselves at all. This line of thought can be traced into the present-day work of sociologists who examine the impact of organizational size on the form of organizations and the behavior of their members (cf. Anderson & Warkov, 1961; Blau, 1972; Durkheim, 1933; Hall, Haas, & Johnson, 1967; Hawley, Boland, & Boland, 1965; Raphael, 1967; Thomas & Fink, 1963) and perhaps to Zimbardo's work on deindividuation (1969).

Simmel made the information-overload hypothesis explicit in his statement from his essay "The Metropolis and Mental Life" (1905/1957): "The psychological basis of the metropolitan type of individuality consists in the intensification of nervous stimulation which results from the swift and uninterrupted change on inner and outer stimuli [p. 48]." Fischer (1976) criticizes urban sociological work based on this assumption by arguing that even though a purely probabilistic account of the impact of size on potential contacts would lead to this conclusion, people do not structure their behavior randomly. He asserts that a subcultural theory of urban life is more accurate—that is, that people experientially live in smaller subgroups in cities and do not actually confront the kind of overload that Simmel described.

This criticism points up an ambiguity in both the sociological and psychological work on the effects of density and population size concerning the relationship between the physical qualities of a setting and cognitive processes. On the one hand, Stokols (1972a, 1978), Freedman (1975), and others have provided evidence that merely being in a high-density environment does not necessarily lead to negative effects, or perhaps to any effects at all. On the other hand, Baum and Koman (1976) and Klein and Harris (1979) found that subjects merely anticipating a crowd displayed coping responses that were similar to those of subjects who were actually crowded. Other variations on this essential ambiguity are explored by Rapoport (1975) in his discussion of cultural and symbolic components of the perception of density, itself a more "objective" quality than crowding, which implies a judgment of how much is too much. As Aiello, Thompson, and Baum remark in their chapter in this volume, (Chapter 21) one of the main conclusions that arises from the work of environmental psychologists on crowding, as well as on other topics, is that the effects of environmental factors are not the products of the environment alone. Having accepted this, however, we are left with the problem of fruitfully conceptualizing the role of environments in human experience.

In understanding the influences of density on cognitive and social processes, there are four sets of variables that we must consider. The first of these are the effective components of a setting—that is, those elements that condition or elicit particular psychosocial responses at any moment in time. Thus, effective components of settings might be thought of as akin to Lewin's idea of "lifespace." The second set of factors involves the dynamic transactions of persons in environments. Here, we must consider (1) the capacities, traits, and tendencies of individuals; (2) the individual's constructs, schemas, memories, expectations, and so on; and (3) the processes that relate the individual to the setting, such as tasks, standing patterns of behavior, and so on. Although it would be possible and perhaps desirable to treat each of these factors separately, I do not do so because of the paucity of data relevant to some of them. Third, we must recognize in our theories and data collection the systemic relationships among the preceding variables.

EFFECTIVE COMPONENTS OF HIGH-DENSITY SETTINGS

Trying to define the effective components of settings for an individual is somewhat like opening a box and finding out it is not only Pandora's box (from the point of view of the researcher), but also that it is only the largest of a set of Chinese boxes. It has become commonplace to observe that density is not a unitary variable but that it has at least two components: the number of people and the amount of space per person. The implications of this statement, however, have barely penetrated the theorizing or research designs of those of us doing work on the topic. Elsewhere, I have discussed the differential impact of these two density variables on cognitive overload (Saegert, 1978). A number of studies have shown differential effects for both actual and anticipated group size and available space (Baum & Koman, 1976; Paulus, McCain, & Cox, 1978; Saegert, 1974). Worchel (1978) hypothesizes that close proximity, not available space nor number of people present, evokes increased arousal. The problem with all of these formulations is that although the researcher may systematically vary some of these environmental dimensions so that they are independent for the purposes of statistical analysis, there is another important sense in which they are not independent. Each aspect of a particular environmental configuration is constrained to some degree by the others. Clearly, the manipulation of group size and space available interact. That bodies take up space is obvious. However, the interdependence of these factors and their different consequences means that density per se can not be said to have any reliable consequences. Nonetheless, the components of density and the ratio itself can in some circumstances be shown to exert a powerful and reasonably predictable influence on a range of human experiences and behaviors.

A second problem emerges when one tries to define the effective components of high-density settings: Different aspects of the setting may be affecting different response systems of individuals and groups. In a reanalysis of some of my past research, this time using path analysis instead of analysis of variance (Saegert & Love, 1979), it was discovered that space per person was affecting the measure of physiological arousal employed, the Palmar Sweat Index, but that group size was more strongly related to task performance. Although in principle such differential effects pose no insurmountable theoretical difficulties, they do contradict the theoretical statements about the effects of density that take the form of Density (or spatial contraint or proximity) → X Mediator → Y Response. The path analysis of my data showed that although two response systems were being affected by the density components of the setting, they were being differentially affected, and it would be a mistake to assume that one mediated the other. In this case, I had begun with the expectation that arousal would mediate task performance but found no support for this using either linear or nonlinear regression paths. This lack of relationship is of particular interest because crowding researchers have often assumed that affective, cognitive, and behavioral effects of density level were mediated by arousal (cf. Evans, 1978; Freedman, Klevansky, & Ehrlich, 1971; Klein & Harris, 1979; Paulus, Annis, Seta, Schkade, & Matthews, 1976).

This reanalysis lends some plausibility to the Worchel–Teddlie hypothesis that proximity, which was surely greater in the smaller spaces, evokes arousal, which is then labeled as one thing or another. In my study, subjects did not converge on a unidirectional self report of feelings, but rather reported more moods of all kinds when they felt aroused. However, the measure of arousal was significantly related to only PSI, not to mood reports, the latter being a *joint* function of initial level of arousal *and* of the experimental condition. In more recent work, Worchel (1978) reports task effects of proximity, as well as self-reports of crowding and stress. Because he used analysis of variance, we cannot tell if arousal mediated the other effects, if perceived crowding mediated both, or if some other form of relationship or disassociation occurred. It should also be noted that group size did not vary, but that the groups consisted of five people. In my study (Saegert, 1974; Saegert & Love, 1979), groups of four performed more poorly than lone individuals and than groups of two. Thus, one might ask whether the same spatial crowding effects would be obtained for groups of two or three. Wolfe (1975) has demonstrated that the social dynamics of room uses vary qualitatively as a function of the number of occupants.

One might use the path analysis previously described and other data (cf. Aiello, Epstein, & Karlin, 1975; Evans, 1980) to argue that spatial constraint more strongly influences arousal, whereas group size has more effect on task performance. However, this approach would, I think, be misleading. Rather, I suggest that we ask the question of how different components of a setting engage various response systems and how these response systems engage each other. The work of Paulus, McCain, and Cox in prison settings supports this approach in that they have found stress effects associated with social crowding in some settings and with total population size and with the inhabitants/space ratio in others (Paulus, McCain, & Cox, 1978). Generally, I would postulate the following as a way of understanding the place of cognitive limitations in crowding experiences:

1. Settings have multiple effective components.

2. People have multiple response systems, only some of which are directly implicated in cognitive overload.

3. Settings limit response systems through a range of qualities including standing behavior patterns, boundaries, layout, number and type of occupants, culturally shared meanings attributed to the setting, multimodal stimulation, and so on.

4. People's response systems are limited by their cognitive capacities, habits, personal preferences, and tolerances, as well as by the interpretive scripts, schemas, strategies, memories, categories, and so on, that they bring to the situation.

5. The unit of interest to us should be the person-in-setting ensemble, which may have some strongly organized subunits in a total ensemble that is itself weakly or tightly integrated.

6. Both settings and people (and groups that are both setting and people) have mechanisms for addressing each other. For settings, some of these would be setting norms, resources for human use, attention-getting stimuli, culturally shared symbols, and so on. People are related to settings by the way they deploy their attention, their purposes, their information-processing strategies, their aesthetic sensibilities, and so on.

7. Some aspects of persons in settings belong to both. People are part of the setting for others. Physical movement, communication, bodily presence, interaction, exchanges, interpretations all have this dual quality.

8. The impact of settings on people is most likely related to the time they spend in the setting, the significance of the setting, and the form of interrelationship among settings temporally, spatially, functionally, and in some kind of valuing or interpretive sense. Stokols (1976, 1978) has developed this idea in his hypotheses that personal thwartings encountered in crowding situations will have stronger effects than neutral thwartings and that crowding in primary settings will have greater impact than in secondary settings. Both time spent in settings and the significance of transactions occurring in them distinguish primary and secondary settings. The effects of primary settings are more likely, Stokols hypothesizes, to be carried over into behavior in other settings.

9. People and settings mutually define each other. This recognition is important in crowding research in that it has been argued that vulnerable populations may be particularly susceptible to the negative effects of crowding (Loo, in press). Thus, the definition and management of settings such as public housing, prison, or luxury housing enter into the definition of the vulnerability of the population.

PERSON–ENVIRONMENT TRANSACTIONS IN HIGH-DENSITY SETTINGS

Given these considerations, various theoretical positions can be seen to address different points of the person-in-setting transaction. My research has emphasized the way the physical qualities of settings run up against the physical and cognitive limitations of their occupants. Certain kinds of transactions and relationships among occupants appear necessary for this to occur. In a number of studies carried out in public spaces, my colleagues and I have found that high densities interfere with the retention of an elaborated, clear, and accurate image of the environment, with tasks that require scanning of and movement through the environment and with complex calculational tasks using information from the environment (Langer & Saegert, 1977; Love & Saegert, 1978; Saegert, 1974; Saegert, Mackintosh, & West, 1975). Negative affect has arisen in high-density settings when the tasks the subjects took to be their main activities were interfered with by the setting, as in the first two studies just cited, but not if that setting was a laboratory (Saegert, 1974). Paulus et al. (1976) also failed to find negative affective reactions in high densities in a series of laboratory studies that did demonstrate task decrements as a result of higher density conditions. This difference between laboratory and field settings may indicate that people's cognitive, behavioral, and affective responses tend to be more integrated in field settings.

Not only is there evidence of decrements in cognitive performance in crowded settings, but there are also data that demonstrate the amelioration of cognitive and affective decrements by cognitive interventions. Langer and Saegert (1977) found that subjects asked to choose the most economical product for specified commodities in a grocery store were less economical in their decisions when the store was crowded, but did better if they were forewarned that the store might become crowded and that crowding sometimes made people anxious and aroused. Forewarned subjects also felt more positive, less interfered with, and less crowded. Interestingly, the subjects in the less-dense conditions who received the warning also did better and felt more positive than those who were neither crowded nor forewarned. We can speculate that the warning induced subjects to use cognitive and behavioral strategies that were both more efficient and less stressful.

In another study (Love & Saegert, 1978), we found that subjects could improve their ability to remember the environment when it was crowded if we told them ahead of time that they would be asked to draw a map of it, to locate items within it, and to estimate the number of people in the setting. However, crowded subjects who received this information, and performed better on the recall tasks, felt very negatively about the experience, more so than crowded subjects who were not told of the task, and more than uncrowded subjects. Wener and Kaminoff (1979) intervened in a prison setting waiting room that regularly became crowded by putting up signs to clarify the location of facilities and procedures for visiting inmates. They discovered that visitors during crowded times reported more positive affect and displayed fewer "lost" behaviors than did visitors at crowded times prior to the installation of the signs. Further, this difference cannot be attributed to visitors' thinking more positively about the prison managers because they bothered to provide signs. Ratings of the prison personnel did not change.

Thus far, all but one of the studies reported, even though they were conducted in field settings, required the participants to engage in tasks set by the experimenter, thus limiting the range of responses that could be observed and also perhaps inducing difficulties that people normally do not experience. Furthermore, we do not know whether the experience of crowding in very different settings leads to different consequences. An interview study of people's perceptions of urban stress helped us address these issues (Roberts & Saegert, 1978). Of the 80 residents of Manhattan questioned in an open-ended manner about urban stress, all but four mentioned crowding as stressful. Distinctive patterns of crowding experiences for different settings emerge from their accounts. They also reported a variety of definitions of crowding, responses to it, reasons for considering it stressful, and coping strategies. Crowding stress was most frequently reported in public settings, particularly on public transportation, in streets and traffic, and in service facilities such as stores, agencies, and entertainment places. In this sample, only seven people mentioned crowding as a problem in their homes. This small number probably reflected sample characteristics. Most respondents were middle class and lived alone or with only one other person. A moderate number of responses involved a general feeling of crowding in the city as a whole.

Crowding in public transportation situations arose, of course, from both the presence of large numbers of others and the limited amount of space available. Predictably, major complaints centered around being pushed and shoved and being too close to other people. These situations, and other high-density settings characterized by many people in a small space, elicited the strongest emotions and the most mentions of physical reactions. Almost all reports of aggressive responses to crowding occurred for transportation settings as did the preponderance of descriptions of coping by fantasizing and ignoring the situation. Fewer coping strategies involving rational problem solving were mentioned for dealing with crowded public transportation than for coping with other crowded settings.

Service facilities were seen as giving rise to crowding stress due to the sheer number of people who used them, as were situations involving automobile traffic and parking. Being delayed and waiting in line were given as the reasons why these settings were stressful when crowded. In respondents' descriptions of crowding stress in which the large number of other people present was the salient dimension, people complained of feeling that extra demands were being made on them. Being with large numbers of people in any setting was also more likely to lead to feelings of alienation and loneliness. Most mentions of feeling confused, mentally overloaded, and so on, were also related to exposure to large numbers of people. Fewer people reported coping strategies for high-number situations than for those involving both limited space and high numbers, perhaps because the former were less stressful. Avoiding using service facilities that tended to be crowded was the most commonly described way to eliminate this kind of crowding stress, although some respondents did then resent the additional constraint this placed on their activities.

Although patterns of crowding stress typical of different kinds of settings did appear, there was also some overlap in descriptions of crowding stress. The more common reasons for why crowding was stressful were given across many different settings. Some reasons also were given about equally in all settings. Table 18.1 lists these reasons and the frequency of mention for each one. There are also some general ways in which respondents' reports of coping with crowding stress differed from those concerning other stresses, such as noise, crime, and so on. People were more likely to avoid crowding settings and less likely to report active coping strategies. Interestingly, respondents were more likely to state that there was nothing they could do about crowding stress than to say this about all other stresses combined.

The findings of this study indicate that (1) city dwellers often experience crowding as stressful; (2) large numbers of people are most often associated with

TABLE 18.1
Reasons for Crowding Stress Reported by
New York City Respondents

	Frequency	Percent
Feeling blocked or delayed	89	.21
Experiencing extra demand	79	.19
Not liking to be pushed and shoved	59	.14
Being irritated by unpleasant strangers	40	.09
Being too close to others	36	.08
Disliking the physical environment	30	.07
Feeling alienated or alone	28	.07
Fear of physical harm	26	.06
Not liking own reactions	16	.04
Feelings of spatial confinement	15	.03
Needing to be alone	5	.01

stressful high-density situations; (3) people are sometimes aware of cognitive overload as an aspect of crowding stress, especially when sheer number of people is a salient component of their experience. Furthermore, the settings my colleagues and I have employed in our studies are ones in which crowding stress frequently occurs. In these ways, then, the hypothesis and studies presented in the earlier part of this chapter appear to be of relevance to people's everyday experiences of crowding.

Interference and behavioral constraint are clearly part of most of the respondents' perceptions of why crowding is stressful. Even though there are some signs that they also experience cognitive overload, this is not frequently named as a cause of crowding stress. This in itself does not necessarily mean that it is not. As Nisbett and Wilson (1977) have persuasively argued, cognitive processes are often not veridically available to introspection. But it does raise some questions about where cognitive overload fits in the total pattern of people's experiences of high-density environments.

Two points emerge from this study that are relevant to the effect of time spent in a setting. First of all, most of the settings described as sites of crowding stress were ones people did not stay in for long periods of time. This may mean that the label "crowding" for a stressor is seen as most appropriate for public settings occupied by strangers, at least in New York City. Second, the sample was composed of half newcomers to the city, who came from smaller towns and had lived in New York an average of 1.8 years, and half long-time residents, who had lived in the city an average of 16.8 years. Yet, the two groups mentioned equal numbers of crowding-stress experiences. There were no differences in the places they felt stress, the reasons they gave for crowding stress, nor their coping responses.

The fact that the settings for crowding stress were chiefly secondary settings in Stokols' typology may have made it easier for respondents to identify crowding as the cause of the stress. Quite possibly, stresses arising from high densities in more primary settings are attributed to characteristics of the people occupying it or of the self. I do not mean to imply that primary settings would not be rated as more crowded when the density is higher, but rather that associated stress may be seen as an inter- or intrapersonal problem. Additionally, the fact that these settings are not very central to people's lives and that they are occupied by strangers may explain the lack of adaptation of either the people or the setting over time. It is likely that behavioral constraint and cognitive capacity limits enter into the effects of high-density primary environments in different and more interactive ways. Thus, density itself may become less of an effective setting variable and other qualities such as the social composition of the group, resources, alternative spaces, personal characteristics, and so on, may become more salient.

One methodological issue this raises concerns the stricture that random assignment of subjects to conditions is necessary in order to test for the effects of a variable alone, like density and its components. This approach regards randomization as a transparent matrix that will reveal the pure effects of an environmental condition. Yet, random assignment itself sets up certain relationships between the occupants of a setting (they have not chosen to be together) and of the occupants to the managers of the setting (the latter have the power to determine what setting the occupants will be in). Therefore, an accurate interpretation of effects of density obtained in these conditions might be that they are the joint effects of random assignment and of density, and therefore generalizable only to similarly unchosen and uncontrollable settings. In thinking about these issues, I have tentatively concluded that in order to understand cognitive and social behavior in the context of the spatial, temporal, cultural, and historical context in which they exist, we will have to be more modest about the degree of certainty we expect to attain.

DENSITY AS A SYSTEMIC VARIABLE

As Altman (1978) has suggested, this recognition leads to the postulation of a circular or systemic model in which all variables may at some time or another serve as causal agents of other variables. Truly thinking through the implications of this analysis would, I believe, take us in the direction of a more cultural, ecological, and historical model of the consequences of high densities. For example, Dennis McCarthy and I have been doing research with families living in public housing who have been randomly assigned to high- or low-rise buildings (McCarthy, 1978; McCarthy & Saegert, 1979). One could hardly argue that building size was caused by the greater perceived crowding and the lesser sense of safety, control, privacy, and social support reported by high-rise building residents. Yet, at an individual level, future choices about where to live are likely to be affected, especially because our data indicate that many inhabitants of the high-rises would prefer to live in low-rises; very few low-rise residents prefer high-rises. On a larger cultural and historical scale, the reporting of research findings like these may enter into decisions about buildings in the future. They may also affect people's evaluations of their own experiences in the buildings they live in. They may lead to management policies that attempt to increase safety, personal control, and social support through the selection of compatible individuals or through social interventions. Over time, the reporting of such research by the communications media may change the attributions people make about their neighbors in public housing from personal attributions to environmental attributions.

Yet, I would not go so far as to suggest that all effects of high density are no more than historical moments. Instead, I suggest that we try to identify tolerances of particular ecological configurations for various activities by human beings and tolerances of various individual and group processes for various environmental configurations. This perspective allows me to assert the validity of some of my hypotheses concerning the consequences of high-density experiences for the past several years and to put them in their place vis-a-vis other theoretical orientations. It also points toward types of investigations that venture further away from the conventions of psychological research, and that require different expectations about what kind of knowledge is to be gained. By focusing on behavioral and cognitive constraints associated with density as explanations of negative effects *and* by choosing settings and person–environment transactions that bring these maximally into play, my colleagues and I have been able to demonstrate certain regularities. We have been slower in developing theoretical explanations about the role of density in less pressing and more adaptable settings. Before going on to consider what kind of research might be able to accomplish this goal, I would like to examine the range of explanatory power of some of the other theoretical formulations concerning the effects of density and to identify the cognitive aspects of these approaches. By using the three loci described previously, I hope to identify significant problems in the person-in-environment transaction that have not been fully studied.

CROWDING THEORIES AND COGNITIVE COMPONENTS

Naturally, it is necessary to approach an attempt to summarize the theoretical perspectives on crowding with a certain amount of humility, because brief paraphrasing always runs some risk of misinterpretation and because there is no definitely finite list of such theories. Yet, I believe that such an effort will highlight some interesting questions that are not being asked.

The first assumption made by social and environmental psychologists about crowding was that it was a stressor, that its effects were mediated by arousal and that they were mainly negative (cf. Altman, 1978; Freedman, 1975; Griffitt & Veitch, 1971). In this framework, cognitive variables were seen as dependent on the mediation of arousal. This turned out to be an oversimplified, underexplicated, and difficult to prove approach (cf. Freedman, 1975; Lawrence, 1974). Evans (1978) reviews both the fairly consistent evidence that subjects in high-density environments show elevated signs of physiological arousal and the much less consistent evidence that such arousal *leads* to decrements in complex, and increments in simple, task performance. He concludes that at present there is no clear way to differentiate the arousal model of the effects of crowding from Cohen's (1978) proposed model, which hypothesizes that environmental stresses are environmental conditions that place a high load on information-processing capacities. Thus, complex tasks, in themselves higher information-processing loads, would show decrements whereas simple ones would not, because cognitive capacity would not have been exceeded. In this paradigm, arousal is seen as a by-product of information overload. The previously mentioned path analysis of my data suggests that perhaps two processes rather than one are involved, a direct arousal-inducing component of high densities and an information-overload component. Second, research has demonstrated, and it seems intuitively obvious, that high densities themselves can make some tasks more difficult without the mediation of arousal (cf. Heller et al., 1977). Third, it is not clear why increased arousal should lead to negative affect or negative interpersonal relationships. Fourth, much evidence suggests that pathological stress reactions are cognitively mediated (cf. Averill, 1973; Langer & Rodin, 1977).

Worchel and Teddlie's (1976) hypothesis that proximity, not density, leads to increased arousal, which then may be labeled as crowding, incorporates a number of significant cognitive variables. They acknowledge Stokols' (1972a) point that crowding is a label that may or may not be applied to a high-density situation and incorporate an approach to understanding crowding stress that derives from Schacter & Singer's (1962) two-factor theory of emotion. Worchel (1978) states the hypothesis that task decrements occur only when subjects attribute their arousal to crowding. In his review chapter, Worchel (1978) provides reasonable support for the significance of proximity in inducing arousal. The reasoning behind attribution-related predictions and evidence obtained is less clear, particularly in the context of other researchers' findings, which Worchel does not discuss. For example, Worchel reports better performance on a cognitive task when subjects are induced to notice their arousal and to attribute it to white noise than when subjects are told there would be white noise that would be relaxing or when they are given no explanation. White noise, arousal-attribution subjects were also more positive to other group members. All of these effects were obtained only when subjects were in close proximity to others; in the far personal-space conditions, attributional condition made little difference. This study is interesting enough in itself but raises a host of questions about what components of attributions are critical in mediating crowding stress. Whereas Worchel and his colleagues (1978) found that telling subjects that an imaginary component of the environment would be arousing made them report more arousal, as well as perform better, Langer and Saegert (1977) did not find this magnification when they told subjects to expect to experience crowding. Langer and Saegert, in fact, found lowered perceptions of crowding even in high-density situations. They also found that subjects forewarned that the store might become crowded and that crowding might be arousing and anxiety provoking performed better on a complex cognitive task and rated the experience as more positive. Thus, I am led to the question of the validity of Worchel's two-factor theory. Indeed, attributions seem to play a part in the experience of crowding stress, but it is not evident that attributing one's arousal to crowding is the significant mediator between crowding and task effects. Further, the veridicality of the suggested attribution needs to be examined and the course of coping responses or behavioral schema it initiates needs to be explored. For example, Baum et al. found that subjects in a field setting led to expect positive effects of crowding became more hostile than subjects led to expect difficulty as a result of crowding. Finally, the path analysis previously described casts doubt on the mediating role of arousal, and thereby also on the arousal-attribution mediation of task performance, at least in some cases.

Worchel's theory and the studies of the other researchers previously reported largely ignore the development of attributions in nonexperimental contexts. Worchel (1978; Worchel & Teddlie, 1976) does suggest that the presence of certain stimuli such as pictures or windows would distract people from the social aspects of the setting and thus reduce crowding attributions. However, he and Teddlie did not directly measure arousal separately from indicators of crowding stress. Therefore, it is possible that the distractor also reduced experienced arousal, rather than simply leading to nonsocial attributions. In settings less controlled by the experimenter, people may consciously seek distractors to reduce stress, but this behavior may have consequences for the performance of other activities by taking their attention away from the social environment (Cohen, 1978; Cohen & Lezak, 1977; Saegert, 1978). Distracted people may become socially insensitive, thus inducing social attributions in those who collide with them. It appears that attributions can influence the course of cognition, behavior, and emotional responses in a high-density setting, What is lacking, though, is a theory of the ecology of attributional salience.

Stokols' theory (1972a, 1972b, 1978) bears some similarity to Worchel's in that it also postulates that crowding stress will not occur unless the label crowding is made salient by the situation. His approach, however, plays greater attention to the nature of the setting and the nature of the interactions within the setting that lead first to attributions of crowding and then to attributions of blame for interference experienced in the setting. He (Stokols, 1978) states that:

(1) the experience of crowding involves the perception of insufficient control over the environment; (2) crowding evokes the desire to augment the physical or psychological space as a means of gaining control over the environment and avoiding actual or anticipated interferences; and (3) feelings of crowding will be most intense, persistent and difficult to resolve when the failure to augment space maximizes security threats [p. 232].

Stokols' position focuses on the transactions of individuals in settings, rather than explicating either capacities of the individual that are influenced by high-density environments or physical qualities of the setting that impinge on individual responses and activities. Thus, even though Stokols provides the most ecologically sensitive analysis of crowding experiences, a more detailed model of the processes relating the four categories of individual-in-setting transactions needs to be developed.

Several other theories of crowding experiences share with Stokols an emphasis on control as the critical issue, and are all informed by the extensive social–psychological research on this topic. Baron and Rodin (1978) attempt to bring all of the variables I listed earlier into their account of the processes by which individuals either establish control in a high-density environment, or fail to do so. Fig. 18.1, taken from their chapter on crowding and control, specifies the relationship phases they predict over time among salient environmental variables, which are not described in detail, and various individual and transactional processes, which they develop to a very useful degree. They thus elaborate the earlier hypothesis of Proshansky et al. (1976) that identified control as the critical problem raised by the presence of large numbers of people in restricted spaces. Altman's boundary-regulation theory of crowding and privacy is seen as describing social transactions and ways of using space that allow an individual to deal with certain difficulties in maintaining control occasioned by high-density settings. Rodin and Baum (1978) extend this analysis of control-related problems experienced in high-density settings to explain the emergence of a "learned helplessness" in the residents of chronically uncontrollable settings. Drawing on the work of Baum and Valins (1977) and Baum's and his colleague's work described in this volume (Chapter 24), they begin to specify architectural, social, and temporal components of the environment that lead to generalized expectations of noncontingency between their own behavior and environmental responses. Thus, they start to spell out a theory of how experiences in one setting shape expectations and responses in other settings.

I think that this selective review of theories and research on crowding demonstrates the way in which environmental psychologists have gone about understanding the role of cognitive limitations in crowding experiences and have also placed them in the context of environmental qualities and individual-in-setting transactions. We have, however, just begun to address the question of how particular person–environment ensembles are formed by effective and responsive components of both the environment and the person. At this point, very little, if any work on the development over time of cultural, environmental, and individual transactions has been undertaken. Another kind of research is also missing from our understanding of crowding experiences. This is a close investigation of how crowding works within various settings and an examination of the ecology of crowding itself.

AN ECOLOGY OF CROWDING EXPERIENCES

The need for descriptive research has been consistently pointed out by environmental psychologists who emphasize the environmental part of that appellation (Winkel, 1977). The aim of such work is not only phenomenological richness, but also an understanding of the interconnectedness and embeddedness of the texture of the environment.

Density and its components are but physical dimensions of settings, as crowding is but one aspect of psychological experiences in them. Not only would we

INSTIGATION PHASE FOR
CROWDING REACTIONS TO DENSITY

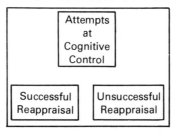

ANTICIPATORY COPING PHASE

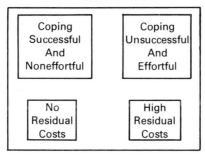

CORRECTIVE COPING

Attempts to Reduce
Demandingness
And/Or Increase
Response Capability

POSTENCOUNTER PHASE

Coping Successful And Noneffortful	Coping Unsuccessful And Effortful
No Residual Costs	High Residual Costs

FIG. 18.1 Sequential–temporal processes in extreme crowding stress. The phases of instigation and coping depicted represent a highly stressful sequence of events for which coping is ineffective at each successive phase. In order to simplify the visual layout of this "flow chart," feedback loops that would allow for "stop" or "exit" messages are omitted.

expect these variables to have differential significance in different settings, but it seems likely that the nature of the setting will organize the way density levels are manifest and how they become psychologically significant. My work with Roberts, described earlier (Roberts & Saegert, 1978), begins to get at these issues by identifying, through self report, setting specific patterns of experiencing crowding stress and coping with it. Barker and his colleagues (cf. Barker, 1960; Barker & Gump, 1964; Wicker, 1968, 1969) have studied the impact of population size in different behavior settings and from that developed the concept of over- and undermanning. Looking at the number of activity roles characteristic of standing patterns of behavior in various settings, they have shown how individuals participate less frequently in these activities when settings have more occupants. Elsewhere, I have sketchily discussed the kinds of demands that the number of occupants and their proximity place on social systems, basing my analysis on the necessity that systems respect the cognitive and behavioral limits of individuals in such circumstances (Saegert, 1978). Yet, none of these efforts really probe the qualities of individual-in-setting transactions that transform the impact of density by setting characteristics and meanings. Baum and his colleagues have revealed two of these qualities in residential environments: limited-occupancy architectural subunits and the presence or absence of existing friendships. Both were found to prevent the development of learned helplessness in high-density dormitory settings. The ameliorating effect of friendship is of particular theoretical interest. Although we could speculate that one has more control over transactions in a setting filled with friends, it is also possible that control is perceived as less necessary because of a general trust in the beneficence of the setting. Thus, in such settings, the emphasis on individual cognitive and behavioral limitations and on problems of control and regulation becomes misplaced.

In closing, I would like to suggest two kinds of research that might be undertaken that would, I think, further our understanding of crowding experiences, and of person-in-setting transactions generally. The first would be to attempt to develop a sort of grounded theory, in the manner of Glaser and Strauss (1967), of the ecology of crowding experiences. This would involve constructing a typology of crowding experiences and settings in which they occur. Winkel (1977) has suggested ways of employing quantitative analysis that are congruent with the intent of the qualitative methods employed by Glaser and Strauss. This ecology of crowding experiences might also involve descriptions and theoretical formulations concerning the distribution of crowded environments in space and time and their differential frequency for various populations. The second kind of research that would be of interest at this time focuses on density as part of a more general understanding of setting dynamics. Thus, for example, we might look at variations in household density as one variable relevant to an understanding of housing environments.

Perhaps my conclusions about desirable directions for crowding research come from a remark made recently in one of my classes—that environmental cognition should be about the way environments think. In an effort to understand the role of cognitive limits in crowding experiences, I suggest we examine these not only from the perspective of the person in the setting, but from the point of view of the setting as well.

REFERENCES

Aiello, J., Epstein, Y., & Karlin, R. The effects of crowding on electrodermal activity. *Sociological Symposium.* 1975, *4,* 43–58.

Altman, I. Crowding: Historical and contemporary trends in crowding research. In A. Baum & Y. Epstein (Eds.), *Human responses to crowding.* Hillsdale, N.J.: Lawrence Erlbaum Associates, 1978.

Anderson, T. R., & Warkov, S. Organizational size and functional complexity. *American Sociological Review,* 1961.

Averill, J. R. Personal control over aversive stimuli and its relationship to stress. *Psychological Bulletin,* 1973, *80,* 286–303.

Barker, R. G. Ecology and Motivation. In M. R. Jones, (Ed.) *Nebraska symposium on motivation.* Lincoln: University of Nebraska Press, 1960.

Barker, R. G., & Gump, R. *Big school, small school.* Stanford, Calif., California University Press, 1964.

Baron, R., & Rodin, S. Personal control and crowding stress: Processes mediating the impact of spatial and social density. In A. Baum, & Y. Epstein, (Ed.). *Human responses to crowding.* Hillsdale, N.J.: Lawrence Erlbaum Associates, 1978.

Baum, A., & Koman, S. Differential response to anticipated crowding: Psychological effects of social and spatial density. *Journal of Personality and Social Psychology,* 1976, *34,* 526–536.

Baum, A., & Valins, S. *Architecture and social behavior: Psychological studies of social density.* Hillsdale, N.J.: Lawrence Erlbaum Associates, 1977.

Blau, P. M. Interdependence and hierarchy in organizations. *Social Science Research,* 1972, *1,* 1–24.

Cohen, S. Environmental load and the allocation of attention. In A. Baum, J. E. Singer, & S. Valins (Eds.), *Advances in environmental psychology,* (Vol. 1), Hillsdale, N.J.: Lawrence Erlbaum Associates, 1978.

Cohen, S., & Lezak, A. Noise and inattentiveness to social cues. *Environment and Behavior,* 1977, *9,* 559–572.

Desor, J. A. Toward a psychological theory of crowding. *Journal of Personality and Social Psychology.* 1972, *21,* 79–83.

Durkheim, E. *The Division of Labor in Society.* New York: Macmillan, 1933.

Evans, G. Human spatial behavior: The arousal model. In A. Baum & Y. Epstein (Eds.), *Human Responses to Crowding.* Hillsdale, N.J.: Lawrence Erlbaum Associates, 1978.

Fischer, C. S. *The Urban Experience.* New York: Harcourt, Brace, Javonovich, 1976.

Freedman, J. L. *Crowding and Behavior.* San Francisco: Freeman, 1975.

Freedman, J., Klevansky, S., & Ehrlich, D. The effects of crowding on human task performance. *Journal of Applied Social Psychology,* 1971, *1,* 7–25.

Glaser, B. G. & Strauss, A. L. *The Discovery of Grounded Theory: Strategies for qualitative research.* Chicago: Aldine, 1967.

Griffitt, N., & Veitch, R. Hot and crowded: Influences of population density and temperature on interpersonal affective behavior. *Journal of Personality and Social Psychology,* 1971, *17,* 92–98.

Hall, R. H., Hass, J. E., & Johnson, N. J. Organizational size, complexity and formalization. *American Sociological Review,* 1967, *32,* 903–912.

Hawley, A. H., Boland, W., & Boland, M. Polulation size and administration in institutions of higher education. *American Sociological Review.* 1965, *30,* 252–254.

Heller, J., Groff, B., & Solomon, S. Toward an understanding of crowding: The role of physical interaction. *Journal of Personality and Social Psychology.* 1977, *35,* 183-190.

Klein, K., & Harris, B. Disruptive effects of disconfirmed expectancies about crowding. *Journal of Personality and Social Psychology.* 1979, *37,* 769-777.

Langer, E., & Rodin, J. The effects of choice and enhanced personal responsibility: A field experiment in an institutional setting. *Journal of Personality and Social Psychology.* 1977, *35,* 897-902.

Langer, E., & Saegert, S. Crowding and cognitive control. *Journal of Personality and Social Psychology.* 1977, *35,* 175-182.

Lawrence, J. E. Science and sentiment: Overview of research on crowding and human behavior. *Psychological Bulletin.* 1974, *81*(10), 712-721.

LeBon, G. *The Crowd: A study of the popular mind.* New York: Ballatine, 1965. (Originally published, 1895.)

Loo, C. Issues in crowding research: Vulnerable participants, assessing perceptions and developmental differences. *Journal of Population,* in press.

Love, K. D., & Saegert, S. *Crowding and Cognitive Limit: Capacity or Strategy?* Paper presented at the annual convention of the American Psychological Association, Toronto, Canada, September 1978.

McCarthy, D. *The Effects of Tenant Population Size on Low-Income Public Housing Residents.* Unpublished doctoral dissertation, City University of New York, 1978.

McCarthy, D., & Saegert, S. Residential density, social overload and social withdrawal. In A. Aiello & A. Baum (Eds.), *Crowding in Residential Environments.* New York: Plenum, 1979.

Milgram, S. The experience of living in cities. *Science,* 1970, *167,* 1461-1468.

Nisbett, R. E., & Wilson, T. D. Telling more than we know: Verbal reports on mental processes. *Psychological Review,* 1977, *84,* 231-259.

Paulus, P. B., Annis, A. B., Seta, J. J., Schkade, J. K., & Matthews, R. W. Crowding does affect task performance. *Journal of Personality and Social Psychology.* 1976, *34,* 248-253.

Paulus, P. B., McCain, G., & Cox, V. C. Death rates, psychiatric commitments, blood pressure and perceived crowding as a function of institutional crowding. *Environmental Psychology and Nonverbal Behavior.* 1978, *3*(2), 107-116.

Proshansky, H., Ittelson, W. H., and Rivlin, L. Freedom of choice and behavior in a physical setting. In Proshansky, H., Ittelson, W. H. and Rivlin, L. (Eds.), *Environmental psychology.* New York: Holt, Rinehart & Winston, 1976.

Raphael, E. E. The Anderson-Warkov hypothesis in local unions: A comparative study. *American Sociological Review.* 1967, *32,* 768-776.

Rapoport, A. Toward a redefinition of density. In S. Saegert, (Ed.) *Crowding in real environments.* Beverly Hills, California: Sage Publications, 1975.

Roberts, C., & Saegert, S. *Phenomenological reports of crowding stress and coping strategies.* Unpublished manuscript, City University of New York, 1978.

Rodin, J., & Baum, A. Crowding and helplessness: Potential consequences of density and loss of control. In A Baum & Epstein (Eds.) *Human responses to crowding.* Hillsdale, N.J. Lawrence Erlbaum Associates, 1978.

Saegert, S. The effects of spatial and social density on arousal, mood, and social orientation. Doctoral dissertation, University of Michigan, Ann Arbor, 1974.

Saegert, S. Crowding: Cognitive overload and behavioral constraint. In W. Preiser (Ed.), *Environmental design research* (Vol. 2). Stroudsberg, PA: Dowden, Hutchinson & Ross, 1973.

Saegert, S. Stress inducing and stress reducing qualities of environments. In H. Proshansky, W. Ittelson, & L. Rivlin (Eds.) *Environmental psychology.* New York: Holt, Rinehart & Winston, 1975.

Seagert, S. High-density environments: Their personal and social consequences. In A. Baum & Y. Epstein (Eds.), *Human responses to crowding.* Hillsdale, N.J. Lawrence Erlbaum Associates, 1978.

Saegert. S., & Love, K. *Differential responses to social and spatial density: Disassociation of arousal and task performance.* Unpublished manuscript, City University of New York, 1979.

Saegert, S., Mackintosh, E., & West, S. Two studies of crowding in urban public spaces. In S. Saegert (Ed.), *Crowding in real environments.* Beverly Hills, California: Sage Publications, 1975.

Schacter, S., & Singer, J. Cognitive, social and physiological determinants of emotional state. *Psychological Review,* 1962, *69,* 379–399.

Scholpler, J., & Stockdale, J. An interference analysis of crowding. *Environmental Psychology and Nonverbal Behavior.* 1977, *1,* 81–88.

Simmel, G. The metropolis and mental life. In P. K. Hatt & A. J. Ross, Jr. (Eds.) *Cities and society.* New York: Free Press, 1957, (Originally published, 1905.)

Stokols, D. On the distinction between density and crowding: Some implications for future research. *Psychological Review.* 1972, *79,* 275–277.(a)

Stokols, D. A social-psychological model of human crowding phenomena. *Journal of American Institute of Planners.* 1972, *38,* 72–84.(b)

Stokols, D. The experience of crowding in primary and secondary environments. *Environment and Behavior.* 1976, *8,* 49–86.

Stokols, D. A typology of crowding experiences. In A. Baum & Y. Epstein (Eds.) *Human responses to crowding.* Hillsdale, N.J.: Lawrence Erlbaum Associates, 1978.

Thomas, E. J. & Fink. C. F. Effects of group size. *Psychological Bulletin,* 1963, *60,* 371–384.

Wener, R. E. & Kaminoff, R. D. *Environmental clarity and perceived crowding.* Proceedings of the 10th annual conference of the Environmental Design Research Association, Buffalo, New York: June 1979.

Wicker, A. Undermanning, performances and students' subjective experience in behavior settings of large and small high schools. *Journal of Personality and Social Psychology.* 1968, *10,* 255–261.

Wicker, A. Size of church membership and members' support of church behavior settings. *Journal of Personality and Social Psychology.* 1969, *13,* 278–288.

Winkel, G. H. The role of ecological validity in environmental research, *Proceedings of the Wisconsin Conference of Behavior-Environment Research Methods.* University of Wisconsin–Madison, October 1977.

Wolfe, M. Room size, group size and density: Behavior patterns in a children's psychiatric facility. *Environment and Behavior.* 1975, *2,* 199–224.

Worchel, S. The experience of crowding: An attributional analysis. In A. Baum & Y. Epstein (Eds.). *Human responses to crowding.* Hillsdale, N.J.: Lawrence Erlbaum Associates, 1978, 327–351.

Worchel, S., & Teddlie, C. Factors affecting the experience of crowding: A two factor theory. *Journal of Personality and Social Psychology.* 1976, *34,* 30–40.

Zimbardo, P. G. The human choice: Individuation, reason and order or deindividuation, impulse and chaos. *Nebraska Symposium on Motivation.* Lincoln: University of Nebraska Press, 1969.

19

A Cognitive Social Learning Approach to the Crossroads of Cognition, Social Behavior, and the Environment

Abraham Wandersman
University of South Carolina

Paul Florin
Peabody College

A major issue in psychology is the investigation of the influences on behavior; predicting behavior has been considered very important. Psychologists have traditionally tended to focus on the contributions made *either* by internal characteristics of the organism (e.g., traits, IQ) or by environmental and treatment influences on behavior. Although over the years advances were made within both internal and external orientations, there was little exchange between orientations. This myopia was noticed many years ago. Newcomb (1951) criticized two social psychologies, which exclusively emphasized either the organism or the environment, for ignoring each other. A few years later, Cronbach (1957, 1975) pointed out that the internal–external schism ran so deep that two distinct disciplines could be identified within scientific psychology. According to Cronbach (1957): "Correlational psychology studies only variance among organisms; experimental psychology studies only variance among treatments [p. 681]." Newcomb and Cronbach, among others, stress the need to develop a psychology that seriously addresses the complexities of studying the "organism-in-situation." Since the 1950's, several fields of psychology have devoted a great deal of energy to such questions as: Which is more important, the person or the situation? Such questions have more recently led to a concern with the interactions between the organism and the environment. The crucial questions now seem to involve: How do the organism and environment influence each other and interact to produce behavior? This question can easily be translated into the central theme of this book—what is the interface between cognition, social behavior, and the environment?

The major purpose of this chapter is to describe a field study that uses a cognitive social learning approach to explore the person in the situation. First, for background purposes, we briefly review the internal–external issue as illustrated by the "person–situation" controversy in personality psychology. We then highlight some of the features of the emerging interactionist position and the key role of cognition in understanding interaction. Next, we discuss a cognitive social learning approach to interactional psychology that can provide an integration of cognitive, social, and environmental variables and use empirical results to illustrate the potential of such an approach.

THE PERSON–SITUATION CONTROVERSY—PERSONALITY PSYCHOLOGY AS AN EXAMPLE

The appearance of *Personality Assessment* by Walter Mischel in 1968 sparked the "person–situation" controversy in personality psychology. Evidence that pointed to a lack of cross-situational consistency challenged the trait concept as a stable personality disposition (Lay, 1977). Empirical results in the 1960's from both the variance components research strategy and the correlational research strategy generally failed to find much consistency (Endler & Edwards, 1978; Mischel, 1968).

The variance components research strategy argued that because more variance in behavior could be explained by person-by-situation interactions than by person or situation variables alone, both strict trait and situationist positions were called into question and the interactionist position was correct (Bowers, 1973; Ekehammar, 1974, Endler & Magnusson, 1976). However, Epstein (1977), Golding (1975), Mischel (1973), Olweus (1977), and Overton and Reese (1973) suggest that the variance components approach is inadequate for addressing consistency issues because it supplies no definitive affirmation of the interactionist position, fails to address how persons and situations interact, and provides little predictive power.

Interactional Psychology

Pervin and Lewis (1978b) indicate that an "interactionist" position is becoming popular in such fields of psychology as personality, social psychology, developmental psychology, genetic psychology, educational psychology, and clinical psychology.

The interactional perspective acknowledges the complex interactions that exist between the organism and environment in producing and sustaining behavior. It recognizes that an exclusive emphasis on either internal or external factors can provide only a one-dimensional and often distorted view of the processes that generate behavior. Magnusson and Endler (1977) have summarized the basic elements in the interactional model as follows:

1. Actual behavior is a function of a continuous process of multidirectional interaction or feedback between the individual and the situations he or she encounters.

2. The individual is an intentional, active agent in this interaction process.

3. On the person side of the interaction, cognitive and motivational factors are essential determinants of behavior.

4. On the situation side, the psychological meaning of situations for the individual is the important determining factor [p. 4].

But even though the interactionist position seems an easy one to adopt (it is taking on the quality of a zeitgeist in some areas [Ekehammar, 1974]), much work remains to be done. For this perspective to provide meaningful contributions, several conceptual and methodological questions need to be answered (Pervin & Lewis, 1978b). What exactly do we mean when we use the term interaction? What is the nature of the processes by which the person and the situation interact? What are the most appropriate units to be employed in interactional research? These issues are discussed in the following sections.

Definitions of Interaction

Several authors (Magnusson & Endler, 1977; Olweus, 1977; Overton & Reese, 1973; Pervin & Lewis, 1978a) have sought to identify various definitions of the term interaction. Olweus (1977) describes four uses of the term:

1. As used in a general sense as the equivalent of combine or connect. "Here it is a question of unidirectional interaction, namely how two or more independent variables (person and situation variables) are combined or connected in their relationship to a dependent variable [p. 225]."

2. As used "to designate the interdependency between the person and his environment, perhaps in particular as regards his perception or cognitive construction of the situation. Here the inseparability of the individual–environment system is emphasized [p. 225]."

3. As used to represent "reciprocal action." "Here the individual and the environment are seen as mutually influencing one another and the emphasis is often on processes over time: Environmental events affect the person's responses, which in turn affect the environment, which again influences the person's responses, etc. [p. 225]."

4. As used in the conventional manner in analysis of variance components technique, illustrated by such statements from Endler and Hunt (1966) as "the interaction of the subjects with situations contributes more of the variance than does either by itself [p. 341]."

Some authors (Endler & Edwards, 1978) suggest that the potential of statistical (also called mechanistic) interaction approaches have not yet been fully explored. They argue that person-by-treatment experimental designs, when based on sound theories that enable one to predict person-by-situation interaction, can contribute to a better understanding of the interaction process. Although such work (e.g., Berkowitz, 1977; Fiedler, 1977; Spielberger, 1977) continues to provide contributions, the fact that it rests on mechanistic approaches (Overton & Reese, 1973) is uncomfortable to a truly interactionist approach. According to Magnusson and Endler (1977): "The main future interest in interactional psychology should be in dynamic interactions, and our understanding of these interactions is not illuminated by the traditional approaches [p. 25]." Magnusson and Endler conclude that the development of new research methods appropriate for investigating dynamic interactions is one of the most urgent needs in interactional psychology.

A COGNITIVE SOCIAL LEARNING APPROACH TO THE "HOW" OF INTERACTION

As the "person–situation" controversy has developed, much of the emphasis has shifted away from questions concerning whether persons or situations are more important determinants of behavior and onto questions that address "how" persons and situations interact (Magnusson & Endler, 1977; Olweus, 1977; Pervin, 1978). Our interest is in the role of cognitive processes as mediating variables in the person–situation interaction. Cognition is important in an interactionist framework because of its role in the construction of what is experienced as reality. It is viewed as an active process and not simply as a passive registering of experiences occurring "out there." Cognitive processes form the crucible in which psychological conditions and environment stimuli produce behavior. They represent the mechanisms whereby an individual constructs and organizes his or her psychological reality in relation to the world. Several authors seeking to further our understanding of the interactional process have suggested cognitive systems as important to consider in personality research (Argyle, 1977; Geis, 1978; Golding, 1978; Peterson, 1977; Reid, 1977; Takala, 1977). One of the most interesting approaches was developed by Walter Mischel (1973, 1976, 1977).

Mischel argues that a full understanding of complex human behaviors must go beyond the study of situational conditions and individual differences to consider the nature of person-by-situation interactions. Thus, although Mischel's work has questioned the utility of the traditional trait approach, he also warns against an overemphasis on classifying environments. Mischel's conceptualization of the mechanism of interaction begins with the recognition that the environment contains a potential flood of stimuli with which the individual must deal. In order to operate efficiently and effectively in the environment, the individual must avoid an overwhelming overload and perceive, process, select, and interpret certain stimuli. For Mischel (1973), these filtering mechanisms are best thought of as cognitive processes, which are the "psychological products within the individual of cognitive development and social learning experiences [p. 265]." The attributes of individuals, according to this formulation, could be linked to these psychological processes rather than traits.

Mischel developed five "cognitive social learning person variables" based on constructs from the areas of cognition and social learning. He stressed that these person variables were *not* intended to be the equivalent of traits; they are not expected to predict accurately broad, cross-situational behavioral differences between persons. "But [according to Mischel, 1977] these variables should suggest useful ways of conceptualizing and studying specifically how the qualities of the person influence the impact of stimuli (environments, situations, treatments) and how each person generates distinctive complex behavior patterns in interaction with the conditions of his or her life [p. 341]." The variables that Mischel identified can be briefly described as follows (for a more detailed description, see Mischel, 1973):

1. *Construction competencies.* This refers to the individual's cognitive and behavioral capabilities, which allow for the successful execution of a particular behavior.

2. *Encoding strategies.* This variable refers to the way the environment or situation is perceived, coded, and categorized by each person. Through selective attention, interpretation, and categorization, the person influences the impact that stimuli exert on his or her behavior.

3. *Expectancies.* This variable deals with the perceived consequences of different behavioral possibilities in the situation. In a given situation, the person selects the response expected to most likely lead to a subjectively valuable outcome.

4. *Subjective stimulus value.* These are the values that the person assigns to expected outcomes. Two persons may have similar expectancies, yet respond differently to a situation because the outcomes have different values for them.

5. *Self-regulatory systems and plans.* This variable reflects the person's regulation of his or her own behavior by self-imposed standards. In addition to externally administered consequences for action, the individual sets personal performance goals and reacts with self-criticism or self-satisfaction, depending on how well behavior corresponds to these criteria.

The number of the variables reflects the important point that behavior is determined by many variables—multiple causation is the rule rather than the exception. Individual differences in behavior within the same situation might be the result of differences on any one variable or combination of variables. A focus on any one particular variable in studying behavior can lead to distortions of understanding and prediction.

Mischel also recognizes differences in the power of situations and the active role of the individual in selecting situations. He conceives of situations as strong or weak to the extent that they allow the idiosyncratic pattern of the psychological mechanisms to emerge. Conversely, the individual not only reacts to environmental stimuli, but often actively selects certain situations and modifies conditions through choices, cognitions, and actions.

An Appropriate Unit of Analysis For Interactional Psychology

In an interactional psychology that stresses the inseparability of person and situation in determining behavior, research approaches that measure each aspect separately are less than satisfying. We believe that the cognitive social learning person variables may have the potential to move us beyond this difficulty. When the cognitive social learning variables are operationalized in terms of a *particular* situation or *type* of situation, they enable us to see the individual's perception, construction, and organization of the situation that is simultaneously influenced by both idiosyncratic factors and the situation. Rather than attempting to identify objective situational factors, the psychologically significant situation for an individual is assessed. Many authors (for example, Endler & Edwards, 1978) agree that "the meaning (perception) that an individual ascribes to a situation seems to be the most influential situation factor affecting the person's behavior [p. 145]." Magnusson and Endler (1977) state that "in an interactional framework, the appropriate level of analysis for situation perception data is often in terms of individual data [p. 29]." Our unit of analysis, then, is an actual person-by-situation unit representing the inseparability of person and situation reflected in Olweus' third use of the term interaction, rather than a statistical interaction in which separate person and situational variables are used. The crucial need for such a unit of analysis has been stressed by several authors (Endler & Magnusson, 1976; Nuttin, 1977; Pervin, 1977).

Aside from some work by Olweus (1977) and experimental work reported by Nuttin (1977), there seem to be few empirical attempts to utilize a person-by-situation interaction variable. Guided by Mischel's advice that an important test for a personality construct is its ability to predict an individual's behavior in a specific situation, we conducted the research described in the next section. It represents the first attempt to operationalize the five cognitive social learning variables in one study and to study them in a field rather than a laboratory setting.

COGNITIVE SOCIAL LEARNING VARIABLES AND NEIGHBORHOOD PARTICIPATION

In the present study, we operationalized the five cognitive social learning variables in relationship to a particular type of situation—specifically, the block and neighborhood environment and participation in neighborhood-type organizations. First, we describe the setting and general purposes of the study and then we discuss some of the results, which use the cognitive social learning variables.

The Neighborhood Participation Project

The Waverly–Belmont neighborhood in Nashville, Tennessee, is typical of many transitional, urban, American neighborhoods. Following a post-World War II exodus to the suburbs by middle-class residents, the neighborhood experienced urban decay—decreasing property values, increasing crime rate, and a general deterioration of the physical environment. Recently, however, there has been a reverse migration to urban areas such as this one, which offer spacious older homes with the conveniences and amenities of an urban location. The neighborhood is racially integrated, with approximately 60% Black and 40% White residents. Individual blocks, however, tend to be more homogeneous, having primarily either White residents or Black residents of varying socioeconomic status. Houses are primarily one- and two-family dwellings with a few multiple (three- to four-family) units interspersed.

In 1975, Neighborhood Housing Services (NHS) began offering services to residents of the neighborhood. NHS is a nonprofit, cooperative organization of citizens, city officials, and local lending institutions designed to assist neighborhood residents in revitalizing their neighborhood. There are over 55 NHS programs operating in 46 cities across the United States. One of the ways that NHS stimulates citizen action is to assist in the development of block organizations. NHS serves as a catalyst for block organization by employing community organizers to work with people in the community, block by block. The block organization serves as a forum for block focus on issues of common concern such as crime, street repairs, street lighting, and so on.

Citizen participation is a popular concept that suffers from a dearth of conceptually based empirical research (Wandersman, 1979a, 1979b). The Neighborhood Participation Project is a prospective longitudinal study designed to add to our understanding of the process of participation and its effects by systematically studying participation in block organizations in the Waverly–Belmont neighborhood. The project is guided by a conceptual framework of participation in community organizations (Wandersman, 1981), and addresses several basic issues that are crucial to understanding participation in block organizations:

1. Which characteristics of individuals and blocks predict who will participate and the degree of involvement in block organizations?
2. What is the range and pattern of effects of different types of participation?
3. How do the processes of participation and their effects change longitudinally?

In this chapter, we are concerned with the first question—Which characteristics of an individual predict who will participate in block organizations? The results reported involve a comparison of traditional individual difference characteristics and cognitive social learning variables in predicting behavioral intention.

The subjects in the study were 384 adult (18 years or older) residents of 11 blocks in a neighborhood in Nashville, Tennessee. The residents of five blocks were predominately (over 90%) Black and of working-class socioeconomic status, and the residents of six blocks were predominately (over 85%) white and of middle-class socioeconomic status.

A 75-item interview questionnaire was administered to the subjects during the period May–September, 1977, *prior* to the organization of some of the blocks by Neighborhood Housing Services. Trained interviewers called on all the houses on the blocks. White interviewers conducted the interviews on the predominately White blocks and Black interviewers on the predominantly Black blocks. The interviewers attempted to interview all adults living in each household.

The items on the questionnaire supplied information concerning such components as demographic variables, satisfaction with the block, neighboring patterns, participation experience, and psychological variables. The items were designed to compose two different sets of independent variables. One set of independent variables, Set *A*, was comprised of more traditional individual difference variables and included: (1) demographic variables (race, sex, age, marital status, family size, education, present activity, and occupation); (2) variables derived from previous research and thought to be potentially related to a decision to participate (home ownership, length of residence, intended length of residence, and degree of social relationships on block) and psychological variables (locus of control and self esteem). The other set of independent variables, Set *B*, were items designed as an attempt to operationalize Mischel's cognitive social learning person variables. Table 19.1 outlines the initial operationalization of Set *B*.

Items specifically related to the focus of the block and participation were designed for each of Mischel's variables. A great deal of thought (and some ingenuity) was needed to operationalize these variables, because they were quite abstract and had never been operationalized for a field study before. Furthermore, we were constrained by the number of questions we could reasonably ask in an interview. We found that several issues had to be confronted in operationalizing the variables. The more basic issues included the following:

1. Objective-subjective—involved whether to use "objective" measures or "subjective" measures (e.g., actual leadership skills or a person's subjective rating of his or her skills). Generally it is difficult to obtain objective measures because of the time it takes to assess them—for example, assessing IQ or demonstrated leadership skills. In addition, the person's own assessment was viewed as easier to obtain and perhaps more influential in influencing behavior than an objective assessment. For example, a person's assessment of his or her own competencies might be more predictive of future participation in an organization than an investigator's behavioral assessment of the person's competencies.

TABLE 19.1
Variables Comprising Set A and Set B

Set A: Individual Difference (Demographic and Personality) Variables

---

1. Race
2. Sex
3. Home ownership
4. Length of residence
5. Intended length of residence
6. Family size
7. Age
8. Marital status
9. Present activity (working, student, retired, etc.)
10. Occupation (Hollingshead Index)
11. Education
12. Social relationships (recognition, social activities, mutual aid giving)
13. Internal locus of control
14. Chance locus of control
15. Powerful others locus of control
16. Self esteem

Set B: Operationalized Cognitive Social Learning Person Variables

---

1. Construction competencies
   — Past leadership experience and perceived personal efficacy in block or neighborhood organization
   — Level of participation in community organizations
   — Perceived competencies related to participation (leading groups, organizing others, ability to persuade others)
2. Encoding
   — General satisfaction with block
   — Satisfaction with specific block aspects
   — Perception of neighbors
   — Attribution of responsibility for working on block problems
   — Attribution of most likely party to undertake action to improve block (state, local government, individuals acting alone, people on block working together)
3. Expectancy
   — Outcome expectancy through group efforts, through individuals
   — Past experience in block or neighborhood organizations
   — Political efficacy
   — Political cynicism
4. Subjective stimulus value
   — Subjective importance of block (environment preference)
   — Subjective importance of sense of community on block
   — Subjective value of working with group of neighbors to improve block
   — Perception of block problems and their degree of severity
5. Self-regulatory system and plans
   — Sense of citizen duty

---

2. Specific–general—involved the degree of specificity of a measure. For example, previous participation experience can be measured in terms of participation in neighborhood organizations or in more general terms of participation in voluntary organizations—e.g., church, bridge club, P.T.A. Although measures that are too general may not predict very well, overly specific measures may have little conceptual utility and generality and also may not predict future behaviors well because a slight change in the situation may make an overly specific measure useless. Therefore, we tended to choose measures that ranged from being general to somewhat specific and occasionally very specific, concentrating on the middle ground.

3. Conceptual level—involved level of analysis investigated—e.g., individual, interpersonal, block, neighborhood, or societal. Because all of these levels were relevant in studying participation in block organizations, we had to decide which levels to focus on for each variable. For example, in exploring the role of expectancies and participation, expectancies about individual action, block action, or neighborhood action could be influential. The extent to which we focused on a particular level was influenced by suggestions from the literature and personal experience about what was important in participation in neighborhoods.

The decisions made in operationalizing the variables were not necessarily either–or decisions. Rather, they tended to be balance and trade-off decisions. We felt that if our first rough operationalization had good predictive value, then a great deal of research would be needed in analyzing how different decisions in operationalizing the foregoing issues (as well as other issues) would influence predictive power. Our present goal was to explore whether the cognitive social learning variables had potential predictive power and would thus influence whether additional research might be fruitful.

The dependent variable for both sets of independent variables, Set A and Set B, was an item measuring behavioral intention to participate in a block association to be organized in the future. The two sets of independent variables were compared for their ability to predict intention to participate using two multiple-regression analyses. The multiple R for Set A was .394 ($F = 11.99$, df, 16,312 $p < .01$), which accounted for about 16% of the variance in the criterion variable, intention to participate. The multiple R for Set B was .564 ($F = 30.44$, df, 7,322 $p < .01$), which accounted for about 32% of the variance in the criterion variable. Further analysis of the sets when combined showed that only 3% of the total variance in intention to participate was uniquely estimated by Set A and could not be estimated by Set B, and 20% of this variance was uniquely estimated by Set B. Testing these differences using the F ratio formula for sets provided by Cohen & Cohen (1975) revealed a highly significant F (12.90) when adding Set B to Set A, and nonsignificance when adding Set A to Set B. Thus, the results indicated that in seeking to predict a behavioral intention to participate, not only were the cognitive social learning variables more powerful predictors, but, furthermore, no significant predictive power was lost in using only these variables without the more traditional individual differences variables, whereas a great deal of significant predictive power was lost when using only the more traditional individual difference variables.

We also analyzed which independent variables from both sets were the best predictors of intention to participate. The four best predictor variables of the combined sets (in order of importance) were: (1) subjective stimulus value—importance of the block environment to the individual; (2) construction competencies—the individual's belief that he or she could produce and successfully execute behaviors relevant to participation; (3) perception of block problems—the individual's assessment of specific block needs; and (4) social relationships—the degree to which the individual engaged in neighborhood behaviors with other block residents. The higher the individual's ratings on these four variables, the more likely he or she was to report an intention to participate. These four variables acting together could account for almost one-third of the variance (31.5%) in behavioral intention to participate.

We view these results with both caution and excitement. This was a first rough operationalization of the cognitive social learning variables in a field setting and yet they predicted behavioral intention much better than the traditional individual difference variables set. Additional research is clearly needed, including research on how the cognitive social learning variables predict behavior (we are in the process of investigating this question using our longitudinal data). We are excited because the cognitive social learning variables relate so clearly to central issues in interactional psychology—they view the person in the situation. The research suggests that they can be operationalized and can have good predictive power. The results also show the importance of using multiple variables for predictive purposes.

The results have considerable potential for practical application. For example, we have been working on a concept called participation potential (see also Wandersman & Giamartino, 1980). Participation potential identifies variables, such as cognitive social learning variables and community characteristics, whose presence indicates a probability of successful participation. The assessment of participation in a particular community might supply policy decision-makers or community organizers with information about whether a program involving citizen participation would be likely to be successful. This could influence a "go or no-go" decision and possibly avoid expenditure of limited resources in futile efforts. Or, if a geographic area was divided into sections (e.g., blocks) and the sections varied on participation potential, community organizing efforts could be initiated in the sections with the most participation potential. Successful block organizations could then be used as a model for other blocks and perhaps serve to increase their participation potential. Finally, participation-potential assessments can be used as a diagnostic tool. For example, if an assessment reveals that participation potential is high in all important areas except construction competencies, organizers could hold workshops, such as those suggested by Wireman (1977), in which individuals could be trained in important skills needed to translate concerns into actions. However, if the assessment revealed that social relationships among neighbors were lacking, then organizers could stimulate social interaction through various means such as block parties.

We close this section by briefly relating this research to the discussion of interaction research presented in the first part of this chapter. There has been very little research on truly interactionist approaches (Olweus' second and third definitions of the inseperability of the individual–environment systems and reciprocal action). Regarding reciprocal action, several approaches are emerging that provide new conceptualizations and methodologies for investigating on-going dynamic interactions over time (Argyle, 1977; Pervin, 1977; Peterson, 1977; Raush, 1977). Even though these contributions are promising, they are somewhat limited in that they have focused primarily on sequential interaction between persons and have only secondarily considered broader situational factors (Endler & Edwards, 1978). They also give very little attention to individual difference characteristics. More research is needed that focuses on dynamic person-by-situation interactions.

The orientation of our research relates to the inseparability of the individual–environment system. In concentrating on the inseparability meaning of interaction, we do not deny and, in fact, we endorse the "reciprocal action" use of the term. As pointed out by Olweus (1977), these two meanings are closely related and the latter is best characterized by its emphasis on processes over time. We view our present research as a cross-sectional slice of the dynamic process. We take this orientation because, although we are interested in the process, we still want to predict (and eventually affect) behavior.

CONCLUDING COMMENTS

There are many promising research directions in a cognitive social learning approach to cognition, social behavior, and the environment. Here, we discuss just a few.

We began this chapter with a discussion of the person–situation controversy. It is clear that there is a great need for research describing *how* people perceive and interact with the environment. We have shown that the cognitive social learning variables represent a useful empirical approach to conceptualize this process. However, as Magnusson and Endler (1977) suggest, an integrated personality theory needs both models of information processing and information about the situation that "can explain the ongoing process in which individual behavior occurs [p. 31]." Therefore, a logical direction for further research would involve linking the cognitive social learning variables to actual characteristics of the environment. What ''objective'' features of the environment are people perceiving, coding, and selecting? There has been little person-environment research of this type performed, and many have criticized the lack of systematic research on the description and assessment of environments as a reason for this. However, in the 1970's, there have been considerable advances made in describing the characteristics of an environment, for example:

1. Moos (e.g., Wandersman & Moos, in press) has developed a multiple approach to assessing characteristics of environments including organizational policy, architectural and physical features, social climate, and the human aggregate.
2. Barker and his colleagues (Barker, 1978) have performed a considerable amount of research on behavior settings.
3. Stokols (1979; Chapter 22 in this volume) has described environments along such dimensions as environmental salience and environmental controllability.

The amount of research in these areas varies, with the most systematic attempts, so far, in the first two areas. However, all of these areas offer a great deal of promise and it will be fascinating to perform research relating the cognitive social learning variables to ''objective'' characteristics of the environment.

The cognitive social learning approach also has a considerable amount to offer other aspects of the interface between cognition, social behavior, and the environment. For example, the promising interface of social cognition has attracted a great deal of attention—for example, Fiske, Chapter 12; Taylor, Chapter 10; Weary, Chapter 11; Wells, Chapter 15; Yarkin, Town, and Harvey, Chapter 14 (all in this volume). Mischel has extended the cognitive social learning approach to the areas of social cognition and person perception. Mischel (1979) discusses research that shows how person categories at different levels of inclusiveness have distinct advantages and disadvantages—for example, in terms of recall of information, prediction, and cognitive economy. In addition, Mischel uses the cognitive social learning person variables to explore the development of cognitive competencies and self-control strategies in young children.

In conclusion, we feel that the cognitive social learning approach has a lot to offer in terms of helping us understand how people select, perceive, and behave in environments and, therefore, has the potential to make a large contribution to the interface of cognition, social behavior, and the environment.

ACKNOWLEDGMENTS

Preparation of this chapter and the research described were supported by National Science Foundation Grant #BNS-78-08827. The authors wish to thank Lois Pall Wandersman and Reuben Baron for their helpful comments and Lynn Walker for her help in operationalizing the cognitive social learning variables.

REFERENCES

Argyle, M. Predictive and generative rules models of P X S interaction. In D. Magnusson & N. S. Endler (Eds.), *Personality at the crossroads: Current issues in interactional psychology*. Hillsdale, N.J.: Lawrence Erlbaum Associates, 1977.

Barker, R. G. *Habitats, environments, and human behavior: Studies in ecological psychology and eco-behavioral science from the Midwest Psychological Field Station, 1947-1972*. San Francisco: Jossey-Bass, 1978.

Berkowitz, L. Situational and personal conditions governing reactions to aggressive cues. In D. Magnusson & N. S. Endler (Eds.), *Personality at the crossroads: Current issue in interactional psychology*. Hillsdale, N.J.: Lawrence Erlbaum Associates, 1977.

Bowers, K. Situationism in psychology: An analysis and a critique. *Psychological Review*, 1973, *80*, 307-336.

Cohen, J., & Cohen, P. *Applied multiple regression/correlation analysis for the behavioral sciences*. Hillsdale, N.J.: Lawrence Erlbaum Associates, 1975.

Cronbach, L.J. The two disciplines of scientific psychology. *American Psychologist*, 1957, *12*, 671-684.

Cronbach, L. J. Beyond the two disciplines of scientific psychology. *American Psychologist*, 1975, *30*, 116-127.

Ekehammar, B. Interactionism in personality from a historical perspective. *Psychological Bulletin*, 1974, *81*, 1026-1048.

Endler, N. S., & Edwards, J. Person by treatment interactions in personality research. In L. A. Pervin & M. Lewis (Eds.), *Perspectives in interactional psychology*. New York: Plenum, 1978.

Endler, N., & Hunt, J. M. V. Sources of behavioral variance as measured by the S-R inventory of awareness. *Psychological Bulletin*, 1966, *65*, 336-346.

Endler, N., & Magnusson, D. (Eds.). *Interactional psychology and personality*. Washington, D.C.: Hemisphere, 1976.

Epstein, S. Traits are alive and well. In D. Magnusson & N. S. Endler (Eds.), *Personality at the crossroads: Current issues in interactional psychology*. Hillsdale, N.J.: Lawrence Erlbaum Associates, 1977.

Fiedler, F. E. What triggers the person-situation interaction in leadership? In D. Magnusson & N. S. Endler (Eds.), *Personality at the crossroads: Current issues in interactional psychology*. Hillsdale, N.J.: Lawrence Erlbaum Associates, 1977.

Geis, F. L. The psychological situation and personality traits in behavior. In H. London (Eds.), *Personality*, New York: Wiley, 1978.

Golding, S. L. Flies in the ointment: Methodological problems in the analysis of percent of variance due to persons and situations. *Psychological Bulletin*, 1975, *82*, 278-288.

Golding, S. L. Toward a more adequate theory of personality: Psychological organizing principles. In H. London (Ed.), *Personality*. New York: Wiley, 1978.

Lay, C. Some notes on the concept of cross-situational consistency. In D. Magnuson & N. S. Endler (Eds.), *Personality at the crossroads: Current issues in interactional psychology*. Hillsdale, N.J.: Lawrence Erlbaum Associates, 1977.

Magnusson, D., & Endler, N. S. Interactional psychology: Present status and future prospects. In D. Magnusson & N. S. Endler (Eds.), *Personality at the crossroads: Current issues in interactional psychology*. Hillsdale, N.J.: Lawrence Erlbaum Associates, 1977.

Mischel, W. *Personality assessment*. New York: Wiley, 1968.

Mischel, W. Toward a cognitive social learning reconceptualization of personality. *Psychological Review*, 1973, *80*, 252-283.

Mischel, W. *The interaction of person and situation*. Draft of paper prepared for the Stockholm Conference on person × environment interaction, 1976.

Mischel, W. The interaction of person and situation. In D. Magnusson & N. S. Endler (Eds.), *Personality at the crossroads: Current issues in interactional psychology*. Hillsdale, N.J.: Lawrence Erlbaum Associates, 1977.

Mischel, W. On the interface of cognition and personality: Beyond the person–situation debate. *American Psychologist,* 1979, *34,* 740–754.

Newcomb, T. M. Social psychological theory: Integrating individual and social approaches. In J. H. Rohrer & M. Sherif (Eds.), *Social psychology at the crossroads.* New York: Harper, 1951.

Nuttin, J. R. A conceptual frame of personality–world interaction: A relational theory. In D. Magnusson & N. S. Endler (Eds.), *Personality at the crossroads: Current issues in interactional psychology.* Hillsdale, N.J.: Lawrence Erlbaum Associates, 1977.

Olweus, D. A critical analysis of the "modern" interactionist position. In D. Magnusson & N. S. Endler (Eds.), *Personality at the crossroads: Current issues in interactional psychology.* Hillsdale, N.J.: Lawrence Erlbaum Associates, 1977.

Overton, W. F., & Reese, H. W. Models of development: Methodological implications. In J. R. Nesselroade & H. W. Reese (Eds.), *Life span developmental psychology.* New York: Academic Press, 1973.

Pervin, L. A. The representative design of person–situation research. In D. Magnusson & N. S. Endler (Eds.), *Personality at the crossroads: Current issues in interactional psychology.* Hillsdale, N.J.: Lawrence Erlbaum Associates, 1977.

Pervin, L. A. Theoretical approaches to the analysis of individual–environment interaction. In L. A. Pervin & M. Lewis (Eds.), *Perspectives in interactional psychology.* New York: Plenum, 1978.

Pervin, L. A., & Lewis, M. Overview of the internal–external issue. In L. A. Pervin & M. Lewis (Eds.), *Perspectives in interactional psychology.* New York: Plenum, 1978.(a)

Pervin, L. A., & Lewis, M. (Eds.), *Perspectives in interactional psychology.* New York: Plenum, 1978.(b)

Peterson, D. R. A functional approach to the study of person–person interactions. In D. Magnusson & N. S. Endler (Eds.), *Personality at the crossroads: Current issues in interactional psychology.* Hillsdale, N.J.: Lawrence Erlbaum Associates, 1977.

Raush, H. L. Paradox levels and junctures in person–situation systems. In D. Magnusson & N. S. Endler (Eds.), *Personality at the crossroads: Current issues in interactional psychology.* Hillsdale, N.J.: Lawrence Erlbaum Associates, 1977.

Reid, D. W. Locus of control as an important concept for an interactionist approach to behavior. In D. Magnusson & N. S. Endler (Eds.), *Personality at the crossroads: Current issues in interactional psychology.* Hillsdale, N.J.: Lawrence Erlbaum Associates, 1977.

Spielberger, C. D. State–trait anxiety and interactional psychology. In D. Magnusson & N. S. Endler (Eds.), *Personality at the crossroads: Current issues in interactional psychology.* Hillsdale, N.J.: Lawrence Erlbaum Associates, 1977.

Stokols, D. A congruence analysis of human stress. In I. G. Sarason & C. D. Spielberger (Eds.), *Stress and anxiety* (Vol. 6). Washington, D. C.: Hemisphere Press, 1979.

Takala, M. Consistencies and perception of consistencies in individual psychomotor behavior. In D. Magnusson & N. S. Endler (Eds.), *Personality at the crossroads: Current issues in interactional psychology.* Hillsdale, N.J.: Lawrence Erlbaum Associates, 1977.

Wandersman, A. User participation: A study of types of participation, effects, mediators, and individual differences. *Environment and Behavior,* 1979, *11*(2), 185–207.(a)

Wandersman, A. User participation in planning environments: A conceptual framework. *Environment and Behavior,* 1979, *11*(4), 465–482.(b)

Wandersman, A. A framework of participation in community organizations. *Journal of Applied Behavioral Sciences,* 1981, *17,* (1).

Wandersman, A., Giamartino, G. A. Community and individual difference characteristics as influences on initial participation. *American Journal of Community Psychology,* 1980, *8,* 2, 217–228.

Wandersman, A. and Moos, R. H. Assessing and evaluating sheltered living environments. *Environment and Behavior,* in press.

Wireman, P. Building good advisory committees: Some important considerations. In P. Marshall (Ed.), *Citizen participation certification for community development: A reader on the citizen participation process.* Washington, D.C.: NAHRO, 1977.

20 Perceived Freedom and Control in the Built Environment

Richard D. Barnes
University of Wisconsin at Madison

In the last decade, a number of articles have appeared in the environmental and architectural literatures that advocate the use of perceived freedom and perceived control as central dimensions for evaluating the built environment (Altman, 1975; Baum, Gatchel, & Aiello, Chapter 24 in this volume; Baron & Rodin, 1978; Chermayeff & Alexander, 1963; Harvey, Harris, & Lightner, 1979; Johnson, 1975; Perin, 1970; Proshansky, Ittelson, & Rivlin, 1970a; Stockdale, 1979). During this same period, empirical work on the antecedents and consequences of perceived freedom and control has been expanding in the social psychology literature. Unfortunately, these events have been occurring in parallel and without much communication between those concerned with environmental applications of perceived freedom and those interested in its origin. As a first step towards bridging this gap, I will briefly review the trend of work in these two areas and then suggest a possibility for developing common ground.

FREEDOM AND CONTROL CONSTRUCTS IN THE DESIGN AND ENVIRONMENTAL LITERATURES

Calls for the use of perceived freedom and perceived control as evaluative dimensions have come in a variety of forms and from a variety of sources. Urban planner Constance Perin, for instance, advocates the use of a measure of "felt sense of competence" (that is, the feeling resulting from fulfillment of behavioral expectations) as an indicator of the success of a built environment. It is assumed (Perin, 1970) that a person is "aware of the outcome he expects from what he is doing and he will be satisfied with his behavior, and with himself, according to the level at which he achieves what he expected [p. 73]." In other words, the extent to which the environment enables a person to successfully achieve plans and goals determines the person's level of satisfaction with himself or herself and with the environment. Perin suggests that this perceived competence information be included at the programming stage of design, along with other, more traditional programming information (engineering criteria and building codes). This kind of concern for behavioral intentions and goals is evident in other behavioral systems approaches to architectural programming, such as Clovis Heimsath's *behavioral architecture* and Christopher Alexander's *pattern language*.

A slightly different approach has been taken by environmental psychologists. While retaining subjective evaluation by the user as the measure of an environment's success, they have focused in more detail on the structure of choices in the built environment. In laying out basic assumptions concerning the influence of environment on behavior, Proshansky et al. (1970b) note that the physical environment serves to define the limits of a user's freedom of choice in a given situation. The environment exerts a continuous constraining influence on behavior by limiting the types of choices and range of options open to the user. Proshansky et al. (1970a) advocate extending the number of options available in built environments (by designing more flexible and malleable environments) as a means of increasing the users' perceived freedom of choice and satisfaction with the setting.

Recently, perceived control has been featured prominently in two discussions of the determinants of crowding. In her integrated framework for crowding research, Stockdale (1979) emphasizes the control-threatening aspects of crowded situations. Control can be lost when the level of stimulus input from physical or social sources is not optimal (loss of input control) or when desired behaviors cannot be performed in a particular behavior setting (loss of output control). Baron & Rodin (1978) also suggest that control is a mediating factor in the experience of crowding. However, in their discussion a distinction is made between *perceived* control (the phenomenal awareness of control), and *personal* control, which they define (Baron & Rodin, 1978) as "the ability to establish a correspondence between intent and the environmental consequences of one's actions [p. 146]." In making this distinction, Baron and Rodin sever the link between the effects of control and the self-conscious realization of one's level of control, reflecting the growing evidence that control does not need to be explicitly present in awareness in order for it to have an effect (Langer & Rodin, 1976; Nisbett & Wilson, 1977; Shiffrin & Schneider, 1977; Turvey, 1977). The presence or absence of control-related effects is separate from the issue of whether subjects can label themselves as having control. When discussing the possible influence of the physical environment on control, this point is particularly relevant, because the built environment often has a background effect on behavior and is seldom the focal point of awareness in everyday experience.

Less explicit allusions to choice and control can be found in the work of other environmental writers. Altman (1975), for instance, says that a general principle of design should be to create *"responsive environments, which permit easy alternation between a state of separateness and a state of togetherness [p. 207]."* In other words, we should provide a choice between privacy and interaction by designing environment that permit differing degrees of access to other people. This theme has been reflected in more applied terms by the architects Chermayeff and Alexander (1963) in their proposals for creating domains of public and private spaces within residences, separated by appropriate filters and transition zones. Other work in the design literature, notably Oscar Newman's (1973) concept of defensible space and Robert Sommer's (1974) discussion of "hard architecture" can be interpreted within a freedom and control framework.

DETERMINANTS AND CONSEQUENCES OF PERCEIVED FREEDOM AND CONTROL

It seems evident that freedom and control concepts are playing an important part in the environment–behavior zeitgeist. They are being used to interpret conflicts between the environment and behavioral goals, and they are being advocated as dimensions for evaluating the built environment. How do these discussions relate to the empirical work on the determinants and consequences of perceived control?

As those promoting a partnership between the social sciences and the design professions are painfully aware, there are few, if any, environment–behavior absolutes that can be presented to designers as guides for their work. If there is something close to an absolute, it is that restriction of the perception of freedom and control leads to negative consequences. Research by Seligman and his colleagues (Seligman, 1975; Seligman, Maier, & Solomon, 1967) on learned helplessness and Glass and Singer's (1972) studies of predictability and control convincingly demonstrate that decrements in perceived control produce undesirable effects. In Seligman's studies, the consequence was passivity and helplessness; in Glass and Singer's work, the result of exposure to an unpredictable and uncontrollable aversive stimulus was increased stress in the form of elevated physiological responses and decreased tolerance for frustration.

Restriction of freedom and control can come about in several ways. In relation to the physical environment, freedom and control have typically been discussed in terms of freedom *from* unwanted outside interference or freedom *to* perform desired behaviors. As previously indicated, Stockdale (1979) notes that perceived control can be lost (1) by restriction of behavioral output; or (2) by an unacceptable level of physical and social input. In both of these cases, there is a loss of control over a desired outcome, but the nature of the threat varies. When a desired behavior is restricted, control over one's ability to act on the external environment is lost, but when the level of input is at an undesirable level, one loses control over one's internal state. Although distinct conceptually, these two kinds of threat have not been teased apart empirically. Research on control has typically not distinguished between the intrusive effects of an aversive stimulus and the effects of an inability to act to prevent or terminate that stimulus.

Although people may initially react strongly against threats to their freedom and control, evidence indicates that over the long term (as in habitation of a residence) repeated exposure to control-threatening experiences leads to passivity and helplessness. Wortman and Brehm (1975) suggest that severe and prolonged decrements in control may have a negative influence on the expectation of control in future situations. Work by Baum and his colleagues (Baum, Aiello, & Calesnick, 1978; Baum, Gatchel, & Aiello, Chapter 24 in this volume; Baum & Valins, 1977) provides empirical support for this prediction. In their studies of crowding and personal control among freshman residences of college dormitories, Baum and his colleagues found that students living in long-corridor dormitories, where crowding was more evident and regulation of social interaction more difficult than in short-corridor dormitories, developed responses indicating an increase in learned helplessness and a decrease in expectation of future control during their term of residence. In laboratory situations and during observations in the dormitories, students living in the long-corridor residences showed a greater tendency to withdraw and avoid social interaction than did students living in the short-corridor or suite-design dormitories.

The other side of the control coin is prevention or reduction of negative effects by the enhancement of perceived freedom and control. Sherrod (1974) has shown enhancement of perceived freedom to be an effective strategy for reducing the effects of crowding. In Sherrod's experiment, subjects who were given the opportunity to escape a crowded situation (even though they did not take advantage of that opportunity) showed higher tolerance for frustration on a subsequent task than did subjects who were not given the privilege of leaving.

Theoretical and empirical work on the determinants of perceived freedom also suggests possibilities for enhancing choice. Mills (1970), for instance, has proposed that perceived choice will be increased in a decision situation if the available alternatives (1) can be distinguished from one another; but (2) are close enough together in attractiveness to generate some uncertainty in the decision maker over which alternative is the best choice. In line with this reasoning, John Harvey and his associates have conducted a series of studies that delineate several factors in the structure of the available alternatives that influence a decision maker's perception of choice. First, and most intuitively, greater choice will be felt when the available options are positively valenced than when they are negatively valenced (Harvey & Harris, 1975). Second, the perception of choice is affected by the similarity in attractiveness of the options. Greater freedom of choice will be experienced when the available options are similar in attractiveness than when they are very different. However, when options are identical in attractiveness, less choice will be felt than when the options are similar, but not equal (Harvey, Barnes, Sperry, & Harris, 1974). Harvey suggests that these effects occur because the greatest uncertainty is experienced when the options are similar, but not equal in attractiveness. A decision maker apparently must hesitate somewhat before making a choice if the decision is to be interpreted as a choice experience.

A third structural influence on the perception of choice is the number of options available to the decision maker. On the surface, it is tempting to equate a large number of available alternatives with a high degree of choice. Discussions of freedom and control in the architectural literature are frequently based on this assumption. Perhaps this is because occasions in which we are confronted with too few alternatives are more common or more prominent in awareness than occasions in which we are faced with a large number of options. Whatever the reason, it seems common to equate the presence of many available options with a high degree of freedom of choice. However, as Harvey and Jellison (1974) found, the presence of a large number of options results in high perceived choice *only* when the options can be easily discriminated from one another. If the options are not clearly distinct from each other, an increase in the number of options does not result in a commensurate increase in perceived choice. As Harvey notes, this limitation on the conventional wisdom of linking perceived choice to the number of options has been reflected in the popular press through Toffler's (1970) concept of *future shock*. Toffler says that when the number of options in a decision situation reaches unmanageable proportions, the freedom associated with an increasing number of alternatives becomes ''unfreedom.'' In terms of Mills' analysis, the uncertainty of choosing between similar alternatives, which enhances perceived choice when the number of options is small, becomes too great when there are many similar alternatives from which to choose. A similar phenomenon noted in the area of leisure studies has been called *overchoice*.

The number of available alternatives interacts with the decision maker's perception of the time he or she took to evaluate the options. Harvey and Jellison (1974) report that when subjects feel that they have rapidly and efficiently evaluated the available alternatives, greater numbers of options result in greater perceived choice. However, when subjects feel they have taken an unusually long time to evaluate the alternatives, the greatest perceived choice is experienced with a moderate number of options. Taken together, these results suggest that when a decision task is not seen as overwhelming, perceived choice will be enhanced by making a large number of alternatives available, but if a decision task is demanding or is coupled with time urgency, increasing the number of options will reduce the perception of choice.

The perception of control has been shown to have both immediate and long-term consequences. Lack of control exacerbates the negative effects of aversive stimuli and can lead to passivity and helplessness, and enhancement of control can at least partially counteract those negative effects. Further, the valence, similarity, and number of the options available to a decision maker have been shown to influence the perception of choice. Given the wealth of information on perceived freedom and control generated by the social sciences and the emphasis on perceived freedom and control in the architectural literature, why have these concepts not been applied to design problems?

PROBLEMS WITH PERCEIVED FREEDOM AND CONTROL CONCEPTS

There are a number of good reasons for the lack of coordination between theoretical and applied work on perceived choice. In spite of the pervasiveness of perceived freedom and control concepts in the architectural and psychological literatures, there are some basic problems in the use of these terms. First among these is the fuzziness of their definitions. In this discussion, as in most earlier work, perceived freedom has been used almost synonymously with perceived control. This lack of precision might be excused as a result of the nascent state of work in the area, but if these concepts are to be useful to the designer, they must be more closely related to decisions made in specific situations and with specific alternatives. Recently, Harvey et al. (1979) have made an initial attempt to distinguish between perceived freedom and perceived control. They propose (Harvey et al., 1979) that the term *perceived freedom* be used to describe the "experience associated with the *act* of deciding upon the alternatives that we will seek [p. 276]." In other words, perceived freedom is linked to the experience of making individual decisions; it is the feeling associated with the act of deciding. In contrast, Harvey et al. reserve the term *perceived control* for the more long-term, on-going belief that one can predict events and cause changes in one's self and in the social and physical environment.

The conceptual separation of perceived freedom and perceived control brings us back to Mills' (1970) analysis of the role of uncertainty in perceived choice. Although perceived freedom and perceived control have been equated in most discussions, the dynamics underlying these experiences seem to be almost opposite. The experience of perceived freedom (that is, the feeling associated with the act of deciding) would seem to be associated with uncertainty. As previously noted, the research on perceived freedom indicates that greater choice will be felt when the decision maker experiences some uneasiness and hesitation before a decision is made. On the other hand, the experience of control seems to be associated with a desire for certainty and predictability. Glass and Singer's (1972) work clearly indicates that greater control is experienced under conditions of high predictability. Perhaps the process underlying perceived freedom is something akin to a desire for variety in options, whereas the process underlying perceived control is a desire for order and stability. It is possible that these processes operate separately; however, it seems more likely that repeated exposure to freedom-enhancing experiences would lead to an increase in more long-term feelings of control. Somewhat paradoxically, then, experiencing a series of minor *un*certainties in the process of making everyday decisions may contribute to greater feelings of certainty and predictability in the long run. From this perspective, control is seen *not* as a global, Gestalt-like perception (as it has been treated in much of the control literature), but as the product of many congruences and incongruences between behavioral goals and the structure of available alternatives in the environment—multiple "efficacy testings," if you will (cf. Bandura, 1977).

In line with this interpretation, Johnson (1975) has characterized personal control as a four-stage decision process involving (1) selection of the desired outcome (outcome choice control); (2) choice of the behaviors that will be employed to reach the desired outcome (behavior selection control); (3) the probability of achieving the outcome (outcome effectance); and (4) subjective interpretation of the outcome (outcome realization control). Depending on personal factors and situational factors such as the structure of alternatives, differing degrees of control (perceived *freedom* in Harvey et al.'s (1979) terms) will be experienced at each stage. Other distinctions have been made between kinds of perceived control (control as a variable state versus control as a relatively invariant trait, active control versus reactive control), but the important point for the present discussion is that the perception of freedom and control can be linked to the experience of making specific decisions in the course of a behavior–environment interaction.

Aside from these problems of definition, there have been other conflicts between theoretical work on perceived freedom and the application of that work. As I have suggested, in order for freedom and control concepts to be useful to designers, they must be related to specific decisions made in specific settings. Given the infinite variety of settings and the lack of an adequate typology of settings, social scientists have generally been unwilling to make educated guesses at a level of specificity that would be useful to designers. Designers, on the other hand, have not systematically considered the cross-situational aspects of their designs. This difference in orientation has been described by Altman (1975) as the "place versus process" conflict.

There is a language problem related to this conflict. In the process of scientific investigation, words taken from common usage gradually are limited in meaning by eliminating as many subjective and ambiguous connotations as possible. In contrast, architects expand on the meaning of words in common usage to describe subtle feelings and relations that are not often expressed in everyday language. Architectural descriptions often include words that attempt to get at the total emotional and cognitive impact, or "feeling," of a space. The advantage of using common words in this way is that holistic impressions that have a reality at some intuitive, gut level can be expressed verbally, but because the language is not broad enough to adequately describe these feelings and impressions, the resulting descriptions are vague and subjective. In this regard, the concepts of perceived freedom and control, simply because they have been identified by both designers and scientists as central concepts, may be useful as linguistic rallying points and catalysts for further dialogue.

If designers are to make reasonable decisions about the kinds of alternatives they will make available in the built environment, there must be a way of measuring the kinds of choices a user faces and the effects that these choices have on his or her perceived freedom. What methods have been employed to measure choice in the physical environment?

MEASURING CHOICE IN THE BUILT ENVIRONMENT

In the majority of work in this area, perceived freedom and control have been assessed by the use of paper-and-pencil self-report measures. Subjects are simply asked, ''How much control did you feel in this setting?'' or are asked to rank the importance of freedom and control along with other aspects of the given settings (as in a procedure described by Canter, 1974).

A more sophisticated version of the paper-and-pencil method has been developed by Rudolf Moos (1972, 1976). Although Moos' scales are more concerned with the individual's global perception of the physical and social ''climate'' of an environment, the subscales do address the issue of control in the environment. Separate scales have been developed for specific settings (work environments, institutions, and family settings) and each scale contains a set of subscales that assess various environmental ''traits'' relevant to the setting. To some extent, these scales reflect the different ways in which an environment is used, but the assumption is made that the configuration of elements that makes up the distinctive quality of an environment will encourage some kinds of interaction and discourage other kinds in a relatively stable and consistent way. In other words, there is an attempt to classify environments according to the kinds of behavioral effects they produce. Those effects may either be congruent or incongruent with the kinds of behavior for which the space has been designed (Moos, 1976).

A number of problems are involved in using self-report measures to assess the effects of the environment. First, if the environment exerts a subtle background effect on behavior, people may not be consciously aware of the elements of the environment that are affecting them. As previously indicated, control-relevant aspects of the environment probably exert an influence without being explicitly present in awareness. Second, self-report measures are subject to all the biases associated with inaccurate recall of experience (Kahneman & Tversky, 1973; Nisbett & Wilson, 1977; Taylor & Fiske, 1978). For these reasons, self-report measures are probably best used when they serve to complement behavioral indicators.

Observational techniques are a somewhat more direct way of assessing the effects of the environment. Although a large number of observational methods have been proposed, only two of the more developed procedures are discussed here: Robert Bechtel's application of Barker's behavior settings to evaluation of built environments, and Christopher Alexander's pattern language.

Using Barker's (1968) method for defining a behavior setting (i.e., "a standing pattern of behavior that occurs over and over again in a given place and at a given time [Bechtel, 1977, p. 22]''), Bechtel is able to organize and catalogue the various behavior–environment interactions that take place in a physical setting, whether that setting is a room, building, or community. Behavior settings are distinguished from one another by the extent to which they share common participants, leaders, action patterns, times, and physical objects and spaces. With this information in hand, a designer has an outline of the various behaviors and patterns of behavior that must be accommodated in the physical setting he or she is about to create. Bechtel claims that through the use of behavior setting surveys, environments can be designed that are more congruent with the behaviors that take place in a given setting. Further, he says that this cataloging of the structure of behavior can be accomplished without imposing the biases and preconceptions of the researcher on the data collected, thus reducing the subjectivity inherent in most questionnaire methods of environmental evaluation.

In contrast to Bechtel's application of behavior settings to programming and evaluation, a method that makes explicit the pattern of behaviors in a given setting, Christopher Alexander's *pattern language* is a technique for objectifying relations between places, things, and activities. Without going into the intricacies of the pattern language technique, which is described in detail by Duffy and Torrey (1970) and by Alexander, Ishikawa, Silverstein, Angel, Jacobson, and Fiksdahl-King (1978), I will say simply that it is a design method for reducing an architectural environment to more definable relationships between geometric elements. A pattern is defined (Duffy and Torrey, 1970) as "a typical arrangement in space of physical objects (or parts) which allow behavioral tendencies of forces to coexist in a context without conflict [p. 262].''

Critical to the pattern language method (and most useful to the present discussion) is Alexander's distinction between *needs* and *tendencies*. Typically, design programs have focused on defining the various needs of clients and users. For instance, office workers may be said to have a need for adequate lighting, an appropriate amount of work space, and fresh air, or more behaviorally, a need for optimal social stimulation and personal control. These needs are often incorporated in the architectural program as design goals. However, as Alexander and Poyner (1970) observe, the concept of need is not well defined. Because needs are conceived to be internal to the person, they are usually unobservable and may even be inaccessible to the person experiencing them. This is particularly true of the need for control with respect to the environment. Alexander proposes replacing the concept of need, for design purposes, with the more testable concept of *tendency.* In effect, a tendency serves as an operational definition of a need. It is what people are trying to do in the environment. So, for example, Alexander proposes relacing the statement, "People working in offices need a view," with the statement, "People working in offices try to get a view." Once these tendencies are made explicit, pattern language suggests configurations of objects and spaces that allow for their expression.

In some ways, Baron and Rodin (1978) take a similar approach to the measurement of perceived control with respect to the environment. Starting from their proposal that control is perceived at a "tacit level of awareness," Baron and Rodin (1978) suggest that the important issue in determining whether or not a individual is experiencing control is not whether he or she can "label a set of stimulus conditions as enhancing or diminishing . . . control. The important criterion is that the organism make a control-relevant response to appropriate stimulus conditions [p. 147]." They propose two ways in which the experience of control might be measured behaviorally. The experience of control may be inferred from behavior (1) when there is covariation between opportunities to establish control and behavior toward that goal; or (2) when there is a shift from smaller to larger units of perceptual organization.

The preceding work leads to this observation: If the concepts of perceived freedom and perceived control are to be meaningfully applied to design problems, there must be a way of linking them to specific decisions made in the course of a person–environment interaction. This means that for design purposes, freedom should be defined less as a *need* and more as a *tendency.* Instead of measuring perceived freedom as a global response to a complex environmental experience, we must begin to tie it to specific decisions made in a goal-directed behavior sequence. In this way, the experience of freedom of choice in the physical environment can be related to decisions and alternatives that the environment either allows or denies, and the investigation of these decisions and alternatives will produce results of sufficient specificity to be used by designers.

ANALYSIS OF CHOICE STRUCTURE

Given that the perceptions of freedom and control are important concepts in evaluation of the built environment (that is, increases in perceived freedom and control lead to increased satisfaction with the environment), and given also that we know some of the determinants of perceived freedom and control, how can we go about constructing environments that enhance these perceptions? The obvious first step is to find a way to make explicit the structure of choices in a built environment, to identify the alternatives that the environment allows the user and those that it denies.

At this point, adaptation of Newtson's (1973, 1976) procedure for identifying meaningful units in the stream of behavior seems the most promising way to identify "choice points" in behavior–environment interactions. Newtson simply asked subjects to observe a film or videotape of a sequence of behavior and press a button whenever they felt the actor stopped doing one thing and started doing something else. In some ways, our problem is similar to the one Newtson faced, Interaction with the environment is a continuous series of choices. The problem lies in identifying those choices that significantly affect perceived freedom and those that are trivial. Once these meaningful choice points are identified, options available at those points can be altered by the designer so that perceived freedom is maximized. In line with the work on the determinant of perceived freedom, this means identifying the number, similarity, and valence of the options available at the choice points and then restructuring these alternatives to increase the perception of choice.

Studies testing the utility of choice-structure analysis are currently under way at the University of Wisconsin. In them, we hope to successfully adapt the procedures used by Newtson to the identification of meaningful choice points in the stream of a behavior–environment interaction. More specifically, we hope to demonstrate (1) that when observers are told the major goals and subgoals of an actor in a filmed presentation of a person–environment interaction, identification of meaningful choice points will be reliable from one observer to another and across time; and (2) that the choice points identified by an actor when viewing a videotape replay of that actor's interaction with the environment will not be significantly different from the choice points identified by observers. Choice points will be defined for subjects as those points at which an actor must interact with the physical environment to accomplish his or her goal and where the environment serves to block or facilitate action toward the goal.

As with any developing method, there are problems with this technique. One of the more obvious criticisms is that multiple goal-oriented behaviors are possible in any given setting. Kitchens, for example, are used not only for cake baking, but also for dishwashing and child tending. Although admitting the validity of this criticism, I should also point out that the number of activities supported by a given setting is not infinite. There are a limited number of activities that are typically observed in a setting. It will not be possible to examine the choices associated with all possible goal-directed behaviors in a setting, but it is reasonable to assume that the most typical, expected behaviors can be studied. At an intuitive level, this is what an architect does when he or she makes a mental inventory of the behaviors expected in a space and then designs a physical structure to accommodate those behaviors.

There are several potential advantages in developing a method to determine choice structure. First, it offers a way of relating work on the determinants of perceived freedom to specific design problems. Although it is widely acknowledged that the freedom allowed a user in a built environment has an important influence on his or her satisfaction with the environment, freedom has not been defined in terms of elements that could be manipulated by a designer. Second, used in conjunction with the methods advocated by Baron and Rodin (1978) for assessing the experience of control behaviorally, an analysis of choice structure may contribute to the validation of self-report measures of perceived control. If, after restructuring the alternatives at choice points, we find that subjects both report an increase in perceived control and show control-relevant responses, we may have increased confidence in the validity of the paper-and-pencil measure. Finally, a choice structure method is compatible with other systems for evaluating the built environment. One of the primary criticisms of Alexander's pattern language has been that no method for systematically measuring tendencies is provided. An observational technique like analysis of choice structure may fill this gap. If the analysis of choice structure proves to be a reliable way of identifying meaningful choices in behavior–environment interactions, it will provide a link between theoretical and applied work on perceived freedom and control and it may be a step toward the goal of designing environments that enhance the users' sense of freedom.

ACKNOWLEDGMENTS

I am indebted to Vernon Allen, John Harvey, Doug Kleiber, Eric Knowles, and Craig Zimring for their thoughtful readings of an earlier version of this chapter. Many of their suggestions have been incorporated in the final draft.

REFERENCES

Alexander, C., Ishikawa, S., Silverstein, M., Angel, S., Jacobson, M., & Fiksdahl-King, I. *A pattern language: Towns, buildings, construction.* Oxford: Oxford University Press, 1978.
Alexander, C., & Poyner, B. The atoms of environmental structure. In G. T. Moore (Ed.). *Emerging methods in environmental design and planning.* Cambridge, Mass.: M.I.T. Press, 1970.
Altman, I. *The environment and social behavior.* Monterey, Calif.: Brooks/Cole, 1975.
Bandura, A. Self efficacy: Toward a unifying theory of behavioral change. *Psychological Review,* 1977, *84,* 191–215.
Barker, R. *Ecological psychology.* Stanford, Calif.: Stanford University Press, 1968.
Baron, R. M., & Rodin, J. Personal control as a mediator of crowding. In A. Baum, J. E. Singer, & S. Valins (Eds.), *Advances in environmental psychology* (Vol. 1). Hillsdale, N.J.: Lawrence Erlbaum Associates, 1978.
Baum, A., Aiello, J., & Calesnick, L. Crowding and personal control: Social density and the development of learned helplessness. *Journal of Personality and Social Psychology,* 1978, *36,* 1000–1011.
Baum, A., & Valins, S. *Architecture and social behavior: Psychological studies of social density.* Hillsdale, N.J.: Lawrence Erlbaum Associates, 1977.
Bechtel, R. *Enclosing behavior.* Stroudsburg, Pa.: Dowden, Hutchinson, & Ross, 1977.
Canter, D. *Psychology for architects.* London: Applied Science Publishers, 1974.
Chermayeff, S., & Alexander, C. *Community and privacy.* Garden City, N.J.: Doubleday, 1963.
Duffy, F., & Torrey, J. A progress report on the pattern language. In G. T. Moore (Ed.), *Emerging methods in environmental design and planning.* Cambridge, Mass.: M.I.T. Press, 1970.

Glass, D. C., & Singer, J. E. *Urban stress*. New York: Academic Press, 1972.

Harvey, J. H., Barnes, R. D., Sperry, D. L., & Harris, B. Perceived choice as a function of internal–external locus of control. *Journal of Personality*, 1974, *42*, 437–452.

Harvey, J. H., & Harris, B. Determinants of perceived choice and the relationship between perceived choice and the expectancy about feelings of internal control. *Journal of Personality and Social Psychology*, 1975, *31*, 101–106.

Harvey, J. H., Harris, B., & Lightner, J. M. Perceived freedom as a central concept in psychological theory and research. In R. A. Monty & L. C. Perlmuter (Eds.), *Choice and perceived control*. Hillsdale, N.J.: Lawrence Erlbaum Associates, 1979.

Harvey, J. H., & Jellison, J. M. Determinants of perceived choice, number of options, and perceived time in making a selection. *Memory & Cognition*, 1974, *32*, 539–544.

Johnson, C. A. *Privacy as personal control*. Unpublished manuscript, National Bureau of Standards, Washington, D.C., 1975.

Kahneman, D., & Tversky, A. On the psychology of prediction. *Psychological Review*, 1973, *80*, 237–251.

Langer, E., & Rodin, J. The effects of choice and enhanced personal responsibility for the aged: A field experiment in an institutional setting. *Journal of Personality and Social Psychology*, 1976, *34*, 191–198.

Mills, J. *Analysis of perceived choice*. Unpublished manuscript, University of Missouri at Columbia, 1970.

Moos, R. H. Assessment of the psychosocial environments of community-oriented psychiatric treatment programs. *Journal of Abnormal Psychology*, 1972, *79*, 9–18.

Moos, R. H. *The human context: Environmental determinants of human behavior*. New York: Wiley, 1976.

Newman, O. *Defensible space: Crime prevention through urban design*. New York: Collier Books, 1973.

Newtson, D. Attribution and the unit of perception of ongoing behavior. *Journal of Personality and Social Psychology*, 1973, *28*, 28–38.

Newtson, D. Foundations of attribution: The perception of ongoing behavior. In J. Harvey, W. Ickes, & R. Kidd (Eds.), *New directions in attribution research*. Hillsdale, N.J.: Lawrence Erlbaum Associates, 1976.

Nisbett, R. E., & Wilson, T. D. Telling more than we can know: Verbal reports on mental processes. *Psychological Review*, 1977, *84*, 231–259.

Perin, C. *With man in mind: An interdisciplinary prospectus for environmental design*. Cambridge, Mass.: M.I.T. Press, 1970.

Proshansky, H. M., Ittelson, W. H., & Rivlin, L. G. Freedom of choice and behavior in a physical setting. In H. Proshansky, W. Ittelson, & L. Rivlin (Eds.), *Environmental psychology* (Vol. 1). New York: Holt, Rinehart, & Winston, 1970. (a)

Proshansky, H. M., Ittelson, W. H., & Rivlin, L. G. The influence of the physical environment on behavior: Some basic assumptions. In H. Proshansky, W. Ittelson, & L. Rivlin (Eds.), *Environmental psychology* (Vol. 1). New York: Holt, Rinehart, & Winston, 1970. (b)

Seligman, M. E. P. *Helplessness: On depression, development, and death*. San Francisco: Freeman, 1975.

Seligman, M. E. P., Maier, S. F., & Solomon, R. L. Failure to escape traumatic shock. *Journal of Experimental Psychology*, 1967, *74*, 1–9.

Sherrod, D. R. Crowding, perceived control, and behavioral aftereffects. *Journal of Applied Social Psychology*, 1974, *4*, 171–186.

Shiffrin, R. M., & Schneider, W. Controlled and automatic human information processing: II. Perceptual learning, automatic attending, and a general theory. *Psychological Review*, 1977, *84*, 127–190.

Sommer, R. *Tight spaces: Hard architecture and how to humanize it*. Englewood Cliffs, N.J.: Prentice-Hall, 1974.

Stockdale, J. E. Crowding: Determinants and effects. In L. Berkowitz (Ed.), *Advances in experimental social psychology* (Vol. 10). New York: Academic Press, 1979.

Taylor, S. F., & Fiske, S. T. Salience, attention, and attribution: Top of the head phenomena. In L. Berkowitz (Ed.), *Advances in experimental social psychology* (Vol. 11). New York: Academic Press, 1978.

Toffler, A. *Future shock*. New York: Bantam Books, 1970.

Turvey, M. T. Preliminaries to a theory of action with reference to vision. In R. Shaw & J. Bransford (Eds.), *Perceiving, acting, and knowing: Toward an ecological psychology*. Hillsdale, N.J.: Lawrence Erlbaum Associates, 1977.

Wortman, C. B., & Brehm, J. W. Responses to uncontrollable outcomes: An integration of reactance theory and the learned helplessness model. In L. Berkowitz (Ed.), *Advances in experimental social psychology* (Vol. 8). New York: Academic Press, 1975.

21

The Symbiotic Relationship Between Social Psychology and Environmental Psychology: Implications from Crowding, Personal Space, and Intimacy Regulation Research

John R. Aiello
Rutgers, The State University

Donna E. Thompson
New York University

Andrew Baum
*Uniformed Services University
of the Health Sciences*

This volume, *Cognition, Social Behavior, and the Environment,* has provided an opportunity for researchers from these three domains to communicate with one another and explore the interface among their respective areas. In the present chapter, we focus on the linkages between environmental psychology and social psychology. As our title suggests, although they represent quite different areas of psychological inquiry, we believe that environmental psychology and social psychology are complementary. Greater interchange between these two subareas would lead to a broader understanding of human behavior. In support of this belief, we draw from our program of research concerned with crowding, personal space, and intimacy regulation. The basic premise of our chapter is that the thoughts, feelings, and behavior of individuals can *best* be understood by including a consideration of the context or setting within which these thoughts, feelings, and behaviors are found. In other words, events and processes are located within the sociophysical environment, which influences the behavior and functioning of individuals and groups.

SOCIAL PSYCHOLOGY

Social psychology and environmental psychology differ with regard to their research content, emphasis on theory, methodology, and research perspective. Although they are both products of the 20th century, social psychology emerged much earlier as an independent area of psychological investigation. The first two textbooks concerned with the study of social behavior were published in 1908 and *Social Psychology,* the first text containing the results of actual experiments was published in 1924 by Floyd Allport. Ever since this early period, social psychology has been concerned with how the behavior of people is influenced by others around them. A more formal, widely accepted definition of social psychology (G. W. Allport, 1968) has been that it is "an attempt to understand how the thoughts, feelings, and behaviors of individuals are influenced by the actual, imagined, or implied presence of others [p. 3]."

During the last two decades, social psychology has been in a state of flux, undergoing a number of significant changes (cf. McGuire, 1973, 1979). Over a dozen new areas of investigation have been established (e.g., altruism, attribution, sexual behavior). Social psychologists have also begun to take a more critical look at the area. Some have argued that social psychology should not even be regarded as a scientific field of inquiry like other more established scientific disciplines. Supporters of this position believe that social psychology should be regarded as "history" because social behavior is affected by the social, political, and economic conditions within which it is observed (cf. Gergen, 1973, 1976). However, the prevailing consensus is that social psychology should be considered a science because the scientific method has consistently been employed to study social behavior (cf. Schlenker, 1974, 1976). Laboratory experimentation, with its emphasis on control and the manipulation of variables characterizes most of social-psychological research.

In general, scientific gains have been believed to result from this type of methodological approach. Over the years, though, there have been some social psychologists who have questioned the generalizability of findings obtained in such laboratory investigations (G. W. Allport, 1968). In fact, at the present time, there is a growing but still nascent awareness on the part of social psychologists of the need for studying social behavior within the context in which it naturally occurs. Another equally important and recurring concern on the part of social psychologists has been that research should be designed to address social problems. Theory has played a central role in social-psychological research because it has been a primary source of testable hypotheses concerning human social behavior. Critics have argued that social psychologists have often allowed a particular paradigm or theoretical framework to determine the topics chosen for investigation.

ENVIRONMENTAL PSYCHOLOGY

It is only within the last two decades that environmental psychology has been established as an independent area of psychology (cf. Proshansky, Ittelson, & Rivlin, 1970; Wohlwill, 1970). Early investigators were primarily concerned with the effects of the built environment on people's behavior, how people manipulate the physical environment during social interaction, and the inclusion of the physical environment in the "life space." Unlike social psychology, environmental psychology is not very easily defined. All agree that the area is concerned with studying environment–behavior relationships, but it has not been possible to find one definition that both encompasses all of the areas of interest to environmental psychologists and yet is able to exclude those areas that are not of any concern. Moreover, this problem is compounded by the fact that during the past decade, the field has grown rapidly, making it even more difficult to delineate its boundaries. Further, as Stokols (1978) points out, one might argue from an historical perspective that the entire domain of psychology has always been concerned with the study of the effects of the environment on behavior. Perhaps the most satisfactory definition of the area at present is still (Proshansky et al., 1970): "environmental psychology is what the environmental psychologists do [p. 5]."

As a unique branch of psychology, environmental psychology does have many distinguishing characteristics. Research in environmental psychology has been characterized by much more methodological eclecticism than other areas of psychology. Multiple-method research strategies are often employed within the same investigation; therefore, in any given experiment one might find both field and laboratory techniques being utilized. The methods or levels of analysis are most often chosen to fit the problem under investigation in environmental psychology. This contrasts sharply with social-psychological research in which the theoretical framework that a researcher adopts often determines what research methods are employed. Environmental psychology is also unique with respect to its social unit by place orientation. Using a systems approach, behavior is studied within the context that it naturally occurs, because complex causal relationships are assumed to exist between the environment and behavior. Lastly, the focus in environmental psychology is problem oriented; theory has played a less central role in the formulation of testable research hypotheses. Although theory is used by environmental psychologists, it is often "imported" from other areas. Because environmental psychology is interdisciplinary in its perspective, environmental psychologists are often exposed more to viewpoints outside of their area.

RELATIONSHIP BETWEEN ENVIRONMENTAL AND SOCIAL PSYCHOLOGY

In recent years, the utility of having any type of interchange between environmental psychology and social psychology has been debated (cf. the 1976 *Personality and Social Psychology Bulletin* series; sec Altman 1976a, 1976b; Proshansky, 1976). Yet, the debate now appears to be superfluous; a sizable proportion of those psychologists studying environmental issues are social psychologists by training and orientation, and the interface of the two is expanding all the time. The fact is that these two subareas share many of their members. In a survey conducted by the Task Force on Environment and Behavior of the American Psychological Association (1976), almost 75% of the individuals who labeled themselves environmental psychologists were also social psychologists. As we have indicated, numerous dissimilarities do exist between the two areas. Nevertheless, there are also a number of commonalities that make the two approaches to psychological inquiry quite complementary. For this reason, we believe that the further development of the linkage between environmental and social psychology will result in benefits for both areas.

The large proportion of social psychologists in the area of environmental psychology has been attributed in part to their dissatisfaction with the area in which they were trained. Even more likely is the fact that many of the same psychological topics are the focus of study for individuals in these two areas. Perception, cognition, attitudes, and group processes represent examples of topics common to both areas. Furthermore, research in crowding and other areas of environmental psychology has demonstrated that sociophysical environmental factors can exert a profound effect on behavior (cf. Aiello & Baum, 1979). Similarly, social-psychological theories such as psychological reactance (Brehm, 1966) and learned helplessness (Seligman, 1975) have proven useful in explaining reactions to overstimulation and uncontrollable events in certain environmental contexts (e.g., Baum, Aiello, & Calesnick, 1978; Rodin & Baum, 1978).

Lewin's Influence

Perhaps the most critical link between the two areas, which we would like to highlight, is the influence of Kurt Lewin. His emphasis on basic, individual psychological processes and the experimental method are clearly reflected in social-psychological research. In fact, Lewin has been posited by many to be the "father" of social psychology. Research in social psychology has also been influenced somewhat by Lewin's field theory, which stressed the interaction of personal and environmental factors in determining behavior. However, as we mentioned earlier, current research in social psychology often fails to consider the effects of both personal and environmental factors on behavior.

Similarly, Lewin's influence on environmental psychology is evident. For example, the emphasis on studying people–environment units and selecting the level of analysis to fit the problem are consistent with Lewin's writings that behavior is a function of *both* personal and environmental factors. Moreover, Lewin's commitment to social relevance and the generalizability of psychological theory and experimentation is reflected in environmental psychology. Lewin's work was also characterized by an emphasis on the interplay between laboratory and field research. In order to fully understand social behavior, Lewin felt that knowledge gained from basic laboratory experiments was needed. At the same time, however, he believed that the social context in which behavior occurred also needed to be considered and that the full value of theories was dependent on their being tested in real-world settings. His often-quoted statement that "there is nothing so practical as a good theory" reflects this belief. A parallel may be drawn between the interface between environmental psychology and social psychology (discussed in this chapter) and the Lewinian emphasis on the interplay between the laboratory and the field (previously presented). We have described social-psychological research as being mostly laboratory in nature, whereas environmental research has been characterized more by field methodologies. Consistent with Lewin, we believe there is a need to develop a system of information exchange between these two areas. Combining knowledge concerning basic human processes obtained from both basic social laboratory experiments and environmental field studies will lead to a greater understanding of how these psychological processes operate under different situations.

Examples for our own program of research might serve to illustrate the utility of a research strategy that combines the benefits of the control attained in the laboratory and the generalizability available from studies performed in their natural settings. The focus of our research has concentrated on how people establish and maintain preferred levels of involvement with others and the conditions under which the attainment of desired degrees of involvement is not possible. More specifically, we have investigated: crowding—one of the psychological consequences of too much involvement with others; personal space—one of the many means of attaining appropriate involvement with others; and intimacy regulation—the dynamic process through which involvement levels are established. Certain themes or key issues are common to these three areas of research. These include: regulation and control; dynamic equilibrium and privacy; and involvement and stimulation levels.

CROWDING

Early correlational studies of population density, done primarily by sociologists, established linkages between higher density levels and various forms of social and physical pathologies (e.g., Lantz, 1953; Schmid, 1969; Schmitt, 1957). Although socioeconomic class and ethnicity variables were unfortunately confounded in these earlier studies, this research nevertheless demonstrated quite clearly that higher density levels are often associated with some severe negative outcomes. Similarly, laboratory studies of animals (e.g., Calhoun, 1962) indicated rather dramatic and devastating consequences of crowded conditions.

Early experimental laboratory studies, however, produced results that were equivocal (e.g., Freedman, Klevansky, & Ehrlich, 1971). As Altman (1978) and others have pointed out, this early human experimental crowding research employing basic laboratory methods often suffered from the use of inappropriate designs and measures for the problem being studied. Further, the use of project-ive measures in the study of crowding—for example, having a person place dolls or clothespins into a scale-model room up to the point where he or she would judge the room to be crowded (Desor, 1972)—is likely to invoke very different judgmental processes than the judgments that would result from their actual participation in settings differing in density level.

The first study in our series of laboratory investigations sought to overcome some of the problems present in early studies in this area (Aiello, Epstein, & Karlin, 1975a). Our goal was to determine whether close physical proximity would produce feelings of discomfort and crowding as well as stress-related arousal. Participants in this experiment, either alone or in groups of six, first experienced either a large (9 ft. by 9 ft.) or a small (4 ft. by 4 ft.) room for a period of 30 minutes. They were told that the experiment was investigating the effects of different environments on physiological responses. Then, after a 5-minute break, they experienced the other of these conditions, thereby enabling them to act as their own controls in a fully counterbalanced design. To overcome the possible confound of a task performed while individuals were under these conditions, distracting them from the close physical proximity and the environ-mental cues present, no task was assigned. As can be seen in Fig. 21.1, partici-pants in groups of six experienced higher levels of stress-related arousal and greater increases of these levels in the small-room condition. Moreover, some residue of these higher levels of stress-related arousal was found when partici-pants were placed in a large room after their experience in the small room. This carry-over effect indicates that high levels of physiological arousal associated with a crowding experience do not dissipate immediately following its termina-tion.

The results of this initial study established that there can be quite potent negative consequences under conditions involving close physical proximity of others, even for relatively brief durations. This type of crowding most closely approximates a transportation analogue in which people are forced into being physically very close to others for many repeated, but brief, episodes (e.g., travelling back and forth to work everyday on a crowded subway or train).

Subsequent investigations have demonstrated similar physiological conse-quences for both children (Aiello, Nicosia, & Thompson, 1979) and for elderly individuals (Aiello, Headly, & Thompson, 1978). It is interesting to note that even though crowded elderly individuals showed the same pattern of higher stress-related arousal levels as younger individuals (see Fig. 21.2), they never-theless labeled the situation as "cozy." In our study of children under these crowded conditions involving close physical proximity, we additionally found that children were more competitive following exposure to crowded conditions, even though they had all to gain and nothing to lose from cooperating.

As we have already discussed, crowding is one of a number of consequences of an inappropriately high-involvement level with others. In one of the studies of

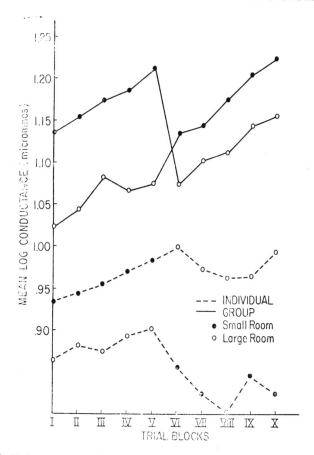

FIG. 21.1.   Mean log skin conductance level of groups and individuals in small and large rooms.

our research program, our objective was to determine whether an individual's personal space preference (one indication of an individual's preferred involvement level) would mediate that person's experience under the crowded conditions previously described (Aiello, DeRisi, Epstein, & Karlin, 1977). As expected, people who preferred to interact with others at larger distances experienced the highest and most rapidly increasing levels of stress-related arousal. All participants, regardless of their personal space preference, however, performed more poorly on a complex cognitive task following exposure to crowding.

Unfortunately, much of the research concerned with the human experience or crowding has failed to differentiate among the various components, present in different environments, that evoke the label "crowded." For example, although close physical proximity is an extremely important component of the type of crowding experienced in transportation settings, in crowded residential settings,

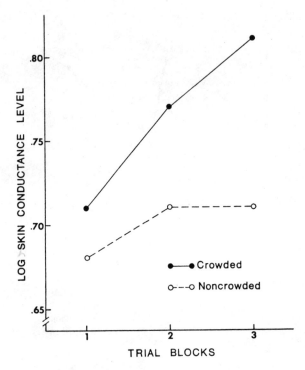

FIG. 21.2. Mean log skin conductance level of crowded and noncrowded groups
of elderly persons.

close physical proximity can be considered less important than the lack of control
over interpersonal interactions and congestion or resource scarcity factors, which
are likely to be more salient in these settings.

In order to more fully understand crowding under residential conditions, we
have conducted a series of studies in college dormitory environments. We describe some of these studies in Chapter 24 in this volume. Consistent with our
call for more than one level of observation to be used in studies of human
crowding (Aiello, Epstein, & Karlin, 1974, 1975a), our studies have employed
multiple dependent measures, which cut across these levels of observation. One
study that we consider here is our investigation at Rutgers University of the
effects of adding a third student to a dormitory room designed for two (Aiello,
Epstein, & Karlin, 1975b; see also Aiello & Baum, 1979, and Karlin, Epstein, &
Aiello, 1978). In addition to feeling more crowded and less satisfied with their
living conditions, tripled students displayed a decreased capacity for handling
complex cognitive problems over the course of a semester. Further, crowded
women were even more negatively affected than crowded men. Unlike the results
obtained in short-term laboratory experiments, in which close physical proximity
is the critical component and in which women have been found to be less

negatively affected than their crowded male counterparts, crowded women under these chronic residential living conditions were found to be in poorer health and reported more physical and psychological problems. Crowded men were found to more frequently escape from their stressful environment. In contrast, crowded women spent more time in their rooms and with each other and became more involved with one another over time (e.g., self disclosed more to each other and approached each other more closely and stood more directly during interactions). Their interdependent coping style, which was so effective under short-term conditions involving close physical proximity, proved maladaptive under prolonged high-residential density conditions. As Lewin noted quite some time ago, an interplay between laboratory and field research is often needed to more fully understand social behavior.

PERSONAL SPACE

A second area of our research has focused upon personal space, one of many variables that acts as a mediator of the involvement level that we maintain with others. Our research in this area has also demonstrated the importance of conducting research in naturalistic field settings, as opposed to solely relying on laboratory studies. In 1963, there were fewer than a dozen studies of personal space. We have now identified over 300 studies to date that have been conducted in the area of personal space (Aiello & Thompson, 1980a).

Several of our studies have examined how personal space behavior develops as children grow older and become socialized into society. In the first of these studies (Aiello & Aiello, 1974), children of varying ages were paired and asked to discuss their favorite television programs. While they were talking, unobtrusive observations of their personal space were made using a "relative" distance scale based on their body sizes. Younger children were found to interact with each other at much closer distances. As can be seen in Fig. 21.3, this behavior changes over time, such that children stand farther and farther apart as they get older until their behavior corresponds to the adult norms by about age 12. Further, although sex differences are minimal for younger children, by age 10 or 12, boys interact at greater distances than girls. A second study (Aiello & Cooper, 1979) varied interactions involving positive and negative affect levels of children at varying age levels. As can be seen in Fig. 21.4, distance once again was found to increase with age, and by age 10, the distance maintained by the children reflects the way they feel about one another; children who dislike one another stand farther apart than children who like one another.

A third study (Pagán & Aiello, 1979) was conducted in Puerto Rico and New York City with Puerto Rican children of varying ages. Consistent with each of the two preceding studies, in both locations, children used larger interaction distances as they grew older (see Fig. 21.5).

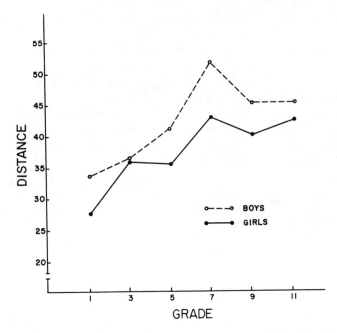

FIG. 21.3. Interaction distances of pairs of boys and girls at six grade levels.

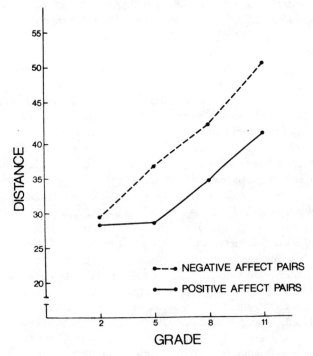

FIG. 21.4. Interaction distances of reciprocated, positive and negative affect pairs at four grade levels.

432

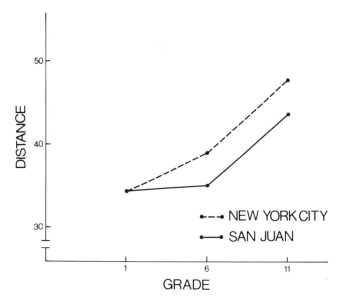

FIG. 21.5.   Interaction distances of Puerto Ricans in New York City and San Juan at three grade levels.

About a decade ago, when we started studying personal space behavior, we included projective and quasiprojective techniques; these techniques require subjects to place figures or dolls representing them "as they would stand during interaction" or to "walk up to another individual" and stand "as close as would feel comfortable." Fortunately, in each of these early studies, we actually observed these same individuals engaged in natural conversation with the person whom they had "walked up to until they felt comfortable" or with whom they had placed a self-referent figure. In those initial studies, we were quite surprised to discover that there was little or no relationship between the more projective behaviors and our observations of actual interpersonal distances. Since these early studies, we have conducted a series of other investigations, all of which have revealed these same results—little or no relationship between projective or quasiprojective measures and actual interpersonal distance behaviors ($\bar{r} = -.02$ to $+ .20$). In fact, we learned in one recent study (Love & Aiello, 1980) that people could not even *replicate* their own interaction distance behavior using these less-direct techniques.

Probably the most dramatic example of the problems of generalizing from these projective or laboratory techniques, which do not include the important proprioceptive (context) cues that individuals draw from during interaction, is the divergent pattern of results obtained by Petri and Huggins (1975). Using a paper-and-pencil measure of interpersonal distance (the Comfortable Interpersonal Distance Scale by Duke & Nowicki, 1972), the authors found children indicating the use of less and less space as they grew older. As our previously summarized studies and many others (e.g., Tennis & Dabbs, 1975) have shown, these results are *just the opposite* of how personal space actually develops. This is another example of how reliance upon results obtained solely under laboratory conditions can be quite misleading. This is particularly true of the personal space literature, in which *over half* of the 300 studies reported to date have used these projective or quasiprojective (laboratory) methods.

Another area of personal space behavior that we have examined concerns how people of different cultural or ethnic backgrounds use space during social interaction. These studies and others, which we have recently summarized (Aiello & Thompson, 1980a), demonstrate that differences between cultures and ethnic and racial groups in the use of space do exist. An important area for future research is how these differences may lead to miscommunication in cross-cultural and cross-subcultural encounters. Attention to the attributional processes that accompany these interactions should prove to be quite valuable for our ability to guard against potential miscommunication.

INTIMACY REGULATION

Intimacy regulation is viewed as the overall process by which individuals attempt to attain and maintain preferred levels of involvement with others and with their environment. We have studied situations within which it is difficult or impossible for people to attain satisfactory involvement levels or to effectively regulate interaction (e.g., encountering unwanted others in a dormitory: Baum et al., 1978; encountering an environmental context that places an individual and someone with whom that person is interacting at too close or too great a distance; Aiello 1972, 1977a, 1977b; Aiello & Thompson, 1980b).

A number of investigators have proposed models for the regulation of social intimacy. Probably the best known is the affiliative conflict theory, or equilibrium theory, proposed by Argyle and Dean (1965). According to this compensatory model, approach and avoidance forces are present in every interpersonal encounter. People arrive at a satisfactory resolution of their preferred levels of involvement through the functioning of numerous verbal and nonverbal behaviors. Once this "equilibrium point" is reached, changes that result in more or less intimacy than is desired produce reciprocal changes in one or more behaviors in order to produce the desired change in intimacy. Under most circumstances, this compensatory process operates outside of the realm of consciousness. An example of a study testing this model was the initial study in our program of research in this area (Aiello, 1972). Individuals were seated at distances that were comfortable (6.5 ft.), too close (2.5 ft.), or too far (10.5 ft.). Observation of the visual behavior maintained at each of these distances was recorded. As can be seen in Fig. 21.6, the amount of looking by both males and females increases

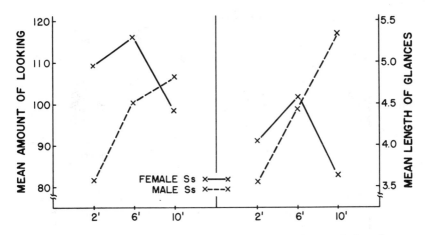

FIG. 21.6. Mean amount of looking and length of glances (in seconds) by male and female subjects at three distances.

when they move from a distance that is too close to one that is comfortable. A similar pattern (more looking) obtains for males when they move from a distance that is comfortable to one that is too far. Women, on the other hand, engage in less looking when they move from a distance that is comfortable to one that is too far.

We have proposed an extension of the equilibrium theory of social intimacy (Aiello & Thompson, 1980b). This extension posits that beyond a critical discomfort level, regulatory processes can no longer be employed easily to reestablish the preferred level of involvement. Avoidance forces therefore outweigh approach forces, which results in an individual's subsequent withdrawal from interaction. As Fig. 21.7 illustrates, males and females generally differ, with females desiring somewhat higher levels of involvement than males. Whereas males are often more uncomfortable at distances that are too close, females are often more uncomfortable at distances that are too far. It is within these critical regions of discomfort, that it is exceedingly difficult, if not impossible, for an individual to utilize any compensatory processes to reduce the discomfort experienced and reestablish the preferred involvement level. A recent study we conducted (Aiello & Thompson, 1980b) provided considerable support for this model. As predicted, females at an extended distance (that is, one that is viewed as "too far") found it more difficult to employ effective coping strategies and displayed greater indications of stress-related arousal as a result of feeling more bothered by the distance. More importantly, females misattributed the source of their discomfort to their interaction partner, whose behavior was standardized across conditions. The physical environment, therefore, exerts its own independent influence on social behavior and needs to be taken into account, along with personal and situational factors, to better understand an interaction context.

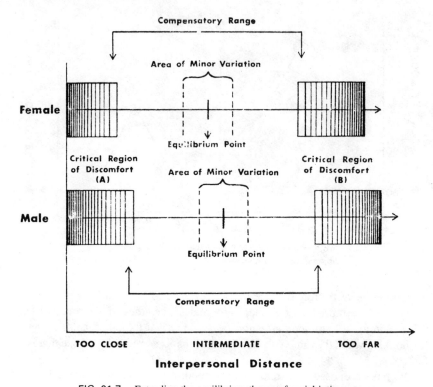

FIG. 21.7.   Extending the equilibrium theory of social intimacy.

SUMMARY

The three areas that we have discussed—crowding, personal space, and intimacy regulation—are considered topics within the domains of both social and environmental psychology. Both environmental and social psychologists have conducted research in these three areas. We feel that the different backgrounds, orientations, and methods that these investigators have brought to these areas have produced beneficial results that are consistent with Lewin's emphasis on the interaction of personal and environmental factors in determining behavior. It is important to consider not only the social but also the environmental factors that impact on an individual. It is also necessary to take into account the way people perceive the behavior of others as well as their environment. Only through the combining of these cognitive, environmental, and social factors will we be able to attain a better understanding of human-interaction processes.

REFERENCES

Aiello, J. R. A test of equilibrium theory: Visual interaction in relation to orientation, distance and sex of interactants. *Psychonomic Science,* 1972, *2,* 335-336.

Aiello, J. R. A further look at equilibrium theory: Visual interaction as a function of interpersonal distance. *Environmental Psychology and Nonverbal Behavior,* 1977, *1,* 122-140. (a)

Aiello, J. R. Visual interaction at extended distances. *Personality and Social Psychology Bulletin,* 1977, *3,* 83-86. (b)

Aiello, J. R., & Aiello, T. D. The development of personal space: Proxemic behavior of children 6 through 16. *Human Ecology,* 1974, *2,* 177-189.

Aiello, J. R., & Baum, A. *Residential crowding and design.* New York: Plenum, 1979.

Aiello, J. R., & Cooper, R. E. *Personal space and social affect: A developmental study.* Paper presented at the meeting of the Society for Research in Child Development, San Francisco, 1979.

Aiello, J. R., DeRisi, D. T., Epstein, Y. M., & Karlin, R. A. Crowding and the role of interpersonal distance preference, *Sociometry,* 1977, *40,* 271-282.

Aiello, J. R., Epstein, Y. M., & Karlin, R. A. *Methodological and conceptual issues in crowding.* Paper presented at the meeting of the Western Psychological Association, San Francisco, 1974.

Aiello, J. R., Epstein, Y. M., & Karlin, R. A. Effects of crowding on electrodermal activity. *Sociological Symposium,* 1975, *14,* 43-57. (a)

Aiello, J. R., Epstein, Y. M., & Karlin, R. A. *Field experimental research on human crowding.* Paper presented at the annual convention of the Eastern Psychological Association, New York City, 1975. (b)

Aiello, J. R., Headly, L. A., & Thompson, D. E. Effects of crowding on the elderly: A preliminary investigation. *Journal of Population,* 1978, *1,* 283-297.

Aiello, J. R., Nicosia, G., & Thompson, D. E. Physiological, social and behavioral consequences of crowding on children and adolescents. *Child Development,* 1979, *50,* 195-202.

Aiello, J. R., & Thompson, D. E. Personal space, crowding, and spatial behavior in a cultural context. In I. Altman, J. F. Wohlwill, & A. Rapoport (Eds.), *Human behavior and environment, Volume 4. Culture and environment.* New York: Plenum, 1980. (a)

Aiello, J. R., & Thompson, D. E. When compensation fails: Mediating effects of sex and locus of control at extended interaction distances. *Basic and Applied Social Psychology,* 1980, *1,* 65-82. (b)

Allport, F. H. *Social psychology.* Boston: Houghton Mifflin, 1924.

Allport, G. W. The historical background of modern social psychology. In G. Lindzey & E. Aronson (Eds.), *The handbook of social psychology* (2nd ed.). Reading, Mass.: Addison-Wesley, 1968.

Altman, I. Environmental psychology and social psychology. *Personality and Social Psychology Bulletin,* 1976, *2,* 96-113. (a)

Altman, I. A response to Epstein, Proshansky, and Stokols. *Personality and Social Psychology Bulletin,* 1976, *2,* 364-370. (b)

Altman, I. Crowding: Historical and contemporary trends in crowding research. In A. Baum & Y. Epstein (Eds.), *Human responses to crowding.* Hillsdale, N.J.: Lawrence Erlbaum Associates, 1978.

Argyle, M., & Dean, J. Eye-contact, distance and affiliation. *Sociometry,* 1965, *28,* 289-304.

Baum, A., Aiello, J. R., & Calesnick, L. E. Crowding and personal control: Social density and the development of learned helplessness. *Journal of Personality and Social Psychology,* 1978, *36,* 1000-1011.

Brehm, J. W. *A theory of psychological reactance.* New York: Academic Press, 1966.

Calhoun, J. B. Population density and social pathology. *Scientific American,* 1962, *206,* 139-148.

Desor, J. A. Toward a psychological theory of crowding. *Journal of Personality and Social Psychology,* 1972, *21,* 79-83.

Duke, M. P., & Nowicki, S. A new measure and social-learning model for interpersonal distance. *Journal of Experimental Research in Personality,* 1972, *6,* 119–132.

Freedman, J. L., Klevansky, S., & Ehrlich, P. I. The effect of crowding on human task performance. *Journal of Applied Social Psychology,* 1971, *1,* 7–26.

Gergen, K. J. Social psychology as history. *Journal of Personality and Social Psychology,* 1973, *26,* 309–320.

Gergen, K. J. Social psychology, science and history. *Personality and Social Psychology Bulletin,* 1976, *2,* 373–383.

Karlin, R. A., Epstein, Y. M., & Aiello, J. R. A setting-specific analysis of crowding. In A. Baum & Y. Epstein (Eds.), *Human response to crowding.* Hillsdale, N.J.: Lawrence Erlbaum Associates, 1978.

Lantz, H. R. Population density and psychiatric diagnosis. *Sociology and Social Research,* 1953, *37,* 322–326.

Love, K. D., & Aiello, J. R. Using projective techniques to measure interaction distance: A methodological note. *Personality and Social Psychology Bulletin,* 1980, *6,* 102–104.

McGuire, W. J. The yin and yang of progress in social psychology: Seven koan. *Journal of Personality and Social Psychology,* 1973, *26,* 446–456.

McGuire, W. J. *Toward social psychology's second century.* Paper presented at the meeting of the American Psychological Association, New York City, September 1979.

Pagán, G., & Aiello, J. R. *Development of personal space among Puerto Ricans.* Unpublished manuscript, Rutgers University, 1979.

Petri, H. L., & Huggins, R. C. *Some developmental characteristics of personal space.* Paper presented at the meetings of the Eastern Psychological Association, New York City, 1975.

Proshansky, H. M. Comment on environmental and social psychology. *Personality and Social Psychology Bulletin,* 1976, *2,* 359–363.

Proshansky, H. M., Ittelson, W., & Rivlin, L. G. (Eds.). *Environmental psychology: Man and his physical setting.* New York: Holt, Rinehart, & Winston, 1970.

Rodin, J., & Baum, A. Crowding and helplessness: Potential consequences of density and loss of control. In A. Baum & Y. Epstein (Eds.), *Human response to crowding.* Hillsdale, N.J.: Lawrence Erlbaum Associates, 1978.

Schlenker, B. R. Social psychology and science. *Journal of Personality and Social Psychology,* 1974, *29,* 1–15.

Schlenker, B. R. Social psychology and science: Another look. *Personality and Social Psychology Bulletin,* 1976, *2,* 384–390.

Schmid, C. Urban crime areas: Part 1. *American Sociological Review,* 1969, *25,* 527–542.

Schmitt, R. C. Density, delinquency, and crime in Honolulu. *Sociology and Social Research,* 1957, *41,* 274–276.

Seligman, M. E. P. *Helplessness.* San Francisco: Freeman, 1975.

Stokols, D. Environmental psychology. *Annual Review of Psychology,* 1978, *29,* 253–295.

Tennis, C. H., & Dabbs, J. M. Sex, setting and personal space: First grade through college. *Sociometry,* 1975, *38,* 385–394.

Wohlwill, J. F. The emerging discipline of environmental psychology. *American Psychologist,* 1970, *25,* 303–312.

V COGNITION, SOCIAL BEHAVIOR, AND THE ENVIRONMENT

Similar to the chapters in the first section, the four papers in this section are quite general in scope. The emphasis, however, is on the interplay of processes all of which in some way relate to the environment-person interaction. The first paper by Daniel Stokols and Sally Shumaker represents an ambitious attempt to develop a conceptualization of settings emphasizing the cognitive and behavioral transactions between people and places and to examine certain policy implications of this line of reasoning. The key terms in Stokols and Shumaker's analysis are ''place'' and ''transaction.'' This analysis is rich in substance, involving, for example, a taxonomy of settings, and represents, in some sense, all of the major concepts considered in our dialogue among cognitive, environmental, and social psychologists.

In the second paper, Gary Winkel presents an analysis of the ways in which an individual's immediate living environment (the home and the neighborhood) contribute to individual and social well being. Winkel suggests that people are embedded in a context that is defined not only by the geographic locale of residence but that also involves primary and secondary social contexts within which they live. Perry Thorndyke, in discussing Winkel's paper at the conference, draws a parallel between Winkel's argument that people's image of environmental deterioration is dependent on their particular experiences in the environment and the so-called representativeness fallacy in decision-making research articulated by Kahneman and Tversky. Thorndyke suggests that if, as Winkel contends, people have no direct experience with environmental deterioration, they tend to view deterioration in idiosyncratic terms, not unlike the tendency for decision-makers to ignore statistical information in favor of anecdotal, personal experiences.

In the next paper, Andrew Baum, Robert Gatchel, and John Aiello present ideas and data within a multi-level perspective emphasizing environmental, social, and cognitive determinants of mood and behavior. Baum et al. take the position that environmental influence will depend on what is going on in the environment and how those people in the setting interpret what is occurring. As the reader also may conclude, the Baum et al. perspective epitomizes a value that is of central import in the development of this conference and the resulting volume. The authors present some intriguing results from studies of subjects in dormitory settings. These results reveal the value (and perhaps necessity) of a multi-level perspective for exploring independent, dependent, and mediating variables in these complex real world settings.

In the final paper in this section, Anthony Greenwald presents one of the most integrative and searching essays in the volume. Relying on evidence about the existence of various cognitive biases, he develops the argument that the self may be regarded as an organization of knowledge and that some cognitive biases can be readily understood only if it is assumed that there exists an organization whose survival they enhance. This argument alone should be a provocative issue for discussion by scholars interested in the self. Greenwald then analyzes cognitive dissonance theory as an example of this type of organization of knowledge. Finally, he extends his analysis to include discussion of how physical environmental structures may be viewed in terms of their functions as social organizers. This is a far-ranging chapter that involves a breadth of inquiry and intellectual challenge that is similar to that found in Proshansky's bold presentation at the beginning of this volume.

22

People in Places: A Transactional View of Settings

Daniel Stokols
Sally Ann Shumaker
University of California, Irvine

INTRODUCTION

The chapters in this volume highlight the current emphasis on the ecological environment in psychological research (cf. White, 1979). The significance of the large-scale environment for behavior and health has been underscored by the contemporary problems of pollution, resource shortages, and urban stress. Yet, the establishment of an ecological orientation among psychologists was prompted as much by challenging theoretical issues as by pragmatic societal concerns. For, after decades of research, it has become increasingly clear that human behavior and well-being cannot be understood solely in terms of psychological processes and the proximate social environment, but must be considered in relation to the broader context as well—the sociocultural and physical milieu in which people are actively involved.

Although the behavioral relevance of the molar environment is widely recognized, systematic studies of the transactions between people and their sociophysical settings have been sparse (see Barker & Associates, 1978; Bronfenbrenner, 1979; and Moos, 1976, for notable exceptions). A major difficulty facing such research is the staggering complexity of the large-scale environment. Unlike the discrete stimuli and cues comprising the microenvironment (cf. Gibson, 1960; Skinner, 1953), the architectural, geographical, and sociocultural components of the molar environment are interdependently arrayed in the form of dynamic, ecological systems (cf. Barker, 1968). In the face of this complexity, it becomes difficult to demarcate the appropriate units of environmental analysis, and to assess their implications for behavior and health.

A crucial challenge facing psychological research is to develop a theoretical basis for describing and categorizing the diverse settings of human behavior. Only by identifying the important dimensions and processes of settings can we begin to assess the comparability of environments and the ecological validity of our research findings and policy decisions (cf. Secord, 1977). Guided by these concerns, the major purposes of the present chapter are (1) to develop a conceptualization of settings emphasizing the cognitive and behavioral transactions between people and places; (2) to delineate a set of theoretical dimensions for describing and categorizing settings; and (3) to derive research hypotheses from the proposed taxonomic dimensions.

The term setting, as it has been used in the psychological literature, typically refers to a common set of interrelated elements—namely, a particular place in which specific individuals share recurring patterns of activity and experience (cf. Argyle, 1977; Barker, 1968; Bronfenbrenner, 1977; Magnusson, 1981; Pervin, 1978; Wicker, 1979b). Among the most comprehensive psychological analyses of settings are Barker's (1960, 1968) theory of "behavior settings" and Bronfenbrenner's (1977, 1979) analysis of the ecology of human development. Although their analyses focus on different psychological and developmental questions, both Barker and Bronfenbrenner construe settings as units of the ecological environment that are characterized by the high degree of interdependence among their physical, social-structural, and personal components.

The conceptualization of settings presented in this chapter extends earlier analyses in at least three respects. First, it gives explicit consideration to the concept of "place"—the geographical and architectural context of behavior. Previous analyses of settings have emphasized the social and behavioral aspects of settings (e.g., processes of under- and overmanning in Barker's theory; transcontextual social networks in Bronfenbrenner's analysis), while neglecting to consider the relationships between these dimensions and the architectural–geographical milieu.[1] Second, a transactional perspective is emphasized in the present analysis, highlighting the reciprocal influence between people and places. Places, thus, are viewed not only as a composite of behavior-shaping forces, but also as the material and symbolic product of human action. Third, our analysis distinguishes among settings that are oriented toward and occupied by single individuals, coacting aggregates, and/or interactive groups. This strategy is in contrast to earlier analyses that have not differentiated among settings in terms of the composition and organization of their occupants. Our approach is based on the assumption that a categorization of settings, reflecting the different levels of social organization and interdependence among occupants offers theoretical leverage for understanding the complex transactions between people and places.

---

[1]Recent chapters by Barker (1979) and Proshansky, Nelson-Shulman, and Kaminoff (1979) are exceptions to this trend.

We should note, however (as becomes apparent in the latter sections of the chapter), that our analysis gives greatest attention to group-occupied settings. We have chosen to emphasize this category of settings because people spend so much of their waking time in groups, and because group-occupied settings afford an opportunity to assess the interrelationships among a wider range of environmental dimensions (e.g., social-structural and organizational as well as psychological and physical dimensions) than do individual- and aggregate-occupied settings.

As a basis for developing the proposed theoretical analysis, it is first necessary to examine in detail the two major components of settings: their physical milieu (places) and their occupants (individuals, aggregates, and groups). Theoretical terms for describing and analyzing the physical milieu and occupants of settings are delineated in the next two sections of the chapter. Throughout these sections, the artificiality of rigidly separating the components of settings becomes apparent, as our analysis arrives at a taxonomy of settings based on transactional or relational terms. Places, for example, are characterized in terms of the predominant orientation of their human functions (e.g., individual-, aggregate-, or group-oriented), whereas people are distinguished by their association or lack of association with particular places (e.g., place-specific and place-nonspecific) and their perceived attachments to those environments (e.g., place-dependent and place-independent). In the final section of the chapter, the proposed taxonomic terms are utilized as a basis for developing a theoretical analysis of the group–environment interface and for deriving hypotheses about the dynamic relationships between people and places.

PLACES: THE PHYSICAL AND SYMBOLIC CONTEXT OF HUMAN ACTION

In 1943, Clark Hull, a leading proponent of behavioral psychology, commented that "... as the behavior sciences evolve the relationships where multiple causes are involved will be expressed more and more precisely in the form of equations; ... It is hardly to be doubted that the behavior sciences are rapidly moving in this direction [p. 288]." Hull's statement summarizes the lofty aspirations of American psychologists during the 1940's, 1950's, and early 1960's—the heyday of behaviorism and the golden age of experimentation—as they rushed into their laboratories in quest of discovering the laws of human behavior.

The experimental search for enduring behavioral laws posed some important implications regarding the proper definition of the environment, on the one hand, and its behavioral consequences, on the other. First, the environment had to be construed in terms of discrete, separable units—that is, *stimuli*—that were amenable to systematic observation within the laboratory. Second, these environmental elements, or stimuli, had to be isolated—that is, examined singly or in small clusters—so that their functional relationships with specific *responses* of the organism could be discerned through experimental manipulation. In the words of Benton Underwood (1957), a highly regarded methodologist, "One may vary more than one stimulus condition in a given experiment . . . but to draw a conclusion about the influence of any given variable, that variable must have been systematically manipulated alone, somewhere in the design [p. 35]."

As psychologists pursued the laws of behavior, their experimentalist fervor gradually gave way to concerns about the external validity or generalizability of laboratory findings (cf. Campbell & Stanley, 1963), and the simplicity of stimulus–response models vis-a-vis the complexity of behavior within naturalistic settings (cf. Gergen, 1973; Ring, 1967; Smith, 1972; Willems & Raush, 1969). In light of these concerns, many psychologists shifted their theoretical focus from the micro to the molar environment in the hope of identifying the contextual moderators of environment–behavior relationships (e.g., Barker, 1963; Chein, 1954; Craik, 1973; Gibson, 1960; Lewin, 1936).

With the emergence of environmental psychology during the late 1960's and early 1970's (cf. Craik, 1973; Wohlwill, 1970), several programs of research emphasizing the large-scale environment were implemented. Research in the areas of environmental cognition, spatial behavior, and stress exemplify this changing research strategy. In the area of environmental cognition, Lynch (1960) developed a conceptualization of cognitive mapping within humans, drawing upon Tolman's (1938) pioneering (but initially neglected) research on "cognitive maps" in rats. Also, Ittelson (1973) contributed a comprehensive analysis of the differences between environment (place) and object (stimulus) perception.

In the areas of spatial behavior and stress, researchers have examined several dimensions of the large-scale environment as they affect human performance and well-being. Studies of personal space, territoriality, and crowding, for example, have established the behavioral and health relevance of variables such as residential density and architectural design (cf. Altman, 1975; Baum & Valins, 1977; Gove, Hughes, & Galle, 1979; Newman, 1973). Other studies have demonstrated the impact of stressors such as community noise, ambient temperature, and air pollution on behavior (cf. Baron & Bell, 1976; Cohen, Glass, & Singer, 1973).

These studies of spatial behavior and stress reflect some significant trends in current research on environment and behavior. First, investigations of the molar environment typically proceed by isolating (via laboratory or field experiments) specific dimensions of the sociophysical milieu—for example, architectural design, noise, density, ambient temperature—and examining their relationships with behavior and health. Although this strategy is consistent with the sequential, experimental strategy favored by Underwood (see the previous quote), it fails to capture the interdependencies among multiple dimensions of the environment and their joint relationships with behavior. One objective of the present analysis is to highlight the interconnections among social-structural and architectural–geographical components of settings.

Second, psychologists typically construe the environment either in terms of its objective, material features or in terms of the individual's subjective impressions of those features. Rarely are the objective and subjective elements of environments considered within the same analysis.[2] In our view, the sociophysical environment is a composite of material and symbolic features. Thus, an attempt is made to integrate the objectivist and subjectivist perspectives within the proposed conceptualization of places. More specifically, the degree to which a place has been transformed by its occupants from a mélange of material elements into a symbolically meaningful setting serves as an important criterion for describing and comparing diverse environments.

Finally, whereas most research on environmental cognition has emphasized the individual's perception of the environment (cf. Moore & Gollege, 1976), the present analysis encompasses the phenomena of social perception—that is, the processes by which setting members collectively perceive and ascribe meaning to their sociophysical milieu. By focusing on the common or widely recognized meanings that become associated with the molar environment, our analysis offers a "middle ground" between subjectivist perspectives, which construe environmental perception as essentially a personal, idiosyncratic phenomenon, and objectivist views of the environment, which avoid reference to perceptual processes altogether.

It is apparent from the preceding discussion that places can be characterized in terms of numerous criteria, including their overt physical attributes, individuals' perceptions of those attributes, and occupants' collective interpretation of place meanings. We have chosen to develop a categorization of places based on their functional, motivational, and evaluative meanings, as reflected in the collective appraisals of their occupants. We believe that an analysis of collectively held place meanings offers conceptual leverage for understanding phenomena such as the degree to which occupants feel dependent on or attached to a particular place, their reactions to abrupt environmental change or relocation, and the conditions under which residents and users will be motivated to improve or withdraw from a given place.

As a basis for identifying the functional, motivational, and evaluative meanings of places, it is necessary to examine the processes of collective perception in more detail. Our discussion of these phenomena builds upon an earlier analysis of group–place transactions presented by Stokols (1981).

---

[2]As examples of the polarity between objectivist and subjectivist viewpoints in psychological research, see Brunswik's (1943) "encapsulation" critique of Lewin's (1936) life-space concept; Gibson's (1977) theory of environmental affordances vis-a-vis Neisser's (1976) constructivist view of perception, and Wohlwill's (1974) article, "The environment is not in the head!"

The Social Perception of Places

The widely recognized images or meanings conveyed by places constitute the nonmaterial properties of the physical milieu—the sociocultural ''residue'' or residual meaning that becomes attached to places as the result of their continuous association with specific patterns of activity. Just as environments can be described in terms of the imageability (or memorability) of their physical elements (Lynch, 1960), they also can be characterized in terms of their *social imageability*—that is, their capacity to evoke vivid and collectively held social meanings among the occupants and users of a place.[3] The sociocultural meanings associated with a place can be thought of as a kind of ''glue'' that binds individuals and groups to a particular environment.

Not all places can be characterized as socially imageable, due to the absence of certain circumstances that foster the development of social imageability. One such factor is the regularlity with which places are occupied. We can distinguish between *patterned-activity* (i.e., regularly occupied) and *nonpatterned-activity* (i.e., unoccupied or sporadically occupied places). Examples of the former include homes, schools, public parks and beaches, and the entire array of behavior settings that have been investigated by Barker and his colleagues (cf. Barker & Associates, 1978). Examples of the latter include empty fields or dilapidated buildings that are neither inhabited nor used by people on a regular basis. A central assumption of this analysis is that places acquire social imageability to the extent that they are regularly and predictably associated with particular patterns of individual and/or collective behavior.

For those places that are associated with recurring patterns of activity, several additional factors may mediate the development of social imageability. For example, the frequency with which community members used a particular place, the number of people in the community who use or know about the place, and the degree to which inhabitants or users of the place communicate with each other about the sociocultural meanings of their environment are all potential determinants of social imageability.

The imageability of a place refers to those features of the environment that are highly salient to its occupants. Kevin Lynch's (1960) discussion of the physical imageability of places, for example, emphasizes the dimension of *perceptual salience*—that is, the number and intensity of highly noticeable features within an environment (cf. Stokols, 1979; Taylor & Fiske, 1978). Among the factors that heighten the perceptual salience of environments are stimulus contrast, novelty, and complexity (cf. Berlyne, 1960; Kaplan, 1975; Wohlwill, 1976).

The concept of social imageability, as used in this analysis, refers not to the perceptual prominence of environments, but rather to their *functional, motivational,* and *evaluative significance.* These dimensions of environmental

---

[3]A glossary of the various terms introduced throughout our analysis is provided at the end of this chapter.

salience encompass collectively held images that relate, respectively, to three basic facets of places: (1) their *functions*—that is, individual- or group-specific activities that occur within places on a regular basis, the norms associated with these activities, as well as descriptive information regarding the identities and social roles of setting members; (2) personal and collective *goals* and purposes, each of which is weighted by its relative importance to the inhabitants or regular users of a place; and (3) *evaluations* of occupants, physical features, and/or social functions typically associated with a place (e.g., the negative stereotypes connected with certain neighborhoods regarding the presumed dangerousness of their occupants; cf. Suttles, 1968).[4]

The actual content of those meanings associated with particular places is referred to in this discussion as the perceived social field of the physical environment. More specifically, the *perceived social field of a place is defined as the totality of functional, motivational, and evaluative meanings conveyed by the physical environment to current or prospective occupants of the place.* This matrix of meanings is essentially a set of collectively held images that evolve as the result of direct or indirect interaction with a particular place.

The evolution of sociocultural meanings within organizations and cultural groups generally has been investigated by sociologists and anthropologists (cf. Agar, Chapter 2 in this volume; Berger & Luckmann, 1966; Garfinkel, 1967; Gerson & Gerson, 1976; Mead, 1934; Tyler, 1969), though more recently psychologists have begun to apply ethnographic methods to the study of social interaction and group structure (e.g., Harré, 1977; Harré & Secord, 1972). The present analysis diverges from these earlier investigations by focusing on place-related meanings (i.e., those attached to a particular environment or category of environments) rather than on the broader set of social rules and meanings (e.g., ethical norms) that are widely held by the members of a community but are not necessarily attached to a specific place.

The notion that physical environments convey information about the sociocultural functions associated with them is similar to Gibson's (1977) "affordance" concept. The affordance of an object or place refers to the potential uses or activities it suggests to observers by virtue of its physical properties (cf. Kaplan, 1978). Gibson has distinguished among physical affordances (those associated with objects and places) and social affordances—the potential forms and consequences of interpersonal encounters available within a social situation (cf. Baron, Chapter 4 in this volume). Whereas physical affordances are presumed to be recognizable by most members of a species, many categories of social affordances are more likely to be perceived by the members of a particular group than by outsiders.

---

[4]The dimensions of functional, motivational, and evaluative salience reflect the three factors of semantic meaning identified by Osgood, Suci, and Tannenbaum (1957): activity, potency, and evaluation.

In the present analysis, the concept of social field subsumes only those social affordances (i.e., functional meanings) that become associated with specific places (e.g., having a drink with one's friends at a local tavern), while excluding those that are not restricted to particular places or types of places (e.g., having a friendly chat). At the same time, it should be noted that the imageability of a place is determined not only by the social affordances it subsumes, but also by those that it precludes (e.g., the difficulty of informal social interaction at a religious service).

The specific meanings associated with places can be described in terms of their content, complexity, clarity, heterogeneity, distortions, and contradictions (cf. Stokols, 1981). For example, the *content* of the social field can be assessed by having a representative sample of occupants list those functional, motivational, and evaluative meanings associated with a given place. This open-ended procedure is similar to Harré and Secord's (1972) notion of "accounting" (i.e., the explication of social action in terms of shared social meanings reflected in individuals' accounts of their social experiences) but pertains more specifically to the sociocultural images attached to the physical environment.

The *complexity* of the social field can be indexed in terms of the number of shared meanings that emerge from the independent listings provided by the different users of a place. The more often a particular meaning is cited by the occupants and users of a place, the greater its *clarity*. An additional criterion for judging the relative clarity of place meanings is the extent to which they are rated by occupants as being highly or slightly characteristic of a particular place.[5]

In some situations, the content and clarity of place meanings may vary according to subgroup membership. Thus, the perceived social field can be characterized in terms of its *heterogeneity,* or the number of subgroups within an environment for whom distinguishable patterns of meaning can be discerned. The social field also can be analyzed in terms of its *distortions.* Distortions are unrecognized discrepancies between the sociocultural images of a place and the nature of the social activities and experiences that actually occur there. Distortions can arise as the result of insufficient exposure to a place (e.g., among outsiders who have never visited the area or among group members who are minimally involved in its activities) or from misinformation about the place.

---

[5]Considering the perceived social field as a whole (i.e., as a composite of multiple meanings), an index of the social imageability of a place can be derived by weighting the diverse meanings of the social field (reflecting its content and complexity) by their relative clarity among setting occupants. An ambiguous social field would be characterized by low imageability—that is, by a lack or small number of vivid images and/or by a lack of agreement among occupants regarding place meanings. See also Jackson's (1965, 1966) analysis of the norm "crystallization" for an alternative approach to the assessment of collectively perceived social meanings, and Milgram and Jodelet's (1976) methods for analyzing collective images of Paris.

Finally, we can characterize place meanings in terms of their *contradictions*—that is, their consistency with or contradiction of the preferences of occupants. Discrepancies between the actual and preferred meanings of a place are exemplified by situations in which people's images of a place are negatively toned as a result of earlier, unpleasant experiences there, or where the actual uses of a place are contradictory to its intended functions (e.g., the presence of a noisy group in a reading room at the library).

The proposed dimensions and measures of place meanings, outlined, previously offer a basis for categorizing environments and for analyzing the reciprocal relationships between people and places. In the remainder of this section, we develop a categorization of places in terms of their functional meanings; in subsequent sections, we examine the processes by which the motivational and evaluative salience of places prompt their occupants to enact structural modifications of the environment.

The Functional Orientation of Places

Our analysis of the perceived social field suggests that places can be categorized in terms of their predominant functional orientations. Earlier, we distinguished between nonpatterned-activity (irregularly occupied) and patterned-activity (regularly occupied) places. In the former, the absence of recurring activity patterns precludes the association of unambiguous, widely recognized functional meanings with the environment. Such places, because they exclude the possibility of occupation or are structured in ways that inhibit the development of sustained activity, remain ambiguous in their functional meanings. Rugged mountain terrains, desert areas, and open fields, for example, are all unlikely places for the development of patterned behaviors. Although people may climb a mountain, explore a desert, or wander through an open field, the probability is low that these behaviors will be repeated or exist independently of a particular person or group. Only in those cases in which people have intervened in these natural environments and have implemented design changes that foster, for instance, hiking, exploring, or wandering (e.g., natural park trails) will clear-cut, functional meanings become associated with the place. In such instances, the places are linked with patterned activities and fall within our second category of place types.

Considering the wide array of functional meanings that evolve within patterned-activity places, it is apparent that such meanings can be categorized according to several different strategies. One such strategy involves a straightforward description of the kinds of activities and behaviors that occur within an environment (e.g., eating, socializing, parenting, political events; cf. Price & Blashfield, 1975). An alternative taxonomic approach is to subsume specific categories of behavior within a smaller set of broader categories (e.g.,

Moos, 1976). Our analysis reflects the second general strategy. Specifically, we categorize the functional meanings of places in terms of the composition and organization of occupants. An advantage of this approach, we believe, is that it provides transactional terms for describing environments that reflect the linkages between physical and social-structural features of places.

Patterned-activity places, thus, are categorized according to whether occupants and users perceive them to be functionally oriented toward single individuals, coacting aggregates, or organized groups. (We are assuming, for the time being, a correspondence between the actual and perceived functional orientations of places. Possible discrepancies between the actual functions and the perceived functional meanings of environments are discussed in a subsequent section of the chapter.)

Individual-oriented places are those typically occupied by a single individual. A private study room or carrel within a library, an individual's bedroom, or the bathroom in a family dwelling exemplify such places. The physical structure and normative properties of these environments either preclude or discourage occupancy by more than one person at a time.

Aggregate-oriented places are those typically occupied by coacting individuals—that is, by collectivities comprised of strangers or minimally related people. Examples of these environments include public subway stations, beaches, pedestrian malls, or parking lots. In these locations, activities are performed by several individuals who are usually unrelated to each other.

Group-oriented places, in contrast with the first two categories of environments, are usually occupied by people who know and interact with each other on a regular basis—that is, by organized groups. The secret meeting place of a neighborhood gang, the headquarters of a business or religious group, the backyard of a family residence, and the practice field of an athletic team exemplify group-oriented places. In each instance, the predominant functions of the environment are geared toward the presence of organized groups. (See Fig. 22.1). (The distinguishing features of groups vis-a-vis coacting aggregates are discussed in the following section of the chapter.)

For several of the examples just mentioned, it is apparent that the main functions associated with a place can be performed by either the same occupants or by different occupants on different occasions. Library study rooms, for instance, might be reserved for use by a specific person, or could be used by several individuals on a rotating basis. Similarly, an athletic practice field might be reserved for use by one team only or could be utilized by different groups at various times. Environments whose functions are performed by the same people on a regular basis we label *same-occupant places;* those whose functions are carried out by different people on a rotating basis we refer to as *variable-occupant places*. The implications of occupant variability for understanding the dynamic relationships between people and their environments are examined in the section of this chapter focusing on settings.

The proposed categories of individual-, aggregate-, and group-oriented places are intended as "ideal types" and, as such, reflect oversimplifications of the actual environment. The meaning and applicability of the proposed place types, therefore, should be qualified in relation to several conceptual issues. First, the suggested categorization of places might imply that environments have singular, rather than multiple, functional orientations. Yet, the constituency of many environments varies over time, as illustrated by offices that support the simultaneous activities of individuals and small groups, or by classrooms that are sometimes used as a study place by individuals and, at other times, as a meeting place by the people enrolled in a course. Thus, a distinction can be drawn between *single-function* and *multiple-function* places. This distinction suggests that any attempt to characterize the functional orientation/s of a place must be carefully bounded with respect to specific time and space coordinates (e.g., the use of Room 432 on Thursday from 1:00 to 2:00 P.M.; the conference meeting area within the executive suite of ACME corporation).

Closely related to the issue of single versus multiple functions of places is the nested or *hierarchical structure of environments* (cf. Barker, 1968). Library study rooms, for example, are located within broader territorial and administrative systems (e.g., the library building, the campus environment). Thus, such places can be characterized not only in terms of the functional meanings associated with individual study, but also with those reflecting the administration of the library (e.g., the maintenance schedule dictating the times at which study rooms must be vacated by readers to permit floor mopping, or the opening and closing hours of the library building).

The functional meanings associated with library study rooms can be assessed from the perspective of individual users or from that of library administrators. In general, our analysis of place meanings emphasizes the perspective of performers within places, but it is important to note that the images of environments can be assessed from the vantage point of administrators and managers, or from the perspective of potential occupants who have had minimal direct exposure to the environment under consideration.

An additional distinction between *geographical* versus *generic places* should be noted.[6] The former refers to a particular geographical area whereas the latter refers to a category of places that are functionally similar. For instance, in attempting to ascertain the functional orientations of BarBQue restaurants, we can query current or potential customers of BarBQue restaurants in general, or we can ask them about "Shorty's BarBQue on Dixie Highway in South Miami, Florida." The level of specificity of the environment poses a number of implications regarding the complexity, clarity, and heterogeneity of place meanings reflected in the respondents' comments. The composite of functional meanings

---

[6]The distinction between particular and generic places was suggested by Stephan Kaplan in a personal communication.

associated with a particular place is likely to be more complex (detailed) than that conveyed by a generic category of environments. Moreover, the place meanings perceived by actual versus potential users of an environment are more likely to diverge when they consider a specific place rather than a more general category of places. For example, people who have never been to a restaurant are more likely to have encountered indirect information about restaurants in general, via the media and friends, than about a specific eating place.

Finally, the relationship between environmental specificity and the characteristics of place meanings (e.g., their complexity, clarity) suggests the importance of distinguishing among *personal, common,* and *shared meanings* of environments. Personal meanings are impressions about places (i.e., their functional, motivational, and evaluative meanings) that are held by single individuals. Personal meanings can be arrived at on an idiosyncratic basis (i.e., through intuition alone), through direct experience with an environment, or through communication with others about their experiences with a place. Personal meanings become part of the perceived social field, described earlier, to the extent that they closely resemble (or are cross-validated by) the place meanings perceived by other users of the environment.

Considering those meanings that are subsumed under the perceived social field (i.e., are jointly held by current or potential occupants of the place), we can distinguish between common and shared meanings. The key difference between these categories of meanings is that the former do not presuppose communication among place users (that is, the commonly held meanings do not arise, intensify, or change as the result of such communication), whereas the latter do. The functional meanings associated with public beaches may arise as the result of each bather's personal experiences with the beach or through communication about the beach with sources other than fellow bathers at the time of occupancy. By contrast, the meanings that become attached to the ''turf'' of a neighborhood gang arise through the joint use of and communication about the area by members of the gang.

Summary

In this section, we have divided places into two general categories: (1) unoccupied or irregularly occupied; and (2) regularly occupied. When places are occupied on a recurring basis, they become associated with widely recognized, sociocultural meanings. These collectively held images of a place—its perceived social field—evolve from the sustained interactions that occur within it. The major components of the perceived social field are the functional, motivational, and evaluative meanings of places.

The patterned activities that occur in regularly occupied places can be oriented toward single individuals, coacting aggregates, or organized groups. These functional orientations are reflected in the physical and normative properties of places. The characterization of places in terms of their functional orientations is proposed as a very general classification scheme; several factors that qualify the proposed categorization are discussed (e.g., variability among occupants.) Having outlined and qualified some of the functional properties of places, we turn now to a more explicit analysis of the composition and organizational attributes of the occupants within places.

OCCUPANTS: THEIR COMPOSITION, ORGANIZATION, AND RELATIONSHIP TO PLACE

The number of ways people vary, both as individuals and in commerce with others, has been studied extensively by social scientists. The results of many of these investigations could be usefully applied to a description of place occupants. Any attempt on our part to review this literature here, however, would both tax our expertise and take the reader far beyond the scope and intended focus of this chapter. Instead, we highlight two features of occupants that critically influence the types of transactions that occur between people and places and are, therefore, particularly relevant to our development of a setting taxonomy. We first consider the composition and organization of occupants, and then discuss the types and degrees of associations that exist between places and people. Our distinctions among occupants along these two dimensions are, primarily, descriptive. However, in the following section of this chapter, the dynamic implications of these distinctions are developed.

Composition and Organization

One of the first things that is obvious when viewing place occupants is simply the number of people present. Is an occupant alone, or are there more than one occupant present in the same place? And, when there is more than one person present, how do the occupants relate to one another? That is, are they individuals who appear to behave independently of one another (e.g., an audience at a Broadway play) or are they more of a unit (e.g., a family picnicking together?) These initial observations produce an unambiguous classification of occupants. People in places act alone, as part of an aggregate, or as members of a group (see Figure 22.2). Before discussing some of the implications of this classification scheme, we would like to clarify our distinction between groups and aggregates.

Definitions of groups are numerous and range from general, inclusive descriptions to very elaborate, precise delineations. This range comes from the number of characteristics used to describe groups, including: internal structure, reciprocal influence of members, amount and form of interaction, degree of real and perceived boundedness, objectives (e.g., work, therapy), size, level of formality, and activities performed (cf. Cartwright & Zander, 1968; Hare, Borgatta, &

Bales, 1965; Kelley & Thibaut, 1978; McGrath, 1964; Shaw, 1976; Steiner, 1972). Because of this variety, and our emphasis on group-occupied places in the next section of this chapter, it is important that we make explicit our meaning of groups vis-a-vis aggregates. Shaw (1976) defines a group as: "... two or more persons who are interacting with one another in such a manner that each person influences and is influenced by each other person [p. 11]." We would like to add to this definition the criterion that members are aware of their interdependence. This expanded definition complements our goal of clearly differentiating groups from aggregates, while simultaneously allowing us flexibility and leverage in our discussion of setting dynamics in the following section. In that section, we discuss a number of group characteristics (e.g., boundedness, formation, structure, etc.) that are not explicitly reflected in the foregoing definition.

Although the classification of occupants by number (single versus multiple) and organization (aggregate versus group) is straightforward, each occupant category has complex implications when the transaction with place is considered. When acting alone, an individual brings to a place a number of personal factors (e.g., values and attitudes, dispositions, history, and behavioral style) that will influence his or her perception and use of the resources within that place. Thus, in conjunction with "collectively held images," there are a number of differences among individuals that impact on the transaction between person and place.

As soon as two or more people transact with the same place at the same time, a number of social factors, in addition to the individual issues, become relevant. For example, social facilitation (Zajonc, 1965), privacy (Altman, 1975), personal space (Evans & Howard, 1973), distribution of resources (Wicker, 1979a, 1979b), and complementarity in personality styles (Altman, 1977) are issues that may influence the person–place interface. When the occupants are a group, these individual and social issues are further complicated by the features that distinguish groups from aggregates (i.e., the interaction and interdependency of members), as well as by other characteristics that are specific to groups (e.g., internal structure and cohesiveness).

On a very general level, variations in occupant numbers and organization influence the sources and kinds of information available to the occupants. The perceived place meaning for a person acting alone derives from his or her personal experience with the place, shared norms, and the widely known and collectively held images of the place. A member of an aggregate has the same sources of information, with the additional input acquired from observing the transactions of others with the place; and, group members' experience is further augmented by the explicit sharing among members of place impressions and images.

One example of the possible impact of information differences on person–place transactions comes from viewing a person who enters a place for the first time and is faced with the immediate task of determining what behaviors are appropriate and how to best use the resources available. If alone, this occupant has no social cues and, therefore, must rely on the physical cues (i.e., affordances) provided by the place, and whatever he or she knows from general norms. If others are present in the place, social cues are available; and, if there is a group of friends present, the individual can enhance his or her commerce with the place by asking them relevant questions.

This example suggests a further nuance in a person's commerce with place that differs because of the number and organization of occupants. Though the presence of others may provide additional information about behavior, it also may restrict behavior. When alone, inappropriate behavior cannot be judged or evaluated by others. However, when in the presence of others, a degree of conformity is a probable outcome and pressures toward conformity are even stronger within a group (cf. Cartwright & Zander, 1968). Thus, even though movement from individual to group increases information, it may concomitantly decrease one's freedom of self expression.

Relationship to Places

Objective Properties of Association: Place specificity.   Whether occupants are acting alone or in the presence of others, their association with place can vary considerably. An individual may walk alone along a beach, join a crowd of people who are watching a sailboat race, and by chance meet some friends who are discussing sailing. In each of these situations, the association between person and place is short-lived and impromptu. Furthermore, the probability is low that the same or similar activities will predictably recur in the same places. When people occupy particular places on a sporadic basis, we describe them in these situations as being *place nonspecific.*

Another situation in which people are place nonspecific is one in which they are members of organizations that rarely (or, perhaps never) meet in a particular place on a regular basis. Members of unions and professional organizations, for example, may be place nonspecific. For them, there is no shared image of a physical place, and though recurring behaviors may occur (e.g., voting by mail for leaders), they do so independently of place.

It is important to emphasize that when we use the term place nonspecific (or, later in this section, place specific), we are not talking about trans-situational traits. Certainly, there are different styles among people in their associations with places and one difference may be the recurring nature of an occupant's association with place. That is, some people may more frequently be place nonspecific than others. However, our application of this term is limited to particular activities associated with distinct places. Limiting the term to a description of specific situations promotes a more ecological perspective than viewing it as a trait. That is, it forces us to consider the multiple factors (including individual differences) that would produce a place-nonspecific (or place-specific) association.

We describe people as *place specific* when they perform particular activities in the same location or in categories of places, on a regular, predictable, basis. To distinguish among situations in which occupants are associated with particular places versus categories of places, we use the terms *geographical* and *generic place specificity,* respectively. Examples of *geographical place specificity* are: the student working in a library carrel over a school year, the businessperson who works in an office each day, the secretary who performs his or her job-related activities at the same desk, and the football team that practices on its home field each week. These associations between people and places are predictable and they recur on a regular basis.

If people perform particular activities at differently located, but functionally similar, places, we describe their association to place as *generically place specific.* For example, a group of friends may meet for lunch, every Monday, but rotate their meeting places among restaurants. Or, a scientific organization might rotate annual convention sites among a number of university campuses. In both of these examples, the people are place specific—that is, the places they occupy are alike in characteristics that are essential to the activities in question (in these examples, eating lunch and exchanging information and ideas).

There are several possible reasons why people are place specific or place nonspecific. For example, activities vary in terms of how place specific the resources are that they require. An individual can hike in a number of places, but playing tennis requires a court, net, and so on. Activities may also differ by how acceptable their performance is in particular places (cf. Price & Bouffard, 1974). Some, for example, may require more privacy or solitude than others. People also differ in how flexible they are in their use of the environment. These variations could evolve from personality traits (e.g., a rigid versus open style), or economic realities including income and mobility (cf. Michelson, 1977). Whatever the antecedents or causes, people do develop different modal styles in their associations with particular activities and places. These styles can be classified into the two broad categories of place specific and place nonspecific. In most instances, this classification is easily done and is based on objectively observable events. Within the set of place-specific occupants, there are two further objective properties of association that merit consideration. These are *endurance* and *frequency.*

A farmer who has worked the same land all of his or her life has an association with place (i.e., the farmland) that has persisted over a lifetime. If the farmer's family has owned and worked this same land for several generations, one might argue that the association that has existed between the family and place has a quality of endurance that goes beyond the experience of the one, current family member. That is, the farmer's sense of endurance is based on his or her actual transactions with the land, and is amplified by the ancestral ties.

The example of the farmer represents one end on a continuum ranging from enduring to transitory place specificity. Individuals, however, may associate with places in less enduring ways. A student's relationship to his or her dormitory room will probably not persist beyond 1 year. Even shorter associations occur between groups that form to solve specific problems in a given period of time and that use the same place for their problem-solving activities. Thus, endurance might range from a lifetime to a few days. In all cases, the people are place specific; but, the quality of their transactions with the environment varies considerably as a function of endurance.

Although frequency of association may relate to endurance, it is not the same property. That is, people may have an infrequent, but enduring association with a place. For example, a group of college alumni may annually reconvene for the homecoming football game. Their transaction with place may endure for several decades, but it occurs only once per year. The problem-solving group described in the earlier example may meet six times per day for 1 month, or only three times during their existence as a group. For the farmer and dormitory student, frequency of transaction with place is very high. Endurance, however, ranges from 1 year to one lifetime.

Subjective Properties of Association: Place Dependence.   In addition to the objective properties of association (i.e., specificity, endurance, and frequency), there is a subjective quality to the relationship between occupants and places. Individuals have differing perceptions of their associations with places—the same person may feel an intense or compelling connection to some places, and very little linkage to others. When occupants perceive themselves as having a strong association with a place, we describe them as *place dependent*. In contrast, when occupants observe a weak connection between themselves and a place, they are characterized as *place independent*. Thus, *place dependence describes an occupant's perceived strength of association between him- or herself and specific places.*[7]

This perceived strength of association can occur at any level of analysis with respect to place. That is, a person may be place dependent on a home, a

---

[7]This presentation of place dependence extends an earlier definition presented in Stokols (1981). In the original definition, place dependence referred to an *on-going setting,* and the degree to which the major functions and actual existence of the setting are linked to a specific physical environment. In addition, the definition was limited to group members' collective perceptions of the connections between setting functions and places.

Our revised definition of place dependence is broader than the initial description, and differs in certain respects. These differences include: (1) an emphasis on the occupants' perceptions of the strength of association between *themselves* and places, as well as between their group and places; (2) the inclusion of individuals and aggregates, as well as groups, as possible setting occupants; (3) a detailed discussion of the processes underlying the development of place dependence and those factors that strengthen people's subjective attachments to places; (4) an extension of the concept by applying it to categorically similar places, as well as to specific geographical areas; and (5) the inclusion of a temporal component of place dependence that extends the concept from present to past and idealized, future places.

neighborhood, or an entire city. Furthermore, the same person may be place dependent for some associations, and place independent for others, (e.g., a person may feel a strong attachment to his or her home, but not to the office in which he or she works).

The place-dependence dimension is descriptive of individuals' (as in the preceding example), aggregates', and groups' relationships to places. A number of surfers, for example, may feel a strong attachment to a beach that they consider the "best" in their area. Though they behave fairly independently of one another (i.e., constitute an aggregate), their perceived association with the place is common. They are all place dependent with respect to that beach. Their commonality in place dependence could produce behaviors that derive strength from the aggregate, as opposed to an individual, perception—a kind of surrogate social support system (cf. Jacobs, 1961). Territorial behavior exemplifies this point. The surfers may have a tacit agreement among themselves as to who has "rights" to use of "their" beach area, and who is an outsider. This implicit understanding could bolster both their coactive and their individual responses to potential encroachments.

Groups have perceived associations with places that transcend the place dependence of individual members. The San Francisco Giants, for example, may, as a team, be place dependent on Candlestick Park. This strong association could evolve from a number of factors. Team members may share perceptions of place meanings, the park may uniquely support the team's activities, they may have a higher success rate at "home," and there may be little opportunity for relocation. Whatever the contributing elements, the outcome is a strong link to a specific place.

Our definition and examples of place dependence provide a general characterization of the concept. In order for place dependence to be usefully applied to settings, however, it is important that we go beyond this imprecise and static description to a more systematic and dynamic analysis. That is, we need to focus on the factors that underlie individual or group assessments of dependency on place. These factors can be organized within a two-component process. Briefly, they include an occupant's assessment of: (1) *the quality of current place;* and (2) *the relative quality of comparable alternative places.*

Before expanding on these components, we should note that although we are conceptualizing place dependence as evolving from occupants' assessments of the quality of places, we are not suggesting that people are continuously and self consciously monitoring their transactions with places. Place dependence is not always salient to occupants. Rather, it becomes relevant when circumstances occur that heighten the occupants' awareness of their associations to places. Periods of abrupt environmental change, relocation, and very pleasant or unpleasant experiences with places are all circumstances that could bring issues of place dependence to the fore (cf. Fried, 1963; Michelson, 1977). Our two components, therefore, merely model the process undergone by occupants when relevant levers cause place dependence to become prominent.

Whatever the particular triggering incident, once people become aware of their association to a place, they will likely assess the place's quality, and the quality of relevant alternatives, in order to determine the strength of their association (i.e., how dependent they are on a particular place). In evaluating the quality of a place, individuals judge how well the place facilitates their goals and activities. This is particularly true of those goals and activities that are most important to them. The result of this evaluation determines an occupant's satisfaction with a place—the better a place meets one's goals, the greater one's satisfaction. This kind of assessment is necessarily subjective and based on some internal standard of the occupant's as to how well a place should meet one's goals. That is, people expect certain outcomes in their transactions with places. These expectations, derived from a person's direct or vicarious experiences with possible outcomes, produces his or her Comparison Level (CL) for places (Thibaut & Kelley, 1959). Thus, degree of satisfaction with place is indexed by the extent to which an existing place's quality diverges from the occupants' CL for places (i.e., their expected level of place quality.)

A number of factors contribute to an assessment of place quality. As noted, a person's CL develops from his or her previous experiences with places. The valence of these experiences will determine current CL. Thus, for example, if individuals historically have had relatively negative outcomes, their CL will be low and they will have lower expectations in their evaluation of place quality. In contrast, a history of positive outcomes with current or comparable, previously experienced places will raise their CL and, concomitantly, the expectations imposed upon their current situation.

Several features of the resources available within a place can affect whether a place facilitates or inhibits goal attainment and, thereby, assessments of place quality. These include the amount of resources in an area, their caliber, and the degree to which they fit the needs of the occupant. The impact of each of these resource characteristics on assessments may vary considerably, and is dependent on the goal in question. For example, a hospital patient whose goal is to become healthier would be more concerned with the caliber or expertise of his or her doctor than with the number and variety of doctors available within that particular hospital.

The value or salience of the goals that are met in a particular place also influence judgments of quality. Although the thwarting of any goal is frustrating, the more important the goal, the more upsetting its blockage (cf. Stokols, 1979; Wortman & Brehm, 1975). Similarly, the achievement of highly valued goals will produce more positive feelings than the attainment of minor ones. Therefore, the value of goals or needs will mediate an occupant's assessment of place quality by influencing the strength of an occupant's reactions to goal facilitation or thwarting.

The second component in the process of assessing place dependence involves the occupants' evaluation of the relative quality of their current situation vis-a-vis alternative comparable places. That is, occupants compare the environment they presently occupy with places that they view as potential locations for their activities. Following Thibaut and Kelley's (1959) formulation of the construct Comparison Level for Alternatives (CLalt), occupants assess the quality of expected outcomes among suitable alternative places. Thus, the issue of place dependence goes beyond a simple assessment of the place currently occupied by focusing on the quality differentials among present place and relevant options.

The identification and evaluation of alternatives is affected by several factors. First, a comparison of possible options is predicated on an occupant's *awareness,* and to a lesser degree *familiarity,* with existing alternatives. Awareness refers to an individual's knowledge of relevant options. Familiarity extends awareness to actual experiences in different places. The more individuals and groups use a variety of places for similar activities, the better able they are to make informed judgments about the relative quality of places. Both awareness and familiarity of potential locations can vary considerably among people. Differences in personality styles may explain why some people are more willing to learn about locational alternatives than others. For example, one couple moving into a new home might actively explore the environment, seeking out accessible recreational facilities and service organizations. Another couple, in the same situation, might be reluctant or uninterested in searching for options, settling quickly on single places for specific activities and never becoming cognizant of other possibilities.

Mobility is another factor that can influence an evaluation of the quality of alternative places. The elderly, physically handicapped, and the poor are often severely limited in their access to different environments and are forced to perform most of their activities in places located within the immediate vicinity of their homes. Although this limited mobility can decrease knowledge of alternatives, this is not necessarily the case. People who lack mobility may be aware of and familiar with alternatives, and even recognize higher quality in places other than the ones they currently occupy. However, as long as places are inaccessible, they are nonviable alternatives.

The resources needed for the performance of some activities may be more specific than for others, thereby limiting the number of alternative places available. Sports activities like golfing and tennis are considerably more *resource specific* than jogging or bicycling. Even more limiting are the resources required by certain types of business establishments. Saw mills, ship builders, and ski resorts all are economically dependent on particular features of the environment.

Our consideration of the elements that influence assessments of current place quality (i.e., CL, resource characteristics, and value of goals), and the quality of relevant options (i.e., awareness of alternatives, mobility, and resource specificity) is not meant to represent an exhaustive list. Rather, these elements are reasonable representations of the kinds of issues that contribute to the two-component process involved in an occupant's assessment of place dependence. In addition to these specific factors, there are a number of more subtle considerations that relate to both components of the assessment process, and account for variations in the essential *character of place dependence*. We consider these variations in place dependence because of their potential implications for the dynamics of settings.

As we have mentioned, place dependence is partially evaluated in terms of how well current and alternative places facilitate the attainment of important goals. The *number and range of needs* met by a particular place will affect judgments of the character of place dependence. Places that satisfy several needs (e.g., primary environments) probably lead to a type of place dependence that can be described as being more embedded, extensive, or deep-seated for the occupants than places in which possible activities (and, therefore, attainable goals) are narrowly defined (cf. Stokols, 1979). In such situations, satisfaction with current place is based on a number of expected outcomes and represents a kind of weighted averaging of all possible effects (i.e., all needs met in one place weighted by value, and averaged across expected outcomes). In addition, the range of possible alternatives may narrow as the range of needs met in one's current environment increases.

The *type of needs* that are met within a particular place can also influence the nature of place dependence. The place dependence that occurs in environments where basic survival needs are met will undoubtedly differ from that that emerges in places where less crucial (e.g., recreational) needs are met (cf. Maslow, 1968). These differences would be most salient when place dependence is strong and occupants are threatened with a loss or disruption of place. The repercussions and impact of such threats would be considerably more serious in places meeting basic subsistence needs then in those associated with less central goals.

Place dependence can occur in situations in which outcomes are *above or below CL*. That is, occupants can be place dependent when their experiences with places are either satisfying or nonsatisfying. In some instances, people will perceive themselves as place dependent when they are satisfied with the quality of their transaction with a particular place, and they believe that this same level of satisfaction cannot be derived from their best comparable alternatives (CLalt). Occupants also can perceive themselves as being strongly linked to a particular place when their transactions with the place are unsatisfactory (below CL) but their best relevant alternative (CLalt) is perceived to be even more negative, or when they feel they have no other alternatives. For example, institutionalized people or those who lack mobility might be dissatisfied with their current place transactions, yet they may still perceive themselves as place dependent because alternatives are inaccessible.

There are several implications for the kind of place dependence that evolves in these very different circumstances. For example, when outcomes are below CL but options are worse or nonexistent, people may react against their environments (e.g., vandalism; cf. Zeisel, 1976; Sommer, 1974), or they may develop a sense of helplessness (Seligman, 1975) and feel unable to act in ways that will improve their lives. Conversely, place dependence that develops because of very positive outcomes may cause people to be very protective of their situations, unwilling to seek out alternatives, and/or resistant to any changes, even those that might improve their current situations (Burton, Kates, & White, 1978).

There are two ways in which the *temporal component* of place dependence affects its general character. As noted, place dependence can occur because of a paucity of relevant options. This lack of alternatives, however, may result from very different factors. In some situations, there may be, from the onset of transaction with place, a limited number of places in which the activity can be performed (e.g., saw mills and ski resorts). In other cases, options may decrease over time. That is, there may have been, initially, a number of viable alternatives for a particular activity but, as occupants spend more time in one place, a narrowing of known alternatives occurs.

A second temporal feature of place dependence relates to the associations people sometimes feel toward places they do not currently occupy. For example, people who are relocated because of business transfers or urban renewal projects may still perceive themselves as strongly linked to their previous or past environment. As long as this perception persists, adaptation to their new environment will most likely be slow. Similarly, people may feel a compelling association toward prospective places. Members of the Palestinian Liberation Organization exemplify this temporal quality of place dependence. That is, they perceive themselves to be linked to, and dependent on, a land that they do not currently occupy. A strong future-oriented place dependence may influence an individual's willingness to adapt to his or her current place transactions, and his or her motivation to alter current activity locations.

In assessing place dependence, occupants evaluate the quality of *perceived place options*. For a variety of reasons (e.g., awareness), there may be discrepancies between these perceived options and *actual place options*. Such inconsistencies would not affect the perception of place dependence, per se. They could, however, have major implications if the occupants become cognizant of the discrepancies. The sudden recognition that one's formerly perceived options do not really exist, or the awareness that more options exist than were initially realized, potentially could affect the long-range survival of settings as well as the short-term stress and well-being of occupants.

A final nuance of place dependence to consider here represents an extension of the CLalt construct, as developed by Thibaut and Kelley (1959). CLalt is the occupant's assessed quality of the single, best alternative. In determining strength of association between oneself and a place, the *number of available* alternatives, as well as the quality of the best alternative, are considered by the occupant. A person perceiving him or herself to have several, qualitatively similar options will probably feel less place dependent than the individual who recognizes only one alternative. Thus, the evaluation of place dependence derives from an assessment of the range or richness of options available, and the quality differentials among all viable options.

Consistent with our earlier distinction between geographical and generic place specificity, it follows that people can be dependent on either a particular place or on a category of places (*geographical* versus *generic place dependence*). People may care deeply about a place that they have never seen and probably never will—because of what it (like generically similar areas) affords. Thus, bird watchers may fight for the preservation of remote, relatively inaccessible places (an example suggested by Stephen Kaplan in a personal communication). People are motivated to preserve their generically similar place options—they care about alternatives that are attractive to them in principle, irrespective of whether they have experienced them in the past or are likely to do so in the future.

We have endeavored to define and characterize place dependence because we consider the concept to be critical in understanding several issues related to settings. Occupants' willingness to alter existing settings or establish new ones, and the impact of settings' termination on occupants, are mediated by the strength of association between place and occupant (cf. Firey, 1945; Fried, 1963). Moreover, the subtle variations in place dependence (e.g., its temporal quality) can be expected to affect the dynamics of settings in several ways. The Palestine Liberation Organization provides an interesting example of how these variations manifest themselves.

The PLO, as a group, is dependent on its current environment (i.e., settlements outside of Israel) because (1) this environment meets the subsistence needs of the members; and (2) the locational alternatives of the group are severely limited. At the same time, the group is dependent on an unrealized future place (i.e., a Palestinian state) that represents an ideal in which the member's subsistence, higher-order personal (e.g., self respect) and group (e.g., collective autonomy as a nation) needs can be met. The incongruity between the outcomes achieved in the current setting (below CL) and those believed to be attainable in the ideal setting (above CL) is stressful, motivating the group to resist adaptation to their current setting and continually strive for their ideal. The PLO is, perhaps, an extreme example of the possible variations in place dependence and the impact of these variations on settings. The more typical ways in which dependence might influence settings are discussed in the following section of this chapter. Before discussing the dynamic interface between people and places (i.e., settings), a brief review of our categorization of occupants may be helpful to the reader.

Summary

People occupy places individually, or as a part of aggregates and groups. The relationship between people and places may be regular or sporadic. When people occupy a particular place on a predictable basis, we describe them as *place specific*. When their relationship to place is irregular, we describe them as *place nonspecific*. Regular relationships between people and places vary objectively with respect to the frequency and enduring nature of the transactions. Subjectively, there may be differences in the degree to which occupants perceive themselves as linked to a particular place (i.e., *place-dependent* versus *place-independent* people).

SETTINGS: THE TRANSACTIONS AMONG PEOPLE AND PLACES

The preceding discussion offers a set of dimensions for categorizing people and places. In general, places have been characterized in terms of their predominant functional orientations, and people in terms of their organization and the type and degree of their associations with places. Although the proposed dimensions are transactional—that is, they reflect the inherent interrelatedness of people and places—we have yet to examine explicitly the dynamic relationships implied by those dimensions. To this point in the discussion, we have neglected questions such as the following: Under what conditions do places acquire a particular functional orientation? To what extent does place dependence mediate people's reactions to abrupt environmental change and to life events involving residential or occupational relocation? What factors prompt people to actively modify their sociophysical environment?

To address these and related questions pertaining to people–place transactions, we begin by delineating a taxonomy of settings based on the dimensions presented in earlier sections of this chapter. Having designated the various types of settings included in our taxonomy, we proceed to examine the dynamic relationships among people and places that are associated with those settings. Our analysis of people–place transactions is organized around a broad set of issues relating to the "life cycles of settings" (cf. Devereux, 1977; Stokols, 1978; Wicker, 1979a)—that is, the conditions under which settings are established, maintained, modified, and/or terminated.

A Taxonomy of Settings

The intersection between categories of places (see Fig. 22.1) and categories of people (see Fig. 22.2) illustrates the distinction between *settings*—that is, patterned-activity places occupied by place-specific people—and *nonsettings*— that is, nonpatterned-activity places that are either unoccupied or sporadically occupied by place-nonspecific people (see Fig. 22.3). Moreover, settings can be partitioned into six major categories on the basis of the composition and organization of their occupants (individuals, aggregates or organized groups) and the

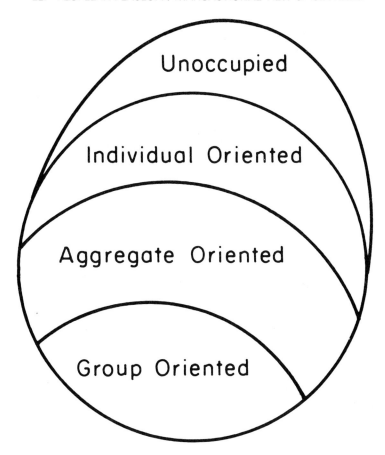

PLACES

FIG. 22.1.   Categories of places according to their functional orientation.

predominant functional meanings associated with their physical milieu (individual, aggregate, or group oriented), as depicted in Fig. 22.4. Thus, the composition and organization of occupants can be either consistent with the predominant, widely recognized orientation of the setting (e.g., an individual studying in a library carrel) or inconsistent with that orientation (e.g., a raucous group that appropriates a library study area as a regular meeting place).

Because the proposed categories of settings represent "ideal types," they necessarily oversimplify a number of inherently complex issues, including situations in which settings are associated with multiple functional orientations (e.g.,

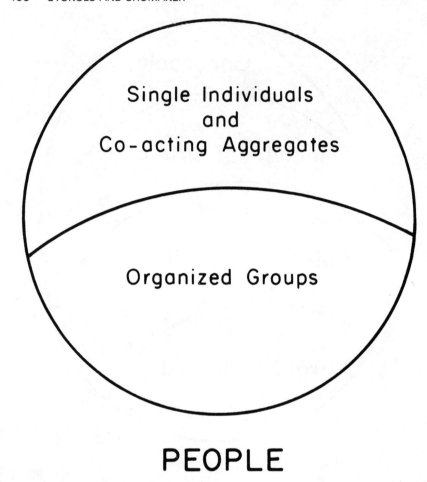

FIG. 22.2. Categories of people according to their composition and organization.

a large company office containing individual work stations, aggregate-oriented reception areas for visitors, and group-oriented conference rooms), and are occupied simultaneously by individuals, aggregates, and groups. Clearly, then, the boundaries between the proposed categories should not be viewed as rigid and impermeable.

The utility of the proposed taxonomy of settings, we believe, resides not so much in its descriptive capacity but rather in the range of theoretical questions and hypotheses that it suggests. As oversimplified as the proposed categories of settings may be, they nonetheless suggest several intriguing questions concerning the etiology, maintenance, modification, and demise of settings. For instance, in what ways do the consistencies or discrepancies among place orientations and occupant organization predispose settings to stability or instability, to internal cohesion or conflict? It is with these kinds of transactional phenomena that we are concerned throughout the remainder of this chapter.

Before turning to an analysis of the life cycle of settings, we should note once again that our discussion focuses on group-occupied rather than on individual- or aggregate-occupied settings. Our reasons for focusing on this subset of our taxonomy are threefold. First, people spend an inordinate amount of their daily routine within group-occupied places, be they family dwellings, classrooms, company offices, or friends' homes. Second, the analysis of group-occupied settings affords the consideration of social-structural as well as personal and architectural–geographical elements of settings. And third, due to space limitations, it is not possible in this discussion to provide a more comprehensive treatment of the full range of settings included within our taxonomy.

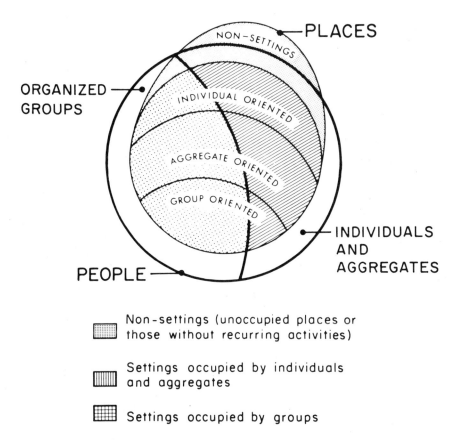

Non-settings (unoccupied places or those without recurring activities)

Settings occupied by individuals and aggregates

Settings occupied by groups

FIG. 22.3.   The intersection of people and place categories.

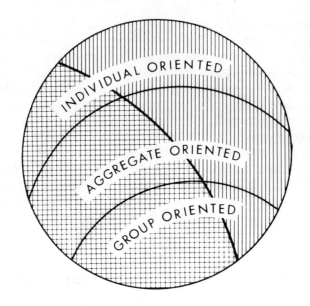

SETTINGS

|||||| Settings occupied by individuals
        and aggregates

:::::: Settings occupied by groups

FIG. 22.4.   A taxonomy of settings.

The Life Cycles of Settings

Factors Affecting the Emergence of Settings.   Edward Devereux, in a recent discussion of the life cycles of settings (Devereux, 1977), has stated that "Behavior settings are nothing more than the swirls and eddies in the flow of motivated human behavior which have become, to some degree, organized, stabilized, localized, recurrent and institutionalized [p. 13]." But what is the nature of those processes by which behavioral "swirls and eddies" are transformed into organized and enduring settings? As a preliminary basis for addressing this question, we distinguish between settings that emerge within previously unoccupied (nonpatterned-activity) places and those that develop within occupied (patterned-activity) areas. Moreover, we distinguish among situations in which the emergence of a setting coincides with the gradual development of a group within a particular place, and those in which a setting emerges as the result of territorial migration or invasion on the part of a preexisting group. These antecedents of setting development are interrelated but not wholly overlapping, and their interaction yields four different sets of conditions under which settings evolve: *unoccupied areas* that either (1) foster the development of a group and, potentially, a setting; or (2) are abruptly appropriated by a preexisting group; and *occupied areas* that either (3) permit or encourage the development of a new group; or (4) are invaded by (or peacefully merge with) an already existing, outside group. In the third and fourth instances, the previous meanings and orientation of the place are altered by the emergence or invasion of the new group.

Before examining the specific factors that influence the emergence of settings within unoccupied or occupied areas, it is necessary to consider the temporal stages reflected in the emergence of settings. At least three such stages can be identified: (1) the *inert (or sporadic-activity) phase;* (2) the *transitional-activity phase;* and (3) the *patterned-activity phase.* The first phase applies only to nonsettings—that is, unoccupied places or those characterized by sporadic occupancy and activities. The second phase describes "transitional places"—that is, occupied areas characterized by preliminary patterns of activity but lacking the clarity of functional orientation and occupant organization that typify structured settings. The emergence of a setting occurs at the outset of phase 3, once the predictability, functional meanings, and occupant structure (e.g., role relationships) associated with patterned activities are recognized and maintained by setting members.

Note that patterned-activity places (i.e., settings) are conceptualized in this analysis as more than the objective "social facts" described by Durkheim (1964). That is, the emergence of settings in our analysis presupposes a subjective dimension involving the recognition among occupants (including previous, current, or prospective occupants) of the stable, functional meanings associated with a place, and of the organizational requirements for maintaining the setting intact. Thus, settings are construed as a category of "perceived social facts"— objective social forces whose existence and impact are collectively recognized.

Having outlined some of the spatial and temporal patterns of setting emergence, we now consider a number of specific circumstances that foster the establishment of settings within unoccupied and occupied areas. Our analysis focuses, first, on conditions favoring the transformation of an initially unoccupied place from a composite of purely physical elements into an organized setting—a mixture of social as well as physical affordances. Second, we consider factors contributing to the evolution of new settings within already existing ones, such that the symbolic meanings (e.g., functional orientation) previously associated with the place undergo fundamental change.

We begin with the assumptions that unoccupied places are differentially suitable for the establishment of settings, and that those areas of greatest latent value to prospective occupants will be most likely to evolve into organized settings. The *latent value of a place* refers to its as-yet unrecognized capacity for accommodating the preferred goals and activities of prospective occupants. To the extent that this supportive capacity of an environment is recognized and, in some cases, actualized by occupants, its value becomes manifest rather than latent. Our earlier discussion of perceived environmental quality and place dependence, for example, emphasized the *manifest value* of environments. That is, environmental quality is judged in terms of the degree to which places are viewed by occupants as congruent or incongruent with their preferred goals and activities (see also the definition of environmental congruence in the glossary of this chapter and in Stokols, 1981). Thus, the distinction between manifest and latent value relates to whether or not potential or current occupants *recognize* the place as congruent with their needs.

The same kinds of factors that determine assessments of manifest value (e.g., the perceived fit between physical affordances of an environment and the activities of its users) offer a basis for estimating the latent value of places. For example, an out-of-the-way, undiscovered pond that remains frozen throughout winter has latent potential value as an outdoor recreational area. Once the pond is discovered by ice-skating enthusiasts, its potential value is recognized and transitional (presetting) activity develops in the area. To the extent that manifest or recognized value is high, the likelihood of a setting emerging (e.g., an outdoor skating rink) is enhanced. Note that in some instances, the recognized potential value of places is not actualized due to physical barriers or normative constraints (e.g., the presence of "no trespassing" signs near the pond).

Any attempt to assess the latent or manifest value of places requires consideration of the potential or actual match between place characteristics and the attributes of a particular set of occupants. The present discussion is not intended to provide a comprehensive listing of the determinants of place value, but it is possible to suggest certain environmental and occupant factors that are relevant to this issue. For instance, places whose supportive physical features are unique (i.e., few comparable areas exist elsewhere or are accessible) are likely to be of high value to prospective or current occupants. Such features might include the esthetic quality of a place, its proximity to transportation and communication facilities, and the degree to which its geographical characteristics offer physical protection and well-demarcated group territory. Among the occupant attributes that are likely to contribute to assessments of place value are the range of alternative environments available to occupants, and the kinds of environmental supports that are required for their accomplishment of desired goals and activities.

Considering the three phases of setting emergence proposed earlier (i.e., inert, transitional activity, and patterned activity), we thus hypothesize that: (1) unoccupied places high in latent value for prospective occupants are more likely to attract and sustain transitional activity than those of low latent value; and that (2) the higher the manifest value of a place either prior or subsequent to occupancy, the greater the probability that patterned activities will be established and a setting will form.

We further hypothesize that: (3) the occupants of settings that emerge gradually within unoccupied areas will ascribe greater symbolic meaning to place than will the members of preexisting groups that migrate to the area. This heightened symbolic meaning of the physical milieu for locally formed versus migratory groups is assumed to result from the greater experience of local groups with a place prior to setting emergence, and the temporal linkage of group formation processes (e.g., the development of cohesion) with the establishment of a setting. At the outset of the patterned-activity phase, then, members of locally formed groups will manifest greater clarity and consensus in their perception of place meanings than will those of migratory groups. Thus, for locally formed groups, the physical environment will be viewed as symbolic of group identity. Accordingly, we predict that: (4) within newly formed settings, assessments of place dependence or independence will be more extreme among local versus migratory groups due to the former's relatively greater experience with the place. Moreover, (5) the direction of occupants' assessments toward either place dependence or independence will be mediated by the quality of their cumulative experiences within that environment.

As our analysis of setting development shifts from initially unoccupied to already-occupied areas, additional conceptual issues arise. Most importantly, the establishment of new settings in occupied areas involves not only a transformation of physical affordances into symbolic meanings, but also the modification of the existing, symbolic meaning by the new occupants. This alteration in the perceived social field of the environment introduces the potential for social conflict, particularly when place meanings associated with the original and newly formed settings are contradictory. Differing perceptions of territorial jurisdiction and ownership rights exemplify sources of conflict among occupant groups who lay claim to the same area.

In many situations, the establishment of a new setting within an already-existing one occurs without social conflict. This is particularly the case when members of a preexisting setting decide voluntarily to subdivide into smaller settings or to merge with the members of an outside group. Examples of subdivision within settings and mergers between them can be found in the research literature of ecological psychology (e.g., Bechtel, 1977; Lozar, 1974; Srivastava, 1974; Wicker & Kauma, 1974). This literature also provides evidence for the impact of subdivisions and mergers on organizational effectiveness and member well-being.

The establishment of a new setting within an occupied area, however, often raises the potential for social conflict, especially when members of the original setting view the impending subdivision or merger as unwanted and involuntary. An attempt by an alienated faction of a teenage gang to develop an alternative setting within an existing one, or the appropriation and alteration of a setting by another gang, exemplify the involuntary or imposed establishment of settings in occupied areas.

The preceding discussion suggests the following, additional hypotheses:

6. The likelihood of a new setting developing within the territorial domain of an already-existing one decreases as the potential for conflict between members of the two settings increases.

7. The potential for intergroup conflict is heightened to the extent that the original setting undergoes involuntary subdivision or merger (particularly when territorial resources are limited and the place meanings perceived by members of the original and new settings are contradictory).

8. Given a high level of potential conflict, active attempts to establish new settings within existing ones will promote overt, intergroup aggression to the degree that the relative power (e.g., membership size, economic resources) of the opposed occupant groups is comparable. Differential power among occupant groups is expected to reduce the likelihood and duration of overt violence, following nonvoluntary subdivisions and mergers of settings (cf. French & Raven, 1959).

Because of our focus on group-occupied settings in this discussion, we have emphasized the role of intergroup conflict as a concomitant of setting emergence in certain situations. We should note, however, that attempts to establish new settings are sometimes accompanied by conflict arising among different categories of occupants (i.e., groups, aggregates, and individuals). The earlier-mentioned examples of a noisy group "hanging out" in a library study area, or a youth gang whose "turf" includes the parking lot of a shopping center, illustrate situations involving potential group-versus-individual and group-versus-aggregate conflicts. Thus, in relation to our proposed typology of settings (see Fig. 22.4), we hypothesize that: (9) the likelihood of a new setting developing within an occupied area decreases to the extent that its membership structure (e.g., group organization) is discrepant with the predominant functional orientation (e.g., individual or aggregate orientation) of the original setting. In those instances in which functionally discrepant settings do emerge, their stability and duration are likely to depend on the rigidity and enforcability of functional meanings associated with the original setting.

Factors Affecting the Maintenance and Modification of Settings.   The three stages of setting emergence previously discussed—that is, the sporadic, transitional, and patterned-activity phases—precede the appearance of those processes by which existing settings are maintained, modified, and terminated. The present section considers some of those processes by focusing on three additional stages in the life cycle of settings—namely, (4) the *stability-maintenance phase;* (5) the *deviation phase;* and (6) the *structural-transformation phase.* In the subsequent section, we examine the (7) *crisis* and (8) *termination phases* marked by the occurrence of events within settings that lead to their deterioration and eventual demise. Crisis events are viewed as a category of severe deviations and transformations whose detrimental impact on the setting is irreversible.

Most conceptualizations of settings deemphasize the emergence, transformation, and termination phases, focusing instead on the ways in which on-going settings maintain their stability and cope with environmentally induced deviations. Barker's (1968) analysis of behavior settings, for example, highlights the synomorphy or fit between recurring patterns of human activity and the sociophysical environment. Deviations from optimal fit between human and environmental resources (e.g., undermanning) are counteracted by setting-protective strategies (e.g., the recruitment of additional members). Thus, the behavior setting is construed as an open system (cf. Katz & Kahn, 1966; von Bertalanffy, 1950) that strives to maintain a stable (equilibrium-like) relationship between itself and the broader environment through internal organization and negative feedback mechanisms.

Our analysis builds upon earlier discussions of setting maintenance and deviation-countering processes. We assume, for example, that settings develop mechanisms for maintaining their stability (e.g., the norms and role structure associated with group-oriented settings), and for resisting internal and external threats to setting operations. The stability-maintenance phase previously mentioned is characterized by the smooth and predictable recurrence of organized activity patterns within the setting. To the extent that perceived or actual departures from typical activity patterns occur, the setting is said to be in a deviation phase. The structural-transformation phase is marked by the occurrence of deviations that result in significant and enduring changes in the setting's activity structure and/or physical milieu.

The present analysis, however, differs from earlier discussions of setting maintenance and deviation in some important respects. First, whereas previous analyses of behavior settings and group dynamics (cf. Barker & Associates, 1978; Cartwright & Zander, 1968) emphasize deviation-countering mechanisms, which serve to preserve equilibrium within groups, we give equal attention to the deviation-amplifying processes (Maruyama, 1963) by which settings are structurally transformed. The phenomenon of overmanning, for example, could be analyzed in terms of occupants' efforts to reduce population pressure by admitting fewer-than-usual new members to the setting (deviation counteraction) or, alternatively, in terms of their initial decision to expand the physical size of the setting, thereby attracting larger numbers of applicants, creating overmanning and stimulating further efforts to expand the physical dimensions of the setting (deviation amplification). We view both of these perspectives as crucial to the analysis of setting maintenance, deviation, and transformation.

Second, earlier discussions of deviations within settings have emphasized the predominant role of the environment in altering stable patterns of setting activities—for example, through the sudden influx of new occupants from outside the setting (cf. Wicker & Kauma, 1974) or through abrupt architectural-geographical changes (cf. Bechtel, 1977). In the face of these events, occupants are usually portrayed as passive responders to environmental problems. Yet, it is often the case that setting members act spontaneously and decisively to refine their activities and surroundings, even in the absence of pressing environmental problems. Thus, we distinguish between *occupant-induced* and *environment-induced deviations* to highlight both the active and responsive roles played by occupants in creating and coping with setting deviations.

Finally, unlike earlier discussions of disequilibrium within settings (e.g., Barker & Associates, 1978), our analysis emphasizes anticipated as well as actual deviations. Whereas the anticipation of deviations will often lead to their actual occurrence, this is not necessarily the case. A company's plans for relocation to a larger office building, for instance, may be delayed or even abandonned due to resource constraints. We, therefore, treat *anticipated* and *actually occurring deviations* within settings as separable phenomena. In the ensuing discussion, we are particularly concerned with those circumstances that prompt occupants first to devise plans for transforming and improving the setting and, subsequently, to actively implement their plans.

Under what conditions are settings likely to shift from stability to deviation and transformation phases? Our attempt to identify some of these conditions begins with an assessment of the *transformational potential* of settings (cf. Stokols, 1981). Transformational potential refers to the motivation of occupants to modify the physical or social structure of their setting in accord with collective preferences. Transformational potential will be high to the degree that existing levels of occupant–environment congruence are lower than the potential level of congruence thought to be available in the best alternative setting. The "best alternative setting" can be either a transformed version of the existing setting or a completely different setting that has not yet been established or experienced.

We noted earlier that when preferred, alternative settings are thought to be available outside of the existing situation, occupants will tend to be place independent rather than place dependent. We, therefore, hypothesize that: (10) when the existing level of environmental congruence is perceived to be low, place-independent occupants will be more motivated to leave rather than attempt to improve the existing setting, whereas place-dependent occupants will be more motivated to transform rather than leave the immediate setting.

In our discussion of place dependence and perceived environmental quality, we mentioned a variety of factors that may contribute to occupants' assessments of actual and potential levels of congruence (e.g., the unique goals and activities of setting occupants; the degree to which these goals are supported by the environment; occupants' awareness of and exposure to alternative settings). The same diversity of factors influences the transformational potential within settings at a given point in time. Changes in the particular goals pursued by occupants, for example, may prompt them to search for more congruent, alternative settings or to restructure their existing environment (occupant-induced deviations). At the same time, sudden shifts in the form and quality of the physical environment may decrease perceived levels of congruence (environment-induced deviations), thereby promoting dissatisfaction with the setting and efforts to improve or withdraw from it.

In general, the perceived gap between actual and potential congruence will be greater to the extent that occupants possess clear images of preferred future environments. Images of preferred settings arise from the collective imagination of occupants within the context of existing environmental conditions. But the salience of preferred environmental arrangements (i.e., a high level of transformational potential) does not necessarily promote structural modification of the setting, even when attractive alternative settings are thought to be unavailable. For, the accomplishment of environmental change requires not only salient images of the future, but also sufficient levels of environmental flexibility, social organization, and behavioral competence among occupants. Thus, assuming that setting members are motivated to improve their environment, the greatest amount of change would be initiated by imaginative individuals and groups within flexible settings, whereas the least change would be accomplished by unimaginative occupants within rigid settings.

The preceding discussion suggests the following specific hypotheses regarding the determinants of setting stability, deviation, and transformation:

11. Place-dependent groups located within group-oriented areas will, in general, maintain settings of greater stability and endurance than will place-independent groups located within group-oriented, aggregate-oriented, or individual-oriented areas. Also, settings established by place-dependent groups within aggregate- or individual-oriented areas will be less stable than those consisting of place-dependent groups within group-oriented areas.

12. Group-oriented places whose physical characteristics favor the development of group identity and cohesion (e.g., "defensible spaces" with well-defined boundaries; cf. Newman, 1973) will be more congruent and, therefore, stable than group-oriented places that do not offer architectural or geographical supports for maintaining group solidarity.

13. Group-occupied settings that have emerged gradually within initially unoccupied areas, or were established voluntarily within previously occupied areas,

will manifest greater stability than those whose establishment was nonvoluntary (i.e., contrary to the preferences of occupants within the original setting).

14. Environmentally induced deviations (e.g., sudden geographical changes or the appearance of unwanted stimuli such as noise and congestion) will be more disruptive to place-dependent than to place-independent groups, due to the former's lack of attractive place options and (consequently) their greater psychological investment in the immediate situation.

14. Deviations from optimal staffing levels within settings (e.g., undermanning and overmanning; cf. Wicker, McGrath, & Armstrong, 1972) will induce greater stress and deviation-countering efforts among place-dependent than among place-independent occupants. In the face of membership shortages, for example, place-independent occupants might be more willing to allow their setting to deteriorate or to merge with other undermanned settings.[8]

15. Given a high level of transformational potential and the lack of better alternative settings elsewhere, structural modifications will more likely be implemented by organized and cohesive groups than by occupants whose disorganization precludes their ability to agree upon and to implement a remedial course of action.

To this point in our analysis, we have ignored the question of whether deviations and transformations within settings are functional or dysfunctional from the occupants' point of view. This issue raises additional, complex questions such as: "functional or dysfunctional in the short run or long run, and for individual occupants or the setting as a whole?" In the remainder of our analysis, we employ two basic criteria for gauging the effectiveness of occupant-induced deviations and transformations within settings—namely, the degree to which these changes raise perceived levels of environmental congruence among occupants, and the degree to which the modifications enacted within settings promote its renewed stability or its eventual demise. The former criterion is essentially one of occupant well-being whereas the latter is more a matter of organizational survival. Depending on the situation, these criteria can be directly, inversely, or negligibly related to each other.

Factors Affecting the Termination of Settings. The present section focuses on the circumstances leading to an irreversible deterioration in the activity patterns of a setting (the *crisis phase*) and, ultimately, to the disappearance of such patterns altogether (the *termination phase*). Our emphasis in this portion of the chapter is on settings of undefined rather than defined duration. *Undefined-duration settings,* such as neighborhood restaurants, churches, and movie theaters, can persist indefinitely, whereas *defined-duration settings,* such as college classes, the campaign headquarters of a presidential candidate, and the yearly

---

[8]This possibility was suggested by Allan Wicker in a personal communication.

convention of a professional group, have prescribed termination dates—for example, the closing of the semester, the presidential election, and the national convention, respectively. Our principal concern, then, is to identify factors that affect the longevity of settings whose duration is indefinite.

Among the various circumstances that can prompt the abrupt and unexpected termination of settings are severe environmental perturbations (e.g., earthquakes and floods forcing migration to safer areas) and events relating to the life cycles of occupants (e.g., increased family size or the death of a spouse necessitating residential relocation). In our analysis of setting crises and termination, we are more concerned with the interplay of environmental and occupant factors than with either of these categories considered alone. For instance, we are more interested in the relative impact of environmental change on place-dependent versus place-independent groups than in the impact of such change on groups in general.

We begin with a series of hypotheses derived from our earlier discussion of environmental congruence, place dependence, and transformational potential:

16. To the extent that occupants' efforts to improve their setting fail to enhance perceived levels of environmental congruence, the setting is more likely to enter the crisis and termination phases, particularly when dissatisfaction among occupants has been prolonged.

17. The abrupt termination of settings following environmental crises and/or occupants' life events will induce greater stress (e.g., mental and physical disorder, social disorganization) among place-dependent vis-a-vis place-independent occupants.

18. Due to their greater psychological ties to their setting, place-dependent groups will take longer to establish new settings following geographical relocation than will place-independent groups.

The concept of place dependence, defined earlier, reflects the perceived strength of association between occupants and their environments. Throughout our analysis, we have emphasized the role of place dependence in affecting the maintenance, modification, and termination of settings. Just as it is possible to assess the dependence of individuals and groups on their environments, it is also conceivable that settings are differentially dependent on particular occupants for maintaining their efficiency and very survival. Prosperous companies, for example, may collapse precipitously following the departure of key executives. Similarly, a neighborhood tennis club may face premature closing as increasing numbers of its members shift their allegiance to raquetball and resign from the club.

Occupant-dependent settings, thus, are defined as those whose continued existence requires the presence of specific occupants or a subset of occupants. *Occupant-independent settings* are those that do not require the presence of specific members for their continuation. In general, variable-occupant settings (or those whose membership varies over time) will be less dependent on specific occupants for their survival than will same-occupant settings (see our earlier discussion of place categories).

On the basis of the preceding definitions, we hypothesize that: (19) occupant-dependent settings are more likely to terminate following the departure of setting members than are occupant-independent settings. Moreover, (20) group-occupied settings characterized by constant rather than rotating members will be more likely to terminate following the departure of key individuals (e.g., charismatic leaders, persons occupying important roles in the organization) than following the loss of less crucial personnel.

In addition to the dimensions of place dependence and occupant dependence, we introduce a final factor into our analysis of setting termination. Emery and Trist (1965) suggest that the environments of organizations vary with respect to their relative ''turbulence''—that is, their complexity and unpredictability. Consistent with their discussion of environmental turbulence, we hypothesize that: (21) the prospects for prolonged survival decrease to the extent that settings exist within turbulent environments. For instance, a housing construction firm may find it increasingly difficult to survive in an economy beset by wildly fluctuating interest rates, spiraling inflation, and a global energy crisis. Furthermore, we predict that: (22) within turbulent environments, settings whose internal organization enables members to forecast environmental changes and to actively initiate self-protective strategies prior to the occurrence of environmental crises (rather than simply responding passively to such events) will be more likely to survive than will less organized and sophisticated settings (cf. Terreberry, 1968; Weick, 1979).

Summary

In this section of the chapter, we have presented a taxonomy of settings based on the intersection of place-specific people and functionally organized places. Additionally, we have outlined eight distinct stages in the life cycles of settings and have offered a series of hypotheses concerning the antecedents and processes associated with setting emergence, maintenance, modification, and termination. Although our analysis of these phenomena is preliminary and incomplete, it may provide a useful framework for future research on the transactions between people and places, and a conceptual basis for designing and improving settings.

SUMMARY AND CONCLUSIONS

In recent years, the focus of psychological research has shifted increasingly from the micro to the molar (ecological) environment. This expanded frame of reference stems from the recognition among social scientists that models based solely on intrapersonal processes and/or social interaction do not adequately explain human behavior. Instead, behavior must be viewed within the context in which it occurs. In this chapter, we have developed a classification framework for describing the sociophysical milieu of behavior. This taxonomy of settings is derived theoretically, and serves as a basis for: (1) conceptualizing the complex transactions between peole and their environment; (2) conducting theory-guided research that focuses on the molar environment; and, (3) developing criteria for assessing the ecological validity of research findings and policy recommendations.

Our theoretical analysis of settings began with a detailed examination of their two major components: places (the physical context of behavior) and occupants (the people who transact with places). After distinguishing between regularly and irregularly occupied places, we discussed aspects of the former that contribute to their social imageability among current and prospective occupants. We further classified regularly occupied places in terms of their predominant functional orientation (i.e., individual, aggregate, and group oriented), and noted certain qualifications of this categorization scheme.

Occupants were described as acting alone, as part of an aggregate, or as members of organized groups. They can be sporadically associated with some places (i.e., place nonspecific), while predictably associated with others (i.e., place specific). When place specific, occupants may develop strong subjective attachments to particular locations. We termed this phenomenon place dependence and discussed, in some detail, its antecedents, subtle qualities, and its role in mediating occupants' reactions to environmental change.

In the last section of the chapter, we examined the interface of place and occupant categories as the basis for developing our taxonomy of settings. We then discussed eight distinct stages in the life cycle of settings and presented several hypotheses derived from our analysis.

Even though the present chapter has not been explicitly policy oriented, we do believe that our analysis of settings is germane to contemporary environmental and political problems. The concept of place dependence, for example, offers a basis for understanding and altering the behavior of people living in hazardous areas who refuse to resettle in different regions, despite the potential for disaster within their current locations. And, in the context of international politics, the place-dependence concept suggests why the fervor of terrorist groups is heightened rather than neutralized by the perception that they have been denied a desired geographical area, or that they have been thwarted in their attempts to transform a currently occupied area into a new setting. These phenomena are exemplified by the efforts of revolutionary groups, such as the PLO and the IRA, to establish independent nations. In these and other instances of social conflict, the place dependence of groups and the collectively perceived contradictions between existing and preferred qualities of an area can have enormous political ramifications.

We have attempted in this chapter to develop a conceptualization of settings that reflects the reciprocal relationship between people and places. Framing behavior within this multicausal model is, admittedly, complex. We believe, however, that taxonomic efforts at describing the large-scale environment, which necessarily reflect the complexity of that environment, are crucial if psychological research is to move effectively from micro to more molar levels of behavioral analysis. As a first step in submitting our conceptualization to empirical test, we are currently evaluating the reliability and validity of an index of place dependence.

DESCRIBING AND CLASSIFYING THE TRANSACTIONS BETWEEN PEOPLE AND PLACES: A GLOSSARY

1. *Aggregate-oriented places (or settings)*. Place (or settings) that are typically designed for and occupied by aggregates of strangers or minimally related people.
2. *Character of place dependence*. Subtle variations in occupants' perception of their attachment to place/s derived from differences on dimensions such as (1) the number and range of needs met by a particular place; (2) temporal aspects of place dependence; and (3) the perceived availability of alternative place options. See also *place dependence*.
3. *Crisis events*. Severe deviations within settings whose detrimental impact on the setting is irreversible. Such events lead to the deterioration and eventual demise of the setting.
4. *Crisis phase of settings*. A stage within the life cycle of settings marked by the occurrence of events that lead to the deterioration and eventual demise of the setting.
5. *Defined-duration settings*. Settings that have a prescribed termination date.
6. *Deviation phase of settings*. A phase within the life cycle of settings marked by the occurrence of perceived or actual changes in the typical activity patterns and/or physical structure of a setting.
7. *Deviations within settings*. Anticipated or actual departures from the typical activity patterns and/or physical structure of a setting.
8. *Environmental congruence*. The degree to which the environment enables occupants to meet their needs and attain their valued goals. (A method for quantifying congruence is presented by Stokols [1979, 1981]. See also Michelson, 1976, for an analysis of environmental congruence).
9. *Environment-induced deviations*. Alterations in the typical activity patterns or physical arrangement of a setting arising from changes in the

external or internal environment of the setting (e.g., abrupt geographical changes within or adjacent to the setting).

10. *Generic place dependence of occupants.* The degree to which occupants perceive themselves to be strongly associated with and dependent on a category of functionally similar places. See also *geographical place dependence of occupants.*

11. *Generic place specificity of occupants.* The degree to which the activities of people are associated with a category of functionally similar places on a regular and predictable basis. See also *geographical place specificity of occupants.*

12. *Geographical place dependence of occupants.* The degree to which occupants perceive themselves to be strongly associated with and dependent on a particular place. See also *place dependence* and *generic place dependence of occupants.*

13. *Geographical place specificity of occupants.* The degree to which the activities of people are associated with a particular place on a regular and predictable basis. See also *place specificity of occupants* and *generic place specificity of occupants.*

14. *Group.* Two or more individuals whose activities and goals are interdependent, and who are aware of their interdependence. See also the definitions of group presented by Cartwright and Zander (1968); Hare, Borgatta, and Bales (1965); McGrath (1964); and Shaw (1976).

15. *Group-oriented places (or settings).* Places (or settings) whose predominant functions are geared toward people who know and interact with each other on a regular basis.

16. *Individual-oriented places (or settings).* Places (or settings) whose physical and normative properties either exclude or discourage occupancy by more than one person at a time.

17. *Inert (or sporadic-activity) phase.* A stage in the life cycle of settings marked by the absence of occupants or by sporadic occupancy and activities.

18. *Irregularly occupied places.* Places characterized by sporadic occupancy and human activities. See also *nonsettings* and *nonpatterned-activity places.*

19. *Latent value of places.* The unrecognized capacity of places to accommodate the preferred goals and activities of prospective or current occupants.

20. *Life cycle of settings.* Processes associated with the establishment, maintenance, modification, and termination of organized settings. As conceptualized in this analysis, the life cycle of settings incorporates the following distinct stages: (1) *inert* (or *sporadic-activity*) *phase;* (2) *transitional-activity phase;* (3) *patterned-activity phase;* (4) *stability-maintenance phase;* (5) *deviation phase;* (6) *structural-transformation*

phase; (7) *crisis phase;* and (8) *termination phase.* See also Devereux's (1977) and Wicker's (1979a) discussions of the life cycle of behavior settings.

21. *Local groups.* Groups whose development coincides with the emergence of an organized, environmental setting. See also *migratory groups.*

22. *Manifest value of places.* The recognized (and sometimes actualized) capacity of places to support the preferred goals and activities of prospective or current occupants. See also *environmental congruence* and *potential congruence.*

23. *Migratory groups.* Preexisting groups that move into a new area and establish a setting there. See also *local groups.*

24. *Nonpatterned-activity places.* Areas characterized by the absence of occupants or by sporadic occupancy and association with human activities. See also *irregularly occupied places* and *nonsettings.*

25. *Nonsettings.* Nonpatterned-activity places that are either unoccupied or sporadically occupied by place-nonspecific people. Nonsettings are characterized by the absence of recurring patterns of behavior and the lack of a clear functional orientation. See also *irregularly occupied places, nonpatterned-activity places,* and *place specificity of occupants.*

26. *Occupant dependence of settings.* The degree to which a setting requires the presence of particular occupants, or a subset of occupants, for its continued existence.

27. *Occupant-induced deviations.* Alterations in the typical activity patterns or physical arrangement of a setting arising from the spontaneous and voluntary actions of setting members.

28. *Patterned-activity phase of settings.* A stage in the life cycle of settings marked by the establishment of stable, recurring patterns of activity and widely recognized place meanings (e.g., the functional orientation of the setting).

29. *Patterned-activity places.* Places in which recurring and predictable patterns of behavior occur. The predominant, functional orientation of such places can be classified as individual oriented, aggregate oriented, or group oriented. See also *settings.*

30. *Perceived social field of the physical environment.* The totality of functional, motivational, and evaluative meanings conveyed by the physical milieu to current or prospective occupants of a place. The specific meanings associated with a place can be described in terms of their content, complexity, clarity, heterogeneity, distortions, and contradictions. (Strategies for quantifying these dimensions are discussed in Stokols, 1981).

31. *Place.* A geographically and/or architecturally delimited area. Places in this analysis are categorized as unoccupied (or sporadically occupied) and regularly occupied. The latter category includes three types of places:

individual oriented, aggregate oriented, and group oriented, depending on the predominant functional orientation associated with the place.

32. *Place dependence.* The degree to which occupants perceive themselves to be strongly associated with and dependent on a particular place, or a category of functionally similar places. The perception of place dependence derives from a two-component process by which occupants assess the quality of their current place, and the relative quality of comparable alternative places. These assessments are influenced by factors such as the importance of occupants' goals, the kinds of resources available within an area, and occupants' awareness of and familiarity with relevant alternative places. See also *geographical place dependence of occupants* and *generic place dependence of occupants.*

33. *Place meanings.* Functional, motivational, and evaluative information and impressions associated with particular places. *Personal meanings* are those held by single individuals. Personal meanings become part of the perceived social field of an environment to the extent that they are held in common with other occupants (*common meanings*), and/or are shared through the interaction and communication among members of organized groups (*shared meanings*). See also the *perceived social field of the physical environment* and *social imageability.*

34. *Place options.* Geographical areas that are perceived by occupants as comparable to their present location and as realistic (accessible) alternatives to their current place. The perceived availability of place options is a crucial factor in determining occupants' assessments of place dependence. See also *place dependence.*

35. *Place specificity of occupants.* The degree to which the activities of people are associated with a particular place, or with a category of functionally similar places, on a regular and predictable basis. See also *geographical place specificity of occupants* and *generic place-specificity of occupants.*

36. *Potential congruence.* The level of goal facilitation perceived by the occupants of a place to be available within their best alternative setting. The best alternative setting can be either a transformed version of the existing setting or a different setting that has not yet been experienced or established.

37. *Regularly occupied places.* Places characterized by stable patterns of occupancy, human activity, and functional orientation. See also *patterned-activity places* and *settings.*

38. *Same-occupant places (or settings).* Places or settings whose functions are performed by the same people on a regular basis. See also *variable-occupant places (or settings).*

39. *Settings.* Patterned-activity places occupied by place-specific people. Settings are characterized by recurring patterns of behavior and by widely

recognized place meanings (e.g., functional orientation). The functional orientation of the physical milieu and the composition and organization of its occupants are used in this analysis to develop a taxonomy of settings. See also the analyses of behavior settings presented by Barker (1968), Barker and Associates (1978), and Wicker (1979b). See also *patterned-activity places, regularly occupied places,* and *place specificity of occupants.*

40. *Social imageability.* The capacity of a place to evoke vivid and collectively held social meanings among its occupants. Places acquire social imageability to the extent that they are regularly and predictably associated with patterns of individual and/or collective behavior. See also the *perceived social field of the physical environment.*

41. *Stability-maintenance phase of settings.* A stage in the life cycle of settings characterized by the smooth and predictable recurrence of organized activity patterns.

42. *Structural-transformation phase of settings.* A stage in the life cycle of settings marked by the occurrence of deviations that result in significant and enduring changes in the setting's activity structure and/or physical milieu. See also *deviations within settings* and *transformations within settings.*

43. *Termination phase of settings.* A stage within the life cycle of settings marked by the cessation of organized activity patterns within an area. See also *crisis events* and the *crisis phase of settings.*

44. *Transformational potential.* The motivation of occupants to modify the physical or social structure of their setting in accord with personal and collective preferences. The actual accomplishment of desired transformations depends not only on motivational factors but also on occupant resources (e.g., imagination, organization) and environmental circumstances (e.g., rigidity or flexibility of the environment).

45. *Transformations within settings.* A category of deviations within settings that result in significant and enduring alterations of the activity structure and/or physical milieu of the setting.

46. *Transitional-activity phase of settings.* A stage in the life cycle of settings marked by the preliminary occurrence of patterned activity within an area that is not yet associated with a clear, functional orientation.

47. *Transitional places.* Occupied areas characterized by preliminary patterns of activity but lacking the clarity of functional orientation and occupant organization associated with structured settings.

48. *Undefined-duration settings.* Settings that do not have a prescribed termination date. See also *defined-duration settings.*

49. *Unoccupied places.* Places that either preclude the possibility of occupation or are structured in ways that inhibit the development of sustained activity and, thereby, remain ambiguous in their functional meaning.

50. *Variable-occupant places (or settings).* Places or settings whose functions are performed by different people on a rotating basis.

ACKNOWLEDGMENTS

We thank Michael Agar, Baruch Fischhoff, Alan Levy, Kelly Shaver, Perry Thorndyke, and Abe Wandersman for their comments on the conference presentation of this manuscript. Also, we are grateful to Irwin Altman, Roger Barker, Dorwin Cartwright, Stephen Kaplan, Joseph McGrath, and Allan Wicker for their helpful suggestions on earlier portions of this chapter. The preparation of this manuscript was supported by funding from the Focused Research Program in Human Stress at the University of California, Irvine, and by postdoctoral grant number F2MH07421A from the National Institute of Mental Health to Sally Ann Shumaker.

REFERENCES

Altman, I. *The environment and social behavior.* Monterey, Calif.: Brooks/Cole, 1975.

Altman, I. Research on environment and behavior: A personal statement of strategy. In D. Stokols (Ed.), *Perspectives on environment and behavior.* New York: Plenum, 1977.

Argyle, M. Predictive and generative rules models of P × S interaction. In D. Magnusson & N. S. Endler (Eds.), *Personality at the crossroads: Current issues in interactional psychology.* Hillsdale, N.J.: Lawrence Erlbaum Associates, 1977.

Barker, R. G. Ecology and motivation. *Nebraska Symposium on Motivation,* 1960, *8,* 1–48.

Barker, R. G. On the nature of the environment. *Journal of Social Issues,* 1963, *19,* 17–34.

Barker, R. G. *Ecological psychology: Concepts and methods for studying the environment of human behavior.* Stanford, Calif.: Stanford University Press, 1968.

Barker, R. G. The influence of frontier environments on behavior. In J. O. Steffen (Ed.), *The American west: New Perspectives, new dimensions.* Norman, Oklahoma: University of Oklahoma Press, 1979.

Barker, R. G., & Associates *Habitats, environments, and human behavior.* San Francisco: Jossey-Bass, 1978.

Baron, R. A., & Bell, P. A. Aggression and heat: The influence of ambient temperature, negative affect and cooling drink on physical aggression. *Journal of Personality and Social Psychology,* 1976, *33,* 245–255.

Baum, A., & Valins, S. (Eds.). *The social psychology of crowding: Studies of the effects of residential group size.* Hillsdale, N.J.: Lawrence Erlbaum Associates, 1977.

Bechtel, R. B. *Enclosing behavior.* Stroudsburg, Pa.: Dowden, Hutchinson, & Ross, 1977.

Berger, P., & Luckmann, T. *The social construction of reality.* Garden City, N.Y.: Doubleday, 1966.

Berlyne, D. E. *Conflict, arousal, and curiosity.* New York: McGraw-Hill, 1960.

Bronfenbrenner, U. Toward an experimental ecology of human development. *American Psychologist,* 1977, *32,* 513–531.

Bronfenbrenner, U. *The ecology of human development.* Cambridge, Mass.: Harvard University Press, 1979.

Brunswik, E. Organismic achievement and environmental probability. *Psychological Review,* 1943, *50,* 255–272.

Burton, I., Kates, R. W., & White, G. F. *The environment as hazard.* New York: Oxford University Press, 1978.

Campbell, D. T., & Stanley, J. C. *Experimental and quasi-experimental designs for research.* Chicago: Rand McNally, 1963.

Cartwright, D., & Zander, A. (Eds.). *Group dynamics* (3rd Ed.). New York: Harper & Row, 1968.

Chein, I. The environment as a determinant of behavior. *Journal of Social Psychology,* 1954, *39,* 115-127.

Cohen, S., Glass, D. C., & Singer, J. E. Apartment noise, auditory discrimination, and reading ability in children. *Journal of Experimental Social Psychology,* 1973, *9,* 407-422.

Craik, K. H. Environmental psychology. *Annual Review of Psychology,* 1973, *24,* 403-422.

Devereux, E. C. *Psychological ecology: A critical analysis and appraisal.* Unpublished manuscript, Department of Human Development and Family Studies, Cornell University, Ithaca, N.Y., 1977.

Durkheim, E. *The rules of sociological method.* New York: Free Press, 1964.

Emery, F. E., & Trist, E. L. The causal texture of organizational environments. *Human Relations,* 1965, *18,* 21-32.

Evans, G. W., & Howard, R. B. Personal space. *Psychological Bulletin,* 1973, *80,* 334-344.

Firey, W. Sentiment and symbolism as ecological variables. *American Sociological Review,* 1945, *10,* 140-148.

French, J. R. P., & Raven, B. H. The bases of social power. In D. Cartwright (Ed.), *Studies in social power.* Ann Arbor, Mich.: University of Michigan Press, 1959.

Fried, M. Grieving for a lost home. In L. J. Duhl (Ed.), *The urban condition.* New York: Basic Books, 1963.

Garfinkel, H. *Studies in ethnomethodology.* Englewood Cliffs, N.J.: Prentice-Hall, 1967.

Gergen, K. J. Social psychology as history. *Journal of Personality and Social Psychology,* 1973, *26,* 309-320.

Gerson, E. M., & Gerson, M. S. The social framework of place perspectives. In G. T. Moore & R. G. Golledge (Eds.), *Environmental knowing.* Stroudsburg, Pa.: Dowden, Hutchinson, & Ross. 1976.

Gibson, J. J. The concept of the stimulus in psychology. American Psychologist, 1960, *15,* 694-703.

Gibson, J. J. The theory of affordances. In R. Shaw & J. Bransford (Eds.), *Perceiving, acting, and knowing.* Hillsdale, N.J.: Lawrence Erlbaum Associates, 1977.

Gove, W. R., Hughes, M., & Galle, O. R. Overcrowding in the home: An empirical investigation of its possible pathological consequences. *American Sociological Review,* 1979, *44,* 59-80.

Hare, A. P., Borgatta, E. F., & Bales, R. F. (Eds.). *Small groups: Studies in social interaction.* New York: Knopf, 1965.

Harré, R. The ethogenic approach: Theory and practice. In L. Berkowitz (Ed.), *Advances in experimental social psychology (Vol. 10).* New York: Academic Press, 1977.

Harré, R., & Secord, P. F. *The explanation of social behavior.* Oxford: Blackwell, 1972.

Hull, C. The problem of intervening variables in molar behavior theory. *Psychological Review,* 1943, *50,* 273-291.

Ittelson, W. H. (Ed.). *Environment and cognition.* New York: Seminar Press, 1973.

Jackson, J. Structural characteristics of norms. In I. D. Steiner & M. Fishbein (Eds.), *Current studies in social psychology.* New York: Holt, Rinehart, & Winston, 1965.

Jackson, J. A conceptual and measurement model for norms and roles. *Pacific Sociological Review,* 1966, *9,* 35-47.

Jacobs, J. *Death and life of great American cities.* New York: Random House, 1961.

Kaplan, S. An informal model for the prediction of preference. In E. H. Zube, R. O. Brush, & J. G. Fabos (Eds.), *Landscape assessment: Values and perceptions, and resources.* Stroudsburg, Pa.: Dowden, Hutchinson, & Ross, 1975.

Kaplan, S. Concerning the power of content-identifying methodologies. In E. H. Zube & T. Daniel (Eds.), *Environmental aesthetics.* Washington, D.C.: U.S. Forest Service, 1978.

Katz, D., & Kahn, R. L. *The social psychology of organizations.* New York: Wiley, 1966.

Kelley, H. H., & Thibaut, J. W. *Interpersonal relations: A theory of interdependence*. New York: Wiley, 1978.

Lewin, K. *Principles of topological psychology*. New York: McGraw-Hill, 1936.

Lozar, C. C. Application of behavior setting analysis and undermanning theory and supermarket design. In D. Carson (Ed.), *Man–environment interactions: Evaluations and applications (Vol. 8)*. Washington, D.C.: Environmental Design Research Association, 1974.

Lynch, K. *The image of the city*. Cambridge, Mass.: M.I.T. Press, 1960.

Magnusson, D. (Ed.). *Toward a psychology of situations: An interactional perspective*. Hillsdale, N.J.: Lawrence Erlbaum Associates, 1981.

Maruyama, M. The second cybernetics: Deviation-amplifying mutual causal processes. *American Scientist*, 1963, *51*, 164–179.

Maslow, A. H. *Toward a psychology of being*. Princeton, N.J.: Van Nostrand, 1968.

McGrath, J. *Social psychology: A brief introduction*. Holt, Rinehart, & Winston, 1964.

Mead, G. H. *Mind, self, and society*. Chicago: University of Chicago Press, 1934.

Michelson, W. *Man and his urban environment: A sociological approach* (2nd ed.). Reading, Mass.: Addison-Wesley, 1976.

Michelson, W. *Environmental choice, human behavior, and residential satisfaction*. New York: Oxford University Press, 1977.

Milgram, S., & Jodelet, D. Psychological maps of Paris. In H. Proshansky, W. Ittelson, & L. Rivlin (Eds.), *Environmental psychology (2nd ed.)*. New York: Holt, Rinehart, & Winston, 1976.

Moore, G. T., & Gollege, R. G. (Eds.). *Environmental knowing: Theories, research and methods*. Stroudsburg, Pa.: Dowden, Hutchinson, & Ross, 1976.

Moos, R. H. *The human context: Environmental determinants of behavior*. New York: Wiley, 1976.

Neisser, U. *Cognition and reality: Principles and implications of cognitive psychology*. San Francisco: Freeman, 1976.

Newman, O. *Defensible space*. New York: Macmillan, 1973.

Osgood, C. E., Suci, G. H., & Tannenbaum, P. H. *The measurement of meaning*. Urbana, Ill.: University of Illinois Press, 1957.

Pervin, L. A. Definitions, measurements, and classifications of stimuli, situations, and environments. *Human Ecology*, 1978, *6*, 71–105.

Price, R., & Blashfield, R. K. Explorations in the taxonomies of behavior settings: An analysis of dimensions and classifications of settings. *American Journal of Community Psychology*, 1975, *3*, 335–351.

Price, R., & Bouffard, D. L. Behavioral appropriateness and situational constraint as dimensions of social behavior. *Journal of Personality and Social Psychology*, 1974, *30*, 579–586.

Proshansky, H. M., Nelson-Shulman, Y., & Kaminoff, R. D. The role of physical settings in life-crisis experiences. In I. G. Sarason & C. D. Spielberger (Eds.), *Stress and anxiety* (Vol. 6). Washington, D.C.: Hemisphere Press, 1979.

Ring, K. Experimental social psychology: Some sober questions about some frivolous values. *Journal of Experimental Social Psychology*, 1967, *3*, 113–123.

Secord, P. F. Social psychology in search of a paradigm. *Personality and Social psychology Bulletin*, 1977, *3*, 41–50.

Seligman, M. E. P. *Helplessness*. San Francisco: Freeman, 1975.

Shaw, M. E. *Group dynamics: The psychology of small group behavior*. New York: McGraw-Hill, 1976.

Skinner, B. F. *Science and human behavior*. New York: Macmillan, 1953.

Smith, M. B. Is experimental social psychology advancing? *Journal of Experimental Social Psychology*, 1972, *8*, 86–96.

Sommer, R. *Tight spaces: Hard architecture and how to humanize it*. Englewood Cliffs, N.J.: Prentice-Hall, 1974.

Srivastava, R. K. Undermanning theory in the context of mental health care environments. In D. Carson (Ed.), *Man–environment interactions: Evaluations and applications* (Vol. 8). Washington, D.C.: Environmental Design Research Association, 1974.

Steiner, I. D. *Group process and productivity.* New York: Academic Press, 1972.

Stokols, D. Environmental psychology. *Annual Review of Psychology,* 1978, *29,* 253-295.

Stokols, D. A congruence analysis of human stress. In I. G. Sarason & C. D. Spielberger (Eds.), *Stress and anxiety* (Vol. 6). Washington, D.C.: Hemisphere Press, 1979, 27-53.

Stokols, D. Group × place transactions: Some neglected issues in psychological research on settings. In D. Magnusson (Ed.), *Toward a psychology of situations: An interactional perspective.* Hillsdale, N.J.: Lawrence Erlbaum Associates, 1981, 393-415.

Suttles, G. D. *The social order of the slum: Ethnicity and territory in the inner city.* Chicago: University of Chicago Press, 1968.

Taylor, S. E., & Fiske, S. T. Salience, attention, and attribution: Top of the head phenomena. In L. Berkowitz (Ed.), *Advances in experimental social psychology* (Vol. 11). New York: Academic Press, 1978.

Terreberry, S. The evolution of organizational environments. *Administrative Science Quarterly,* 1968, *12,* 590-613.

Thibaut, J., & Kelley, H. *The social psychology of groups.* New York: Wiley, 1959.

Tolman, E. C. The determiners of behavior at a choice point. *Psychological Review,* 1938, *45,* 1-41.

Tyler, S. A. (Ed.). *Cognitive anthropology.* New York: Holt, Rinehart, & Winston, 1969.

Underwood, B. *Psychological research.* New York: Appleton-Century-Crofts, 1957.

von Bertalanffy, L. The theory of open systems in physics and biology. *Science,* 1950, *111,* 23-29.

Weick, K. *The social psychology of organizing* (2nd ed.). Reading, Mass.: Addison-Wesley, 1979.

White, W. P. *Resources in environment and behavior.* Washington, D.C.: American Psychological Association, 1979.

Wicker, A. W. Ecological psychology: Some recent and prospective developments. *American Psychologist,* 1979, *34,* 755-765. (a)

Wicker, A. W. *An introduction to ecological psychology.* Monterrey, Calif.: Brooks/Cole, 1979. (b)

Wicker, A. W., & Kauma, C. E. Effects of a merger of a small and a large organization on members' behaviors and experiences. *Journal of Applied Psychology,* 1974, *59,* 24-30.

Wicker, A. W., McGrath, J. E., & Armstrong, G. E. Organization size and behavior setting capacity as determinants of member participation. *Behavioral Science,* 1972, *17,* 499-513.

Willems, E. P., & Raush, H. L. (Eds.). *Naturalistic viewpoints in psychological research.* New York: Holt, Rinehart, & Winston, 1969.

Wohlwill, J. F. The emerging discipline of environmental psychology. *American Psychologist,* 1970, *25,* 303-312.

Wohlwill, J. F. The environment is not in the head. In W. F. E. Preiser (Ed.), *Environmental Design Research: Volume 2, Symposia and Workshops.* Stroudsburg, Pennsylvania: Dowden, Hutchinson, and Ross, 1974, 166-81.

Wohlwill, J. F. Environmental aesthetics. The environment as a source of affect. In I. Altman & J. F. Wohlwill (Eds.), *Human behavior and environment: Advances in theory and research* (Vol. 1). New York: Plenum, 1976.

Wortman, C. B., & Brehm, J. W. Responses to uncontrollable outcomes: An integration of reactance theory and the learned helplessness model. In L. Berkowitz (Ed.), *Advances in experimental social psychology* (Vol. 8). New York: Academic Press, 1975.

Zajonc, R. B. Social facilitation. *Science,* 1965, *149,* 269-274.

Zeisel, J. *Stopping school property damage.* Boston: American Association of School Administrators and Educational Facilities Laboratories in collaboration with City of Boston Public Facilities Department, 1976.

23

The Perception
of Neighborhood Change

Gary H. Winkel
City University of New York

INTRODUCTION

Over the course of its brief history, environmental psychology has been dominated with a concern for the role that the large-scale physical environment may
play in understanding the diverse forms of human behavior that psychology takes
as its explanatory focus (Ittelson, Proshansky, Rivlin, & Winkel, 1974). Although not wishing to disregard the contents of other specializations in psychology, it is fair to say that these early years have been marked by efforts to
differentiate components of the physical environments in which people pursue
their goals, purposes, and objectives and to develop a set of research strategies
that might be more sensitive to the empirical realities of on-going lives within
ecologically diverse settings (Craik, 1973; Stokols, 1978).

If there was a guiding scheme that characterized the work of environmental
researchers during these early years, it was the belief that explanations of human
behavior (consider in the broadest sense of that term) would require a much
greater sensitivity to the problems of context, situational demands, and the
understanding of the interconnections that existed between and among the different settings within which people typically operated.

Given the complexity of these issues, however, early research was to a significant extent more descriptive than analytical and more likely to employ exploratory research strategies rather than the formalistic canons of experimental design
that had come to be characteristic of the better established specialities within
psychology.

As we enter the second decade of behaviorally oriented environmental research, it has become increasingly clear that environmental psychologists must

reexamine their relationships to other investigators who are working on cognate problems of decided relevance to the concerns of environmentalists. At the same time, we must continue to insist upon the importance of recognizing that the quest for the understanding of human behavior will not be satisfied by a reduction to purely psychological analysis nor by an arbitrary decision to limit our research designs to the unyielding requirements of a puristic definition of acceptable and unacceptable procedures for generating knowledge.

The possibilities for rapprochement among different psychological specializations seem particularly promising at present, in large part because of recent trends in the behavioral sciences toward a greater sensitivity to the problems of context and situation in dealing with human activity systems. Environmental psychologists have long pointed out that there is every reason to believe that the sociophysical characteristics of diverse settings create different contextual demands upon people and that these factors must be considered when efforts are made to evolve explanations of human behavior.

If one were to consider the possible contributions that environmental psychology might make to the problems of related specialities, it would be to suggest the kinds of issues that we have encountered when involved in our descriptive analyses of people and environments. Many of these are directly related to the concerns of cognitive and social psychology and it is my belief that the theoretical frameworks developed by researchers in these areas can suggest some fruitful forms of theoretical analysis, which are sorely lacking in much of existing environmental research.

The present chapter represents an effort to illuminate the nature of these potential interconnections within the context of a problem having both theoretical and practical importance to environmental psychologists—namely, the ways in which the person's immediate living environment (the home and neighborhood) contribute to individual and social well being.

BACKGROUND

There can be little doubt that home and neighborhood play an important role in the quality of people's lives (Campbell, Converse, & Rodgers, 1976). For most people, these two settings are closely interrelated and serve as a locale in which a variety of important human transactions occur. Stability or relative stability in these contexts is essential if the person is to work out a satisfying set of relationships both to other people and to whatever qualities he or she may deem important about the physical environment that defines his or her place of residence.

One does not need to search very extensively in the literature on neighborhood change to realize quickly that there are a variety of circumstances under which threats to the continued stability of a person's place of residence and general neighborhood bring about psychological reactions that are sometimes profound and occasionally socially disruptive. Two of the more dramatic instances of these events are associated with large-scale alterations in the fabric of the physical environment resulting from urban-renewal activities or with changes in the social and racial composition of neighborhoods (Fried, 1963; Fried & Gleicher, 1961; Gans, 1962; Molotch, 1972; Rapkin & Grigsby, 1960; Taeuber & Taeuber, 1965).

It is not necessary to assume, however, that depth of reaction is related solely to the size or pervasiveness of the changes that occur in a neighborhood. Anyone who has ever attended community meetings can easily recall instances in which even the most seemingly minor changes under discussion can unleash deeply felt emotions regarding the effects of such alterations on the quality of community life. Almost daily, community officials, planning staffs, planning boards, and others involved in the daily commerce of neighborhood life become embroiled in issues that are highly charged and often unsettling for the people involved. Of course, not all these interchanges have any necessarily long-lasting effects on the participants. But the fact that the character and quality of the built environment can be the basis for the expression of such deeply felt affective responses cannot and should not be ignored.

Our task in this chapter involves the development of a conceptual framework that might serve as a guide to the investigation of the nature of the transactions that people have with their immediate living environments and/or with their idealized visions of an appropriate setting within which they might pursue their desires for what they consider a fulfilling way of life. I plan to address the problem of neighborhood change and stability as a focus for this effort. Before I consider this issue, however, it would be helpful to describe the conceptual framework I plan to employ, because this may clarify some of the observations and assertions made in the Introduction to this chapter.

In the analysis that follows, I view the person operating in a sociophysical context from a systemic perspective. Specifically, this orientation implies that people are embedded in a context that is defined not only by the geographical locale of his or her place of residence, but that demands of the primary and secondary social contexts within which they live must be considered as well (Stokols, 1976). In addition, people may be expected to play different roles in different settings, and these requirements could conceivably influence both their concern for and evaluation of the characteristics of their environment. One of the immediate consequences of this embedded quality of experience is that there will be variation among people in terms of the importance they attach to the quality of their immediate living environment and that the evaluation of neighborhood change and stability must be tempered by the contingent nature of one's place in the context of different setting experiences and role requirements.

I also assume that people are bound differentially to the demands of the environments they encounter largely as a consequence of the degree of access they have to the material and psychological resources that would provide them with a greater range of options to choose a satisfying residential locale. There are two interrelated implications of this assumption. The first of these is that the content and directions of the types of inferential evaluations that are employed in assessments of neighborhood environmental quality will vary as a direct function of perceptually available resources. Secondly, I expect that the structural quality of the evaluations that people provide when discussing the neighborhood environment will vary. These variations in structural quality will be expressed in terms of the degree to which people make differentiations among elements of the neighborhood environment, the elements that are selected for purposes of differentiation, the structural coherence of the presumed relationships among elements that are differentiated, and the extent to which people even attempt to develop causal explanations for the changes that might be occurring in a neighborhood.

I further think that aspects of the residential and neighborhood sociophysical milieu will influence resident perceptions and experiences, but that these may not necessarily be reported as influential in affecting judgments of neighborhood quality. Nonetheless, the "naive" theories or inferential systems employed to explain change or stability are of interest in themselves and because they may serve as either a basis for or justification of actions taken with respect to the environment. In addition, these "explanations" may be shaped by environmental characteristics residents tend to ignore.

In the latter context, I am especially interested in the relationships among residents' inferential systems, their evaluations of changes in neighborhoods, and the extent to which perceived changes are linked to more "objective" measures such as land value, population characteristics, crime statistics, traffic volume, pedestrian activities, building code violations, and so on. These connections are of interest, in part because of their obvious policy implications and because of the enduring controversy in the social-indicators literature concerning the role of "objective" and "subjective" indicators as predictors of environmental quality assessments.

Finally, I believe that a comprehensive theory of the nature and consequences of neighborhood change and stability must be particularly sensitive to both social and physical context. This position implies that I must adopt a systemic analysis in which both the person's perceptions of the neighborhood and those elements of the sociophysical environment to which little attention may be paid are seen as potential transactive codeterminants of the future state of the neighborhood. No one aspect is viewed as conceptually independent in this analysis. On the other hand, I am well aware of the possibility that at various times in the course of a neighborhood's history, alternative configurations of person–situation transactions may assume importance and may lead to different types of futures for an area. For example, I might find that land-use changes become particularly significant at some points in the temporal progression of a neighborhood. At other times, the character of the people who move into an area will yield a different set of responses. In trying to assess relative impact, therefore, researchers must examine the qualities of the physical environment, environmentally related values and goals that people bring to the situation, and characteristics of the person and the social groupings within which he or she is located.

With these considerations as background, I can now turn to one of the central problems being addressed in the chapter—change and stability in neighborhood settings.

CHANGE, STABILITY, AND ENVIRONMENTAL MANAGEABILITY

Although the relative changes that the immediate living environment may undergo differ depending on the geographical locale under investigation, change or stability is probably not the central issue that arouses residents' concern about their environment. Indeed, in many cases, at least some neighborhood residents actively seek to initiate and bring about changes. When considering the full range of such transactions, one is tempted to say that the issue concerns not change per se but control of change. Yet, I believe that the concept of control places too much emphasis on the person as separate from or in conflict with the environment. The ways in which the environment may be trustworthy or beneficial are thus neglected as are the limitations on the person's ability or desire to monitor and control the environment. Further, the neighborhood is composed of an aggregation of individuals engaged in explicit and tacit transactions with the environment and with one another. So, the issue of control becomes even more problematic.

For these reasons, I believe that the concept of *environmental manageability* better expresses the kind of relationship that residents and users seek to obtain among themselves and with the physical environment. A manageable environment is one in which the residents of an area are able to organize information from their immediate sociophysical environment in such a way that they can develop a predictive system that allows them to judge whether a setting supports their goals and purposes. Carr and Lynch (1968) tried to describe what would be required at an urban scale to allow people to better understand how their city worked. I believe that at the neighborhood scale, people will try, depending on their interests and activities, to know how land and space are used and by whom so that they can achieve their objectives. For example, they need to know what goods and services are available, how accessible they are to life-support systems such as police, fire, and hospitals, what formal and informal organizations exist that might be of use to them, what kinds of people live in the neighborhood or might be attracted to it, what information resources are available, what opportunities exist for children, how many and what kind of recreational and cultural facilities are present, and so on. Finally, residents may find it important to understand what action possibilities are available to them, both individually and collectively, should certain changes occur that they feel would be either detrimental or desirable for their neighborhood.

We know, of course, that people differ considerably in terms of their knowledge of these issues and even their concerns about whether this form of knowledge is worthy of pursuit. One of my tasks, therefore, becomes the development of an explanatory system that might account for these differences. In the material that follows, I attempt to show how environmental, social, and cognitive factors may influence people's varying orientations to their immediate residential environments.

ENVIRONMENTAL MANAGEABILITY AND VALUE ORIENTATIONS

One of the important ways in which people experience their neighborhoods is in terms of their evaluations of them. In the transactive connections between person and environment, the person's values with respect to the meaning and importance of the neighborhood both influence the nature of the evaluations attached to change and, in turn, are influenced by the characteristics of the environment itself. I view the dimensions of person–environment transactions that are particularly salient to the values residents seek to maximize in their neighborhoods as belonging to both the person and the environment. For example, the extent to which the friendliness of other residents is used as an evluative criterion may be primarily a function of the person. The actual friendliness of other residents, however, is also likely to be related to the person's satisfaction, which in turn may exert an influence on the place that this value has in the person's criterion set. Unlike neighborhood structural features (i.e., the arrangement of people and spaces), which I discuss later, I expect people to consciously perceive the value-related aspects of their neighborhoods. Their perceptions of these characteristics, however, may or may not reflect physical and social conditions as they exist— that is, most residents may, in fact, behave in a friendly fashion, but a particular person may not experience their behavior in this way. Further, as previously indicated, the inferential systems people use in evaluating their neighborhoods may be inaccurate. For example, attentional overload has been shown to lead to withdrawn social behavior. Residents of an area, however, may attribute such behavior to the internal or personality characteristics of their neighbors. Even if such attributions do not best explain the state of affairs, they may affect behavior and compound the effects of the structural characteristics of the neighborhood that gave rise to the withdrawn social behavior in the first place.

It should be clear that the work of social psychologists concerned with attributional phenomena would be instructive for environmentalists who wish to explain how people isolate features of their environment as plausible sources of cues for the events they perceive (Nisbett & Wilson, 1977; Taylor & Fiske, 1978). It is my feeling, however, that the content of such attributional processes in the neighborhood context must be understood in terms of the overall assessments that people make of the quality of their immediate residential environments. This is particularly true in cases in which the neighborhood either has a reputation for being especially attractive or desirable and, conversely, in places known as "unsafe" or particularly undesirable. These evaluations relate to the social and physical characteristics of an area as well as to the activities that occur there. Historically, planners have tended to concentrate more heavily on the physical and land-use properties of the environment to account for these evaluations, whereas sociologists have emphasized the social characteristics of the residents. Given the framework being developed in this chapter, however, I am interested in a wider range of sociophysical characteristics that may be used to describe the neighborhood environment on the supposition that the structure of the attributional systems that are employed in explanations of the reasons for neighborhood change and stability may vary depending on the values that people use in assessments of neighborhood quality.

One fruitful source of such descriptions may be obtained from open-ended but structured interviews in which people are asked to describe features and conditions of their current living environments and the types of settings that they would consider as potential places of residence. In this connection, I have thus far relied on an extensive series of open-ended interviews conducted by Birch and his associates at the Harvard-M.I.T. Joint Center for Urban Studies and on interview and questionnaire data gathered by various members of the Environmental Psychology Program at the City University of New York.[1] I have examined this material from two perspectives: (1) an analysis of the major thematic elements that appear in the protocols; and (2) the identification of the cues that are employed when assessing the quality of the person's living environment.

---

[1]The research conducted by David Birch and his colleagues at the Harvard-M.I.T. Joint Center for Urban Studies was funded by the United States Department of Housing and Urban Development. Its mandate involved the development of a computer simulation model of the factors that influenced neighborhood evolution and decline in terms of the various actors who were responsible for these events. One aspect of this research involved gathering data from open-ended interviews regarding patterns of residential mobility and the attitudes and motivations that guided such mobility. In general, the researchers were interested in discovering the factors that pushed people over the moving threshold, what households sought in the new residence, and what process they followed in finding a new home. Specific topics included attitudes toward neighborhoods, investments in housing maintenance, the role of employment opportunities in the search for a new residence, and the role of schools in neighborhood evaluation.

In 1971, 600 residents of metropolitan Boston were interviewed. In 1972, 300 men and women in the greater Kansas City area were surveyed. In 1975, findings were updated through interviews with 100 residents of the Houston, Texas, area. In the summer and fall of 1976, 900 men and women living in Houston, Dayton, Ohio, and Rochester, New York, were also interviewed.

Because the perspectives guiding the design of these interviews and questionnaires were not the same as those being developed in this chapter, it is not
possible to use the results of these investigations to evaluate the adequacy of our
model. Nonetheless, there are some aspects of these self reports that are of
interest in this context.

In the first place, it is certainly possible to detect rather constant references to
the notion of the manageability of one's living environment. At the same time,
the adequacy of the person's material and psychological resources has a direct
bearing on their manageability assessments.

For example, upper- and upper-middle income families place great emphasis
on settings in which both people and environments are congruent with the values
they believe should be appropriate to their status. Status homogeneity, basic
similarities in housing style, and the desire that the neighborhood represent a
sound investment are all stressed as important issues. At the same time, one
senses that there is no question but that the setting will be manageable. Thus,
these families do not mention the more obvious aspects of manageability, such as
safety and easy access to needed goods and services, largely because these
requirements are taken as a given. The environment is considered to be presumptively manageable.

The aspects of manageability mentioned by middle-income families are best
understood within a comparative perspective. Desirable environments are
evaluated largely in terms of their ability to reduce the number of demands that
are placed on the person. Thus, suburban settings are preferred to urban settings
because the greater homogeneity in activities, architecture, and people are more
likely to ensure that fewer coping strategies must be employed in the commerce
of daily life. Because the resources of middle-income people are not unlimited,
however, they are less likely to assume that any environment to which they move
will be manageable even though there appears to be little doubt that their basic
security needs will be met. From a manageability perspective, middle-income
people assume that their living environment will be manageable but they are also
likely to recognize that there may be specific areas of concern in which they feel
that it is essential to seek more information about the environment before making
a commitment to it. These concerns have to do largely with the adequacy of the
school system, the degree of safety associated with areas that their children may
be expected to use, and the presence of other children with whom they can
socialize.

Recall that I assumed that differential access to resources should have a
bearing on neighborhood evaluations. I have just mentioned how social-class
standing and its correspondent ease of access to resources will influence environmental values. Also note that even within social class, sex-role differences
are becoming increasingly important as factors in choice of living environment.
Saegert and Winkel (in press) have found that middle- and upper-middle income
men are much more likely to stress the qualities of suburban living just men-

tioned than are women. Women who are living in urban settings are much more uncertain about the likelihood that they will be able to find suburban settings that will meet their needs for educational, cultural, and economic development, particularly if these needs are currently being met within an urban setting. These trends are likely to persist in the future; with changes in family structure and female employment patterns, the future of the suburbs becomes even more problematic (Saegert, 1980).

Working-class respondents are also heavily dependent on shifting access to resources. They are less likely to feel the necessity to move to a suburb as a way of achieving a manageable environment than are middle- and upper-middle income people. The complexity that may characterize their current urban residential locations is not considered as problematic, particularly if social networks exist that may be used to offset the multiple demands required of urban residents. On the other hand, many working-class residents are quite well aware of the changes that cities have undergone and are now undergoing and they are particularly sensitive to the avoidance of environments and people who symbolically or actually imply unmanageability. Working-class residents stress the importance of environmental maintenance, the avoidance of contact with people whose values or backgrounds they cannot understand or that they believe to be incompatible with their own, physical safety, and the presence of a stable population.

From a manageability perspective, they feel that the environment is often problematic in these regards, and they are less inclined to speak of those environmental elements they find attractive or desirable in a positive sense and are much more prone to assume that what they now possess is vulnerable to changes over which they have no control.

Lower-class residents are generally pessimistic about their options for environmental stability and are much more likely to assume that the settings in which they find themselves are unmanageable. For these people, manageability is precarious at best and there is no sense that they feel they have any control over the events that transpire in their immediate living environments. In short, the environment is presumptively unmanageable and one just tries to "make do."

What these findings tend to suggest, then, is that control becomes a question mainly for middle- and working-class people and that control is important in the environment largely because the issue of manageability is problematic. Upper-income people assume that their environments are manageable. Thus, control is a less salient concept largely because the controls are already embedded within the settings they inhabit.

If these observations are correct, one of the implications for an understanding of the relationship of values to manageability is that it might be easy to overlook variables that are indeed important to neighborhood residents in their assessments. In order to handle this potential problem, I have analyzed the interview and questionnaire material in terms of the social and environmental cues that different groups employ as plausible indicators of the quality of their living environments. I assume that these cues are intimately related to the basic value orientations that people use when considering various environments and serve as a descriptive vocabulary for the assessment process.

Because no one working on the problems of neighborhood dynamics has yet developed a comprehensive set of environmental descriptors, I have set this task as a high-priority research problem. Content analyses of the material previously described yielded an initial set of 600 items describing neighborhood characteristics. After elimination based on duplications and highly idiosyncratic responses, I have narrowed the variables down to 118 phrases that reflect different aspects of neighborhood evaluation. Selection criteria for these items were guided by the desire to conform, where possible, to the phraseology of the respondents who were originally interviewed on the expectation that I would improve the ecological validity of the final instrument and to ensure that I covered major thematic elements that frequently appeared in the responses that people gave.[2]

At present, I am completing a study in which these items were used to evaluate both urban and suburban neighborhoods that varied in terms of their quality, social and environmental characteristics, and the range of people who live in them. I expect the results of these analyses to provide the first systematic information about the structural characteristics of the cue systems that people employ in the assessment process.

The next problem becomes how these cues (and the values that are presumably associated with them) relate to the manageability notion. It is to this issue that I would next like to turn.

THE JUDGMENTAL CONTEXT FOR MANAGEABILITY ASSESSMENTS

Earlier, I mentioned that there were differences in the ways in which neighborhood residents who varied in social class responded to the types of living envi-

---

[2]In the final instrument, respondents were instructed to evaluate their current neighborhoods in the following areas: safety and security needs, availability and quality of life-support systems (e.g., police, fire, emergency services), environmental pollutants, availability of needed goods and services, educational resources, recreational facilities and programs, status needs, resident characteristics, behavioral characteristics of those people who used the neighborhood, esthetic and cultural needs, desires and possibilities for neighborhood socializing, availability and adequacy of transportation facilities, economic opportunities, family-rearing requirements, religious needs, availability and adequacy of programs and facilities for children, school characteristics, opportunities for political action, responsiveness of public officials, and degree of resident involvement.

These issues were rated using Likert-type scales. Respondents were then asked to indicate the relative importance they attached to having neighborhood qualities as they now existed either change or stay the same. Two hundred and fifty respondents living in both urban and suburban areas and representing different socioeconomic levels as well as different stages in the life cycle were given these questionnaires. These data are now in the process of being analyzed in an effort to determine the dimensions of manageability.

rons in which they currently resided or might consider for future residence. I indicated that the degree of manageability might vary from neighborhood to neighborhood and would change depending on the material, psychological, social, and political resources possessed by different segments of the population. Although in principle it should be possible to differentiate among neighborhoods depending on the degree of change associated with them, it would be very difficult to identify all levels of change that might impact on an area's residents.

At this point, I am inclined to believe that values with respect to manageability become salient when the person is placed within a decision-making context brought about either by an internally motivated desire to change residence or by events in the environment that require some form of response. In this sense, I do not believe that people typically operate as "naive" scientists if that terminology is meant to imply that individuals engage in a relatively constant search for information guided largely by their curiosity. Rather, it is more likely that the assessment process occurs in an episodic fashion against a backdrop of potential decisions to leave one setting and search for a new place of residence, or attempts to engage in organized activity designed to forestall or initiate change. In the final analysis, however, environmental values are differentially activated within the context of potential or actual moves from one locale to another.

The manner in which environmental change becomes an issue for decision making is partially dependent on events occurring in the environment, as is indicated later, and is also related to the person's location on a continuum of prospective moving behavior.

In the case of relatively permanent residents (i.e., people who are not seeking a new place of residence), we would hypothesize that their relationship to the present condition of their immediate living environment involves only an episodic monitoring for purposes of updating information. Under these circumstances, there are no particular incentives for vigilance regarding the sociophysical environment. Changes that do occur are more often than not considered only as background shifts, which may or may not call to attention particular impacts on the different functions that are currently being transacted in the setting. As long as whatever changes that do occur do not create conflicts with important values that the residents feel are central to the stability of their living spaces, it is unlikely that changes will even be noticed, or if they are, their impacts will tend to be ignored or discounted.

The analysis of the interview and questionnaire material previously mentioned would suggest that only a limited range of conditions would have to exist before there would be an increase in the amount of monitoring. These involve: (1) a deterioration in the maintenance of the physical environment, assuming that it is now well maintained; (2) a gradual but steady or dramatic shift in the characteristics of the population who may be living in an area (these changes would be confined mainly to the socioeconomic status and/or race of new residents); (3) the appearance of people whose behavior is considered to be unpredictable or potentially dangerous, even if the absolute numbers of such people are small compared to the population as a whole (this category would include individuals who, from society's perspective, would be considered stigmatized; obvious candidates would include mental patients, exoffenders undergoing rehabilitation, addicts who are receiving medical treatment and/or psychological counseling, the developmentally disabled, and drifters, bums, or panhandlers); (4) the appearance of service facilities in the community that would be expected to draw upon an audience that is either in a lower socioeconomic class and/or who are among the stigmatized; and (5) alterations in activity patterns in a community that could be expected to disrupt habitual patterns of behavior (e.g., the introduction of facilities that would serve people not now living in a particular area and that would be expected to put strains on the carrying capacity of the neighborhood; examples would include large department stores, trendy boutiques, stores depending on high-use volumes, and so on).

The critical dimension that underlies the types of changes just enumerated involves the extent to which change brings into the resident's attentional frame questions about the person's basic self and primary-group definition or what might be called, for want of a better term, ''a way of life.'' The greater the probability that any alteration in the environment creates that sort of question, the more likely there will be a dramatic response to the proposed change.

If the immediate living environment is not characterized by the conditions just enumerated, and a resident is considering the possibility of a move to a new location, ambient environmental conditions are less likely to be the source of reasons for the move. Data gathered by Rossi (1955) and others would indicate that the characteristics of the house as a dwelling unit become the major focus of attention. These findings have been replicated by Mackintosh, Olsen, and Wentworth (1977) and would suggest that the search for more space in the home and immediately outside the home become the basis for the decision to leave. This is not to say that neighborhood conditions are totally irrelevant, but they are less important and seem to figure in the decision process to the extent that the person experiences approach–avoidance conflicts to the prospect of a new residence. To the extent that such conflicts exist, Birch's data support the view that people can be characterized by what might be called ''inertial adaptation'' to present neighborhood conditions (Birch et al., 1977). If the moving threshold is finally passed, the factors that prompted the decision are often not immediately obvious from an analysis of the ambient environmental conditions that exist. It is only when the decision becomes consolidated that reasons and explanations are sought to justify the move. In these instances, the person does not seem to monitor the environment actively in such a way that there is a ''rational'' and considered match between way of life and external conditions. The utilization of a set of requirements that must be met in the environment becomes prominent only in the consideration of the potential place of residence.

Although the question of the psychological consequences associated with a move from one locale to another is a fascinating issue within environmental psychology, that is not the intent of this chapter. I am more concerned with how relatively permanent residents in an area assess change and stability within the neighborhood.

In that context, then, I would argue that the set of 118 descriptors mentioned earlier serve as surrogate expressions of particular views that people have of the types of lives they would like to live. They are concrete indicators of the various dimensions that people consider important in the assessment of the quality of the living environment. The different configurations of these valuational factors, along with the importance attached to them, are influenced by the person's life-goal priorities, the shared goals that grow out of the primary social relationships they have with intimate others, and by the environmental-setting characteristics within which they pursue their day-to-day lives. It is the latter issue to which I now wish to turn, because of my belief that the assessment of change and stability is as much influenced by factors within the person as by setting characteristics that influence the nature and rate of information potentially available to the person.

NEIGHBORHOOD STRUCTURAL CHARACTERISTICS AND MANAGEABILITY

Certain sociophysical qualities of a neighborhood environment are expected to influence the ease with which residents can form a reasonably accurate understanding of the possibilities and options available in their neighborhoods. These qualities may also affect the extensiveness of people's knowledge and, under some circumstances, their central concerns such as security, predictability, and a sense of belongingness. My premise is that the physical configuration and social organization of a neighborhood present to the resident potential information in ways and quantities that will differentially facilitate the person's perception and organization of such information. The person may not identify those qualities of the sociophysical environment as directly important, but rather their significance may be mediated by perceptions of insecurity, lack of control, difficulty in making friends, unpredictability, or the converse of these conditions.

The four concepts we use to relate the person's perceptions to the neighborhood environment in this way are *sociophysical heterogeneity,* the extent to which a bounded environment possesses mixes of both people types and activities; *attentional overload,* the extent to which potentially relevant elements in a situation exceed the person's ability to attend to them; *environmental permeability,* a condition in which significant elements in the environment are so changeable, unstable, or hard to identify that the person has difficulty in forming a reasonably stable set of categories and expectations for the neighborhood; and the concept of *unit formation,* which plays a role both as an attenuating mediator of the effects of attentional overload and of environmental permeability as well as functioning in its own right. The latter notion, drawn from Heider (1956), grows out of the Gestalt tradition in psychology with its emphasis on perceptual closure as a property of certain forms. As it applies to environmental perception, unit formation has much in common with Lynch's (1960) concept of the "imageability" of the environment.

Sociophysical Heterogeneity

A basic component of any geographical locale that provides the contextual background for manageability judgments involves the degree of similarity or dissimilarity of its residents, the range of activities (e.g., commercial–retail, institutional, cultural, recreational uses, and so on) and the compactness or separation of these components.

As far as the people living in any neighborhood are concerned, the interview and questionnaire material referred to earlier indicate clearly that the broadest categorical distinctions that people draw in relation to their fellow residents or users of the environment are based on their social-class standing and/or racial–ethnic backgrounds. Somewhat finer discriminations are introduced when respondents described the values, ages, familial structures, sociopolitical orientations, and, to a much lesser extent, the religious preferences of an area's inhabitants.

Of course, these labels are not that informative and are used by respondents as shorthand summaries of the behavioral and attitudinal characteristics they believe are associated with people who are classified within the system previously summarized. Upon probing, it is clear that the real issues of concern to residents involve the nature and types of social interactions they can expect from their neighbors, how others use the environment in ways that may facilitate or interfere with the respondent's goals, how others do or do not relate to children, the amount of care that others give to the maintenance of their homes and the areas immediately surrounding them, others' tolerance for social and physical diversity in the environment, and their willingness to take responsibility for community affairs.

I believe that the basic dimension underlying these specific aspects of neighborhood life is cognitive in nature. Operating within frameworks that vary in uncertainty, I think that people try to make subjective probability assessments concerning the likelihood that the people with whom one has contact will exhibit behaviors whose parameters are known and, if not known with certainty, may be assumed to lie within an acceptable range of predictability. As social heterogeneity increases and the degree of spatial separation among people decreases, I anticipate that judgments of manageability would become more problematic. This hypothesis must be tempered by the realization that the person's degree of familiarity with heterogeneity must be taken into account. In addition, one must be aware of the mechanisms that may exist within a neighborhood to deal with heterogeneity and its demands. Thus, community organizations, both formal and informal, may exist that allow flexibility to community residents in dealing with the requirements of different people. In general, however, it is possible to argue that changes in the social composition of an area will be a decisive factor in affecting manageability assessments, particularly if those changes exceed the adaptive responsiveness of neighborhood resources.

Social homogeneity or heterogeneity clearly operates within an environmental context, and the neighborhood researcher must be sensitive to the ways in which the physical environment itself may be used to affect manageability assessments. Neighborhoods vary in terms of the location and proximity of different types of settings that give them their peculiar ambience. In view of the relatively close association that exists between different populations and the types of facilities that serve their needs (Aldrich, 1975; Rams, 1976), it should not be surprising to learn that the physical environment and its components have been used to control the social characteristics of different neighborhoods.

One of the central preoccupations of land-use planners has been the development of regulatory mechanisms that will allow municipalities control over the types and locations of land-use activities in various areas. A key element in many of these schemes has been the notion of use compatibility and concurrently the conditions under which there should be use separation. It has been generally true that in areas that are basically residential, these uses should take priority and that for concomitant activities, such as commercial–retail, entertainment, cultural, industrial, and institutional use, location should be adjusted depending on residential requirements. The extent to which such separation has been successful depends, in large part, on the age of the area in which such plans have been implemented. Obviously, newer housing developments are more likely to be planned according to the principle of use separation.

In general, the presence of multiple activities under conditions of increasing compactness will increase the informational-processing requirements for a resident, which in turn will affect manageability judgments. There are two levels at which this condition operates: (1) the immediate environmental requirements associated with the different uses (e.g., the amount of traffic they generate, the extent to which they may contribute to various forms of pollution, their effects on the nature and types of pedestrian traffic in the area, and so on); and (2) the range of people that they serve and the visibility and impact of the behaviors of these users on the surrounding area. Both factors may be very directly related to the question of whether conflicts will arise in a neighborhood and are directly related to manageability in terms of the demands that different developmental patterns will exert on residents.

These patterns also function in another capacity. They may serve as a source of cues for both longer-term residents and potential newcomers when they monitor the environment in an effort to determine its livability. In this context, land-use activities and related physical indicators (such as maintenance, decoration, the presence of security devices, the amount of street litter, and so on) are closely related to the value assessments discussed earlier. Environmental elements carry with them social–symbolic implications, provide information about the people and uses to which they may be put, and differentially impact the ambient quality of the living environment.

The question of how the built environment operates in this fashion represents a potentially rich source of research possibilities that would be germane to both environmental psychologists and to social psychologists who are working in the area of impression formation. To my knowledge, however, very little data exist that would illuminate the nature of these relationships. In the one limited study I was able to locate, Taylor, Brower, and Stough (1976) demonstrated that various physical indicators in an environment were associated with inferences about the types of people who might be found there, some types of behaviors that could be expected from the area's residents, and the presence of organized social systems designed to increase the manageability of the setting.

I suspect, however, that the major impact of sociophysical heterogeneity will be found in investigations of its effects on information-processing strategies and their behavioral consequences. It is to this topic that I would now like to turn.

Attentional Overload

The overload concept has been employed primarily to explain the effects of high densities on people's experiences (cf. Milgram, 1970; Saegert, 1973, 1978), although it has also been used to understand the effects of other environmental characteristics such as excessive noise (cf. Cohen, 1977; Cohen & Lezak, 1977). Potential and actual overload have been considered a possible source of the indifference urban dwellers often exhibit to each other's plights (Milgram, 1970). What is often called "social" overload occurs when the number of people in a given area exceeds the number that a person can come to know or even recognize as familiar or at least "legitimate" users of an area; potential overload exists when a person, for example, a resident of a high-rise building, does not actually come in contact with all the other residents, but cannot select a subset of these people with whom to become familiar because there is no physical or social structure that allows repeated contact with a knowable subset of the total population.

Research has suggested that randomly assigned public-housing residents living in high-rise buildings, compared to residents living in low-rise structures, are more subject to overload, that they know fewer other people, that they do not establish supportive networks of aid and surveillance, that they have less control over the residential environment and decisions of management, that they are less satisfied with and feel less of a sense of belongingness to their project, and even that they are less likely to belong to organizations outside the project (McCarthy & Saegert, 1977). Roberts and Saegert (1977) found that when urban dwellers described their experiences of stress in the city, almost all of them include crowding as a major stressor; further, those experiences in which large numbers of others are seen as the primary source of difficulty were also likely to make the person feel alienated and mentally confused. Saegert (1978) has developed more fully a theoretical treatment of the circumstances in which high density may occasion experiences of overload and the factors that may ameliorate such experiences.

It is my hypothesis that both social and physical structures that allow people to become familiar with a reasonable number of others (but not too many) with whom they regularly come in visual contact increases the likelihood that people will have a sense of security associated with that contact. Visual contact, however, is not enough. There must be some agreement among the people regarding the importance of and actual experience with mutual assistance before visual contact will operate in the manner specified. Here, I think that the absolute number of people involved must not be extremely great, or alternatively, the selection of people into the environment must lead others to feel that anyone in it would be trustworthy.

Density, however, is not the only factor that we would expect to lead to overload. In a study of seven Dutch cities and towns, Korte, Ypma, and Toppen (1975) found impacts from the environment measured by sound level, traffic and pedestrian count, and number of buildings to be negatively related to the helpfulness of passersby. A plausible explanation, and one supported by Cohen and Lezak's (1977) study of attentional determinants of decreased helping behavior in noisy environments, is that any environmental qualities that interfere with a person's ability to obtain a fairly accurate sense of the information field will lead to overload, and to its consequences, such as social withdrawal or a sense of alienation. Thus, land uses and building types can contribute to overload by increasing noise level, number of users, or visual complexity, although not all of these variables have equal impact. For example, the circumstances in which visual complexity would interfere with the acquisition of important information may be fewer than those in which noise or number of users might do so, because it may be easier to ignore visual stimuli. It is also expected that formal qualities of the environment, such as those Lynch (1960) describes, that contribute to clearer edges and categories in the environment as well as land use mixes that have the same effects would decrease the probability of experiencing overload. The establishment of cognitive units is expected to reduce the number of environmental elements that require separate attention.

In this sense, anything that increases environmental heterogeneity may also increase attentional demands, at least for some users and some purposes. It is important, however, to remember that environmental richness and number of options may also arise from these conditions. Thus, we believe that when the environmental elements that might lead to overload are people, places, or things that the person views as pleasant, trustworthy, and/or relatively beneficial, the effect may be a sense of increased possibilities rather than overload. For example, Mackintosh et al. (1977) have found that young mothers living in relatively homogeneous and very clearly bounded high-density urban residential developments, in which management is believed to carefully select responsible tenants, experience the density as a source of diversity and a satisfying social life.

These housing developments, however, have existed since the years following World War II and many of the residents have lived there for extended periods of time. In the majority of urban settlements, on the other hand, change rather than stability is the rule; under these conditions, we expect that in areas of greater density, the development of a stable sense of manageability will be more problematic.

In considering the relationships that density has to manageability, it is important to distinguish between the role that density plays in altering the information field that is relevant to other types of changes that might be occurring in the neighborhood environment and the role that density as a factor itself plays as part of judgments about the desirability of changes that may either increase or decrease density levels in an area. In the discussion that follows, density is considered in terms of the density of the environment within which the person who makes judgments currently resides, the density of the neighborhood as a whole, and the density associated with any particular changes that might occur within the neighborhood.

If I am willing to accept the proposition that sociophysical changes in the neighborhood environment will vary both in terms of the number and importance of their possible impacts on the setting, I would argue first that as density increases, the threshold of what are considered to be undesirable changes will increase and that for those changes that are considered undesirable, there will be a corresponding decrease both in the differentiation of the range of possible impacts and in assessments of their significance for the neighborhood. In addition, I would anticipate that as the geographical distance of whatever changes occur that would be considered undesirable events for a neighborhood increase, the perceived impacts would decline much more dramatically as the density of the residential environment of the perceiver increases.

I would also expect that as the heterogeneity of the ambient neighborhood environment increases, there will be a corresponding increase in the demands placed upon the attentional capacities of the resident such that the predictions made for the effects of the density of the current living environment in the previous paragraph will continue to hold, but to a somewhat lesser extent than would be the case for a person living in a heterogeneous neighborhood and in a high-density dwelling unit.

I believe these hypotheses are appropriate because of the implications of the overload notion. More specifically, I think that as the attentional demands required by the immediate and extended living environment increase, the range of the person's ability to process that information decreases to the point where their concerns about change tend to recede into the immediate day-to-day living space.

The consideration of density factors would not be complete unless I also addressed the question of the density of those land uses that might replace other activities in an area. In those instances in which the changes that might occur in a neighborhood involve alterations in existing density levels, we would anticipate that if density increases above existing levels, the effects would be seen to detract from neighborhood quality even if the activities to be accommodated by the new density levels were considered to be desirable. If it should turn out that the activities are considered undesirable within manageability terms, and if increases in density are associated with these changes, the effects on quality will be affected multiplicatively rather than in an additive fashion.

I would argue that these hypotheses are defensible on the grounds that density itself is a factor that contributes to a loss in the ability to manage the environment. Thus, any aspect of neighborhood change that is associated with increasing density will be evaluated negatively because of the strain that this change places on neighborhood resources and on the informational processing capabilities of neighborhood residents.

Environmental Permeability

Difficulty in establishing a satisfactory sense of understanding environmental conditions may arise not only from the number and organization of elements requiring one's attention, but from the instability of the elements themselves. This is expected to interfere with residents in their efforts to form a clear image of the significant characteristics in the environment. Unlike the problem of attentional overload, which involves limitations of the perceiver, the degree of environmental permeability is related to the extent of change in the environment itself. These *changes* themselves place increasing burdens on the person's capacity to know the environment and its users. Neighborhoods are permeable to varying extents depending on population shifts, changes in public policy, the stringency of zoning and building regulations, and the flow of economic market forces. It is often the case, however, that regulations governing the nature and rate of change in many municipalities are broadly interpreted so that change is relatively easy to bring about. Thus, in the abstract at least, neighborhoods are more likely to be permeable than impermeable.

Permeability is a somewhat difficult concept to operationalize because it can only be understood in a temporal context. This context involves both the rate of change and the temporal duration of any meaningful investigation. I cannot at present offer any definitive guidelines for what might constitute an appropriate duration. For example, Smith (1963), in his study of the process of racial succession, found that racial changes were evident only when statistics from a 20-year period were examined. Rossi's (1955) study of residential turnover relied on statistical information derived from the decennial census. It has been my experience in talking with professional planners that "rapid change" is often conceptualized in terms of 3- to 5-year segments. For any neighborhood, resident change will obviously be related to each resident's own point of entry into the neighborhood. It is clear that one area of research that definitely requires attention involves the investigation of resident perceptions of the time frames within which they evaluate neighborhood stability and change. Preferred research designs for permeability assessments would be longitudinal, although it is certainly possible to use comparative designs as well.

If one wishes to examine the degree of change, it is obviously necessary to take into account the rate of change prior to the time of the initiation of the investigation. This may be done by an examination both of resident perceptions and public records documenting the types of changes that have occurred. I anticipate that the major impact of rate of change would appear to occur in situations in which there was some perceivable break in the continuity of change. In such cases, the increased or decreased permeability of an area will be expected to affect judgments of the desirability and/or acceptability of shifts in both populations and land-use activity in an area, as well as impacting on manageability estimates.

The general hypotheses that follow are based on the assumption that a neighborhood is characterized by a low degree of permeability prior to the initiation of an investigation, but that the neighborhood is moving in the direction of increased permeability. Under these conditions, I would expect that if the neighborhood were considered to be manageable and desirable, positive changes in population and land-use activity would have little effect except for the expression of some uneasiness over the rate of change. If population shifts and land-use activity changes involved both positive and negative components or were all considered to be negative, the neighborhood would be judged as going into decline. If the area were considered to be initially unmanageable and undesirable, positive changes would lead to an increased sense of manageability, but this relationship would be expected to be curvilinear rather than linear. If the changes were both positive and negative, this would have little effect on manageability assessments, at least in the short run. Negative changes would simply reinforce the notion that the area was unstable and undesirable.

If an area under study were moving from a state of high permeability to one involving reduced rates of change and were judged to be manageable and desirable, any further positive changes would be taken as indicators of a decrease in potential danger for the neighborhood's future. If the changes represented a mix of positive and negative or all negative elements, the area would be assessed as entering into a slow decline. On the other hand, if the setting were considered initially undesirable and unmanageable, positive changes would be viewed as contributing to a slow improvement. A mix of positive and negative shifts would likely be considered as signs of stabilization, whereas all negative changes would lead to an assessment that the area was stagnating.

Aside from the general hypotheses just summarized, I would anticipate that there would be interactions between permeability, density levels, and the sociophysical heterogeneity of an area. Limitations of space prevent a discussion of these in detail, but I can say that as there are increases in these three aspects of neighborhood structural quality, greater strains will be placed on the residents' ability to understand the nature of changes in the setting. In addition, manageability will be affected depending on the valences of the changes that are occurring. To some extent, these effects may be altered by one further aspect of structural quality, and that is unit formation.

Unit Formation

The physical structuring of the environment as it may influence the organization of information about an area is an essential component in understanding neighborhood-change perceptions. Unit formation is a concept that involves the ways in which parts of the environment are defined as perceptually distinct or as related to one another. Neighborhoods differ in the degree to which they are perceived as bounded units and the extent to which residents share in the definition of a unit. All neighborhoods, however, do have some boundaries and the assessment of the meaning of change is very much dependent on residents' perceptions of these boundaries.

There are different properties of the environment that lead to the definition of a unit. Lynch (1960) has identified some of the qualities that are apparently related to clarity of image for areas, such as the presence of landmarks, edges, paths, nodes, and consensually agreed-upon districts. I expect that edges, paths, and districts play a part in what is considered to be a neighborhood boundary. I see these elements as related to Gestalt-like properties such as proximity, closure, contiguity, similarity, and simplicity of form. In addition, within a more broadly defined neighborhood, there may be smaller areas that are identified as units based upon site characteristics as well as upon the physical form of the buildings comprising that location. For example, site configurations involving town squares, clearly identified edges, circular arrangements, or homogeneous building types surrounded by contrasting building forms are expected to be seen as closer or more related to one another.

Unit formation primarily plays the role of an informational organizing device within the environment. Its success depends to a significant extent on the strength of the boundary conditions that allow the identification of a unit. Other things being equal, a change that might occur in a neighborhood will have less impact on a resident if it occurs outside a bounded unit than inside. Within the unit, distance from the locus of a change event is less relevant as a factor that might influence the perceived manageability of an area than it would be if such a unit did not exist. In some ways, it is possible to think of unit formation as analogous to a chunking strategy that assists in the differentiation of an information field. Rather than being a characteristic of the perceiver, however, unit formation is a configural property of the environment that affects the interpretation given by any perceiver of those changes that might or might not be germane to stability and manageability assessments.

Although unit formation can assist in organizing information about an environment, it obviously has a double-edged quality about it. The effects of sociophysical heterogeneity, density, and permeability discussed earlier may be expected to be much more pronounced when these variables operate in a negative fashion within a bounded unit. The critical question then becomes whether the unit has operated to allow the resident to have access to the means whereby change can be controlled effectively by the resident working in conjunction with others living in the unit. Perhaps the most fruitful way of considering unit formation within the context of neighborhood change and stability would be to say that unit formation may be a necessary but certainly not sufficient condition to improve the manageability of the environment.

CONCLUDING REMARKS

In this admittedly brief consideration of the factors that I believe may help explain the perception and evaluation of neighborhood change, I have stressed the importance of both person-related and environmentally related factors. Although it was not possible to draw out completely the implications of the various assumptions and hypotheses put forward here, I hope that the reader has been convinced of the importance and utility of considering environmental, social, and cognitive issues that have a bearing on neighborhood evaluation. One of the major tasks that lies before us involves the elucidation of the manner in which the factors discussed here operate in the complicated ecology of the sociophysical environment within which we all live.

ACKNOWLEDGMENTS

The present chapter has been adapted from a monograph by G. Winkel and S. Saegert entitled *A Theoretical Approach to the Perception of Neighborhood Change,* available from the Center for Human Environments, Graduate School and University Center, City University of New York, 33 West 42nd Street, New York, New York, 10036. Some of the research discussed in this chapter was supported by a Faculty Research Award Grant (No. 11829) to G. Winkel from the PSC–BHE Grant Award Program at the City University of New York.

REFERENCES

Aldrich, H. Ecological succession in racially changing neighborhoods: A review of the literature. *Urban Affairs Quarterly,* 1975, *10,* 327–348.

Birch, D., Brown, E., Coleman, R., DaLomba, D., Parsons, W., Sharpe, L., & Weber, S. *A Behavioral Model of Neighborhood Change.* Cambridge, Mass.: Joint Center for Urban Studies of M.I.T. & Harvard, 1977.

Campbell, A., Converse, P., & Rodgers, W. *The quality of American life.* New York: Russell Sage Foundation, 1976.

Carr, S., & Lynch, K. Where learning happens. *Daedulus: Journal of the American Academy of Arts and Sciences,* 1968, *97,* 1277–1291.

Cohen, S. Environmental load and the allocation of attention. In A. Baum, J. Singer, & S. Valins (Eds.), *Advances in environmental psychology.* Hillsdale, N.J.: Lawrence Erlbaum Associates, 1977.

Cohen, S., & Lezak, A. Noise and inattentiveness to social cues. *Environment and Behavior,* 1977, *9,* 559–572.

Craik, K. H. Environmental psychology. *Annual Review of Psychology,* 1973, *24,* 403–422.

Fried, M. Grieving for a lost home. In L. I. Duhl (Ed.), *The urban condition.* New York: Basic Books, 1963.

Fried, M., & Gleicher, P. Some sources of residential satisfaction in an urban slum. *Journal of the American Institute of Planners,* 1961, *27,* 305–315.

Gans, H. *The urban villagers.* New York: Free Press, 1962.

Heider, F. *The psychology of interpersonal relations.* New York: Wiley, 1956.

Ittelson, W., Proshansky, H., Rivlin, L., & Winkel, G. *An introduction to environmental psychology.* New York: Holt, Rinehart, & Winston, 1974.

Korte, C., Ypma, I., & Toppen, A. Helpfulness in Dutch society as a function of urbanization and environmental input level. *Journal of Personality and Social Psychology,* 1975, *32,* 996–1003.

Lynch, K. *The image of the city.* Cambridge, Mass.: M.I.T. Press, 1960.

McCarthy, D., & Saegert, S. Residential density, social overload and social withdrawal. In A. Aiello & A. Baum (Eds.), *Crowding in residential environments.* New York: Plenum, 1977.

Mackintosh, E., Olsen, R., & Wentworth, W. *The middle-income family's experience in an urban high-rise complex and the suburban single family home.* New York: Center for Human Environments, Graduate School of City University of New York, 1977.

Milgram, S. The experience of living in cities. *Science,* 1970, *167,* 1461–1468.

Molotch, H. *Managed integration.* Berkeley and Los Angeles: University of California Press, 1972.

Nisbett, R., & Wilson, T. Telling more than we can know: Verbal reports on mental processes. *Psychological Review,* 1977, *84,* 231–259.

Rams, E. *Analysis and valuation of retail locations.* Reston, Va.: Reston, 1976.

Rapkin, C., & Grigsby, W. The demand for housing in racially mixed areas. Berkeley and Los Angeles: University of California Press, 1960.

Roberts, C., & Saegert, S. *Crowding in the big city: Urbanites descriptions of crowding stress.* New York: Center for Human Environments, City University of New York, Graduate School and University Center, 1977.

Rossi, P. H. *Why families move: A study in the social psychology of urban residential mobility.* New York: Free Press, 1955.

Saegert, S. Crowding: Cognitive overload and behavioral constraint. In W. Preiser (Ed.), *Environmental design research* (Vol. 2). Stroudsberg, Pa.: Dowden, Hutchinson, & Ross, 1973.

Saegert, S. High-density environments: Their Personal and social consequences. In A. Baum & Y. Epstein (Eds.), *Human response to crowding.* Hillside, N.J.: Lawrence Erlbaum Associates, 1978.

Saegert, S. Feminine Suburbs and Masculine Cities. *Signs,* 1980, *5,* 96–111.

Saegert, S., & Winkel, G. The home: A critical problem for changing sex roles. In G. Wekerle, R. Peterson, & D. Morley (Eds.), *New space for women.* Boulder, Colo.: Westview Press, in press.

Smith, W. Forecasting neighborhood change. *Land Economics,* 1963, *39,* 292–297.

Stokols, D. The experience of crowding in primary and secondary environments. *Environment and Behavior,* 1976, *8,* 49–86.

Stokols, D. Environmental psychology. *Annual Review of Psychology,* 1978, *29,* 253–295.

Taylor, R., Brower, S., & Stough, R. User-generated visual features as signs in the urban residential environment. In P. Suedfeld & J. Russell (Eds.), *the behavioral basis of design.* Stroudsberg, Pa.: Dowden, Hutchinson, & Ross, 1976.

Taylor, S., & Fiske, S. Salience, attention and attribution: Top of the head phenomena. In L. Berkowitz (Ed.). *Advances in experimental social psychology* (Vol. 11). New York: Academic Press, 1978.

Taeuber, K., & Taeuber, A. *Negroes in cities.* Chicago: Aldine, 1965.

24 Cognitive Mediation of Environmental Stress

Andrew Baum
Robert J. Gatchel
Uniformed Services University of the Health Sciences

John R. Aiello
Rutgers, The State University

Donna Thompson
New York University

Because this volume is concerned with the interface among cognitive, social, and environmental psychology, we thought it best to make our point by presenting the findings of some research we have conducted over the past 2 years. Our point is a simple one: The best understanding of human response to anything can be achieved by viewing it from a multilevel perspective, emphasizing environmental, social, and cognitive determinants of mood and behavior. This point has been made before (e.g., Barker, 1960; Ittelson, Proshansky, Rivlin, & Winkel, 1974; Lewin, 1951), and environmental psychologists have typically described environmental influences on behavior in terms of their impact on social processes and their interpretation by cognitive processes. In other words, environmental influence will depend on what is going on in the environment and how those people in the setting interpret what is occurring.

This is a simple enough point. Sometimes, however, this kind of simplicity is misleading. One of the hallmarks of the recent development of an environmental psychology has been the rejection of the radical behaviorist notion of "architectural determinism" (cf. Lee, 1971). The notion that environments could directly influence behavior was not an easy one to dislodge, and a good part of research in environmental psychology has been concerned, more or less directly, with demonstrating the mediating influence of social and cognitive factors. We now know that these factors are crucial in determining the extent and nature of an environment's effect on people. But some persist in viewing environment and behavior in a direct, one-to-one fashion, as illustrated by reliance upon one-to-one density–pathology indices to illustrate the effects of crowding (e.g., Freedman, 1975).

The research that is considered in this chapter is drawn from a program of research considering architectural and psychosocial determinants of environmental stress (cf. Baum & Valins, 1977). More specifically, we have been concerned with the determinants of crowding stress in college dormitory settings. Essentially, our findings have indicated that architectural designs that vary the number of residents sharing common areas in the dormitory are associated with different levels of stress and withdrawal. In the summary that follows, we trace the role of environmental, social, and cognitive factors in the development of crowding stress, withdrawal, and helplessness. One fact immediately becomes clear: The architectural designs we have studied do not act directly on residents. Rather, the consequences of living in a building with a given design are manifest in the unfolding of a complex array of social and cognitive factors. Expectations and group-based achievements mediate the influence of building design.

SOCIAL DENSITY AND REGULATORY CONTROL

Social density represents the group-size component of density, reflecting the consequences of increasing numbers of people. Experimentally, this is manipulated by varying group size, and descriptively, it is a translation of the nonspatial effects of density. Over the past 8 years, we have been studying naturalistically manipulated social density by considering the effects of architectural designs that varied the size of groups sharing common space. Consistent with laboratory study (cf. Sundstrom, 1978), we found that increasing social density was associated with discomfort and withdrawal. But we were able to learn more about the processes involved in response to high social density because of our on-going naturalistic settings.

One of the dormitory designs that we studied can be called a long-corridor design; in it, 32–40 residents are grouped around a common hallway, lounge, and bathroom spaces. The others, which are suite or short-corridor–design residences, group fewer residents (6–20) around common areas. So, beyond the constant roommate dyad, the group sizes in these dormitories are different. These designs are presented in Figs. 24.1–24.4.

We were initially interested in how these different design-authored group sizes affected the development of social structure in the dormitories. Physical densities were comparable across settings, and residents were either haphazardly (early studies) or randomly (later studies) assigned to residence. Yet, clear differences between the two kinds of environments were quickly apparent. Long-corridor design dormitories were not characterized by the development of small local groups beyond the roommate dyad, whereas suite- and short-corridor–design housing were. Long-corridor residents had fewer friends in the dormitory,

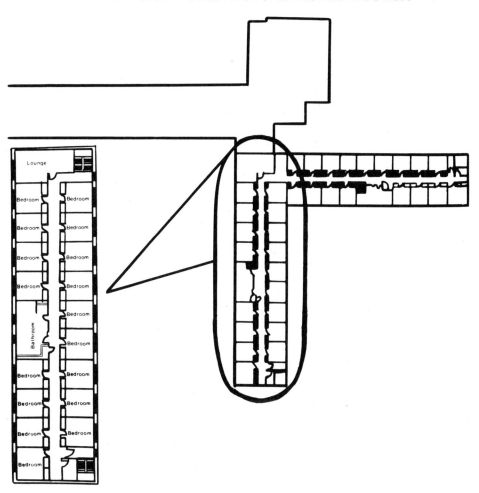

FIG. 24.1.   Floor plan of a corridor-design dormitory (from Baum & Valins, 1977).

and tended to leave more often. Their primary groups tended to be based else-where, whereas corridor/suite residents' primary groups were local.

Long-corridor residents also reported knowing fewer of their neighbors well than did short-corridor/suite residents. As a result, they more often encountered people they did not know very well, and because of the large number of people sharing the common spaces, more frequently interacted with all neighbors, both known and unknown. This situation was associated with heightened perceptions of crowding, loss of control, and more frequent complaints about unwanted interaction in the dormitory. The large group size apparently inhibited both the exercise of regulatory control (determining when, where, and with whom interac-

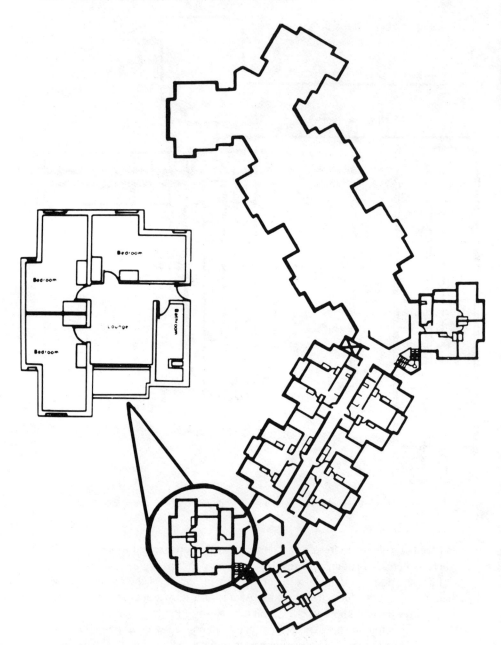

FIG. 24.2.   Floor plan of a suite-design dormitory (from Baum & Valins, 1977).

tion would occur) and the development of groups (which can provide a structure that supports individual regulatory control). The long-corridor environments, then, were characterized by loss of control and distress.

Residents of these crowded dormitories responded to this stress by withdrawing from social interaction. Observation of behavior in the dormitory settings indicated that long-corridor residents avoided contact with neighbors and spent more time elsewhere than did short-corridor/suite residents. Further, when brought to a neutral laboratory and introduced to a relative stranger, long-corridor residents persisted in avoiding contact.

The large residential group sizes of the long-corridor dormitories were also associated with a form of helplessness. Under most conditions, helplessness can be conditioned by repeated or prolonged exposure to uncontrollable situations. As an individual learns that responses and outcomes are not contingent, motivation to control decreases and cognitive deficits may occur. Presumably, helplessness training began when residents recognized that they could not control interaction with one another. Residents of these dormitories exhibited, in several settings, a reduced motivation to control outcomes. In one experiment (Baum & Valins, 1977), subjects were told they could choose the experimental condition in which they would participate. Residents of long-corridor dormitory settings were less likely to respond to this choice by seeking additional information or attempting to choose than were residents of short-corridor dormitory groups.

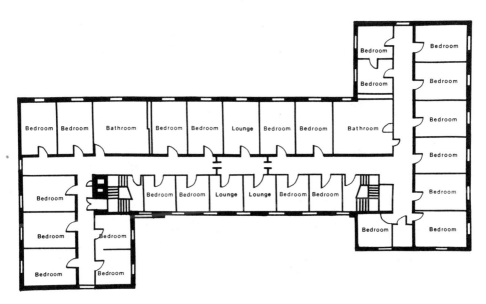

FIG. 24.3.   Floor plan of a long-corridor–design dormitory (from Baum & Valins, 1977).

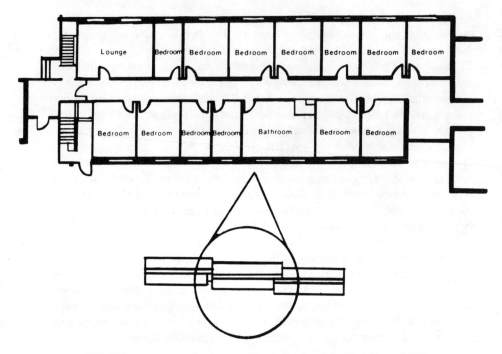

FIG. 24.4.   Floor plan of a short-corridor–design dormitory (from Baum & Valins, 1977).

A second study assessed responses to a modified prisoners-dilemma (PD) game. The game provided a withdrawal option as well as the more traditional competitive and cooperative choices. This game has been used to assess motivation deficit following helplessness training (e.g., Seligman, 1975) and our studies of it have indicated that students interpret the third (withdrawal) response category as one best suited when "you don't care what happens in the game." The competitive choice, on the other hand, has been rated as a response best suited for asserting control over the game. The results of this study indicated that when interaction with the other player was unlikely, long-corridor residents selected more withdrawal responses than did short-corridor residents, suggesting reduced motivation to influence the game.

The studies that we now consider in detail take these findings as their point of departure. Because of the on-going nature of the setting, it was possible to observe the processes involved in helplessness conditioning. In addition, inconsistencies in earlier data suggested that this conditioning was sequential in a way approximating that described by Wortman and Brehm (1975); consequently, two longer-term studies were conducted.

SOCIAL DENSITY AND THE DEVELOPMENT OF
LEARNED HELPLESSNESS

Briefly, Wortman and Brehm have argued that loss of control is initially associated with reactance and attempts to reestablish control. As expectations for control diminish with repeated exposure, reactance fades and behavior becomes more helpless. Response to loss or lack of personal control is therefore mediated by one's expectancies. In our particular environment, given that students arrived on campus expecting to be able to control their social experience, it can be argued that the violation of these expectancies aroused reactance among long-corridor residents. As these residents become aware of the relatively uncontrollable nature of contact in the dormitories, however, purposive control-oriented behavior would decrease.

A study conducted during the first semester of the academic year at Trinity College in Connecticut (Baum, Aiello, & Calesnick, 1978) shed some light on these issues. Specifically, the study was concerned with the applicability of Wortman and Brehm's analysis of helplessness of the social dynamics of these

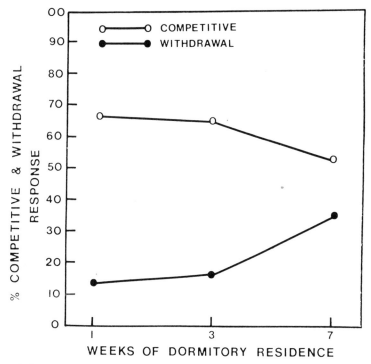

FIG. 24.5. Long-corridor dormitory residents' competitive and withdrawal responses over time.

dormitories. Residence (long- and short-corridor dormitory) and length of residence (1, 3, or 7 weeks) were considered. Groups of 10 experimental and 10 survey subjects from each dormitory type were tested at each interval. Samples were drawn so that each subject participated in only one mode and at only one testing time.

Three major dependent variables were assessed during the experimental session: frequency of competitive, cooperative, and withdrawal responding in the modified PD situations. Additional information about goals during the game was obtained by having subjects complete a brief questionnaire at the end of the experimental game. Survey subjects answered 42 questions about their satisfaction with campus life and dormitory life, the ways in which they spent their time, problems associated with dormitory living, their perceptions of crowding, feelings about roommates, and their motivation to assume control over certain situations.

Results of this study indicated that long-corridor residents played a noncooperative strategy whereas short-corridor residents approached balance by playing cooperative and competitive choices nearly equally. As can be seen in Fig. 24.5, long-corridor residents' strategies varied with length of exposure: During the first two test periods, they responded competitively, but by the third, this responding had fallen off in favor of sharply increased withdrawal.

Those goals selected by long-corridor residents reflected their response choices; during the first and second testings, they were likely to identify negative interpersonal goals and attempts to control as reflective of their own, but by the final testing identification of this goal, had yielded to reduced motivation in the game (see Fig. 24.6).

Survey findings provided further evidence of divergent mood and behavior in the two residential environments, and suggested that our control-based explanations of these differences were tenable. Long-corridor residents were generally less satisfied with residential experience, were less positive about fellow students, and reported greater dislike for neighbors than did short-corridor residents. However, this negativity began to decrease after 3 weeks of residence and, by the 7th week, had become largely neutral. At the same time, perceptions of control in the dormitories rapidly decreased; by the 3rd week, long-corridor residents had begun to complain about the frequency and uncontrollability of dormitory interaction and to express doubts about their ability to control experience in these settings. These control problems intensified over time, paralleling reports of unwanted interaction with neighbors and increasing desire to avoid contact with other residents of the dormitory. Finally, long-corridor residents reported less confidence in their ability to control in general; by the 7th week of residence, they reported less perceived value in exerting effort to change things than did short-corridor residents.

These findings indicate that withdrawal and purposive avoidance behavior are modal responses to prolonged exposure to crowding stress but that a form of helplessness is also conditioned. In addition, they suggest that helplessness is

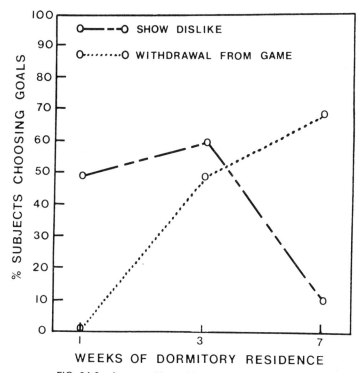

FIG. 24.6. Long-corridor residents' game goals over time.

mediated by expectation for control, emerging only after repeated attempts to reestablish control have proven unsuccessful. Whereas short-corridor residents showed few effects of length of exposure to residential conditions, long-corridor residents reported an intensification of control-relevant problems in their dormitory as length of residence increased. Their responses to the experimental game and survey items show trends that suggest dramatic shifts in mood and behavior as such problems become more salient. Competition and control-oriented behaviors fade in favor of a helpless kind of response *after* problems with regulation of interaction become apparent *and* expectations for control are diminished.

COGNITIVE MEDIATION OF HELPLESSNESS CONDITIONING

One problem raised by this study is the possibility of even more fine-grained dynamics occurring during this sequential pattern of loss of control, reactance, and helplessness. A closer examination of the data, for instance, indicates that behavioral symptoms of helplessness do not appear until the 7th week of residence, even though students report loss of control after 3 weeks. Findings of another study of these residential environments (Baum & Davis, in press) reflect this same pattern. In this study, control-relevant complaints were clearly apparent by the 5th week of residence, but decrements in persistence on difficult problem-solving tasks did not appear until 2 or 3 weeks later. These "lags" highlight the fact that in the study of any behavioral phenomenon, one must consider a complex of responses consisting of three broad components of behavior: (1) subjective or self-report measures; (2) overt somatic-motor measures such as actual performance on some task; and (3) physiological measures. One cannot always assume that these three behavioral components will be highly correlated (Gatchel, 1979). For example, a person may verbally report that he or she is not anxious, but yet be observed trembling and stuttering and displaying a greatly accelerated heart rate; or, the opposite might be the case. In the present study, therefore, the "lag" finding that at 3 weeks subjects provide *self reports* of loss of control, but do not display *overt behavioral* signs of helplessness until the 7th week of residence should not be viewed as a particularly unusual or peculiar finding. Indeed, more and more behavioral scientists have been emphasizing the importance of assessing all three components of behavior in specific situations whenever possible with the expectation that there may be complex interactions between components that may differ from one situation to the next.

A second study conducted at Trinity College (Baum & Gatchel, 1980) suggested that attributed responsibility for failure to control may be a heuristic explanation of the lag between reported and overt behaviors. This study was originally intended to be a simple replication of the first, looking at behavior over a longer period of time. In addition, we presented subjects with a list of 12 problems commonly encountered in the dormitory, and asked them to indicate: (1) whether they had solved these problems; and (2) if they remained unsolved, whether this was due to their failure to find a solution or to the fact that the dormitory environment did not afford a solution. Thus, residents were asked to attribute responsibility for unsolved problems. Of special interest were four of the problems listed, all dealing with control in the dormitory. Responses to these items allowed us to study the attributional processes involved in loss of control in these settings.

The study was conducted in the same way as the first, using the same game and similar questions on the survey. Some changes in procedure were made, however. Assessment of response to the experimental game was conducted during the 2nd through tenth weeks of residence, allowing a more detailed view of changing response choices. Brief questionnaires were administered during first-year students' orientation, before students had had any appreciable experience living in the dormitories, and more detailed surveys were completed by residents after 3, 5, and 10 weeks of residence. Unlike earlier studies, this one was longitudinal; subjects were asked to complete all four surveys and participate (one session) in the laboratory phase of the study. For each subject, then, self-report data were obtained for four different time intervals and response to the experimental game was sampled once.

The data from this study are interesting from three perspectives. First, they support the findings obtained in the first study indicating that the development of helplessness is sequential and is mediated by expectations for control. As can be seen in Fig. 24.7, responses to the PD game among long- and short-corridor residents followed the same pattern as previously observed, with competitive responding falling off by weeks 6–7 in favor of increasing withdrawal responding. Survey findings were also similar to earlier data; expectations for control began to diminish around the 5th week of residence as the predictability and controllability of dormitory life decreased.

The second implication of our findings concerns attribution of responsibility for control-relevant problems. In general, long-corridor residents reported more

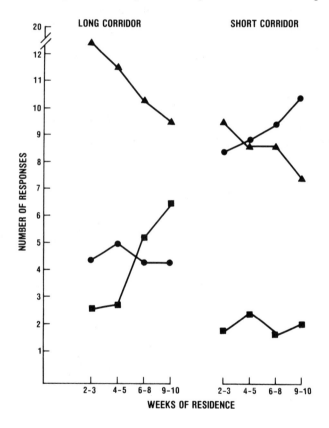

FIG. 24.7.   Response to the PD game over time, by long- and short-corridor dormitory residents.

unsolved problems than did short-corridor residents. Interestingly, however, long-corridor residents attributed unsolved problems to different causes over time. As length of residence increased, long-corridor residents attributed unsolved problems decreasingly to personal factors and increasingly to environmental factors. This can be illustrated by the data for the four control-relevant items in the list of problems presented to subjects. The first, "determining when I talk to people in the dormitory" did not produce significant differences between residential groups. However, the others clearly show increasingly external attributions for control problems among long-corridor residents over the course of the semester (see Fig. 24.8).

What is surprising about this finding is not just that attributions become more external over time, but that this trend parallels increasingly helpless behavior. As attributions for loss of control become more external, expectations for control diminish and behavior becomes more indicative of helplessness.

The degree to which these problems were attributed to environmental factors, especially during the 5th and 10th weeks, was highly correlated with game responses and survey responses during these weeks. The more these problems were attributed to the environment, the more withdrawal responses and fewer competitive responses were played during the PD game, and the more severe were perceptions of control-related problems. In addition, expectation for control decreased as attribution of control problems became more external.

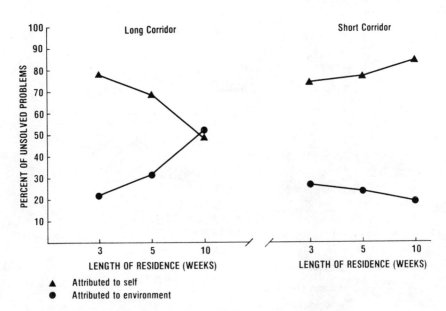

FIG. 24.8.   Unsolved dormitory problems attributed to personal and environmental causes over time.

This suggests that the categorization of personal and universal helplessness provided by Abramson, Seligman, and Teasdale (1978) may be incomplete—that these situations may be sequentially linked to each other rather than standing alone as end products of loss of control. In their recent reformulation of the learned helplessness phenomenon, Abramson et al. have argued that a complex attributional schema can be applied to the conditioning of helplessness. Once people perceive failure or a loss of control, they make attributions relating this loss to a cause, which can be internal or external, stable or unstable, or global or specific. Each of these dimensions will affect the kind of response people make to loss of control. Once an attribution is chosen, it influences whether the expectation of future helplessness will be acute or chronic, or narrow or broad.

Personal attributions for failure or loss of control involve placing the responsibility or blame on oneself. Here, people perceive others as being able to solve a problem or achieve a degree of control, but are unable to do so themselves. Hence, they decide that the difficulties they are experiencing are their own fault. Universal or external attributions for failure or loss of control involve placing the blame on an environmental variable—be it the setting one is in or the people one is with. Here, others are not seen as able to solve the problem either and the loss of control or failure to solve is seen as more extensive. In the former case, people seem to be saying "I cannot solve this," whereas in the latter, they seem to believe that "This cannot be solved."

Inherent in the differences between these statements is a possible distinction between personal and universal helplessness that Abramson et al. did not draw. Universal helplessness seems to involve a more definitive judgment that a situation is not solvable or controllable. It is an endpoint—a judgment of conclusion—such that when made, efforts to solve or control should cease. The belief that no one else can solve a problem either should convince us that a problem is not solvable—an attribution to the problem rather than the person.

Personal helplessness, on the other hand, carries with it no such excuse. It is not clearly an endpoint—people who attribute failure to themselves do not believe that the problem is unsolvable, nor do they believe that an environmental factor is involved. Rather, they believe that they have failed to find the solution to the problem. This can be exacerbated if it is known that others have successfully solved it. The question in this case becomes one of expectation. Clearly, when attributed externally, expectation for eventually solving the problem is low. What kind of expectations do people have when they attribute failure or loss of control to personal causes?

Our data suggest that people do not readily give up when they attribute loss of control to themselves; as long as they see it as their own fault, they seem to believe that they can eventually solve the situation and establish the kind of control they want. When long-corridor residents do attribute control-related difficulties to themselves, they are reactant rather than helpless. Their expectations for control are still present at this time and their behavior remains directed at some kind of goal. It is only when attributions for loss of control have become external that helplessness seems to emerge. Apparently, long-corridor residents do not give up even though attributing failure to themselves. Yielding to the situation (i.e., concluding that a solution is unattainable) is associated with a change of attribution from personal to environmental factors.

Thus, we are arguing that personal attributions for loss of control or failure may be expected to precede environmental attributions, and that the stage characterized by personal attributions may be more like reactance than helplessness. Rather than considering the two as separate and distinct, it may be more heuristic to consider the time course of attributions for loss of control. However these are viewed, it is clear that loss of control attributed to personal and environmental factors do not seem to lead to the same behavior or mood.

The actual reasons for these differences are not clear, but the finding that taking personal responsibility for failure to control outcomes is associated with more persistent and less helpless behavior is consistent with several studies of helplessness. For example, Dweck and Reppucci (1973) found that subjects who assumed personal responsibility for failure were more persistent than subjects who blamed external causes for their failure. The more helpless individuals were those who assumed less personal responsibility for outcomes. Similarly, Wortman, Panciera, Shusterman, and Hibscher (1976) found that subjects led to attribute failure to external factors were less motivated on subsequent tasks than were subjects given personal attributions for failure. Hanusa and Schulz (1977) have found better performance among subjects who blamed themselves for failure. All of these studies suggest that when personal responsibility is assumed, repeated failure results in persistence rather than helplessness. When failure is attributed to external causes, persistent responding is less evident. The present findings also suggest that attribution of loss of control to environmental conditions is associated with mood and behavior characteristic of helplessness, whereas attributions to personal factors are more closely associated with the reactance phase of response to loss of control and *not* the helplessness phase.

GENERALIZATION OF LEARNED HELPLESSNESS

This also raises questions about how helplessness generalizes. The weight of theory and research in this area suggests that internally attributed phenomena are more easily generalized. If long-corridor residents are convinced that they are personally responsible for their control problems, they should be more likely to carry around with them the expectation that they will not be able to control things. Here, helplessness should generalize to other settings. Conversely, if long-corridor residents believe that the dormitory environment is responsible for their inability to regulate experience, they should exhibit helplessness only in that setting or in settings very much like the dormitory. Yet, much of our data pertain to behavior in laboratory settings, and indicates that generalization of helplessness to the experimental game is linked with externally attributed failure. Externally attributed failure to control generalized to the laboratory PD game, whereas personally attributed failure did not.

This finding is consistent with the notion that different things may be learned as helplessness is conditioned. For example, personally attributed loss of control should be associated with conditioned beliefs regarding one's ability to exert control (e.g., "I cannot control what happens to me"). Environmentally attributed helplessness, on the other hand, should be associated with learning that some environments are uncontrollable. In the former case, generalization is easily explained. In the latter case, however, people should acquire the expectancy that a fairly limited range of outcomes in a specific setting are uncontrollable. If so, this expectancy should not generalize as readily as it seems to have done in our research. What may be occurring instead is a sensitization to noncontingent environments such that, when control is not immediately available, people who attribute loss of control to an environmental factor may make premature judgments regarding controllability and may give up trying to control outcomes more readily. Rather than carrying around the belief that they cannot control things, they bring to each new situation an expectation that the situation may not be controllable. As a result, they may be *more* motivated to control new situations at the outset. However, if control is not immediately forthcoming, they may jump to the conclusion that, "This is another uncontrollable situation" and cease control attempts prematurely.[1]

By considering response choices over the 20 trials of the experimental game, we obtained some evidence of these kinds of processes. In order to do this, we divided the game into five-trial quarters and analyzed response choices in each of these periods. These analyses indicated that:

1. During the first 5 weeks of residence, long-corridor residents generally increased competitive responding over trials.

2. Abruptly, during the 6th week, response patterns shifted such that long-corridor residents increased competitive responding through the first half of the game, but dramatically ceased playing competitively and greatly increased withdrawal–helplessness responses over the last 10 trials.

3. Short-corridor residents played a fairly consistent strategy across time.

These differences are illustrated in Fig. 24.9. Three things are immediately evident: First, the change from increasingly competitive responding through the

---

[1]When control is available in the setting but a judgment of noncontingency is made before this can be perceived, cessation of control attempts will be premature and maladaptive. If, on the other hand, a new situation is uncontrollable, such behavior can be considered adaptive.

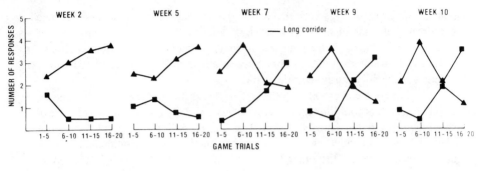

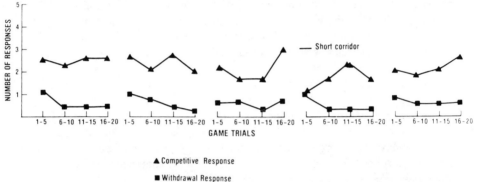

▲ Competitive Response

■ Withdrawal Response

FIG. 24.9.   Competitive and withdrawal responding across the 20 trials of the PD game, for selected weeks of residence.

PD game to an initially competitive but subsequently helpless pattern occurs as expectations for control decreased (around week 5). Second, these behavioral and cognitive changes parallel residents' increasing tendency to attribute them to environmental factors. Finally, the response curve for long-corridor residents' choices across trial blocks in the game are very similar to the one for response across weeks of residence. Instead of weeks of residence, however, trials in the game appear to mediate response; over the first 10 trials, subjects appear to be attempting to control the game (reactance), whereas after the midway point, they appear to give up and play more helplessly. Response across trials, especially after 2 months of residence, also conformed to the reactance–helplessness pattern described by Wortman and Brehm (1975).

These findings can be interpreted as support for the hypothesis derived earlier. During the 1st month of residence, long-corridor residents appear to experience reactance, their expectations for control have been disconfirmed, and they are oriented toward regaining control over social experience. By the end of the 2nd month of residence, however, they appear to have decided that the dormitory setting is inherently uncontrollable, and are highly motivated to control the new

PD situation during the first half of the game. However, control is not readily apparent in this game, and long-corridor residents appear to give up midway through the game.

ENVIRONMENT, COGNITION, AND BEHAVIOR

The results of these two experiments demonstrate the necessity of considering different levels of behavior influence in understanding social phenomena. The complexity of the environment, its effects on social structure, and the impact of different cognitive interpretations of these events are all underscored. They also demonstrate one value of considering the processes by which behavior develops in the context of naturally occurring settings. The on-going nature of the settings studied, for example, allowed research to be conducted that ultimately provided us with alternative perspectives on the development of learned helplessness.

Briefly, we have interpreted these findings as indicative of a heightened sensitivity to noncontingency or lack of control. By the 6th week of residence, long-corridor residents have begun to show symptoms of helplessness and to attribute loss of control to the environment. Thus, they may become sensitive to contingencies in other environments. As they enter into new situations, they may anticipate control-relevant problems and, as a result, try harder to control these situations than students who do not live in environments characterized by lack of control. This reactance is generated by their expectation of problems controlling the situation and their concomitant desire to control it in some manner. However, because they are actually playing themselves, contingencies are not immediately apparent and, by the third quarter, they may have made an attribution of uncontrollability to the new situation. Hence, competitive, control-oriented responding fades and withdrawal/helpless responding increases. We feel that these data indicate that helplessness may involve *more* than learning that one cannot control outcomes—that it also involves learning that some environments cannot be controlled. People who have come to learn that environments can be uncontrollable and are sensitized to that fact by prolonged exposure to an uncontrollable setting may make premature judgments about new settings. They may jump to the conclusion that this is just another uncontrollable environment. Thus, each new setting will be approached, and if control is not readily apparent, response will approximate a reactance–helplessness sequence all over again.

These results also highlight the potential importance of taking into account an expectancy construct in order to more fully understand the helplessness phenomenon. Indeed, Rotter (1966) has long emphasized the importance of subjective expectancy as a mediating variable in understanding behavior. He assumes that expectancies vary in terms of their generality. Individuals may require generalized expectancies that operate across a wide variety of situations, as well as expectancies specific to a particular situation. Specific expectancies can be modified by even small changes in the persons' situations, but generalized expectancies are more consistent and stable across situations. Our findings suggest that the early traces of a trait-like generalized expectancy of helplessness (based on the belief that environments are uncontrollable) may have been kindled in our long-corridor residents. One might speculate that in the real world, if these individuals continued to encounter uncontrollable situations, the trait-like disposition might be further developed and solidified.

An interesting area for future investigation is the evaluation of individual differences in expectancy associated with this phenomenon. The effects of reinforcement on behavior depend on whether individuals habitually perceive events as contingent on their behavior or independent of it. Those who perceive rewards as being contingent on their own behavior have a high degree of perceived personal control, and should respond differently to failure than should external locus-of-control individuals, who perceive rewards as independent of their behavior. This locus-of-control construct has been shown by Rotter to significantly differentiate subjects on a variety of performance tasks. In terms of the learned helplessness literature, Hiroto (1974) has shown that external locus-of-control subjects are more sensitive to learned helplessness manipulations than are internal locus-of-control subjects. Finally, a number of studies have indicated that these generalized expectancies influence response to stressful environments (e.g., Schopler & Walton, 1974).

It should also be noted that there is an accumulating amount of evidence that the Internal–External Locus of Control Scale is not a unidimensional measure but rather a multidimensional one, consisting of several components. For example, perceived externality may refer to an individual's feeling that "powerful others" dominate and control the world, or to a person's belief that the world is such a complex place that any significant comprehension and control of it are impossible. Lao (1970), moreover, has suggested that it is helpful to distinguish between locus of control at the self or personal level and at the social or ideological level. Thus, for example, it was found that in a sample of Black college students in the deep South, an *internal* belief in self or personal control was, as expected, significantly related to general competence and knowledge of the environment. More importantly, an *external* belief in the social system, in which the "system" was blamed for the Blacks' disadvantage in society (attributions to factors such as discrimination, rather than to the self), was also related to competences such as creative and innovative occupational goals. Thus, as Lao suggests, a certain type of externality may often be adaptive for an individual. It allows individuals to focus on external societal barriers rather than blame themselves for their current social status and behavior. Our findings in college dormitories may parallel these, in that attributions to internal or external events in these settings may be very complex and mean more than they appear to on the surface. Clearly, quick judgments of uncontrollability can be adaptive. The degree to which the helplessness demonstrated by long-corridor residents is adaptive or maladaptive remains to be studied.

Finally, these results may be of use in explaining the "facilitation" effect observed by Wortman et al. (1976) and by Hanusa and Schulz (1977). As we noted earlier, subjects in these studies who made ability attributions for failure to control outcomes performed better on subsequent tasks than did those subjects attributing lack of control to environmental factors. Wortman and Dintzer (1978) interpret this as evidence for an information-seeking aspect of exposure to non-contingent outcomes; people who have come to doubt their abilities may desire additional information about their performance in other settings and may therefore try harder. This is consistent with Bandura's (1977) assertion that when expectations regarding standard of performance are inconsistent with actual performance, reevaluation is necessary. Studies have considered an "hypothesis-testing" explanation in which subjects making ability attributions for failure seek to determine the persistence of failure in other situations (e.g., Hanusa & Schulz, 1977; Wortman & Dintzer, 1978). However, support for these assertions has been equivocal.

It is possible that facilitation of response by attribution of previous failure to control to internal factors may reflect a desire not to test abilities so much as to test the environment. In order to dismiss environmental factors entirely, it may be necessary to "challenge" the setting, to see whether it is ultimately controllable or not. Thus, people may initially try harder on subsequent tasks, not to test the hypothesis that their abilities are suspect but to determine first whether the environment holds the prospect for control. The expectation that environments are uncontrollable is a more desirable one than the expectation that one cannot control things, and it is possible that when abilities are implicated as a potential cause, attention is turned toward gaining evidence that situations are instead responsible.

SUMMARY

Whatever the eventual implications or interpretations of these findings turn out to be, these studies highlight the complexity of environmental and cognitive mediation of social behavior and shed some new light on helplessness phenomena. Expectations for control mediated naturalistic conditioning of helplessness, and these expectations were ultimately related to the effects of social density on group formation and regulatory control. External attributions for control problems were associated with more persistent helpless responding, whereas internal attributions were associated with more reactant, control-seeking behavior. Clearly, the relationships between environment and behavior are far more complex than the earlier espoused behavioral–deterministic theory would have us believe. As additional research is conducted, these relationships will hopefully be more clearly delineated.

REFERENCES

Abramson, L. Y., Seligman, M. E. P., & Teasdale, J. D. Learned helplessness in humans: Critique and reformulation. *Journal of Abnormal Psychology*, 1978, *87*, 49–74.

Bandura, A. *Social learning theory*. Englewood Cliffs, N.J.: Prentice-Hall, 1977.

Barker, R. G. Ecology and motivation. In M. R. Jones (Ed.), *Nebraska symposium on motivation* (Vol. 8). Lincoln: University of Nebraska Press, 1960.

Baum, A., Aiello, J. R., & Calesnick, L. E. Crowding and personal control, social density and the development of learned helplessness. *Journal of Personality and Social Psychology*, 1978, *36*, 1000–1011.

Baum A., & Davis, G. E. Reducing the stress of high density living. *Journal of Personality and Social Psychology*, 1980, *38*, 471–478.

Baum, A., & Gatchel, R. J. *Locus of attribution and learned helplessness*. Unpublished manuscript, 1980.

Baum, A., & Valins, S. *Architecture and social behavior: Psychological studies of social density*. Hillsdale, N.J.: Lawrence Erlbaum Associates, 1977.

Dweck, C., & Reppucci, N. D. Learned helplessness and reinforcement responsibility in children. *Journal of Personality and Social Psychology*, 1973, *25*, 109–116.

Freedman, J. L. *Crowding and behavior*. San Francisco: Freeman, 1975.

Gatchel, R. J. Biofeedback and the treatment of fear and anxiety. In R. Gatchel & K. Price (Eds.) *Clinical application of biofeedback: Appraisal and status*. New York: Pergamon Press, 1979.

Hanusa, B. H., & Schulz, R. Attributional mediators of learned helplessness. *Journal of Personality and Social Psychology*, 1977, *35*, 602–611.

Hiroto, D. Locus of control and learned helplessness. *Journal of Experimental Psychology*, 1974, *102*, 187–193.

Ittelson, W. H., Proshansky, H. M., Rivlin, L. G., & Winkel, G. H. *An introduction to environmental psychology*. New York: Holt, Rinehart, & Winston, 1974.

Lao, R. C. Internal–external control and competent and innovative behavior among Negro college students. *Journal of Personality and Social Psychology*, 1970, *14*, 263–270.

Lee, T. R. Psychology and architectural determinism. *Architects Journal*, 1971, *154*, 253–262; 475–483; and 651–659.

Lewin, K. Formalization and progress in psychology. In D. Cartwright (Ed.), *Field theory in social science*. New York: Harper, 1951.

Rotter, J. P. Generalized expectancies for internal versus external control of reinforcement. *Psychological Monographs*, 1966, *80*(1), Whole #609.

Schopler, J., & Walton, M. *The effects of expected structure, expected enjoyment and participant's internality–externality upon feelings of being crowded*. Unpublished manuscript, University of North Carolina, 1974.

Seligman, M. E. P. *Helplessness: On depression, development, and death*. San Francisco: Freeman, 1975.

Sundstrom, E. Crowding as a sequential process: Review of research on the effects of population density on humans. In A. Baum & Y. Epstein (Eds.), *Human response to crowding*. Hillsdale, N.J.: Lawrence Erlbaum Associates, 1978.

Wortman, C. B., & Brehm, J. W. Responses to uncontrollable outcomes: An integration of reactance theory and the learned helplessness model. In L. Berkowitz (Ed.), *Advances in experimental social psychology*, 1975, *8*, 277–336.

Wortman, C. B., & Dintzer, L. Is an attributional analysis of the learned helplessness phenomenon viable? A critique of the Abramson–Seligman–Teasdale reformulation. *Journal of Abnormal Psychology,* 1978, *87,* 75–90.

Wortman, C. B., Panciera, L., Shusterman, L., & Hibscher, Jr. Attributions of causality and reactions to uncontrollable outcomes. *Journal of Experimental and Social Psychology,* 1976, *12,* 301–316.

25 Environmental Structure and Cognitive Structure

Anthony G. Greenwald
Ohio State University

Introduction

The term cognition is used so frequently in contemporary psychology that it may be in danger of losing its meaning. That is sufficient excuse to note that I am using cognition as an equivalent of knowledge. A cognitive structure is thus a knowledge structure, or a memory. Knowledge structures exist not only inside the head. Many outside-the-head structures—not just obvious ones such as books or computers—can function as memories or knowledge structures.

This chapter is in three parts. Part I concerns a particularly important knowledge structure, the human self. I argue that self is usefully regarded as an *organization* of knowledge, rather than, say, as an unstructured collection of information. The major evidence for this conception of self as organization is the existence of some cognitive biases that are readily understandable only if it is assumed that there exists an organization whose survival they enhance. Part II analyzes the evolution of cognitive dissonance theory as an organization of knowledge. Dissonance theory is of particular interest because the theory's content deals with the cognitive biases that operate in the self system and that may also operate in the theory itself as a body of knowledge. Part III extends the analysis of knowledge organization to outside-the-head structures that are not commonly thought of as memory structures.

I. THE SELF AS AN ORGANIZATION OF KNOWLEDGE

The Totalitarian Ego

In a recent paper (Greenwald, 1980), I have summarized evidence concerning the pervasiveness of three biases in self knowledge in the average normal adult of (at least) our North American culture. These cognitive biases include *egocentricity*, the tendency for judgment and memory to be focused on self, *"beneffectance"* (see also below), the tendency for self to be perceived as effective in achieving desired ends while avoiding undesired ones, and *cognitive conservatism*, the tendency to resist cognitive change. I have referred to this constellation of biases as the "totalitarian ego," a label chosen because the three biases match ones that are considered to be characteristics of the information control apparatus of a totalitarian dictatorship. The totalitarian epithet is therefore intended to be provocative, a challenge to understand why biases that we disparage in a political system may be just the ones that are used in managing our more personal flow of information. The next three subsections give a brief overview of the evidence for the three cognitive biases of the totalitarian ego.

The Egocentric Character of Knowledge

"The past is remembered as if it were a drama in which self was the leading player" (Greenwald, 1980, p. 604). In part, this observation is a reference to the autobiographical or episodic character of much of memory—that is, the tendency for events to be encoded in terms of the person's location (in time and space) during the original experience. However, the egocentric character of knowledge involves much more. It is reflected in the well-replicated finding (first reported by Rogers, Kuiper, & Kirker, 1977) that information is especially well remembered if the person considers the relation of the information to self at the time of initial experience. It is reflected in Brenner's (1973) finding that, in a group setting, subjects focus on their own performance at the expense of retaining information from just-preceding or just-following performances of others.[1] It also is reflected in the results of a series of experiments by Ross and Sicoly (1979), who found their subjects to have an exaggerated recall of their own relative contributions to group activities such as conversations or household chores. An additional component of cognitive egocentricity is the tendency to insert self into perceived causal sequences, either as influencing agent (cf. Langer's 1975, illusion of control) or as influenced object (cf. Jervis, 1976, Chapter 9).

The "Beneffectance" of Self

"Beneffectance" is a compound of beneficence (being good) and effectance (being competent; see White, 1959). I ask to be forgiven for this contribution to

---

[1] An interesting sidelight of these findings is that similar, although weaker, effects occur in relation to well-liked others. For example, Brenner (1976) found a secondary focus on the performance of the subject's dating partner. The extent to which familiar others participate in the self as an organization of knowledge is left, for the moment, as an interesting but unanswered question.

jargon. The term was coined chiefly to establish a concept that could be compared with a few other contemporary concepts (see below). Beneffectance designates a tendency, in both judgment and memory, for self to be credited for achieving desired outcomes, but not to be blamed for undesired outcomes. Some of the earlier experimental demonstrations of this phenomenon were provided in Rosensweig's (1943) and Glixman's (1949) variations of the Zeigarnik-effect research (see review in de Rivera, 1976). Zeigarnik's research had shown that subjects who perform a series of laboratory tasks, being interrupted on some while being allowed to complete others, typically recalled more of the interrupted tasks. However, when interruption was a signal of failure, and completion was a signal of success, as in Rosenweig's and Glixman's studies, the usual effect was reversed such that more completed than interrupted tasks were remembered. In a variation of Milgram's (1963) well-known obedience experiment, Harvey, Harris, and Barnes (1975) showed that shock-administering subjects accorded themselves less responsibility for the recipient's (apparent) distress when that distress was severe as compared to mild, and also blamed themselves less for the recipient's severe distress than did third-person observers. Cialdini, Borden, Thorne, Walker, Freeman, and Sloan (1976) demonstrated that college students extend their use of first-person grammatical forms to include their university and are more likely to wear clothing bearing the university name in the context of a positive achievement of the university (a football victory) than a negative one (a loss).

Other experimental studies of self-serving distortions in perceived responsibility for desirable or undesirable outcomes have been reviewed recently by Miller and Ross (1975), Wortman (1976), and Weary (Bradley, 1978). These distortions in perception of responsibility are pervasive and powerful processes. They can be applied to understanding such things as money-making power of slot machines and the reluctance of drivers to acknowledge that they caused automobile accidents. In the case of slot machines, it appears that players manage to perceive some ability to control the machine amidst a random pattern of successes and failures—that is, they perceive themselves as having done something to obtain the occasional payoffs, while not being responsible for the more frequent losses. Thus, the gambling task becomes reconstructed as a solvable learning task, with the result that substantial investments may be made. In the case of automobile accidents, a recent collection of explanations provided in accident reports to police (*San Francisco Sunday Examiner and Chronicle,* April 22, 1979, p. 35) illustrates the imaginativeness of drivers in displacing responsibility away from the self—for example, ''The telephone pole was approaching. I was attempting to swerve out of its way when it struck my front end.''

The term ''beneffectance'' combines the notions of beneficence (goodness) and effectance (competence) that are represented in the tendency for perceived responsibility to covary with desirability of outcomes. This label may facilitate distinguishing this concept of cognitive bias from some other recently developed and influential concepts of responsibility attribution—particularly Langer's (1975) concept of illusion of control and Jones and Nisbett's (1971) account of actor–observer differences in attributed responsibility. Interestingly, at first reading, Langer's and Jones and Nisbett's analyses seem to imply a contradiction with one another—a contradiction that disappears when each of their analyses is considered in the context of the beneffectance notion. To elaborate: Langer's concept of illusion of control refers to the tendency for people to perceive that outcomes are contingent on their own behavior in situations that minimally support such perceptions (for example, the arm of the slot machine may be a critical prop to permit the illusion of control over its spinning dials). On the other hand, Jones and Nisbett claim that people typically transfer perceived responsibility *away* from themselves, onto the situation. Applying the Jones and Nisbett actor–observer analyses to slot machines, we should expect people to credit themselves less for slot machine payoffs than would uninvolved bystanders. We can resolve the apparent contradiction between Langer's and Jones and Nisbett's analyses by proposing that the Jones and Nisbett analysis is prototypically applicable to undesired outcomes (such as automobile accidents), whereas Langer's analysis is prototypically applicable to desired outcomes (such as slot machine payoffs). This resolution achieves exactly the synthesis contained in the principle of beneffectance as a cognitive bias. That is, the perception of self versus external force as the controlling agent covaries with the desirability of the outcome that is being explained. (Examination of Langer's [1975] and Jones & Nisbett's [1971] articles confirms that the former concerns mostly situations involving desirable or potentially desirable outcomes, whereas the latter reports its strongest supporting evidence from experiments dealing with undesired outcomes.)

Cognitive Conservatism

Conservatism is, in general, the disposition to preserve what is already established. At the most elementary level, cognitive conservatism includes well-known processes of *object conservation* (perceptual constancy) and *assimilation* (reuse of existing categories). Both of these processes often function in the service of veridical knowledge. Two other conservative (change-resisting) processes, *confirmation bias* and *rewriting of memory,* appear to serve the interests of perceptual accuracy less well.

Confirmation bias designates a tendency to manage knowledge so as to promote the selective availability of information that confirms judgments already arrived at. The variety of evidence for this bias includes: selection of interview questions that prejudice an interview toward confirmation of a planted hypothesis about the interviewee (Snyder & Swann, 1978); selective recall of information that confirms experimentally established beliefs (Mischel, Ebbesen, & Zeiss, 1976; Snyder & Uranowitz, 1978); selective generation of arguments that support existing opinions when these are under attack (Greenwald, 1968; Petty,

Ostrom, & Brock, 1981), and researchers' selective evaluation of their own data as a function of the data's agreement with their hypotheses (Greenwald, 1975).

The concept of *rewriting of memory* is a descendant of Bartlett's (1932) conception of memory's constructive processes:

> The construction that is effected is [one] that would justify the observer's "attitude"... [which is] very largely a matter of feeling or affect.... When a subject is being asked to remember, very often the first thing that emerges is something of the nature of an attitude. The recall is then a construction, made largely on the basis of this attitude, and its general effect is that of justification of the attitude [pp. 206-207].

Bartlett's evidence for this constructive process came from experiments showing that subjects introduced distortions into repeated reproductions of stories or pictures. Recent studies have provided sufficient additional evidence of alterations of memory to have prompted a characterization of their findings as showing "fabrication and revision of personal history" (Greenwald, 1980). Examples include systematic misrecall of prior opinions so as to obscure the occurrence of opinion change (Bem & McConnell, 1970); believing that newly acquired facts have had lengthy residence in memory (Fischhoff, 1977; Loftus, Miller, & Burns, 1978); and overestimating the validity of inaccurate memories (Trope, 1978).

Confirmation bias and rewriting of memory are conservative processes in the sense that they protect against major cognitive change. Rewriting of memory has the interesting characteristic of allowing the content of memory actually to change (for example, opinions may change or new facts may be acquired), even though the larger system maintains an illusion of no change. The conservative function of this illusion may be likened to the adaptation of a sizable business organization to a change in one of its key personnel. The new incumbent may have many characteristics that differ from those of the predecessor, but because the label of the position in the corporate structure is unchanged, others are not obliged to adjust to a new person; they can deal instead with the person's (unchanged) role.

Organization of Self

In a characterization of totalitarian information control, George Orwell (1949) summarized the function of information control by saying:

> It is not merely that speeches, statistics, and records of every kind must be constantly brought up to date in order to show that the predictions of the Party were in all cases right. It is also that no change of doctrine or in political alignment can ever be admitted. For to change one's mind, or even one's policy, is a confession of weakness [p. 175].

Thus, information control at the societal level was assumed by Orwell to function as a necessary means of safeguarding the continued power of the totalitarian dictatorship—in other words, it served the function of preserving an organization. By analogy, it can be suggested that the biases in self knowledge that comprise the totalitarian ego play a similar organization-protecting function. Accordingly, an important argument for the conception of self as an *organization* of knowledge is the observation that self knowledge is characterized by biases that may be understandable partly by assuming that there is an organization whose dominance and integrity is protected by those biases.

There are two other lines of argument for self as organization that I mention only briefly. One is the class of phenomena that are often referred to as evidences of ego-involvement (Allport, 1943; Sherif & Cantril, 1947; Greenwald, in press). Ego-involvement phenomena take the form of demonstrations that the relationship between two variables is markedly affected, sometimes being reversed, by the use of procedures that establish personal importance of the experimental task. One illustration is the reversal of the Zeigarnik effect, mentioned previously, when the tasks performed in the experiment are presented as assessments of important abilities. Another such effect of ego-involvement is the reversal in the relation between communication discrepancy and opinion change (from positive to negative) when the opinion issue is changed from an uninvolving one to one that is relevant to important values (e.g., Rhine & Severance, 1970).

These alterations in relationships among psychological variables as personal importance is increased may reflect the dependence of those relationships on the *level of organization* that is being observed; as importance increases, higher levels of organization become involved. The finding that consistency among cognitions increases as their perceived importance increases (cf. Festinger, 1957, p. 16; Greenwald, 1980) also supports the view that ego-involvement can be interpreted as the *involvement of an organized system* that is not engaged under conditions of less importance (see also Allport, 1943, p. 460).

A final set of arguments for regarding self as an organization of knowledge can be based on consideration of what experience and memory should be expected to be like if there were no organization of knowledge that encompassed much of the content of memory. (The absence of a functional, large-scale organization of knowledge may be simulated by the experience of sudden wakening from a deep sleep, at which time it may be several seconds before a clear impression of personal identity or location is achieved. A more extended loss of contact with the dominant organization of personal knowledge may be associated with a concussion injury, such as the case described by Koffka (1935, pp. 323–324), as well as with various pathological conditions, such as amnesia, fugue, or depersonalization. See Claparède's description of a Korsakow-syndrome patient in Rapaport, 1951.)

One of the most remarkable aspects of normal human memory, even though it is very much a taken-for-granted characteristic, is the temporal reach of memory. We remember not only the immediate past, but also experiences from various times going back to within a few years of the beginning of our lives. At the same time, it is apparent that a great deal of what is experienced is forgotten. (Indeed, we may vastly underestimate the amount that is forgotten due to the facility with which we can construct recollections, as shown by Bartlett.) It may be suggested that successfully retained long-term memories are ones that participate in the continuing self organization. A related explanation has been offered by Schachtel (1959) in his account of the loss of memories of early childhood, although his is by no means a generally accepted explanation. Schachtel has suggested that the adult cognitive organization lacks the categories that were used by the young child to organize experience and, therefore, the adult is effectively separated from those early memories.

An extension of the preceding analysis of very-long-term memory can provide a partial explanation of the cognitive conservatism bias. Consider that long-term survival of memories requires the use of stable cognitive categories. Memories associated with unstable categories will necessarily be lost. Therefore, the surviving collection of memories necessarily is associated with long-term stable categories, possibly ones that have achieved a certain degree of artificial stability, by means of the cognitive conservatism bias.

Summary of Part I

The assertion that self is an organization of knowledge has been supported first by noticing that the cognitive system has pervasive biases that can be given sensible interpretations if it is assumed that they function to preserve the integrity of the dominant organization of knowledge; that is, the organization might not have been able to establish itself as dominant unless it possessed such characteristics. Second, experimental phenomena of ego-involvement were interpreted as indicating the engagement of an organized system that may be disengaged when experimental tasks are of only minor personal importance. Lastly, it was suggested that long-term memory may depend on the integrity of a large-scale knowledge organization, rather than being an inevitable consequence of associative experience.[2]

II. CASE STUDY OF A SCIENTIFIC THEORY AS A KNOWLEDGE ORGANIZATION

In George Kelly's *The Psychology of Personal Constructs* (Kelly, 1955), the thesis of the human personality functioning as a scientist constructing a theory of

---

[2]The present view of self as an organization, or system, has many precedents in psychological and psychoanalytic theory (e.g., Allport, 1960; Freud, 1923/1961; Koffka, 1935). The chief innovation in the present analysis of organization is the role attributed to cognitive biases in maintaining the self's organization.

the world was developed systematically. Seymour Epstein (1973) extended this type of analysis in presenting the view that what we call ''self'' should be conceived as the theory one possesses about oneself. Jane Loevinger (1976) presented a developmental analysis in which the progression of ego through stages of development was likened to the establishment and overthrow of successive theoretical paradigms—that is, the abandonment of old theories in favor of new ones. In these works, the case for regarding self as an organization of knowledge that resembles the organization of knowledge embodied in a scientific theory has already been well made. In a recent article, Greenwald and Ronis (1978) have attempted to characterize the evolution of cognitive dissonance theory as a body of knowledge. In the following pages, the analogy between self and theory that is found in the works of Kelly, Epstein, and Loevinger is merged with Greenwald and Ronis's account of cognitive dissonance theory. This analysis leads to the conclusion that a scientific theory may protect its status as an organization knowledge by using some of the same devices that are used by self as a knowledge organization (see also Greenwald, 1980). Cognitive dissonance theory provides a particularly informative example because the theory itself concerns these organization-protective devices.

A Brief History of Cognitive Dissonance Theory

Festinger's (1957) original statement of cognitive dissonance theory defined dissonance as an aversive motivational state evoked when two simultaneously experienced ideas deviated from a relationship of logic-like consistency. (Festinger, 1957, wrote: ''Two elements are in a dissonant relation if, considering these two alone, the obverse of one element would follow from the other [p. 13].'') After intermediate theoretical stages in which moderator variables of choice, commitment, expectancy, and self-relevance were accorded important theoretical roles, the most recent detailed statement of dissonance theory (Wicklund & Brehm, 1976) presents a definition of dissonance in which the dissonant relation between two ideas depends on the cognizer's perception of personal responsibility for aversive consequences stemming from some aspect of the two ideas' juxtaposition (cf. Greenwald & Ronis, 1978, p. 54). Greenwald and Ronis noted that this alteration has modified dissonance theory so that some of the important original (Festinger, 1957) illustrations of dissonance are not encompassed by the present definition. Another aspect of dissonance theory's gradual evolution has been the deemphasis of one of its original major hypotheses—that people should expose themselves selectively to information that can be expected to be consistent with their preexisting beliefs.

The changes just described comprise only a very simplified characterization of the evolution of dissonance theory over a 20-year period. A detailed study would show that the theory has branched, at different times during this period, in several different conceptual directions, in the hands of different theorists and researchers. Thus, the personal-responsibility-for-aversive-consequences definition is the most successful survivor among the variations within dissonance theory that have arisen in recent years. The literature of the past few years shows dissonance theory making tentative evolutionary variations in still new directions (e.g., Fazio, Zanna, & Cooper, 1977; Cooper, Fazio, & Rhodewalt, 1978).

Functions of the Evolutionary Process within Dissonance Theory

In their discussion of the changes in dissonance theory, Greenwald and Ronis observed that the theory had changed to a point at which it might be regarded as a different theory. The present context promotes consideration of the opposing view—that there is value in *preserving* dissonance theory despite its changes in response to the evolutionary pressures of continually accumulating research evidence. That view can be justified when it is recognized that the theory plays the role of *organizing,* and thereby enabling access to, a large body of research knowledge. Thus, the concepts of cognitive dissonance theory remain useful in enabling access to the data of a long series of experiments on counterattitudinal role playing, on selective exposure to opinion-relevant information (even though several of those experiments have been inconsistent with the theory; cf. Freedman & Sears, 1965), and on postdecisional "spreading" of decision alternatives. Without the theory's mnemonic help, much of this research literature might be effectively lost to researchers. However, even with the theory, there can be substantial loss in access to the research literature; specifically, findings that deal with problems of concern to the theory, but that have no particular relevance to the theory, can easily drop out of the collective memory of the field. For example, the theory presently offers no particular interpretation of experiments done in the mid-1960s that showed "incentive" effects in the counterattitudinal role playing situation. These findings (e.g., Elms & Janis, 1965; Janis & Gilmore, 1965; Rosenberg, 1965) tend not to be mentioned in introductions to recent empirical studies that deal with counterattitudinal role playing and, therefore, their accessibility for recently trained researchers is declining.

Parallels Between Evolving Theory and Self as Cognitive Organizations

Although the details are not presented here fully, a case can be made for the conclusion that in the course of its evolution, cognitive dissonance theory (which is intended to designate a body of knowledge that includes both published literature and the activities of researchers who contribute to and use that literature):

1. has been egocentric in the sense of claiming to accommodate a greater domain of psychological phenomena than is accorded to it by competing paradigms (such as self-perception theory). (Dissonance theory, at present, seems no longer to be egocentric in this sense.)

2. has been beneffectant in the sense of accepting responsibility for desired outcomes (i.e., confirmed hypotheses) while denying responsibility for undesired outcomes (disconfirmed hypotheses); and

3. has been cognitively conservative, preserving the existence of its central concept, dissonance, by revising its operational definition as needed to accommodate the accumulating findings of theory-inspired research. (This revision has been away from operations corresponding to logic-like inconsistency between ideas, and toward ones based on perceived responsibility for aversive consequences.)

The conclusion of this argument, put briefly, is that dissonance theory's success as an organization of scientific knowledge may be due to characteristics that resemble ones that make self viable as an organization of personal knowledge.

Cognitive Dissonance Theory as a Theory About Self

Greenwald and Ronis (1978) suggested that, in its present form, cognitive dissonance theory can be interpreted as a theory about ego defense, perhaps more so than as a theory about maintenance of logic-like consistency among ideas. It can be suggested, further, that the essence of present dissonance theory is a psychological principle very much like that described here as beneffectance. In experiments that are now accepted as most representative of dissonance processes, subjects revise evaluations of choice alternatives postdecisionally and change attitudes after counterattitudinal role playing. These cognitive changes can be interpreted, respectively, as increasing perceived credit for a desirable outcome (by increasing the chosen outcome's perceived desirability) and reducing perceived responsibility for an undesired outcome (by opinion change that reduces the perceived undesirability of the position espoused in counterattitudinal role playing).

At the same time that dissonance theory has evolved toward apparent agreement with a beneffectance principle, it has not emphasized a cognitive conservatism principle of the sort that seems useful for understanding the Bem and McConnell (1970) finding. In discussing the counterattitudinal role-playing procedure of the sort that Bem and McConnell used, dissonance theorists offer an account of the attitude change result, but have not developed any treatment of the most striking aspect of the Bem and McConnell findings—that is, their subjects' lack of perceived change in attitude. This bypassing of the phenomenon of cognitive conservatism is at least mildly ironic, for two reasons. First, the notion of cognitive conservatism (in the form of consistency of belief over time) would seem to be easily integrated with the original statement of dissonance theory. Second, cognitive conservatism is characteristic of the behavior of dissonance theorists in the course of the theory's evolution, as noted previously (but no more so than it is characteristic of advocates of other successful theories, of course).

To repeat a conclusion stated earlier, cognitive dissonance theory's success as a paradigm in contemporary psychology may be a manifestation of the same processes that make the normal self successful as an organization of personal knowledge. This analysis therefore supports the definition of self as an organization of knowledge—that is, it seems reasonable to regard self as an organization of knowledge in the same sense that it seems reasonable to regard cognitive dissonance theory as an organization of knowledge.

III. ENVIRONMENTAL STRUCTURE AND MEMORY STRUCTURE

We commonly think of memory, insofar as that word denotes an area of research within psychology, as the study of information storage within the central nervous system. However, if memory is defined more generally as the deposition of records that may subsequently be deciphered, then we can recognize that people use a great variety of external media in mnemonic fashion—that is, as legible records. Recognition of the ubiquity of these outside-the-head memories may both improve understanding of the characteristic environmental impact of human behavior, and help to generate principles that are useful in environmental design.

The Sock-Drawer Problem

When one tries to think of environmental objects that serve memory functions, one may first think of things that use writing to serve a reference function, such as dictionaries, textbooks, or telephone books. These external reference memories are revised or written into relatively infrequently compared to some other records, such as diaries, course notebooks, or date books. External memories need not use words, as exemplified by phonograph recording of music or photographic records of visual images.

Memory structures, such as the ones just noted, vary in their modes of access (they may be accessible in fixed sequential order, or accessible without any sequential restrictions, or content-addressable, etc.) and in their modifiability (that is, they may be permanent or "read only," at one extreme, or may be completely modifiable, at the other). As students of artificial intelligence have been aware for many years, memories are potentially powerful devices when they are user modifiable, or programmable.

The point to be made here is that many unlikely seeming environmental objects have the powerful properties of user-modifiable memories. Take a particularly homely example—a dresser drawer that contains socks. The drawer has minimal properties of a memory, in the sense that the contents provide a legible record of what was put in. Further, this memory is user modifiable in easily discernible ways, by variations in the selection of socks that are put in and their arrangements within the drawer. The sock drawer has one property that is not shared by all memories; specifically, items are regularly removed for use and are usually returned, possibly to a new place. A series of snapshots of the sock drawer's contents will reveal temporal patterns that are critically dependent on what can be called restorage responses—the method of returning socks to the drawer. Consider the different time series that are produced by the following three strategies of removal and restorage responses:

1. Socks are removed from any location and are always returned to their original location—in other words "a place for everything and everything in its place." The time series for this removal–restorage combination is static, except, of course, for absences of currently in-use socks.

2. Socks are removed from the front of the drawer and are returned to the back. The time series reveals a continuous rotational pattern, which incidentally guarantees equal use of all socks.

Of course, people do not use such tidy strategies. They use ones that are both less precise and more interesting analytically, such as:

3. Socks can be removed from any location but are returned to the front of the drawer. The time series of this third strategy is not immediately obvious, and bears further analysis.

An important difference of the third strategy from the first two is that the first two strategies, when applied in a rigid fashion, produce a time series that is entirely predictable from the initial configuration of socks in the drawer. The third strategy, however, will arrive at a structure that depends on the user's removal responses, rather than on the initial configuration. After a period of use, the average closeness to the front of the drawer for any pair of socks will be a direct function of its frequency of use. This could be a very convenient state of affairs if, as is likely, it is easier to remove socks from the front than the back—that is, the most often used socks will be easiest to get at.

The difference of the third strategy from the first two may be summarized by observing that the third strategy has the characteristics of a user-modifiable memory, and has the potential of evolving to a stable *user-compatible structure*. This is a case of an outside-the-head structure—that is, the sock drawer—evolving toward compatibility with an inside-the-head structure—the user's preference ordering of socks. In a proper sense, this is an instance of an outside-the-head structure *being* a cognitive structure.

Some Other Examples of Memory Structures

Many external structures may preserve legible records of the past. The discovery of such records is an enterprise that affords much opportunity for ingenuity, as documented by Webb, Campbell, Schwartz, and Sechrest (1966) in their book on *Unobtrusive Measures*. The deciphering of such records as the differential erosion of flooring in a museum or the distribution of fingerprints on pages in magazines requires an understanding of the process by which these traces are written into their media.

Especially interesting are memories that have the potential for evolving toward user-compatible structures, which can be defined as an arrangement of complementarity or matching between the external structure and the user's knowledge (cf. Shepard, 1981). Such memories are likely to be in active use rather than being fossilized remains of extinct species. A useful way to proceed toward development of the understanding of outside-the-head memory structures may be to consider several more examples. What follows is a sampler of incompletely analyzed examples of outside-the-head memories.

More Structured Containers.   The sock drawer is one of a group of container memories, which share the characteristic of having objects put into them for storage, and then having them removed temporarily for use (or perhaps permanently for consumption or discarding). Examples are wallets, purses, and desk tops, in addition to all sorts of drawers, cupboards, and closets. Especially interesting for analysis are containers that are used socially, such as the family refrigerator. Here, there is a problem due to different users having different restorage strategies, which can interfere with evolution to a user-compatible structure. Arrival at a user-compatible structure is also problematic for containers such as uncompartmented purses, which allow the contents to rearrange themselves during storage.

Paths and Highways.   A path is an environmental structure that records the route from one place to another. Because paths are user modifiable, they have a ready potential to adapt to user-compatible form. For example, repeated use of a newly cut path through wilderness will enlarge the path by destroying adjacent vegetation. Disuse of the path will lead to its overgrowth and disappearance. Recently, I encountered an interesting televised example of a user-modified path—during qualification trials at the Indianapolis Motor Speedway. After several race cars had made high-speed trial runs, there was a visible path of rubber left behind by their tires, marking the most frequently used path, which—given the skill of the drivers—was also an optimal path.

Most paved highways deteriorate, rather than improve, with use. When a political system responds to worn highways by budgeting funds for their enlargement, then there is an opportunity for a positive relationship between frequency of use and ease of use. In a system that has evolved to the point of having roads that vary substantially in capacity, the information that is recorded in the structure of the road system is not only the route between places, but also the frequency of travel to and from the places so connected.

Social Groups and Committees.   A common social response to a problem is to form a committee. The committee is, literally, a monument to the problem—a structure created so as not to forget the problem. If the committee's problem can be divided into subproblems, there may be subcommittees or, at least, distinct roles within the committee. The committee as a social organization, therefore, comes to have a structure that can match the structure of the problem. The committee functions as a mnemonic in the sense that its existence is a continuous or recurring reminder to its members of their obligation to deal with the task for which it was set up; without this social structure to provide reminders, the individuals might easily forget their common task. The information recorded in the structure of social groups is thus potentially informative about task motivations of group members.

Buildings.   Perhaps in the same sense that social organizations such as committees or professional societies are monuments to persisting tasks, buildings are monuments to social organizations. The permanence of a building may support the continued existence both of the social organization that uses it and of memory for the group's task by group members. Historical monuments, such as the ruins of ancient cities, serve to connect the memories of those presently alive with the past of their social groups. (The injunction for Texans to "Remember the Alamo" acknowledges the mnemonic function of that particular building.) The relationships among individual memories, social groups, and buildings are almost certainly important enough to be given fundamental consideration in architectural design. In planning to build a high-rise building, for example, it should be considered that each group housed in the building might benefit from being associated with a distinct substructure. This form of physical recognition of the group's identity may facilitate the group's continued existence.

Computers.   The preceding comments have minimized attention to the impact of external, or outside-the-head, structures on the organization of internal, or inside-the-head, knowledge. This relative neglect is perhaps justified only because the external-to-internal direction of causation is the only direction considered in most existing work on the organization of memory. It is particularly consistent with the spirit of the present analysis, however, to consider the impact of *human-created* external structures on the structure of internal memory. Already noted has been the potential effect of social and physical structures to provide an external mnemonic that supports long-term persistence of memories. In turning to consideration of that most complex of human artifacts, the computer, the analysis now addresses the question of more profound effects of external structure on internal structure.

At present, computer and information scientists are busily designing "user-oriented" programing and information retrieval systems. There are tremendous selection pressures operating in the design of these systems, in that user inconveniences can often be detected readily, and it is often easy to generate system modifications that improve convenience. Inconvenient systems have little survival potential and, thus, long-surviving systems may represent optimal fits between computer software structure and internal knowledge structure. In this sense, the viability of FORTRAN as a programing language for computation may be taken as a clue that inside-the-head computational machinery may correspond closely to the computational devices of FORTRAN programs.

Computers and the Future of Human Knowledge Organization

Having just contemplated a convenient future of computerized comfort, let us consider also that there will come a time, perhaps within a few decades, when computers are better able than humans to evaluate the success of new computer programs. A consequence of that very significant programing achievement is that computers, rather than humans, will take over the job of writing programs. At that time, the balance of selection pressures in regard to knowledge organization between human and computer memories should reverse. That is, instead of program structures being selected for compatibility with existing human memory structures, the reverse will be true. Knowledge structures within the human memory will be selected for compatibility with the design principles of superhuman computer memories. It will be convenient for people to have such computer-compatible knowledge structures in the same sense that it is presently convenient for computers to have people-compatible knowledge structures.

Prediction of the consequences for human or computer knowledge structures of the reversal of human-versus-computer selection pressures is at best a speculative enterprise. The following speculations are limited to consideration of the organizational aspects of knowledge:

1. It is already happening that computers are becoming organized into networks of processors. As computers become interdependent in this fashion—and therefore as their usefulness to people depends on maintaining the integrity of *their* organization—it can be expected that programmers will devise increasingly sophisticated methods of protecting the integrity of the network organization.

2. As computers take over the function of designing and maintaining their own network protection devices, they will come to seem much more ''alive'' and ''human.'' It may be that their network protection devices will have characteristics resembling the constellation that has been identified here as the totalitarian ego, which is hypothesized to serve an organization-maintaining function for the self.

3. The subservience of humans to computers should be a quiet revolution in that it will be accompanied by increased material comforts. Therefore, we may not recognize that the revolution, in the form of a reversal of selection pressures, has occurred.

4. One might ask how far along this quiet revolution is right now. In increasing numbers, we welcome computer terminals and memories into our homes, in the form of sophisticated telephone instruments, interactive cable television, and home computers. The revolution may be practically complete when we connect our home computer terminals to the telephone network, assuming that there is coincident development of the ability for computers to write their own programs.

5. How will selection pressures operate on human knowledge organizations once computer knowledge organizations become dominant? It seems possible that human knowledge organizations in the near future may be as different from those characteristic of the present as present knowledge organizations are different from those of 3000 years ago, about which Jaynes (1977) wrote in his book on the bicameral mind. One possibility is that computers may deliberately program human memories, thereby "domesticating" the human species. This programing might be done partly by techniques descended from what is now called programed learning, but it might also involve genetic engineering, which should be within the eventual grasp of a computerized technology. Such deliberate engineering of humans, in addition to various, more accidental evolutionary changes, might well result in human knowledge structures that lack the organization-protecting devices of the totalitarian ego—namely, egocentrism, beneffectance, and conservatism. Future human knowledge structures might thus lack some of the features that we now consider most characteristically human.

This chapter started by trying to integrate a variety of research results as evidence for self as a dominant organization of human knowledge. From being thus firmly rooted in data, it proceeded to a speculative analysis of cognitive dissonance theory as an evolving organization of knowledge. Finally, it concluded by considering a variety of outside-the-head structures that are of interest because they, too, have characteristics of evolving knowledge structures. It is not entirely clear at what point I entered the realm of science fiction, but I have provided all the evidence necessary to conclude that science fiction has been a major source of inspiration, from Orwell's analysis of thought control in *1984* as a model for the organization of self, to Huxley's genetic and psychological programing in *Brave New World,* to Clarke's vision of the computer as a self-protective knowledge structure in *2001.* One of the major charms of science fiction is that some of it turns out, after all, not to be fiction.

ACKNOWLEDGMENTS

Preparation of this chapter was facilitated by grants from the National Institute of Mental Health (MH–31762, MH–32317, and MH–07669). The author is grateful to John T. Cacioppo, Susan T. Fiske, John H. Harvey, and M. Brewster Smith for their comments on an earlier draft.

REFERENCES

Allport, G. W. The ego in contemporary psychology. *Psychological Review,* 1943, *50,* 451–478.

Allport, G. W. *Personality and social encounter.* Boston: Beacon, 1960.

Bartlett, F. C. *Remembering: A study in experimental and social psychology.* Cambridge, England: Cambridge University Press, 1932.

Bem, D. J., & McConnell, H. K. Testing the self-perception explanation of dissonance phenomena: On the salience of premanipulation attitudes. *Journal of Personality and Social Psychology,* 1970, *14,* 23–31.

Bradley, G. W. Self-serving biases in the attribution process: A reexamination of the fact or fiction question. *Journal of Personality and Social Psychology,* 1978, *36,* 56–71.

Brenner, M. The next-in-line effect. *Journal of Verbal Learning and Verbal Behavior,* 1973, *12,* 320–323.

Brenner, M. W. *Memory and interpersonal relations.* Unpublished doctoral dissertation, University of Michigan, 1976.

Cialdini, R. B., Borden, R. J., Thorne, A., Walker, M. R., Freeman, S., & Sloan, L. R. Basking in reflected glory: Three (football) field studies. *Journal of Personality and Social Psychology,* 1976, *34,* 366–375.

Clarke, A. C. *2001: A space odyssey.* New York: New American Library, 1968.

Cooper, J., Fazio, R. H., & Rhodewalt, F. Dissonance and humor: Evidence for the undifferentiated nature of dissonance arousal. *Journal of Personality and Social Psychology,* 1978, *36,* 280–285.

de Rivera, J. *Field theory as human-science.* New York: Gardner, 1976.

Elms, A. C., & Janis, I. L. Counternorm attitudes induced by consonant versus dissonant conditions of role playing. *Journal of Experimental Research in Personality,* 1965, *1,* 50–60.

Epstein, S. The self-concept revisited: Or a theory of a theory. *American Psychologist,* 1973, *28,* 404–416.

Fazio, R. H., Zanna, M. P., & Cooper, J. Dissonance and self perception: An integrative view of each theory's proper domain of application. *Journal of Experimental Social Psychology,* 1977, *13,* 464–479.

Festinger, L. *A theory of cognitive dissonance.* Stanford, Calif.: Stanford University Press, 1957.

Fischhoff, B. Perceived informativeness of facts. *Journal of Experimental Psychology: Human Perception and Performance,* 1977, *3,* 349–358.

Freedman, J. L., & Sears, D. O. Selective exposure. In L. Berkowitz (Ed.), *Advances in experimental social psychology* (Vol. 2). New York: Academic Press, 1965.

Freud, S. *The ego and the id.* In *Standard Edition* (Vol. 19). London: Hogarth, 1961. (Originally published, 1923.)

Glixman, A. F. Recall of completed and uncompleted activities under varying degress of stress. *Journal of Experimental Psychology,* 1949, *39,* 281–296.

Greenwald, A. G. Cognitive learning, cognitive response to persuasion and attitude change. In A. G. Greenwald, T. C. Brock, & T. M. Ostrom (Eds.), *Psychological foundations of attitudes.* New York: Academic Press, 1968.

Greenwald, A. G. Consequences of prejudice against the null hypothesis. *Psychological Bulletin,* 1975, *82,* 1–20.

Greenwald, A. G. The totalitarian ego: Fabrication and revision of personal history. *American Psychologist,* 1980, *35,* 603–618.

Greenwald, A. G. Ego task analysis: An integration of research on ego-involvement and self-awareness. In A. Hastorf & A. Isen (Eds.), *Cognitive social psychology.* Amsterdam: Elsevier/North-Holland, in press.

Greenwald, A. G., & Ronis, D. L. Twenty years of cognitive dissonance: Case study of the evolution of a theory. *Psychological Review.* 1978, *85,* 53–57.

Harvey, J. H., Harris, B., & Barnes, R. D. Actor-observer differences in the perceptions of responsibility and freedom. *Journal of Personality and Social Psychology,* 1975, *32,* 22–28.

Huxley, A. *Brave new world*. New York: Harper, 1932.

Janis, I. L., & Gilmore J. B. The influence of incentive conditions on the success of role playing in modifying attitudes. *Journal of Personality and Social Psychology*, 1965, *1*, 17–27.

Jaynes, J. *The origin of consciousness in the breakdown of the bicameral mind*. Boston: Houghton Mifflin, 1977.

Jervis, R. *Perception and misperception in international politics*. Princeton, N.J.: Princeton University Press, 1976.

Jones, E. E., & Nisbett, R. E. The actor and the observer: Divergent perceptions of the causes of behavior. In E. E. Jones, D. E. Kanouse, H. H. Kelley, R. E. Nisbett, S. Valins, & B. Weiner et al., *Attribution: Perceiving the causes of behavior*. Morristown, N.J.: General Learning Press, 1971.

Kelly, G. A. *The psychology of personal constructs* (Vol. 1). New York: Norton, 1955.

Koffka, K. *Principles of gestalt psychology*. New York: Harcourt, 1935.

Langer, E. J. The illusion of control. *Journal of Personality and Social Psychology*, 1975, *32*, 311–329.

Loevinger, J. *Ego development*. San Francisco: Jossey-Bass, 1976.

Loftus, E. F., Miller, D. G., & Burns, H. J. Semantic integration of verbal information into a visual memory. *Journal of Experimental Psychology: Human Learning and Memory*, 1978, *4*, 19–31.

Milgram, S. Behavioral study of obedience. *Journal of Abnormal and Social Psychology*, 1963, *67*, 371–378.

Miller, D. T., & Ross, M. Self-serving biases in the attribution of causality: Fact or fiction? *Psychological Bulletin*, 1975, *82*, 213–225.

Mischel, W., Ebbesen, E. B., & Zeiss, A. M. Determinants of selective memory about the self. *Journal of Consulting and Clinical Psychology*, 1976, *44*, 92–103.

Orwell, G. *1984*. New York: Harcourt, Brace, Jovanovich, 1949.

Petty, R. E., Ostrom, T. M., & Brock, T. C. (Eds.). *Cognitive responses in persuasion*. Hillsdale, N.J.: Lawrence Erlbaum Associates, 1981.

Rapaport, D. *Organization and pathology of thought*. New York: Columbia University Press, 1951.

Rhine, R., & Severance, L. Ego-involvement, discrepancy, source credibility, and attitude change. *Journal of Personality and Social Psychology*, 1970, *16*, 175–190.

Rogers, T. B., Kuiper, N. A., & Kirker, W. S. Self-reference and the encoding of personal information. *Journal of Personality and Social Psychology*, 1977, *35*, 677–688.

Rosenberg, M. J. When dissonance fails: On eliminating evaluation apprehension from attitude measurement. *Journal of Personality and Social Psychology*, 1965, *1*, 23–42.

Rosensweig, S. An experimental study of "repression" with special reference to need-persistive and ego-defensive reactions to frustration. *Journal of Experimental Psychology*, 1943, *32*, 64–74.

Ross, M., & Sicoly, F. Egocentric biases in availability and attribution. *Journal of Personality and Social Psychology*, 1979, *37*, 322–336.

Schachtel, E. G. *Metamorphosis*. New York: Basic Books, 1959.

Shepard, R. N. Psychophysical complementarity. In M. Kubovy and J. R. Pomerantz (Eds.), *Perceptual organization*. Hillsdale, N.J.: Lawrence Erlbaum Associates, 1981.

Sherif, M., & Cantril, H. *The psychology of ego-involvements*. New York: Wiley, 1947.

Snyder, M., & Swann, W. B. Hypothesis-testing processes in social interaction. *Journal of Personality and Social Psychology*, 1978, *36*, 1202–1212.

Snyder, M., & Uranowitz, S. W. Reconstructing the past: Some cognitive consequences of person perception. *Journal of Personality and Social Psychology*, 1978, *36*, 941–950.

Trope, Y. Inferences of personal characteristics on the basis of information retrieved from one's memory. *Journal of Personality and Social Psychology*, 1978, *36*, 93–106.

Webb, E. J., Campbell, D. T., Schwartz, R. D., & Sechrest, L. *Unobtrusive measures: Nonreactive research in the social sciences*. Chicago: Rand-McNally, 1966.

White, R. W. Motivation reconsidered: The concept of competence. *Psychological Review*, 1959, *66*, 297–333.

Wicklund, R. A., & Brehm, J. W. *Perspectives on cognitive dissonance*. Hillsdale, N.J.: Lawrence Erlbaum Associates, 1976.

Wortman, C. B. Causal attributions and personal control. In J. H. Harvey, W. J. Ickes, & R. F. Kidd (Eds.), *New directions in attribution research* (Vol. 1). New York: Lawrence Erlbaum Associates, 1976.

VI FINAL COMMENTARIES

The following four commentaries represent a set of concluding remarks on the conference and issues germane to interdisciplinary work. Other scholars participated in the final discussions from which these commentaries derived. Their conclusions generally are included in the various chapters in this volume.

In the first commentary, John Bransford presents a searching discussion of issues that a cognitive psychologist might consider after considerable dialogue with environmental and social psychologists and anthropologists. In focusing on concepts such as experimentation and social contracts and rapport with subjects, Bransford is raising questions that rarely if ever have been probed by contemporary cognitive researchers. He also develops the concept of ecological analysis that should pique the interest of various types of scholars, certainly including environmental and social psychologists.

The brief presentations by Roy Freedle and Michael Agar emphasize the need for more of a cross-cultural perspective in the field and the value of an ethnographic approach, respectively. These commentaries reflect further the breadth of inquiry Freedle and Agar displayed in their individual chapters. Also, Agar provides some useful information about anthropology journals and writings that may articulate well with the goals of psychologists concerned with the integration of ideas drawn from various fields.

In the final commentary, Baruch Fischhoff presents an engaging discussion of issues pertaining to the question "if interdisciplinary work is so good, why is there so little of it?" These remarks are invaluable because they come from a seasoned professional whose work is at the forefront of both basic and practical integrative endeavors involving the social sciences.

26 Social Cultural Prerequisites for Cognitive Research

John D. Bransford
Vanderbilt University

Interdisciplinary conferences are reminiscent of the famous bar scene in Star Wars, in which creatures of all shapes, sizes, and languages intermingle. There is a strong tendency to "seek one's own kind" and to settle into familiar conversation. Even so, the experience has some impact; one is prompted to ask how "one's kind" fits into the larger scheme of things.

There are important differences between wanting to see the bigger picture and knowing what to do to gain admittance. As a cognitive psychologist, how do I develop the ability to see the world through the eyes of a social psychologist, anthropologist, environmental psychologist, and so forth? Why do they see certain issues as being more important than others? Why do they do the strange research that they do? How does "my kind" look from their perspective? The problem here is fascinating: What can one do in order to understand things he or she does not currently understand, or to understand things in new ways?

I am not going to tackle the problem of "learning to think like an anthropologist or social or environmental psychologist." The only solution to this problem may be to work in each of these areas for a number of years. My goal is more limited: to focus on some of the questions that cognitive psychologists might ask themselves in order to gain a clearer picture of how others might view their research activities. Because many environmental and social psychologists at this conference have stated that they borrow heavily from cognitive psychology, this exercise might be relevant to them, too.

The exercise begins with a caricature of cognitive researchers whose primary mode of understanding people is to design, conduct, and analyze laboratory experiments involving human, college-age subjects. What kinds of issues do researchers worry about and what sets of questions are left unasked? Our imagi-

nary researchers ask themselves all kinds of questions about their work—
questions about how to analyze and interpret their experimental data, for example. What they fail to analyze are the processes necessary in order for the
experiment to be conducted in the first place. The experiments depend on the
cooperation of human subjects, so the researchers must design them a suitable
environment, convince them to accept the role of subject, make sure they are able
to understand what they are supposed to do, and so forth. These activities are
necessary in order to conduct the research in the first place, but they are so
mundane that they are effectively ignored. Our cognitive researchers do not have
to worry about these types of issues because they, and their subjects, are embedded in a shared, social–cultural matrix that supports mutual cooperation and
interaction. Our cognitive researchers also do not *want* to be bothered with these
issues; they want to get on with the business of experimentation. Caricatures are
easily manipulated, however, so ours have agreed to ask themselves about
social–cultural constraints that are necessary in order to perform their experimentation. This topic is discussed next.

EXPERIMENTATION AND SOCIAL CONTRACTS

The purpose of this section is to analyze aspects of the *social contract* (I am
borrowing this concept from John Locke, 1632–1704) that must be developed in
order for experimentation to proceed smoothly. The essential ingredient of this
contract is that people agree to be subjects who allow the experimenter to
"rule." Four aspects of social contracts are considered: (1) environmental design; (2) the development of rapport; (3) procedures for ensuring comprehension;
and (4) the resources that participants are permitted to utilize. Each of these areas
is discussed from two points of view. First, it is argued that laboratory researchers must deal with each of these factors; however, the problems these
researchers face with respect to environmental design, rapport, and so forth, are
quite minor and not particularly challenging. The second part of each discussion
therefore looks at each aspect of the social contract and discusses issues that arise
when this part of the contract is changed or broken. It is at these junctures that
other disciplines and areas of specialization operate. One goal of this discussion
is to illustrate how one group of specialists (e.g., cognitive psychologists) may
fail to appreciate the issues raised by a second group (e.g., environmental psychologists, classroom teachers) because members of the first group never have to
face particular issues as they go about their business of understanding people. By
becoming aware of the social–cultural constraints under which they operate, it
may be possible for researchers to develop a more accurate picture of their role in
the scheme of things. A second goal of this discussion is to relate the concept of
social contract to the concept of ecological validity. By understanding how
constraints in one's experimental environment affect the behavior of subjects,
one stands a better chance of evaluating the significance of experimental results.

LABORATORY RESEARCH AND ENVIRONMENTAL DESIGN

Imagine a simple ''cognitive'' experiment in which subjects are read lists of words or sentences and are then asked to recall them. To conduct such a study, an experimenter must create a physical and social setting within which the experiment can take place. Consider first the physical environment for the study; few cognitive theorists analyze this explicitly, but it seems clear that they make many intuitively based assumptions about appropriate physical settings. The laboratory must look ''sufficiently scientific,'' the experimenter will probably be dressed ''properly'' and will be positioned in the room in a manner that reinforces his or her status. Even chairs and tables play an important role. They may be arranged differently depending on whether subjects are to work as individuals or as small cooperative groups, or on whether the experimenter wants to encourage or discourage social comparison, and so forth. Whether explicitly acknowledged or not, cognitive psychologists must make decisions about environmental design.

I do not mean to imply that cognitive theorists frequently obtain questionable experimental results because they use their intuitions to design laboratory environments; and, I am definitely not advocating research that manipulates the arrangement of chairs and tables and assesses the effects on cognitive processes such as memorizing. The purpose of the discussion is to compare the design problems of the laboratory researcher with those faced by environmental psychologists. Note that the researcher's laboratory design is appropriate *only* given certain social contracts. Experimental subjects agree only to visit for a while, not to live there for long periods of time. The task of designing cities, campuses, and so forth, is very different from designing a special-purpose lab. These differences in design problems would be uninteresting if they simply involved differences in knowledge about various styles of buildings, landscapes, furniture, and so forth. The major difference is that environmental psychologists are forced to ask many kinds of questions about people that cognitive psychologists might not ask.

As an illustration, imagine designing offices for a research institute. This task requires one to ask questions about ways that people act as individuals as well as groups. One of the first things that becomes apparent is that laboratories for running experiments are only part of the requirements for an institute. Researchers spend a lot of time in the laboratory, but by no means do they spend all their time there. Laboratories provide environmental support for a specialized subset of activities, but researchers are people who engage in a wider variety of activities, some of which are incompatible with one another. For example, researchers often need to consult with their colleagues who are experts in certain areas; the environment must therefore support ease of access so that these interactions can take place. On the other hand, the researchers often need privacy so that they can think, write, and so forth. It is relatively easy to design an environment that supports *either* interaction *or* privacy; it is much more difficult to design one that allows both.

The Haskins laboratory in New Haven provides an excellent example of a research institute designed with an eye toward the dynamics of human interaction. The design (at least this was the design when I visited a few years ago) involved a room full of offices (labs were elsewhere) surrounded by walls approximately chest height. If a researcher wanted to talk with a colleague in another office, he or she could stand up and make eye contact with the person; social interaction was therefore facilitated. If the colleague was absorbed in a personal project (reading, writing), this was also apparent; personal privacy was therefore preserved (note that this office design assumes the cooperation of the inhabitants). I know nothing about environmental design, so I have no basis for evaluating this particular environmental solution. The reason for discussing it is to emphasize how the problem of design forces one to acknowledge the dynamics and complexities of human adaptation. Individuals engage in many types of specialized activities that are frequently incompatible with one another. Adaptation requires the coordination of these specialities; the environment can either support these efforts at coordination or block them. The researcher who implicitly focuses only on "adaptation in the laboratory" can obtain a narrow view of "being in the world."

LABORATORY RESEARCH AND RAPPORT

The cognitive researcher not only designs environments, but must also create an acceptable social climate; an experimenter who fails to develop rapport with subjects can expect suspicious-looking results. Once again, most cognitive theorists rely on their intuitions in order to develop rapport and these usually work quite well. However, how much of a challenge is it to develop rapport with people who have already agreed to accept the role of "subject in a psychological experiment"? One way to examine this question is to imagine some moderately bizarre behaviors that would probably be accepted in a laboratory context but that would be reacted to differently somewhere else.

Imagine an experimenter who reads his or her instructions in a dull monotone. This will seem strange to subjects, but most will probably accept it as "the way some experiments are done." Imagine the same experimenter soliciting volunteers for a forthcoming experiment by speaking in a monotone to a class of potential subjects; the volunteer rate will probably be low. If the experimenter approaches people on the street in this manner, the rate of acceptance will be lower still (the experimenter may also be detained for psychiatric examination). The point is that researchers who work almost exclusively with college students do not have to confront serious problems of rapport; most of the problem has evaporated once subjects enter the laboratory because they have already agreed to participate. Besides, most experiments occupy only a few minutes or hours of a person's life. Imagine talking with an educator who is trying to teach a required course to a group of high-school students who are waiting for their next birthday so that they can drop out of school. Now the problem of developing a climate of mutual cooperation becomes very real.

LABORATORY EXPERIMENTS AND COMPREHENSION

Once the experimenter solves the (usually easy) problem of developing rapport, he or she must still ensure that the subjects understand what they are supposed to do in the experiment. A theorist who works almost exclusively with American college sophomores can use his or her intuitions to create comprehensible instructions; it is a relatively safe bet that the sophomores possess background knowledge that is at least *reasonably* congruent with the experimenter's. Try working with young children and see what it does to one's intuitions about "comprehensible instructions." When one begins working with people from different cultures (e.g., see Agar, Chapter 2 in this volume; Cole, 1977; Cole & Scribner, 1974; Scribner, 1977), it becomes even more imperative to question one's intuitions about probable interpretations of instructions; tasks that seem straightforward to the experimenter can seem extremely bizarre relative to the cultural background of many groups (e.g., "We don't make inferences about people we don't know"). Many anthropologists argue that it can be highly valuable to see someone reacting to an "intuitively obvious" statement or idea in an unexpected manner; one is forced to question a number of previously unarticulated assumptions. The researcher who works exclusively with "similar-minded" college students is denied opportunities such as these.

The content of the stimulus materials selected by the researcher can also affect the need to question tacit assumptions. There is nothing particularly controversial about asking people to comprehend and remember "The boy hit the ball." However, try discussing some of John Holt's (1964) indictments against the educational system with college students versus veteran teachers. The former will generally say, "Yes, these things happen," whereas the teachers will often get angry (some get defensive) and say, "That's unfair, he doesn't understand the problems teachers face today." It is noteworthy that cognitive theorists who have studied people's comprehension of stories (rather than word lists, for example) have placed more and more emphasis on the importance of viewing performance as being a function of the *relationship* between the stimulus materials and the cognitive schemata (e.g., discourse frames, story grammars) available to different people (see Freedle, Chapter 3 in this volume; Grueneich & Trabasso, Chapter 13 in this volume). What about the emotional and motivational "schemata" that affect people's reactions to events? Few cognitive researchers have to face these kinds of issues because we "control them" from our experiments (partly for ethical reasons, of course). Professional arbitrators and clinicians could undoubtedly teach us a great deal about processes that split opposing groups (or two individuals) further apart versus prompt them to compromise in effective ways.

One of the reasons researchers usually do not have to deal with powerful emotional and evaluative issues is that peoples' reactions to experimental materials are affected by the social contract formed during the experiment. To illustrate, assume that subjects in our prototypical cognitive experiment decide to cooperate and that they understand their task, which is to comprehend words and sentences and to recall them later. The to-be-remembered stimuli might include "Paper," "Lee has a red car," "The cat ran across the floor," and so on. All English-speaking subjects will rate these stimuli as "comprehensible," but the meaning of "comprehensible" is affected by the experimental task. In particular, the experimenter is asking subjects to accept a social contract that assumes that the statements to be heard might be uttered by *someone,* at *some* time and place, for *some* purpose; the stimuli are therefore perceived as examples of possible English utterances. Try walking up to a friend (or a stranger, if you dare) and simply utter "Paper" or "Lee has a red car." The person will be startled; he or she will know what you said but will not understand what you mean (see Bransford, 1979; Bransford & Nitsch, 1978). Similarly, try teaching language to infants by restricting their exposure to situations in which you sit down with them and say, "O.K. kids, here are some English words and sentences: 'Paper'; 'Lee has a red car,'" and so one. It is highly doubtful that children could acquire language under conditions such as this (e.g., Bransford, 1979; Chapman, 1978; MacNamara, 1972; Nelson, 1974).

As a thought experiment, imagine someone's designing a typical memory experiment to test my earlier assertion that college students will tend to accept many of Holt's (1964) statements about problems of education, whereas veteran teachers will often get angry. If the experimenter simply states that the task is to listen to a list of Holt's assertions and then recall them, it is not clear that one would expect any differences in experimental results. The experimenter is asking people to treat each statement as an object to be remembered, he or she is not actually asserting the truth value of these statements. It is possible that evaluative and emotional reactions will play some role given this social contract, but the effects may well be attenuated. An alternative way to approach this issue is to act as if one believes in each of John Holt's arguments and present them to groups of students versus teachers in nonlaboratory settings (e.g., at a teachers' conference). If one does this, I predict that the major focus of attention will be on people's reactions rather than on their memory scores per se.

LABORATORY RESEARCH AND ENVIRONMENTAL RESOURCES

An important function of the social contract formed between experimenter and subject is to control the resources available to the subject. For example, subjects in a memory experiment are not allowed to write down each stimulus item as they hear it, nor to ask others in the experiment to tell them answers during a memory test (note that even "group" experiments therefore frequently require people to act as individuals). An experimenter also limits subjects' abilities to use him or her as a resource; for example, subjects cannot ask the researcher for answers during a memory test. There is nothing wrong with limiting the resources available to subjects; indeed, this is necessary for experimental precision. Problems arise when researchers restrict the range of potential resources without explicitly realizing that there are other options available. This can result in a limited view of ways in which people react and adapt.

To illustrate, consider once again a prototypical cognitive experiment on memory. How does the social contract limit subjects' abilities to adapt to the situation; for example, what kinds of questions are they allowed to ask? Most experimenters encourage subjects to ask questions immediately after the instructions are presented. However, subjects can ask only certain types of questions, *not* "What's the purpose of this study?" "What's your hypothesis?", and so forth. Once the experiment actually begins, questions are discouraged. Subjects are expected to listen to the stimulus materials, try their best to learn them, and then take some type of retention test. Perhaps this is one of the reasons we often call them "subjects" rather than "participants" or "people."

An ethologist might ask us to imagine holding conferences such as this one in an analogous manner. Participants (nobody called them "subjects") are instructed that they are to understand and remember the paper presented by each speaker. Immediately after each presentation, certain participants are asked to recall what they heard. (Discussants, for example, might be asked to recall the paper in front of the rest of the participants.) I suspect that most of us would hesitate to attend conferences under these types of conditions. The social contract would restrict our abilities to understand and learn (not to mention make us very anxious).

Participants at this conference have been very active learners. They ask speakers to repeat statements, to provide examples, to define ambiguous terms, and so forth. Of course, participants also frequently disagree with one another, but valid disagreement presupposes that one person understands the other's point of view. Discussants at this conference frequently used coffee breaks to question speakers whose papers they were to discuss, request written copies of presentations, take notes, and so forth. The point is that effective comprehenders (learners) are generally proficient at knowing when they need more information, study time, and so forth, and at deciding what to do in order to gain it. However, these activities are permissible only given certain social contracts; our prototypical "cognitive" experiment does not encourage activities such as these.

Michael Cole (1979) provides an illuminating illustration of adaptive behavior that could not be observed given certain types of environments and social contracts. He focuses on a cooking class in which children can work together in order to bake a cake. One of the boys cannot read and hence is unable to decipher the written recipe. He is nevertheless an excellent organizer and knows when to call on a person who can read during each step of preparing the cake. In contrast to the nonreader, the reader is easily distracted and keeps getting off task; the organizer prompts him to perform his speciality (reading) at the appropriate times. Cole's argument is not that the ability to read is unimportant. The point is that the two boys form an adaptive *system* that functions beautifully; the cake gets baked.

When sociologists, systems theorists, historians, and many others look at the world, it must seem obvious that an analysis of human adaptation must focus on systems rather than on isolated individuals. The president of General Motors functions well only because he can rely on specialists in assembly, engine design, marketing, and so forth; his skill is in knowing what he needs to know and then coordinating resources that are potentially available. The nonreader in Cole's cooking class exhibits a similar kind of skill. Indeed, the remarkable accomplishments of human culture seem to revolve around people's ability to specialize in ways that can still be coordinated (needless to say, humans do not always reach this goal of coordination). When individuals fail to mesh with the more general scheme of things, we often speak of "thinkers who were ahead of their times" and "scientific discoveries that were premature."

Successful adaptation requires the availability of various resources; yet experimentalists place restrictions on the resources that can be utilized. This is fine as long as the researcher is aware of these restrictions and realizes the possibility of other "possible worlds."

THE CONCEPT OF ECOLOGICAL VALIDITY

The preceding section sets the stage for discussing a concept that was very popular at this conference and hence appears to have gained "interdisciplinary acceptance": the concept of ecological validity. This is the kind of concept that seems highly desirable; no one has boasted that he or she is engaged in ecologically *in*valid theorizing and research. However, there are potential dangers when a concept is embraced with such enthusiasm; the affective loading can be so positive that we neglect to ask ourselves what we mean by the term. For example, it would be easy to interpret my previous remarks as support for the ecological *in*validity of "artificial laboratory experiments" and the ecological validity of research in "real-world settings." This is not the argument I wish to make.

Note first that the contrast between "laboratory settings" and "real-world settings" is puzzling because it implies that laboratories are not part of the "real world." As argued earlier, laboratory environments are human creations; so are schools, cities, novels, texts, and so forth. Some of these creations are undoubtedly better (for certain purposes) than others; some texts are written more effectively, some schools are designed more efficiently, some laboratory experiments are more informative, and so forth. The challenge for the theorist is to *analyze* these structures in order to gain a more precise understanding of why things happen as they do. I therefore prefer the term *ecological analysis* to ecological validity. The former term may help inhibit the tendency to apply a label ("ecologically valid") simply on the basis of the surface characteristics of the events under investigation. Ecological analysis refers to something that must be done before decisions about ecological validity are made.

There are some obvious problems with a view that equates ecological validity with "research in real-world settings." What does one say about physicists' experiments with objects in a vacuum? Are the studies of sensory deprivation in humans examples of ecologically invalid research? A particular laboratory situation may be very different from typical "real world" environments, but this fact alone by no means warrants the label "ecologically invalid." Indeed, experimentation derives its power from people's abilities to create relatively novel environments that are particularly informative. However, such environments need to be analyzed and theoretically motivated rather than relegated to the domain of "intuitively obvious lab lore" or "historical precedent in the literature." For example, the physicists and sensory-deprivation researchers analyzed the similarities and differences between their laboratory settings and other possible settings (e.g., environments without a vacuum). They created unique environments that were particularly informative, but the results would be meaningless if the researchers had failed to analyze the ways in which their environments were unique.

I am reminded of a study I read several years ago but have been unable to find again in the literature. If my memory serves me correctly, it went something like this: Some ethologists studied the habits of a relatively rare species of bird in the wild in order to design a setting in a zoo that would allow these birds to survive and propagate. Their goal was to duplicate features such as climate, nest-building materials, food, and so forth. They designed their zoo environment, imported a male and female of the species, and anxiously awaited spring. The birds did indeed have babies but these were soon found dead on the ground; they seemed to have been pushed out of the nest prematurely.

Subsequent analysis revealed the problem. In the wild, the parent birds discarded unwanted objects from their nest—broken eggshells, for example. The parents in the zoo setting seemed to be discarding their babies as well. In the wild, parents spent considerable time searching for food so the babies were usually hungry at feeding time. The babies were therefore active and animated. In the zoo, however, there was too much food available at close distances. Because the babies were usually full, they were relatively docile and seemed inanimate; the parents therefore discarded them from the nest.

How might we characterize the ethologists' initial attempt to design the zoo environment? Was this an ecologically valid experiment or not? The answer to this question depends on the conclusions one attempts to draw from the experiment. Imagine that the ethologists had observed the birds only in the zoo environment and had concluded that birds of this species were horrible parents. Most of us would question this conclusion; because this species has survived this long, it makes no sense to assume that they kill their young. A more reasonable assumption is that the zoo environment constituted an ecologically invalid test of the potential of the birds. However, there are other perspectives that render the zoo experiment highly informative. The ethologists were not trying to assess the birds' potential as parents, they were trying to understand the conditions necessary in order for this potential to be realized. Their initial failure to create an appropriate zoo environment therefore prompted them to attend to various conditions in the wild that they had failed to notice when first observing the natural behavior of the birds.

The task of designing the birds' environment in the zoo is analogous to designing a laboratory research environment. The researcher chooses a physical setting, designs instructions, creates materials, and controls the resources available to the subjects. The results that occur are never a function of the subjects in isolation; the latter are embedded within a social–cultural setting that places constraints on the way that they behave. As researchers, we often seem to overlook the potential importance of this organism–environment relationship. We often make general claims about the nature of organisms without considering the importance of environmental constraints. The ethologists who designed the zoo setting did not forget the importance of organism–environment relationships; they asked themselves what was wrong with their setting rather than attribute the failure to the birds per se. When we work with human subjects, however, we often seem to attribute failure to the people rather than to the experimental environment we create.

Grueneich and Trabasso's chapter (Chapter 13 in this volume) provides one illustration of this problem. They note that earlier researchers attempted to assess children's moral development by measuring their interpretations of various stories. If this aspect of the environment (i.e., the text structure) is not carefully analyzed (which it was not), the conclusions one reaches can be as ludicrous as the claim that the parent birds discussed earlier were terrible parents. The developmental literature includes many other illustrations that are similar. For example, a researcher may claim that children of a certain age cannot remember well, perform certain "cognitive operations," and so forth. Someone else may then design a different experimental environment and show that the children can indeed perform activities such as these (e.g., Chi, 1978; Odom, 1978). Similar problems have arisen in anthropology; people were often deemed "primitive, and so on," because they performed strangely given particular types of tasks (see Cole, 1977; Freedle, Chapter 3 in this volume; Scribner, 1977, for a discussion of these problems). An analogous error is to conclude that college sophomores "reason improperly" without analyzing the nature of the questions one is aking them to answer during the experimental task (see Smith, Chapter 16 in this volume).

It seems to me that there are two general ways to attempt to understand organisms. One is to create a task environment (e.g., a memory experiment, intelligence test) and to ask oneself whether particular organisms can or cannot adapt to that environment. An alternate method is to assume that particular organisms are capable of certain adaptive activities (e.g., caring for babies, remembering, reasoning) and to ask oneself about the environmental conditions that are necessary in order to bring this potential to the fore. In the first instance, the subject is expected to accommodate to the task environment created by the experimenter; in the second, the experimenter takes responsibility for accommodating to the subjects with whom he or she works. Both of these methods of investigation are valid and any particular investigation probably involves each of them to some degree. Nevertheless, researchers seem more likely to expect subjects to adapt to their environments than to ask themselves how to design an environment that can bring the subjects' potential to the fore.

Labov's (1978) comments are highly relevant in this context. Educational researchers often claim that many Black children come to kindergarten without knowing the words for knife, fork and spoon. Labov (1978) states: ''From my research in Newark and South Harlem, I have reason to doubt these statements [p. 437].'' He argues that the educational researchers and test makers do not know how to gain access to the lexical knowledge of the child. This argument can be extended, to problems with intelligence tests, for example. Traditional measures of intelligence require people to adapt to the testing instrument. Feuerstein (1979) takes a different approach to intelligence; he tries to determine what is needed in order to help people learn to deal with various problems. The purpose of his testing is to assess their potential to learn. Cole's analysis of the boys baking a cake (discussed earlier) also emphasized the importance of designing environments that reveal people's potential. If forced to function on his own, the nonreader in Cole's investigation would have been unable to bake the cake because he could not read the recipe. When allowed to use others as a resource, however, the boy's skill as an excellent organizer came to the fore.

SUMMARY AND CONCLUSIONS

This chapter began by asking how the behavior of ''my kind,'' cognitive psychologists, might be viewed from the perspective of other areas of specialization. This prompted an analysis of various prerequisites for experimentation; experimentalists have to form a social contract with subjects in order for the research to proceed. Researchers must: (1) design an appropriate physical setting; (2) develop rapport; (3) make the task instructions comprehensible; and (4) decide how to control the resources available to the subjects. These sets of activities help define a social–cultural framework within which the experiment takes place.

There are several reasons for analyzing the social–cultural framework within which both subject and experimenter are embedded. First, it may help researchers become aware of problems that they do and do not confront—help them define the limits of their expertise. For example, as a cognitive researcher, I rarely confront serious problems of rapport and motivation with my college-age subjects and I had better be aware of this fact. Imagine trying to sell a cognitive model of learning to elementary and high-school teachers saying nothing about problems of motivation, interest, defensiveness, and so forth. They would have good reason to be skeptical of my ''solution'' to learning problems. My typical laboratory environment is very different from their everyday teaching environment; I had better do a lot of listening in order to gain some idea of the problems they face.

A second reason for analyzing social–cultural frameworks is to gain some sense of the ecological validity of particular experiments and conclusions. A laboratory experiment can be very different from typical real-world environments yet yield results that are highly informative and relevant. The important point is that one attempt to analyze the similarities and differences between a particular research environment and other ''possible worlds.'' The major reason why this is important is that behavior is never a function of the organism in isolation. Everyone acknowledges this at some level, yet the point is easy to forget.

This emphasis on organism–environment relationships set the stage for discussing two general ways to attempt to understand organisms. One is to assess their abilities to adapt to particular situations; the other is to assume that they have particular potentials and to attempt to design environments that bring these to the fore. Both methods of investigation have the potential to yield ecologically valid information but the second seems to be employed much less frequently than the first. These two methods of investigation become particularly powerful when used in conjunction with one another. For example, 1-year-old children may be quite adept at understanding verbal utterances when their parents speak them in context, yet they may fail miserably in a decontextualized setting (e.g., Chapman, 1978). A great deal can be learned by observing them in environments in which they do show their potential and by noting how this breaks down when contextual support is removed. One can then go beyond the observation stage and attempt to design environments that support certain activities. This is analogous to the ethologists' work with the birds in the zoo environment; they learned a great deal by their initial failure to design an environment that was appropriate for the birds. It seems to be very productive to explore the conditions under which organisms behave adaptively. Adaptation is a two-way street, however; we tend to overemphasize people's abilities to accommodate to our situations (standardized laboratory tasks, intelligence tests, etc.) and to underemphasize the importance of trying to accommodate to them.

ACKNOWLEDGMENTS

Preparation of this chapter was supported in part by grant NIE-G-79-0017 and by a University Research Council Fellowship from Vanderbilt University.

REFERENCES

Bransford, J. D. *Human cognition: Learning understanding and remembering.* Belmont, Calif.: Wadsworth, 1979.

Bransford, J. D., & Nitsch, K. E. Coming to understand things we could not previously understand. In J. F. Kavanagh & W. Strange (Eds.), *Speech and language in the laboratory, school and clinic.* Cambridge, Mass.: M.I.T. Press, 1978.

Chapman, R. S. Comprehension strategies in children. In J. Kavanagh & W. Strange (Eds.), *Speech and language in the laboratory, school and clinic.* Cambridge, Mass.: M.I.T. Press, 1978.

Chi, M. T. H. Knowledge structure and memory development. In R. Siegler (Ed.), *Children's thinking: What develops?* Hillsdale, N.J.: Lawrence Erlbaum Associates, 1978.

Cole, M. An ethnographic psychology of cognition. In P. N. Johnson-Laird & P. C. Wason (Eds.), *Thinking: Readings in cognitive science.* Cambridge, England: Cambridge University Press, 1977.

Cole, M. *Metacognition outside the laboratory.* Symposium paper presented at the Society for Research in Child Development, March 1979.

Cole, M., & Scribner, S. *Culture and thought: A psychological introduction.* New York: Wiley, 1974.

Feuerstein, R. *The dynamic assessment of retarded performers.* Baltimore Md.: University Park Press, 1979.

Holt, J. *How children fail.* New York: Dell, 1964.

Labov, W. Gaining access to the dictionary. In J. F. Kavanagh & W. Strange (Eds.), *Speech and language in the laboratory, school and clinic.* Cambridge, Mass.: M.I.T. Press, 1978.

Locke, J. *Of civil government.* Chicago: Henry Regnery, 1955.

MacNamara, J. Cognitive basis of language learning in infants. *Psychological Review,* 1972, *79,* 1–13.

Nelson, K. Concept, word and sentence: Interrelations in acquisition and development. *Psychological Review,* 1974, *81,* 267–285.

Odom, R. A perceptual-salience account of décalage relations and developmental change. In L. S. Siegel & C. J. Brainerd (Eds.), *Alternative to Piaget: Critical essays on the theory.* New York: Academic Press, 1978.

Scribner, S. Modes of thinking and ways of speaking: Culture and logic reconsidered. In P. N. Johnson-Laird & P. C. Wason (Eds.), *Thinking: Readings in cognitive science.* Cambridge, England: Cambridge University Press, 1977.

27

The Need for
a Cross-Cultural Perspective

Roy Freedle
Educational Testing Service,
Princeton, N.J.

Several results reported at the conference suggest the need to seriously pursue cross-cultural work on how societies differ in assigning attributes to different person constructs. After all, the range and categorizations of person types may differ across cultures. How children come to learn these distinctions would certainly be a fascinating research topic. Are the types learned in some settings first? Do children from bicultural backgrounds learn some *mixture* of these person types or do they keep the two sets cognitively separate with each type foregrounded as the setting demands? One reason for taking such a cross-cultural framework seriously is that McDermott and Pratt (1976) have already suggested that the Zapotec Indians of Mexico place a more salient emphasis on role playing as an explanation for why people act in a certain way—and place less emphasis on presumed individual personality attributes. Thus, role schemata *dominate* individual-personality schemata in these societies. It appears that Western societies may reverse this pattern of schema dominance. If so, how are these distinctions learned? If a person knows both cultures, how does he or she negotiate any conflicts in social perception that might result from this difference in dominance patterns? Explorations in this topic would represent a new frontier of cognitive social psychology. A multidisciplinary conference brings such topics to the foreground.

Another reason for taking cross-cultural work seriously is that it may alter the form of equation we use to describe how elements of a schema interact. In story grammars, we can represent the proportion of key categories (categories such as setting, main character, episode's beginning, outcomes, etc.) that are remembered by a subject by just using a simple *sum* (divided by the total possible categories that could be recalled). Each term in the sum would be either a 0 or 1, with 1 meaning the particular category was remembered and 0 meaning it was not recalled. A subject's recall proportion could then reasonably be any value *between* and including 0 and 1. This may work fine as a description of Westerners' recall of stories, but it is certainly not an adequate representation of the rule that underlies native Americans' recall of a cherished tribal story or myth.

Many native Americans (e.g., the Pomo Indians) will say they do not "know" a story if *any element of the story has been forgotten*. Thus, a simple sum does not represent how what they know is related to what they recall. Instead, the *product* of every category (either a 0 or 1 for each category) determines the recall. Thus, if a 0 occurs any place in the product, the person will say "I do not know the story." Such a person will get a 0% recall score, even though such a person may very well have known all category information but one. The implication is that a Pomo Indian's recall will either be perfect or null. In contrast, using the sum equation, Westerners will give you many *gradients* of recall from 0 through totally correct. Hence, cross-culturally, an additive formula describes one population whereas a product formula describes another population.[1] This is surely not a trivial piece of information as we attempt to construct cognitive models of how individuals comprehend and recall text information. If we study only Westerners, we shall probably arrive at a highly biased set of rules for describing cognitive performance.

The result for native Americans can be understood as a prevailing attitude they have about the form of knowledge and the rules that govern when it is *appropriate* to speak (see Hymes, 1974, on sociolinguistics). Generally, native Americans consider it bad form to speak on any topic if one is not an expert. If there are defects in one's knowledge, it is best to remain *silent*. Because of this, cultures can differ in which model best represents the relationship between story memory and story recall. One might reply: A *probe* for specific category information may get around this; maybe. But we do not know whether the social *context* in which the probe takes place would still constrain the subject's willingness to give any information if the whole set of categories is not known. For example, if the subject does not consider himself or herself an expert, he or she may choose to remain silent even though he or she knows the answer for a specific probe question. If so, this would show that experimental techniques *cannot be selected in ignorance of cultural norms for when it is appropriate to speak*. If it is selected in ignorance, the wrong conclusions are likely to be reached concerning the mental competence of non-Western populations.

---

[1]Actually, the equation for Western recall is probably more complicated than just a simple sum. Kintsch and Greene (1978) present data that suggest that entire episodes can be deleted if only a few fragments of the episode are known; this suggests the possibility that *within* an episode, the categories may be better represented by a multiplicative equation, but *across* episodes, the information is represented additively. This refinement does not obviate the general distinction I have made contrasting native American recall patterns with Western recall patterns.

In a related vein, Deborah Tannen (1979) has found that the social perceptions of intentions differ in Greek and American communities. Subjects from both groups watched a silent film and then verbally reconstructed what they saw. Although many differences were found, the one of greatest interest here is that the Greeks read into the actions of the film more of a moralizing characteristic than the Americans did. Thus, perception of social intentions and social guilt as person attributes of the characters in the film were clearly different across these cultures. This also shows that some of the social-psychological conclusions we may be tempted to reach on the basis of testing only North American subjects may be in need of revision when cross-cultural work is conducted.

Multidisciplinary conferences are extremely valuable in bringing tolerant scholars together for intelligent discussion. It is a natural way to break down old academic distinctions, and it is a healthy trend if we are to unify knowledge and increase its relevance to everyday problems.

REFERENCES

Hymes, D. Ways of speaking. In R. Bauman & J. Sherzer (Eds.), *Explorations in the ethnography of speaking.* Cambridge, England: Cambridge University Press, 1974.

Kintsch, W., & Greene, E. The role of culture-specific schemata in the comprehension and recall of stories. *Discourse Processes,* 1978, *1,* 1–13.

McDermott, R. P., & Pratt, M. Attribution theory and social interaction: Some ethnographic accounts. *Quarterly Newsletter of the Institute for Comparative Human Development,* 1976, *1*(1), 3–5.

Tannen, D. What's in a frame? Surface evidence for underlying expectations. In R. Freedle (Ed.), *New directions in discourse processing.* Norwood, N.J.: Ablex, 1979.

28 Benediction by an Anthropologist

Michael H. Agar
University of Houston

It is time to debrief you. I am actually an anthropologist doing a study of psychologists as a quasitribe, but you are very difficult informants because you keep negotiating your culture.

I have two metaphors for my experience of the conference. The first is that I have been trying to build a schema out of scotch tape and cardboard. It is difficult to listen to you talk about your area and at the same time try to figure out what the underlying premises are that guide how you talk about it. That is called doing ethnography and it can drive you crazy if you try to do it in 3½ days.

The second metaphor is that being at this conference is like trying to drink a bucket of Hollandaise sauce. It was just too much, too rich, too quick, and I needed to slow it down to have some time to dwell on the issues that were raised. In almost every paper that I have heard, there have been two or three ideas that I would love to take to the field, using them as a beginning orientation for an ethnographic study that could be done to interact with the kinds of problems raised in the papers. Some of you, in fact, have already done that sort of thing even if only on an informal basis.

One trend that I heard, which of course I was listening for—evidence for some of the points in earlier papers—was the idea of the extension of research contexts, applying the things you are talking about to a broader range of situations and people than characterizes most of the data bases that you usually operate with. A second trend was the idea of enriching subdisciplinary perspectives, the classic case here being the integration of cognition and affect.

An ethnographic orientation offers an approach that is particularly compatible with both of those tasks. Roy Freedle mentioned cross-cultural applications in his comments. Let me give you a hypothetical example. Consider the finding of *self*

575

attribution for favorable outcomes and *situational* attribution for unfavorable outcomes. I find that fascinating and would like to go out and play with that idea in some ethnographic work. But, as soon as I start doing some thought experiments to try to think of counterexamples that are possible or that I happen to know about, I can immediately think of possible cultures where that might not hold—where one is not supposed to take personal credit for favorable outcomes, at least in some situations. I also think of individuals I know who panic at the thought of taking credit for favorable outcomes and love taking the blame for unfavorable outcomes. In fact, most everything that you talked about leads me to think about variation—variation across and within cultures, and across and within individuals.

The second trend, the enrichment of subdisciplinary perspectives, would also be aided by an ethnographic orientation. Because that was the theme of my paper for the conference, I do not elaborate any further on it here. There are some other comments I would like to make, though.

First, you should hear more ethnographers talk. At a conference with anthropologists more adequately represented, you could hear us fight and find out what a mess our field is. You are getting much too consistent a presentation from your lone anthropologist, as if there is agreement on what we do. There are many anthropologists I can think of who, had they been invited, would be criticizing me after I had given my paper.

There is also another paper I was going to give on the history of anthropological–psychological interaction. There is a rather elaborate one that some of you may not be aware of. For example, the field of ''culture and personality'' was perhaps the mainstream of American cultural anthropology for several years. There is also a field called ''cognitive anthropology.'' Some linguistic anthropologists who enjoyed doing ethnography took some ideas from Bruner, Goodnow, and Austin, and others, and developed ways of more carefully talking about and doing the study of culture. Cognitive anthropology has dispersed now as people have gone on different trails.

Some of the trails are very compatible with the issues discussed in this conference. For example, some anthropologists are interacting with psychologists around the issue of story structure. There is also some interest in recent work in artificial intelligence. There are suggestions there for the development of an ethnographic language. If you look at culture as cognition as some anthropologists do, then you must wonder how to describe it and talk about it in a theoretically interesting way. Schank and Abelson's work, to take one example, suggests some of the properties such a language must have.

Another striking aspect of the conference is that some psychologists who frequently work with anthropologists did not seem to come in for much discussion. For example, Michael Cole and Sylvia Scribner talk to anthropologists a good deal and, in fact, have always included them in their research on learning and thinking. Eleanor Rosch's work on category structure is influential in some current work in cognitive anthropology.

I would also like to mention that there is a new journal called *Ethos,* which has only been out a few years. It is a publication of the Society for Psychological Anthropology. Should you have some spare time in the library, you might enjoy going through it to see what kinds of things anthropologists who consider themselves psychological anthropologists talk about.

On the issue of fieldwork, some of you asked me for references. There are some personal accounts of the field experience if you want to get a flavor of how ethnographers work. One example is by Hortense Powdermaker and is called *Stranger and Friend;* another is *Doing Fieldwork* by Rosalie Wax. There are not many comprehensive treatments of the actual doing of ethnography, especially the earlier inductive pattern-finding parts. It is a difficult process to specifiy at any rate.

There are numerous articles scattered through the literature in anthropology and sociology. James Spradley has two books that just came out, one entitled *The Ethnographic Interview,* the other called *Participant Observation.* My own introductory treatment of ethnography is called *The Professional Stranger.* Other book-length discussions of ethnography have appeared in the last few years in sociology as well. Some additional references are cited in my paper (Chapter 2 in this volume).

John Harvey asked me to close the conference with a benediction. I would like to read a sort of Tennessee haiku that is intended as a compliment to the conference. I was inspired during a walk in the city park where they have the replica of the Parthenon. I have to explain before I read it that it is not insulting to the term ''schema,'' because one of my hobbies is looking for correspondences between street talk and social-science talk.

A schema, a scheme, a scam for the Parthenon
Rebirth of a classic in Nashville to bluegrass echoes.

I am not sure what that means, but I think it has got something to do with the conference.

29 No Man Is a Discipline

Baruch Fischhoff
Decision Research, A Branch of Perceptronics

If interdisciplinary research is so good, why is there so little of it?

One reason is that no one is trained to do it. Rather, the interested parties are trained in their respective professions and are drawn to interaction via involvement in some substantive problem. The nascent fields that result tend to be strong on commitment and on the sort of fresh ideas produced by rubbing strange disciplines together. Weaknesses lie in decreasing quality control and conceptual clarity as one leaves traditional fields, with their strongly developed sense of "what good is" in the way of research.

Established disciplines promote individuals who adhere to a set of ritualistic procedures developed by trial and error over a considerable period of time. The recipient of this seal of approval will neither fall prey to mistakes discovered by the discipline nor address more than a slice of any real-life problem. Similarly, practitioners are likely to use terms in a systematic and conscious manner, although perhaps without much awareness of their range of applicability, underlying assumptions, or cognates in other disciplines. Thus, although the potential pay-offs are large in interdisciplinary research, so are the problems and pitfalls.

A second reason why so few people take the interdisciplinary plunge is that there are often rather meager rewards for doing so. University departments like people who can teach the traditional courses and be evaluated by the usual criteria. Joint appointments often leave one doubly orphaned. The notion that "those who can't hack it in basic research tackle applied problems" is rampant in many quarters. Real-life problems calling for many perspectives are often in the lock of one discipline (i.e., economics, engineering) that is unwilling to give more than lip service to sharing attention or resources. Those who are shunted aside may feel an unsatisfying temptation to oversell their own wares in order to gain a hearing. Although debates do not necessarily go to the shrillest, hearing the confident, unqualified testimony of, say, economists could lead a psychologist to go a generalization too far.

An additional deterrent from interdisciplinary work for those who do not like a fight is that not only the research business, but also its public context are often heavily politicized. Real problems involve real stakes, beside which the prestige games of scholarly disputes pale. Many academics are loath to think about the ideological underpinnings of their own pursuits, much less venture into polarized debates and contend with the dirty tricks, doctored data, and name calling that are often involved.

A final problem is the lack of persuasive models for how interdisciplinary research might be conducted. On this score, the present conference offers a number of interesting examples.

MODES OF INTERDISCIPLINARY WORK

The simplest mode of interaction is to compare terminology to reveal the hidden assumptions in frames of reference. Consider, for example, the apparent (and productive) conflict between Wandersman and Florin's and Winkel's chapters (Chapters 19 and 23, respectively) in this volume over whether neighborhood or block organizations should be assumed to be more natural social units. If we do not clarify such assumptions, we risk ethnocentric misconceptualizations and the attendant dangers of (1) not realizing that the terms we used have different interpretations in the populations we are studying (and with whom we must communicate); (2) deluding ourselves into thinking that the focus of our research life is also the focus of our respondents' lives; (3) misinterpreting our subjects' lives by failing to see their internal logic. For example, we might take the failure of neighborhood organizations as a sign of general apathy, when in fact it was due to active involvement in groups that provide a "neighborhood" without a geographical base (e.g., the PTL Club or feminist organizations or Masons). Clarifying the assumptions our psychological work makes about the world in which behavior is embedded is a first step toward establishing the generalizability of our results and thus developing a theory of context to complement our more evolved theories of the individual.

A second level of interaction is to add a dimension from another domain to our disciplinary work. For example, although no economists or political scientists attended this conference, their issues appeared again and again. Suburban neighborhoods can only be understood in the context of the urban blight that is slowly creeping over them (Winkel, Chapter 23 in this volume). The need for neighborhood groups and the prospects for their prosperity may depend on exogenous factors like the presence or absence of redlining (Wandersman & Florin, Chapter 19 in this volume). One might argue that meaningful public participation cannot be given but must be taken, hence people's attitudes toward neighborhood groups may reflect their political savvy or cynicism (Kasperson & Breitbart, 1974). The right to choose between dozens of breakfast cereals may confer an illusion of control over one's environment that mutes the need to assert real control (Barnes, Chapter 20 in this volume). Indeed, one of the secrets of political manipulation may be to make people's control over events seem larger than it actually is.

One limit to this mode of interdisciplinary awareness is that it may be uninformed. The fact that we know the technical term for redlining is no guarantee that we are aware of its intricacies. A second limit is being forced to rely on handouts from other disciplines. If they have failed to study boundary topics or have not conceptualized them in terms compatible with our own interests, awareness of context may be hygienic without being therapeutic.

A further escalation in interdisciplinary contact is criticizing one another's work. Barnes' questioning of architects' presumptions regarding human behavior is one example of keeping another field honest. Testing any of the outrageously definitive statements about how people interact with buildings found in *The Pattern Language* (Alexander, Ishikawa, Silberstein, Jacobson, Fiksdahl-King, & Angel, 1977) might be another. Agar's chapter (Chapter 2 in this volume) told us something about psychologists' naivete from an anthropologist's perspective.

A higher level of contact can be seen in sorties across disciplinary boundaries, returning with bounty in the form of stolen methodologies. Many major advances have been the result of such appropriation. Kates (1962) transformed geography by introducing attitude measurement, thereby freeing the field from reliance on purely physical measures. Fiske (Chapter 12 in this volume) has changed our understanding of the relationship between affect and cognition through the use of tools developed in econometrics and sociology. Heider (1958) invigorated social psychology with a breath of contemporary philosophy. One practical problem with such forays is that they are often one-time efforts. As the loot is passed on from one generation of scientists to another, it gradually loses its fidelity and vitality until the intellectual capital it created is exhausted.

A generic limitation in such contact is that the relationship between the fields involved is unequal, with the borrower being in an unnecessarily subservient role. As Taylor (Chapter 10 in this volume) noted, one result of social cognition's heavy reliance on designs borrowed from cognitive psychology is a failure to convince cognitive people that they have anything to learn from considering social context. This imbalance is exacerbated by the tendency in social cognition to apply cognitive designs in settings most likely to replicate original results. Although this strategy increases the likelihood of getting interesting, publishable results, it fails to produce the sort of contradictory conclusions that might make cognitive psychologists worry about how far their results generalize beyond laboratory settings.

If social cognition did produce discrepant results, they could be interpreted in one of two ways, depending on one's philosophy of science. Disconfirming results may be seen as an attack on the original researchers, leading them to draw around their wagons and the upstarts to snipe from the outside, hoping to discredit the entire enterprise with one well-placed shot. Or, one can acknowledge that all behavior takes place in context, that results from well-done research are valid in at least some contexts, and that discrepancies should be valued for helping to delineate relevant aspects of context.

More dangerous than pointless rancor is borrowing tools from another domain without the full appreciation of their limitations that comes from extended professional socialization in that domain.[1] Hexter (1971) characterized those "leaders of fashion in history" who were borrowing notions from the analytic philosophy of science just as philosophers were becoming disillusioned with analytic methods as "leaping aboard intellectually sinking ships and drowning their innocent followers along with them [p. 110]." Similar criticisms might be leveled against psychohistorians embracing psychoanalysis as an analytical tool just as psychologists were giving up on it as a research methodology, or cliometricians applying economic analysis to historical settings just as economists are questioning the validity of their measures.

The highest form of interdisciplinary work is actually working together with people from other disciplines. Although full collaboration is rare, its salutary effects are widely enough acknowledged for working together to be regarded as virtuous. For example, only by extended interaction can we learn to incorporate other disciplinary perspectives in our own work. The pitfall of collaboration is a sophisticated version of the blind leading the blind. My colleagues in geography must trust my psychology, as I must trust their geography. It may be very tempting to become a prophet in someone else's field, going well beyond the limits of one's data in the absence of corrective criticism. Furthermore, because most collaborative works are unique products of the interactions between the perspectives and personalities brought to bear on a particular subject, there are no firm standards or systematic means to ensure quality control. Disciplines progress by trial and error. Active collaborations attempt to create new, integrative disciplines in whole cloth at first crack. They cannot always do it and may not always be able to assess the validity of their attempt.

An alternative goal for collaboration is not to create a new discipline, with the capacity for getting the right answers to a newly, but narrowly, defined set of questions. Rather, one can acknowledge that there are no "right" answers (or at least no way to be certain that we have come across them) to questions rich enough to draw talents from a variety of fields. What one can hope for is to avoid getting the wrong answers, with each discipline helping to avoid particular kinds of errors.

---

[1]While writing this, I received a telephone call from an engineer at a major industrial concern asking for a reference book that would teach him how to conduct attitude surveys.

REFERENCES

Alexander, C., Ishikawa, H., Silberstein, M., Jacobson, M., Fiksdahl-King, I., & Angel, S. *The pattern language*. New York: Oxford Press, 1977.

Hexter, J. H. *The history primer*. New York: Basic Books, 1971.

Heider, F. *The psychology of interpersonal relations*. New York: Wiley, 1958.

Kasperson, R. E., & Breitbart, M. *Participation, decentralization, and advocacy planning* (Resource Paper 25). Washington D.C.: Association of American Geographers, 1974.

Kates, R. W. *Hazard and choice in perception in flood plain management*. Chicago: University of Chicago, 1962. (Department of Geography, Research Paper No. 78).

VII EPILOGUE

We present one last discussion. This discussion focuses not only on some final conclusions, but also importantly on criticisms regarding the funding of conferences such as this one by federal agencies; we present both some of the criticisms and our counter-arguments.

30

An Editorial Commentary on Interfaces in Psychology and the Social Sciences

John H. Harvey
Jerri P. Town
Kerry L. Yarkin
Vanderbilt University

GENERAL CONCLUSIONS

Many of the writers in this volume have presented summary perspectives regarding the current status of interdisciplinary work both within psychology and between psychology and other fields. Our own view is that although there is a substantial interfacial dialogue now underway, much more ''interfacing'' will be necessary before the strands of interlocking ideas and paradigms become more substantial in the field and before the value of integration is well recognized. There is an obvious paradox that interdisciplinary work must confront—namely: If the work is too general, it will not appeal to the scholar who searches for detail and order in the constituent processes of phenomena (a point that Trabasso stressed at the conference). If, however, the work is too specific, it will not appeal to the scholar who would persistently advance the matter of the real world as a touchstone for progress in such inquiry (a point emphasized by Agar, Fischhoff, and Wandersman among others). The confrontation cannot be avoided because both types of scholars represent an essential element in cross-disciplinary work.

We believe that the dialogue at this conference bodes well for an eventual resolution or effective mediation of these antagonistic tendencies. One example is the social and environmental concepts woven into the statements by cognitive investigators such as Lappin, Grueneich and Trabasso, and Bransford, Stein, Shelton, and Owings; another is the attention given to basic comprehension processes displayed by social and environmental investigators such as Taylor, Fiske, Smith, Wells, Saegert, Aiello, Thompson, and Baum, Gatchel, Aiello, and Thompson. In these treatments, at least, the loss of in-depth specification and precision is minimal. Consider, also, the interplay between social and environmental research that Aiello et al. articulate in their chapter; remarkably, it is only recently that this interplay has been recognized and addressed in the literature. The statements by Baum et al., Greenwald, Stokols and Shumaker, and Winkel are particularly useful as representative of emerging interdisciplinary work because they involve different levels of analysis, a combination of theory and research, and meldings of concepts from cognitive, environmental, and social psychology. Finally, it is apparent that some of the scholars who have contributed to this volume (e.g., Agar, Baron, Freedle and Fischhoff) have been pursuing balanced interdisciplinary programs without apology for level of specificity for many years now.

DIRECTIONS FOR FUTURE INTERDISCIPLINARY DIALOGUE AND CONFERENCES

As we write, future directions for interdisciplinary work are being forged in diverse ways by diverse sets of scholars. Some trends emerging from these proceedings include: (1) systematic blending of social cognition and developmental work (e.g., Grueneich and Trabasso's research); (2) examination of the overlap between social and clinical psychology (Harvey & Weary, 1979), of the interrelationships among motivation, emotion, cognition, and the environment (Weary and Fiske sensitized us to some of the issues that deserve cross-disciplinary address); the so-called strong motivations and emotions and their connections to other phenomena certainly cannot be disregarded if we wish our interdisciplinary efforts to provide a very realistic reflection of the human condition; (3) further consideration of the self in various domains of work (Greenwald's contribution was unique and stimulating in suggesting many linkages); and (4) exploration of the interface of the type of cognitive mapping work discussed by Chase and Chi, Clayton and Woodyard, and Thorndyke, and the concept of "psychological space" formulated by scholars of an earlier era like Tolman and Lewin (a point emphasized by Saegert in her comments at the conference).

Any of these types of endeavors might be enriched by input from basic perception–cognition theorists or anthropologists. We should remember that our lone anthropologist, Michael Agar, could only represent a small area of anthropology,—namely, cognitive anthropology. Without suggesting that all sciences be thrown together in one grand conference or set of meetings, our bias is toward integration, wherever meaningful and feasible. We believe that much greater advance will occur in the social sciences as a consequence of such integration. As this volume appears in print, a tangible manifestation of our optimism about this type of advance is the development of further proposals (by John C. Masters and John H. Harvey) to continue this series focusing on boundary areas in psychology and between psychology and other social sciences.

To close this section, we present the following quotes from other scholars with similar convictions. First, from Neisser (1976):

> Lacking in ecological validity, indifferent to culture, even missing some of the main features of perception and memory that occur in ordinary life, such a psychology [cognitive] could become a narrow and uninteresting specialized field [p. 7].

Next, from Petrinovich (1979):

> Since all behavior takes place in some medium with which the organism must interact, all psychological analysis is, in essence, at the level of social psychology. The medium might consist only of ecological variables, which are multiple, changing and complex in their influence, or it might involve other organisms. The mode of analysis is the same in either case: The organism is actively sifting stimuli, translating them into ''meanings,'' and acting in a constant interaction with a dynamic world [p. 378].

And last, from Luria (1976):

> It has become a basic principle of materialistic psychology that mental processes depend on active life forms in appropriate environments. Such a psychology also assumes that human action changes the environment so that human mental life is a product of continually *new* activities manifest in social practice [p. 29].

FUNDING OF INTERDISCIPLINARY CONFERENCES

A final topic that must be addressed is how interdisciplinary conferences can be sponsored in the future. In the main, federal agencies provide the most flexible and ample source of funds for these endeavors. But to fund an interdisciplinary venture, an agency must consider a number of general and often well-taken objections made by critics of such conferences. Presented here are a few of the objections to the present meeting, as paraphrased or quoted from anonymous reviews of our proposal, along with a brief reply to each.

1. *Objection:* Representatives of different areas often *talk at* rather than *with* each other. As a result, positions tend to polarize, thus reducing the likelihood of synthesis. Such a mishmash of things will be presented that participants will be discouraged about further cross-disciplinary efforts. ''For example, can a social psychologist or an anthropologist really make many meaningful comments on the work in comprehension and memory?'' *Reply:* Yes, there may have been

some "talking at" and polarization at our meeting. But to whatever degree these tendencies emerged, it seemed clear that much "talking with" also occurred, with a salutary impact on the participants and their input to the meeting. Further, in large conferences such as this one, some implementation of what we know about psychology (especially in the realm of environmental–social interaction tendencies) may work to obviate the "talking at" tendency. That is, planning regarding likely interaction patterns during times when formal sessions are not planned can stimulate dialogue among participants who otherwise might not have that much informal contact with one another. From this volume, the reader can be the judge whether a mishmash of ideas resulted; we are satisfied. The fact that a social psychologist or an anthropologist can make meaningful comments about work in comprehension and memory is attested to not only chapters found in this volume, but also by works such as Abelson (1976), Rosch and Lloyd (1978), and Whorf (1956).

2. *Objection:* There is greater pay-off associated with funding individual researchers' programs of work than with funding conferences. *Reply:* We would not argue that conferences per se should, in general, receive a higher funding priority than individual research programs. Rather, we argue that conferences are important *because they can enrich the work of individual investigators.* Also, as at our conference, participants who are early in their careers will be among the most influential senior investigators in their fields in the near future. Thus, the merit of conferences such as this one in having a long-term intellectual impact on the work of young investigators cannot be underestimated, nor easily translated into a dollar value.

3. *Objection:* Meetings such as this should be held only when they reflect "something in the air that hasn't jelled." *Reply:* It appears to us that the jelling process is well under way and that we would be remiss as social scientists if we did not recognize this process and, as we are able, to give it a hand.

ACKNOWLEDGMENTS

We are grateful to Baruch Fischhoff and Gifford Weary for comments on an earlier version of this chapter.

REFERENCES

Abelson, R. P. Script processing in attitude formation and decision making. In J. S. Carroll & J. W. Payne (Eds.), *Cognition and social behavior.* Hillsdale, N. J.: Lawrence Erlbaum Associates, 1976.

Harvey, J. H., & Weary, G. The integration of social and clinical psychology training programs. *Personality and Social Psychology Bulletin,* 1979, *5,* 511-515.

Luria, A. R. *Cognitive development.* Cambridge, Mass.: Harvard University Press, 1976.

Neisser, U. *Cognition and reality*. San Francisco: Freeman, 1976.

Petrinovich, L. Probabilistic functionalism: A conception of research method. *American Psychologist*, 1979, *34*, 373–390.

Rosch, E., & Lloyd, B. B. (Eds.). *Cognition and categorization*. Hillsdale N.J.: Lawrence Erlbaum Associates, 1978.

Whorf, B. L. *Language, thought, and reality* (J. B. Carroll, Ed.). Cambridge, Mass.: M.I.T. Press and New York: Wiley, 1956.

Author Index

Italics denote pages with complete bibliographic information.

A

Abelson, H., 354, *368*
Abelson, R. P., 197, 206, *210,* 229, 234, 253, 257, *259, 262, 263,* 590, *590*
Abramson, L. Y., 202, *208,* 525, *532*
Adams, R., 23, *32*
Adesman, P., 115, *135*
Agar, M. H., 23, *32,* 40, 42, 58, *58,* 197, *208*
Aiello, J. R., 376, *389,* 412, *420,* 426, 428, 429, 430, 431, 433, 434, 435, *437, 438,* 519, *532*
Aiello, T. D., 431, *437*
Ajzen, I., 314, *321,* 351, *368*
Akin, O., 117, *135*
Albert, M. L., 48, *58*
Albert, S., 61, *86*
Aldrich, H., 503, *511*
Alexander, C., 409, 411, 417, *420,* 581, *583*
Allen, G. L., 138, *148*
Allen, R. B., 74, *87*
Alley, T. R., 68, *86*
Allport, F. H., 292, *306*
Allport, G. W., 191, *208,* 424, *437,* 540, 541, *551*
Altman, I., 13, *19,* 382, 383, *389,* 409, 411, 415, *420,* 425, 427, *437,* 444, 454, *485*

Amabile, T. M., 314, *322*
Anderson, C., 199, 200, *211,* 237, 245, *263*
Anderson, E., 47, *58*
Anderson, J. E., 151, *161*
Anderson, J. R., 228, 229, *259,* 343, *368*
Anderson, N. H., 203, *208,* 229, 241, 242, 243, 249, 254, *259*
Anderson, R. C., 94, *109,* 240, *259*
Anderson, T. R., 374, *389*
Andrews, L., 281, *287*
Angel, S., 417, *420,* 581, *583*
Annis, A. B., 376, 378, *390*
Appleyard, D., 139, *148*
Apsler, R., 291, *306*
Argyle, M., 396, 404, *406,* 434, *437,* 442, *485*
Arkin, R. M., 310, *322*
Arkin, R. W., 318, *321*
Armstrong, G. E., 476, *488*
Arnold, M. B., 233, 240, 242, *259*
Aronson, E., 191, *208*
Asch, S. E., 16, *19,* 74, *86,* 304, *306*
Ashmore, R. D., 253, *259*
Asp, S., 279, *286*
Averill, J. R., 234, 240, 242, 257, *262,* 384, *389*
Ax, A. F., 237, *262*

B

Babbitt, M., 345, *368*
Bacastow, R. B., 163, *182*
Bales, R. F., 234, *259*, 453, 481, *486*
Bandura, A., 74, *86*, 201, *208*, 414, *420*, 531, 532
Barclay, C. R., 108, *110*
Barclay, J. R., 154, *161*
Barenboim, C., 277, 278, *286*
Barnes, R. D., 213, *224*, 293, *307*, 318, *322*, 413, *421*, 537, *551*
Barker, R. G., 388, *389*, 405, *406*, 417, *420*, 441, 442, 444, 446, 451, 473, 474, 484, *485*, 513, *532*
Baron, R. A., 385, *389*, 444, *485*
Baron, R. M., 80, 82, *86*, *87*, 409, 410, 418, 420, *420*
Barsky, A. J., 202, *208*
Bartlett, F. C., 265, *286*, 293, 294, *306*, 539, *551*
Bassili, J. N., 71, 72, 81, *86*
Bates, E., 290, *307*, *308*
Baum, A., 374, 375, 386, *389*, *390*, 412, *420*, 426, 430, 434, *437*, *438*, 444, *485*, 514, 515, 516, 517, 518, 519, 522, *532*
Beach, L. R., 174, *184*
Bearison, D. J., 278, *286*
Bechtel, R. B., 417, *420*, 471, 474, *485*
Behrens, W. W., 179, *183*
Bell, H. H., 355, 356, 357, *368*, *369*
Bell, P. A., 444, *485*
Bem, D. J., 193, *208*, 305, *307*, 310, *321*, 539, 544, *551*
Benner, L. A., 327, *339*
Berger, P., 447, *485*
Berkowitz, L., 396, *406*
Berlyne, D. E., 446, *485*
Berlyne, D. W., 247, *259*
Berndt, E. G., 269, 278, 280, *286*
Berndt, T. J., 269, 278, 280, 281, *286*
Berscheid, E., 10, *19*, 229, 248, *259*, 290, *307*
Birch, D., 500, *511*
Birdsall, T. G., 366, *369*
Black, J. B., 197, *208*, 248, *260*
Blackmer, E., 281, *287*
Blalock, B., 191, *208*
Blaney, P. H., 236, *260*
Blashfield, R. K., 449, *487*
Blau, P. M., 374, *389*
Bobrow, D. G., 240, *259*
Bogdan, R., 23, *32*

Boland, M., 374, *389*
Boland, W., 374, *389*
Borden, R. J., 537, *551*
Borgatta, E. F., 453, 481, *486*
Borgida, E., 195, *210*, 314, 318, 319, *323*
Borkan, B., 176, *183*
Borkowski, J. G., 108, *110*
Bouffard, D. L., 456, *487*
Bower, G. H., 96, *109*, *110*, 197, *208*, 231, 248, 250, *259*, *260*, 289, 292, 305, *307*, 343, *368*
Bowers, K., 394, *406*
Bradley, G. W., 236, *260*, 537, *551*
Bransford, J. D., 62, 89, 94, 96, 98, 99, 101, 108, *110*, 153, 154, *161*, 293, *307*, 562, *569*
Bregman, A. S., 289, *307*
Brehm, J. W., 412, *422*, 426, *437*, 459, *488*, 518, 528, *532*, 542
Breitbart, M., 581, *583*
Brenner, M. W., 536, *551*
Brewer, M. B., 192, *208*
Brock, T. C., 291, *308*, 538, *552*
Bronfenbrenner, U., 441, 442, *485*
Brower, S., 504, *512*
Brown, A. L., 108, *110*
Brown, D., 240, *262*
Brown, E., 500, *511*
Brown, E. R., 345, *368*
Bruner, J. S., 190, *208*, 292, 304, *307*, 361, *368*
Brunswik, E., 18, *19*, 445, *485*
Bryant, K. J., 138, 143, *148*
Bryson, R. A., 175, *182*
Buck, R., 80, 82, *86*, *87*
Buckhout, R., 360, *368*
Bukstel, L., 116, *135*
Bulman, R. J., 200, *208*
Burke, W. P., 108, *110*
Burns, H. J., 539, *552*
Burton, I., 174, *182*, *183*, 462, *485*
Buss, A. R., 82, *86*
Butkowsky, I., 77, *89*
Butzine, K. W., 327, 331, *339*
Byers, H., 42, *58*
Byers, P., 42, *58*
Byrne, D., 191, *208*

C

Caelli, T. M., 345, *368*
Calesnick, L. E., 412, *420*, 426, 434, *437*, 519, 532

Calhoun, J. B., 427, *437*
Campbell, A., 490, *511*
Campbell, D. T., 444, *486*, 547, *552*
Campione, J. D., 108, *110*
Canter, D., 160, *161*, 416, *420*
Cantor, N., 199, *209*, 228, 248, *260*
Cantril, H., 540, *552*
Caputo, C., 213, *225*
Carello, C., 65, *88*
Carlsmith, J. M., 191, *208*
Carlston, D., 228, *261*
Caroll, J. S., 314, *321*
Carr, S., 493, *511*
Cartwright, D., 453, 455, 473, 481, *486*
Carver, C. S., 216, 220, 224, *225*, 236, *260*, *263*
Cassirer, E., 343, 360, *368*
Cazden, C. B., 43, 44, *58*, *59*
Chafe, W., 43, *59*
Chaiken, A. L., 293, *307*
Chandler, M. J., 277, 278, *286*
Chanowitz, B., 196, *210*, 245, *262*
Chapman, L. J., 316, *321*
Chapman, R. S., 562, 568, *569*
Charness, N., 115, 116, *135*
Chase, W. G., 112, 113, 114, 117, 120, 128, 129, *135*, *136*
Chein, I., 444, *486*
Chermayeff, S., 409, 411, *420*
Chi, M. T. H., 115, 116, 118, *135*, 566, *569*
Chiesi, H. L., 118, *135*
Christensen, A., 10, *19*
Churchman, C. W., 53, *59*
Cialdini, R. B., 537, *551*
Clark, H. H., 128, *135*
Clark, M. C., 96, *110*
Clark, M. S., 219, 220, *224*, 231, 232, *260*, *261*, 305, *307*
Clarke, A. C., 550, *551*
Close, M., 199, 200, *211*, 237, 245, *263*
Cohen, C. E., 78, *86*, 253, *260*
Cohen, J., 402, *406*
Cohen, P., 402, *406*
Cohen, S., 373, 383, 385, *389*, 444, *486*, 504, 505, *511*
Cole, J. D., 268, 270, *286*
Cole, M., 53, *59*, 561, 563, 566, *569*
Coleman, R., 500, *511*
Collins, A. M., 256, *260*
Collins, B. E., 191, *209*, 291, *307*
Collins, W. A., 281, *286*
Combs, B., 172, 174, *183*, *184*

Condon, W. S., 42, *59*
Converse, P., 490, *511*
Cooper, J., 327, 331, *339*, 543, *551*
Cooper, R. E., 431, *437*
Cornsweet, T. N., 357, *368*
Corrigan, B., 172, *184*
Costanzo, P. R., 268, 270, *286*, 310, *324*
Coupe, P., 128, 131, *136*, 138, 142, *149*
Cox, V. C., 375, 377, *390*
Craik, F. I. M., 84, *86*
Craik, K. H., 444, *486*, 489, *511*
Crandall, R., 319, *323*
Crocker, J., 79, *89*, 198, *211*, 228, 230, 240, 244, 249, 251, 253, *263*
Cronbach, L. J., 393, *406*
Crossman, E. R. F. W., 121, *135*
Cutting, J. E., 71, 72, 81, *86*, *87*, 359, *369*

D

Dabbs, J. M., 61, *86*, 434, *438*
Dabek, R. F., 273, *286*
DaLomba, D., 500, *511*
Darley, J. M., 293, *307*
Darwin, C., 80, *87*
Davis, G. E., 522, *532*
Davis, J. A., 334, *339*
Davis, K. E., 193, *209*, 213, *224*, 269, 272, *286*, 310, *322*
Davitz, J. R., 234, *260*
Dawes, R., 194, 195, *209*
Dawes, R. M., 172, *182*
Dean, J., 434, *437*
Deaux, K., 305, *307*
de Groot, A., 112, *135*, *136*
Del Boca, F. K., 253, *259*
DeRisi, D. T., 429, *437*
de Rivera, J., 537, *551*
Dermer, M., 247, 248, *259*, 290, 307
Derry, P. A., 236, 253, *261*
Desor, J. A., 373, *389*, 428, *437*
Devereux, E. C., 464, 468, 482, *486*
Dimberg, V., 80, *88*
Dintzer, L., 202, *211*, 531, *533*
Doner, J., 357, *369*
Dooling, D. J., 293, *307*
Downs, R. M., 131, 132, *135*, 138, *148*, 156, *161*
Dreben, E. K., 203, *209*, 249, *260*
Duffy, F., 417, *420*
Duffy, R., 82, *86*
Duke, M. P., 433, *437*

Dunkel-Schetter, C., 247, *264*
Dunn, D., 253, *260*
Durkheim, E., 374, *389*, 469, *486*
Duval, S., 214, 215, 217, 218, 220, *224*, 253, *260*, 318, *321*
Dweck, C., 526, *532*
Dyck, R. J., 310, *322*

E

Eagly, A. H., 228, *261*
Easterbrook, J. A., 238, *260*
Ebbesen, E., 74, 78, *86, 87*, 219, 220, *224*, 228, *261*, 538, *552*
Edwards, J., 394, 395, 398, 404, *406*
Edwards, W., 175, *184*, 314, *322*
Egan, D. E., 118, *135*
Ehrlich, D., 376, *389*
Ehrlich, P. I., 427, *438*
Einhorn, H. J., 168, 175, *182*
Eisenstadt, M., 115, *135*
Ekehammar, B., 394, 395, *406*
Ekman, P., 76, 80, *87*, 233, *260*
Elkind, D., 273, *286*
Ellis, S. H., 115, *135*
Ellsworth, 80, *87*
Ellsworth, P. C., 84, *88*, 228, 234, 237, *263*
Elms, A. C., 543, *551*
Elo, A. E., 121, *135*
Emery, F. E., 478, *486*
Endler, N. S., 394, 395, 396, 398, 404, *406*
Engle, R. W., 116, *135*
Engquist, G., 240, *262*
Enquist, G., 78, *87*
Enzle, M. E., 318, *322*
Epstein, S., 394, *406*, 542, *551*
Epstein, Y. M., 376, *389*, 428, 429, 430, *437*, *438*
Erickson, F., 41, *59*
Ericsson, K. A., 120, *135*, 233, *260*
Estes, W., 204, *209*
Etcoff, N. L., 192, 203, *209, 211*, 250, 253, *261, 263*, 302, *307*
Evans, G. H., 376, 383, *389*, 454, *486*
Ewert, O., 231, *260*
Exline, R. V., 305, *307*

F

Farber, J., 310, 318, *323*
Farkas, A. J., 249, *259*
Farnill, D., 268, 270, 273, *286*
Fazio, R. H., 543, *551*

Feather, N. T., 318, *322*
Federoff, N. A., 215, 216, 217, 220, *224, 236*, *260*
Feigenbaum, R., 310, *322*
Feldman, N. S., 315, *322*
Feltovich, P., 116, 118, *135*
Fencil-Morse, E., 221, *224*
Ferguson, T. J., 317, *322*
Festinger, L., 176, *182*, 191, *209*, 228, *260*, 325, 326, 327, 332, *339*, 540, 542, *551*
Feuerstein, R., 108, *110*, 567, *569*
Fiedler, F. E., 396, *406*
Fiksdahl-King, I., 417, *420*, 581, *583*
Fink, C. F., 374, *391*
Firey, W., 463, *486*
Fischer, C. S., 374, *389*
Fischhoff, B., 171, 172, 174, 176, 178, 180, *182, 183, 184*, 339, *339*, 539, *551*
Fishbein, N., 351, *368*
Fiske, S. T., 61, 64, 73, 75, 78, 79, 84, *89*, 192, 195, 196, 197, 198, 199, 200, 203, *209*, *210, 211*, 214, 218, 219, 220, 223, *224*, 236, 237, 244, 245, 246, 247, 249, 250, 251, 253, 257, *260, 261, 262, 263*, 289, 302, 305, *307, 308*, 310, 316, *323*, 416, *422*, 446, *488*, 495, *512*
Fitts, P. M., 36, *59*, 122, *135*
Flapan, D., 265, 274, 279, *286*
Flavell, J. H., 265, *286*
Fleishman, E. A., 122, *135*
Fodor, J. A., 362, *368*
Forrester, J. W., 179, *183*
Fox, J., 305, *307*
Frake, C. O., 40, *59*
Franks, J. J., 153, 154, *161*
Freedle, R. O., 47, 51, 55, *59*
Freedman, J., 376, *389*
Freedman, J. L., 374, 383, *389*, 427, *438*, 514, *532*, 543, *551*
Freeman, S., 537, *551*
Frieze, I., 253, *264*, 305, *308*
Freize, I. H., 253, *261*
French, J. R. P., 472, *486*
Freud, S., 541, *551*
Frey, D., 217, *224*
Frey, P. W., 115, *135*
Fried, M., 458, 463, *486*, 491, *511*
Friesen, W. V., 76, 80, *87*

G

Galanter, E., 257, *262*
Galle, O. R., 444, *486*

Gans, H., 491, *511*
Garfinkel, H., 61, *87,* 197, *209,* 447, *486*
Garland, H., 196, *209*
Garner, W. R., 364, *368*
Gatchel, R. J., 522, *532*
Gazzaniga, M. S., 85, *87*
Geertz, C., 26, *32*
Geis, F. L., 396, *406*
Gerard, H. B., 78, *89*
Gergen, K. J., 8, *19,* 310, *322,* 424, *438,* 444, *486*
Gerson, E. M., 447, *486*
Gerson, M. S., 447, *486*
Gettys, C. F., 172, *183*
Giamartino, G. A., 403, *407*
Gibbs, J. C., 8, 11, *20*
Gibson, J. J., 62, 65, 66, 68, 73, 75, 81, *87,* 354, 362, *368,* 441, 444, 445, 447, *486*
Gifford, R. K., 199, *209,* 316, *322*
Gilbert, E. N., 345, *368*
Gillen, B., 314, *323*
Gilligan, S. G., 231, *260*
Gilmore, J. B., 543, *552*
Ginsberg, R., 176, *183*
Glantz, M. H., 164, *183*
Galser, B. G., 21, *32,* 205, *209,* 388, *389*
Glaser, R., 116, 118, *135*
Glass, D. C., 411, 414, *421,* 444, *486*
Gleason, J. M., 310, *322*
Gleicher, P., 491, *511*
Glenn, C. G., 267, 268, 269, 270, 280, 282, *287*
Glixman, A. F., 537, *551*
Goethals, G. R., 249, *261,* 327, 331, *339*
Goffman, E., 75, *87*
Goldin, S. E., 115, *135,* 231, *260*
Golding, S. L., 394, 396, *406*
Golledge, R. G., 138, *148*
Gollege, R. G., 445, *487*
Goodman, C. C., 190, *208,* 292, *307*
Goodman, N., 80, *87*
Gove, W. R., 444, *486*
Graham, N., 357, *368*
Graziano, W., 247, 248, *259,* 290, *307*
Green, D. M., 365, 366, *369*
Greene, E., 572, *573*
Greeno, J. G., 117, *136,* 345, *369*
Greenspan, S., 277, 278, *286*
Greenwald, A. G., 197, 199, *209,* 291, *307,* 535, 536, 538, 539, 540, 542, 544, *551, 552*
Griffin, M., 293, 294, *307*
Griffitt, N., 383, *389*
Grigsby, W., 491, *511*

Groff, B., 373, 384, *390*
Gross, B. M., 281, *286*
Gruder, C. L., 327, 331, *339*
Grumet, J. F., 268, 270, *286*
Gump, R., 388, *389*
Gumperz, J. J., 26, *32,* 38, 39, *59*
Gyr, J. W., 65, *87*

H

Hakmiller, K. L., 327, *339*
Hall, R. H., 374, *389*
Hall, W. S., 55, *59*
Hamill, R., 195, *209*
Hamilton, D. L., 74, 87, 196, 199, *209,* 228, 253, *261,* 316, *322*
Hansen, R. D., 77, *87,* 314, 318, *322*
Hanson, L. R., 232, 246, *261*
Hanusa, B. H., 526, 531, *532*
Hardy, A., 196, *209*
Hare, A. P., 453, 481, *486*
Harkins, S. D., 310, 317, *323*
Harkins, S. G., 290, 292, *307*
Harre, H., 21, *32*
Harré, R., 447, 448, *486*
Harris, B., 213, *224,* 277, *286,* 293, *307,* 318, *322,* 374, 376, *390,* 409, 412, 413, 414, 415, *421,* 537, *551*
Hart, R. A., 129, *136*
Harvey, J., 10, *19*
Harvey, J. H., 6, *20,* 213, 215, 216, 217, *224,* 225, 236, *260,* 290, 292, 293, *307,* 310, 311, 317, 318, *322, 323,* 409, 412, 413, 414, 415, *421,* 537, *551,* 588, *590*
Hasher, L., 293, 294, *307*
Hass, J. E., 374, *389*
Hastie, R., 203, *209,* 228, 230, 249, 257, *260, 261, 262*
Hastorf, A. H., 84, *88,* 228, 234, 237, *263*
Hawley, A. H., 374, *389*
Hayes, J. R., 116, *136*
Hayes-Roth B., 143, *149,* 228, *264*
Hayes-Roth, F., 229, *261*
Haywood, H. C., 108, *110*
Headly, L. A., 428, *437*
Heider, F., 63, 64, 73, 75, 77, *87,* 191, *209,* 265, 269, 272, 273, 277, *286,* 290, *307,* 363, 364, *369,* 501, *511,* 581, *583*
Heim, M., 200, 201, *210*
Heller, J., 373, 384, *390*
Hensley, V., 217, 218, *224,* 253, *260*
Herman, C. P., 228, *261*
Hess, V. L., 281, *286*

Hewitt, K., 174, *183*
Hewitt, L. S., 271, *286*
Hexter, J. H., 582, *583*
Hibscher, Jr., 526, 531, *533*
Higgins, E. T., 206, *209*, 228, 238, *261, 264*, 315, *322*
Hill, J. F., 327, *339*
Himmelfarb, S., 228, *261*
Hinsley, D. A., 116, *136*
Hiroto, D., 530, *532*
Hogarth, R., 175, *182*
Holt, J., 561, 562, *569*
Hovland, C. I., 228, *261*, 291, *308*
Howard, R. B., 454, *486*
Hubbard, M., 78, *88*, 304, *308*
Hubert, S., 203, *208*, 249, *259*
Hughes, M., 444, *486*
Huggins, R. C., 433, *438*
Hull, C., 443, *486*
Hull, J. G., 216, 217, 223, *224*, 236, *261*
Hunt, J. M. V., 395, *406*
Hunter, I. M. L., 119, *136*
Huston, T., 10, *19*
Huxley, A., *552*
Hymes, D., 38, 44, *59*, 572, *573*

I

Ingram, M. J., 178, *183*
Inhelder, B., 139, *148*
Irwin, F. W., 331, *339*
Isaacs, L., 278, *286*
Isen, A. M., 219, 220, *224*, 231, 232, *260, 261*, 305, *307*
Ishikawa, S., 417, *420*, 581, *583*
Ittelson, W. H., 138, *148*, 386, *390*, 409, 410, *421*, 424, 425, *438*, 444, *486*, 489, *511*, 513, *532*
Izard, C. E., 80, *87*, 233, 237, 242, 257, *261*, 305, *307*

J

Jackson, J., 448, *486*
Jacobs, J., 458, *486*
Jacobson, M., 417, *420*, 581, *583*
James, W., 232, 233, *261*
Janis, I. L., 228, *261*, 543, *551, 552*
Jaynes, J., 85, *87*, 550, *552*
Jellison, J. M., 413, *421*
Jenkins, J., 82, *87*
Jennings, D., 314, *322*

Jervis, R., 536, *552*
Jimenez-Pabon, E., 82, *87*
Jodelet, D., 123, 126, 127, 133, *136*, 448, *487*
Johansson, G., 71, *87*, 359, *369*
John, V. P., 43, 44, *58, 59*
Johnson, C. A., 409, 415, *421*
Johnson, J., 201, *209*
Johnson, L., 279, *286*
Johnson, M., 200, *210*
Johnson, M. K., 293, *307*
Johnson, N. J., 374, *389*
Johnson, N. S., 267, *287*
Johnson, S., 310, *322*
Johnson, T. J., 310, *322*
Jones, E. E., 63, 64, 75, *87*, 193, *209*, 213, *224*, 249, 254, *261, 262*, 269, 272, *286*, 310, *322*, 538, *552*
Jones, P. D., 175, *184*
Jones, R. A., 327, 331, *339*
Jones, S. C., 325, 327, 328, 329, *339*
Jöreskog, K. G., 252, *261*
Julesz, B., 345, 355, *368, 369*

K

Kagehiro, D. K., 290, *307*, 310, 317, *323*
Kahn, R. L., 473, *486*
Kahneman, D., 168, 172, *184*, 195, 199, *209*, *211*, 238, 252, *261, 264*, 315, *322, 323*, 334, 336, 337, *339*, 416, *421*
Kail, R. V., 139, *149*
Kaminoff, R. D., 379, *391*, 442, *487*
Kanouse, D. E., 232, 246, *261*
Kaplan, S., 446, 447, *486*
Kareev, Y., 115, *135*
Karlin, R. A., 376, *389*, 428, 429, 430, *437*, *438*
Karlovac, M., 315, *322*
Karp, L., 219, 220, *224*, 231, *261*, 305, *307*
Kasperson, R. E., 581, *583*
Kassin, S. M., 64, 77, *87*, 311, *322*
Kastenberg, W. E., 175, *183*
Kates, R. W., 174, 175, *182, 183*, 462, *485*, 581, *583*
Katz, D., 473, *486*
Katz, L. B., 196, 199, *209*
Katz, N., 176, *183*
Kauma, C. E., 472, 474, *488*
Keasey, C. B., 266, 269, 270, *286*
Keeling, C. D., 163, *182*
Keithly, L., 290, 292, *307*
Kelley, C. W., 172, *183*

Kelley, G. A., 541, *552*
Kelley, H. H., 10, *19,* 77, *87,* 193, 197, 200, *209,* 228, *261,* 269, 274, *286,* 304, 305, *307* 310, 311, 313, 317, 319, 321, *322,* 336, *339,* 454, 459, 460, 462, *487, 488*
Kellogg, W. W., 163, *183*
Kelly, P. M., 175, *184*
Kempton, 41, *59*
Kenny, D. A., 197, *209,* 250, 252, *260, 261,* 305, *307,* 316, *322*
Kestner, J., 108, *110*
Kidd, R., 206, *209*
Kiesler, C. A., 191, *209,* 291, *307*
Kihlstrom, J. F., 228, *260*
Kinchla, R. A., 366, *369*
Kinder, D. R., 198, *209,* 235, 257, *260, 261*
Kintsch, W., 290, *307, 308,* 572, *573*
Kiraşic, K. C., 139, *149*
Kirker, W. S., 536, *552*
Klein, D. C., 221, *224*
Klein, G. S., 361, *368*
Klein, K., 374, 376, *390*
Klevansky, S., 376, *389,* 427, *438*
Knowles, E. S., 305, *308*
Kobben, A. J. F., 24, *32*
Koffka, K., 540, 541, *552*
Koivumaki, J. H., 318, *323*
Kolers, P. A., 84, *87*
Koman, S., 374, 375, *389*
Koptsik, V. A., 345, *369*
Korenz, K., *88*
Korte, C., 505, *511*
Koslowski, L. T., 71, 72, 81, *86, 87*
Kosslyn, S. M., 128, *136*
Kotovsky, K., 345, *369*
Kottas, B. L., 356, 357, *369*
Kozlowski, L. T., 138, 143, *148,* 359, *369*
Kriss, M., 196, *210,* 289, *308*
Kruglanski, A. W., 269, 275, *287*
Kuiper, N. A., 222, *224,* 228, 236, 253, *261* 536, *552*
Kuipers, B. J., 123, 127, 129, 130, 131, 132, *136,* 153, *161*
Kukla, A., 253, *264,* 305, *308*
Kunreuther, H., 176, *183*

L

Labov, W., 567, *569*
LaCross, K., 78, *87, 88*
Lane, D. M., 115, *136*

Langer, E. J., 84, *87,* 195, 196, 200, 201, *209, 210,* 245, *262,* 373, 378, 384, 390, 410, *421,* 536, 538, *552*
Lantz, H. R., 427, *438*
Lao, R. C., 530, *532*
Laosa, L., 47, *59*
Lappin, J. S., 355, 356, 357, 360, 365, 366, 367, *368, 369, 370*
Larkin, J. H., 116, *136*
Larson, R. W., 304, *308*
Laufer, J. K., 203, *209,* 250, *261,* 302, *307*
Lawrence, J. E., 383, *390*
Lay, C., 394, *406*
Layman, M., 173, 174, *183*
Lazarus, R. S., 234, 240, 242, 257, *262*
Leach, E. R., 23, *32*
LeBon, G., 374, *390*
Lee, T. R., 513, *532*
Legant, P., 213, *225*
Lehnert, W., 229, *262*
Leifer, A. D., 281, *286*
Leirer, V. O., 74, *87,* 196, 199, *209*
Leon, M., 276, 277, 278, *287*
Leone, C., 254, *264*
Lerman, D., 236, 244, 253, *264*
Lesgold, A. M., 94, *110*
Leventhal, H., 201, *209,* 240, *262*
Levinger, G., 10, *19,* 61, *88*
Levy, A. S., 216, 217, 223, *224,* 236, *261*
Lewin, K., 190, *210,* 312, *322,* 363, *369,* 444, 445, *487,* 513, *532*
Lewis, C. W., 121, *136*
Lewis, M., 47, *59,* 394, 395, *407*
Lezak, A., 385, *389,* 504, 505, *511*
Lichtenstein, S., 171, 172, 174, 176, 180, *183, 184,* 197, *210*
Lightner, J. M., 409, 414, 415, *421*
Lingle, J. H., 196, *210*
Linville, P., 254, *262*
Lloyd, B. B., 590, *591*
Locke, J., 558, *569*
Lodge, J. P., 173, *183*
Loevinger, J., 542, *552*
Loftus, E. F., 256, *260,* 539, *552*
Loo, C., 378, *390*
Love, K. D., 373, 376, 378, 379, *390, 391,* 433, *438*
Lowe, C. A., 64, 77, *87,* 314, 318, *322*
Lozar, C. C., 471, *487*
Luce, R. D., 48, *59*
Luckmann, T., 447, *485*
Luria, A. R., 589, *590*

Lynch, K., 132, *136,* 138, *148,* 155, *161,* 444, 446, *487,* 493, 502, 505, 509, *511*

M

Mace, W. M., 65, 68, *88, 89,* 360, 362, *369*
Mackintosh, E., 373, 378, *391,* 500, 506, *511*
MacNamara, J., 562, *569*
Magnusson, D., 394, 395, 396, 398, 404, *406,* 442, *487*
Maier, S. F., 411, *421*
Manabe, S., 163, *183*
Mandler, G., 232, 233, 238, 239, 242, 248, *262*
Mandler, J. M., 267, *287*
Manis, M., 315, *322*
Maracek, J., 213, *225*
Mark, L. S., 70, 71, 81, *88, 89*
Marshall, G. D., 237, *262*
Marteniuk, R. G., 122, *136*
Martens, R., 327, *339*
Maruyama, M., 473, *487*
Marx, M. H., 309, *322*
Maslach, C., 237, *262*
Masling, M., 290, *307*
Maslow, A. H., 461, *487*
Massad, C. M., 77, *88,* 304, *308*
Matthews, R. W., 376, 378, *390*
McArthur, L. A., 311, *323*
McArthur, L. Z., 62, 78, 83, 84, *88,* 203, *210,* 236, 245, *262*
McCain, G., 375, 377, *390*
McCall, G. J., 23, *33*
McCarthy, D., 382, *390,* 504, *511*
McCaul, K. D., 222, 223, *225*
McClintock, E., 10, *19*
McConnell, H. K., 539, 544, 551
McCraw, B., 101, *110*
McDermott, J., 116, *136*
McDermott, R. P., 571, *573*
McDougall, W., 232, *262*
McGrath, J., 454, 481, *487*
McGrath, J. E., 476, *488*
McGuire, W. J., 192, *210,* 305, *308,* 424, *438*
McIntyre, M., 68, *89,* 360, *369*
McKone, T. E., 175, *183*
Mead, G. H., 447, *487*
Meadows, D., 179, *183*
Meadows, D. H., 179, *183*
Mesirow, L. E., 175, *184*
Messé, L. A., 304, *308*
Mettee, D. R., 191, *208*

Michaels, C., 65, *88*
Michaels, G. Y., 304, *308*
Michelson, W., 456, 458, 480, *487*
Michotte, A., 73, *88*
Milgram, S., 123, 126, 127, 133, *136,* 373, *390,* 448, *487,* 504, *511,* 537, *552*
Miller, A. G., 314, 318, *323*
Miller, D. G., 539, *552*
Miller, D. T., 194, *210,* 214, 222, *224,* 537, *552*
Miller, F. D., 196, *211,* 302, *308*
Miller, G. A., 36, *60,* 168, *183,* 257, *262*
Miller, K., Sr., 293, *308*
Miller, L., 176, *183*
Miller, N., 191, *209,* 291, *307*
Mills, J., 412, 414, *421*
Minsky, M., 354, *369*
Mischel, W., 199, *209,* 219, 220, *224,* 248, *260,* 311, *323,* 394, 396, 397, 405, *406, 407,* 538, *552*
Mitroff, I., 57, *60*
Molotoch, H., 491, *511*
Monson, T., 213, *225,* 247, 248, *259,* 290, *307*
Monteiro, K. P., 231, *260*
Moore, G. T., 129, *136,* 445, *487*
Moore, T. T., 138, *148*
Moos, R. H., 405, *407,* 416, *421,* 441, 450, *487*
Moreland, R. L., 242, *262*
Morris, C. D., 96, 98, *110*
Mullet, R. L., 293, *307*

N

Nagler, S., 305, *307*
Nebergall, R. E., 291, *308*
Neisser, U., 21, *33, 292, 308,* 352, 362, *369,* 445, *487,* 589, *591*
Neisser, V., 65, 84, *88*
Nelson, K., 562, *569*
Nelson-Shulman, Y., 442, *487*
Newcomb, T. M., 393, *407*
Newell, A., 197, *210*
Newman, J. R., 176, *183*
Newman, O., 411, *421,* 444, 475, *487*
Newston, D., 62, 63, 69, 73, 75, 77, 78, *87, 88,* 304, *308,* 310, *323,* 418, *421*
Nezworski, T., 282, 284, *287*
Nicholas, D. W., 267, 277, *286*
Nicholls, J. G., 221, *225*
Nicosia, G., 428, *437*

Nisbett, R. E., 195, 202, 207, *209, 210,* 213, *224,* 233, *262,* 310, 314, 318, 319, *322, 323,* 381, *390,* 410, 416, *421,* 495, *511,* 538, *552*
Nitsch, K. E., 153, *161,* 562, *569*
Nix, D., 39, *60*
Norman, D. A., 154, *161,* 238, 240, *259, 262*
Norman, S. A., 222, *224*
Nowicki, S., 433, *437*
Nowlis, V., 231, *262*
Nuttin, J. R., 398, *407*

O

Obler, L. K., 48, *58*
Odom, R. D., 84, *88* 566, *569*
Ohman, A., 80, *88*
Okrent, D., 175, *183*
Olsen, R., 500, 506, *511*
Olson, C. T., 217, *225*
Olson, J. M., 228, *261*
Olweus, D., 394, 395, 396, 398, 404, *407*
Omanson, R. C., *287*
Opie, J., 175, *183*
Opton, E. M., 234, 240, 242, 257, *262*
Orne, M. T., 301, *308*
Ortony, A., 228, 240, *263,* 316, *323*
Orwell, G., 539, *552*
Osgood, C. E., 191, *210,* 234, *262,* 447, *487*
Ostrom, T. M., 196, *210,* 228, *261,* 538, *552*
Overton, W. F., 394, 395, 396, *407*
Owings, R. A., 99, 101, *110*

P

Pagán, C., 431, *438*
Paivio, A., 96, *110*
Panciera, L., 526, 531, *533*
Papert, S., 354, *369*
Parsons, W., 500, *511*
Paulus, P. B., 375, 376, 377, 378, *390*
Pearce, J. W., 77, *89*
Pennebaker, J. W., 200, *210*
Penrod, S., 257, *262*
Peplau, L. A., 10, *19,* 200, 201, *210*
Perfetti, C. A., 94, *110*
Perin, C., 409, *421*
Perloff, R., 217, *225*
Pervin, L. A., 394, 395, 398, 404, *407* 442, *487*
Peterson, C. R., 172, 174, *183, 184*
Petersen, G., 99, *110*

Peterson, D. R., 10, *19,* 396, 404, *407*
Petri, H. L., 433, *438*
Petrinovich, L., 11, *20,* 589, *591*
Pettigrew, T. F., 334, *339*
Petty, R. E., 291, *308,* 310, 317, *323,* 538, *552*
Philips, S. U., 44, *60*
Phillips, L. D., 177, *183*
Piaget, A., 253, *260*
Piaget, J., 139, *148,* 266, 272, 275, *287*
Pittenger, J. B., 65, 68, 70, 81, 83, *88, 89*
Plutchik, R., 233, 234, 237, *262*
Polanyi, M., *88*
Posner, M. I., 122, *135*
Post, D. L., 64, 78, *88,* 236, *262*
Poulton, E. C., 174, *184*
Powerdermaker, H., 23, *33*
Poyner, B., 417, *420*
Pratt, M., 571, *573*
Preiss, J. J., 23, *32*
Pribram, K., 257, *262*
Price, R., 449, 456, *487*
Proffitt, D. R., 71, 72, 81, *87*
Proshansky, H. M., 8, 11, *20,* 138, *148,* 386, *390,* 409, 410, *421,* 424, 425, *438,* 442, *487,* 489, *511,* 513, *532*
Pryor, J. B., 196, *210,* 289, *308*
Pylyshyn, Z. W., 229, *262*

R

Radlove, S., 314, *323*
Rams, E., 503, *511*
Randall, D., 305, *307*
Randers, J., 179, *183*
Rapaport, D., 540, *552*
Raphael, E. E., 374, *390*
Rapkin, C., 491, *511*
Rapoport, A., 374, *390*
Ratliff, F., 357, *368*
Raush, H. L., 404, *407,* 444, *488*
Raven, B. H., 472, *486*
Rayner, E. H., 120, *136*
Reed, H., 319, *323*
Reed, L., 253, *264,* 305, *308*
Reed, S. K., 343, *369*
Reese, H. W., 394, 395, 396, *407*
Regan, D. T., 325, 327, 328, 329, *339*
Reid, D. W., 396, *407*
Reitman, J., 115, *136*
Reppucci, N. D., 526, *532*
Rest, S., 253, *264,* 305, *308*

Restle, F., 345, *369*
Rhine, R., 540, *552*
Rhodewalt, F., 228, 238, *261, * 543, *551*
Rich, M., 290, 292, *307*
Riemer, B. S., 221, *225*
Rinder, R., *88*
Ring, K., 444, *487*
Rivlin, L. G., 138, *148, * 386, *390, * 409, 410, *421, * 489, *511, * 513, *532*
Roberts, C., 379, 388, *390, * 504, *511*
Robertson, L., 115, *136*
Robinson, J. E., 327, 331, *339*
Rodgers, W., 490, *511*
Rodin, J., 200, 201, *209, * 210, 384, 386, *390, * 409, 410, 418, 420, *420, 421, * 426, *438*
Rodin, S., 385, *389*
Rogers, C. R., 221, *225*
Rogers, T. B., 536, *552*
Rohwer, W. D., Jr., 96, *110*
Ronis, D. L., 310, *323, * 542, 544, *551*
Rosch, E., 590, *591*
Rose, T., 253, *261*
Roseman, I., 229, 234, 257, *262*
Rosenbaum, R. M., 253, *264, * 305, *308*
Rosenberg, M. J., 543, *552*
Rosenfield, D., 310, *323*
Rosenweig, S., 537, *552*
Rosinski, R. R., 138, *148*
Ross, L., 194, 198, 201, *210, * 213, 214, 223, *225, * 236, *263, * 314, *322*
Ross, M., 194, *210, * 214, 218, 219, 220, 223, *224, * 236, *263, * 536, 537, *552*
Rossi, P. H., 500, 507, *511*
Rotter, J. B., 193, *210, * 529, *532*
Ruble, D. N., 315, *322*
Ruble, T. L., 318, *323*
Ruderman, A. J., 192, 199, 200, *211, * 237, 245, 253, *263*
Rule, B. G., 310, *322*
Rumelhart, D. E., 228, 240, *263, * 267, *287*
Runeson, S., 71, 77, *88*
Rushton, G., 138, *148*
Russell, B. R., 61, *88*
Russell, D., 200, 201, *210, * 236, 244, 253, *264*
Russell, J. A., 234, *263*
Russell, J. U., 78, *88*

S

Sackett, G. R., *88*
Saegert, S., 373, 375, 376, 378, 379, 382, 384, 385, 388, *390, 391, * 496, 497, 504, 505, *511, 512*

Sagan, C., 85, *88*
Sagasti, F., 57, *60*
Sagi, P., 176, *183*
Sander, L. W., 42, *59*
Schachtel, E. G., 541, *552*
Schachter, S., 193, *210, * 237, 238, *263, * 384, *391*
Schank, R., 197, 206, *210, * 234, *263*
Scheier, M. F., 216, 220, *224, 225, * 236, *260, 263*
Schenker, C., 314, *323*
Schkade, J. K., 376, 378, *390*
Schlenker, B. R., 424, *438*
Schlosberg, H., 234, *263*
Schmid, C., 427, *438*
Schmitt, R. C., 427, *438*
Schneider, D. J., 84, *88, * 228, 234, 237, *263*
Schneider, S., 166, *184*
Schneider, S. H., 175, *184*
Schneider, W., 410, *421*
Scholpler, J., 373, *391, * 530, *532*
Schulz, R., 200, 201, *210, * 526, 531, *532*
Schuman, H., 200, *210*
Schwartz, B. J., 118, *135*
Schwartz, J. M., 330, *339*
Schwartz, R. D., 547, *552*
Schwartz, S. P., 128, *136*
Schwarz, M., 39, *60*
Schweiger, P. K., 217, *225*
Schweitzer, G. C., 173, *184*
Scribner, S., 53, *59, * 561, 566, *569*
Sears, D. O., 291, *306, * 543, *551*
Sechrest, L., 547, *552*
Secord, P. F., 21, *32, * 442, 447, 448, *486, 487*
Sedlak, A. J., 277, *287*
Sefen, J., 82, *87*
Sekuler, R., 357, *369*
Seligman, M. E. P., 80, *88, * 202, *208, * 221, *224, * 411, *421, * 426, *438, * 461, *487, * 518, 525, *532*
Seta, J. J., 376, 378, *390*
Severance, L., 540, *552*
Shacham, S., 240, *262*
Shalker, T. E., 219, 220, *224, * 231, *261, * 305, *307*
Shantz, C. U., 265, 267, 269, *287*
Shapiro, B., 80, *87*
Sharpe, L., 500, *511*
Shaver, K. E., 327, 331, *339*
Shaver, K. G., 65, *89, * 193, *210, * 214, *225, * 237, *263*
Shaw, M. E., 454, 481, *487*

Shaw, R. E., 62, 68, 70, 71, 72, 81, 82, 83, *87,* *88, 89,* 360, 362, *369*
Sheil, B. A., 194, *210*
Shemyakin, F. N., 139, *149*
Shepard, R. N., 547, *551*
Sherif, C. W., 291, *308*
Sherif, M., 291, *308, 540, 552*
Sherman, S. J., 310, *324*
Sherrod, D. R., 310, 318, *323,* 412, *421*
Shiffrin, R. M., 410, *421*
Shor, R. E., 78, *89*
Shubnikov, A. V., 345, *369*
Shultz, T. R., 77, *89*
Shusterman, L., 526, 531, *533*
Sicoly, F., 218, 220, 223, *225,* 236, *263,* 536, *552*
Siegal, A. W., 129, *136,* 138, 139, *148, 149*
Siegler, R. S., 314, *321*
Sierad, G., 221, *225*
Silberstein, M., 581, *583*
Silverstein, M., 417, *420*
Simmel, G., 374, *391*
Simmel, M., 64, 73, 77, *87*
Simmons, J. L., 23, *33*
Simon, D. P., 116, *136*
Simon, H. A., 112, 113, 114, 116, 117, *135, 136,* 168, *184,* 195, 197, *210,* 231, 233, 239, *260, 263,* 345, *369*
Simon, J. G., 318, *322*
Singer, J., 193, *210,* 237, 238, *263,* 325, *339,* 384, *391,* 411, 414, *421,* 444, *486*
Singer, R. N., 122, *136*
Skelton, J. A., 200, *210*
Skinner, B. F., 441, *487*
Sloan, L. R., 537, *551*
Slovic, P., 171, 172, 174, 176, 180, *183, 184,* 197, *210*
Smith, E. R., 196, *211,* 302, *308*
Smith, M. B., 444, *487*
Smith, R. J., 305, *308*
Smith, W., 507, *512*
Smith, W. A. S., 331, *339*
Smith, W. P., 330, *339*
Snyder, M. L., 213, *225,* 253, *263,* 290, 293, 305, *308,* 310, *323,* 538, *552*
Solomon, R. L., 411, *421*
Solomon, S., 318, *323,* 373, 384, *390*
Sommer, R., 411, *421,* 461, *487*
Spence, K. W., 152, *161*
Sperry, D. L., 413, *421*
Spielberger, C. D., 396, *407*
Spilich, G. J., 118, *135*
Spradley, J., 23, *33*

Sprinzen, M., 79, *89,* 244, 251, *263*
Srivastava, R. K., 471, *488*
Staller, J. D., 367, *370*
Stanfield, H., 77, *89*
Stanley, J. C., 444, *486*
Stasz, C., 138, 142, 145, *149*
Stea, D., 131, 132, *135,* 138, *148*
Stea, M., 156, *161*
Stein, B. S., 96, 98, 99, 101, *110*
Stein, N., 269, 282, 284, *287*
Stein, N. L., 267, 268, 269, 270, 280, 282, *287*
Steiner, I. D., 454, *488*
Stephan, W. G., 310, *323*
Stephenson, L., 196, *209*
Stevens, A., 128, 131, *136,* 138, 142, *149*
Stockdale, J., 373, *391*
Stockdale, J. E., 409, 410, 411, *422*
Stoeckle, J. D., 202, *208*
Stokols, D., 373, 374, 377, 385, *391,* 405, *407,* 425, *438,* 445, 446, 448, 459, 461, 464, 470, 474, 480, 482, *488,* 489, 491, *512*
Stollak, G. E., 304, *308*
Storms, M. D., 222, 223, *225,* 317, *323*
Stough, R., 504, *512*
Strauss, A. L., 21, *32,* 205, *209,* 388, *389*
Streufert, S., 310, *323*
Streufert, S. C., 310, *323*
Strongman, K. T., 231, 235, *263*
Suci, G. H., 447, *487*
Suci, G. J., 234, *262*
Sumner, R. K., 345, *369*
Sundstrom, E., 514, *532*
Suttles, G. D., 447, *488*
Swann, W. B., 538, *552*
Swets, J. A., 351, 365, *369, 370*
Szeminska, A., 139, *148*

T

Taeuber, A., 491, *512*
Taeuber, K., 491, *512*
Tagg, S., 160, *161*
Tajfel, H., 192, *211*
Takala, M., 396, *407*
Tannen, D., 42, 58, *60,* 573, *573*
Tannenbaum, P. H., 191, *210,* 234, *262,* 447, *487*
Taves, P. A., 228, 238, *264*
Taylor, P. H., 281, *286*
Taylor, R., 504, *512*
Taylor, S. E., 61, 64, 73, 75, 78, 79, 84, *89,* 189, 192, 195, 196, 197, 198, 199, 200, 203, *209, 210, 211,* 214, 218, 219, 220, 223, *224,*

Taylor, S. E. (*cont.*)
228, 230, 235, 236, 237, 240, 244, 245, 247,
249, 250, 251, 253, 257, *260, 261, 262, 263,*
289, 302, 305, *307, 308,* 310, *316, 318, 322,*
323, 416, *422,* 446, *488,* 495, *511*
Taylor, S. J., 23, *32*
Teasdale, J. D., 202, *208,* 525, *532*
Teddlie, C., 373, 384, 385, *391*
Tennis, C. H., 434, *438*
Terreberry, S., 478, *488*
Tesser, A., 254, *263, 264*
Thibault, J. W., 63, 64, 75, *87,* 454, 459, 460,
462, *487, 488*
Thomas, E. J., 374, *391*
Thompson, D. A. W., 70, *89*
Thompson, D. E., 428, 431, 434, 435, *437,*
438
Thomson, D. M., 155, *161*
Thorndyke, P. W., 138, 142, 143, 145, *149,*
228, *264,* 267, *287*
Thorne, A., 537, *551*
Till, A., 310, *324*
Todd, J. T., 71, *89*
Toffler, A., 413, *422*
Tolman, E. C., 132, 134, *136,* 138, 143, *149,*
151, 152, *161,* 444, *488*
Tomkins, S. S., 233, *264*
Toppen, A., 505, *511*
Torrey, J., 417, *420*
Trabasso, T., 94, *110,* 267, 277, 279, 282, 284,
286, 287
Trist, E. L., 478, *486*
Trope, Y., 539, *552*
Trowbridge, C. C., 138, 145, *149*
Tulving, E., 155, *161*
Turner, T. J., 197, *208,* 248, *260*
Turvey, M. T., *89,* 362, *369,* 410, *422*
Tversky, A., 168, 172, *184,* 195, *209, 211,*
252, *261, 264,* 315, *322, 323,* 334, 336,
337, *339,* 416, *421*
Tyler, S. A., 447, *488*
Tyler, S. R., 26, *33*

U

Underhill, D. J., 178, *183*
Underwood, B. J., 294, *308,* 444, *488*
Uranowitz, S. W., 253, *263,* 290, 293, *308,*
538, *552*
Uttal, W. R., 366, *369*

V

Valins, S., 202, *210,* 386, *389,* 412, *420,* 444,
485, 514, 515, 516, 517, 518, *532*
Veitch, R., 383, *389*
Verbrugge, R. R., 85, *89*
von Bertalanffy, L., 473, *488*
von Winterfeldt, D., 175, *184*
Voss, J. F., 118, *135*

W

Walker, M. R., 537, *551*
Walster, E. H., 229, *259*
Walton, M., 530, *532*
Wandersman, A., 399, 403, 405, *407*
Warkov, S., 374, *389*
Warren, W. H., 267, 277, *286, 287*
Watkins, M. J., 155, *161*
Wax, R., 23, *33*
Weary, G., 6, *20,* 216, 217, 221, *225,* 236,
264, 588, *590*
Weary Bradley, G., 214, 222, 223, *225*
Webb, E. J., 547, *552*
Weber, S., 500, *511*
Weeks, T. E., 45, *60*
Weiby, M., 310, *322*
Weick, K., 478, *488*
Weiner, B., 200, *211,* 221, *225,* 236, 244, 253,
264, 290, 305, *308*
Weinstein, C. E., 96, *110*
Wells, G. L., 291, *308,* 310, 311, 316, 317,
322, 323
Wener, R. E., 379, *391*
Wentworth, W., 500, 506, *511*
Wertheimer, M., 292, *308*
West, S., 373, 378, *391*
Wetherald, R. T., 163, *183*
Weyl, H., 345, *370*
Wheeler, L., 327, 331, *339*
Whipple, C., 171, *184*
White, G. F., 174, *182,* 462, *485*
White, R. W., 536, *552*
White, S. H., 129, *136,* 139, *149*
White, V., 327, *339*
White, W. P., 441, *488*
Whorf, B. L., 590, *591*
Wicker, A. W., 388, *391,* 442, 454, 464, 472,
474, 476, 482, 484, *488*
Wicklund, R. A., 214, 215, 216, 217, 218, 220,
223, *224, 225,* 236, *264,* 318, *321,* 542, *553*

Wigley, T. M. L., 175, 178, *183, 184*
Wilder, D. A., 192, *211*
Willems, E. P., 444, *488*
Wilson, S. R., 327, *339*
Wilson, T. D., 195, 207, *209, 210,* 233, *262,* 381, *390,* 410, 416, 421, 495, *511*
Winkel, G. H., 386, 388, *391,* 489, 496, *511, 512,* 513, *532*
Winkler, J. D., 79, *89,* 244, 251, *263*
Winters, L. C., 305, *307*
Wireman, P., 404, *407*
Witkin, H. A., 138, *149*
Witt, T. R., 310, *324*
Wohlwill, J. F., 424, *438,* 444, 445, 446, *488*
Wolfe, M., 376, *391*
Wolosin, R. J., 310, *324*
Wong, P. T., 290, *308*
Worchel, S., 373, 375, 376, 384, 385, *391*
Wortman, C. B., 200, 202, *208, 211,* 222, *225,* 257, *264,* 310, *324,* 412, *422,* 459, *488,* 518, 531, *532, 533,* 537, *553*

Wortman, C. V., 526, 528, 531, *533*
Wundt, W. C. H., 234, *264*
Wyer, R., 228, *261*

Y, Z

Ypma, I., 505, *511*
Zajonc, R. B., 203, *211,* 228, 229, 241, 242, 249, *262, 264,* 290, 304, *308,* 454, *488*
Zander, A., 453, 455, 473, 481, *486*
Zadney, J., 78, *89*
Zanna, M. P., 228, 238, *261, 264,* 327, *339,* 543, *551*
Zeiss, A. M., 219, 220, *224,* 538, *552*
Zeissel, J., 461, *488*
Zimbardo, P. G., 201, *210,* 237, *262,* 291, *308,* 374, *391*
Zuckerman, M., 314, *324*

Subject Index

A,B

Affordance, 66–68
Attention, 247–248
Attributions,
  as an epistemic act, 76–80
  and recall, 301–302
Beneffectance, 536–538

C

Casual force, 311–312, 317–320
Chess Mastery, 112–122
Climatic change and catastrophe, 166–180
Cognitive medication of helplessness conditioning, 521–526
Cognitive politics, 181–182
Cognitive sets, 292–306
Cognitive social,
  learning approach, 396–398
  for neighborhood participation, 398–404
Crowding,
  theories of, 383–386
  an echology of crowding experiences, 386–
  389
  research on, 427–431

E

Ecological validity or ecological analysis, 564–
  567

Emotions,
  from an ecological-event perspective, 80–84
  cognition and affect, 231–258
Environmental and social psychology, relationship between, 425–427
Environmental manageability,
  features of, 493–501
  and neighborhood structural characteristics,
  501–510
Environmental structure and memory structures,
  545–550
Ethnography, nature of, 22–29
Ethnographic language, 29–32
Experimental-laboratory, model, 7–13, 17
Experimentation and social contracts, 558

F

Focus of attention, as a determinant of attributions, 215–221
Freedom and control,
  in design and environmental literatures, 409–
  411
  determinants of, 411–414
  measuring in the built environment, 416–418
  analysis of choice structure, 418–420

G,H,I

Grammar to account for motives and intentions,
  269–275

High density settings,
    analysis of, 375–378
    person-environment transactions in, 378–382
Individual differences in spatial cognition,
    145–147
Interface of social-cognitive psychology, 198–
    205

L

Laboratory research and rapport, 560–561
Learned helplessness, generalization of, 526–
    529
Learning to learn, 102–109

M,O

Map drawing, 122–129
Miscommunication, 38–43
Modes of interdisciplinary work, 580–582
Moral-judgment, 277–281
Occupants, nature and relationship to place,
    453–463

P

Perception, perception-based knowing, 64–68
    and cognitive-based knowing, 73–76
    in dynamic stimulus patterns, 353–360
    prior knowledge in, 361–368
Person,
    as information processor, 192–194
    as cognitive miser, 194–196, 227–230
Person-situation, controversy, 394–396

Personal space, 431–436
Place, physical and symbolic context, 443–453
Psychological process, versus content, 14–17

R,S,U

Relativity of choice, behavior, 349–353
Relativity of knowledge, 342–349
Schemata,
    cognitive bias of, 36–37
    for modeling miscommunications, 51–56
    schema-based interpretation, 248–255
Self,
    organization of knowledge, 535–541
    cognitive dissonance theory as a theory about
        self, 544–545
Self-serving attributions, 221–223
Settings, transactions among people and places,
    464–478
Social density and regulatory control, 514–521
Social comparison,
    Festinger theory, 326–328
    questions social comparison can answer,
        328–339
Spatial knowledge,
    and cognitive maps, 129–133
    types of, 139–142
    utilization of, 152–160
Story—grammar,
    analysis 267–269
    research on, 281–285
Successful and less successful learners, 99–109
Unsolicited attribution, 290–291, 300